Bureau of the American Republics

Commercial Directory of Latin America

Bureau of the American Republics

Commercial Directory of Latin America

ISBN/EAN: 9783743393462

Manufactured in Europe, USA, Canada, Australia, Japa

Cover: Foto ©Andreas Hilbeck / pixelio.de

Manufactured and distributed by brebook publishing software (www.brebook.com)

Bureau of the American Republics

Commercial Directory of Latin America

COMMERCIAL DIRECTORY

OF

LATIN AMERICA.

BUREAU OF THE AMERICAN REPUBLICS,

1892.

II

In compliance with the requests of many merchants and manufacturers who desire to send Catalogues and Circulars to importers and dealers in Mexico, Central and South America, the Bureau of the American Republics has undertaken to publish a series of Commercial Directories of the several countries and colonies. The difficulty of securing the names and addresses of merchants has been greater than was anticipated, particularly those in cities and towns where there are no consular officers of the United States, and the lists herein given will be found incomplete. They are, however, as complete and accurate as the Bureau can make them with the present facilities at its command, and will doubtless be found useful to those who desire to introduce their wares to the knowledge of buyers on the southern continent. Any additions and corrections for subsequent publications will be appreciated.

III

CONTENTS.

III

Argentine Republic.

BAHIA BLANCA.

Banks.

Banco de la Provincia.

Merchants.

Belloni, Manuel, iron, timber, etc.

Chabaneau, Paris & Co., comestibles, wines, and spirits.

Duprat, Cárlos, comestibles and soft goods.

Ferro y Hnos, J., timber and iron.

Forgues & Ca., P., paints, varnish, etc.

Garay, Lorenzo, comestibles and soft goods.

Goodhall, E. P., explosives.

Goodhall Hnos., private bankers and general agents.

Helguera, Gerardo, comestibles and soft goods.

Mayo y Leiton, soft goods.

Muggeridge & Co., saw mill and timber yard.

Parte, Manuel de la, comestibles and soft goods.

Tardieu, A., chemist.

Raiteri, saddler and harness-maker.

BUENOS AYRES.

Bankers.

Daguerre & Co.

Fernandez, José.

Hale' & Co., S. B.

Hogg & Co., David.

Santiago & Co., Miguel.

Banks.

Banco Nacional.

Banco de la Provincia.

Banco Hipotecario Nacional.

Banco Hipotecario de la Capital.

Banco Municipal de Préstamos y Caja Municipal.

Banco Agricola Comercial del Rio de la Plata.

Banco Aleman Transatlántico.

Banco de Buenos Aires.

Banco Carabassa y Ca.

Banco de Cobranzas y Anticipos.

Banco Colonizador Nacional.

Banco Comercial de la Plata.

Banco del Comercio.

Banco Crédito Real.

Banco Constructor de la Plata.

Banco Español del Rio de la Plata.

BUENOS AYRES—Continued.

Banks—Continued.

Banco Francés de Montevideo.

Banco Francés del Rio de la Plata.

Banco Industrial y Constructor.

Banco Inmobiliario.

Banco Inglés del Rio de la Plata.

Banco Inglés de Rio de Janeiro.

Banco de Italia y Rio de la Plata.

Banco Popular Argentino.

Banco Provincial de Entre Rios.

Banco Sud-Americano.

Caja de Descuentos.

Nuevo Banco Italiano.

Bazars.

Aleman y Hnos.

Almeida, Roberto.

André, Jules.

Anglade ó Hijos, Juan.

Baron ó Hijo, Vda. de.

Barnes y Ca., A.

Barusso, Nicolás.

Bazan, Lorenzo.

Benza y Pagliono.

Bertuzzi, Domingo.

Bisotti Hnos.

Bondschedler, R.

Bono y Bruschi.

Bouché, Victor.

Bourcier y Ca.

Braun, Alberto.

Buireo, Roque.

Bullrich, Rodolfo.

Calderon, Meliton.

Canciello, Antonio.

Cánepa, Miguel.

Cazalas y Ca., Alfredo.

Castelletti, Luis.

Castiella y Cisneros.

Castro, Ramon.

Contreda, Francisco.

Costa y Ca., Fco.

Cotta, José.

Datey, J.

Dardignac y Torassa.

Donis, Pedro.

BUENOS AYRES—Continued.

Bazars—Continued.
Escajadillo, ManueL
Espiasse, Isidoro.
Evrard, Cárlos.
Galan Hnos.
Galli, Jerónimo.
Geslin, Viuda de.
Giacometti, Luis.
Graña y Ca., F. M.
Guilbert, Enrique.
Hanrie y Ca.
Japi Hnos. y Ca.
Kern, Jorge.
Laborde, Adolfo.
Lacaille, A.
Larese, Antonio.
Lorenzone é Hijo, Clemente.
Lusardi, A.
Lutcher, A. E.
Marengo, José.
Martínez, Robustiano.
Mazéres, F.
Menière Hnos.
Milet, José.
Miranda, Daniel.
Moreno, S.
Naris, Pedro.
Neira, C.
Novoa. José.
Nye, Jorge A.
Ojam, Cárlos.
Ouielhe, Domingo.
Paganani, Vicente.
Peltzer, J. A.
Penco y Hnos., J.
Peñaforte. Ricardo B.
Pesado, Nicolás.
Puig, G. F.
Rivero, Orlando.
Rocha, Ant. M.
Rodriguez, José.
Roldan, N.
Rouger, P.
Saché Hnos.
Sanguines, Antonio.
Santafé y Hno., Benito.
Simons y Cia., C. R.
Soneira Casanegra Hnos. y Ca.
Soucy y Ca.
Souza, Cándido de.
Tatlock, Alfredo.
Taurel, Agustin P.
Thenon, Marta.
Ugarte, Antonio.
Vega y Ca., J.

BUENOS AYRES—Continued.

Bazars—Continued.
Vidal y Camelino.
Vieira y Ca., Ernesto.
Vignes y Ca., Alberto.
Weyl, Eduardo.
Wilkes y Ca.
Boot and shoe dealers.
Balaguer, Antonio.
Beltram é Hijo, Benedict.
Cersosimo, Vicente.
Dausa y Costa.
Del Bueno, Pascual.
Kauert, R.
Loisel, J.
Lorini y Hno., F.
Prunnell, Antonio.
Richard, Celestino.
Rodriguez y Pico.
Smart, James.
Solcá Hnos.
Temaghi y Ca.
Chemists and druggists.
Aceti y Cirelli.
Aiardi, Juan.
Ambrosioni, L.
Amoedo, Rafael E.
Anfosso, Cornelio.
Ardy, José.
Arizábalo y Minicucci
Assorati, Pablo.
Astiz, Cárlos.
Ayestaran, Joaquim.
Bacigalupo y Vattuone
Badia y Almató, L.
Balzari, P.
Banon, Teófilo.
Barabino, Nicolás.
Barth, Cárlos G.
Battillana, Agustin.
Battilana, Federico.
Battilana, Luis M.
Bellati, Cárlos.
Berretti, Arnaldo.
Balze, E. de la.
Berri y Hno., C.
Beruti, José.
Berronelli, Héctor.
Bosio, F.
Besson, Luis.
Bessono Pedro y Cárlos, Camoloeth.
Bianchi, Giovanni.
Boeri, Silvia.
Bottari, J.
Bozzetti, Domingo.

BUENOS AYRES—Continued.

Chemists and druggists—Continued.

Cardalda, J.
Carlevero Hnos.
Carro, Pablo.
Cattaneo, Luis E.
Cella, Eugenio.
Cobos, F.
Cobos, S.
Cobos, Francisco.
Colombato, José.
Conforti llnos.
Converse, Francisco.
Couget, L.
Cranwell y Ca., G. A.
Cranwell, E. E.
Criscuolo, L.
Curutchet, Macedonio.
Danusso, C. A.
De Paula, Héctor.
Demarchi y Ca., Parodi.
Denevi, Ernesto A.
Dentone, E.
Dillon, Juan.
Di Marino, Luis.
Diosdado, José.
Duca, Giacomo.
Dupuitren, J.
Faggiotti, Constantino.
Felizia, Luis.
Fernandez, Frco.
Ferris, C.
Fillia, F.
Fiorini, Anacleto.
Follet, J.
Fontana, Manuel.
Francés, A.
Franzoni y Ca.
Galleri, Pedro.
Gallo, Segundo T.
Galvan, H.
Garbisco, Martin V.
Garofalo, M. A.
Gensana, César.
Gentile, A.
Gibson, Rolon y Ca.
Gil, Pascual.
Gilardi, C.
Goulo y Ca.
Grandinetti y Barberia.
Graña, Tomás.
Guillen y Harismendy.
Hammer.
Harlucea y Ca., R.
Hermida y Diaz.
Hermida, Manuel M.

BUENOS AYRES—Continued.

Chemists and druggists—Continued.

Hospital Italiano.
Ibarlucea y Ca.
Imperiale, José.
Imperiale, Cárlos.
Kelly, Enrique S.
Krauss, Enrique.
Lascarte, Tomás.
Lascano, C. F.
Lavarino, Cárlos.
Lopez, Enrique.
Luca y Galdi.
Magnasco, Cárlos.
Magnasco y Ca., M.
Magnasco, Márcos.
Magri, Ejidio.
Maione, Arturo.
Malatesta, Pablo.
Malvagne, Cárlos.
Malvigne, Pedro.
Malvigne Hermanos.
Mariani, Ventura.
Marino, Luis Di.
Marrazo, R.
Marsan, M.
Martinez, Faustino.
Maspero, Francisco R.
Mermier, José.
Mey y Ca., J.
Misuraco, R.
Moetzel, V.
Moine Hijos, Soulignac y Ca.
Monzini, Bellezza e Ca.
Morales, Florencio M.
Mosquera, Juan P.
Mujica, Adolfo.
Mujica Hnos.
Mujica, R.
Murray y Aikens.
Murray y Seedorff.
Navarro, Manuel F.
Neyer, Adolfo.
Olombrada, Matias.
Oneto, Juan.
Orsini, Nicolás.
Paganini, F.
Paquien y Ca., A.
Pastor, Vicente.
Perez, Norberto.
Perrone y Ca., L.
Petray, C. C.
Pianavia, P. A.
Piantelli, E. F.
Pisa, Manuel.
Popolizo, José.

4 ARGENTINE REPUBLIC.

BUENOS AYRES—Continued.

Chemists and druggists—Continued.
Ragozza, José.
Rauch, Guillermo.
Ravetta y Ca., Eugenio.
. Roble, José J.
Rueda, Eduardo.
Ruiz, Francisco.
Saintagne y Ca., P.
Salgueiro, Ramon.
Sanabria, R. Lujan.
Sanchez, Adolfo.
Sanchez, Cárlos.
Santini, Julio.
Sagastume, J.
Savaris, Serafin.
Sicardi, Jacinto.
Spangenberg, E.
Tebaldi, A.
Teganni, Alfonso.
Vaccaro, A.
Vaccaro, Juan F.
Vacarro, Julio D.
Vallebella, Jerónimo.
Vallebella, José A.
Veronelli y Fillia.
Vidali, Evasio.
Volger y Gnedcke.
Weissenbach, A.
Ynurrigarro, N.
Zanchi, Julio D.
Zumarraga, A.

Cigar dealers and manufacturers.
Alvarez y Ca., M. Cortes.
Amilis, Luis.
Brisson, J.
Canter, Juan.
Capra, Domingo.
Cruz, Juan.
Delbaso, José.
Dirube y Ca., B.
Duran, M.
Duran y Ca., M.
Fernandez, Manuel.
Fossati, Felix.
Fuster, Manuel.
Krauel y Ca., Augusto.
Leon y Ca., J.
Mendez de Andes.
Nadelmann, S
Naya, Vicente.
Nogués, J.
Patiño, Juan D.
Planos Hnos.
Parry & Co.
Peñelva, Francisco.

Cigar dealers and manufacturers—Continued.
Piñeyro, Pujadas y Ca.
Posse y Ca., J.
Reuther Oitale y Ca.
Ravenscroft & Rowland.
Schüren, Guillermo.
Sociedad Fábrica Nacional de Tabacos "El Telégrafo."
Somay y Ca., Pedro.
Steenkel y Ca., Adolfo.
Tarando, Antonio.
Terbeck, A.
Volkmann, Adolfo.
Wasinski, Adolfo.
Wiese, Claudio.
Zozay y Ca., F.

Commission merchants.
Acosta y Alkaine.
Aguirre, Pedro.
Aicardi, Heynes y Ca.
Albaicero, P. M.
Albert, Luis F.
Alvarez, A. F.
Alvarez, Domingo.
Amaral, Santiago.
Arau, Mariano.
Arginloau, M.
Arias y Ca., A.
Arias, Francisco.
Arias, Rafael.
Arvigo, Lorenzo.
Arzeno, B. D.
Ayos, Simon.
Baraldo, Antonio.
Barruti, Manuel.
Basail, Eduardo.
Beaumarie, Marqués y Ca.
Becher, E. C.
Beduwe y Wathelet.
Beltran y Calvo.
Benguria, Francisco.
Benguria, M.
Benso, Fco. L.
Bergia, Jorge.
Bernardo y Hno., D.
Bilbao y Cornjo Hnos.
Bilbao, Lavieja y Ca.
Biscati Hermanos.
Bista, Andrés.
Blanche y Ca., E.
Bohm, B.
Bollini y Alkaine.
Bonnement, J. B.
Bóveda Hnos.

BUENOS AYRES—Continued.

Commission merchants—Continued.

Bozzo y Cia.
Bradley y Ca., B.
Braly, C. A.
Broullon, Juan M.
Bruzzone y Bozzo.
Buhigas, Ramon.
Burgos, Juan L.
Bustamente, F.
Cabrero, Ensebio.
Calvo, Julio.
Campis y Dresco.
Cánepa y Pezzo.
Canfield y Thompson.
Cardoso, A.
Carozzi, Uises.
Carreño, J. T.
Casaban, Alejandro.
Castaño, José F.
Castellani y Cabrera.
Clarfeld, Federico.
Coulon, J.
Culloli, J.
Curto, Pascual.
Dallmann y Ca., F.
Daoust, J. M.
Daries, M.
Demaria, P. M.
Descalzo.
Despoy, B.
Dewey, Enrique D.
Diaz, M. N.
Dominguez y Aguirre.
Donnewald, B. G.
Dufour, A.
Duplan y Ca.
Durante y Roca.
Eborall, Arturo E.
Elizalde y Fernandez Hnos.
Espinosa, Luis E.
Fabis y Ca., J.
Fascia y Degalles.
Ferrari Hnos.
Ferrari y Ca., E.
Ferreira, A. José.
Figarol, Juan.
Fiorini y Ca., L.
Fogel Cailliat y Ca.
France, Peña y Ca.
Franck, Alberto.
Franco, Rómulo.
Frestes, F.
Frias Hnos.
Furst, Ch.
Fusoni, Pedro.

BUENOS AYRES—Continued.

Commission merchants—Continued.

Galan, F. C.
Galbiati Hnos.
Games y Dewitz.
Gandelfo y Ca., D.
Garcia, L. G.
Garibay y Ca., M. N.
Gamand Frères.
Gibelli, E. G.
Godoy y Zabala, A.
Gomez, Alfredo.
Gondra y Ca., A.
Gonzalez, Dimas.
Gonzalez, E. R.
Gonzalez y Ca., Piro E.
Gonzalez, Tomás.
Golba y Ca., A.
Guimaraes, A.
Gutierrez Hnos. y Ca.
Haimes, J.
Hastiguera, S.
Hill, Pascual.
Hodgett y Adelson.
Hoerle y Franhein.
Huergo, M.
Jacobs y Ca.
Jamardo, José M.
Jofre y Hno., J.
Johnson Hnos. y Ca.
Keny, Eduardo.
Kierman, B.
Knees y Villate.
Kraemer, F. F.
Lagerio y Lossi.
Lanusse, J. J.
Larrosa, P.
Lascano Hnos.
Laurencena y Plot.
Levington, F. C.
Lichtenhahn, E.
Limiñana, Pascual.
Lodia, Feo. W. N.
Lombardi Hnos.
Lopez, Isidoro.
Loubet, G. B.
Loy, Cárlos.
Macchiavelli, Juan.
MacLennan y Ca., J.
Magnanif, G.
Mango, Roberto C.
Maquiovelli, S.
Marcenaro y Ca., B.
Marinovich, Justo.
Mariscotti y Landuci.
Mariott, B.

BUENOS AYRES—Continued.

Commission merchants—Continued.

Marti y Font.
Martin, E.
Massini, Publio.
Máthot y Ca., B.
Medica, Adolfo.
Meili y Roesli.
Mendiondou, E.
Mendizabal, R. E.
Méry, Rout y Ca.
Miguenz, A. B.
Milhas, Bernardo.
Miranda, Pedro F.
Mohr-Bell, J.
Moleres, Marcoartio y Ca.
Molinari, A.
Montes de Oca, A.
Moro, C. A.
Muller, Juan S.
Muñoz y Lara.
Mussich y Diaz Velez.
Naon y Nicholson.
Nopp y Meyer.
Neumann, Julio.
Nicolau Hnos.
Niño, J. M.
Nocett, Angel.
Nocolás, Nicola.
Nowel y Harms.
Obejero, J.
Ocampo y Ca.
Ochoa, E.
Oderigo y Ca.
Olazabal, M. J.
Oliveira, J. R.
Ortix, Antonio.
Ortuño, Gregorio.
Ottolenghi, M.
Pacz, J. A.
Palazuelos y Ca.
Papuccio y Ca., L.
Parise, Aquiles.
Pein y Ca., A.
Peltzer y Praeger.
Peretti y Pestagalli.
Pereyra, Ximenes y Lowengard.
Perrera, José.
Perugorria y Ca., G.
Piera, Manuel.
Popper, Máximo.
Portela, Gonzales y Ca.
Porth y Ca., N. F.
Puccio, R.
Querencio y Ca., C.
Quintana, Manuel.

BUENOS AYRES—Continued.

Commission merchants—Continued.

Ricart, Nemesio.
Rigle, Miguel J.
Risso, Patron P.
Ristempart, Enrique.
Robinson, E.
Rocamora, José.
Rocatagliata, B.
Rock, Cárlos.
Roldan y Kiernan.
Roman Hnos., J.
Romer, R. W. W.
Rosales, Pedro.
Rosas y Ca., Juan.
Ruette y Ca.
Ruggeroni y Ca.
Saenz y Loza.
Salguero y Ca., F.
Salinger, G.
Sanchez, P. E.
Sansoni y Ca., F.
Sarmiento, H. P.
Satgé, Luis.
Sauerbeck y Hoffmann.
Saval, J. E.
Schiaffino y Ca.
Scotti, Manuel.
Scotti, Pedro.
Segarra, José.
Serrahima, Torent.
Smith, Lion.
Solari y Andreis.
Somoza y Ca., E.
Sosa, F. R.
Sosa, Juan B.
Soto y Calvo.
Surra y Ca.
Sussman, M. L.
Tartarone, P.
Tatloch Hnos.
Terr y Ca., E.
Tito y Carrere.
Torres, Agüero y Ca.
Tuber y Ca., A.
Trinnmer, A.
Trucco-Fabarro, M.
Tucker, Diego.
Underwood, Alfredo.
Van Harpen y Ca.
Vasques, D. R.
Vecchio, Oscar L.
Velasques, J. M.
Vercollino, E.
Vernet, L. Emilio.
Vidal, Agustin.

BUENOS AYRES—Continued.

Commission merchants—Continued.
Videla, Gregorio.
Villar, H. Deljo.
Viter, H.
Vinay y Ca.
Viola y Ca.
Valle, Gaston.
Vucinas y Ca.
Ximenes.
Yaniz, Ricardo.

Consignees.
Acebal, Diaz y Ca.
Acevedo y Pinto.
Aicardi y Heynes.
Atgelt y Ca., H.
Alvarez, M.
Aspita, Bernardo.
Balestrasa, A.
Balleto y Bidart.
Basavilbaso, Rufino.
Benitez Hnos.
Biondi y Magnelli.
Boerr, Juan C.
Bonnesserre, J. C.
Bouquet, Roldan y Guiñazu.
Bóveda Hnos.
Bradley, Ricardo.
Bunge, Emilio.
Burgos, L.
Carboni, José.
Casal y Hno., E.
Cascallari y Olazabal.
Castagnino y Flores.
Catoni y Ca., F.
Ceballos, Manuel.
Cernadas, Pedro M.
Costa, Galindez.
Costa y Diaz.
Costa Quirno y Martinez.
Cuffui, Juan.
Cutiellos, Manuel.
De Alberti Hnos.
De Andreis, Richini y Ca.
Delpiano y Gotusso.
Devotó y Ca., B.
Diaz, M. José.
Dickinson.
Dimas, Gonzalez.
Elordi, José.
Esquivel, Dionisio.
Etchegaray y Ca., L.
Fábregas y Forreira.
Fernandez, Máximo.
Fernandez y Ca., N.
Franchi, J.

BUENOS AYRES—Continued.

Consignees—Continued.
Franes, Juan.
Fuentes, José.
Furtado y Butler.
Galarce y Ca., V.
Garbino, Domingo.
Garcia, Manuel E.
Genoud, Martelli y Ca., B.
Ghiraldo y Murature.
Ghigliazza, M. A.
Ginochio y Podestá.
Gonzalez, Dimas.
Gowlard, Máximo.
Gramajo, W.
Gutierrez y Muñoz.
Ham, P.
Herrera, Onagoity y Ca., R.
Hoz, Martinez de.
Kelsey y Ca., G.
Koch y Haesloop.
Laguerre, Paul.
Laportilla y Ca., R. R.
Lasso, Eloy y Ca.
Lastra, José R.
Leguerio y Rossi.
Loubet, G. B.
MacKean, Cecelio.
Maderna, Alejandro.
Maltheus, Richards y Ca.
Matthey, P. T. E.
Mussich y Diaz Veles.
Nolte, German.
Ocampo. Samanés, M.
O'Connor y Ca., J.
Paz, Fuentes.
Paz y Ca., Max.
Paz y Roselló.
Peluffo, B.
Perez y Cueto.
Pettigrew, F. P.
Peyredier, J.
Piaggio, Juan.
Piera y Ca.
Pietranera, Tancredi.
Piñero, Juan.
Pocamora, José.
Podesta, H.
Pommez y Ca.
Porthé, F.
Porto, Juan.
Ratti, A. M.
Reepen y Ca., F.
Reinojo, Lucio.
Repetto, Lázaro.
Richerl y Ca.

BUENOS AYRES—Continued.

Consignees—Continued.
Rivera 6 Hijos, J.
Rodriguez y Ferrer.
Rojas y Ca., F.
Rojas y Ca., M. Z.
Rothes y Kern.
Sañchez y Roca.
Sansinena, F.
Sardá, Rafael.
Schiaffino y Ca., Nic.
Selasco y Derta.
Serantes, A.
Soage y Ca., S.
Sobrado, B.
Soriano, F. Garcia.
Soulignac y Ca.
Surra y Ca.
Torres, Agüero y Gascon.
Udaondo, M.
Unzué, Sat., é Hijos.
Uriburo, F.
Vazquez, Juan.
Vela, Angel.
Vela, Pedro.
Velardo y Naon.
Videla, M.
Viejobueno, Anot.
Weisieke, J.
Weisieke, Teodoro.
Yofre y Labarrière.
Ysern y Garibay.
Zanatta, I.
Zorraquin, J. R.

Consignees of vessels.
Acuña, Cabral y Ca.
Mosso, Santiago.
Shaw Hnos.

Dealer in church supplies.
Froc, Robert.

Dealers in explosives.
Evans, Livock & Co.
Moore & Tudor.

Dealers in shoe findings.
Adamo y Dellepiane, H.
Astraldi, Mariano.
Blestcher y Ca.
Bollo, F.
Bollo, Sebastian.
Brunacci y Ca., Ricardo.
Cailloux, A.
Cetráncolo, Vicente.
Ciappe, B.
Colombe y Ca.
Curuchet, Pedro.

BUENOS AYRES—Continued.

Dealers in shoe findings—Continued.
Dardagnol. Pablo.
Etcheto, Estevan.
Etchevers, Graciano.
Fortunato, Francisco.
Giusto, Juan.
Irigaray y Campori.
Irigaray, Lopez y Ca.
Iraola, Miguel.
Laborde, J. M.
Jost y Ca., Teofilo.
Montagna, A., y Brunacci, R.
Montagna, B.
Pecoraro, Victor.
Ste. Marie, Simon.
Videla, Juan.

Dry goods and notions.
Aldalzabal, B.
Ambrosetti, Fratelli.
Arijon, Froncoso Castaneda.
Auld, A.
Barreiro y Ca.
Bates, Stokes y Ca.
Bemberg, Otto y Ca.
Bindschedler.
Blanco, Bazteriga.
Bradford & Co., G.
Brambilla, Conjugl.
Brandes, E., y Ca.
Costa y Piola.
Del' Acqua e Cia.
Echevarria Hnos.
Engelberdt, Hardt y Ca.
Erana Hnos.
Fels y Ca.
Fernandez, J. R.
Garcia, Lapuente Guinca.
Gebbie, Albert & Co.
Gudenswager, Ressler y Ca.
Hardy y Ca.
Hortal, Torroba.
Jalck Hnos.
Labaqui Hnos.
Laclaustra, A.
Luders y Ca.
Luxardo, Costaguta y Ca.
Mahler.
Martinez y Pascual.
Martinez y Taladrid.
Menet y Ca.
Miers Laudaburo y Ca.
Naveira y Carro.
Olasso Castet C.
Olasso Hnos.
Quintana Hnos Ca.

BUENOS AYRES—Continued.

Dry goods and notions—Continued.
Repetto, Francesco.
Rivera, Ganuza y Ca.
Roccatagliata, Costa y Ca.
Rullan, Irazu y Ca.
San Pedro, A.
Schlieper, Herm.
Verrazzi y Larco.
Villar, A.
Wedekind, Fehr y Ca.
Zaldivar, Martinez y Ca.
Zuberbühler y Ca.

Exporters.
Armeingaud, E.
Arning, Brauss y Ca.
Azevedo, José P. de.
Barrozo y Ca.
Bates, Stokes y Ca.
Bean y Ca., Andrew C.
Bechem, Andrew y Ca.
Benausse, A.
Bertram, Wilhelm.
Best y Hnos., Juan.
Bonich y Ca., Luis P.
Bonnaffé, P.
Borzone y Ca.
Bossis y Camoyrano.
Bowers y Ca., C. S.
Bracht y Ca., Th.
Brandt, Eduardo.
Bunge, E. A. y T. B.
Burgos y Ca.
Burmeister, German.
Buschmann y Ca.
Çamartino y Hno., Francisco.
Canosa y Ca., J. M.
Caprile, Enrique.
Carboni, Cattó y Ca.
Caude y Ca., Decaussin Th.
Caulliez, Henry.
Cholat, Victor.
Cibils, Buxareo Jaime.
Cinzano y Ca., F.
Cohen, Giacomo.
Collins y Ca., Fraser T.
Coplane y Ca., Juan.
Corbellini, Carlo.
Daguino y Ca., Federico.
Delavigne y Ca., I.
Desplanques.
Drabble Hnos. y Ca.
Dreyfus Frères y Ca., J.
Duquennoy, Adolfo.
Eicken, H. H. von.
Etchegaray y Ca., C.

BUENOS AYRES—Continued.

Exporters—Continued.
Funck y Ca., Th.
Fuhrmann y Ca., H.
Galibert, J.
Ginouves y Ca., B.
Greffier, E.
Greffier Fils.
Hardt, Engelbert y Ca.
Hill, Bellamy y Ca.
Koch y Haesloop.
Lahusen y Ca.
Lamarque y Ca., A.
Ledesma Hnos.
Lernoud, E.
Lombardini Hnos.
Lopez y Ca., Antonio.
Lothiois Hnos.
Lothiois Frères.
Louet, S.
Lloreda y Ca., Mayner.
Mallmann y Ca.
Marco del Pont, A.
Masurel Fils.
Mendez y Ca., Francisco.
Milhas y Ca., Bernardo.
Moller y Ca.
Moores, H. G.
Navas, Rafael de.
Negrinelli, A. Remo.
Nery y Ca., F.
Nogues, Ninet y Ca.
Northmann y Ca., M.
Ortuño, Gregorio.
Ostwald y Ca., S.
Paterson y Ca., R. C.
Payrás, F.
Peltzer y Fils.
Perea y Navas.
Perry, Gardner B.
Pettis y Calzado.
Piaggio, Ernesto.
Podestá, Giacomo.
Ponzini, Ercole.
Quatrefages y l'aillard.
Reye Hnos. y Ca.
Rigal, R.
Roberts y Ca., C. F.
Roca y Santamaría.
Rollei, Domingo.
Rossi, Francisco.
Schumann y Zernik.
Solari, Cárlos.
Standt y Ca.
Steen y Ca.
Surra, Aurel N. de.

10 ARGENTINE REPUBLIC.

BUENOS AYRES—Continued.

Exporters—Continued.
Tay, Henry.
Tay, William H.
Theobald y Ca., J. K.
Tiéman y Ca., Cols.
Tornquist y Ca., E.
Torre, Ernesto.
Trinquier y Ca., G.
Villaté Hnos.
Waetge y Schlief.
Wattinne, Bossut & Fils.
Wens y Ca.
Wiengreen y Ca.

Furniture dealers and manufacturers.
Adamoli, Bernard.
Ader, Bernardo.
Allemandi, Constancio.
Alpini Quirino y Ca.
Amibale, Santo.
Baccaro, Juan.
Bancalari, José.
Barceló, Mariano.
Barsellini, Leopoldo.
Batista, Pascual.
Bergadá, José.
Bernardo, Luigi.
Berri, Juan.
Binaghi y Ca., Antonia.
Bó, José.
Bogni y Hno., Alejandro.
Bolcelli, Mariano.
Bosch, Antonio.
Botelli, Victor.
Bottaro, Antonio.
. Burghi, Angel.
Bristow & French.
Calachati, Juan.
Calcatera, J.
Cámpora, Antonio.
Campos, Anto.
Carraffa, Miguel.
Carlevari, S., y Gustavino, N.
Caró, Juan.
Carai, José.
Casale, S.
Casamiquela, J.
Casella, Emilia M. de.
Cassajus, Alejandro.
Cussina, José.
Castagnino, Bernardo A.
Castillone, Pascual Catoira Manuel.
Coruti, J.
Changhea, Cárlos.
Chiodi, Juan.
Chirelle, Cesare.

BUENOS AYRES—Continued.

Furniture dealers and manufacturers—Continued.
Ciolina, Emilio M. de.
Ciovino, A.
Cipolla Hnos., Froo.
Cipolla, Juan.
Cirelli, Agustin.
Colombari, Francisco.
Colombo, Antonio.
Confolonieri, P.
Copello y Hno., J.
Correge, Felipe.
Cortés y Ca., Francisco.
Costa, Jaime.
Costa, José.
Craviotto y Ca., Bartolomé.
Davi, Amalia.
Debot, Celestino.
Debatista, Ambrosio.
Debernava, José.
Dedini y Ca.
Dedini, Julio.
Dejean y Ca., D. C.
Delavela, Luis.
Delbueno, José.
Delean, Fernando.
Delfino Hnos.
Del Rio, Andrés.
Denevi, Juan B.
Descotte, Máximo.
De Vita, Crisando.
Devoto y Ca., B.
Didore, Augustino.
Do Mato, Manuel.
Dominguez y Ca., Roque.
Farnetano, Angel.
Ferrari, Angel.
Ferrigno, Juan.
Fialo, Joaquin.
Fideres, Roqué.
Florentino y Lecourse.
Fontan, Manuel.
Fonterosa, Manuel.
Forns, Feliciano.
Fortunato, Vicente.
Gandolfo, Pedro.
Garcia y Ca., Luis.
Genovesio, Leonor.
Ghirolle, Cesare.
Giachetti, Juan.
Gilardi, Enrique.
Giliberti, Pascual.
Ginepro, Victorio.
Gonzalez, Manuel.
Grampa, Miguel.
Grampa y Radios.

BUENOS AYRES—Continued.

Furniture dealers and manufacturers—Continued.
Granett, A.
Greco, Leonardo.
Green & Co., Juan.
Griet Hnos.
Gritti, Francisco.
Gross, Francisco.
Guanziroli, José.
Guastavino, Nicola.
Guido, Tomás.
Herment y Ca., A.
Jacob, Pedro y Vicente.
Jacod, J.
Jürgenson, Pedro.
Juillera y Ca.
Klein, Felipe.
Laborandi, Angel.
Lanata, Bartolo.
Lanatta, Juan.
Laurent, Augustina de.
Lavang, José.
Lerca, Juan.
Lorenzini y Peretti.
Maggione, D.
Marasco, José.
Marcolli, Cárlos.
Marcora, José.
Marrone, Benito.
Marsico, José.
Martindale, W. G.
Marzorati y Maccio.
Mascazzini, A.
Mascheroni, José.
Mastai, José.
Mattaldi, Leandro.
Meretta, José.
Mohimont, Viuda de P.
Molera, R.
Molteni, Lucas.
Molteni, Luis.
McDonald, J. J.
Molteni, Pedro.
Monaco, Vicente.
Moneta, A.
Monier, Juan.
Moreau, L.
Mounier, Juan.
Murino, Vicente.
Musso, Benito.
Navarrete, Ramon.
Naveiro y Parada.
Nicolello, Juan.
Nicolini, S.
Nocera, Domingo.
Novas, M. R.

BUENOS AYRES—Continued.

Furniture dealers and manufacturers—Continued.
Novo, Cedlio.
Nulli, Oreste.
Olivos, Juan.
Osorio, Ricardo.
Ottonello, Miguel.
Pacano, Rafael.
Paez, Jacinto C.
Pagani, Ramon.
Pagano, R.
Palacio, Pascual.
Palazzo, J. P.
Pallares, Gabriel.
Parenti, Santo y Hno.
Pasel y Ca., M.
Pastore, Antonio.
Pazos y Aznar.
Pazos, Pascual A.
Pech, Marius y Carranza.
Peretti y Hnos.
Pinoli, Cárlos.
Pisani, Rocco.
Pisano, J.
Ponti, José.
Popa, José.
Porro, Napoleon.
Pozos, Pascual Arturo.
Preller, Guillermo.
Prevost, V.
Rabollini, Angel.
Radice, Enrique.
Rebuffo, A. F.
Rilla, Francisco.
Rimoldi, Cesar.
Rivera y Ca.
Rocca y Ca., Tomás Rodés Sovero.
Rodriguez, Francisco.
Roiz y Cortés.
Rosiano, B.
Rotta, Antonio.
Rubio y Merlo.
Rubio, Salustiano.
Ruggero, Onofrio.
Ruiz, Anto.
Ruiz y Ca., José.
Saenz, Sandalio y Ca.
Salvador, Teodoro.
Santoparenti y Hno.
Santoyanni, Pascual.
Scarpati, A.
Scarpati Vicente.
Scarsi, Vda. de M.
Schmeil é Hijo, H.
Seng é Hijo, J. D.
Serrat y Ca.

BUENOS AYRES—Continued.

Furniture dealers and manufacturers—Continued.
Silvetti y Hnos., J. B.
Simonetti Hnos.
Sociedad Fca. de Muebles.
Solares, Antonio.
Solei y Ca., Hebert.
Souza, Antonio.
Spadaforo y Ca., S.
Spinetto, Luis.
Sueyro, Juan.
Tavelli, Pablo.
Tettamanti, Viuda de.
Texo y Ca.
Thompson y Ca., H. C.
Tigles y Amor.
Tonelli Hnos.
Toppi y Maffiolini.
Trazando, Benito.
Vadone, Francisco.
Vaggi y Rossi.
Valenté, Luis u.
Vannoni y Ca., P.
Vazquez, José.
Veghi, Angel.
Veroni, Domingo.
Vicano y Hno.
Vierci, Juan.
Vincent, J.
Viola, Luis.
Vismara Hnos.
Viz y Ca.
Zancarini, Elias.
Zara, José.
Zucchi, Luis.
Zucchi y Molteni.
Zurutuza, José,

*Importers of—
books and paper.*
Castex, Luis.
Chollat y Guillot.
Escary, J.
Espiasso, Jolly y Ca.
Lajouane, F.
Mackern y McLean.
Parellada, Juan.

brewery fixtures.
Aischmann, L.
Bua y Bachmann.
Heinemann, Kloy y Ca.

builders' materials.
Ginouvés y Ca., B.
Mirey y Ca.
Ribó y Hno., Augosto.
Van Harpon y Ca.

BUENOS AYRES—Continued.

*Importers of—
carpets.*
Romero, Diaz y Toresano.
chemicals.
Savelkoul y. Ca.
chicory coffee.
Caude, Decaussin y Ca., Th.
cider.
Cueli, Eduardo.
cigars and tobacco.
Aparicio y Ca.
Parellada, Juan.
Bello, Abelardo D.
Bonani y Ca.
Charro y Ca.. F. de.
Noceti, Cesar.
Romani y Ca., J.
Van Harpen y Ca.
cloths, clothes, etc.
Blotte, Saturnino.
Bonnaud y Goffre.
Bullrich, Rodolfo.
Figueroa y Ca., N.
Hira, José N.
Liguex y Ca., C.
MacCallum y Ca.
Portes y Benquez.
Molinero y Ca.
Schlieper, Herm.
Seligman y Baudon.
Staudt y Ca.
Viademonte, Harguindey.
Vidiella y Ca.
Zuberbuhler y Ca.
coal, coke, etc.
Roma, Duo y Ca.
corks.
Molinas y Ca., T.
diamonds, jewelry, and clocks.
Anezin Hnos.
Benchimol, J.
Black y Ca., William.
Bompet y Hnos., F.
Campodónico, Leonardi y Ca
Franchi, A.
Gerson y Hnos., A.
Hoch, J., jeune.
Imbert, R.
Jacard y Ca., H. E.
Lambert, Levy y Ca.
Levaillant y Ca., A.
Levy, Oscar.
Matthey Hnos.
Roulina, Ch.

BUENOS AYRES—Continued.

Importers of—
diamonds, jewelry, and clocks—Continued.
Seguinguan.
Silberberg, Muhlrad y Pozmanski.
Sotto y Ca., Joseph.
Steinhener, Jacobo.
Tabernig, Dussauet.
Wuille, Billey Bloch.
fancy notions.
Clarfeld, Federico.
Gass, Luis.
Greenway y Ca., D.
Haurie y Ca.
Jowey Frères.
Kaufmann, R.
Kruger y Ca., R.
Penco y Hnos., Juan.
Repetto Nocetti y Ca.
Weyl, Eduardo.
furniture.
Ader, B.
Green y Ca., Juan.
Griet Hnos.
Solei, Hebert y Ca.
Thompson y Ca., H. H.
Wilkes y Ca.
gas fixtures.
Cerini y Heinlein.
Gass, Luis.
Ribó y Hno., Agustin.
Sanchez y Vilá.
Storni Hnos. y Ca
general merchandise.
Acevedo y Ca.
Acherley y Ca., E.
Alzaga, Cárlos de.
Ancizar Hnos. y Ca.
Apesteguy Frères.
Apheca y Suzanne.
Arambarri, Rodriguez, Gonsalez y Ca.
Aretz y Ca.
Arizmendi y Ca., M.
Arning, Brauss y Ca.
Artagaveytia Hnos. y Ca.
Artaza y Landera.
Asworth y Ca.
Baratty Hnos.
Barclay, Mackintosh y Ca.
Barros y Lafont.
Bates, Stokes y Ca.
Beligard, Leopoldo.
Bemberg y Ca., Otto.
Ben y Brusch.
Bennet y Ca., J. A.
Berisso Hnos. y Scala.

BUENOS AYRES—Continued.

Importers of—
general merchandise—Continued.
Berliner, Horacio.
Bernheim, J. A.
Benkelaer y Ca.
Bianchetti y Ca.
Bianchi y Ca., E.
Bianchi y Ca.
Blanchard, P.
Blanchereau.
Blanco, M. Ramon.
Boie Hnos. y Ca.
Bonani y Ca., A.
Bonnaud y Goffre.
Borel, L.
Borro, Lorenzo.
Borzone y Ca.
Boyd, John P.
Bozzo, Antonio.
Brambilla, C.
Brandos y Ca., E.
Brownell y Ca., R. P.
Burgaud, Senet y Portes.
Camino y Ferrer.
Carbone, Pio.
Carboni, Catto y Ca.
Cardinali y Ca., P.
Carlisle y Ca., R. J.
Castiella y Cisneros.
Caude, Decaussin y Ca., Th.
Cazalás y Ca., A.
Chaldneto, Figari y Ca.
Charost y Ca.
Chás é Hijos, F.
Chatril y Ca.
Chauvel, Saul.
Chavanne y Roux.
Chaves, Fazio y Ca.
Chayla y Ca., E.
Checchini, A. P.
Chevrot y Ca., R.
Chide y Philipot.
Clark y Ca., Juan N.
Cobas, Benito.
Cobos, R.
Codina, Bartolomé.
Codino Hnos. y Ca.
Coelho y Halbach.
Collins y Ca., T. Fraser.
Cordero y Ca., V.
Corradi, Arturo.
Costa y Ca., S.
lagnino y Ca.
Dájaer Frères.
Delaye y Ca., A.

BUENOS AYRES—Continued.

Importers of—
general merchandise—Continued.
Della Cha, E.
Dell' Acqua y Hno., E.
Dematteis y Ca., C.
Denis y Ca.
Descours, A.
Deville y Ca., J. A.
Devotto y Hno., A.
Devotto y Ca., S. F.
Devotto y Ca., S.
Dieckmann y Malher.
Dillenius y Ca., O.
Donato y Ca., B.
Drabble Hnos. y Ca.
Drouet, Camille y Ca.
Dussddorp y Ca., M. H.
Englebert y Ca.
Fels y Ca.
Ferrer, V.
Font, J. Juan.
Friedmann, Mauricio.
Furt, Emilio.
Funn, Butler y Ca.
Galli Hnos.
Galup, S.
Gamble y Ca., M.
Garbarcino y Ca., A.
Garbolino, Cárlos.
Garcia y Ca., N.
Garcia y Soro.
Garibaldi, Fratelli.
Garibaldi y Tilll.
Garré y Ca., J. B.
Gaulhiac, Eduardo.
Getting y Ca.
Giuliani Hnos.
Goicoechea y Ca.
Gomez y Rodriguez.
Gondret, Juan.
Gonzalez y Ca., E.
Gramblin y Ca., A.
Hale y Ca., Samuel B.
Hall y Ca., Juan O.
Hardy y Ca.
Hegenbarth, T.
Helguera y Ca.
Herrmann, E.
Hill, Bellamy y Ca.
Hodsoll, John.
Hollmann y Müller.
Hopmann y Ca., A.
Jagmetti, Luis G.
Jardon y Ca., J. M.
Jones y Herschel.

BUENOS AYRES—Continued.

Importers of—
general merchandise—Continued.
Joseph, Henri.
Josué y Ca., C.
Kalko, Th. Hilarius.
Kauert, R.
Kirschbaum Hnos.
Krabes y Ca., H.
Kristofec y Ca.
Kuliche y Ca., Cárlos.
Lacaille, Alejandro.
Lacanette y Ca., J.
Lacau y Ca., A.
Laclaustra, Saenz y Ca.
Lafont, Camille.
Lahusen y Ca.
Lamarque y Ca.
Lapedagne y Soropon.
Lara y Ca., F. G.
Larco, Verrazz.
Larrouy y Ca., J.
Lavagno, Gregorio.
Lavallée y Ca., J.
Lawson y Ca.
Ledesma Hnos.
Lenguas y Ca., H.
Levy, Oscar.
Link y Ca., A. C.
Lohmann y Ca.
Lopez y Ca., A.
Loubet, G. B.
Lozano, Emilio.
Luders y Ca.
Macgregor, Aitken y Ca.
MacKechnie, G.
Mahler, D.
Maine, A.
Malatesta y Ca., P.
Marcosi y Vandervée.
Margenat y Ca., José.
Marguerie, L.
Martinez, Roberto.
Martinez y Ca., G.
Martini y Rossi.
Massuco, Cárlos R.
Matheron, A.
Matthews y Ca., R.
Matthey, P. T. E.
Mendez y Ca., F.
Menet y Ca.
Meyer y Schaub.
Milligan y Williamson.
Miranda, Matias J.
Molina y Ca., J. Juan.
Molina, M. E.

BUENOS AYRES—Continued.

Importers of—
general merchandise —Continued.
Molino, Alfredo.
Monsegur y Ca.
Montes y Ca.
Montesino, J. S.
Moreno, Manuel J.
Moreno y Fernandez.
Munyo, Manuel.
Naveira y Carro.
Neel, Le Bas y Ca.
Negrao, Vidarte y Ca.
Negrevernis y Ca.
Negrinelli, A., Remo.
Nery y Ca.. F.
Nothmann y Ca., M.
Nouche, Vilaplana y Ca.
Novaré, Tomás.
Oddo, Raja y Ca.
Oest, J. W.
Olcott y Ca.
Olivari y Ca., T.
Orlando y Ca., R.
Orsolini, Miguel.
Pages, G. F.
Palma y Bernasconi.
Palma, Feijo y Garcia.
Parlane, Graham y Ca.
Pearson y Ca.
Peck, William E.
Pellerano y Ca., B.
Perea y Navas.
Perez Mendoza, H. y J.
Perez, Serra y Ca.
Perez y Ca.
Perissé, Chiquirrin y Barra.
Perotti, José.
Petero Hnos.
Petri y Valenti.
Pettis y Calzada.
Pietranera, G. y A.
Pietranera, T.
Porth y Ca., N. F. L.
Prieur, Poput, Taran y Ca.
Queirolo, F. G.
Ramirez, V. A.
Ramos, A. F.
Rasche, R. S.
Rathje, A.
Rehn, Ernesto.
Rey y Ca., L.
Reynecke, B.
Reyre Hnos. y Ca.
Rhotes y Kern.
Ribero y Ca., O.

BUENOS AYRES—Continued.

Importers of—
general merchandise—Continued.
Rigal, R.
Roca Hnos. y Rivarola.
Rocha Hnos. y Ca.
Rocha, J. P.
Rodes, E. F.
Rodriguez, Javier M.
Rodriguez y Ca., M.
Rohner ó Hijos.
Roig y Ca., L.
Rolleri y Ca., D.
Ropes, Franklin S.
Rosas, A. G. de.
Rosciano y Piriz.
Rosenthal, G. y C.
Rossi, F.
Rousseau, P.
Roux y Ninet.
Robelle, G.
Ruiz, Garcia ó Hijos.
Rusca, A.
Ruscheweyh, G.
Rusconi, A.
Sabatté y Ca., J. F.
Salterain y Ca.
Samper y Ca., A.
Savernier, P. R.
Scherff Hnos.
Schiavoni, Juan.
Schneidewind y Ca., W.
Schulte, Roberto.
Segarra, José R.
Seaniglia y Crovetto.
Sehlmeyer y Vogt.
Senillosa y Romero, P.
Sequeira y Rosa.
Shaw Hnos.
Shaw y Ca., Juan.
Shaw, Miller y Ca.
Snell y Ca.
Sola y Ca., R.
Sotto y Ca., Joseph.
Spring y Ca.
Stefano, Questa.
Steier y Rosenstein.
Stevens, Corwin y Ca.
Storni, Traverso y Ca.
Sturla Hnos. y Torres.
Sueguin, Juan.
Sundblad y Ca., C.
Surra, Aurelio N. de.
Tatlock Hnos.
Theobald y Ca., J. K.
Thompson y Ca.

Importers of—
general merchandise—Continued.
Thompson y Torras.
Trager y Ca., H.
Troncoso y Ca.
Uribe y Ca., J. A.
Urrutia, Magdalena.
Valentin, Pedro.
Verazzi y Larco.
Vergara ó Hijos.
Vidal y Ca., B.
Vidal y Ca., M. G.
Vives, J.
Vulbeno, S.
Watson y Ca., C.
Widenmayer, Romero y Ca.
Widmer y Saintot.
Williams, Gaudencio y Ca.
Williams y Cichero.
Wipperling, Kirchhofer y Ca.
Wolff, Adolfo.
Wolff, Sigismundo y Ca.
Wood y Ca., Tomás.
Woolley y Ca.

glassware, chinaware, and porcelain.
Arredondo y Ca., R.—
Clarfeld, Federico.
Kruger y Ca., R.
Penco y Hnos., Juan.
Wilkes y Ca.

groceries and provisions.
Arabchety, J.
Ayarragaray y Capdepont.
Barnes, Hulcar.
Bianchi, Angelo.
Borzone, Stefano.
Camere, Fratelli ó Ca.
Cannale y Rusca.
Caride Hnos. y Ca.
Caride, Manuel.
Castiglioni, Luigi.
Caude, Decaussin.
Cima, Giuseppe.
Chapar, J.
Charost.
Crespi, Eugenio.
Croce y Pisani.
Crovetto y Ca.
Debussy, L.
De Nicola, Angelo.
Devoto, Podesta.
Devoto, Rocha ó Ca.
Dussaud, J.
Emmanuele, F., y Ca.

Importers of—
groceries and provisions—Continued.
Escutary, P.
Friedmann, M.
Gaminara, L., y Com.
Gandolfi, Moss y Ca.
Garcia, Fernandez y Ca.
Ginocchio ó Podesta.
Girou, Omer.
Gonzales, F.
Gonzales y Ferradaz Hnos.
Goyenechea, Bilbao y Ca.
Gutierrez y Ca.
Kruger y Ca.
Labarthe, R.
Laguerre, Paul.
Lalanne, S.
Lanusse, Pedro y A.
Lanus y Ca., J.
Lavagno e Comp.
Lavie, Serna y Ca.
Levi, G. A.
Linck y Ca.
Logan, Beatty y Ca.
Loguegaray.
Lopez y Ca.
Marco del Ponte.
Marini y Ca.
Martinez y Ca.
Martini y Rossi.
Maupas y Ca.
Mazzini e Repetto.
Morales y Castro.
Narice, Giuseppe.
Necol Hnos. y Ca.
Necol, V.
Neinmann, Kley y Ca.
Olivart y Ca.
Orsolini.
Ottone, Fratelli ó Cia.
Paats y Ca., W.
Parry y Ca.
Pavero, Felix.
Paz y Ca., J. F. de.
Pesagno, Silvestre.
Peters Hnos.
Pietranera, G. A.
Polledo, Candia y Ca.
Ponzini, Cav. Ercole.
Profumo e Comp.
Raimondo e Comp.
Repetto, l'arpaglione y Ca.
Reyre Hnos. y Ca.
Rezzo, Santiago.
Rigal, R.

BUENOS AYRES—Continued.

Importers of—
*groceries and provisions—*Continued.
Roig y Ca.
Rolleri, Giacomo, e Fratello.
Roncoroni, Giovanni.
Roviralta Hnos.
Samele, Vito.
Saralegui y Mascias.
Saulie, J.
Sgrosso, G.
Soages, S.
Spinetto y Ca.
Staudt y Ca.
Tabusso, Felice.
Trager y Ca.

hatters' articles.
Franchini y Ca., C.
Pesissé y Jardon.

household goods, paints, and hardware.
Belloni é Induni.
Cassels, King y Ca.
Demerengo é Hijo, J.
Dillemann y Ca., P.
Dellazoppa.
Font, Juan y Jaime.
Hasenclever y Ca.
Homps y Ca., A.
Lysaght, John.
Mieres, Forres y Ca.
Nicholson, Barnetche y Ca.
Pini y Roca.

iron.
Bell é Hijos, Jorge.
Cassels, King y Ca.
Descours, A.
Medina, Antonio.
Steen y Ca.

leather.
Blescher y Ca.
Fábrica Nacional de Calzado, Sociedad Anónima.
Fontan Frères.
Graff, A.
Levi, G. A.

machinery.
Adde, A. E.
Agar, Cross y Ca.
Barnetche, P.
Bertuch y Ca., F.
Carmen, Diego M.
Chauanard, G.
Dilleman fils.
Drysdalo y Ca., Juan y José.

BUENOS AYRES—Continued.

Importers of—
*machinery—*Continued.
Drysdale y Ca., Tomás.
Earnest, W.
Eberteins, L., y Ca.
Forquez.
Greenway y Ca.
Hasenclever y Ca.
Heinemann, Kley y Ca.
Hornsby & Sons, R.
Lanari y Ca., C.
Lanus, M.
Lejeune y Dutrois.
Mecks y Ca., S. J.
Menditeguy.
Moore y Tudor.
Osborne y Ca.
Portalis Frères.
Santos Hnos.
Shanks Hijos y Ca., A.
Shaw é Hijos, Juan.
Villafañe, G.
Walsh, Lovett y Ca.
York y Ca.. Samuel.
Wyssmann y Prevot.

men's articles.
Gath y Chaves.
Manicot y Perissé.

mosaics.
Allende, Santiago.
Arechavalena y Ca., M. J.

naval stores.
Bossi, Rugero y Ca.
Fullé y Ca., E.
Pini y Roncoroni Hnos.
Repett, Noceti y Ca.

paints, paper, and glass.
Aubine y Despaux.
Bonnemort, B.
Quesnel é Hijos, P.
Savelkoul y Ca.
Van Harpen y Ca.

perfumery.
Caude, Decaussin y Ca., Th.
Bianchi y Sobrinho, F.
Lafontaine y Ca., L.
Monreu, H.
Rivera, Ganuza y Ca.
Sabatté y Ca., J. F.

photographers' supplies.
Boote, Samuel.
Demarchi, A.
Stein, H.

BUENOS AYRES—Continued.

Importers of—
plantation supplies.
Alzaga, C.

printers' supplies.
Demarchi, A.
Estrada y Ca.
Hoffmann, Gotardo.
Ostwald y Ca., S.
Wiengreen y Ca.

ranges, fireplaces, and stoves.
Cassels, King y Ca.
Green y Ca., Juan.
Jones, Latimer E.
Wilkes y Ca.

saddlery and harness.
Astoul Hnos.
Irigaray y Barnetche.
Widner y Saintot.

small wares and notions.
Amant y Doublet.
Belgrano y Ca., J. B.
Bellon y Challe.
Berdoy, Calle y Ca.
Beye Hnos.
Burnichon y Ca., J.
Carrera y Ca., J.
Capdevile, A.
Caplane Hnos.
Challe, J. M.
Challe, José.
Charles Frères.
Chiappara, Tencone y Ca.
Coquetcaux, A.
Darte y Ca., Julio.
Delaye y Ca.
Echevarria, J. P.
Esquerré y Ca.
Fernandez, Glorialdo y Segundo.
Furt et Fils.
Goffre, Bonneau.
Gomez y Migone.
Grunhut y Ragozza.
Gudenschwager, Kessler y Ca.
Guenón, Gustavo.
Herbin Frères.
Lafontaine.
Laserre, C.
Liguex.
Maurcill & Co.
Moureau, H.
Menet y Ca.
Milan, Eusebio.
Nothmann, M.

BUENOS AYRES—Continued.

Importers of—
*small wares and notions—*Continued.
Portes, Benquez.
Puy, P. G.
Schnickel, José.
Seligman, Baudon.
Siegrist, Baader Hijos y Ca.
Sommer, Christian.
Villanueva, Leguineche y Ca.
Zorraquin, Cárlos.

tailors' articles.
Deville y Ca., J. A.

white clothing.
Adhemar y Ca., L.
Baño y Ca., M.

wines and liquors.
Alinari, Francisco.
Allec, J. P.
Allende Santiago.
Amadeo, Joly y Ca.
Aparico y Ca.
Aymar, Marti y Ca.
Barca y Peñasco.
Bazille, J.
Bazzoni, A. G.
Bonomi, Josué.
Bossany, Julio, y Ca.
Breuer y Hnos., Gustavo M.
Brunelli y Gatti.
Burnichon y Ca., J. B.
Bussaud Frères.
Charpentier y Ca., A.
Campbell, Colin.
Cinzano y Ca., Frco.
Conceição, A. J.
Dagnino, Federico.
Dell' Acqua y Hno., E.
Domanico, Taconianni y Ca.
Domenech, Baudillo.
Echezarreta y Fernandez.
Fernandez, Gayol S.
Fernandez y Ca., Ricardo.
Gandolfi, Moss y Ca.
Jolly y Ca., A.
Jones y Ca., S. H.
Kristufec, Julio.
Laborde, Auras J.
Laborde, Alexis.
Lesina y Bajetto.
Levi, G. A.
Loma y Ca.
Magnano y Ca.
Mantegazza y Ca.
Marino y Ca., E.

BUENOS AYRES—Continued.

Importers of—
*wines and liquors—*Continued.
Ortega, Beovide, Cibeira y Ca.
Piscione, Monaco D.
Portais y Ca., E. R.
Pressiani y Ca., J. B.
Queirolo y Ca., J. L.
Ramos y Ca., B.
Romat é Hijos, M.
Saborido Hnos.
Staudt y Ca.
Steiner-Richter. A. C.
Tonazzi y Hno., A.
Van Harpen y Ca.
Zeppi y Ca., A.

Liquor merchants.
Campbell, Colin.
Fraser & Co.. T. Collins.
Lafont, Brutus.
MacLean & Mulvany.
Manini, Ciarlotti y Ca.
Moore & Tudor.
Paats & Co., Wm.
Parry & Co.
Pontais, Calvert & Co.

Machinery depots.
Agar, Cross & Co.
Bertuch y Ca., F.
Bash, Hnos. y Ca.
Blanch, Pedro.
Chouanard, G., "Aux Forges de Vulcain."
Drysdale & Co., John & Joseph.
Earnest, W.
Eberstein y Ca., L.
Foley y Cia., Thomas G.
Hasenclever y Ca.
Heinemann, Kley y Ca.
Hornsby & Sons, R.
Lanari y Ca., C.
Lanus, Miguel.
Moore & Tudor.
Phillips, E. T.
Reinard, Julio.
Serra Mateo Hnos.
Shanks é Hijo, Alejandro.
Sociedad Casa Amarilla.
Shanks Sons & Co.
Shaw é Hijo, Juan,
Symes y Ca., Enrique.
Turner, Juan E.
Walsh, Lovett y Ca.
York y Ca, Samuel.
Autheman, Gustavo.
Boote, Samuel.

BUENOS AYRES—Continued.

Manufacturers of photographers' apparatus.
Da Costa, Gaston.

Merchants, general.
Acosta, Gardosse Manuel.
Acuña, Francisco.
Acuña, Juan N.
Andrew, F. E.
Aribas, Alberto.
Arrufo, Javier.
Arseno, Manuel.
Arzeno, Juan.
Bacigalupo, Luis.
Balcarce, Jose.
Bagley & Co.. M. S., grocers.
Baker, Edward L.
Ballauf, Ernesto.
Barcelo, Domingo F.
Barras, Lorenzo.
Barreiro, Juan.
Barrera, Antonio.
Barrios, José de.
Barserque, M.
Bartram, W. B.
Baumann, G.
Belaustegui, Francisco.
Bell & Sons, George.
Berasategui, Martin.
Bemberg & Co., O.
Bergalleni, Juan.
Bernasconi, Ernesto S.
Bieckert's Brewery Co.
Binaghi, Julio M.
Bissone, P.
Bolla, Vicente P.
Bonorino, Martiniano.
Boote, Samuel, paints.
Borzone, Esteban.
Bowers & Co., Charles S.
Bradford & Co., J., manufacturers of boys' clothing.
Bradley, Ernesto.
Brillabrille, Apolinario.
Broucas, B.
Burmester, I. W.
Burzaco, A., hardware.
Busana, David.
Cadret, Manuel.
Cafferata, N.
Calvino, José.
Camozzi, Juan B.
Carballo, M. José.
Carranza, Acosta Adolfo.
Carreras, Manuel de las.
Carreras, Sábas P.

BUENOS AYRES—Continued.

Merchants, general—Continued.
Casanova, Cayetano.
Casanovas, José.
Casaretto, Juan.
Cassels, King & Co., stoves, coal, etc.
Castillo, Manuel.
Caulliez, Henry.
Cayol, E.
Cestaro Hnos.
Childs, Saunders y Ca., cutlery.
Chiquierin, Francisco.
Cildoz y Ca, Martinez.
Clarfeld, Federico.
Close & Son, J. H.
Coll, Fco.
Conazzi, Cárlos.
Contritti, Pedro, jewelry.
Cook, Federico A. M.
Cornejo, Luis F.
Cornejo, Pedro.
Cowes & Browne.
Crassiello, A.
Crocé, Santiago.
Crother & Co.
Curtin, J. Clark, petroleum.
D'Acosta, M.
Debat, Pedro.
Delfino, A. M.
Devoto, Rocha & Co.
Diaz. José A.
Diego de Castro.
Drysdale, Thomas, general hardware.
Duhalde, Santiago J.
Duprat, Cárlos.
Duprat. Luis.
Durno, Jorge.
Earnshaw y Ca.
English Book Exchange.
Fernandez, Baldomero.
Fernandez, Enrique.
Fernandez, Manuel.
Ferro, José.
Figueroa, Juan.
Fortune, M. G.
Gambaudi, Sebastiano.
Garat, Luciano.
Gerlach, Eugenio.
Gomez, Gerardo.
Gonzales, Agustin.
Goth, G., arms and ammunition.
Grandolfi & Moss.
Grünbein, A.
Haltze, Juan B.
Hale & Co., S. B.
Hall & Ca., Juan O., teas.

Merchants, general—Continued.
Hamonet, Gustave, florist.
Harilaos, R. y H.
Hasselmann, Enrique L.
Henry, Fay & Co.
Hernes, Apesteguy.
Hodsall, John, hardware.
Hornes, Acebal & Co.
Howard, L. F.
Hoymer. Juan.
Hoecker, Maximo.
Isla, J. Juan.
Jerran, Eduardo.
Kaufman, Gustave.
Krabbé, Higgins y Ca.
Lafont, Brutus, teas and coffees.
Lamarque, Juan.
Lanus, Miguel.
Lanusse, A.
Lara, Pedro.
Lascano, Benito.
Lasso, Eloy.
Lastagaray Hnos., hardware.
Lauth. Juan P.
Lazaro, P.
Leslie, A.
Lockwood, Cárlos.
Lopez, Alejo.
Lopez, Daniel.
Lopez, José.
Luaces, Manuel.
Luque, Honorio F.
MacKeghnie, Guillermo.
Makern, Wm., stationer.
Maffei, Luis.
Malbran, Tristan A.
Malm, Cárlos.
Malvicini, Bartolo.
Marenco & Co.
Martin, Francisco.
Martin, Matias.
Martinez, Barrutti y Ca.
Martinez, José C.
Martinez, Pedro.
Massini, Esteban.
Mata, José.
Mattaldi, Torenato.
Matthews, Richards y Ca.
Maxuach, José T.
Merlo, Francisco.
Mertens y Ca.
Meyer, Leopoldo A.
Meyer, Nicolás A.
Miranda, Miguel.
Moine, Eduardo.

BUENOS AYRES—Continued.

Merchants, general—Continued.
Morkill y Ca., W. L.
Muñoz, Gervasio.
Murray & Lanman, perfumeries.
Navarro, E.
Negbaur & Co., Julius, stationers.
Neild y Ca.
Neri, Domingo.
Nicholson, Barnetche & Co.
Nogueras, E.
Novetti, Frco.
Nogues y Ca.
Ochoa, Indalesio.
Ocampo, Sackman & Co., lumber.
Oliven, Manuel.
Ortiz, José M.
Paez, Pastor B.
Palacios, Sastre Ignacio.
Parpaglioni, Juan.
Pascual, Pablo.
Pearson's Piano Store.
Perea y Navas.
Perez, Fernando.
Perez, Patricio.
Perfumo & Co., F.
Périssé, Luis.
Philipps, J.
Pichot, Emilio.
Piñero, Melchor.
Pingel, Juan.
Pita y Amenedo, hardware.
Pitkin, J. R. S.
Podestá, S.
Portalis Frères & Charbonier.
Puig, Antonio.
Puig, Martin.
Queiro, Alberto G.
Rabicini, Antonio.
Raggio, Lorenzo.
Ramirez, V.
Rasche, R. S.
Ravenscroft & Rowland.
Rebello, Cesar.
Recht Hnos.
Regunaga, Manuel.
Reyna, Toribia B.
Richards y Cia., M.
Riglos, Javier.
Rillo, Bonifacio.
Roas, Francisco.
Roca, Ataliva.
Rocca, Manuel.
Rocca, Juan.
Rocca, Santiago.
Rodger, G. D.

BUENOS AYRES—Continued.

Merchants, general—Continued.
Rodriguez, Gabriel.
Rodriguez, Gregorio.
Rodriguez, Luis C.
Rodriguez, Tomás.
Rojas, Luis.
Rotassi, Fco.
Roviralta, Teodoro.
Ruiz, L.
Runciman y Ca.
Ruscheweyh, G.
Saligeri, Zucchi N.
Salterain & Co.
Sanford, C. H.
Schiff y Ca., L.
Schnable & Co.
Schröder, Guillermo.
Semeria, Bernardo.
Servais, Lonhienne.
Shaw Bros.
Sifredi, Modesta.
Silva, Federico.
Silva, Garreton Cárlos.
Silveyra, Augustin.
Smits, Cárlos.
Spinetto, Andrés.
Spraggon, Guillermo.
Stagno Bacigalupo, Cárlos.
Stevens, Corwin & Co.
Strong, William.
Tao, Francisco.
Torrado, Francisco.
Trella, Juan.
Tronconi, José.
Turner y Ca., Juan E., builders' supplies.
The Gourock Ropework Co.
Viejobueno, Aatolio.
Vignale, Juan.
Nilaró, Juan Fco.
Vilatte Hnos.
Vitale, José.
Vivar, Cárlos.
Volpe, Luis, umbrellas and canes.
Wilkes y Ca.
Wood & Co., Thomas, engineers and contractors' stores.
Zwingen, Antonio.

Representatives of foreign houses.
Adde, E. A.
Allard, E.
Bazzoni, Giunio.
Boisot, C. V.
Bouwer, N.
Burmester, William.

BUENOS AYRES—Continued.

Representatives of foreign houses—Continued.
Busch, Walther.
Carbados, Eugenio.
Carassiano y Ca., A.
Clemente, M. de, filtros Pasteur.
Caillon y Ca., Ernesto.
Catuna, M.
Collins, J. H.
Coquet et fils, James.
Costa, Pablo.
Coulon, F., y Crèvecœur, E.
Duplaquet, Comptoirs Commerciaux Français.
Dupont et Fils, P.
Favrot, Ch.
Fischer, M.
Fischer y Schlatter.
Forgues, L. D.
Groenewoud, S.
Hauck, Emilio.
Hauser, Ricardo.
Höchel, German.
Hollman y Müller.
Howard, L. F.
Hupfeld, C. F.
India Rubber, Gutta-Percha and Telegraph
   Works.
Joubert, Pablo.
Lassaletta y Mariobalar.
Kaufmann, G.
Kristufeck, Julio.
Leech, J.
Letzgus y Ca.
Lloyd, Ernesto H.
Lottermoser, Guillermo.
MacCracken, William H.
Malm, Godofredo.
Mitau, J. y E.
Naar, F. F.
Ortuno, Gregorio.
Ovando y Ca.
Payton y Ca.
Peck, William F.
Perrel, C.
Pietsch y Ca.
Plaut, George.
Potter, Eduardo.
Ramell, J.
Rodriguez, Marcos.
Sattler, L.
Scharnitz, H. y Alejandro.
Schneider y Ca.
Schuerer Stollo, Juan.
Schwob Hnos.
Sgrosso, G. y I. Martiguetti.
Stoarn, F.

BUENOS AYRES—Continued.

Representatives of foreign houses—Continued.
Sternberg, Luis.
Stevens, Corwin y Ca.
Surra, A. N. de.
Symes y Ca., Enrique.
Tatlock Hnos.
Thomson, C. G.
Torrella, Pedro.
Vaucher y Pachon.
Wauer, William.
Weil y Ca., Hugo.
Wollwerber, W.
Woodgate, G. M.
Zeppi y Ca., A.
Sandal manufacturers.
Andia, F.
Apesteguia, Domingo.
Arnal, Dionisio.
Ascarat, Martino.
Asco, Manuel.
Avendaño, Fermin.
Barueche, Salvador.
Bidondo, Bernardo.
Campolongo, Sra. Rechela.
Carasa, Francisco.
Carrique, Simon.
Casamayor, P.
Cesario y Cia., M.
Courtes, Bernardo.
De Diego, Francisco.
Dominguez Hnos.
Echave, Martin.
Esnola, José Maria.
Etchegaray y Fraser.
Fourcade, Bautista.
Furnoda, Clemente.
Grela, Andrés.
Hernandez y Mira.
Lafuente, J.
Lastiri, Pedro J.
Marañon, Jenaro.
Marti, Prudencio.
Marton, B.
Marton, Pedro.
Morea, Aniceto.
Moreno, Fernando.
Otamondi, J. M.
Otamondi, José.
Redondo, Maria.
Rendo, Domingo.
Rivera, Evanis.
San Gil, Ubaldo.
Senteler, L.
Sociedad Anónima.
Sotres, Salvador.

BUENOS AYRES—Continued.

Sandal manufacturers—Continued.
Ugaldia, Juan.
Vega, Servando.
Zubillaga, Blas.

Ship chandlers.
Badaracco é Hijos, José.
Blanch, Pedro.
Bruzzone, Juan.
Canova Hnos.
Cicosi, Ruggero y Ca.
Cichero, Domingo.
Deacon, T. T.
Francioni, Francisco.
Fulle y Ca., Emilio.
Guizzetti y Garrone.
Maranga, J.
Massone, Cárlos.
Meincke é Hijo, Enrique.
Mortola, Canevari.
Pini, J., y Roncoroni Hermanos.
Pitre, Francisco.
Repetto, Noceti y Ca.
Rizzi, José.

Silversmiths.
Batrica, J.
Benassi, Luis.
Benatar, L.
Biondi, Beneditto.
Biondi, B., y J. Sauciat.
Bonthoux, P. y E.
Cantalupi, Salvador.
Capra, J., y Fagioli, G. A.
Costa, Julio.
Cubelli é Hijo.
Cuomo, Felipe.
D'Atri, Carmelo.
Diaz, Melanio.
Fernandez y Casal.
Ferrari, Agustin.
Franco, Máximo.
Frugoni, D.
Fuchs, Cárlos y Frco. Pomi.
Krämer, Simon.
Krämer, Isaac.
Kempter y Straube.
Macucho, Domingo.
Marinelli, José.
Mégalo y Cia., B. J.
Mina, A. G.
Molinari, Vicente.
Nasso, D., y G. Dezcalzo.
Odoricio, Felipe.
Ornstein, R.
Petragnani, José.

BUENOS AYRES—Continued.

Silversmiths—Continued.
Pietrafesa, Antonio.
Pietrafesa, Juan.
Pietrafesa, Miguel.
Podestá, A.
Podestá, Enrique.
Pomi, Frco.
Rachetti, César.
Puiz, Leonardo.
Putra, Miguel.
San Martino, Angel.
Servi, José de.
Suviria, Eusebio.

Surgical instrument manufacturer.
Belleza, A.

Tailors.
Amillis, Luis.
Ash, Henry.
Brown, J.
Damas, A.
McMillan & Co., J.
Murray, A.
Smart, James.

Wool depositories.
Beautemps, F.
Bécat, Eugenio P.
Casado, P.
De Barrera, Masia y Ca.
Fongue y Dhios.
Guirand, Emilio.
Jalabert, Fermin.
Mañi, Domingo.
Marcou, Calisto..
Orbiscay, Cárlos.
Perez, Jerónimo.
Sanchez, Pedro.
Taullard, A.
Urrutia, G., y Durrati, J.

Wool and produce.
Garrahan & Bros., L.
Kelsey & Co., G.
Kenny, Eduardo.
Ramsay, James T.

CATAMARCA.

Banks.
Banco Nacional, Sucursal del.
Banco de Sta. Fé, Sucursal del.

Merchants, general.
Abarra, Miguel.
Bazan, Luna.
Caravati, Luis.
Carranza, Mauricio.

CATAMARCA—Continued.

Merchants, general—Continued.
Carreras, Cipriano.
Cisneros, Juan.
Cubos, Francisco.
Ferruro, Calixto.
Figueroa, Casto.
Figueroa, Molax & Co.
Franco, Luis.
Lascano Hermanos.
Mescado, Wellington.
Molax Hermauos.
Molina Hermanos.
Navarro, Manuel.
Navarro, O.
Rodriguez, Severo.
Terum, A.

CORDOBA.

Banks.
Banco Agricola Comercial del Rio de la Plata.
Banco Hipotecario de la Provincia.
Banco Nacional, Sucursal del.
Allende y Ca., José.
Castro, V.
Cordeiro, Abelardo, ó Hijo.
Debreza y Ca., E.
Flandin, T.
Peñolosa y Velez.
Pitt, J.J.
Salvarezza y Giachino.
Sanguinet, E.

Dry goods and notions.
Bourlier, P.
Canelo, E.
Flandin, T.
Silva, Torres.
Taboada, P.

Groceries and provisions.
Bas, Tomás.
Caballero, F.
Caratala, J.
Ferreyra, F.
Figueroa, E.
Gaiviso, Lencina. Silvia y Ca.
Leiva, T.

Iron and machinery.
Conde, J.
Fernaudez, J.
Leudeadorf y Ca.
Llovet y Ca., J.
Obregon, Severan.
Oranto, Zuraldo.
Santiago, Pascual de.

CORDOBA—Continued.

Merchants, commission.
Garfagnoli, Petracchi y Ca.
Gonzalez y Martinez.
Muñoz, Perea A.

Merchants, importers.
Abarca, Jaime.
Accssat y Fary.
Acosta y Argüello.
Acroza, Ortiz y Ca.
Allende, Pedro.
Alvarez, Javier.
Boggild y Petersen.
Bressler, A.
Caeiro, P.
Carranza, N.
Carranza, P.
Castro, V.
David y Antenor Carreras.
Deanda Hnos.
Deheza, Eduardo.
Damarcet, José.
Ferdinand Givaudant.
Fernandez, José.
Flandin, Theod.
Gairer Cia., E.
Gavier, Enrique.
Gavier, Pedro.
Goicohechea, Mariano J. de.
• Heina, Kurth y Ca.
Karna Pablo y Ca.
Lapierre, A.
Lasl, L.
Lazcano y Ca.
Leila, Teodomiro.
Martinez Rogelio y Ca.
Mendez, José Me
Michieli Huos.
Montenegro Huos.
Obregon, S.
Oulier y Darlay.
Pietro, Franzoni.
Prieto y Ca.
Rodriguez, F.
Ronnan y Hermanos, J.
Romillon, Marin y Ca.
Tagliaferri, G.
Thome, John M.

CORRIENTES.

Banks and bankers.
Agricola.
Banco Nacional, Sucursal del.
Nacional.
Oneiva, Desiderio.

CORRIENTES—Continued.

Banks and bankers—Continued.
Provincial.
Scotte, Augusto L.
Territorial.

Groceries and provisions.
Bustradny, Borjas. ˋ
Biondi, Cataldo.
Vaccaro Hnos.

Iron.
Gotusso, J.
Luraschi. E.
Vible, Luis.

Merchants, commission.
Agueret, Hipolito.
Billinguret & Sotero.
Corin, P.
Desimoni, Nicolini.
Fontana, Manuel.
Laffont, A.
Odena, Antonio.
Resoagli y Ca.
Vaque, M., y Ca.

Merchants, general.
Aguirre & Co.
Birrastain, Pedro.
Cremente & Queirel.
Decoud, Antonio.
Elena & Co., José.
Figueroa & Co., L.
Giorgeti, Viuda de.
Gustuzo & Guerell.
Moreno, Francisco.
Persini Hermanos.
Sala & Co.
Santa Marina, Narciso.
Vages & Co., Juan.
Villa, Luis.

JUJUY.

Banks.
Constructor.
Sucursal del Banco Hipotecario.
Sucursal del Banco Nacional.

Importers and exporters.
Dellepiagge, Bidondo.
. Lopez, Antonio.
Montero, Garcia y Ca.
Solana, Aragon y Ca.
Tezanos, Pintos Alvina y Ca.

LA PLATA.

Bankers.
Banco Comercial de La Plata.
Banco de Italia y Rio de La Plata.

LA PLATA—Continued.

Bankers—Continued.
Banco de la Provincia.
Banco Hipotecario de la Provincia.
Banco Hipotecario Nacional.
Banco Mercantil del Rio de la Plata.
Banco Nuevo Italiano.

Merchants.
Ahr & Olivera, timber.
Alvarez, Desidero, paving contractor.
Ambrosis ó Hijos, timber.
Amoretti, Cárlos, vermicelli factory.
Angauuzzi, Baltasar, iron foundry.
Arechavaleta & Ca., mosaics.
Artigue, Enrique, artificial stone factory, bricks, and mosaics.
Asnaghi, Luis, timber and general merchant.
Attillo, Rafael, marble works.
Barbero, José R., carriage factory.
Basset Frères, nursery gardens.
Bianchi, Spont, Delpino y Ca., timber and general import merchants.
Bianchi, Esteban y Ca., wholesale grocery and import house.
Bizzozero Hermanos, furniture-makers.
Boggiano, V. M., wholesale grocery.
Botel & Cia., Felipe, furniture and general hardware importers.
Carbone Maesani & Cia., timber.
Casseli Hnos., piano factory.
Cassels, Francis, electric-light deposit works.
Cereale, Juan, wholesale grocery.
Chalier, Augusto, lithographing establishment.
Cisneros, José, timber.
Colomb, C., dyeing works.
Colombo Hermanos, brewers.
Corderiola Hnos. & Ca., grain merchants.
Deydier & Küttner, millers.
Diaz de Vivar, R., lime factory.
Etchart, Geronimo, cigars.
Fablet, Julio, wines.
Ferrari, Esteban, timber.
Florini, Pedro, contractor.
Gentile, Manuel, silk factory.
Giani, Angel E., harness and saddlery factory.
Giussani y Tainana, brewers.
Guardo, Daniel, cattle dealer.
Guichon ó Hijos, grocery importers and brewers.
Lanteri, Geronimo, corn merchant.
Lanusse & Ca., J. J., private bankers and commission agents.
Lanusse y Mendes, maritime agents.
Lanza, Domingo, general importer.

LA PLATA—Continued.

Merchants—Continued.

Llobet ó Hijo, timber and ironmongery.
Manri, Salvador, building contractor.
Manzoni, Virgilio, leather and general merchant.
Maull, Jorge, corn and hay.
Mendizabel Hnos., ironmongery.
Moroni y Tonesi, furniture-makers.
Nocetti y Gallino, paving contractors.
Palma y Zappettini, timber.
Pedemonte ó Hijo y Ca., building contractors.
Pedemonte y Rupprich, steam carpentry works.
Perez, Roque, dry goods.
Petit, Teófilo, shipping contractor.
Penser, Jacobo, stationery and printing works.
Puleston, E. T., general commission agent.
Rezabal, Ricardo, general grocery.
Riosa, Francisco, furniture factory.
Rozas, Insmaralde & Co., general hardware.
Sciurano y Ca., Manuel F., timber.
Segovia & Co., J. M., contractors and general merchants.
Serra, Leopoldo, hats and dry goods.
Szelagowski, Miguel, cloth merchant.
Tewes, Adolfo, corn and hay.
Toyos Hnos. & Ca., grocery importers.
Urrea & Ca., match factory.
Valarché & Ca., wine merchants.
Valle, Nocetti y Vila, Italian warehousemen.
Veneroni, C., notion warehouseman.
Zunda y Beranger, barge-owners.

PARANÁ.

Banks.

Banco Hipotecario Nacional.
Banco Nacional.

Commission merchants.

Amaret, Alexis.
Badello Hermanos.
Brugs & Hijos, Angel.
Gaura, Dionisio.
Guarri & Co.
Palmo & Hijos.
Perez & Co.
Predolini y Nuñez.

Merchants, general.

Amestegul, Guillermo.
Coll, Mariano.
Comas, Justo.
Cortaveria, Juan.
Dalurzzo, Juan.
Gaureguiza, Escolástico.

PARANÁ—Continued.

Merchants, general—Continued.

Otaño, Joaquin.
Palma, Gerónimo.
Palma, Pedro.
Palma, Santiago.
Pianello, José.
Pietro, Mariano.
Raffo, Santiago.
Scheaffini, Luis.
Solari, Juan.
Torres, Baltasar.
Vinas, Pedro.

ROSARIO.

Banks.

Banco de España y Rio de la Plata.
Banco de Italia y Rio de la Plata.
English Bank of River Plate, limited.
National Bank.
Provincial Bank.

Commission brokers.

Bates, Stokes y Ca.
Dolcini, Guiordano.
Pereyra, L.
Shaw, Turnbull.
Shon y Ca.

Commission merchants.

Alvarado y Puccio.
Frugoni, Juan.
Hertz & Minvielle.
Lorzano, Federico.
Machain & Co.
McKern & McLean, stationers, importers.
Muñoz & Co., Rodriguez.
Orgaz, Florentino & Co.
Palacios & Co.
Paz & Co., José.
Paz & Co., Manuel F.
Rodriguez, Enrique.
Tietjen & Co.
Zulder & Co., A.

Exporters.

Davies & Co., E., general produce, wheat, maize, hides, bones, etc.
Lodesma Bros., exporters of produce.
Machain & Co., exporters of produce.
Maspoli, Chiesa & Co., exporters of produce.
Omarini Bros., exporters of produce.

Groceries and provisions.

Berdaguer y Ca.
Borzone, B. y E.
Copello, Berllugieri.
Frugoni, Parpaglioni.

ROSARIO—Continued.

Groceries and provisions—Continued.

Paz, Brusterlot y Ca.
Paz y Ca., Manuel.
Recagno, Alceste.
. Sabathie et fils.
Crosta, Borelly & Co.
Day Hermanos, drugs.
Deurer & Co., hardware.
Dimarchi, Parodi & Co., drugs.
Eggington, John, dry goods.
Gay & Co., E., drainage, water, and gas materials.
Kropf, Enrique, crockery and fancy wares.
Lindesdorf & Co., Martin, machinery for agriculture.
Mantels & Pfeiffer.
Maspoli, Chiesa & Co., machinery and general hardware.
Ortiz & Co., Emilio.
Ottone é Hijo, Giorgio, dry goods.
Pinasco & Castignino, ship purveyors.
Schiffner & Co., general hardware.
Schlieper & Co., Herman, dry goods.
Senac & Co., Adolfo.
Sociedad Cooperativa, groceries.
Travella & Ghirlanda.

Iron and machinery.

Agar, Cross y Ca.
Bancoro, F., y Ca.
Chiesa Hnos.
Hopf, E.
Lenenweber y Ca.
Moore y Tudor.
Pinasco, Castagnino.

Merchants, general.

Acevedo y Pintos, importers of provisions and liquors.
Abbaladejo, Cárlos, dealer in produce.
Allendo, Miguel, importer of provisions and liquors.
Alvarado y Pucio, commission agents.
Amelong y Ca., importers of dry goods.
Barnett & Co., Lloyds' agents.
Barraco, Domingo, general importer.
Baker, Willis E.
Bernasconi, José, importer of pianos.
Berganini, H., architect.
Bianchi, A., gilder.
Bianchi, S., furniture importer.
Blythe & Co., general importers of machinery, hardware, crockery, fancy notions.
Brignardello é Hijo, Ventura.
Broqua, Scholberg & Co., gunsmiths and plate wares.

ROSARIO—Continued.

Merchants, general—Continued.

Browning, Robert, florist.
Caberja, Rossi y Ca., importers of boots and shoes.
Cafferena, E., ship broker and agent.
Canals, Dam & Co., contractors and commission agents.
Chiesa Hermanos, general importers and exporters.
Clark & Walker, brokers.
Cautero, Juan, tailor.
Chute & Brooks, photographers.
Coffin, H. B., commission agent and exporter of produce.
Colombres & Co., commission agents and exporters of produce.
Coutteret, Luiz.
Curry, H. F., stationer.
Davis & Co., E.
Day, Hermano, chemist and druggist.
Deroto, M., importer of furniture.
Deurer & Co., importers of provisions and liquors.
Diary, Joaquin, receiver of produce.
Dimarchi, Parodi y Ca., wholesale druggists.
Dreyfus Frères, importers, exporters, and general commission merchants.
Eggington, John, importer of dry goods-wholesale.
Egurvide y Vallarino, importers of dry goods, wholesale and retail.
Etchesortu y Casas, commission agents.
Ferguson, H. S., steamship agent.
Firmat, Ignacio.
Fisher, Henckler & Co., wholesale and retail ironmongers and agricultural implements.
Frey, E., carriage-builder.
Frugoni, Pagaglioni & Co., wholesale importers of provisions and liquors.
Garcia, F., dealer in produce.
Gay & Co., E., plumbers.
Gillies, A., pianos, etc.
Gogeascoechea & Co.
Gomez y Teran, retail dry goods.
Hall & Co., Alanson S.
Heurich, Marquadt & Co., grain brokers and shippers of grain.
Homan, E., broker.
Horler. Schultz & Co., wholesale importers of dry goods.
Hume Bros., railway contractors.
Kropf y Ca., E., importers of general merchandise, hardware.
Lao Prugent, J., consignee.
· Lavarello & Co., shipping agents.

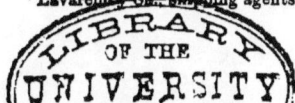

ROSARIO—Continued.

Merchants, general—Continued.

Lavendera, A., wholesale importer of provisions and liquors.
Leinenweber & Co., general importers.
McCallum & McCrae, importers of dry goods.
McKern, R., bookseller and general stationer.
Machado & Co., J., wholesale merchants and importers of provisions.
Machain & Co.
Mallet, H., land and commission agent.
Maristany & Co., wine merchants.
Marmol, Lanus & Co.
Maumas y Dodero, ship brokers.
Mayor, Pedro, foundry works.
Meigg, Son & Co., engineers and contractors.
Moore & Tudor, explosives.
Obieta, Torello & Co., bag manufacturers.
Omarini Bros., shippers of produce and consignees.
Orgaz & Co., general commission merchants.
Ortiz, C., provision merchant.
Ortiz, E. D., general importer and exporter.
Otero & Co., José.
Paul, William Taylor, pharmacist.
Paz, José F., commission merchant.
Paz & Co., M. J., commission merchants and exporters.
Pinto, Nicolás, y Hermano.
Poirano & Co., Andrade, confectioners.
Portalis Frères, general importers and exporters.
Puente & Co., Alonso, dry goods.
Recagno, Olcese & Cazeneuve.
Rivas & Co., Fernando, hardware.
Rouillon, Martini & Co.
Rufener & Co.
Sabathie, Juan.
Sampson & Co., shipping agents and brokers.
Santiago & Co., Alonso, grocers.
Schiffener & Co., agricultural machinery and general hardware.
Schelhas, J., opticians' materials.
Schlieper & Co., importers of dry goods.
Sel & Iñarra, flour and grain.
Senac & Co., A., importers.
Servine Bonifacio & Co., dry goods.
Sixbixthie ó Hijos, I.
Tietjen & Co., general importers of hardware, exporters of produce, and commission merchants.
Thomas & Davis, provisions.
Tixier, Armando, watches, clocks, and jewels.
Travella & Ghirlandor, ironmongers.
Vila, Nicasio & Co., importers general provisions.

ROSARIO—Continued.

Merchants, general—Continued.

Vizcaya Hermanos, jewel and diamond merchants.
Wildermuth Bros., dealers and exporters of grain.
Wolff, Schorr, bazar and fancy knickknacks.
Zimmermann & Co., jewelers.

Tobacco.

Barcia y Blanco.
Chozas, Urtuboy y Ca.

SANTA FÉ.

Banks.

Banco de la Provincia de Santa Fé.

Merchants.

Casser, R.
Foster & Co.
Gonzalez, Bergmann.
Perret, Gasser.
Reyes, J. M.
Sigel Bros.
Videla Hnos.

Groceries and provisions.

Aldao, E. R.
Colina, M.
Pinacco y Ca., J.

Iron and machinery.

Bonnazola, L.
Navarro, Gullen.

Dry goods and notions.

Rodrigues, Sandaza y Ca.

TUCUMAN.

Banks.

Banco Comercial de Mendez y Ca.
Provincial.

Bazars.

Avallone y Ca.
Carbonelli y Ca.
Casalas y Ca.
Pomo, P.

Groceries and provisions.

Estape, Nomos J.
Lopez, Adolfo.
Lopez, J. J.
Sesini, J.

Importers.

Correa, L. S.
Daffis, A.
Garcia y Ca., M.

TUCUMAN—Continued.

Importers—Continued.
Lindesdorf & Co., M.
Longo, F.
Molina, Segundo.
Navoni, F. R.
Perez, Moises.
Puigcero.
Riera, G

TUCUMAN—Continued.

Importers--Continued.
Soler y Julia.
Testo, Pampeo.
Zamora, C. y Ca.
Iron and machinery.
Fonteula y Ca.
Lindesdorf & Co., M.
Paverini, Barcia y Ca.

Bolivia.

CHUQUISACA.

Banks.
Banco Hypotecario.
Banco Nacional.

Merchants, commission and general.
Alvarez & Arana.
Arana, V.
Beckrich, M.
Bleichner, A.
Boeto & Hermano.
Dorado.
Duviels, Ibarnegaray & Co.
Gomez, J. B.
Gutierrez, D.
Herrero, José Ens.
Lora, Manuel.
Lora, N.
Prudencio, U.
Ramirez, M. J.
Saravia & Fernandez, J. M.
Urioste & Suarez.
Urriolagoitio & Hermanos.
Villa, Bernardó.
Williams & Co., G.

COCHABAMBA.

Agents, commercial.
Blackud, Ernesto.
Blanco Hijo, Benj.
Lafuente, Balbino.
Ramirez, Severo.
Urquidi, Rafael.

Banks.
Sucursal del Banco Nacional de Bolivia.
Sucursal del Banco Potosi.
Sucursal del Crédito Hipotecario.

Importers of European goods.
Bebin Hermanos.
Bomchard y Cia., Th.
Bubeck y Cia.

COCHABAMBA—Continued.

Importer of European goods –Continued.
Cavagnaro y Cia.
Fricke, German y Cia.
Hellmann. Guillermo.
Pullkammer, Jorge.
Read, Juan Guillermo.
Reinecke y Cia., Roberto.
Schwab y Cia., Manuel.
Schultze, Adolfo.
Torres y Hermano.

Importers of South American products.
Arego y Hermano.
Barrenechea y Cia.
Cosio, Manuel del Transito.
Cusicanqui y Cia.
Forseca, Juan Climaco.
Guzman, Victor A.
Levy, Adolfo.
Levy, Gabriel.
Morales & Bertrand.
Pacieri, Antonio.

LA PAZ.

Banks.
Banco Nacional.
Crédito Hipotecario de Bolivia.

Merchants, commission.
Antequera & Co., Eduard.
Louiza, Victor.
Santibañez & Co., M.
Solis, Leonardo.

Merchants, importers.
Alexander & Co.
Aliaga, José.
Anderson, Thomas H.
Caruncho, Juan de Mata.
Castagné y Cia.
Chinel y Cia.
Cusicanqui, Fermin.
Farvan & Co., V.

LA PAZ—Continued.

Merchants, importers—Continued.
Friberry, Harrison & Co.
Gerdes & Co., F.
Reinecke & Co., Rob.
Richter, Otto.
Schultze & Co., Ernst.
Segura & Arenas.
Todd, George L.

Novelties.
Club de la Pas.
Schultze & Co., Ernst.
Segala, Antonio.
Sibtner, Emilio.

Provision merchants.
Cueto, Vidaurre & Co.
Eduardo, Maximo.
Farfan & Co., V.
Peñarando, Juad.
Perez, Francisco.
Saenz, San Martin José B.

POTOSI.

Banks.
Banco de Potosi.
Sucursal del Banco Nacional.

Merchants, wholesale.
Behin Hermanos.
Cavagnaro y Ca., A.
Lieks & Schenor.
Fernandez, Juan Ant.
Ibarragaray, Juan.
Leitoy & Co.
Levy Hermanos.
Nava, Morales José.
Palmero, Salvador.
Richter, Otto.
Santa, Cruz Ameller.
Uriolagoitia y Ca.
Urioste & Co.
Zelmab, Manuel.

SANTA CRUZ DE LA SIERRA.

Banks.
Banco Nacional.
Banco del Potosi.

Merchants, importers.
Antelo & Co.
Bauzer, Jorge.
Carreno, Miguel.
Costas, Juan Manuel.
Chalot, Cárlos.
Landivar, Gumersindo.
Moreno, Isaac.
Peña, Manuel.
Roca, Cristanto.
Sancedo, Lucas.

SANTA CRUZ DE LA SIERRA—Continued.

Merchants, importers—Continued.
Torres Bros.
Vega, Pedro.
Vespa Bros.

Sugar manufacturers.
Antelo, Rosendo.
Chaves, Napoleon.
Gutierrez, Franc.
Gutierrez, Pastor.
Justiano & Sons, B.
Medina, Juan M.
Oliva & Morris.
Parada, Mariano.
Suarez, Manuel.
Suarez, Ricardo.
Suarez, Sixto.
Suvirana, Juan M.
Suvirana, Romulo,
Zambrana, Zoilo.

SUCRE.

Merchants.
Arana, Nictor & Julio.
Urriolagoitia y Ca.
Ybarnegaray, Juan.

TARIJA.

Banks.
Banco Nacional.

Merchants.
Araaz é Hijos, M.
Arenas, Teresa.
Echazu, Delio.
Jonnashon, José.
Krüger & Co.
Maldonado, Juan.
Maldonado & Sons, M.
Morales, Luis.
Moreno Bros., C.
Pacheco, B.
Pacheco, Hermogenes.
Valdivieso, Simon.
Vargas, Josefa.
Vargas, Ruperto.

Merchants, importers.
Araos & Sons, M.
Arce Bros.
Extensoro, Rosendo.
Jofre Hermanos.
Navajas & Sons.
Paz Bros.
Reyes, J.
Romero & Co.
Trigo Bros.

Brazil.

ALAGOAS.

Fancy goods.
Aguiar, José Candido de.
Almeida, Anna de Messias.
Maia, Ignacio Francisco.
Portello, José.
Rosa, Manoel Marques da.

Merchants, general.
Almeida, Anna de Messias
Caniana, João de Araujo.
Cunha, Manoel Esteves da.
Espirito Santo, Anacleto José do.
Gouvea, Manoel Francisco.
Lima, Marcos José de.
Oliveira, Belarmino José de.
Valente, Alcebiades Monteiro de Cerqueira.
Vasconcellos, M. Francisco Tourinho.

ANGRA DOS REIS.

Coffee merchants.
Jungueiros, Barão de.
Silva, Manoel Antonio Rodrigues da.

Hardware.
Soares Filho & Co.

Merchants, general.
Araujo Campos, Antonio José de.
Bittencourt, Antonio Placido.
Coutinho, Victorino José
Galindo, Oliveira, & Co.
Silva, Antonio José da, jr.
Silva, Coelho & Cardoso.
Soares Filho & Co.
Silva, Antoni) da, & Sá.

Tinware.
Belloni, Adão.
Paulo, Luiz Pedro.

ARACAJÚ.

Cotton factory.
Cruz & Co. (Lim.), proprietors of "Sergipe Industrial," spinning and weaving.

ARACAJÚ—Continued.

Druggists and chemists.
Motta, Pedro Amancio d'Almeida.
Rabello, Simeão Motta.

Foundry, iron.
Adams, James, & Co.

Merchants, import and export.
Brown, Robert, sugar, cotton, etc.
Coelho, José Roiz, salt, etc.
Costa, José Álves da, sundries.
Cruz, João Rodrigues da, sugar. cotton, etc.
Machado & Monteiro, sugar, cotton, etc.
Schramm & Co., sugar, cotton, etc.

Shopkeepers, general stores.
Coelho, Estevão Pereira, dry goods.
Coelho, João Pereira, dry goods.
Coelho, José Roiz. Bastos, dry goods and groceries.
Costa, José Alves da, grocery.
Felisola, João, dry goods.
Guilherme José Vieira, & Irmão, dry goods and hardware.
Maia, Gervasio Freitas, dry goods.
Mattos, João Victor de, dry goods and hardware.
Pungitori, Nicoláo, dry goods.

Soap works.
Espinheira & Irmão.

Unclassified merchant.
Schmidt, L.

ARACATY.

Candle manufacturers.
Martins, Francisco.
Ramos, José Candido.
Souza, Ramalho João Barboza de.

Cotton manufacturers.
Amaral, José Augusto Gurgel do.
Santos, Caminha Andre Ferreira dos.

34 BRAZIL.

ARACATY—Continued.

Dry goods.
- Brito, José Pereira de.
- Caminha, Alexandra Ferreira.
- Carvalho, Joaquim.
- Costa Lima & Irmão.
- Cunha & Irmão.
- Fernandes Manoel Alves.
- Figueiredo, Antonio Rodrigues da Silva.
- Fiuza Lima, Antonio de Fontes.
- Graca, Antonio Pereira da.
- Levy Bros.
- Oliveira, José Cicero Maria de.
- Pereira, José Alexandre.
- Pinto, Diasco.
- Pinto, Dias de.
- Possidonio, Solon, & Co.
- Ramos, Francisco Candido.
- Ramos, Francisco José.

Hardware.
- Gurgel & Figueiredo.

Soap manufacturers.
- Astudillo & Bussoms, Clemente.
- Astudillo & Bussoms, João.
- Possidonio, Solon, & Co.

Wax dealers.
- Levy Bros.
- Figuerido, Antonio Rodrigues da Silva.

BAHIA.

Dry goods.
- Cardoso & Baroco.
- Conde, Filho & Co.
- Costa, Pinto & Filhos.
- Fortunato, Pinho, Avellar & Co.
- Gomes & Ferreira.
- José Ferreira Pontes.
- Lefèvre & Son, Étienne.
- Mendonça de Athayde & Co.
- Moraes Irmão & Co.
- Nogueira & Filho.
- Oliveira, Domingos de, & Alves.
- Pedro Souza & Leite.
- Pontes, José Ferreira.

Exporters.
- Arkenoe, Franz, tobacco and coffee.
- Belchior, José Gonçalves, piassava and woods.
- Benn, Edward, & Son.
- Böving & Schröter, tobacco, sugar, and coffee.
- Briscoe, Finney & Co. piassava, cocoa, and coffee.
- Catlina & Co.
- Dennis, Blair & Co., diamonds.

BAHIA—Continued.

Exporters—Continued.
- Duder, G. H., cocoa, piassava, wood, and coffee
- Fisher & Co., sugar.
- Gunter & Mundt, piassava.
- Heineken, Meyer & Co., tobacco and coffee.
- Hirsch & Hers, skins, woods, and rubber.
- Keller, C. F., & Co., coffee.
- Lages & Co.
- Laporte & Co., sugar and tobacco.
- Lima & Amaral, Lopez da Silva.
- Oldach & De Hose, coffee, tobacco, piassava, and rubber.
- Ottens, F. H., tobacco, coffee, and cocoa.
- Rode & Pope, piassava, native curiosities, feathers, and flowers.
- Rossbach & Co. skins, hides, and rubber.
- Schindler, S. S., rubber, piassava, coquilho, nuts, medicinal plants, cane handles and sticks.
- Schramm, Stade & Co., coffee, sugar, cocoa, tobacco, and hides.
- Souza, Francisco de Assiz, coffee, cocoa, woods, hides, and tapioca.
- Stevenson, F., & Co., piassava, coffee, cocoa, sugar, hides, rubber, and woods.
- Vaughan, McNair & Co., coffee, cocoa, sugar, and carbonate.
- Williamson & Co., local produce, principally hides.
- Willison, George, Succ., piassava.
- Winkel, F. W., sugar, coffee, tobacco, piassava, rubber, and coquilho.

Furniture dealers.
- Alcantara, Pedro Joaquim de.
- Canuto & Irmão.
- Carmo, Nicolas Tolentino do.
- Ferrão, Francisco Luiz.
- Pereira, Victorino, jr.
- Santos, Sabino José dos.

Importers of books and stationery.
- Bernardes, José Evaristo.
- Cantolino, Moyses.
- Catalina & Co.
- Gallo, jr., & Co.
- Kock, Fernando.
- Magalhaes, José Luiz da Fonseca.
- Silva, Eduardo Pereira da.
- Silva, Lima & Amaral.

Importers of boots and shoes.
- Adelino, Fernandes, & Co.
- Alves & Co.
- Braga, José Joaquim de Araujo.
- Campos & Pontes.
- Clark & Co.

BAHIA—Continued.

Importers of boots and shoes—Continued.
Cunha, Joaquim da Silva.
Figueredo, Rocha & Co.
Gomes & Pinto.
Mangaba, Manuel Ricardo.
Motta & Co.
Oliveira & Baptista.
Pinheiro & Monteiro.
Placidi Dini.
Souza, Vianna & Co.
Teixeira, Leal & Co.
Voz, Agostinho, & Co.

Importers of coal and general merchandise.
Benn, Edward, & Son.

Importers of codfish.
Carvalho, Manoel Joaquin de.
Conde, Filho & Co.
Loureira, Vianna & Co.

Importers of dry goods in general.
Affonso, Henrique, & Trinidad.
Barrette & Sampeio.
Barros, Domingos Rodrigues de.
Belchior, Antonio Gonçalves.
Bessa, Ribeiro & Co.
Bompet, Samuel.
Borges, José Antonio.
Braga, Sampaio & Co.
Brandão, Antonio Francisco, & Co.
Brandão, Marques & Co.
Bruderer & Co.
Caldas, Fràncisco Pires.
Cardoso & Barroco.
Carvalho, João Maria, & Co.
Cerqueira & Fonseca.
Costa, Irmão & Co.
Costa & Co., Manuel Gomes.
Della-Cella, Virgilio.
Dias & Irmão.
Dutra, Antonio Ferreira.
Fernandes, Anselmo de Azevedo.
Ferreira, Santos & Costa.
Floro, Pinheiro & Requião.
Freitas Manuel Ferreira Guimarões.
Goes, José Oliveira.
Guimaraes, Affonso, & Co.
Hasselmann, F. A.
Jesurino, Sobrinho & Co.
Keller, C. F., & Co.
Kleinschmidt, Adolpho.
Lima, João Baptista de.
Luquino, François Henri.
Maltez, Francisco.
Massena & Co.

BAHIA—Continued.

Importers of dry goods in general—Continued.
Meister, Zoll & Co.
Mello, J., & Co.
Mello, Manoel Freire de.
Menezes, Eduardo de, & Co.
Miranda, Francisco de.
Moraes, Rodrigues de, & Co.
Moura, Guerra & Frazão.
Muller & Frey.
Nathan & Levy.
Novaes & Co.
Oldach & de Hasse.
Pedreira & Maudim.
Pinto, Costa & Co.
Pinto & Ferreira.
Podesta, Irmão & Co.
Ramos & Irmão.
Rocha & Irmão.
Ruas, Joaquim da Silva, & Co.
Sá, Pereira & Co.
Santos, A. J. Ferreira dos.
Silva, Junior, & Co.
Silva, Francisco Pinto da.
Silva, Guilherme Pinto da.
Silva, Lima & Carvalho.
Silva, Moreira & Souza.
Stevenson, F., & Co.
Teixerra, José Jacintho Rodrigues.
Tuvo, José Alexandre.
Vasconcellos, Frederico Pinto de.
Vaughan, McNair & Co.
Yates & Co.

Importers of drugs.
Aguiar, Irmãos & Co.
Araujo, Falceo & Co.
Barros, Francisco de, & Co.
Dias, da Rocha & Co.
Domingos, Gomes Borges.
Fernandes & Co.
Fonseca, Antonio Faria da.
Lima, Irmãos & Co.
Silva, Galdino Fernandes da.

Importers of earthenware and glassware.
Adelino, Veigas & Co.
Almeida, Correira de, & Co.
Alves, João Tolentino, & Co.
Amorim & Campos.
Azevedo, Chaves & Co.
Lacerda, João Ribeiro de.
Leite, Borges & Irmão.
Maria, José, & Co.
Oliveira & Cardoso.
Paraiso, Sigismundo.

BAHIA—Continued.

Importers of fancy goods.
Almeida, Antonio Bernardino de, & Co.
Ameida, Sampaio & Co.
Barretto & Sampeio.
Carvalho, Guilherme de, & Co.
Cunha, João, & Co.
Duarte, Costa & Co.
Ferreira, João Bispo.
Ferreira, Santos & Costa.
Fortuna, Francisco José da Silva.
Gomes, Cabral & Co.
Gunter & Mundt.
Magalhães & Martins.
Maria & Maltez.
Menezes, Ramos & Co.
Mello, Manoel Freire de.
Moreira, Manoel Pinto, & Co.
Moraes & Martins.
Oliveira, Antonio Marques de.
Palacio de Crystal.
Pedroso, Junior, & Co.
Pitombo, Francisco Alves.
Pontes, Henrique Ferreira.
Resende, José Coelho de.
Rezende, Soares & Co.
Ribeiro & Lopes.
Rodrigues, Antonio José, & Co.
Rodringues, Cardoso & Co.
Souza, Alexandre Cardoso de.
Souza, Francisco Fadigas de.

Importers of food products.
Avellar & Co.
Azevedo, Irmãos & Co.
Bastos & Co.
Belchior, José Gonçalves, & Co.
Benn, E., & Son.
Cardoso e Silva, Francisco.
Cardoso, José Ferreira.
Carvalho, Manoel Joaquim de, & Co.
Carvalho, M. M. de.
Castello, Branco e Ferreira.
Conde, Filho & Co.
Costa & Filhos.
Costa, Pinto & Lopes.
Costa, Junior, Antonio José da.
Couto, Antonio Luiz do, & Co.
Ferreira, Antonio, & Co.
Feria, Augusto.
Ferreira, Irmãos & Co.
Ferreira, Pedro, & Co.
Figueiredo, Simões de Oliveira.
Frazão & Co.
Freitas, Amencio de.
Ferreira, Fresco & Co.

BAHIA—Continued.

Importers of food products—Continued.
Lacerda, Augusto Francisco de.
Leitão, Nunes Antonio Vierra.
Lima, Brazeleiro, & Co.
Magarão & Co.
Miguel, Geraldo.
Machado, Albano Dias.
Marceline, José da Cunha.
Marques, João B. B., & Irmão.
Motta, Silva & Co.
Oliveira, Antonio de.
Pereira, Antonio Leite.
Pereira, Manuel Gomes, & Irmão.
Pereira, Mattos & Co.
Pimento & Co.
Pinto, Fortunato.
Sá, João Teixeira, & Co.
Santos, Manuel Pinto dos.
Santos, Matheus dos, & Co.
Silva & Co.
Schram, Stade & Co.
Stevenson, Frank, & Co.
Turinho, Eduardo, & Co.
Willison, George, Succ.
Wilson Sons & Co.

Importers of hardware.
Barbosa, Eduardo.
Costa, Santos & Co.
Fernando, Pinto & Co.
Gama & Co.
Machado, Soares & Co.
Perry, H. B.
Marinhos & Co.
Monteiro, Murça & Co.
Moreira & Co.
Oliveira, Antonio Fernandes de.
Pinto, Manuel Gomes de Sá.
Santos & Co.
Souza, M. J. Nevez de.
Vieira, Lima & Co.

Importers of jewelry, clocks, and watches.
Bompet, Samuel.
Gallo, Junior.
Maia, Francisco José de Araujo.
Ribeiro, Victor Soares.
Silva, Valeriano Tiburcio da.
Soares, Ferreira & Giunino.
Souza, Gonçalo Luiz de.

Iron founders.
Azevedo, Irmão & Leite.
Companhia Bahiana.
Cox, Irmãos & Co.
Moreira, Oliveira & Co.

BAHIA—Continued.

Manufacturers.
Brandão & Co., cotton goods.
Catalina & Dutra, cotton goods.
Coimbra, Manoel Luiz Pinto, cotton goods.
Costa, David & Co., cotton goods.
Danneman & Co., cigars.
Guendeville & Co., snuff.
Martinho Fernandes & Co., cigars.
Meuron & Co., snuff.
Moreira, Andrade & Co., cotton goods.
Moreira, Oliveira & Co., cotton goods.
Ramos & Co., Francisco, cotton goods.
Sampaio & Co., hats.

Marble dealers.
Oliveira, Plinio Celso de.
Palma, Thomaz Pereira.

Merchants.
Albuquerque, A. P.
Bastos Sobrinho.
Benn & Son.
Blanchet & Barboza.
Bolde, Kattemkamp & Co.
Böving & Schrötter.
Bruderer & Co.
Caldas, M. J. P.
Cardoso & Baroco.
Chuchu, A.
Colombo, Gust.
Conde, Filho & Co.
Costa, B., & Co.
Cramer, Frey & Co.
Cuigini Podest.
Cunha de Fetal.
Dutton Bros.
Espineira, J. C. R.
Ferraro & Figli.
Gavazza Bros.
Gomes, T. T.
Gunter & Co.
Gunter & Meindt.
Heiniken, Meyer & Co.
Hirsch, Coulon & Hanau.
Hoffmann & Co.
Keller, C. F., & Co.
Kelsch, Tib.
Lacerda, A. de.
Laporte & Co.
Lima, Diaz A.
Lohmann & Co.
Marinhos & Co.
Meister Zollel.
Mendonça d'Atthay.
Meuron & Co.

BAHIA—Continued.

*Merchants—*Continued.
Mira, E., & Co.
Moraes & Co.
Moreira, Irmãos & Co.
Moura, Guerra, Fiazão & Co.
Nathan & Levy.
Oldach & de Hose.
Oliveira & Irmãos.
Pereira, Marinho J.
Pereira & Monteiro.
Pinto, Novaes M.
Rumpf, M. H., & Co.
Santos, Miva & Co.
Santos, A. G. dos, & Co.
Saunders & Co.
Schirm, Wyhl & Co.
Silva, Moreira & Souza.
Simpson & Co.
Simon & Co.
Souza, A. T.
Steel, F. F.
Steffin & Co.
Stevenson & Co.
Teixeira & Hasselman.
Vaughan, C., & Co.
Vaughan, McNair & Co.
Vianna, Jounão, Hathan, Berke & Co.
Wilson, Hett & Co.
Yates & Co.

Photographers.
Gaensly & Lindermann.
Mendes, Ignacio.
Silva, Pedro Gonçalves da.

Pictures, frames and wall paper.
Alvares, João Tolentino.
Bosquet, Emilio.
Veigas, Adileno.
Vianna, Carlos.

Soap makers.
Araujo Motta & Co.
Ferreira Martins & Co.
Oliveira & Filho.

Sugar refiners.
Costa Lopes & Co.

Trunks, etc.
Conceição, Angelo Alves da.
Cotias, José Rufino dos Santos.
Fernandes, Ignez Maria, & Co.
Guimarães, Antonio José de Souza.
Jacob, Lucio.
Maria, Mauricio Antonio.
Pereira, Elesbão Francisco.

BAHIA—Continued.

Umbrella dealers.
Conde, Filho & Co.
Costa & Co., Manoel Gomes.
Lima, Araujo & Co.
Lima, José Perreira.
Lupin, Henri.
Messena & Co.
Moraes, Julio.
Solari, Agostinho
Undertakers.
Alcino & Co.
Brandão, Julio.
Caetano & Mattos.
Gouveia, Rosalino de Almeida.
Lacerda, José Bonifacio de.
Silva, Miguel Paulo da.

BARRA DE S. JOÃO.

Cigar manufacturers.
Andrade & Silva, Carlos Freire.
Castro, Guimarães João Antunes de.
Merchants.
Alves & Rocha.
Araujo, Odylo Domingues de.
Bastos, Fontes, Rabo & Co.
Bastos, M. A. T., & Co.
Carvalho, Miguel Monteiro de.
Cordeiro Zeferino, José.
Costa, Joaquim José da.
Fonseca, João Xavier da.
Gonçalves & Irmão.
Lopes, Paulo, & Irmão.
Mello, Ignacio Xavier de, & Co.
Moreira, Joaquim Alves, junior.
Motta, Julio Barbosa de.
Oliveira, Manoel Joaquim do.
Pereira, Antonio David.
Pereira, Domingos Ribeiro.
Pereira, Joaquim David.
Pinto Marcellino, D., & Co.
Peixoto & Lima.
Prata & Rocha.
Real & Irmão.
Ramos, Manoel Gonçalves.
Rebello Henrique Xavier.
Silva, Albino Rodrigues da.
Souza, José Ferreira de.

CABO FRIO.

Merchants, general.
Alves, Luiz Henrique.
Beranger, Adolpho.
Beranger, Ernesto.
Barbosa, Jeronymo José.

CABO FRIO—Continued.

Merchants, general—Continued.
Bragança, Fernandes, & Co.
Costa, Leopoldo Lopes.
Cruz, Manoel Joaquim da, & Silva.
Coelho, Antonio Alves.
Dias, Samuel José.
Gomes, Gualter Antonio.
Gomez, Joaquim.
Gouvêa, José Maria de.
Marques, João da Silva.
Motta, Joaquim José Baptista da.
Novelino, Vicente Ant.
Rocha, José Fr. Gomes da.
Souza, Antonio Jorge de.
Souza, Valente Francisco de.

CAMPOS.

Boots and shoes.
Corrêa & Sobrinho.
Couret Irmão & Pessanha.
Esberard & Julio.
Figueiredo, Miguel.
Guimarães, Domingos Antonio Teixeira.
Guimarães, José Gomes.
Luiz, Candido de.
Nunes, José Gonçalves.
Oliveira & Monteiro.
Pereira & Cardoso.
Pereira, Albino Joaquim.
Rosa, Miguel.
Silva, Vasco Machado da.
Souza, Figueiredo.
Cabinetmakers.
Andrade, José Christovão de.
Carneiro, Leonardo Caetano.
Carvalho, José Joaquim Pinto de.
Nascimento, José Rangel do.
Oliveira, Manoel Gomes de.
Paula Neves, Francisco de.
Serbas, Nicolau.
Cigar and tobacco manufacturers.
Antunes, Antonio Manoel.
Barrobino, Miguel.
Guimarães & Antunes.
Lisboa, Santos & Co.
Macedo, J. J. Rodrigues de.
Meira, José Alves.
Santa Rita, José Francisco.
Country produce exporters.
Carvalho, Cezar Augusto de.
Castro, José Fernandes de.
Costa, Antonio Rodrigues da.
Costa, Boaventura Peixoto.
Guimarães, Antonio Leite de Freitas.

CAMPOS—Continued.

Country produce merchants—Continued.
Merelles, Sobrinho José Riberio de.
Silva, Castro Antonio Ferreira da.
Souza, Vianna Guilherme Candido de.
Torres, José Alves.

Druggists.
Campos, Antonio M. dos.
Delgado & Co.
Oliveira, Aurelio Carvalho de.
Reis, João Rodrigues dos.
Sampaio, Esequiel Pinto de.
Santa Caza de Misericordia.
Silva & Irmão, Venancio de.
Silva, Joaquim Manoel Venancio de.
Souza Matta, José Joaquim de.
Teidyl & Cruz.

Foundries.
Thompson, Block & Co.
Torres, Francisco Eugenio.
Victor & Co.

Hardware.
Campos, Felippe Alexandrino de Oliveira.
Machado, Vianna & Daniel Sampaio.
Magalhães, Antonio Vicente de.
Oliveira, Santos Manoel.
Rocha & Co.

Machinery.
Lima, Antonio José Monteiro.
Rochert, Arthur.
Spilstu, Henrique.
Zulckner, Antonio.

Watchmakers.
Costa, Antonio Teixeira da.
Fritz, G.
Leite, José Rodrigúes.
Rauff, João.

CEARÁ.

Alimentary products.
Albuquerque, Antonio Alfonso
Geraldo, Antonio Domingo.
Pinheiro, Dias & Co.
Rego, Candido Gomes do.
Simões, Irmão & Co.

Cigar manufacturers.
Lopes, Silva & Co.
Silva, Marques da, & Co.

CEARA—Continued.

Cotton factory.
Guijão, Hollando & Co.
Pompeu & Irmãos.

Earthenware and china merchants.
Confucio Pamplona & Co.
Da Costa Bastos, João.
Joaquim Felicio d'Oliveira Lima & Irmão.

Export merchants, general.
Abreu, Gomes & Co.
Albano & Irmão.
Barrozo & Irmão.
Boris frères.
Bruno, I. Abdon & Co.
Cunha, Narciso, Primos & Co.
Cunha, S. R., & Co.
Faria & Sobrinho.
Gomes do Rego, Candido.
Gradvohl Frères.
Justa, Antonio G. da, & Co.
Levy Frères.
Machado, Coelho & Co.
Marcal, José, & Co.
Possidonio, Porto & Co.
Rocha, Dias da, & Co.
Rossbach Bros., skins and rubber.
Singlehurst & Co.

Stein, Abe, & Co., skins and rubber.

Gunpowder importers.
Araujo, Motta & Co.
Boris Frères.
Singlehurst & Co.

Import merchants, general.
Albano & Irmão.
Araujo, Motta & Co.
Areas & Co.
Barbarosa, Gomes & Co.
Boris Frères.
Braga, Filho & Co.
Bruno, I. Abdon & Co.
Chagas Nabor A. & Co.
Cunha, Narciso, Primos & Co.
Cunha, S. R.. & Co.
D'Albuquerque, A. Alfonso.
Gomes do Rego, Candido.
Gradvohl Frères.
Justa, Antonio Gonçalves da, & Co.
Maia & Irmãos.
Perreira, Bernardo José.
Singlehurst & Co.

CEARÁ—Continued.

Ironmongers.
Amaral, João Antonio do, & Co.
Cabral, Conrado.
Villar, João da Silva.

Sugar refiners.
Costa & Co.

Wholesale drugs and paints.
Rocha, Guilherme, & Co.

DESTERRO.

Dry goods.
Bainha, Ernesto.
Boeker, Emilio.
Costa Campinas, Innocencio José da.
Faria & Malheiros.
Goeldner & Regis, Germano.
Habenbeck, Catharina.
Haenschecke, Fernanda.
Haensecke, Francisco.
Pereira, Severo Francisco.
Silva, Xavier Antonio Ramalho da.
Wendhausen, A., & Co.

Hardware.
Cabral, José Luis Alvares, & Co.
Cosia, Jacques Joaquim Martins, & Co.
Moltman & Filho.
Souza, Junior, Anastacio Silveira de.

Importers and exporters, foreign goods.
Capeker, Car, & Co.
Demaria, João Bonfant.
Fison, H. W., & Co.
Moltmann & Filho.
Trompowsky & Brandt.
Wilhal & Co., Ernesto.

Merchants, native produce.
Bronhoza, Veiga & Co.
Costa, Boaventura da, wines.
Costa, Domingo José da.
Lemos, João de Prado, & Co.

Soap and candle manufacturers.
Vieira, Mollo & Co.

MACAHÉ.

Cigar and tobacco manufacturers.
Oliveira, Luiz Carvalho de.
Silva, Feliciano Antonio da.

Merchants, general.
Almeida, Monteiro de, & Co.
Almeida & Co.

MACAHE—Continued.

Merchants, general—Continued.
Carvalho Torres, Antonio José da.
Rosario & Motta.
Santos, Costa & Co.
Soares & Irmão.

MACEIÓ.

China and glassware.
Costa, Nicolau Tolentino da.
Guimarães, Manoel Ferreira.

Commission merchants.
Achilles, Americo, & Irmão.
Carneiro, Tiririca & Co.
Cruz, Mattos Serra, João da.
Leite & Ferreira.

Hardware.
Coelho & Filhos, Viuva.
Caldes, Antonio Pereira.
Leite, Jacintho José Nunes.
Martins, Gonçalves & Co.
Montenegro, Vincente Bezerra.

Exporters and importers.
Aguiar, Vicente Alves de.
Almeida, Guimarães & Co.
Bandeira, Coutinho & Co.
Baxwell, Jn. H., & Co.
Borghesi Irmão & Terri.
Borstelmann & Co.
Carneiro Tiririca & Co.
Carvalho & Co.
Carvalho, Tiburcio Alves de.
Carvalho & Filho.
Cruz Mattos.
Fontan, Manoel, & Co.
Ferreira, João Martins.
Guimarães, José Antonio de Almeida.
Gonçalves, Guimarães & Co.
Leite & Ferreira.
Leite, Francisco Nunes.
Leite, Jacinto José.
Machado, José Teixeira.
Medeiros, Viuva, & Filhos.
Pohlman & Co.
Ramalho, Manoel.
Ribeiro, Agostinho, & Cazal.
Serra, João da.
Silva Braga, Manoel José da.
Silva Leão & Filhos.
Silva, Rego Antonio da.
Silva, Rego Taciano da.

MACEIÓ—Continued.

Exporters and importers—Continued.
Torres Irmãos.
Vasconcellos, Guimarães & Co.
Vandeval, Pedro.
Venancio, Candido & Co.
Wucherer, Gustavo Guilherme.

Sugar refiners.
Almeida Monteiro, João de.
Carvalho, Joaquim Gomes de.
Costa, Victor Estanislau de Andrada.
Leite, Ferreira & Co.
Nunes Leite, Francisco.
Sampaio, Miranda de, & Co.

Tobacco and cigar manufacturers.
Moraes & Co.
Silva, Lins & Co.
Vasconcellos, Joaquim de Rego.

Umbrella manufacturers.
Bertolmy Pedro.
Gouvêo, Manoel Francisco.
Lima, Marcos José de.
Vaudavel, Pedro.

MANÁOS.

Merchants.
Andresen, J. H.
Bernardo Bockris & Co.
Booth & Co.
Brocklehurst & Co.
Campos & Co.
Candido, C. S. Roza, & Co.
Freitas, Bic ι & Co.
Kahn, Polack & Co.
Moucheiro & Co.
Pedrosa, Motta & Antongini.
Potey, G. Rabert, & Co.
Rodrigues Vieira & Co.
Santos, G. M., & Co.
Schill, L., & Irmão.
Silva, Freitas & Co.
Vaz, J. da Costa.

MANGARATIBA.

Coffee and sugar merchants.
Botelho, Pedro.
Corrêa, Pio José.
Custodio, Antonio José.
Gennel, Eugenio.
Godinho, Felisberto.
Lopes, Viuva, & Filhos.

MANGARATIBA—Continued.

Coffee and sugar merchants—Continued.
Maciel, José Francisco.
Sveder, Pedro.
Speltz, Alexandre.
Steckler, Frederico Antonio.
Pieira, Francisco Antonio.

Merchants, general.
Affonso, Antonio Joaquim.
Affonso, A. J., & Co.
Abreu, José Maria Marques de.
Barbosa, Frederico Antonio.
Barrocas, José Rodrigues.
Costa, Alexandro Netto da.
Costa, Velho M. J. da.
Guerra, Antonio Narciso.
Lopes & Telles.
Lopes, João Francisco.
Mello, José Corrêa de.
Mello, Francisco Corrêa de.
Rubião, Joaquim G. A. M.
Silva Braga, José Antonio Herdeiros de.
Souza, José Joaquim de.
Souza, Telles J. J. de.
Silva, Manoel Gomes da.
Vasconcellos & Filhos.

MARANHAM.

Commission merchants.
Airlie, Henry.
Ribeiro, José Pedro, & Co.
Santos, Luiz Ferreira da Silva.

Export merchants—cotton, sugar, hides.
Airlie, Henry.
Castro, Manoel Martins de, & Co.
Guimarães, Bastos & Co.
Lima, Antonio Joaquim de, & Co.
Lima, Francisco Antonio de, & Co.
Maia Sobrinhos & Co.
Moreira & Saraiva.
Ribeiro, José Pedro, & Co.
Thomson, Rosa, & Co.

Grain merchants.
Jorge & Santos.
Irmãos Martins.
Nogueira, Alves & Co.
Oliveira, Santos & Co.

General import merchants.
Almeida, junior, & Co.
Almeida, Marcelino Gernes d'.
Almeida, Santos & Teixeira.
Almeida & Co.
Borralho & Co.

MARANHAM—Continued.

General import merchants—Continued.
Castro, Manoel Lopes de, Irmão & Co.
Castro, Manuel Martins de, & Co.
Correia, José Julio, & Co.
Dias, Bento, Irmão & Co.
Fernandes, Luiz Manoel, & Irmão.
Fragoso & Co.
Gomes, Nogueira & Co.
Graca & Co.
Guimarães, Bastos & Co.
Guimarães, Novaes & Co.
Lima, Antonio Joaquim de, & Co.
Lima, Francisco Antonio de, & Co.
Lopes. Antonio da Costa.
Maia, Sobrinhos & Co.
Moreira & Saraiva.
Moreira, José Domingues, Filho & Co.
Moura, José Antonio Rodrigues de.
Martins, Ferreira & Co.
Pereira, Britto & Irmão.
Pires & Ferreira.
Santos & Irmão.
Santos, Crispim, A., & Co.
Silva, Bernadino, Filho & Co.
Silva, José Joaquim Lopes da, & Filho.
Souza, José Moreira de, & Co.
Souza, José Luiz de, filho.
Thomson, Rosa & Co.
Valente Trajano & Co.
Vinhaes & Couto.
Youle, William.

Ironmongers.
Broadbent, William.
Cunha, Santos & Co.
Graid & Co.
Maia, Oliveira & Co.
Peixoto, Dias & Co.

Ship chandlers.
Valle & Co.

Unclassified merchant.
Tavares, J. J.

NATAL

Chemists.
Garcia, Gervazio.
Madeiros, José de.
Soares, Henriques.

General merchants.
Domingues de Oliveira.
Ferreira de Mello.
Graf, J. N., & Co.
Macedo Lapa.

NATAL—Continued.

Merchants, general—Continued.
Pereira, Joaquim Ignacio.
Sampaio, Daniel.

PARÁ.

Importers and exporters.
Andrade & Co.
Aguiar & Co.
D'Aguiar, Silva & Co.
Almeida & Filho.
Amaral, Maria de, & Co.
Amorim, Tavares & Co.
Antunes, A., & Co.
Araujo & Co.
Aréas, T. F.
Azevedo, Castro, & Co.
Bastos, Gonçalves & Co.
Bastos & Irmão.
Calheiros & Co.
Calheiros & Oliveira.
Carvalho & Irmão.
Casanova & Irmão.
Castro, L., & Co.
Cerqueira, Lima & Co.
Cintra, Joaquim, & Co.
Coimbra, Cunha & Co.
Condurcé & Co.
Costa, Dias da, & Co.
Cronan, Deniz, & Co.
Cullire, Deniz, & Co.
Ferreira, Ant. Balt.
Ferro, Morão & Co.
Fonseca & Co.
Fonseca, Coutinho & Co.
Goes & Co.
Hollanda, B. J., & Co.
Ivo, Joaquim dos Sautos.
Kingdom & Co.
Leite, Alberto, & Co.
Leite, Manoel Mandes & Co.
Levy, J., & Alb.
Lima, Cerqueira & Co.
Lima & Hollanda.
Lobo, A., & Co.
Martins & Co.
Menezes, junior, & Co.
Miranda, C. de, & Co.
Oliveira, junior, D. de.
Oliveira, F. de, & Irmãos.
Oliveira, M. d', & Co.
Paiva & Co.
Pedrozo, Motta & Autongini.
Pereira, da Silva, & Co.

PARÁ—Continued.

Importers and exporters—Continued.
Pinho, A. de.
Righils, A., & Co.
Rocha, Machado & Co.
Saldanha & Co.
Salza, F., & Co.
Sampaio, G., & Co.
Schramm & Co.
Silva, A. da, & Co.
Silva, F. da, & Co.
Silva, G., & Co.
Silva, J. da Costa.
Silva, J. Nunes da, & Co.
Silva, N. da.
Silva, Ribeiro da, & Co.
Singlehurst, Brocklehurst & Co.
Sinha, M. da.
Soares, A., & Co.
Souza, A. L., & Co.
Souza, D. de, & Co.
Teixeira Bastos Irmãos.
Vianna, J. C. G., & Co.
Vieira da Cunha, F. A., & Co.
Watrin & Co.

Merchants, general.
Almeida Irmãos & Co.
Alves, Gerardo Ant., & Filho.
Araujo, João Pinto d', & Filho.
Brenner & Co.
Campbell, A., & Co.
Carvalho, Manoel José de, & Co.
Cornaings, Moran & Co.
Corrêa & Co.
Cristiansen, Aug., & Co.
Costa, Gaudencio da, & Filhos.
Cronan, Denis, & Co.
Cullerre Bros.
Duiheiro, Manoel, & Co.
Elias, José Nunes da Silva, & Co.
Freitas, Manoel de, & Irmão.
Furlad & Irmão.
Gäensby Jacques.
Iglezias, José Maria.
Jam, Ristrop & Co.
Jeffries & Co.
Levy, J. & A.
Martins, Nicolao.
Mouraille, P., & Hermano.
Oliveira, José Corréa d', & Co.
Parisa, Manoel Im. de, & Co.
Raio, Miguel José, & Co.
Ribeiro, Gualter José.
Saraiva & Co.
Sinay & Lion.
Singlehurst, Brocklehurst & Co.

PARÁ—Continued.

Merchants, general—Continued.
Tappenbeck, Brambeer & Co.
Zeller & Co.

Sugar refiners.
Almeida, Nunes de, & Co.
Bonçon & Co.
Carreira, Joaquim Francisco, & Co.
Castro, Souza & Co.
Ferreira, Francisco, & Co.
Gomes, José Joaquim, & Co.
Ivo, Santos & Irmão.
Leal, Pedro Nunes.
Maciel & Gomes.
Oterêllo & Almoêdo.
Pires, André, & Camanho.
Pontes, Fernando, & Barreiros.
Pinho, João Antonio.
Pimenta, Joaquim Mendes.
Pereira & Gonçalves.
Pinho & Co.
Pires, Soares & Irmão.
Ruão, José Moreira.
Ruiz, Julião Augusto.
Silva, M. Pinto da, & Co.
Teixeira, João Manoel P., & Co.
Vigia, Pedro Fernandes.

Unclassified merchants.
Amazon Steam Navigation Co., Ltd.
Amorim & Co.
Antonio Brito & Co.
Antonio Couto & Co.
Bastos, Araujo & Co.
Bastos, M., & Co.
Bernard, A., & Co.
Booth & Co.
Castro, Irmão & Co.
Cesar Figueiredo & Co.
Chermont, Aguiar & Co.
Christiano Suhl & Co.
Compania Mercantil do Pará.
Carvalho & Co.
Coimbra, J., & Co.
Compª. Estrada de Ferro Paraense.
Coutinho, Braga & Co.
Correia, M. J. da Rocha, & Co.
Diogo, Manoel de Souza, & Co.
Domingos, José de Carvalho, & Co.
Fco. Jm. Pereira & Có.
Fernandes d'Oliveira & Co.
Ferreira Salgado & Co.
Figueiredo & Co.
Fortunato, junior, & Mendes.
Francellino Lopes de Azevedo.
Freire, Castro & Co.
Gil, J. R., & Co.

PARÁ—Continued.

Unclassified merchants—Continued.
Ignacio, José da Silva, & Co.
Jm. Nunes da Silva Matta & Co.
João José de Freitas & Co.
Julio Bastos & Co.
Klantão, H.
La Rocque & Co.
La Rocque, da Costa & Co.
La Rocque, Rocha & Co.
La Rocque, Veiga & Co.
Lemos & Leite.
Marques, Braga & Co.
Mel. J. Pereira Leite & Co.
Mello & Co.
Mesquita & Co.
d'Oliveira, A. F., & Co.
Norton & Co.
Paes de Carvalho, Dr.
Pedroso, Motta & Antongini.
Pereira, Lima & Co.
Pereira Purcell & Co.
Pires, Teixeira & Co.
Rebello, M. J., junior, & Co.
Ricardo José da Cruz & Co.
Robinson & Norton.
Rodrigues Vieira & Co.
Rudolph Zietz.
Santos, Z. Y. dos, & Co.
Silva, Matta & Co.
Silva, Sá & Co.
Solheiro, H., & Co.
Souza Irmãos & Co.
Sulzer & Co.
Teixeira de Mesquita & Co.
Well & Mendell.

PARAHIBA.

Merchants, produce.
Carvalho, Caetano Daniel de.
Figueiredo & Irmão.
Motta, Jeremias Isaias da.
Oliveira Filho & Co.
Pires & Co.
Veigas, Manoel Martins.

Merchants, stuffs.
Brito, Lyra & Co.
Castro, Irmão & Co.
Maia, José de Azevedo.
Soares, Adolfo Eugenio.
Silva, Ferreira & Co.
Vinagre & Co.

Unclassified merchants.
Cahn Frères & Co.
Paiva, Valente & Co.
Santos, Gomes & Co.

PARANAGUÁ.

Importers.
Balster, A. L., & Co.
Costa, C. M. da, & Co.
Drusina & Co.
Gomes, Joaquim Soares.
Leite & Co.

Importers and exporters, general.
Balster, Arthur B.
Correia & Co.
De Nacar, Visconde, & Filho.
Gomes, Joaquim Soares.
Gomes, Antonio Henrique.
Leite & Co.
Mendes, Cunha & Co.
Soares & Co.
Stolle, Drusina & Co.

PELOTAS.

Breweries.
Eifler, Ernest.
Frank, Carl.
Heartel, Leopoldo.
Oliveiro & Ca.

Commission agents.
Hislop, L. W., ships, salt, etc.
Konow, Gustav, dry goods.
Madureira, José Pinto de, machines, etc.
Silva, Julio J. da, wines, etc.

Merchants, exporters—hides, etc.
Granja & Nogueira.
Leite, Paulino T. C.
Maurell, Filho & Co.
Rocha & Co.
Souza, Francisco Nunes de.
Trapaga & Zórrilla.

Merchants, importers.
Borges, Alsina & Co., wines, provisions, etc.
Condeixa, A., & Co., dry goods.
Castro, Antonio Dias de, dry goods.
Conceição & Co., hardware.
Gomes, Otero & Co., wines, provisions, etc.
Levy Irmãos & Co., jewelry.
Leite, Irmão & Co., wines, provisions, etc.
Lupi Irmãos, dry goods.
Main, Santos & Co., wines.
Mausch & Co., wines, provisions.
Moyses, Gompertz, French goods.
Olive & Zamorano, wines, provisions.
Pinheiro, João, & Co., hardware.
Ramos, Antonio Ferreira, d y goods.
Rech & Co., hardware, etc.
Rios, Lopez & Co., dry goods.

PELOTAS—Continued.

Merchants, importers—Continued.
Rocha, Theodozio da, & Co., wines, provisions, etc.
Sequeira & Co., hardware.
Scholberg, Jouclá & Silva, firearms, etc.
Sequeira, Eduardo C., drugs, etc.
Souza, Bernardo José de, crockery, etc.
Trápaga, Ramon & Co., dry goods.
Traeb & Co., hardware.
Warncke & Dörken, hardware.

Unclassified merchants.
Granja & Voqueira.
Leite, Irmão & Co.
Paulino Teixeira da Costa Leite.

PERNAMBUCO.

Cigars and tobacco, manufacturers and merchants.
Azevedo & Co.
Augusto José & Co.
Bourgard & Co.
Braga, Antonio Lopes.
Cruz, Antonio Francisco da.
Costa & Pereira.
Esnaty, Isaac.
Falcão & Pires.
Faria, Rodrigues de, & Co.
Ferreira & Co.
Figueiredo, José Antonio Dominguez de.
Freitas, Joanna Joaquina de.
Gonçalves & Co.
Gomes, Coimbra & Co.
Gomes, Manoel, & Co.
Leal & Co.
Lopes, Moreira & Co.
Mello, Araujo & Co.
Meurón & Co.
Neves & Costa.
Oliveira, Manoel Rodrigues de, & Co.
Pereira, Faria & Co.
Pereira & Carvalho.
Pessoa & Co.
Ramos, José Machado.
Santos & Co.
Santos, Mello & Co.
Seve, Domingo F., & Co.
Villaverde, Joaquim Gonçalves, & Co.

Importers, food products.
Almeida Machado & Co.
Amorim, Joaquim & Co.
Araujo, Guedes and Fº. de.
Bastos Amorim & Co.
Druzina, R. de.
Esnaty, Rodrigues & Co.
Fernandes & Irmão.

PERNAMBUCO—Continued.

Importers, food products—Continued.
Fonseca Irmãos & Co.
Fraga, Rocha & Co.
Gonçalves, Rosa & Fernandes.
Guimarães, Rocha & Co.
Loureiro, Antonio, & Co.
Nuesch, H., & Co.
Paiva, Valente & Co.
Soares do Amaral & Irmão.
Souza, Antonio Alves de.

Importers, stuffs.
Bernet & Co.
Burle, H., & Co.
Cramer, Frey & Co.
Lima, Rodrigues & Co.
Machado & Pereira.
Olinto, Jardim & Co.
Sequeira, Antonio de.
Wild, D. P.

Merchants, commission.
Alves, Miguel José.
Borstelman & Co.
Brown & Co.
Burle, H., & Co.
Forster, H., & Co.
Johnston, Pater & Co.
Julio & Irmão.
Labile, Augusto.
Laporte & Co.
Niemeyer, Cahn & Co.
Pereira, Carneiro & Co.
Sulzer, Kaufmann & Co.
Tavares de Mello Genro & Co.
Travassos, Orestes, & Co.
Wild, D. P.

Merchants, general.
Albuquerque & Filhos.
Alencar, José Franklin de.
Amorim Irmãos & Co.
Antunes, Pedro, & Co.
Azevedo, Alfredo Soares de.
Baltar & Irmão & Co.
Bernet & Co.
Blackburn, Needham & Co.
Borstelman & Co.
Boxwell, J. H.
Brown & Co.
Burle, H., & Co.
Cascão, Eugenio Gonçalves.
Calaça, Dr. Francisco José Gomes.
Christiansen, Theodoro.
Coelho, Eugenio, & Vieira.
Coelho, José Ferreira.
Cramer, Trey & Co.
Cunha, A. P. da.

PERNAMBUCO—Continued.

Merchants, general—Continued.
Drummond, Gaspar de.
Foster, Henry, & Co.
Garcia, Alfredo Henrique.
Gonçalves Irmãos & Co.
Guimarães, Francisco Ribeiro.
Halliday, William, & Co.
Joaquim, R. T. de.
Johnston, Pater & Co.
Labile, Augusto Lima.
Leal, Antonio Gomes Miranda.
Leal & Irmão.
Lidstone, N. J.
Lobo & Filho, José da Silva.
Lustosa, Arruda & Co.
Maia, Pacheco & Co.
Maia & Rezendo.
Mattos Irmãos, Gomes de.
Medeiros, Antonio Ignacio do Rego.
Mehão, Leopoldo Borges Galvão.
Mello, Genro & Co.
Monhard, Huber & Co.
Nüesch, H., & Co.
Olinto Jardim & Co.
Oliveira, Maia Antonio de.
Pereira, Carneiro & Co.
Rodrigues, Lima & Co.
Sulzer, Henry.
Silva, Francisco Manoel da, & Co.
Vianna, Antonio Duarte C.
Vieira, A., & Co.
Waschmann, Conrado.
Wild, D. P.
Wilson, Sons & Co. (Limited).

Sugar merchants, commission.
Accioly, Adolpho Targino.
Azevedo, Alfredo Soares de.
Albuquerque & Filho.
Amorim Irmãos & Co.
Baltar Irmãos & Co.
Beltrão, David Ferreira, & Co.
Benicio & Co.
Barbosa, Bruno Alves.
Burle & Co.
Corrêa & Co.
Cascão, Francisco, & Filho.
Castro, J. J., & Co.
Carvalho, Moraes João José de.
Cruz, Joaquim Monteiro da.
Castro, Moura, José Joaquim de.
Cruz, Manoel, & Co.
Furtado, Antonio João.
Gonçalves, José Lourenço.
Guimarães, Francisco.
Leal & Irmão.

PERNAMBUCO—Continued.

Sugar merchants, commission—Continued.
Leite, Francisco José.
Moutinho, João Pereira.
Moura & Filhos.
Paula, Amorim Francisco de.
Ribeiro, Pinto.
Saraiva & Mello, Henrique Xavier de A.
Souza, Augusto Octaviano de.
Souza Pinheiro & Co.
Travassos, Orestes, & Co.
Wanderley & Bastos.

Sugar refiners.
Albuquerque, Manoel Alves Laurenço, & Co.
Alves, Pinto & Co.
Baptista & Alves.
Bastos, B. Antonio Pereira.
Bernardino Manoel Pereira & Co.
Barros, Viuva de M. Gonçalves de.
Costa & Co.
Corrêa, Gonçalves & Co.
Carneiro, João Alves Lima.
Costa, José Antonio Siqueira da.
Guimarães, José Joaquim Gonçalves.
Sena, Manoel Alves de, & Co.
Silva, Luiz Ferreira da, & Co.
Silva, Salgueiral Joaquim da.
Valente, Irmão & Co.
Vasconcellos, Luiz de, & Co.
Viamonte, Antonio Alves.

Unclassified merchants.
Alves Irmãos.
Amorim & Co.
Araujo, Castro & Co.
Beltrão & Costa.
Bernardino Duarte de Campos & Co.
Bernardo Joaquim Gomes & Co.
Borstel, Henry C.
Carlos Alves Barboza.
Carvalho & Co.
Castro, Lemos & Co.
Costa & Medeiros.
Costa, Lima & Co.
Dias Fernandes & Co.
Domingo, Cruz & Co.
Domingos, Ferreira da Silva & Co.
Fernandes da Costa & Co.
Fernandes & Irmãos.
Ferreira, Rodrigues & Co.
Figueiredo, Costa & Co.
Gibson, Charles.
Gonçalves, Rosa & Fernandes.
Guedes de Araujo & Co.
Guimarães & Valente.
Jm. Alves da Silva Santos.
Jm. Ferreira de Carvalho & Co.

BRAZIL.

PERNAMBUCO—Continued.

Unclassified merchants—Continued.
João de Aquino Fonseca.
João Ferreira da Costa.
João F. Ferreira & Co.
João Fernandes d'Almeida.
Joaquim Duarte Simões & Co.
Joaquim Philippe & Aguiar.
José Barboza de Carvalho.
José Joaquim Alves & Co.
José Rufino Climaco da Silva.
Lopes Irmãos.
Lopes, Magalhães & Co.
Lopes, Alheiro & Co.
Machado, Lopes & Co.
Manoel dos Santos Araujo.
Manoel Martins Ribeiro.
Miguel Joaquim Carlos Cardozo.
Niemeyer, Gomes & Co.
Parente, Vianna & Co.
Pereira de Faria & Co.
Ramos & Co.
Seixas & Co.
Seixas Irmãos.
Silva, Fernandes & Co.
Silva, Guimarães & Co.
Silva, Marques & Co.
Soares & Co.
Souza Bastos, Amorim & Co.
Souza, Soares & Co., A. P. de.
Times, Thomas.

PORTO ALEGRE.
Breweries.
Alves, Joaquim de Oliveira.
Becker, Guilherme.
Bobb, Carlos.
Campini, A.
Christoble & Ca., succ.
Huble, Henrique.
Kauffman, A.
Lackmann, João.
Schmidt, Frederico.

Carriage builders.
Hannemann, Carlos, & Neilsen, Frederico P.
Uhrig & Mesterlin, G.

Commercial organizations.
Praço do Commercio.
Junta Commercial.

Dry goods, wholesale.
Barros, Sebastião de.
Bartian & Meyer.
Becker, Carlos.
Blanth, Guilherme.
Brito & Neves.
Carvalho, Gonçalo H. de.

PORTO ALEGRE—Continued.

Dry goods, wholesale—Continued.
Chaves e Filhos.
Ely & Co.
Fontoura, Ernesto, & Co.
Fontoura, Antonio Carneiro da.
Jacobi & Co.
Jung, Pedro, e Filho.
Magnus, J. G.
Schell, Guilherme.
Tollens & Kleuzer.

Merchants.
Aaron, Ed. & Em.
Almeida & Travassos.
Armishaw, G. W., & Co.
Aydes, Dies dos, & Co.
Backhäuser, Alfredo.
Bruggen da Silva, A. H., & Co.
Calcaquo & Co.
Carvalho, Bastos & Vieira.
Cunha, Reis & Co.
Emmerich Berto, Barbosa, Esteves & Co.
Folzer & Co.
Fonseca & Oliveira.
Fonseca, Antonio Maria da.
Fraed, H., & Co.
Freitag Arnol & Co.
Gonçalves & Pereira.
Heinsen, M.
Holtzweisig & Co.
Huch & Co.
Jung & Dreher.
Kourath, João, & Co.
Kuhn & Duval.
Lartigan, J., & Irmão.
Lorenz & Co.
Maiz, Joaquim Antonio de Oliveira.
Manoel da Silva Pauperio.
Manoel da Silva Sá & Co.
Marques, Alfama & Co.
Marques da Silva.
Martel Vicente Porto.
Oliveira, Braga J. M. de.
Ozorio Nunes Irmão.
Pinto, Carlos, & Co.
Pinto da Motta, G.
Peterscn, H., & Co.
Rocha, Antonio dos Santos.
Rocha, Manoel.
Santos Paranhos.
Silva, Bastos & Filha.
Warncke & Dörken.

Merchants, importers and exporters.
Archer & Co.
Aydes, A. Dias dos, & Co.
Aydos, João.

48   BRAZIL.

PORTO ALEGRE—Continued.

Merchants, importers and exporters—Cont'd,
Barbosa, E., & Co.
Barreto, Bastos & Co.
Barros, Sebastião de.
Bastos, Antonio Jm. de Carvalho.
Bastos, Carvalho & Vieira.
Becker, Felippe.
Beneke, Ernesto, & Co.
Bina, José, & Co.
Bins & Friederichs.
Boeira, Vergilino, & Ca.
Caetano, Pinto & Franco.
Carvalho, Nogueira de, & Co.
Chaves & Almeida.
Chaves & Filhos.
Claussen, Viuda, & Ca., suc.
Cuna, Reis & Co.
Dias, I. J.
Dörken & Co.
Edwards, Cooper & Co.
Fletcher & Bartian.
Fontoura, Antonio Carneira da.
Fontoura, Ernesto, & Co.
Fraeb & Co.
Freytag, Junqueira & Co.
Frisoni & Cademartori.
Hasche, Otto.
Heinicke & Livonius.
Huch & Daniel Victor.
Jouvin, A.
Jung & Dreher.
Kessler, Felix H.
Kohler, Nicolan & Co.
Lartigan & Irmão.
Lopes, Candido, & Co.
Lopes, Martiniano & Co.
Luce & Co.
Luderitz, H.
Macedo & Azevedo, Suc.
Marques da Silva, Boaventura.
Menke, C. H.
Mostardeiro & Luchsinger.
Motta, Gabriel.
Nauro & Irmão.
Pereira de Souza, Lionel.
Pereira, José Luiz, & Co.
Peixoto, A. C. S., suc.
Pietzcher, G.. & Co.
Py, Manoel.
Rech y Co.
Reuter, Chr., & Co.
Rocha, Antonio dos Santos.
Santos, José Franc. dos.
Schilling & Co.
Schröder, Ebbesen & Co.
Schult, A., & Co.

PORTO ALEGRE—Continued.

Merchants, importers and exporters—Continued.
Sperb, José Luiz, & Co.
Tavares & Co.
Tellscher & Bastian.
Torres, C., & Co.
Warlich, Bernardo.

Merchants, importers and exporters, produce.
Alscher & Co.
Carneiro & Irmão.
Carvalho, Bastos & Vieira.
Caetano, Pinto & Franco.
Issler, Julio.
Jung & Dreher.
Macedo & Azevedo.
Pereira, José Luiz, & Co.
Tavares, Antonio R., & Co.

Sugar refiners.
Chana, B.
Silva Paranhos, Antonio P.
Tavares, R., & Co.

Unclassified merchants.
Edwards, A. H.
Ernesto Beneke, Rech & Co.

Wholesale druggists.
Hallawell & Co.
Martel V. Porto.

RIO DE JANEIRO.

Bazaars.
Abramant, Moritz.
Azevedo, José Augusto de.
Barifouse, J.
Bittencourt, Joaquim Ignacio de.
Botelho, Antonio Alves.
Cabral & Co.
Carneiro, Santos & Co.
Carvalho, Antonio Augusto.
Castro, Francisco José da Silva.
Fernandes, Simões & Co.
Fonseca, A., & Co.
Fonseca & Cruz.
Gonçalves, Manoel Fagundes.
Goulart & Irmão.
Ibrotsmy, Clemente.
Ilia, José.
Macieira & Soares.
Menezes, Antonio da Costa.
Migueis, Manoel, & Ribeiro.
Moura, Paulino de, & Co.
Oliveira, C. L. de, & Co.
Oliveira, João José da Costa, & Co.
Penafiel, José Vieira da Silva.
Pestana, Raymundo & Co.
Regis & Co.
Ribeiro, Theodoro Lorenzo.

RIO DE JANEIRO—Continued.

Bazaars—Continued.
Romano & Irmão.
Santos & Costa.
Simas, Antonio Xavies de.
Trindade, Alexandre José da.

Beer brewers, merchants.
Almeida, Antonio Fernandes de.
Alves, Paula de Souza, & Co.
Alves & Stoffels.
Backheuser & Co.
Baptista, Joaquim de Souza.
Bayer Viuva, Luiz.
Carneiro, D. S.
Casenave & Beson.
Couto, Manoel do.
Fernandes & Co.
Friederizi, John B.
Gabel Viuva & Co.
Garai, Emilio.
Glecias, Peres & Co.
Hecksher. Chr., & Co.
Kremer, Augusto, & Co.
Leiden, Léon.
Lima, Alves & Co.
Lindscheid, Frederico Guilherme.
Logos & Co.
Mentges, F., & Co.
Metzger, Alfred.
Miranda, Boucher & Soares.
Miranda, José de.
Paz & Tambouri.
Peixoto, Guimarães & Co.
Penedo & Rodrigues.
Pereira & Silva.
Petzold, H., & Co.
Petzold, O. & H.
Pinho & Leite.
Pinto & Braga.
Rangel & Co.
Rodrigues, Manoel Ventura.
Silveira, Machado da, & Co.
Stampa, J. F.
Teixeira, Manoel Joaquim.
Torres & Rodrigues.
Torres, José.
Veloso, Joaquim José.
Villiger & Co.

Billiard table manufacturers and merchants
Carnone & Ribeiro.
Espinola, Viuva & Co.
Tujague, Eduardo.

Boot and shoe manufacturers.
Abreu. Carneiro de, & Co.
Agnello, Domingos.
Almeida, Antonio José Joaquim de.

RIO DE JANEIRO—Continued.

Boot and shoe manufacturers—Continued.
Almeida, Francisco Soares de.
Andrade & Co.
Areas, João Dias.
Arnaldo, Fonseca & Co.
Avila, Amorim & Co.
Baptista Domingos da Costa.
Barbosa, Antonio Domingos.
Barbosa, José de Souza.
Bastos, Abreu & Co.
Bastos, Antonio José da Graça.
Bastos & Baptista.
Benedicto, Affonso.
Bettencourt, Antonio Gomes.
Biar, João Gonçalves.
Bittencourt, Antonio & Co.
Bonifacio, Antonio.
Borga, Felippe.
Borges & Almeida.
Borges, Antonio Manoel & Co.
Borges, Albino Pinto.
Braga, Azevedo.
Braga & Barbosa.
Braga, Souza & Co.
Braga, Bernardo José de L.
Brandão, José Luiz.
Braune Braz.
Brum, Francisco Antonio.
Campello, Jesuino de Souza.
Carmo, Vicente Maria do.
Carvalho, Andrade & Co.
Carvalho, Chagas & Co.
Carvalho, Guimarães & Co.
Carvalho, Henrique de, & Co.
Casimiro, Ribeiro & Co.
Castilho & Co.
Castro & Coelho.
Castro, José Barros de, & Co.
Castro, José Malbar.
Castro, Minervino Dantas.
Cathiard & Alaphilippe.
Clark & Co.
Coelho, José Ignacio.
Conceição, João de Deus Ladislau da.
Corrêa, Alfredo Augusto.
Costa, Carlos Avila da.
Costa, João de Araujo.
Costa, José Luiz da.
Costa, Manoel Ignacio da.
Covett, Manoel Cesar.
Crashley & Co.
Creculy, Angelo.
Crescencio, João.
Cunha, José Antonio da, & Co.
Cunha, Antonio Augusto da
Cunha, Carlos Alberto da

50

BRAZIL.

RIO DE JANEIRO—Continued.

Boot and shoe manufacturers—Continued.
Cunha, J. A. Pereira da.
Damasio, Joaquim de Freitas.
Dantas & Bastos.
Dias & Filhos.
Dias & Irmãos.
Elias, Antonio.
Esteves, José Gomes.
Eusebio & Souza.
Fagundes, Armando Luiz, & Co.
Faria, José Barbosa de.
Faria, José Luiz de.
Ferreira, Nicolau, & Co.
Ferreira & Gomes.
Ferreira & Co.
Ferreira, A. J.
Ferreira, Antonio.
Ferreira, Manoel da Silva, junior.
Figueiredo, Irmão & Co.
Figueiredo, Joaquim de.
Fonseca, Francisco Soares da.
Fonseca, Manoel Pinto da.
Fontes, Antonio Joaquim Gonçalves.
Fontes, Joaquim Moreira Souza.
Fontes, José Luiz Ferreira.
Freitas Almeida & Co.
Freitas, Ricardo de, & Co.
Friza, Malho & Co.
Gallipoli, Luiz.
Garcia, Hygino José.
Gonçalves, Venancio.
Guimarães, Abreu & Co.
Guimarães, Ant. de Abreu.
Guimarães, Ignacio da Silva.
Guimarães, Manoel M. da C.
Guimarães, Manoel S.
Guimarães, Pedro D.
Guimaraes, Pereira.
Lage, Martins & Co.
Lima & Irmão.
Lima, José de Amorim, & Co.
Lima, José Bernardino de.
Lisbôa, Romão Peres.
Lisbôa, Theo. José da Costa.
Lopes, Manoel da Rosa.
Louzada, Antonio Baptista.
Luiz, Manoel d'Avila.
Machado, Manoel T., & Co.
Machado, J. T.
Machado, Tomaz Joaquim.
Madeira, A. Ferreira.
Malavar, Agostinho.
Malheiros & Araujo.
Marciano & Cunha.
Marques, Francisco F., junior.
Martinez, Manoel Francisco.

RIO DE JANEIRO—Continued.

Boot and shoe manufacturers—Continued.
Martins, Coriolano & Co.
Martins, Antonio Alves.
Mattos & Coelho.
Mattos, Fonseca & Co.
Mauricio, Bernardo Teixeira.
Mesquita & Carvalhal.
Montes & Gayoso.
Moraes & Irmão.
Moraes, Raymundo Nonato do.
Moreira, Pereira & Co.
Moreira, Silva & Co.
Nasti, Nicolau.
Neves & Rocha.
Nicolau, Geo.
Nunes, Manoel Machado.
Oliveira, Alberto de, & Co.
Oliveira, Bento de.
Oliveira, Joaquim P C. de.
Paiva, J. M. de Oliveira.
Paiva, João Marques de Oliveira.
Paschoal Passarelli.
Pedroso, José Manoel de Carvalho.
Peixoto, Antonio J., junior.
Pereira, José Joaquim, junior.
Pereira, Baptista, & Co.
Pereira, Garcia & Co.
Pereira, Moreira & Co.
Pereira, Ant. Jm. Dias de Castro.
Pereira, Augusto Cesar.
Pereira, João Manoel.
Pereira, Manoel Luiz.
Pereira, Zephirino.
Pimentel, José d'Alvia.
Pimentel, José Maria de Carvalho.
Pinhão, Joaquim F. da Silva.
Pinheiro & Lisbôa.
Pinto & Oliveira.
Pinto, Alexandro de Paula.
Pinto, Ant. Fco. da S.
Pizarro & Irmão.
Porto & Filho.
Porto, Silva & Co.
Porto, J. P. da Fonseca.
Praça Guimarães & Co.
Prados & Filho.
Queiroz & Co.
Quintella, Francisco José.
Ramos, José Augusto.
Ramos & Irmão.
Rapyo, Domingos Soares da.
Ribeiro, J. Ferreira, & Co.
Ribeiro, Souza & Co.
Ribeiro, José.
Ribeiro, Vaz da Silva.
Ricaldoni, João Baptista.

RIO DE JANEIRO—Continued.

Boot and shoe manufacturers—Continued.
Risso, Raphael.
Rocha, Justiniano de F.
Rodrigues, Luiz, & Co.
Rodrigues, Eusebio José.
Rodrigues, José Pereira.
Salazar, João Alves.
Sancho, João Antonio.
Santos, A., & Co.
Santos, Custodio José dos, & Co.
Santos, João Gonçalves dos.
Santos, Silvino J. N. dos.
Savedra, Bernardo G.
Schubnel, Lourenço.
Silva, Antunes da, & Co.
Silva, Carvalho & Co.
Silva & Garcia.
Silva, Joaquim D. da, & Co.
Silva, Antonio Teixeira da.
Silva, Augusto José da.
Silva, Francisco A. da.
Silva, Francisco Ferreira da.
Silva, João Antonio da.
Silva, M. Joaquim da.
Silva, Manoel da.
Silva, Modesto Goulart da.
Soares, Domingos da Feira.
Souto, Ferreira & Co.
Souza, Braz, F. de, & Co.
Souza, J. Dias de
Souza, Vasco Ferreira de.
Speyer & Co.
Tavares, Antonio Clemente.
Tavares, Manoel José
Teixeira, Antonio.
Tinoco, Jeronymo, & Co.
Vasconcellos & Coelho.
Vieira, junior, & Co.
Vianna, Rodrigo & Co.
Viguier, H.
Villela, Fernandes & Co.
Villela, José Luiz Fernandes.
Xavier & Co.
Young, Hugh.

Butter merchant.
Leboucher, Ernest.

Carpet manufacturers and merchants.
Brito, Castro & Abreu.
Doux & Ferreira.
Guimarães, Cunha & Co.
Martins, J. J.
Martins, Leandro & Alexandro.
Miranda, Costa & Co.
Netto, J., junior.
Novaes, A. C. dos Santos.

RIO DE JANEIRO—Continued.

Carpet manufacturers and merchants—Cont'd.
Pinto & Madureira.
Regis, Julio, & Co.
Regis, Frederico.
Silva, José, & Co.
Sucena, J. R.
Villaverde & Co.
Vianna, Rodrigo, & Co.

Church furniture dealers.
Azevedo, Coelho de, & Co.
Azevedo, Manoel Tavares Coelho de, & Co.
Castello, Ricardo Alfredo de Souza.
Driendl, Thomaz.
Guimarães Cunha & Co.
Instituto Artistico de Munich.
Leite & Nunes.
Sucena, J. R.

Cigar and tobacco manufacturers and merchants.
Almeida & Martins.
Alves, Casnes & Ramos.
Araujo, Souza & Co.
Brazil & Neves.
Carvalho, Ribeiro & Co.
Faria & Rocha.
Gonçalves & Ribeiro.
Leite & Alves.
Leite & Gonçalves.
Lima & Co.
Lopes, Sá & Co.
Machado, Carvalho & Co.
Moreira, Ponto & Salles.
Neves & Vieira.
Oliveira & Guimarães & Castro.
Pinto & Irmão.
Silva & Lima.
Soares de Oliveira.
Simões, Irmãos & Co.
Souza & Fernandez.
Vianna Irmãos.
Viuva Magalhães & Bittencourt.

Coffee, commission.
Abrahão & Co.
Abreu, Leite de, & Co.
Abreu, Sobrinho & Quartim.
Alegria, Ferreira & Co.
Alexandre, Castro & Co.
Almeida & Paiva.
Alves & Avellar.
Alves, Oliveira & Co.
Amorim, Adolpho, & Co.
Amorim, H. Hatje & Co.
Andrade, Cabral & Mattos.
Araujo, Maia & Irmão.

BRAZIL.

Coffee, commission—Continued.
Araujo, Vianna & Costa.
Avellar, Barcellos & Co.
Avellar & Co.
Baptista, Belfort & Co.
Barbosa, José Fernandes, junior.
Barboza junior, & Co.
Barros & Coutinho.
Barros, Narciso & Costa.
Bastos & Co.
Botelho junior, & Co.
Bastos, Camara, Cunha & Co.
Bastos, Carvalho & Co.
Berla & Co.
Borges, F., & Co.
Braga, Lafayette & Co.
Brandão, Faro & Co.
Brandão, Carneiro.
Brandão, Saraiva & Co.
Brandão, Souza & Co.
Brandão, A.
Breves & Josué.
Brito, Machado & Co.
Bruno & Co.
Camara, João, & Co.
Caminada, José Luiz.
Campos, Francisco de Almeida.
Campos, Leite de, & Co.
Cardoso, Custodio & Co.
Cardoso, José Augusto Rodrigues.
Carneiro & Monteiro.
Carneiro, Peixoto & Co.
Carregal & Co.
Carvalho, Gomes de, & Co.
Carvalho & Pinho.
Carvalho, Raul de, & Co.
Castanheira & Vargas.
Castro, Albano de, & Co.
Castro, Filho & Co.
Castro, Teixeira de, & Co.
Cerqueira, Machado & Co.
Chagas, Duprat & Co.
Coelho & Navarro.
Cornelio & Co.
Costa & Filho.
Costa, Pedro Lopes da.
Costa, Vaz da, & Co.
Coutinho, Belisario & Co.
Coutinho, D. F.
Cruz, Werneck & Mattos.
Cunha & Co.
Cunha, Machado & Co.
Custodio & Guimarães Machado.
Delgado, Limas & Velloso.
Duarte & Costa.
Duarte. Lima & Co.

Coffee, commission—Continued.
Duque Estrada, Cesar & Co.
Esteves & Filho.
Faria, Cunha & Co.
Faria, Domingos Miguel de Andrade Rego.
Fernandes, A. M., & Co.
Fernandes & Irmão.
Fernandes, N., & Co.
Ferraz, Araujo & Co.
Ferraz, Soares & Graça.
Ferreira, Duarte & Co.
Ferreira, Eduardo Gomes, & Co.
Ferreira, Martins & Co.
Ferreira, Augusto Mendes.
Figueiredo, Leite & Co.
Figueira, Marcondes & Co.
Filgueiras, M., & Co.
Franco Joaquim de Mello.
Friburgo & Filhos.
Góes & Mendes.
Gomes, Domingos, & Co.
Gomes, Fraga & Azevedo.
Gonçalves, A. M., junior, & Co.
Gonçalves, Filho & Co.
Gracie, Ferreira & Co.
Guedes, Oliveira, Castro & Mendes.
Guimarães & Sampaio.
Guimarães, João, & Co.
Guimarães, Leite & Co.
Henriques, Feliciano José.
Iguassú & Co.
Ipanema, Barão de.
Jalles, Mascarenhas & Co.
Johnston, Edward, & Co.
Joppert, Furquim & Co.
Jordão, Miranda & Co.
Lemos junior, & Pinheiro.
Lacerda, Saturnino de, & Co.
Lima, Dourado & Ladeira.
Leite & Cortes.
Leite & Co.
Leite, Augusto Xavier.
Lemgruber, Moreira & Co.
Lemgruber & Co.
Lemos, João P. de.
Linger, B., & Co.
Lourenço, José, & Co.
Lourical & Quartin.
Machado, Araujo & Co.
Botelho Machado & Co.
Magalhães, João Paulo de Almeida.
Malafaia & Co.
Maldonado, Almeida.
Marinhas, Antonio Martins, & Co.
Marques, Carvalho & Co.
Martins, Andrade & Souza

RIO DE JANEIRO—Continued.

*Coffee, commission—*Continued.

Menezes, Laranja & Oliveira.
Miranda, João & Co.
Miranda & Villela.
Monteiro, Almeida & Co.
Monteiro, Miranda & Co.
Monteiro, Oliveira & Co.
Moraes, Pedroso & Co.
Moura & Tenente.
Mourão, Francisco da Silva.
Nascimento, José Theodoro do, & Co.
Nascimento, Maia & Costa.
Neff, Raymundo, & Co.
Netto, Corrêa & Co.
Nobrega, A. Alves.
Nogueira, Francisco Pedro, & Co.
Nogueira & Co.
O'Kell, Mourão & Wilson.
Oliveira, Vaz de, & Co.
Ortigão & Co.
Padua & Co.
Pereira, A., & Co.
Pereira, M. J. Gonçalves, & Co.
Pereira, Dias & Co.
Pereira & Valentim.
Pereira, Aureliano Augusto da Costa.
Pinheiro, F., & Co.
Pinto, Francisco, & Co.
Pinto, Irmão & Co.
Pires & Pinheiro.
Porto, Joaquim P. R., & Co.
Porto, Manoel P. R.
Portugal & Co.
Ramos, Almeida & Co.
Ramos, Mariani & Co.
Ramos, Peixoto & Co.
Ramos & Co.
Rebello, Irmão & Co.
Rebello & Silva.
Reis, Henriques Costa, & Co.
Ribeiro, A. B., & Co.
Ribeiro, Esteves, & Co.
Ribeiro, Leite & Co.
Rodrigues, J., & Co.
Rodrigues, Ramão.
Roque, Victorino, & Co.
Roxo, Lemos & Co.
Santos & Serra.
Santos, Aureliano Monteiro dos.
Silva, Corrêa da, & Co.
Silva, Manoel Cardoso da.
Silveira, Frederico da, & Co.
Soares, Quartim, Silveira & Co.
Soccorro, Moraes & Irmão.
Souto, Francisco José Alves.
Souza, Cerqueira & Co.

RIO DE JANEIRO—Continued.

*Coffee, commission—*Continued.

Souza, Irmão, Queiros & Filho.
Souza, M. J. Pereira, & Co.
Teixeira junior, & Pinto.
Teixeira, Eduardo, & Co.
Telles, Moura & Co.
Tobias, Ignacio, & Co.
Torres, A. J. Rodrigues, & Co.
Torres, Alves & Co.
Torres, J., & Co.
Valverde & Co.
Vianna, Castro & Co.
Vianna, Moreira de Rezende & Co.
Vianna, Manoel F. de Araujo.
Vieira & Co.
Viggiano, Costa & Macedo.
Vilhena & Mendes.
Villela Gomes & Co.
Villela & Miranda.

Commission agents.

Abreu, Daguerre & Co.
Francisco Lumay.
Barandier, Georges.
Behrend, Schmidt & Co
Bouchet, Ch.
Braga, Carlos, & Co.
Bueno, Manoel Antonio Pimenta.
Cahen & Guilherme.
Conteville, Carlos.
Deans, H. Cowan, & Co.
Deming, William B.
Diamantino, Francisco.
Dias, Victor.
Estienne, Gustavo E. L.
Favraud, François.
Feldmann & Oppenheimer.
Fischer, Schlatter & Augliker.
Fuentes, Baldomero Carqueja de.
Géraud, Jules.
Guerra, Salles & Co.
Guimarães, Wenceslau & Co.
Hall, J. V., & Co.
Hanriot, Gustavo.
Hasenclever & Co.
Hatje, Amorim H., & Co.
Jessop, William John.
Kastrup, Arthur, & Co.
Kunhardt, Carlos João.
Lévy, Joseph, & frère.
Lumay, Francisco.
Machado Fonseca & Irmão.
Mello, José de.
Metzger, Alfredo.
Meyer, Alfredo.
Ribeiro Barros & Braga.
Ridgway, John.

RIO DE JANEIRO—Continued.

Commission agents—Continued.
Rochefort, Bertram.
Rodde, Ferdinand.
Souza, Eduardo Braga de.
Spann, Adolph.
Taylor, Carlos Frederico.
Theiner, B.
Wetmore, Henry S.
Zschockel, Ernst.

Druggists.
Adolpho, Veiga & Co.
Almeida, F. Ribeiro de, & Co.
Alves, João Luiz, & Co.
Andrade, Barbosa de, & Co.
Araujo, Silva & Co.
Barbosa & Co.
Baruel, Soares & Co.
Berrini & Co.
Camara, Pedro Perestrello da.
Cardoso, Manoel Teixeira.
Carneiro, J. W., & Co.
Carvalho, Alfredo de, & Co.
Carvalho, Filho & Co.
Carvalho, Luiz Augusto de.
Dias, Lourenço, & Co.
Diniz & Pinheiro.
Ferreira, Carlos Alberto, & Co.
Foglia, Hercules.
Fonseca, Domingos da, & Co.
Forzani Viuva & Co.
Freire & Martins.
Freitas, Araujo & Co.
Freitas, F. Paulo de.
Gouvêa & Quirino.
Granado & Co.
Guilherme Guimarães & Co.
Guimarães, José Antonio da Silva.
Guimarães & Pereira.
Guimarães, A. Pereira.
Hellot, Dr. E.
Araujo Irmãos & Co.
Costa junior, & Co.
Klingelhoefer & Co.
Leite & Irmãos.
Lima, Hargreaves & Co.
Lopes, Domingos da Silva.
Macedo & Gonzalez.
Macedo, L. de, & Co.
Miranda, Ferreira de.
Monteiro, Cardoso & Co.
Oliveira & Gad.
Oliveira, José Luiz Paes de, & Co.
Peckolt, Dr. Theodoro.
Pedro, Irmão & Co.
Pereira, Antonio, & Co.
Pinto, Silva & Co.

RIO DE JANEIRO—Continued.

Druggists—Continued.
Puget, A.
Rasina, Giovianni.
Rodrigues & Pinheiro.
Rodrigues, Justino José.
Santos, Paschoal & Co.
Silva, Gomes & Co.
Silva, J. C. da.
Smart, Eduardo John.
Soares, Adriano Pereira.
Vautelet & Duceux.
Werneck, Leoni & Co.
Werneck, A. Furquim.

Earthenware, china, etc.
Almeida, Anardino Borges de.
Almeida, Augusto Carlos de.
Alves, João & Ribeiro.
Azevedo, Joaquim Alves de.
Batalha, Thereza Lodi.
Berutti, Luiz & Co.
Bittencourt, Joaquim Ignacio.
Canejo, João Francisco.
Carvalho, José Augusto de.
Casalta, João Luiz.
Clapp, João, & Filhos.
Cruz, Alfonso, & Co.
Cunha, Bernardo Ribeiro da.
Cypriano, J., & Co.
Dias, M. A. Braga.
Esberard, F. A. M.
Estella & Co.
Faria, Luiz José de, & Co.
Farinha, Leonardo, & Co.
Fernandes, Francisco José.
Ferreira, A. C. Mondego, & Co.
Fonseca & Cruz.
Goulart & Co.
Hampshire, Harold José.
Januario, Coelho & Co.
Jessop, William J.
Kallenbach, Philipp.
Leitão, M. C., & Co.
Lion, Alfred.
Lomba, Manoel Genaro.
Malheiros, Domingos, & Co.
Martins, Custodio & Co.
Martins, Manoel Joaquim.
Mello, João Manoel Pereira de, & Co.
Mendes, Antonio Daniel.
Meyer & Vaz.
Muniz & Oo.
Notto, Seraphim Corrêa.
Noellner, Carl.
Oliveira, C. L. de, & Co.
Oliveira, João José da Costa, & Co.
Oliveira, Luiz da Rocha.

RIO DE JANEIRO—Continued

Earthenware, china, etc.—Continued.
Oliveira, M. J. de Figueiredo.
Oliveira, Manoel Joaquim Martins de.
Pagani, Constantino.
Patto, Ezequiel Rodrigues.
Peixoto, Nogueira & Cc
Pereira, Antonio Joaquim Dias de Castro.
Pereira, Heitor Adriano.
Pinto, Castro & Co.
Queiroz, José Luiz de.
Rocha, Carneiro & Co.
Rogers, Henry, Sons & Co.
Sampaio & Co.
Sampaio, Silva & Co.
Santos, Ferreira dos & Co.
Saraiva, Felix, & Co.
Silva, Eusebio Luiz da.
Silva, Gomes da, & Co.
Silva, Joaquim Pereira Martinho da.
Silva, José Alves da, & Co.
Siqueira, Manoel de Silveira.
Tavares, Amaral & Co.
Teixeira, José de Lemos.
Torres, Vianna.
Trindade, Manoel Correa da.
Veiga, Joaquim Rodrigues.
Villaca & Co.

Electric apparatus.
Barbosa & Co.
Bazin & Co.
Borlido, Barbosa & Co.
Braga & Co.
Chaves, A. R.
Companhia União Telephonica do Brazil.
Conteville, Carlos.
Fraga, Francisco Ferreira.
Haupt & Co.
Oliveira & Gad.
Penfold, W.
Rodde, Ferdinand.
Torres, Francisco.

Embroidery merchants and dealers.
Andrade, A. P. de, & Co.
Araujo, Coque & Co.
Barbosa, Freitas & Co.
Couto, Juvanon & Domingos.
Sučena, J. R.

Fruit merchants.
Dias, A. M., & Co.
Bernardino Ferreira da Costa & Souza.
Dias & Silva.
José Amoretti F. & Co.
Ferminich & Co.
Leão & Co.
Silva, Araujo & Machado.
Vignolo, Teixeira & Co.

RIO DE JANEIRO—Continued.

General stores.
Abreu, J. M. de, & Co.
Almeida & Fernandes.
Almeida, Joaquim de, & Co.
Almeida, Manoel Luiz de, junior.
Almeida & Mesquita.
Almeida, Lourenço de.
Alves, Felisberto José.
Andrade, Abilio José, & Co.
Amorim, Antonio José de Araujo.
Araujo, Antonio José Lopes de.
Araujo Irmão & Co.
Araujo, Pereira & Co.
Araujo, Tavares & Co.
Araujo, Manoel Joaquim Soares de.
Araujo, Pinto de, & Co.
Araujo, Pinto de, & Sampaio.
Attademo, B. A.
Auleta & Santis.
Azevedo, Francisco de Souza.
Azevedo, Martins de, & Machado.
Azevedo, José Augusto de.
Azevedo, Monteiro de, & Co.
Azevedo & Co.
Azevedo & Campos.
Azevedo & Taveira.
Barreiros, M. A., & Co.
Barros, M. de Souza.
Bastos, Miguel Augusto.
Bastos, João Cesar.
Bastos, Oliveira & Co.
Bastos & Moreira.
Bastos, Sousa & Gomide.
Beirão & Co.
Bittencourt, Antonio Guedes de.
Botelho, Antonio Alves.
Boucher, Miranda & Soares.
Braga, Gomes & Co.
Brandão, Antonio de Souza.
Brazão, Lopes de, & Irmão.
Cabral, Teixeira & Co.
Cabrita, Jacinto Pereira.
Cambiaso & Co.
Campello, José Pereira.
Canario, Marques & Co.
Cardoso, B. P., & Co.
Cardoso, Francisco do Nascimento.
Carneiro & Gomes.
Carrazedo Santos & Co.
Carvalhal & Coelho.
Carvalho, A. Dias de, & Co.
Carvalho, Dias de, Mattos & Co.
Carvalho & Irmão.
Carvalho, Agostinho Ferreira de.
Carvalho, Antonio Joaquim de.
Carvalho, Antonio Rodrigues de.

RIO DE JANEIRO—Continued.

General stores—Continued.
Carvalho, Bernardino Marinho de.
Carvalho, João, & Co.
Carvalho, João de Almeida.
Carvalho, José Bento Alves de.
Carvalho J. F. Rodrigues de.
Carvalho, Thomaz Alves de.
Castro, Antonio Martins Alves de.
Castro, José de.
Catão, Casimiro Rodrigues.
Cerqueira, A. Adriano de.
Cesario, Pires & Co.
Chaves, Augusto Cesar.
Coelho, Manoel Diniz Ferreira.
Coimbra, Silva & Coelho.
Coelho, Silva & Co.
Cordeiro, Almeida & Co.
Cordeiro & Amaral.
Corrêa & Co.
Corrêa, José Francisco Antonio.
Costa, Azevedo & Co.
Costa, Marcellino da, & Co.
Costa, Menezes da, & Co.
Costa, Albino Maria da.
Costa, J. F. Lopes da.
Costa, Joaquim José da.
Couto, J. G. Pereira de, & Co.
Couto & Co.
Couto, Francisco Figuereido do.
Couto, Seraphim Mendes.
Cruz, Pereira da, & Rosa.
Cruz, Joaquim Manoel Pereira da.
Cunha, Caldeira & Co.
Cunha, A., Caldeira & Co.
Cunha, Bernardo Corrêa da.
Escaleira, Manoel Calvo, & Co.
Fernandes, A. J. Leite, & Co.
Fernandes, João José.
Fernandes, José Antonio.
Ferreira, A. Pavia.
Ferreira, João Antonio d'Orvil.
Ferreira, José Antonio.
Ferro, Victorino & Co.
Figueira, A. Barros.
Freire, Antonio Lennox da Rocha.
Freire, L. de Barros.
Freire de Andrade & Irmão.
Freitas, Antonio de Abreu.
Fróes & Co.
Garcia, A. J., & Co.
Garcia, Ribeiro & Co.
Gil, F., & Co.
Gomes, Daniel Ribeiro.
Gomes, João Coelho & Sobrinho.
Gomes, José Ribeiro.
Gonçalves, Carlos, & Guimarães.

RIO DE JANEIRO—Continued.

General stores—Continued.
Gonçalves, Constantino José.
Gonçalves, H., & Co.
Gonçalves, Irmão & Costa.
Gonçalves, Lino & Co.
Gonçalves, Penna & Co.
Gonçalves, Julio Francisco.
Gonçalves, Lino de Moraes.
Guedes & Souza.
Guerra, Antunes & Co.
Guilherme, José & Co.
Guilherme & Co.
Guimarães, Alberto da Fonseca, & Co.
Guimarães, Augusto, & Co.
Guimarães, Leopoldo Leite, & Co.
Guimarães, Machado, Fernandes, & Co.
Guimarães, Sampaio & Co.
Guimarães, Francisco de Oliveira.
Guimarães, João Leite.
Guimarães, Manoel Ribeiro da Costa.
Joppert, Guilherme.
Ketele, J.
Lacerda & Co.
Lacurte Irmãos.
Leal, Gomes, Guedes & Co.
Leitão, Irmão & Co.
Leite, Ramos & Co.
Lima, Miguel Luiz Sequeira de.
Lisbôa, M. V., & Co.
Loureiro, J., & Co.
Louzada, Antonio José Pereira.
Machado, A., & Co.
Machado, Antonio Seraphim Pinto, & Co.
Machado & Co.
Machado, Antonio Gonçalves.
Magalhães & Silva.
Magalhães, M. J. de.
Marques, Monteiro & Oliveira.
Martinez, José Benito.
Martins, Carneiro & Pires.
Martins, Duarte Ferreira.
Mattos, Carvalho & Co.
Mattos, Joaquim Antonio de.
Mello, Antonio Corrêa de, & Co.
Mello, Bernardo de, & Co.
Mello, José de Freitas Couto.
Mendes & Rocha.
Mendes, Santos & Co.
Mendes, Sobrinho & Co.
Mendonça, Cardoso de, & Co.
Mendonça & Co.
Menezes, Vieira de, & Co.
Merelim, José da Rocha.
Miranda, Francisco José da Costa.
Monteiro, Antonio Gomes.
Monteiro, Christovão Dias.

RIO DE JANEIRO—Continued.

General stores—Continued.

Moraes, Irmão & Co.
Moreira, Estevão Fernandes.
Moreira, José Gonçalves, & Co.
Motta & Co.
Moura, Marcondes de, & Co.
Moura, Joaquim dos Santos.
Moura, Miguel da Silva.
Neff, Ayrosa & Juvenal.
Nobrega, M., Alves da, & Co.
Nobrega & Co.
Novaes, A. T. de Amorim.
Nunes, A., & Co.
Nunes, Silva & Co.
Oliveira, G. H. de, & Co.
Oliveira, Joaquim de, & Co.
Oliveira, José Carlos de.
Oliveira, J. Marques de.
Ortigão, Antonio, & Co.
Osorio, Arthur, & Co.
Pacheco, Antonio da Silva.
Pacheco, Francisco José Rodrigues.
Paranhos, Santos & Co.
Paula e Silva, Joaquim Francisco de.
Penafiel, José Vieira da Silva.
Penna, José Joaquim da.
Pereira, Alves & Co.
Pereira, Carneiro & Co.
Pereira, Rodrigues & Co.
Pereira & Valentim.
Pereira, José de Faria.
Pereira, Luiz Francisco.
Pereira, Manoel Antonio.
Perez André.
Pimentel & Lopes.
Pinheiro & Magalhães.
Pinho, F. J. de.
Pinto, Antonio Francisca da Silva.
Pinto, Joaquim Marques.
Pinto & Guimarães.
Pinto, Rodrigues & Co.
Pinto, Werneck & Oliveira.
Pontes, Oliveira & Irmão.
Portella, Rabello & Co.
Porto, Thomaz & Paes.
Porto, Joaquim Rodrigues de Almeida.
Possinba, Casimiro de Almeida.
Queiroz, Manoel Soares de.
Raphael & Co.
Ribeiro, Antonio José Gonçalves, & Co.
Rocha, Irmão & Seabra.
Rocha, Francisco José da.
Rocha, Justiniano de Figueiredo.
Rodrigues, José Manoel.
Rosado, José Mascarenhas.
Russo, João Marques.

RIO DE JANEIRO—Continued.

General stores—Continued.

Sampaio, Avelino & Graça.
Sampaio, J. Rodrigues, & Co.
Santos, Antonio Alves dos.
Santos, Antonio Pereira dos.
Santos, João Diogo dos.
Santos, Joaquim Francisco dos.
Santos, João Rodrigues Cardoso dos.
Santos, Paulo dos, & Montes.
Santos, Antonio Eduardo da Silva.
Sicoli, Lopes & Co.
Silva, Francisco Antonio da.
Silva, Carvalho da, & Co.
Silva & Lima.
Silva, J. A. da, & Co.
Silva, Joaquim Domingues da.
Silva, José Custodio Teixeira da.
Silva, Pereira da, & Irmão.
Simão, João Pereira de.
Simonetti, A., & Irmão.
Soares, Marcos & Co.
Soares, Antonio da Costa.
Soares, J. S.
Soares, Joaquim Gonçalves.
Souza & Barbosa.
Souza, J. de.
Souza, Benjamin Leite de.
Souza, J. P. de.
Spirito, P. Petrosini & Co.
Spolydoro & Co.
Sprenger, F. W.
Teixeira & Martinez.
Teixeira, José Augusto.
Teixeira, M., & Co.
Tinoco, Rodrigues, & Co.
Torres, Joaquim, & Co.
Torres & Pacheco.
Valle, J., & Co.
Valle, José Gomes do, & Co.
Vasconcellos, Seraphim Ayres de, & Co.
Vasconcellos & Coelho.
Vieira, Rebello & Co.
Vieira, Francisco José Gonçalves.
Villan & Co.

Hardware dealers.

Cardoso, Antonio F.
Costa, Paulo.
Ferreira, Manoel da Silva.
Freitas, José de.
Gomes, João de A.
Guimarães, José F. M.
Jorge, Domingos D.
Machado, Antonio I.
Magalhães, Antonio C. de.
Marques, Ignacio F.
Pedrosa & Carvalho.

RIO DE JANEIRO—Continued.

Hardware dealers—Continued.
Pereira, Paulino G.
Ribeiro, Manoel Ant. P.
Rocha, Joaquim M. da.

Hardware manufacturers and merchants.
Brandão, Henrique P. A., & Co.
Gomes, C.
Gomes, Oliveira & Co.
Magalhães & Co.

Hat (felt and silk) manufacturers and dealers.
Andrade, Manoel J. P. de.
Araldo, Lourenço.
Araujo, Coque & Co.
Barandier, G.
Barra, Alberto.
Braga & Co.
Calvão, Pinto & Co.
Calvão & Co.
Carvalho, M. Marques de.
Ciuffo, Miguel.
Clement, P. A.
Coelho, João de Souza & Co.
Costa, Manoel Baptista da.
Gelardi & Filho.
Loubet & Irmão.
Lyra & Co.
Martins & Barbosa.
Martins, J. P., & Co.
Menna, Maria da Gloria.
Narciso, Manoel.
Noé Irmãos & Co.
Paranhos, Santos & Co.
Pereira, J. A.
Pinto, Braulio & Co.
Possas, Gonçalves, & Co.
Ribeiro, Henrique, & Co.
Ribeiro, J. J. da Rocha.
Rodrigues de Almeida.
Ruch, F.
Silveira & Souza.
Thomé, Claudemiro F., & Co.
Torteroli, Roque & Co.
Villan, Colomb & Co.

Hat merchants (gentlemen's).
Alt, Henrique, junior, & Co.
Andrade, Manoel J. P. D. de.
Araujo, José Goursand.
Armada, Joaquim Alvaro d', & Co.
Armada & Co.
Barros, Antonio Madeira de, junior.
Braga, Bento & Co.
Braga Viuva & Co.
Cambiaso & Co.
Cardoso, Gabriella S., & Co.
Carneiro & Gomes.

RIO DE JANEIRO—Continued.

Hat merchants (gentlemen's)—Continued.
Carvalho, A. M. de, & Co.
Carvalho junior, & Co.
Carvalho, M. Marques de.
Castro & Coelho.
Castro & Filho.
Clement, P. A.
Costa, Braga & Co.
Cunha, A. J. da, & Co.
Esteves, Victorino José.
Feraudy, Filho & Pereira.
Granja & Guimarães.
Guedes, J. C.
Guimarães, Fernandes, & Co.
Guimarães, Manoel da Costa, & Co.
Guimarães & Ribeira.
Guimarães, Silva & Co.
Guimarães, J. C. M., junior.
Leite, D. I. Affonso, & Co.
Leite, Silva & Co.
Lima, Costa & Co.
Lopes, Jacintho Ferreira.
Machado Assis & Co.
Meirelles, D. F. A.
Mounier & Filho.
Netto, Oliveira, Luiz de & Irmão.
Osorio, Joaquim T.
Paiva, J. F. de, & Co.
Pereira, M. A., & Co.
Portella, Rabella & Co.
Possas & Co.
Ribeiro & Bordallo.
Ruch, F.
Sampaio & Co.
Santoro Avelino Puga.
Simonetti & Irmão.
Souza, Araujo & Co.
Souza, Pereira de, & Co.
Souza, Leonardo Barboza de.
Teixeira & Co.
Teixeira, Arantes & Co.
Torres & Co.
Vianna, C. J. Alvares.
Victorino & Co.
Vieira, Manoel Martins.

Hide and skin merchants and dealers.
Abreu, Gregorio de, & Co.
Bastos, G., & Co.
Breissan, J. B., & Co.
Bret, Paulo & Co.
Carneiro, Ant. G.
Cathiard & Alaphilippe.
Cerqueira, Cardoso de, & Co.
Coelho, A. A.
Conteville, Carlos.

BRAZIL.

RIO DE JANEIRO—Continued.

Hide and skin merchants and dealers—Continued.
Cordeiro, Manoel Esteves, & Co.
Costa, Antonio M. da, & Co.
Couto, Guimarães & Co.
Esteves, Ant. J.
Garai, Emilio.
Guimarães, Pinto & Sampaio.
Lévy, Joseph frère.
Lima, Araujo & Co.
Marques, J. F., & Co.
Novaes, A. C. dos Santos.
Oliveira, Airoza de, & Co.
Pereira, Joaquim José.
Regis, Julio, & Co.
Regis, Frederico.
Ribeiro, José Maria, & Co.
Saint-Denis, E. de, & Co.
Silva, José, & Co.
Silva, Francisco da.
Vianna, Rodrigo & Co.
Villela, Jeronymo, & Co.
House furniture dealers.
Azevedo, Coelho de, & Co.
Azevedo, Manoel Tavares Coelho de, & Co.
Bernachot, Serraria.
Boiteux, Eugenio.
Brito & Abreu.
Doux & Ferreira.
Eloy, Alfredo.
Faria, M. J. de, & Irmão.
Fischer, H. W.
Guignard, Gaston.
Kingston, Henry.
Laleuf Viuva.
Leite & Nunes.
Lima, Souza.
Martins, J.
Marturier, Jean Joseph.
Pinto & Madureira.
Rebello & Co.
Souza, Antonio Silveira de.
Sucena, J. R.
Vianna, Rodrigo, & Co.
Vieira, Seraphim Martins.
Vasconcellos, Netto & Co.
Importers and exporters.
Abrahão & Co.
Abrantes, C., & Co.
Abreu, A., & Co.
Abreu, Irmão & Co.
Abreu, Leite de, & Co.
Abreu, M. S. de.
Abreu, Sobrinho & Quartin.
Amorim, Adolpho, & Co.
Aguiar & Estrelita

RIO DE JANEIRO—Continued.

Importers and exporters—Continued.
Alegria, Ferreira & Co.
Alexandro Castro & Co.
Almeida, Alberto de, & Co.
Almeida & Malheiros.
Almeida, C. de, & Co.
Almeida, Gudim & Paiva.
Almeida, Joaquim de, & Co.
Almeida, Manoel Dias de, & Co.
Almeida, Monteiro & Co.
Almeida & Paiva.
Almeida, Paschoal de, & Co.
Aloti & Co.
Alt, Henrique, junior, & Co.
Alvarenga, J. P. da Silva, & Co.
Alvares, Franklin.
Alvarez, Fernandez y.
Alves & Avellar.
Alves da Silva, José, & Co.
Alves & Ribeiro.
Alves Oliveira & Co.
Alves & Co.
Alves, José Luiz.
Amares, Fernando, & Co.
Amorim, H. Hatze, & Co.
Amorim, Joaquim A. D. de.
Amoroso, Costa & Co.
Anachoreta & Frazão.
Andrade, Barbosa de, & Co.
Andrade, Cabral & Mattos.
Andrade, Candido Luiz de.
Andrade, José Martins de.
Andrade & Souza.
Araujo, Antonio José R. de, & Co.
Arbuckle Irmãos.
Arens Irmãos.
Antunes & Pestana.
Arantes & Rebello.
Araujo, Coque & Co.
Araujo, José Goursand & Co.
Araujo, Machado & Co.
Araujo, Maia & Irmão.
Araujo, Santos & Co.
Araujo, Vianna & Costa.
Araujo, Bernardino José de.
Araujo, Bonifacio do Rego.
Araujo, J. J. Vieira de.
Araujo, Joaquim.
Armada, Joaquim A. d', & Co.
Armada & Co.
Arnade, Rocha & Co.
Aron, A., & Co.
Ashworth, Edward, & Co.
Aspinwall, Jones & Co.
Assumpção, Gomes & Co.
Augé Ribeiro & Co.

RIO DE JANEIRO—Continued.

Impoiters and exporters—Continued.

Augusto Vaz & Co.
Avellar, Barcellos & Co.
Avellar & Co.
Avellar, João G. Ribeiro de.
Avellar, Manoel Duarte de.
Avenier, Dale & Co.
Alves & Carvalho.
Azambuja Irmãos.
Azevedo, Luiz, & Co.
Azevedo, Mayrink de, & Co.
Azevedo, Paiva & Co.
Azevedo, Pimenta & Co.
Azevedo & Silva.
Backheuser & Co.
Bahia, Manoel F. de S.
Bandeira, Adriano Corrêa.
Baptista, Belfort & Co.
Baptista, Figueiredo & Co.
Baptista & Ferreira.
Baptista, Ramos & Co.
Baptista, Libencio Lupercio.
Barbosa, A., & Co.
Barbosa, Costa & Co.
Barbosa, Coutinho & Co.
Barbosa, Emilio, & Co.
Barbosa junior, & Co.
Barbosa, Maya & Co.
Barbosa & Co.
Barbosa, José J. de O.
Barbosa, Luiz Rodrigues.
Barbosa, Silverio.
Barreiros, Bruno & Co.
Barros, Antonio A. M. de.
Barros & Coutinho.
Barros, Narcizo & Costa.
Barros, Emilio de.
Barth & Co.
Bastos & Queiroz.
Bastos, B. T. de M., & Co.
Bastos, G., & Co.
Bastos & Guimarães.
Bastos, Oliveira & Guimarães.
Bastos, Pinheiro.
Bastos & Valentim.
Bastos, Antonio José Gomes P.
Bastos, Bernardino, & Co.
Bastos, J. L. Teixeira.
Bastos, José dos Santos P.
Bastos, José Ribeiro.
Bastos, Salvador G. da Cunha
Baumann & Gonnet.
Bazin, C., & Co.
Babo, Joaquim da Costa.
Bebianno & Irmão.
Behrend, Schmidt & Co.

RIO DE JANEIRO—Continued.

Importers and exporters—Continued.

Bellamy, John H., & Co.
Berger, Henry.
Berla & Co.
Bernardes & Ribeiro.
Berthalo, Domingos Fernandes.
Bestial, Dominique.
Beuttenmüller, G. J.
Biedekarcken, Henry.
Bittencourt, Joaquim Ignacio de.
Bloch & Angelo.
Bonança, J. F.
Bonniard fères.
Bonniard, A.
Bordallo & Co.
Borges, F., & Co.
Borlido, J. J. Gonçalves.
Bouchaud, J. H., & Co.
Bourbon, Julio.
Bradshaw, John, & Co.
Braga, Araujo & Co.
Braga, B., & Co.
Braga, Bôa & Co.
Braga, Coutinho & Co.
Braga & Filho.
Braga, Lafayette & Co.
Braga, Souza & Co.
Braga, Diogo Luiz Peixoto.
Bragança, Alves & Co.
Branca, Clemente Castello.
Brandão & Alves.
Brandão, Carneiro & Co.
Brandão, Carvalho & Co.
Brandão & Moreira.
Brandão, Rocha & Co.
Brandão, Saraiva & Co.
Brandão, Antonio José Gomes.
Brandão, Felisberto Coelho.
Brandão, Joaquim F. P.
Brandon, F. M.
Bravo, Fernandes, & Co.
Breissan, J. B., & Co.
Breves & Josué.
Brito & Abreu.
Brito, Duarte & Co.
Brito, Geraldes & Co.
Brito, Miranda & Almeida.
Brito, Machado & Co.
Brito, Miranda & Co.
Brito, Antonio P. e, junior.
Brito, Jeronymo M. da R.
Bruno & Co.
Butler, Antonio Ferreira.
Caldas, Bastos & Co.
Calogeras Irmãos & Co.
Camacho & Guilbaud.

RIO DE JANEIRO—Continued.

RIO DE JANEIRO—Continued.

Importers and exporters—Continued.

Camara, Cunha Bastos & Co.
Camara & Gomes.
Camara, João, & Co
Camarão & Co.
Cambiaso & Co.
Campo Verde & Mattos.
Campos, Antunes de, & Co.
Campos, Leite de, & Co.
Camuyrano, Luiz.
Cardoso Almeida & Co.
Cardoso, Arthur, & Co.
Cardoso & Brito.
Cardoso, Custodio & Co.
Cardoso, Gonçalves & Fernandes.
Cardoso, M. de Mesquita, & Co.
Cardoso, Pereira de Lima & Co.
Cardoso, José Augusto Rodrigues.
Cardozo & Guimarães.
Conteville, Carlos.
Carvalho, Carlos Teixeira de.
Carneiro, A. J., & Co.
Carneiro, Caldeira & Co.
Carneiro & Guimarães.
Carneiro & Irmão.
Carneiro & Monteiro.
Carneiro, Peixoto & Co.
Carneiro, Teixeira & Co.
Carneiro, Xavier, & Co.
Carneiro, Antonio Gonçalves.
Carneiro, Bernardino Martins.
Carneiro, Joaquim Alves Torres.
Carrazedo, Santos & Co.
Carregal, Bastos & Guimarães.
Carregal & Co.
Carvalho, Mattos & Co.
Carvalho, Filho & Co.
Carvalho, Freitas & Co.
Carvalho, Gomes de, & Co.
Carvalho, Affonso Henriques de, & Co.
Carvalho & Almeida.
Carvalho, Leonel de, & Co.
Carvalho, Libano & Mascarenhas.
Carvalho, Moreira & Co.
Carvalho & Olegerio junior.
Carvalho & Pinho.
Carvalho & Rocha.
Carvalho, Silva & Co.
Carvalho, A. Augusto da Silva.
Carvalho, Augusto Hortense de.
Carvalho, J. J. Ferreira de.
Carvalho, José Leite Teixeira de.
Carvalho, Samuel Cesar de Pinho.
Carvalho, Thomaz Alves de.
Casenave & Boson.
Cassels, W. R., & Co.

Importers and exporters—Continued.

Castanheira & Vargas.
Castro, Adriano de, & Co.
Castro, Albano de, & Co.
Castro & Oliveira.
Castro, Gonçalo de, & Co.
Castro, Filho, & Co.
Castro, Irmão & Co.
Castro, Teixeira de, & Co.
Castro, Antonio Ribeiro de.
Castro, J. B. de.
Castro, Luiz José da Silva.
Cathiard & Alaphilppe.
Cerf, Dale & Co.
Chagas, Duprat & Co.
Chaves, Braga & Co.
Clemente & Ferreira.
Clemente, Francisco, & Co.
Coelho, Duarte & Irmão.
Coelho & Martins.
Coelho & Navarro.
Coelho, Pinto & Co.
Coelho, José Joaquim.
Coggin, William John.
Colucci, Benjamin.
Companhia União Mercantil.
Conceição & Cunha.
Cordeiro & Filho.
Cordeiro, Manoel Esteves, & Co.
Cornelio & Co.
Corrêa, Francisco Fernandes.
Costa, Honorio Hermeto Corrêa da.
Corrêa, José Francisco & Co.
Cortico, José Antonio dos Santos.
Costa, Ant. M. dos Santos, & Co.
Costa, Domingos, & Co.
Costa, Irmão & Soares.
Costa & Leal.
Costa & Martins.
Costa & Irmão.
Costa, Pacheco & Co.
Costa, Souza & Co.
Costa, B. F. da, & Souza.
Costa, Bernardino Dias da.
Costa & Sá, José M. da.
Costa, Pedro Lopes da.
Coutinho de Souza & A. Abreu.
Coutinho, Francisco, & Co.
Coutinho, Belisario, & Co.
Coutinho, Domingos F.
Couto, J. S., & Co.
Cox, George E.
Cruz, Gomes & Co.
Cruz & Filho.
Cruz, Werneck & Mattos.
Cruz, Manoel Rodrigues da.

62 BRAZIL.

RIO DE JANEIRO—Continued.

Importers and exporters—Continued.

Cruz, Irmão & Co.
Cruzeiro, Vasconcellos.
Cunha, Alves & Souza.
Cunha, Fortunato P. da, & Co.
Cunha, Machado da, & Co.
Cunha, Marques & Co.
Cunha & Co.
Cunha, Augusto Ferreira da.
Cunha, Bernardo Ribeiro da.
Cunha, D. J. da Silva.
Cunha, João Candido F. da.
Cunha, Joaquim Antonio da.
Custodio & Machado Guimarães.
Daguerre & Co.
Dalmer & Schmidt.
Daniel & Camarinha.
Dannecker, Jacobson & Co.
Dantas, Paulo, & Co.
Deans, H. Cowan, & Co.
Decap, Nöel.
Delgado, Limas & Velloso.
Deming, William B.
Deserbelles, Prosper.
Dias, Gonçalves, Pereira & Co.
Dias, Manoel Joaquim, & Co.
Diniz & Pinheiro.
Doane, J. W., & Co.
Duarte & Costa.
Duarte, Lima & Co.
Duque-Estrada & Co.
Duvivier & Co.
Eichborn, Guilherme.
Ennes & Co.
Ennes & Silva.
Espinola Viuva & Co.
Estella, & Co.
Esteves & Filho.
Esteves, Antonio José.
*Esteves, Francisco José.
Evora, Antonio Vieira Miranda
Farani & Sobrinhos.
Faria, Chaves & Co.
Faria, Cunha & Co.
Faria & Lopes.
Faria, Xavier de, & Co.
Faria, Barão de.
Faria, Eduardo Ferreira de.
Faria, Urbano da Cunha.
Faro, Joaquim de Mattos.
Fechner, Rodolpho.
Feldmann & Oppenheimer.
Feraudy, Filho, & Pereira.
Fernandes, A. M., & Co.
Fernandes, Barbosa & Co.
Fernandes & Irmão.

RIO DE JANEIRO—Continued.

Importers and exporters—Continued.

Fernandes & Nascimento.
Fernandes, Sá & Co.
Fernandes, Caetano Antunes.
Fernandes, José Antonio.
Ferraz, Araujo & Co.
Ferraz, Soares & Graça.
Ferraz, Sobrinho & Co.
Ferreira, Antonio da Silva, & Co.
Ferreira & Carvalheira.
Ferreira, Carlos Alberto, & Co.
Ferreira, Duarte & Co.
Ferreira, Guia & Co.
Ferreira, Henrique, & Co.
Ferreira, José Passos, & Co.
Ferreira, Martins & Co.
Ferreira, Alfredo Rodrigues.
Ferreira, Heitor A.
Ferreira, João Francisco da Costa.
Ferreira, Joaquim José Gonçalves.
Fiebrig, G., & Co.
Figueiredo, Leite & Co.
Figueiredo, M. J. d'Oliveira.
Filgueiras, Mello & Co.
Filipponi & Filha.
Finnie Irmãos & Co.
Fiorita, A., & Co.
Fischer, Schlatter & Angliker.
Fonseca, Barbosa da, & Co.
Fonseca & Cunha.
Fonseca, Domingos da, & Co.
Fonseca, Ribeiro da, & Co,
Fonseca, Silva & Co.
Fonseca, João Baptista da.
Fonseca, Braga & Co.
Fontes, Bento & Co.
Fontes & Pinheiro.
Fontes, Rodrigues & Co.
Fox & Co.
Franco & Benjamin.
Franco, Joaquim de Mello.
Freire & Martins.
Freitas, A. J. de, & Co.
Freitas, Brandão & Co.
Freitas, J. A. Pinto, & Co.
Freitas, Oliveira & Co.
Freitas, Silva & Pereira.
Frey, Cramer & Co.
Friburgo & Filhos.
Fritz, Mack & Co.
Fróes & Co.
Gabriel, Dénis François.
Gallo, Adriano, & Co.
Gama, Fernando, & Co.
Garai, Emilio.
Garcia & Braga.

RIO DE JANEIRO—Continued.

Importers and exporters—Continued.

Garnier, B. L.
Garcia, Luiz Antonio, junior.
Géraud, Jules.
Gerson & Co.
Gil & Co.
Góes & Mendes.
Gomes, Franco & Co.
Gomes, Fraga & Azevedo.
Gomes, Moura & Co.
Gomes, Evaristo Luiz.
Gomes, Eugenio, & Co.
Gonçalves & Guimarães.
Gonçalves, Costa, Rocha & Menézes.
Gonçalves, Joaquim José, & Co.
Gonçalves & Ribeiro.
Gonçalves, Filho & Co.
Gonçalves & Co.
Gonçalves, A. M., junior, & Co.
Gonçalves, Custodio Baptista.
Gondolo, Carlos.
Gonella, Amadeo.
Gordon, William Ainslie.
Goulart, Arthur.
Gracie, Ferreira & Co.
Granado & Co.
Granja, J. J. Lima & Co.
Granja, José F., & Co.
Granja, Domingos F.
Grelle, Carl F. A., & Co.
Grillo & Moreira.
Gross, C. W., & Co.
Gudgeon, Gustavus, & Co.
Guedes & Costa.
Guedes, Domingos de Souza, & Co.
Guedes, Oliveira, Castro & Mendes.
Gueffier, Ritter & Co.
Gueffier, Paulo.
Guerra, Salles & Co.
Guidão, Braulio & Co.
Guimarães & Soares.
Guimarães, Cardoso & Co.
Guimarães, Carneiro & Co.
Guimarães, Cunha & Co.
Guimarães, Dantas & Co.
Guimarães, Francisco, & Co.
Guimarães, Guilherme, & Co.
Guimarães, Henriques & Co.
Guimarães, J., & Co.
Guimarães & Pereira.
Guimarães, João, & Co.
Guimarães, junior, & Co.
Guimarães, Lopes, & Co.
Guimarães, Machado & Co.
Guimarães, Manoel da Costa, & Co.
Guimarães & Castro.

RIO DE JANEIRO—Continued.

Importers and exporters—Continued.

Guimarães, Monteiro & Co.
Guimarães, Pinto & Sampaio.
Guimarães & Pereira.
Guimarães, Wenceslau, & Co.
Guimarães, Antonio José Alves.
Guimarães, Augusto Cesar da Costa.
Guimarães, J. F. de Freitas.
Guimarães, José Ferreira Machado.
Guimarães, José J. da Silva.
Guimarães, Manoel José de Souza.
Haas, Isidore.
Hall, J. V., & Co.
Hamann & Co.
Hamilton & Co.
Hanriot, Gustavo.
Harberts & Co.
Hard, Rand & Co.
Hampshire, Harold José.
Hasenclever & Co.
Haupt & Co.
Hecksher, Chr., & Co.
Hellot, E.
Hederström, Henning.
Hermanny, Louis, & Co.
Hermanos Frias & Co.
Hirsch, Coulon & Hanau.
Hirsch, H., & Co.
Honold, Luiz.
Hopkins, Causer & Hopkins.
Iguassú & Co.
Ipanema, Barão de.
Jacintho & Rebello.
Jalles, Mascarenhas & Co.
Janacopulos, George Constantino.
Janowitzer, Veit & Co.
Januario, Coelho & Co.
Janvrot & Macedo.
Jeroloni & Co.
Jessop, William J.
Johnston, Edward, & Co.
Joppert, Furquim & Co.
Joppert, G., & Co.
Jordão, Miranda & Co.
Jorge, J., & Co.
Jorge, Manoel M.
Kastrup, Arthur, & Co.
Klingelhoefer & Co.
Lacerda, J. F. de, & Co.
Lacerda, Rodrigues & Co.
Lacerda Saturnino & Co.
Lachaud, P., & Co.
Lacombe, D. L.
Laemmert & Co.
Laforcade, P., & Co.
Lage Irmãos.

RIO DE JANEIRO—Continued.

Importers and exporters—Continued.

Lagôa, Barão da Ant.
Lahmeyer, João Alex.
Lambert, Émile.
Laport, G., & Co.
Laport, Henrique, & Co.
Laureys & Co.
Lazary, C., & Co.
Lecocq, Oliveira & Co.
Leal, Oliveira & Silva.
Lehéricy, A., & Co.
Leitão, Machado & Co.
Leite & Alves.
Leite, Corrêa & Co.
Leite, Dourado & Co.
Leite & Nunes.
Leite, Pinto & Co.
Leite & Raymundó.
Leite, S. de Sampaio & Co.
Leite, Eduardo.
Leite & Cortes.
Leite & Co.
Leite, Augusto Xavier.
Lemgruber & Lemgruber.
Lemgruber, Moreira & Co.
Lemos, Faria & Co.
Lemos, João Pereira de.
Lemos, junior, & Pinheiro.
Leonardos Othon.
Leuba, Aug., & Co.
Leuba Montandon & Co.
Leuba, Henrique.
Leuzinger & Filhos.
Lévy & Frère.
Levy Irmãos & Co.
Lidgerwood Manufacturing Machine Co.
Liebmann, Gustavo, & Co.
Liebmann, E.
Lima, Araujo & Co.
Lima, Dourado & Ladeira.
Lima, Pinto & Co.
Lima & Guimarães.
Lima, João Antonio Santos.
Linger, B., & Co.
Lisbôa, M. V., & Co.
Lixa & Dias.
Lopes, Antonio, & Co.
Lopes, Faceiro & Co.
Lopes & Irmão.
Lopes, Teixeira & Co.
Loureiro, F., & Co.
Lourical & Quartin.
Lumay, Francisco.
Luquet, F. L.
Lutz, Gustavo.
Lyra, junior, & Co.

RIO DE JANEIRO—Continued.

Importers and exporters—Continued.

Macedo, junior, & Co.
Macedo, L. de, & Co.
Macedo, M., & Co.
Macedo, Sepulveda & Co.
Macedo, Teixeira de, & Co.
Machado & Carvalho.
Machado, Cerqueira & Co.
Machado & Irmão.
Machado, Meira & Co.
Machado, Souza & Co.
Machado, José R. de A.
Mackenzie, P. A. C.
McKinnell & Co.
Magalhães & Bastos.
Magalhães & Veiga.
Magalhães, João José F.
Magalhães, João Paulo de A.
Maia, Ant. de A., & Co.
Maia, Antonio de Castilho.
Maior, Sotto & Co.
Malafaia & Co.
Mansell & Carré.
Marie, Arthur.
Marinhas, Antonio Martins, & Co.
Marinho, Reis & Co.
Marinho, João Ant, L.
Marques, J. F., & Co.
Marques, Manoel Antunes.
Marti & Co.
Marti, H.
Martins, Caetano & Co.
Martins, Custodio & Co.
Martins & Menezes.
Martins, Moreira & Co.
Martins, Diogo Candido.
Martins, J.
Mascarenhas, Gontijo & Co.
Matthew, James, & Co.
Mattos, Carvalho & Co.
Mattos, Dias & Co.
Mattos, Fernandes de, & Co.
Mattos & Santos.
Mattos, V. J. de, & Co.
Maury, Pedro M.
May, E. W.
Mayrink, Abreu & Co.
Meirelles & Co.
Mello & Alves.
Mello, Souza & Co.
Mello, Alfredo Luiz de.
Mello, Vicente L. F. de.
Mendes & Braga.
Mendes, Gonçalves & Co.
Mendes & Rocha.
Mendes, Victor.

RIO DE JANEIRO—Continued.

Importers and exporters—Continued.
Mendonça & Lima.
Menezes, Laranja & Oliveira.
Mentges, F., & Co.
Merino & Loureiro.
Merker, A.
Merlin, Ernest.
Mertens, L.
Mesquita, Firmino de O.
Mesquita, José dos Santos.
Metzger, Alfred.
Meyer, Eugenio & Co.
Meyer & Vaz.
Meyer, Alfredo.
Migliora, V., & Co.
Miranda, Boucher & Soares.
Miranda & Soares.
Miranda & Dias.
Miranda, José de, & Co.
Miranda & Villela.
Miranda, Bernardo Affonso de.
Miranda, Joaquim Bueno de.
Mocker, Carlos.
Moitinho, Domingos.
Monarcha & Fonseca.
Monteiro, Cardoso & Co.
Monteiro, Francisco Ant., & Co.
Monteiro, Guimarães & Belmiro.
Monteiro & Hime.
Monteiro, Joaquim Manoel, & Co.
Monteiro, Luiz de Andrade. Monteiro, junior, & Co.
Monteiro, Miranda & Co.
Montenegro, Fernando, & Co.
Moore, John, & Co.
Mora, Henrique.
Moraes, Castro & Co.
Moraes, J. J. Pereira de, & Co.
Moraes, José M. P. de.
Moraes, José da Costa, junior.
Moreira, Manoel J., & Co.
Moreira, Pinho & Co.
Moreira, Pinto & Co.
Moreira, José Maria Rodrigues.
Morrissy Brothers.
Morrissy, Guilherme.
Morrissy, Martin.
Motta, Fraga & Azevedo.
Motta, José G. da, & Co.
Motta, Souza & Co.
Mounier & Filho.
Moura, Braga & Co.
Moura, de, & Tenente.
Moura & Co.
Mourão, Cunha & Co.
Mourão & Gomes.

S. Ex. 8, pt. 11——5

RIO DE JANEIRO—Continued.

Importers and exporters—Continued.
Mourão, Rebello & Co.
Mourão, Victorino, & Co.
Mourão, Francisco da Silva.
Muniz, A., & Co.
Myohl, H., & Co.
Narciso, Ribeiro, Leite & Co.
Nascimento, José T. do, & Co.
Nascimento & Maia.
Nascimento, Maia & Costa.
Natividade & Co.
Neff, Raymundo & Co.
Neves, Silva & Co.
Nicolson, P. S., & Co.
Nicoud, G. Alfred.
Nielsen, E., & Co.
Netto, Victorino Alves, & Co.
Newlands Irmãos & Co.
Nobrega Lino, Rodrigues.
Noé Irmãos & Co.
Noellner, Carl.
Nogueira, Dias & Co.
Nogueira, José Amaro.
Norton, Megaw & Co.
Northmann, Max, & Co.
Novaes, Souza & Co.
Novaes, P. A. de Mello.
Novella, Lucas.
Nunes, Mercadante & Co.
Nunes, J. A., & Co.
Nunes & Co.
Okell, Mourão & Wilson.
Oliveira, Antonio de, & Co.
Oliveira, filho & Co.
Oliveira, J. F. de, & Co.
Oliveira, João Antonio de, & Co.
Oliveira, Magalhães & Co.
Oliveira, Soares de, & Co.
Oliveira, Valle & Co.
Oliveira & Gonçalves.
Oliveira, Bernardino Luiz de.
Oliveira, Joaquim Coelho de.
Oliveira, José Pinto de.
Ortigão & Co.
Pacheco, João Corrêa, & Co.
Padua & Co.
Paranhos, José P. da S.
Paradeda, Jaime.
Pareto, Claviez & Co.
Paridant, L.
Parisot & Rufler.
Passos Fernando, & Co.
Peake, J. & J.
Pecher, Ed. & Co.
Pedemonte, Salvador.
Pedro, Irmão & Co.

RIO DE JANEIRO—Continued.

Importers and exporters –Continued.

Pedroso, Moraes & Co.
Peixoto, Marques & Co.
Peixoto, Mora & Co.
Penfold, W.
Pentagna, N., & Co.
Pereira, A., & Co.
Pereira & Bens.
Pereira, Costa & Co.
Pereira & Almeida.
Pereira, Ferraz & Co.
Pereira, Gonçalves & Co.
Pereira, Lobato & Co.
Pereira, Pinto & Vieira.
Pereira & Ramalho.
Pereira & Sobrinhos.
Pereira, Silva & Co.
Pereira & Valentim.
Pereira, Luiz Gomes.
Petersen, Herm., & Co.
Petzold, H., & Co.
Petzold, O. & H.
Pfaltzgraff, Carlos Augusto.
Pfuhl, Carl.
Philippi, Oscar, & Co.
Phipps Irmãos & Co.
Pimenta, Jeronymo, & Co.
Pimenta, Silva & Co.
Pimenta, Luiz Antonio.
Pinheiro, Silva & Co.
Pinheiro, F. A. Xavier.
Pinho, Martins de, & Co.
Pinho, Sebiastião.
Pinto, Francisco, & Co.
Pinto, José Neves, & Co.
Pinto & Madureira.
Pinto, Motta & Co.
Pinto, Braulio & Co.
Pinto & Co.
Pinto Teixeira & Co.
Pinto, Irmão & Co.
Pinto, Antonio José.
Pinto, Joaquim Pereira.
Pires, Ferreira & Co.
Pires & Faria.
Pires & Pinheiro.
Pires, Rios & Co.
Pires, Antonio Nunes.
Pollery, Alvares & Co.
Portelinha & Co.
Porto, J. P. R., & Co.
Porto, L. A. da Silva.
Portugal & Co.
Potey, Rabert & Co.
Pradez & Fils.
Prado, Marinho & Co.

RIO DE JANEIRO—Continued.

Importers and exporters—Continued.

Proença & Co.
Purchas, J. W. B.
Queiroz & Caplionch.
Queiroz, Moreira & Co.
Queiroz & Co.
Quirino Irmãos & Co.
Rabello, Portella & Co.
Rahm, Guilherme.
Ramiro, Vieira & Co.
Ramos, Almeida & Co.
Ramos, Irmão & Rocha.
Ramos, M., & Co.
Ramos, Peixoto & Co.
Ramos, Sobrinho & Co.
Ramos, Rodrigues & Co.
Ramos, Varzim & Co.
Ramos & Co.
Ramos, P. A. de Andrade.
Raposo, João Gonçalves.
Raynsford, Carlos Alexandra.
Rebello & Bastos, junior.
Rebello, Irmão & Co.
Rebello, M., & Co.
Rebello & Silva.
Rée frères.
Reis, Brandão & Co.
Reis & Nogueira.
Reis, Henriques Costa, & Co.
Reis, João José dos, & Co.
Reis, Machado & Co.
Reis & Saraiva.
Reis, M. da Silva.
Repsold, J. Georg.,
Reys, F. J. Freitas dos.
Rezende Luiz de, & Co.
Rezende, Manoel Duarte.
Rhind, C. B.
Ribeiro & Gonçalves.
Ribeiro, Alves & Co.
Ribeiro, Augusto, & Co.
Ribeiro, Barros & Braga.
Ribeiro, Esteves & Co.
Ribeiro, Irmão & Co
Ribeiro, José Maria, & Co.
Ribeiro, Souza & Co.
Ribeiro, José Paulino.
Ribeiro, Paiva & Bernardes.
Ricões, Antonio José.
Riechers, Richard, & Co.
Rocha, Barros & Moreira.
Rocha, Carneiro & Co.
Rocha, Ribeiro & Co.
Rocha, Roque & Co.
Rocha & Saldanha.
Rocha, José M. C. da.

RIO DE JANEIRO—Continued.

Importers and exporters—Continued.
Rocha & Souza.
Rodrigues, Belmiro & Co.
Rodrigues & Pinheiro.
Rodrigues, Leopoldo.
Rogers, Henry, Sons & Co.
Röhe, Henrique Christiano.
Romaguera & Co.
Romaguera, José.
Romariz & Co.
Rombauer & Co.
Roque, Victorino, & Co.
Rosario, Oliveira & Co.
Rossi, Luiz.
Roth, Schanz & Co.
Roul'na, Ch.
Rôxo, Fonseca & Santos.
Rôxo, Lemos & Co.
Ruch, F.
Ruchon Irmãos.
Sá, Carvalhos & Co.
Sá, Cunha & Co.
Sá, Santos & Co.
Saboia & Guimarães.
Saint-Denis, E. de, & Co.
Francisco, Visconde de S.
Saint Martin, C.
Saldanha & Co.
Sampaio & Faria.
Sampaio & Co.
Sampaio, Irmãos & Sobrinho.
Sampaio, Fred. de F.
Samuel & Vianna.
Samuel Irmãos & Co.
Santiago, Manoel J. P.
Santos, Abreu & Co.
Santos & Serra.
Santos, José A. G., & Co.
Santos, Mendes & Co.
Santos, Nunes dos, & Co.
Santos, A. M. dos.
Santos, Bartholomeu Soares dos.
Santos, D. J. de Oliveira.
Santos Irmãos.
Santos, João M. C. dos.
Santos, José da Silva.
Santos, Manoel Pinto dos.
Santos, Venancio dos.
Banville, George, & Co.
Saraiva, Delphim Rodrigues.
Sauwen, F., & Co.
Schindler & Co.
Schloss, Philippe, & fils.
Schmidt & Irmão.
Schmidt, F., & Co.
Schmidt, Symons & MacKinlay.

RIO DE JANEIRO—Continued.

Importers and exporters—Continued.
Schmidt, Frederico Augusto.
Seabra, G. Garcia.
Sederstrom & Guimarães.
Sequeira Dias Irmãos.
Sequeira & Irmãos.
Silberberg, Muhlrad Poznanski.
Silva, Azevedo & Co.
Silva, Braga & Marques.
Silva, Carvalho & Coelho.
Silva & Corrêa.
Silva, Corrêa da, & Co.
Silva, Francisco Gomes da, & Co.
Silva, Gaspar da, & Co.
Silva, Lowndes & Co.
Silva, Pereira da, & Co.
Silva & Pinna.
Silva & Rocha.
Silva, da, & Marques.
Silva, Vieira & Co.
Silva & Co.
Silva, Alfredo Augusto da.
Silva, Cardosa, filho, & Co.
Silva, Carlos G. da.
Silva, Claudio José da.
Silva, Delphim R. da.
Silva, E. L. da.
Silva, Joaquim P. da.
Silva, Manoel D. da.
Silva, Manoel F. Dias da, junior.
Silveira, Frederico da, & Co.
Silveira, Antonio J. C. da.
Silveira, M. G. da.
Simões, Costa & Co.
Simões, José Joaquim da Costa.
Simonard, H.
Simonetti, A., & Co.
The Singer Manufacturing Co.
Soares, Araujo & Santos.
Soares, Coelho & Co.
Soares & Lavrador.
Soares & Martins.
Soares, Quartin, Silveira & Co.
Soares, Manoel José.
Soccorro, Moraes & Irmão.
Soccorro, Vinceute Alves do.
Souza, Antonio Gonçalves de, & Co.
Souza, Antonio Leandro de.
Souza, Assumpcão & Co.
Souza, Cerqueira & Co.
Souza, Fonseca & Co.
Souza G. Irmãos.
Souza Irmãos & Co.
Souza, Irmão, Queiroz & Filho.
Souza, J. de, & Co.
Souza, Carlos M. de.

68

BRAZIL.

RIO DE JANEIRO—Continued.

Importers and exporters—Continued.
Souza, Ignacio T. de.
Souza, M. José de.
Smart, Edward J.
Smith & Youle.
Spolydoro & Co.
Steele, Andrew, & Co.
Stoltz, Herm., & Co.
Struve, Proença & Co.
Sucena, J. R.
- Swanwick & Gordon.
Tavares, J., & Co.
Taves, Paul.
Teixeira & Borges.
Teixeira, Eduardo, & Co.
Teixeira, José Augusto.
Teixeira junior, & Pinto.
Terra, Ludovico E. K. de.
Thiago & Filhos.
Teixeira, Ferraz & Pinto.
Tobias, Ignacio & Co.
Topin, Francisco B. M.
Torres, A. J. Rodrigues, & Co.
Torres, Alves & Co.
Torres, Arthur, & Co.
Torres, J. J, & Co,
Torres, Mattos & Camarão.
Torres & Pacheco.
Torres, Vianna & Co.
Torres, João da S.
Totta, Barão de Mendes.
Tribolet, Frederico.
Trinks, Gustav, & Co.
Valle & Oliveira.
Valais, Karl, & Co.
Valle & Silva.
Valle, Silveira & Co.
Valverde & Co.
Van Erven Irmãos.
Vasconcellos, Jacintho Leal de.
Vasconcellos, José Smith de, junior.
Vautelet & Duceux.
Veiga & Co.
Veiga, Pinto & Co.
Velloso, Manoel Joaquim Pimenta.
Villaverde & Co.
Vianna, Castro & Co.
Vianna, de Rezende & Co.
Vianna, A. J. de Araujo.
Vianna, Manoel José Gonçalves.
Vieira, Dantas & Co.
Vieira, Menezes & Co.
Vieira, Mattos & Albano.
Vieira, Rebello & Co.
Vieira, José Maria Fernandes.
Vierling, Frederico, & Co.

RIO DE JANEIRO—Continued.

Importers and exporters—Continued.
Viggiano, Dangelo & Co.
Villela, Gomes & Co.
Villela & Miranda.
Villela, José Luiz Fernandes.
Vincenzi & Filho.
Vincenzi, Claudio S. do.
Wagner, E., & Co.
Walter, Hime & Co.
Watson, Ritchie & Co.
Wellisch & Irmão.
Werneck & Oliveira.
Wille, Schmilinsky & Co.
Wilson, Sons & Co.
Wyatt, James H.
Xavier, Fernando Gomes & Co.
Xerez, Francisco de.
Young, Hugh.
Yzurzun, Gregorio, & Co.
Zenha, Ramos & Co.
Zenha & Silveira.
Zenha, Salgado & Co.

Iron furniture and bed manufacturers and mer-
chants.
Costa, Oliveira & Co.
Costa & Silva.
Campos, Adão da Costa, & Boher.
Erven, João van.
Guimarães. J. C., & Co.
Magalhães, Rodrigo Camillo de Souza, & Co.
Oliveira, Leal, & Silva.
Porto, Joaquim Pinto Ribeiro.
Valle & Silva.

Iron, safe and balance manufacturers and mer-
chants.
Caussat, C. A.
Conteville, Carlos.
Domèrs, H.
Guimarães, Wenceslau & Co
Haffner, Pierre.
Isnard, J. B.
Petzold, O. & H.

Jewelry, etc., merchants.
Aderne, Theodolina Caroline.
Aguiar, Francisco Ignacio de Oliveira, & Co
Aguiar, João Ignacio de Oliveira
Aguiar & Porto.
Almeida, Abilio Manoel de.
Amaral, Francisco, & Co.
Avila, Wilfrid Josué de.
Baker, William Gore.
Barbosa & Co.
Barbosa, Francisco de Paula.
Barbosa, Silverio José.
Barros, F. Ribeiro de.

RIO DE JANEIRO—Continued.

Jewelry, etc., merchants—Continued.
Bastos, Seraphim da Motta.
Bastos, João Meirelles.
Borges, Antonio Gonçalves de Oliveira.
Bove, Achille.
Braga, Manoel Antonio Gomes.
Branco, Manoel Alves.
Bubois, Augusto, & filhos.
Carvalho, Honorio de, & Co.
Carvalho, Manoel José da Silva.
Cassella, A. P.
Castro, Antonio Alves Vieira de.
Coelho, José Pinheiro.
Colucci, Benjamin.
Comte, E. Bailly.
Costa, Antonio Teixera da.
Costa Ayres.
Cruz, Antonio Gonçalves.
Cunha, Antonio Gonçalves da.
Dantas, Antonio José.
Deserbelles, Prosper.
Diederich, A., & Co.
Doti, Miguel.
Du Bois, Charles Damien Maeder.
Duque, Camillo, & Co.
Esmeriz & Avila.
Faller, Francisco de Salles.
Farani & Sobrinhos.
Faria & Lopes.
Ferraz, José Gonçalves.
Ferreira, José Manoel.
Ferreira, José Miguel.
Ferreira, Pedro Lourenço dos Santos.
Ferreira, Vicente Francisco.
Fonseca, Thiago Pinheiro da.
Freitas & Alves.
Freitas, Antonio Rodrigues de.
Gabriel, Viuva.
Gama, Figueiredo.
Garbeirou, E.
Germain, Francisco José, & Co.
Germain & Co.
Germann, F. J.
Gerson & Co.
Gomes, Francisco José.
Gonçalves, Antonio José.
Gondolo, Carlos.
Guimarães, Casimiro José Monteiro.
Guimarães, Joaquina Fiusa.
Guimarães, Manoel da Cruz Freitas.
Guimarães, Manoel Gonçalves.
Gurgin, Domingos.
Haas, G.
Hanriot, Victor, & Filho.
Hermany, Louis, & Co.
Hirsch, Coulon & Hanau.

RIO DE JANEIRO—Continued.

Jewelry, etc., merchants—Continued.
Hivernat & Co.
Horta, José de Oliveira.
Jacques, Luiz.
Krussmann, F., & Co.
Lacroix, Julio.
Laforcade, P., & Co.
Lecouflé, Augusto, & Co.
Lévy, Irmãos & Co.
Liebmann, E.
Lima, João F. de.
Lommez, Carlos.
Magalhães, Faustino Taveira de.
Magalhães, Francisco Taveira de.
Marciano, Domingos.
Marques, Luiz Teixeira & Irmão.
Martin, C. Saint.
Masson, Jacintho Prudencio.
Menezes, José Maria Barreto de.
Menezes, Barreto de.
Merlin, Ernst.
Mesquita, Wenceslau Antonio de.
Miranda & Dias.
Monteiro, José Moreira.
Moraes, Henrique Cardoso de.
Moreira, Francisco Alves.
Morrot, Eugenio.
Motta, Azuil Augusto da.
Nascimento, Albino do.
Nemettzass, C. A.
Norris & Co.
Oliveira, Candido José Fernandes de.
Pedemonte, Salvador.
Pelissier, François.
Pereira, José Duarte.
Pernod, Emilio.
Perriraz, Alberto Marcos.
Pfallzgraff, Pedro, & Co.
Pimentel, Carlos Frederico.
Pinho, Viuva.
Pinto, Joaquim Ferraz de Souza.
Puissegur, José Frederico.
Rego, Antonio de Castro.
Resse, Victor, Filho, & Irmão.
Reys, I. G., & Co.
Rezende, João Luiz de.
Rezende, Luiz de, & Co.
Ribeiro & Fanzeres.
Rocha, Alvaro & Co.
Rocha, Antonio Alves da.
Romano, Victor Roque.
Rosas, Antonio Joaquim.
Roulina, Ch.
Santa Anna, Celestina M.
Santos, Viuva, Pereira dos, & Moreira.
Santos, Antonio de Oliveira.

RIO DE JANEIRO—Continued.

Jewelry, etc., merchants—Continued.
Santos, Clarimundo Barreto dos.
Sarrat, Felix Manot.
Seidmann, David
Silberberg, Muhlrad & Poznanski.
Silberberg, Salomon.
Silva, Pedro Pereira da.
Silveira, A. M. da.
Silveira, Alfredo Cesar da.
Silveira, Francisco José da.
Silveira, José Gonçalves da.
Silveira, Manoel José da.
Soares & Loureiro.
Souza, José Vicente de.
Tempette, Hector.
Torres, Irmãos & Carneiro.
Ulysses & Pinho.
Valentim, M. J.
Vasconcellos, Antonio Rosario Rodrigues de.
Vasconcellos, Augusto de Araujo.
Vasconcellos, João Araujo de.
Vernaut, Guilherme.
Vianna, João Candido Martins.
Vianna, José Gonçalves.
Vieira, D.
Walther, João Gottlieb.
Walther, João Henrique.
Wöllner, Severino.
Worms, Emilio.
Worms, José.

Kitchen utensil manufacturers.
Affonso, Cruz & Co.
Affonso & Lima.
Agostinho, Gabriel & Freitas.
Aguiar, João & Co.
Alberto & Co.
Almeida, Alberto de, & Co.
Almeida & Silva.
Almeida, J. J., junior.
Amorim & Irmão.
Araujo, Martins & Co.
Araujo, Avila de.
Aspinall, Jones & Co.
Azarias, Antão & Co.
Azevedo, Joaquim Alves de.
Azevedo, José G. de, & Co.
Barbosa, José Joaquim.
Bastos & Guimarães.
Bifano & Rocha.
Botelho, Irmão & Andrade.
Botelho & Co.
Brandão, Freitas & Co.
Brandão, Jeremias de Carvalho & Co.
Brandão, L., & Co.
Brando & Irmão.
Breissan, J. B., & Co.

RIO DE JANEIRO—Continued.

Kitchen utensil manufacturers—Continued.
Brito, Francisco A. da Silva.
Campo-Verde & Mattos.
Campos, Castro & Co.
Canejo, João Francisco.
Carneiro & Co.
Carvalho, Mello & Co.
Carvalho, Silva & Co.
Carvalho, Soares de, & Co.
Carvalho, José Bento Alves da.
Cassels, W. R., & Co.
Castro, Adriano de, & Co.
Castro, Gonçalo de, & Co.
Castro, Monteiro de, & Co.
Castro, Rocha & Co.
Castro & Oliveira.
Costa, A. G., junior.
Costa, Antonio Martins da, & Co.
Costa & Figueiredo.
Costa, Manoel da Silva.
Costa & Costa.
Couto, Fernandes & Co.
Cunha, Ildefonso de Souza.
Dantas, Freitas & Co.
Dias, João Antonio.
Domingues & Rodrigues.
Ennes & Silva.
Ennes & Co.
Fernandes, Sá & Co.
Fernandes, Francisco José.
Ferraz, Lopes & Co.
Ferreira, A. Sobrinho & Co.
Ferreira, Antonio da Silva & Co.
Ferreira, Manoel, C. B., junior.
Fonseca & Vieira.
Fontes, Domingos & Co.
Fontes, Firmino & Co.
Gama, Fernando & Co.
Gazio & Sampaio.
Gomes de Castro Sobrinho & Co.
Gonçalves, José Antonio, & Co.
Gonçalves, Reis & Co.
Gonçalves, Luiz José.
Gontijo, Mascarenhas & Co.
Guerra, José Tavares.
Guerra, Luiz Ribeiro.
Guillobel & Co.
Guimarães, Antonio de Freitas.
Guimarães, M. J. da Costa, & Co.
Guimarães, Fernandes, & Co.
Guimarães & Ferreira.
Guimarães, João Antunes de Oliveira.
Guimarães, José F. C., & Co.
Guimarães, Moutinho & Co.
Guimarães & Co.
Guimaraes, Eduardo Pereira.

RIO DE JANEIRO—Continued.

Kitchen utensil manufacturers—Continued.
Hampshire, Harold José.
Jessop, William J.
Klingelhoefer & Co.
Lazary, C., & Co.
Leitão, Borges & Co.
Lima, Pinto & Co.
Lima & Guimarães.
Lobo & Abilio.
Machado, Faria & Co.
Machado, Antonio.
Machado, João da Gama.
Magalhães & Irmãos.
Maia, Calazans & Co.
Maia, Antonio de C.
Maia, Mendes & Co.
Mano, Costa & Co.
Marinho, Antonio.
Marques, Antunes & Co.
Menezes, J. de, & Co.
Monteiro, Antonio G. P.
Montenegro, Fernando, & Co.
Montenegro & Co.
Moraes, Luciano Pereira de, & Co.
Moreira & Ferreira.
Moreira, Joaquim Rodrigues.
Netto, Pereira & Co.
Nobre, Souza & Co.
Noellner, Carl.
Nunes, Antonio Ferreira.
Oliveira, Costa & Co.
Oliveira, C. L. de, & Co.
Oliveira, João José da Costa, & Co.
Oliveira, José Agusto de, & Co.
Oliveira, João F. de.
Pacheco, Antonio Pereira.
Pagani, Constantino.
Paredes, Joaquim José de Almeida.
Pedreira, João Baptista.
Pereira, Antonio, & Co.
Quartin & Co.
Ramos & Pereira.
Ramos, Irmão & Rocha.
Ribeiro, Abel Costa.
Rocha & Oliveira.
Rogers, Henry Sons, & Co.
Rodrigues, Francisco, & Co.
Rodrigues, M. M.
Santos, Paschoal & Co.
Santos, Thomaz Rodrigues dos
Sanville, George, & Co.
Silva & Ferreira.
Silva, Santos & Co.
Silva, Abel Joaquim da.
Silva, José J. P. da.
Silva, Manoel M. da.

RIO DE JANEIRO—Continued.

Kitchen utensil manufacturers—Continued.
Silveira, Manoel G.
Simões, Manoel Antonio.
Simonard, H.
Soares & Irmãos.
Souza & Barboza.
Souza, Fonseca & Co.
Souza & Quirino.
Sucena, J. R.
Tavares & Costa.
Tavares, J., & Co.
Tavares, A. Pinto.
Vianna, Alexandre Martins.
Vianna, Francisco Martins.
Victorino, Cordosa Valente Sobrinho.
Victorino & Fontes.

Liquor merchants and manufacturers.
Agostinho Rodrigues Ramos.
Antonio da Cunha Magalhaes Sobrinho.
Antonio Ferreira da Silva Santos.
Benjamin do Carmo Braga.
Braga, Irmãos & Co.
Carmo Braga, Salgado & Co.
Courréges & Jean.
Drouhins, Noth & Co.
Ernesto Gomes de Oliveira & Co.
Esteves & Plamplona.
Fontana & Portilho.
Fortunato Pereira da Cunha & Co.
Francisco da Silva Sepulveda.
José Coffarema & Co.
José de Sousa & Silva Braga.
Juan Ollivella.
Machado, Irmão & Co.
Macedo, Reis & Co.
Mourão & Gomez.
Rodrigues de Sá & Co.
Santos & Costa.
Santos & Pedroso.
Santos, Pinto & Teixeira.
Schumann, C., & Co.

Machine manufacturers and merchants.
Alegria & Co.
Alves, Severino Silvestre.
Amoretti, Viuva Leocadia.
Araujo, Joaquim.
Arens, Irmãos.
Aspinall, Jones & Co.
Bastos, José Ribeiro.
Bouchet, Ch.
Braga, Anto. José Rodrigues.
Carvalho, Moreira & Co.
Companhia Constructora.
Conteville, Carlos.
Coral, A. M., & Co.

RIO DE JANEIRO—Continued.

Machine manufacturers and merchants—Cont'd.
Couto, Small & Co.
Cunha, Faustino José da.
Delforge, H. Ulique.
Erven, João van.
. Ennes & Co.
Faro, Joaquim de Mattos.
Fechner, Rodolpho.
Ferreira, Costa & Co.
Ferreira & Co.
Grande, G. F.
Hampshire, Harold José.
Haupt & Co.
Hopkins, Causer & Hopkins.
Jessop, William J.
Krupp, Friederich.
Lambert, Émile.
Leal, Oliveira & Silva.
Lidgerwood Manufacturing Co.
Lemgruber & Lemgruber.
Loureira, Marques & Co.
Mansell & Carré.
Marques, J. F., & Co.
Marques, Teixeira & Co.
Mattos, A. G. de, & Co.
Mello & Costa.
Mello, José Pimenta de.
Middleton & Lancaster.
Moreira, Manoel Joaquim, & Co.
Northmann. Max., & Co.
Olveira & Colomb.
Pasos, Antonio da Rocha.
Repsold, J. Georg.
Rocha, Carneiro & Co.
Rogers, Henry, Sons & Co.
Sanville, George, & Co.
Sauwen, F., & Co.
Soares, José Bernardo Pereira.
Souza, Albano de, & Co.
Tavares, A. Pinto.
Van Erven & Irmãos.
Vierling, Frederico, & Co.
Music publishers.
Mackar & Noël.
Novelties and fancy goods.
Agostinho, Gabriel & Freitas.
Alfredo & Co.
Almeida, Alberto de, & Co.
Almeida, João de.
Almeida, M., & Co.
Alves, Felisberto José & Co.
Amaral, Manoel Gonçalves de.
Andrade, A. P. de, & Co.
Antão, Azarias & Co.
Antão, Carlos & Co.
Araujo, Avila de.

RIO DE JANEIRO—Continued.

Novelties and fancy goods—Continued.
Araujo, Coque & Co.
Araujo, Francisco José Leite de.
Araujo, Manoel Lopes de.
Araujo, Martins & Co.
Armada, Joaquim Alvaro d', & Co.
Augusto, Vaz & Co.
Avila, Francisco Coelho de.
Ayres, José Thomaz.
Azevedo, José Caetano de.
Azevedo, Joaquim Alves de,
Azevedo, José Gonçalves de, & Co.
Azevedo & Pereira.
Azevedo, M. P. de, junior.
Bahia Irmãos.
Baltar, Manoel F. C., junior.
Baltar & Pinho.
Baptista, A., & Co.
Baptista, João & Co.
Barbosa & Co.
Barbosa, Freitas & Co.
Barbosa, Gomes & Co.
Barbosa, Julio Antonio.
Barboza & Angelo.
Barboza, Maya & Co.
Bastos, A. J. da Motta.
Bastos & Moreira.
Bastos, F. F. Pinto & Co.
Bastos, Oliveira & Co.
Bifano & Rocha.
Bittencourt, Joaquim Ignacio de.
Borges, Luiz Martins.
Botelho, Irmão & Andrade.
Braga, Coutinho & Co.
Braga, José de Macedo Manso.
Branco, Pedro Castello.
Brando & Irmão.
Bruno, José.
Caldas, José da Silva.
Caldeira & Co.
Campos & Teixeira.
Cardoso, B. P., & Co.
Cardoso & Brito.
Cardoso, M. de Mesquita, & Co.
Carmo, Manoel & Co.
Carneiro & Gomes
Carvalhaes, Epiphanio A. B.
Carvalhaes, José de Barros.
Carvalho, Agostinho Ferreira de.
Carvalho, Antonio Augusto de.
Carvalho, Antonio Joaquim de.
Carvalho, Bernardino Marinho de.
Carvalho, Mello & Co.
Carvalho, Silva & Co.
Casaes & Ramos.
Castro & Oliveira.

RIO DE JANEIRO- -Continued.

Novelties and fancy goods—Continued.
Castro, Antonio José de.
Cesario, Pires & Co.
Chagas, Osorio & Co.
Conceição & Cunha.
Corrêa & Freitas.
Corrêa, José Francisco Antonio.
Costa, Antonio A. da.
Costa, Antonio Martins da, & Co.
Costa, Francisco José da, & Co.
Costa, Marcellino da, & Co.
Costa, Pacheco & Co.
Costa, Souza & Co.
Couto, Domingos Ribeiro do.
Cruz, Antonio José da.
Cruz & Rosa.
Cunh , Ildefonso de Souza.
Dantas, Freitas & Co.
Dias, A. C. Loureiro.
Dias, José Francisco de Souza.
Duarte & Vaz.
Eduardo & Co.
Elias, José.
Elsten, Affonso Manoel Tavares.
Faria, Bernardes & Co.
Faria, Luiz da Costa & Co.
Feitoso, José & Co.
Feraudy, Filho & Pereira.
Fernandes, Barroso & Co.
Fernandes, Couto & Co.
Fernandes, Sá & Co.
Fernandes, Sebastião.
Ferreira, Alves Sobrinho & Co.
Ferreira, Antonio da Silva & Co.
Ferreira, Francisco P.
Ferreira, Joaquim dos Santos.
Figueiredo, Vianna & Co.
Fonseca, João Mendes da.
Fontes, Domingos & Co.
França, Luiz Carlos da.
Franco, Abel Gomes & Co.
Freire, Souza & Co.
Freitas, Brandão & Co.
Frigit, Augusto.
Furiati, Braz Antonio.
Garcia & Braga.
Garai, Emilio.
Gaspar & Irmão.
Geslin, Mme.
Gomes & Co.
Gomes de C., Sobrinho & Co.
Gomes, J. J., & Co.
Gomes, Rufino & Co.
Gomes, Torres & Co.
Gonçalves, Candido & Co.
Gonçalves, Luiz José & Co.

RIO DE JANEIRO—Continued.

Novelties and fancy goods—Continued.
Gonçalves, Reis & Co.
Gonçalves, Francisco Ribeiro.
Gonçalves, João Marcellino.
Gontejo, Mascarenhas & Co.
Goulart & Irmão.
Graça, Quartin, Guerra & Co.
Graça, Soares Quartin & Co.
Guerra, Antunes & Co.
Guerra, C. J. da Fonesca.
Guimarães & Co.
Guimarães, Bastos & Fernando.
Guimarães, Edylio.
Guimarães & Ferreira.
Guimarães & Irmão.
Guimarães, J.
Guimarães, José Carlos de Oliveira.
Guimarães, José Ferreira C., & Co.
Guimarães, M. J. da Costa.
Guimarães, Manoel Ribeiro da Costa.
Guimarães, Montinho & Co.
Guimarães, Sampaio & Co.
Guimarães & Soares.
Juvanon & Couto.
Klingelhoe'er & Co.
Lago, J. L. P. do, & Co.
Leite, Francisco, & Co.
Lima, Antonio Hygino do.
Lima, Antonio J. de C.
Lima & Guimarães.
Lima, Miguel L. S. de.
Lima, Pinto & Co.
Linhares, José B.
Lobo, Ant. J.
Lontra & Irmão.
Macedo, Teixeira de, & Co.
Machado, Albano D.
Machado, Antonio, G., & Co.
Madahil, Augusto dos Santos.
Magalhães, Graça & Co.
Magalhães & Irmão.
Maia, Mendes & Co.
Mano, Costa & Co.
Mansur & Antonio.
Marinho, Antonio.
Marinho, João Borges.
Martins, Caetano & Co.
Martins, Feliciano José.
Martins, Joaquim Antonio.
Mattos, Maia & Co.
Medella & Co.
Mello, Bernardo de, & Co.
Mendes & Pinto.
Merelim, José da Rocha.
Miranda, Francisco José de, & Co.
Mocker, Celestina Caire.

RIO DE JANEIRO—Continued.

Novelties and fancy goods—Continued.

Monteiro, Campos & Co.
Monteiro, Christovão Dias.
Monteiro, Francisco Antonio.
Monteiro, Joaquim Dias.
Montenegro, Fernando & Co.
Moraes, Irmão & Co.
Moraes, J. J. Pereira de, & Co.
Moraes, Sequeira de, & Co.
Moreira, A. J., & Co.
Moreira & Ferreira.
Moreira, J. F., & Co.
Motta & Irmão.
Mounier & Filho.
Moura, José Firmo de.
Nery, José Rodrigues Cabral.
Netto, José Joaquim.
Neves, Carneiro & Co.
Nobre, Souza & Co.
Noellner, Carl.
Nogueira, José Armaro & Co.
Northmann, Max., & Co.
Novella, Lucas.
Nunes, A., & Co.
Nunes, M , & Co.
Oliveira & Co
Oliveira, C. L. de, & Co.
Penafiel, José Vieira da Silva.
Pacheco, Francisco José Rodrigues.
Paula e Silva.
Peixoto, Mora & Co.
Pereira, Antonio Joaquim D. de O.
Pereira, Costa & Co.
Pereira, José.
Pereira, José B. A.
Pereira, José de Araujo.
Pereira, Manoel José.
Pereira, Netto & Co.
Perez, André.
Perú, Casado.
Petrosini, Vicente.
Pimentel, Candida Amarinho da Madama.
Pinheiro, Silva & Co.
Pinto, Almeida & Co.
Pinto, Antonio Francisco da Silveira.
Pinto, Dias & Co.
Pinto, Silva & Co.
Pinto, José Antonio.
Pires, F., & Co.
Ponte, Thomaz José da.
Prestano, Affonso.
Quartin, Guerra & Co.
Quartin & Co.
Queiroz, Manoel Teixeira de.
Ramalho, Thereza de Oliveira.
Ramos, Irmão & Rocha.

RIO DE JANEIRO—Continued.

Novelties and fancy goods—Continued.

Ramos, Sobrinho & Co.
Rafael & Co.
Reis, Manoel Sá dos.
Reis, Silva.
Rodrigues, Fructuoso & Co.
Rodrigues, Antonio Lourenço.
Rodrigues, José Manoel.
Rodrigues, Martinho José.
Rodrigues, M. L., Coelho.
Rodrigues, M. M.
Rolla, Costa & Co.
Roth, Schanz & Co.
Russo, Domingos.
Salomão, José & Co.
Sampaio, Reginaldo & Co.
Santos, Antonio Eduardo da Silva.
Santos, Paschoal & Co.
Santos, Silva & Co.
Santos, Antonio Alves dos.
Santos, João Diogo dos.
Santos, João Gonçalves dos.
Santos, João Rodrigues Cardoso dos.
Santos, Oliveira.
Santos, Thomaz Rodrigues dos.
Saraiva, Felix, & Co.
Serpa, M. F., & Co.
Settas, Maria Augusta.
Silva, Agostinho Joaquim Lopez da, & Co.
Silva, Jorge da, & Co.
Silva, Manoel Gomes da, & Co.
Silva, Alfredo Augusto da.
Silva, José Augusto da.
Silva, José Custodio Teixeira da.
Silva, Joaquim Domingues da.
Silva, Joaquim José Alves da.
Silva, Joaquim Rodrigues da.
Silva, Manoel A. Marques da.
Silva, Manoel Pereira Gomes da.
Silva, Brown José Joaquim da.
Simas, João Pereira de.
Souza & Barbosa.
Souza, Carvalho & Co.
Souza, Ferreira & Benjamin.
Souza, Fonseca & Co.
Souza & Monteiro.
Souza & Quirino.
Souza, Alfredo Teixeira de.
Souza, Antonio Joaquim de.
Souza, J. M. J.
Souza, Joaquim Pereira de.
Souza, Manoel Thomaz de.
Sucena, J. R.
Terra, A. Garcia.
Trindade, Alexandre José da.
Vasconcellos & Coelho.

RIO DE JANEIRO—Continued.

Novelties and fancy goods—Continued.
Vasconcellos, Netto & Co.
Verde, Villa & Co.
Verdilhão Viuva.
Vetromile, Francisco, & Co.
Vianna, E., & Co.
Vianna, J., & Co.
Vianna, José Ribeiro da Cunha.
Vieira, M., & Co.
Vieira, Aleixo M. dos Santos.
Vieira, João Baptista.
Vieira, João Jacintho.
Viggiano, N., & Co.
Villaça, Antonio da Silva.
Viveiros, Manoeldo Rego.
Wellisch & Irmão.
Willische, M., & Co.

Piano, organ, etc., manufacturers and merchants.
Araujo & Filho.
Aydes, Francisco.
Barbosa, J. M., & Co.
Barreto, J. S. Oliveira.
Bevilacqua, Izidoro.
Bourret, Affonso.
Buschmann & Guimarães.
Caldeira, J. A.
Caminha, Manoel Luiz.
Cardoso & Co.
Diederichs, João Frederico Francisco.
Dsiesch, Guilherme Carlos.
Ermida, Ribeiro & Co.
Figueiredo, M. J. d'Oliveira.
Filipponi, Viuva & Filha.
Gomes, José Antonio, & Co.
Gomes & Oliveira.
Guigon, Frederico.
Guimarães, João Antunes de Oliveira.
Luciano, Montenegro, junior.
Lebreton, Alfredo.
Leonardo, Victorino José.
Macieira Silva.
Madeira, João Braziel.
Napoleão, Arthur, & Co.
Paes, Antonio José, & Irmão.
Paranhos, Manoel Nunes Moreira.
Pires, A. M. Affonso.
Stanen, A.
Sucena, J. R.
Taborda, Miguel Antonio.
Vanniero, Hipplyto.
Vasconcellos, A. Fertin de.
Wehrs, C. Carlos F.

Precious stones, merchants.
Avenier, Dale & Co.

RIO DE JANEIRO—Continued.

Precious stones, merchants—Continued.
Cerf, Dale & Co.
Rezende, Luiz de, & Co.
Roulina, Ch.
Souza, José Vicente de.

Ship builders.
Araujo, Joaquim.
Delforge, H. Ulique.
Duarte, Vieira.
Fernandes, Antonio F.
Flôres & Chagas.
Mattos, A. G. de, & Co.
Moraes, Augusto G. de.
Pimentel, J. P., & Co.
Santos, Manoel Francisco dos.
Silva, Luiz Gomes de.
Vierling, Frederico, & Co.

Sugar refiners and merchants.
Affonso, José Antonio.
Azevedo, Antonio Rodrigues de.
Barbosa, José Joaquim de Oliveira.
Bastos, Joaquim de Carvalho, & Co.
Bezerra, Manoel Alves Carneiro, & Co.
Borges, José Joaquim Pereira.
Braga, Custodio & Co.
Braga, Domingos José Fernandes.
Carneiro, Ferreira & Co.
Carrapatoso & Co.
Castro, José Maria de.
Costa & Leal.
Costa, Agostinho José Alves.
Coutinho, Francisco, & Co.
Cruzeiro, Vasconcellos & Co.
Cunha, Fortunato Pereira da, & Co.
Dias, M. Duarte.
Duos, Francisco Izidoro.
Fernandes, Sobrinho & Co.
Ferreira, José Joaquim da Costa.
Fins, João, & Co.
Fonseca, Emygdio Fortunato da, & Co.
Franco, Henrique Ferreira, & Co.
Gonçalves, Costa, Rocha & Menezes.
Gorçalves, Fernandes, & Co.
Gracie, Ferreira & Co.
Guimarães & Soares.
Lacerda, Rodrigues, & Co.
Lara, Neves & Silva.
Lopes, João Soares.
Macedo, Sobrinho & Co.
Machado, Costa & Co.
Magalhães & Silva.
Monarca & Fonseca.
Motta, João G. da.
Oliveira, Rodrigues, & Co.
Oliveira, Antonio José Ramos de.

RIO DE JANEIRO—Continued.

Sugar refiners and merchants—Continued.
Pinheiro, Mattos & Co.
Pontes, Augusto S. de Oliveira.
Portelinha & Co.
Rocha, Costa & Co.
Rocha, junior, & Araujo.
Tavares & Co.
Torres, Francisco Alves.
Vaz, Francisco Ferreira, & Co.
Vieira, Mattos & Albano.

Toy merchants.
Araujo, Coque & Co.
Bazin, C., & Co.
Borges, Gustavo.
Caresch, Paul.
Couto & Co.
Estella & Co.
Ferreira, junior, A. J.
Figueiredo, M. J. d'Oliveira.
Graça, junior, & Co.
Lauro, Pedro.
Lopes, Miguel, & Irmão.
Martins, Joaquin Antonio.
Rodriguez, Leopoldo.
Roussiaux, João Jacques.
Valle, Silveira & Co.
Valle, M. M. do, & Co.

Unclassified merchants.
Alvaro, Moreira & Co.
Bazaar Americano.
Carlos Joppert & Co.
Carlos Tromont.
Cranelli & Co.
Crashley & Co.
Fernandes, Tavares & Co.
Fonseca, Machado & Co.
Gibson, A. M.
Levy Lawson, S.
Liebermann & Co.
Lopez, Silva & Co.
Mendez, J. C. V.
Pinheiro, Trout.
Ramos, Soares & Co.
Tavares, L.
Teixeira, Bastos y Gerades.
Wilson, E. P., & Co.

Underwear merchants.
Albernaz & Co.
Araujo, Coque & Co.
Azevedo, José Maria Teixeira da.
Barboza & Co.
Bittencourt. Joaquim Ignacio de.
Bonnlard Frères.
Braga, Costa & Fonseca.
Braga, Alvaro.
Brando, Pedro, & Irmão.
Brito, José Mendes de.

RIO DE JANEIRO—Continued.

Underwear merchants—Continued.
Caldeira, Cunha & Co.
Caldeira & Co.
Cambiaso & Co.
Camillo & Magalhães.
Cardoso & Ruão.
Cardozo, Pereira de Lima & Co.
Carmo, Manoel, & Co.
Coulon, Marie, Mme.
Cunha. Caldeira & Co.
Decap, Noël.
Dreyffus Filho & Co.
Emporio Commercial.
Escobar, Luiz Martins.
Fontes, Adolpho de Oliveira.
Garai, Emilio.
Gonçalves, Victorino A. de S.
Kallenbach, Philipp.
Lacurte Irmãos.
Lefebre, Paulina, & Filha.
Lemos, Jeronymo de.
Marques, Mme., & Co.
Mercier, Célestine, Mme.
Moraes, Irmão & Co.
Moreira, Alvaro da Fonseca.
Neves, Carneiro & Co.
Nicoud, G. Alfredo.
Portella, Rabello & Co.
Possas, Gonçalves & Co.
Praça, Guimarães & Co.
Ramos, Sobrinho & Co.
Ramos, Ricardo, & Co.
Regal & Oliveira.
Sá, Couto A. J. de.
Sicoli, Lopes & Co.
Silva & Co.
Souza, Alfredo Teixeira de.
Torquato, Felix, & Irmão.
Velloso, junior, Francisco José da Silva.
Victorino, P.
Villan & Co.
Werneck & Judice.

RIO GRANDE DO SUL.

Brewers.
Jonge, Frederico J. de.
Klinger, Antonio.
Roberts & Heutges.
Schmidt, Pedro.

China, glass and earthenware dealers.
Alves & Co.
Buhle, Carlos.
Costa, Antonio José.
Ferreira, Antonio José.
Mendonça & Co.
Mutti, Pedro.

RIO GRANDE DO SUL—Continued.

Commission merchants.
Arnaldo, Pereira, Ashlin & Co.
Barão de São José do Norte.
Buhle, C.
Claussen, Viuva, & Co.
Fraeb, H.
Gosch & Co.
Heidtmann, W.
Kettenburg, Herm.
Lawson, Huxham & Co.
Luchsinger & Co.
Martins, Cardoso & Bormann.
Moreira Irmãos.
Otero, Gomes & Co.
Pietzcker, Guilherme, & Co.
Sinclair, Robinson & Co.
Thomsen & Co.
Vianna, João Luiz.
Exporters.
Borgallo & Dimarchi.
Claussen, Viuva, & Co.
Fraeb, H.
Frisoni, Cademartoir & Co.
Lawson, Huxham & Co.
Pinto, Carlos, & Co.
Sinclair, Robinson & Co.
Thomsen & Co.
Grocers, wholesale.
Araujo & Co.
Barros, João de, & Co.
Campos, Moraes & Co.
Cintra, J. J. da Silva.
Cirne & Co.
Cunha, Albino J., & Co.
Leite, Antonio T., & Co.
Luchsinger & Co.
Martins, Cardoso & Bormann.
Mendes & Filhos.
Mendes & Guimarães.
Miranda & Silva.
Moreira Irmãos.
Pereira, Joaquim D.
Piedade, Antonio d'O.
Importers.
Arnaldo, Pereira, Ashlin & Co.
Buhle, C.
Borgallo & Dimarchi.
Bornhorst, chemicals.
Campos, Moraes & Co.
Claussen, Viuva, & Co.
Corne & Costa.
Cunha & Co.
Fraeb, H.
Frisoni, Cademartoir & Co.
Godoy, J. J., chemicals.
Gosch & Co.
Hallwell & Co.
Hechler, C., dry goods.
Kettenburg, Herm.

RIO GRANDE DO SUL—Continued.

Importers—Continued.
Leivas, Augusto, & Co., groceries and wines.
Luchsinger, F.
Martins, Cardoso & Bormann.
Masseron & Ca., chemicals.
Mena & Co., dry goods.
Monteiro & Co., chemicals.
Montinho, S.
Moreira Irmãos.
Otero Gomes & Co.
Pietzcker, G., & Co.
Rech & Co., hardware.
Silva, Manoel R. da, chemicals.
Sinclair, Robinson & Co.
Thomsen & Co.
Tricate & Leite, iron, cement, etc.
Vieira, Mendes & Filhos.
Urbano Martins Garcia.
Unclassified merchants.
Bennington, Lebbens G.
Cadermatori, A., & Co.
Manoel Luiz de Mesquita.
Marques & Costa.
Rasteiro, F., & Co.

SANTA CATHARINA.

Candle manufacturers.
Almeida, Alfredo Augusto.
Druggists.
Barbedo, Joaquim Urbano Pereira.
Mineida, Salathiel Pires de.
Dry goods.
Almeida, Alfredo Augusto de.
Aprigio, José de.
Pereira, Faustino de Alcantara.
Paiva, José Flauzino.
Paiva, Tertuliano José de.
Souza, Augusto Pereira.
Saddlers.
Nascimento, Manoel Ferreira do.
Silva, Ignacio Pedro.
Unclassified merchants.
Gorrisen, Viuva, & Filho.

SÃO PAULO.

Banana exporter.
Costa, Luiz A. R. da.
Billiard-ball manufacturer.
Silva, Domingos J. C. da.
Billiard-table manufacturers.
Cunha & Sastre.
Zanchi, Angelo João.
Carriage manufacturers and merchants.
Bühler, Alberto, & Co.
Camps & Irmão.
Coelho, Joaquim Matheus.
Hinze, João.
Kuhlmann, Alberto.
Salvador & Co.

SÃO PAULO—Continued.

Chemists.
Baruel & Co:
Borges, A. A. Mendes.
Botelho, Carlos de Meira.
Bourroul, Camillo.
Camara, Alves & Co.
Carvalho, Antonio Pires de.
Castro, Francisco José Calassancio de.
Costa, Adelino Correira da, & Co.
Faraut, Felix.
Fernandes, Moraes & Co.
Hoffmann, G. Th.
Martins, João Macario de Paula, & Co.
Mendes, Arruda & Pinto.
Pereira & Co.
Queiroz, José de Paula.
Ramos, Dr. Leopoldo.
Romeo & Mello.
Sampaio, Antonio Gomes da Silveira.
Soares, Macedo & Anhaia.

China, glass, and earthenware.
Granja, Manoel José.
Guerra & Carneiro.
Leite, Guimarães & Co..
Leite, Sampaio & Co.
Souza & Co.

Commer ial agents.
Almeida, Manoel Nobrega de.
Andrade, Galvão & Co.
Badaró, Antonio Ferreira da Silva.
Boanova, Francisco de Paula.
Borba, Menezes & Co.
Castro, J. P. de.
Chagas junior, João Baptista das.
Coelho, Antonio José.
Drouet, Luiz, & Co.
Ferreira & Menezes.
Flach, J.
Freitas & Co.
Jordão, D., & Co.
Lima, Amador José de.
Lima, Joaquim Eugenio de.
Magalhães, Ernesto Henrique Pereira de.
Orozimbo, Paulo, & Co.
Pestana, Emilio Rangel.
Philegrete, Augusto, & Co.
Ralston & Fonseca.
Sá & Andrade.
Santos, João dos.
Schmidt, Augusto.
Soares, Antonio Bernardino Gonçalves.
Urioste, A., & Co.
Wilhelmi, Bruno.

Commission merchants.
Americano, Luiz, & Co.

SÃO PAULO—Continued.

Commission merchants —Continued.
Anderson, Pedro, & Co.
Arantes & Co.
Borges, Pedro, & Co.
Braga, Manoel Garcia.
Calderaro, D.
Cardozo, José Pinto Magalhães.
Carmillo, Victorino Gonçalves.
Coelho. José Augusto.
Eisenbach, Jorge, & Co.
Ferreira, Antonio, junior, & Irmãos.
Gonçalves, Costa & Co.
Guimarães, Joaquim Barbosa.
Guerra & Ozorio.
Lemcke, Emilio.
Leonhardt, Max.
Levy, M. V., frères, & Co.
Lima, Henrique dos Santos, & Co.
Machado, Porfirio.
Mesquita, Manoel Luiz de.
Oliveira, Antonio Branco Miranda de.
Paiva, Verrissimo F. de.
Payão, Silveira & Co.
Prado, Chaves & Co.
Rabello, Manoel Joaquim Pereira.
Rodovalho, Joaquim Proost, & Co.
Rosa, Eugenio.
Santos, José Ferreira dos.
Santos, Paulo, & Co.
Schmidt & Trost.
Schulz, Carlos.
Silva, J., & Co.
Silva, João Mendes da, & Co.
Souto, José Calbo, & Co.
Taylor, Ribeiro & Co.
Toledo, João Pacheco de.
Upton, F.
Urioste, A., Co.
Vianna, Araujo & Co.
Vianna, Santos & Co.

Dealers and manufacturers of pianos.
Castro, J. P. de, & Co.
Gonçalves & Leal.
Levy, H. L.
Roedder, Leopoldo.
Weith, Carlos.

Druggists.
Anderson, Pedro A.
Geraldis, V. de, & Mellis.
Lima, Amarante & Co.
Peixoto, Estella & Co.
Silveira & Co.

Embroidery manufacturers.
Albuquerque & Co.

SÃO PAULO—Continued.

Flower (artificial) manufacturers.
Caldas, Marcelina Gomes.
Chiarugi, Manovela D.
Weltmann, Carlos.

Gun manufacturer.
Kleeberg, G.

Hardware merchants.
Bahia & Co.
Bertani, João.
Geist, Rodolpho.
Heincke, E., & Co.
Kern, Eugenio.
Lima, Pereira, J. J.
Lima, Pereira & Co.
Mendes & Co.
Pereira, Alberto, & Co.
Queiroz & Co.
Rispoli, Achilles.
Vieira, Felicio.

Iron foundry.
Fabrica de ferro de S. João de Ypanema.

Jewelers.
Abrate, B. & J.
Calabrese, Antonio.
Calderaro, D.
Carvalho, Manoel Borges de.
Chiquet, Pedro.
Collet, Étienne.
Deutsch, Henrique & Irmão.
Levy, Jacob.
Lucien & Co.
Maia, Guilherme da Silva.
Mendes, Eugenio Orsario.
Migliara, Martin.
Raphael & Meclis.
Rispoli, Achilles.
Silberberg, Muhlrad & Poznanski,
Sansone, Silvio & Co.
Suplicy, Hippolyto.
Vieira, J. A., & Co.

Lithographers.
Lichtenberger, Philippina.
Martin, Junior.

Manufacturers and merchants (piano).
Bosio, Heitor.
Nardelli, Isidore.
Pastore, Antonio.
Ponsio, Luiz.
Weith, Carlos.

Manufacturers of animal fat.
Americano & Co.
França, Adolpho A.
Loureiro, Adolpho, & Co.
Salles, Joaquim de, & Co.
Schultz, Carlos.

SÃO PAULO—Continued.

Manufacturers of matches.
Eisenbach, Jorge, & Co.
Seckler, Jorge, & Co.

Manufacturer of printed cotton.
Bolidair, E. M.

Merchants—Seed.
Coelho & Co.
Garcia, M.
Joly, Julio.
Nogueira, J. B. Marques.
Sarafana & Co.
Sarafana, A. F.

Soap manufacturers.
Gonçalves, Costa & Co.
Loureiro, Adolpho & Co.
Pamplona, J. C.

Stationery.
Secklen, Jorge, & Co.
Toledo, Pauperio & Co.

Sugar refiners.
Carvalho, J., & Irmão.
Flosi, José, & Co.
Franzoi, Antonio.
Gallo, David.
Pereira, Irmão & Co.
Pardini, Joaquim Luiz, & Co.
Paturan, A.
Thomaz, Augusto.

Tobacco and cigar merchants.
Abreu, José Monteiro d', & Co.
Arruda & Co.
Cascão, Francisco José, & Co.
Fontes, Joaquim Ferreira.
Gomes, Paulo.
Gonçalves, José.
Guilherme Fernando Jures.
Hants, Augusto.
Kanz & Bicudo.
Loureira & Co.
Mattos, Joaquim de.
Netto, Ferreira & Co.
Rocha, Manoel Oliveira.
Sarmento, E.
Seide & Co.
Viuva Pinto, Gonçalves & Co.

Unclassified merchants.
Schmidt & Frost.

Underwear and tableware.
Abreu, Bernardino de, & Filho.
Abreu, Bernardino Monteiro de.
Azambuja, Justo Nogueira de.
Bloch, frère & Co.
Bloch, Achilles.
Costa, Moreira & Co.

80

BRAZIL.

SÃO PAULO—Continued.

Underwear and tableware—Continued.
Dalton, J., & Co.
Esteves, José, & Co.
Fernandes, Patricio, & Co.
Fonseca, Alfredo.
Freire, Barros & Co.
Guerra, Valentim & Irmão.
Leite, Teixeira & Comp.
Lino, A., & Co.
Machado & Co.
Peres, Barroso & Co.

SANTOS.

Carriage builders.
Emmerich & Albas.
Grossenbacker, Christ.
Pinto, Motta João.
Pinto da Silva, Franc.

Coffee exporters.
Admezyk, E., & Co.
Alfaia & Filho.
Alves Lima & Co.
Aranha & Irmão.
Arbuckle Bros.
Arruda, Botelho & Magalhães.
Arruda, Luiz, & Co.
Bastos, Antonio da Silva.
Behrens, Landsberg & Co.
Bento de Souza & Co.
Berla, Cotrim & Co.
Bittencourt, Manuel Antonio.
Bradshaw, J., & Co.
Braga junior, & Co.
Brügmann, H.
Bueno, Claudio Marçolino da Silva.
Caiuby, Belisario Soares.
Camargo, Andrade Floriano Ferreira Je.
Coelho, Francisco de Paulo.
Coelho, José Guedes.
Coimbra, Cesario.
Costa, Silveira & Co.
Costa, A., & Co.
Costa, João Domingues da.
Costa & Santos Matt.
Cruz, F., & Co.
Curvello & Corrêa.
Ferraz & Barbosa.
Ford, John, & Co.
Fortunato, Lucas Alves, & Co.
Freitas, Gregorio Innocencio da.
Freitas & Mattos.
Freitas Guimarães.
Guerra junior, & Moraes.
Hampshire, F. S., & Co.
Hard, Rand & Co.

SANTOS—Continued.

Coffee export rs—Continued.
Hermann Hayn.
Holworthy & Ellis.
Iden, H., & Co.
Johnston, Ed., & Co.
Lacerda, J. F. de, & Co.
Lecocq, Gardner & Co.
Leomil, Valencio Augusto Teixeira.
Leuba, Augusto, & Co.
Levreiro, Domenico.
Lima & Carvalho.
Lopez de Azevedo & Co.
Lucas, Alves, Fortunato, & Co.
Marques, Antonio Carvalho de.
Mattos, Luiz de, & Co.
Mello, José Vaz Pinto de, & Co.
Montenegro & Co..
Moraes, Guimarães & Co.
Narcizo, Benedicto, & Silveira.
Pacheco, Irmão & Jordão.
Pedro, O. H. de.
Pesoldt, Hafus & Co.
Pinto, Gomes & Cardoso.
Prates & Filho.
Quirino, Riteiro & Co.
Ribas & Lima.
Rocha, Soares & Co.
Rodovalho, Antonio Proost
Salles, Oliveira & Sá.
Sarmento & Couto.
Sauwen, F., & Co.
Schwinger, H.
Silva, C. da, & Pereira.
Silvarinho, João.
Soares, Candido.
Souza, José Proost de, & Co.
Souza, Guimarães & Co.
Souza, Queiros & Vergueiro.
Teixeira, Coelho.
Toledo, José Carlos de.
Trommel, A., & Co.
Valais, Karl, & Co.
Vasconcellos & Co.
Vianna, Bento Thomaz.
Vianna, Bueno.
Vianna, Manoel F. de Araujo.
Wille, Th., & Co.
Wright, W. T.
Wursten, R., & Co.
Zerrenner, Bülow & Co.

Commission merchants.
Alfaya, Rodrigues Manoel.
Arruda, J. M.
Azevedo & Co.
Bastos, M. Car.

SANTOS—Continued.

Commission merchants—Continued.
Bittencourt, Ant. M.
Cardozo, Seraph. & Co.
Coelho, Paula.
Conceição, Julio, & Arruda Lima.
Da Silva, A. Ferreira.
Da Silva, Braga, J. F.
Da Silva, M. & F., & Co.
De Freitas, Guimarães, A.
Dias Nuno & Motta.
Dos Santos, J. O.
Forus & Sa.
Henrique, Pedro.
Innocencio de Freitas, G.
Martinho, Prado & Co.
Pizzaro, J. L.
Prates & Filho.
Quirino, Gomes & Co.
Rocha, Soares da.
Salles, Oliveira & Sa.

Earthenware and china merchants.
Ameido, Simoes de, & Co.
Backhäuser, Fernandes & Co.
Manoel Alfaia Rodrigues, João.

Exporters.
Alfaia, Rodrigues J. Mel.
Lecoq, Gardner & Co.
Pezold, D., & Co.
Wockorod & Co.

Exporters and importers.
Backhauser, Gustave.
Berla, Cotrim & Co.
Bradshaw & Co.
Ford, J., & Co.
Helm, Otto, & Co.
Holtworthy, W. T., & Co.
Leuba, Aug., & Co.
Schwenger & Co.
Wille, T. L., & Co.
Wright, W. T.
Vianna, Manoel F. Araujo.

General merchants.
Aguiar de Barros.
Andrade & Bros.
Azevedo, J.
Barbalero, José.
Barreiros, J. S.
Brandão, A. P.
Brande, A.
Constantino, Aguiar.
Da Costa, Carneiro Anto.
Da Cunha, J. A.
Da Silveira, M. B.
De Campos, Maura J.
De Castro & Silva, J.

SANTOS—Continued.

General merchants—Continued.
Dos Santos, J. P.
Dreyfus, H. N.
Esteves & Bros.
Eugenio & Oliveira.
Filho Martins & Silveira.
Freitas & Co.
Guimarães, M. J. L.
Lacerda, J. F. de, & Co.
Lopes, M.
Marques, A.
Montaudon, Hauldi & Co.
Paiva, D.
Peixoto, A., & Co.
Proost, Rodwaldo A.
Proost, Souza & Co.
Rebello, J. L.
Reis, Maria J. dos.
Rosmann, George.
Santos & Co.
Santos, Pereira & Co.
Schmidt & Co.
Schwinger, C.
Silva, J., & Co.

Importers.
Alba da Silva, J., & Co.
Backhauser, L.
Barriere & Oliveira, C.
Ferreira de Souza & Peixoto.
Manoel Abreu Ferreira da Silva & Co.
Manoel Alfa Rodrigues, João.
Marques & Queiroz.
Miller & Co.
Monteiro, Fontes & Villar.
Schaar, E. B., & Co.
Schmidt, J. W., & Co.

Unclassified merchants.
Broad, Henry.
Gomes, Pinto & Cardozo.
João Octavio dos Santos.
Naumann, Geff & Co.
Pezold, Hofer & Co.
Zerenner, Bulow & Co.

SAO LUIZ DE CACER (State of Matto Grosso).

Merchants.
Dulce & Villanova.

SOROCABA.

Commission merchants.
Bastos & Co.
Rocha, Camargo Manoel da.
Souza, Antonio Manoel de.

SOROCABA—Continued.

Merchants, general.
Almeida, Adolpho Claro de.
Almeida, Antonio Pires de.
Amaral, Antonio Nunes de.
Almeida, Amancio José de.
Almeida, Santos Antonio de.
Athanagildo, José Pedro.
Aquaviva, Paschoal.
Azevedo, Antonio Egodio.
Augusta, Flori na Maria.
Almeida, Francisco Ferreira de.
Almeida, Germano Loureira de.
Astori, Gustavo.
Almeida, Jeronymo Ribeiro de.
Almeida, João Benedicto de.
Azevedo, Joaquim Rodrigues de.
Barros, Camillo Rodrigues de.
Bastos, Gonçalves.
Barros, Manoel José M. de.
Canizo, Roque.
Camargo, Amancio Antonio de.
Camargo, Antonio Pedro Correa de.
Conceição, Rosa Ambrosina Maria da.
Camargo, Francisco Evarista de.
Camargo, Jose Padilha de.
Campos, Barbara Ferras de.
Cardoso, José Manoel.
Cassiano e Silva, Hipolito.
Costa, Hortino Jose da.
Costa, Manoel José da.
Costa & Silva, Antonio Elesbão.
Cruz, Cardozo Antonio da.
Cunha, Vieira Luiz da.
Espirito Santo, Antonio Maria do.
Ferreira, Antonio Joaquim.
Firmo, José.
Flores, Manoel Rodrigues.
Fogaça, Felisbena Angelo.
Fogaça, Francisco de Souza.
Fontoura, João Baptista.
Franca, Albino de Almeida.
Freitas, Antonio Francisco de.
Gaspar, Timotheo Antonio.
Goes, Luiz Antunes de.
Guimarães, João Fernandes.
Guimarães, Joaquim Pereira.
Joel, Fernando Augusto.
Jorge, Domingos.
Labre, João Baptista.
Leão, Sobrinho José Ferreira.
Lopes, Domingos Ildefonso.
Maciel, João Antunes.
Marco, Roque di.
Marinho, Damaso.
Marinho, José Gonçalves.
Mario, Manoel.

SOROCABA—Continued.

Merchants, general—Continued.
Marques, João Fernandes.
Mastrandei, Pascoal.
Mattos, Estanislau de Almeida.
Mendes, José Evaristo.
Narducci, Luiz.
Nelli, Luiz.
Oliveira, Agapilo Luiz José de.
Oliveira, Antonio Angelo de.
Oliveira, Antonio Francisco de.
Oliveira, Coelho Joaquim Mendes de.
Oliveira Filho, Francisco de Paula.
Oliveira Guimarães, João Fernandes.
Oliveira, Ribas Lourenço Pinto.
Optz, Carlos.
Padua, Almeida Antonio de.
Paranhos, Domingos Fernandes.
Paschoal, Domingos.
Pasquini, Daniel & Angelo.
Paula, João Amancio.
Pedrusqui, Gaudencio.
Pinto, Manoel Camargo.
Pontes, Dimetrio Vieira.
Pontrimoli, Antonio.
Proenca, Antonio José.
Proenca, Francisco dos Santos.
Rey, Jacob.
Ribeiro, Pedro João.
Rosa, Antonio Bernardo da.
Salles, Anna Joaquim de.
Salustiano, Zeferino de.
Santos, Bernardo.
Santos, Elias Machado dos.
Santos, Joaquim Antonio dos.
Sewaibriker, João Pedro Jacob.
Silva, Antonio Pedro Correa da.
Silva, Domingues da.
Silva, João José da.
Silva, Joaquim Gregorio da.
Silva, José Francisco da.
Silva, José Penta da.
Silva, Paulino Bento da.
Soares, José Antunes.
Sofredini, Fernando.
Solla, João.
Souza, Antonio Martins da.
Souza, Constancio Maria de.
Souza, Floriano Lima de.
Souza, Pinto Antonio de.
Tonheti, Pedro.
Valento, Manoel Pereira.
Vasconcellos, Manoel A. de Castro.
Vieira, Manoel Antonio.
Vieira, Manoel José.
Weneraik junior, Phillppo.
Wey, Roberto.

URUGUAYANA.

Merchants, general.
Barbara, João.
Barbosa, Joaquim Pedro.
Carbalido, José.
Carvalho, Vasco Henrique.
Castro & Irmão.
Codorruz junior, Francisco M.
Curtoy, Antonio, & Co.
Demaria, Antonio Tito Augusto de A.
Eguia, Carmelo.
Fernandes, Francisco, & Co.
Fernandes, Manoel J.
Garcia, José, & Co.
Girall Irmaos.
Gomes, Liberato.
Gulierres Irmãos.
Irala, Manoel de.
Mendes, Guilherme.
Monjardim, Erasmo.
Oliveira, João M. de.
Oliveira, José Servio de.
Oliveira, Pedro de.
Perry, James, & Co.
Podesta, Eugenio.
Pratz, Miguel.
Ronco & Co.
Soler, Paulo, & Co.
Souza, João M. de.
Souza, João Pedro de.
Souza, Luiz M. de.
Surrean, Luiz.
Valente, João.
Venrone, Caetano.
Zenon, Junau.

VICTORIA.

Merchants, general, importers and exporters.
Aguiar, Augusto Manoel de.
Alves, Rebello & Co.
Andrade, Manoel Ferreira de.
Angelo, Mercadonte.
Antonio, Inverruze.
Braga, Manoel da Rocha.
Braulio, Jayme Muniz Cordeiro, junior.
Brazilio, Carvalho Damon.
Borges & Ramos.
Cabral & Co.
Canoce, Alexandre.
Caparica, Indro José.
Cassilhas, Antonio José Pereira.
Christofiorte, Benjamin, Cruz & Irmão.
Coelho, Calisto Ribeiro.
Coitinho, Aulero da Silva.
Coronel, Henrique Soares.
Costa, Antonio Ferreira Ribeiro.

VICTORIA—Continued.

Merchants, general, importers and exporters—
Continued.
Costa, Antonio Joaquim Pereira.
Curto, João da Costa.
Debrasi, João.
Dianno, Antonio.
Espendolo, Christiano José.
Franco, Gonçalo da Rocha.
Frederico, Guilherme & Co
Goffoni, Domingos.
Guimarães, Antonio Ferreira Ribeiro.
Hoffmann, Federico.
Jacome, José Francisco.
Lopes, Antonio Nogueira.
Luiz, Francisco.
Madeira, Domingos da Costa.
Madeira, Pimento, Barreto & Cruz.
Manoel, Pinto Netto, & Filho.
Maria, Philippe de, junior.
Marques, Manoel Pedro.
Marques & Rebello.
Mendes, João Ferreira.
Monteiro da Silva, A. F.
Monteiro, Ramão José.
Moreira & Co.
Moraes, Juvencio Pereira de.
Motta, José Custodio Alves.
Nagre, Domingo.
Nascimento, Aureliano Manoel de.
Nascimento, Aureliano Pinto de.
Netto, Couto & Co.
Oliveira, Victor Carlos de.
Parase, João.
Pedro Marques, Pinto & Co.
Pessoa junior, João Antonio.
Povoas, Francisco da Rocha.
Povoas, Francisco Thomas Ribeiro.
Prado, W.
Pyiani, Angelo.
Reis, Bastos, José Antonio dos.
Ribeiro, José Francisco.
Ribeiro, Miguel Botelho.
Rocha, Galdino das Chagas.
Rodrigues, Francisco Pinto de.
Sandro, Domingos.
Santos, Maria Vedigal dos.
Silva, José Ignacio da.
Sinderle, Luiz.
Souza, José Goulart de.
Teixeira, João Luiz.
Tesh, João Jacob.
Togano, Francisco da Rocha.
Tristão, Manoel Ferreira de.
Victor Freline.
Victoria, João Seraphim da.
Wetzel & Co.

Brazilian Banks and Bankers.

Bahia.
Banco da Bahia.
Banco Mercantil.
Caixa Economica.
Caixa Hypothecaria.
London & Brazilian Bank, Ltd.
Schramm, Stade & Co.
Sociedade do Commercio.
Marinhos & Co.
Vaughan, McNair & Co.

Campos.
Banco de Campos.
Banco Commercial & Hypothecario.

Macahé.
Banco da Povoa de Portugal.

Maceió.
Caixa Commercial.
Caixa Economica e Monte do Soccorro.
Companhia União Mercantil.

Maranham.
Banco Nacional do Brazil.
English Bank of Rio de Janeiro, Ltd.
London & Brazilian Bank, Ltd.

Pará.
Banco Commercial do Para.
Banco de Belem do Para.
Banco do Para.
Banco Nacional do Brazil.
English Bank of Rio de Janeiro, Ltd.
London & Brazilian Bank, Ltd.
Lisbon & Açores Bank.

Paranagud.
Banco de Credito Publico.

Pelotas.
London & Brazilian Bank, Ltd.
Banco Emissor do Sul.

Pernambuco.
Banco Sud Americano.
Banco Internacionali.
English Bank of Rio de Janeiro, Ltd.

Pernambuco—Continued.
London & Brazilian Bank, Ltd.
Oliveira, Augusto Frederico, & Co.

Porto Alegre.
Bank of Rio Grande do Sul.
Bank Confiance Rio Grande do Sul.
English Bank of Rio de Janeiro, Ltd.
London & Brazilian Bank, Ltd.
Mostardeiro & Luchsinger.
Provincial Bank.

Rio de Janeiro.
Agency of the Banco Alliança do Porto.
Banco Auxiliar, r. da Quintanda 89.
Banco do Commercio e Industria do Porto.
Banco de Credito Real do Brazil r. do Gene
 Camara 6.
Banco de Credito Real de S Paulo, Largo
 Palacio 8.
Banco Industrial & Mercantil do Rio de
 neiro.
Banco Commercial do Rio de Janeiro.
Banco do Commercio.
Banco do Minho.
Banco do Brazil.
Banco Nacional do Brazil.
English Bank of Rio de Janeiro, Ltd.
London & Brazilian Bank, Ltd.
Banco Predial, r. da Quintanda 78.
Banco de Portugal.
Banco Mercantil de Santos.
Brasilianische Bank für Deutschland.
Banco Rural e Hypothecario do Rio de Jane
 r. da Quitanda 103.

Rio Grande do Sul.
London & Brazilian Bank, Ltd.
Banco do Brazil.
Banco do Minho, Oporto.
Luchsinger & Co.

Santos.
English Bank of Rio de Janeiro, Ltd.
London & Brazilian Bank, Ltd.

Santos—Continued.
Banco Mercantil.
Agency of the Banco do Brazil.
Nielson & Co.
Banco Commercial.
Banco da Lavoura.
Banco do Minho.
Banco de São Paulo.
São Paulo.
Banco de Credito Real.

São Paulo—Continued.
Banco Provincial.
Bank of St. Paulo.
Brazilian Bank.
Commercial Bank.
English Bank of Rio de Janeiro, Ltd.
London & Brazilian Bank, Ltd.
Mercantile Bank.
National Bank.

Chile.

ANTOFAGASTA.

Banks.
London Bank of Mexico and South America, limited.
Sucursal del Banco de Valparaiso (Benigno Barril, Mgr.).

Coal merchants.
Felin, César O.
Orchard, Eduardo.

Merchants, general.
Leiton, L., & Co.
Winoste, A. de, y Ca.

Merchants, importers.
Barnett & Co.
Bella Vista, E. F. de.
Hodgkinson, Brierley & Co.
Imria, Santiago.
Koster, Federico.
Llopar & Rossell.
Meyer & Pinnan.
Pero & Co.
Turio, Santiago.

Metal merchant.
Bella Vista, E. F. de.

Shipping and commission agents.
Barbajelata & Co.
Barnett & Co.
López, Tapia & Co.
Radbruch, Cárlos, Suc.

ARICA.

Banks.
London Bank of Mexico and South America, limited.

Merchants, importers.
Canepa Bros.
Casey, Nap.
Danelsberg & Co.
Dominguez y Lacalle.
Laurien, Emilio.
MacLean, A. R.
Nugent & Co.

ARICA—Continued.

Merchants, importers—Continued.
Pescetti & Trabucco.
Rei, J., & Co.
Serra, C. J.
Visscher & Co.

CALDERA.

General agents.
Beazley, H. B.
Piedra & Co.
Stahmer & Co.

Merchants, import.
Arestizabel Hos.
Burran, J. van.
Copiapo Mining Co.
Copiapo Railroad Co.
Finger, T.
Gusita & Gratti.
Mitchell, J. H.
Morong, J. T.
Rosser, J.
Sociedad Industrial de Atacama.
Tomini & Locatelli.
Vigil, H. R., & Co.

Merchants, export.
Copiapo Mining Co.
Maq. de Totoralilo.
Sociedad Industrial de Atacama.

CHILLAN.

Druggist.
Arrán, Cárlos.

CONCEPCIÓN.

Agents, commercial and shipping.
Campo & Grant.
Ibieta, Ignacio.
Van Ingen, John T.
Mulgren, P. N.

Agents, general.
McKay, William.
Watson & Co.

88 CHILE.

CONCEPCIÓN—Continued.

Banks.
National Bank of Chile.
Banco Comercial de Chile.
Banco de Concepción.
Banco Gor de Valores del Sur.
Banco de Santiago.
Banco de Valparaiso.

Druggist.
Ramdohre, G., Hijo.

Importers.
Castro, J. M., & Co., hardware.
Cockbain, Roxburgh & Co., general.
Duncan, Fox & Co., general.
Gleisner, M., & Co., general.
Goyoneche, Eug., & Co., general.
Grace & Co., hardware.
Guerin Frères, general.
Hardt, E. & W., cloths.
Heineken, Schwartz & Co., general.
Huth & Co., general.
Mauger & Haran, general.
Mathews, Richards & Co., hardware.
Stachow & Eickenrodt, general.
Stockmeyer & Von Borries, general.
Tanck, Herbst & Co., general.
Vermehren, A., general.
Voelker Hermanos & Co., fancy goods.
Von Borries, A., & Co., general.
Williamson, Balfour & Co., general.

COPIAPO.

Bankers.
Edwards, A., & Co.

Merchants.
Asmussin, F.
Arestizabel Hos.
Buger, J.
Bugnoh, J.
Cabrera, V.
Cena, P.
Copiapo Mining Co.
Escola Hos.
Frademann, T.
García, A.
García, T.
Guerra, Guarta & Guggiani.
Gonzales, R.
Lacazette, J.
Marco, J.
Mitchell, T. H.
Romero, R.
Sagri, A.
Van Burren, J. M.
Vigil, II. R., & Co.
Villanueva, L.

COPIAPO—Continued.

Producers of metals.
Echeveria, M., silver.
Edwards, A., & Co., copper, silver, and gold.
García, I. E., silver.
Mano, J., gold.
Sanctrey, J. R., gold.
Soto, M. P., silver.

COQUIMBO.

Bankers.
Astataburuaga Hermanos.
Muñoz, Juan y P. P.
Marin, S. Eduardo.
Steel, Alfredo.
Sociedad Santos.

Dry goods stores.
Badal, Tomás.
Baquedano, Guillermo.
Batifoule, Felipe.
Blamy, Santiago.
Bleicht, Estanislao.
Bowden, Juan.
Castillo, Matías.
Cortez, Zenon.
Gerardo, Adolfo.
Godoy, Jorge.
Inostrosa, Estefania V. de.
James, Guillermo,
Jopia, Hilaro.
Jopie, Manuel Antonio.
Landa, Tomás.
Norrea & Rios.
Olivares, Eliodoro.
Raby, Isabel.
Raby é Hijos, Isabel.
River Hermanos.
Rivera, Pedro.
Rojas, José N.
Stephens, José, & Co.
Treveno, Guillermo.
Venegas, Pedro.
Vergara, Manuel J.
Vicuña, José del C.

Merchants, general.
Ireland & Co.
Jenkins & Co.
John, Robert.
Palassie & Leste.
Steel, A., & Co.
Virgilio, Baron & Co.

Merchants, import.
Cabellaro, Alejandre.
Carcason, Julio.
Carmona, F. de P., & Co.
Cuevas, V. Francisco.

COQUIMBO—Continued.

Merchants, import—Continued.
Diaz, Genaro.
Espinosa, José E.
Grierson, Joseph.
Jhon, Roberto.
Jenkins & Co.
Miltee, David R.
Neuneborn, Ricardo.
Palassie & Lesté.
Steel, A., & Co.
Trelweck & Co.
Virgilio, Baron & Tiffon.

CORONEL.

Merchants.
Brunn, Ernesto.
Damendrall & Arostegui.
Duhart Bros.
Gervasame Bros.

IQUIQUE.

Agents, commercial and general.
Ayala y Geerken.
Buffet, Emilio.
Christie, George.
Groothoff, A.
Jackson y Pelle.
Polastri, Aug. V.
Reyes, J. Adolfo.
Richardson, D., y Ca.
Wertheimer, Cárlos.
Wieber, Cárlos.

Amalgamation works (silver).
Beneficiadora de Iquique.
Sociedad Internacional Minera y Beneficiadora de Huantajaya.

Banks.
Banco Comercial.
Banco Internacional.
Banco Nacional de Chile.
Banco de Tarapaca y Lóndres.
Banco de Valparaiso.

Drugs and druggists.
Botica Alemana, E. Schwarstan.
Botica Central, A. F. Gariazzo.
Botica de El Pueblo, R. Miguel.
Botica Española, V. Reszezynski.
Botica Roma, A. A. Gariazzo.
Sucursal de la Botica Alemana.
Botica Valparaiso, Rafael Simon.
Botica Waliana, Adelaida Gianolo B.

Importers.
Coquelet, Guillermo.
Rola Hermanos.
Vatin, A.

IQUIQUE—Continued.

Manufacturers, miscellaneous.
Arimany, Alberto, soap.
Fundición del Morro, iron.
Fundición de Tarapaca.
Mocbis, Pablo.
Pallerano y Ca.
Polastri y Ca.

Manufacturers, nitrates.
Banco Mobiliario.
Chinchilla y Ca.
Devescovi, José.
Drew, Santiago.
Folsch y Martin.
Granja, Dominguez y Lacalle.
The Colorado Nitrate Co., limited.
The Liverpool Nitrate Co., limited.
The London Nitrate Co., limited.
The Paccha Nitrate Co., limited.
The Primitiva Nitrate Co., limited.
The Rosario Nitrate Co., limited.
The San Jorje Nitrate Co., limited.
The Santa Elena Nitrate Co., limited.

Merchants, general.
Aliband, Sucesión de la Víuda de.
Carcasson, Estevan.
Cuneo, Salvador.
Chinchilla Hermanos.
Hahn, A. M.
Hesse, Cárlos A.
Fuenzalida Hermanos.
Landeta, Nemesio.
Malinarich Hermanos.
Polastri, Augusto V.
Rodil, Enrique.
Rodriguez y Lacalle.
Varas, Valentin.
Zanelli Hermanos.

Merchants, hardware.
Brain Hermanos.
Mitrovich Hermanos.
Perramon y Puig.
Santich, Estevan.
Voduizza, Juan.
Zavala, Cosme.

Merchants, miscellaneous.
Anthony, C. E., Sucesión de, groceries.
Armengol, Guasch y Ca., dry goods.
Balart, Juan, dry goods.
Barsby, F. W., tailors' supplies.
Beperet Hermanos, dry goods.
Boivin, Rudolfo, lumber.
Bremer, Augustin, hatter.
Brescia, Anjel, groceries.
Candina, José, dry goods.
Capella Hermanos, groceries.

IQUIQUE—Continued.

● *Merchants, miscellaneous—Continued.*
Caralpo, Francisco, y Ca., dry goods.
Caranzano, Victor, jewelry.
Chinchilla Hermanos, lumber.
Echeverria, A., stationery.
Farnes, Sebastian, dry goods.
Frank, Julio, jewelry.
Gamon, M., ó Hijo, stationery.
Garcia, Francisco, y Ca., dry goods.
Gildemeister, J., y Cía.
Jacobs, David, jewelry.
Lenenroth, T., hatter and tailors' supplies.
McDonald, groceries.
Merani, Emanuel, jewelry.
Nienhuser & Thompson, ship supplies.
Northcote y Ca., ship supplies.
Ochoa, Prudencio, dry goods.
Osterloh, A., jewelry.
Petersen, Juan L., jewelry.
Petersen, Lorenzo, stationery.
Pirreta. Salvador, y Ca., dry goods.
Williams, G. W., ship supplies.
Wilson, Cárlos, lumber.
Zanetti Hermanos, lumber.
Zimmermann, Otto, ship supplies.

Photographers.
Marcich, Miguel.
Odds, Luis.
Richardson, V. L.

LOTA.
Merchants, exporters.
Compañía Esplotadora de Lota y Coronel,
bar copper and coal.
Mauricio, Gleisner & Co., half hides, tanned.

PISAGUA.
Banks.
Bank of Tarapaca & London, limited.
Bank of Valparaiso.

Shipping agents, import and export merchants.
Blair & Co.
Gamble, North.
James, Inglis & Co.
Loayza & Pascal.
Perfetti, Pedro.
Watters Brothers.

SANTIAGO DE CHILE.
Banks.
Banco Nacional de Chile.
Banco Crédito Unido.
Banco Garantizador de Valores.
Banco Matte & Co.
Banco Agrícola.

SANTIAGO DE CHILE—Continued.

Banks—Continued.
Banco Hipotecario.
Banco Mobilario.
Banco Santiago.
Banco de la Union.
Banco de Valparaiso.
Hipotecario Popular.
London Bank of Mexico and South America.
limited.
Nacional Hipotecario.

Beer brewers.
Arancibia, Pedro.
Brandau, V.
Bustorf, E.
Carbonell, Ant.
Ebner, Andrés.
Ebner, Ant.
Knofler & Liebee.
Passig, Enrique.
Remedi Herm.
Salinas, Micaela.
Werth, Th.

Brokers and commission merchants.
Carmona, B.
Claro, Gualterio.
Diaz, B. J.
Edwards, Ed.
Errazuriz, M.
Fernandez, B. Joaquim.
Galino, Rafael.
Garfias, Manuel.
Guiñazu, David.
Gamercio Hermanos & Co.
Infante, F. Javier.
Lecaros, I.
Morande, P.
Moreno, N.
Mundt, S.
Orrego, E.
Puerta de Vera, J.
Sanfuentes, J. L.
Seco, J. A.
Shanklin, F. B.
Sotomayer, B.
Valdes. L. J.
Valdirieso, Est.
Vail, M. C.
Vicuna, N.
Walker, M. J.

Drugs and druggists.
Hidalgo, Juan.
Mourgues, Daniel.
Puyó, Luis, y Ca.

SANTIAGO DE CHILE—Continued.

Furniture merchants.
Alvarez, B.
Araya, R.
Beltran, A.
Carmona, Fernando.
Dolg, D.
Donoso & Kirman.
Eyzaguirre, C.
Guillet, Andrés.
Molfato, C.
Ricci, L.
Rojas, J. N.

General storekeepers.
Bazare Español.
Bazare Santiago.
Krauss, Cárlos.
Moreno & Co.
Steinfort, Martin.
Velasco, Isidro.

Hat merchants.
Cohé, A.
Dumas, A.
Leron, H
Levean, M.
Massaben, V.
Placier, L.
Rodanet, L.
Voigt & Co.
Wegener & Co.

Importers.
Asquett, Angel.
Briceño, J. D.
Cariola Bros.
Costa, Lázaro & Benito.
García, Pio A.
Gómez, Manuel.
Ricu, J.
Saint-Macary Hermanos.
Silva, Alejandro.
Silva, J. D.
Zuleta, Marcus J. D.

Importers and exporters.
Claro, José Luis.
Davis, Enrique.
Egan, Patrick.
Hillman, Chas. F.
Nuñez, José Adelarde.
Rei, A. Thompson, & Co.
Solar, Luis Claro.
Swinburne & Co.

Leather manufacturers.
Aguerreverri, J.
Allamand, F.

SANTIAGO DE CHILE—Continued.

Leather manufacturers—Continued.
Arenas, J. A.
Arrate, Iturvide.
Bustos, M.
Echegoyen, P.
Elissegarey, Alf.
Etchipare, J. M.
Graciet, Augner.
Hempell, G.
Leal, Magdalena.
Magnare, A. G.
Marinot, Alb.
Marinot, J.
Sepulveda, P. J.
Tiffon Hermanos.

Marble merchants.
Manneci, H.
Vignolo & Co.

Wood merchants.
Bolton, J.
Barahona, N.
Bravo, D.
Calderon, José M.
Castro, M.
Cornejo, B.
Cornejo, F.
Cruchága, R.
Cuellar, M. J.
Curti, En.
Fresno & Co.
Gonzales, Santos.
Guerrero, P. R.
Marcham, José.
Martinez, R.
Molina, T.
Montero, Sant.
Morales, J.
Moya, Cam.
Muñoz, J. M.
Pacheco, M.
Pulgie, J.
Pinochet, J.
Quesada, J. E.
Salas, Fr.
Salvatierra, J.
Vazques, P.

TACNA.

Merchants.
Cavagner, A., & Co.
Cusicanqui Hos.
Giezols, Brieger & Co.
Richter, Lehue & Co.

TALCA.

Merchant.
Santiago, Vaccaro.

TALCAHUANO.

Merchants, importers, and commission agents.
Applegarth, A. O., commission agents.
Cornou Herm., commission agents.
Duncan, Fox & Co., importers, etc.
Elton, Fred., commission agent.
Fuentès, David, commission agent.
Gleisner, C. & M., general.
Jehovich & Co., commission agents.
Klug, M., commission agent.
Mathieu, Brañas & Co., commission agents.
Merlet, Pablo, commission agent.
McKay & Co., G., commission agents.
Von der Heyde, T.

Ship chandlers.
Cook, Robinson & Co.
Van Ingen, J. F.

TONGOY.

Grain merchants.
Evans, David.
Melgorejo, Lorenzo.

Merchants, exporters.
Sociedad Chilena de Fundiciones.

Wood merchants.
Jenkins & Co.

VALPARAISO.

Agents, commercial.
Cano, Emilio.
Chaigneau Hermanos.
Chaigneau, Adrian.
Edmonson, J. E.
Merlet, Julio.
Navarro, Federico.
Nieto, Danor.
Rojas, A. Lisandro.
Schmidt, Ern. G.
Stoss, Emilio.
Titus Hermanos.
Vera, Juan C.
Walther, Federico.

Agricultural implements.
Clark & Co.
Grace & Co.
Gunston, Edmonson & Co.
Martin, Santiago.
Mathews, Richards.
Rattray & Co.
Rose, Innes & Co.

VALPARAISO—Continued.

Bankers.
Edwards, A., & Co.
Vorwark & Co.

Banks.
Banco Hipotecario.
Banco Nacional de Chile.
Banco de Valparaiso.
Banco Mobiliaro.
Bank of Tarapaca and London, limited.
London Bank of Mexico and South America, limited.

Cigar manufacturers.
Betancourt, Francisco.
Lagos, Cortés Mariano.
Mackes & Co.
Phillips & Liebes.
Sanchez, Eucarpio.
Torres & Co.

Drugs and druggists.
Diaz de la Vega, C.
Eissele, Emilio.
Hengstenberg & Co.
Hochteteter y Ca.
Teichmann & Co.
Zilleruelo, Aurelio.

Exporters of nitrate of soda, wool, goatskins, etc.
Browne, Beeche & Co.
Compton, John.
Cooper & Co.
Doll & Co.
Grace & Co.
Granja, Domingues & Lacalle.
Huth & Co.
Titus Hermanos.
Verdugo, J. A.
Weber & Co.
Williamson, Balfour & Co.

Hardware merchants.
Betteley & Co.
Burmeister & Co.
Caro & Co.
Clark, J. E.
Commentz, Cárlos.
Dimalow & Co.
Dupré, Pedro.
Gunther & Co.
Katz, José.
Lee. A. J.
Limozin & Co.
Matthews, R., & Co.
Rattray & Co.
Schoenemann & Eberhardt.

Importers and exporters.
Bates, Stokes & Co.

VALPARAISO—Continued.

Importers and exporters—Continued.
Campbell, Jones & Co.
Cariola Hos.
Delano, Dr. Jorge.
Dugenne & Co., Le Chevalier.
Engstenberg, H., & Co.
Gibbs & Co.
Graham, Rowe & Co.
Hardie & Co.
Herrera, Oscar.
Huth & Co.
Macary, V. St., & Co.
Milne & Williamson.
Morgan, Guy S.
Paton, Wm. G., & Co.
Rattray & Co.
Rogers & Co.
Romeyn, James W.
Salinas, P. J.
Sanguinetti Hos.
Schuchard, Gruner & Co.
Stevens, Corwin & Co.
Weber & Co.
Weir, Scott & Co.
Importers of cigars.
Cervero & Co.
Edwards Hermanos.
Herrero, Oscar.
Kirchhoff, H.
Lagos, Cortés Mariano.
Oscar, Herrera & Co.
Schilling & Co.
Soltau & Co.
Importers of cloths.
Haunziker, Gubler & Co.
Laven, Manuel.
Luttermersk, Winbelhagen & Co.
Moller & Co.
Ode, Leoncio.
Polamo, Benigno.
Prieto, Gonzalez & Valencia.
Puelma, R., & Hijo
Sahr & Co.
Schele, H., & Co.
Tanck, Herbst.
Thiele, Errald & Co.
Importers of cutlery and lamps.
Tillmanns, R.
Importers of drugs and mineral waters.
Teichmann & Co.
Importers of fancy goods.
Baird & Co.
Burmeister & Co.
Gordon, Deuderson.
Kirsinguer, C., & Co.

VALPARAISO—Continued.

Importers of farm and railroad machinery.
Clark, Juan E.
Grace & Co.
Rosenberg, G.
Saavedra & Co., Bernard.
Schuchard, Grisard & Co.
Importers of general merchandise.
Aguilar y Sobrinos.
Huth & Co.
Herrera, Oscar, & Co.
Williamson, Balfour & Co.
Importers of glass.
Maldin & Co.
Importers of hardware and spirits.
Günther, Ocheus & Co.
Lazomby, Campbell.
Limozin A., & Co.
Matthews, Richards & Co.
Rattray & Co.
Swinglehurst & Co.
Importers of jewelry.
Gross, Cárlos, & Co.
Hepp, H. G., & Co.
Labourian, H., & Co.
Naegeli, Sinn & Co.
Importers of linen goods.
Bennett & Co.
Importers of machinery, agricultural implements, locomotives, railway plants, hardware, dry goods, furniture, groceries, lumber, paints and oils, cordage, tar, pitch, rosin, salt meats, etc.
Browne, Beeche & Co.
Compton, John.
Grace & Co.
Rose, Junes & Co.
Importer of pottery.
Schneider, Guillermo.
Importers of sewing machines.
Bassett, Guillermo, & Co.
Jenkins, Guillermo, & Co.
Importers of small ware.
Hermann, G. A., & Co.
Herveró & Co.
Gervasoni Hermanos.
Greulich, Adam.
Hengstenberg & Co.
Luttjens Hermanos.
Importers of sugar.
Besa & Co.
Hancurray, Beeche & Co.
Importers of tailors' furnishings.
Grote, Teodoro.
Simon & Co.

VALPARAISO—Continued.

Importer of tobacco.
.Carson, Daniel. .

Iron founders.
Balfour, Lyon & Co.
Harper, Almendral.
Lever, Murphy & Co.
Compañía Nacional.

VALPARAISO—Continued.

Iron founders—Continued.
Compañía de la República.
Compañía de la Victoria.
Iron-tool merchants.
Balfour, Lyon & Co.
Lazomby & Campbell.
Swinglehurst & Co.
Williamson, Balfour & Co.

Colombia.

AGRADO, TOLIMO.

Merchant.
Lemonete, Luis A.

ANAPOIMA.

Merchant.
Duran, L. Fructuoso

BARBACOAS.

Merchant.
Costillo, Daniel de.

BARRANQUILLA.

Banks and bankers.
Banco de Barranquilla.
Fergusson, Noguera & Co.
Gonzalez Zapata, Juan.
Marquez Esteban.

Commission merchants.
Alzamora Hermanos & Co., J.
Carbonell & Co.
Castallano, Carvajalino & Co.
Echeverria, R. E.
Fergusson, Noguera & Co.
Gonzalez & Co.
Senior & Co., S. P. de.
Strunz, August.
Vengoethea & Co.
Vengoechea y Hijos

Importers and exporters, general.
Aepli, Eberbach & Co.
Berne & Co., O.
Carbonell & Co.
Coria & Co., A. M.
Correa & Co., A. A.
Dagand, Julio.
Davila, Demetrio.
De la Hoz Hermanos.
Giesiken & Held.

BARRANQUILLA—Continued.

Importers and exporters, general—Continued.
Glen, J. A.
Henriquez & Mathieu.
Infante & Co.
Magri, T.
Mayans, C. M.
Meek, John, jr.
Müller, Siefkin & Co.
Naar & Malabet.
Nuñez, Santiago.
Olier & Co., Lopez.
Rosa, F. Perez.
Senior, De Sola & Co.
Villan, Bell & Co.
Wehdeking, Focke & Co.

Merchants, general.
Aepli, Eberbach & Co.
Alzamora & Co., J. Hermanos.
Angulo, Pedro Celestino.
Arjona, Ricardo.
Batlle é Hijo.
Batlle, Ribot José.
Berne & Co., O.
Carbonell & Co.
Castellano & Co., Julio.
Cisneros, F. J.
Conde, M. T.
Correa & Co., A. M.
Dagand, Julio.
Danonille. Alejandro.
Dávila, Demetrio.
De la Hoz Hermanos.
De la Torre ó Hijos.
Echeverria, R. E.
Fergusson, Flirken y Sarda.
Fergusson, Noguera & Co., druggists.
Ferrau Hermanos.
Fuenmayor & Hermano.
Giesken & Geld.

95

BARRANQUILLA—Continued.

Merchants, general—Continued.
Glen, J. A.
Gonzalez & Co.
Gonzalez, José Manuel.
Helm & Co., J.
Henriquez, Jacobo, jr.
Henriquez & Mathieu.
Infante & Co.
Insignaris, Sierra, Roca & Co.
Isaac, D. H., sr.
Jimeno Hermanos.
Llamas Hermanos.
Lleras, Mariano.
Lopez, Olier & Co.
Magri, T.
Martinez, J. S.
Martinez, S. Mercado.
Mayans, C. M.
Mayans & Gual.
Meek, John, jr.
Müller, Siefken & Co.
Naar & Malabet.
Noguerra & Co.
Nuñez, Santiago.
Obregon, E.
Palacio, Virginia M. de.
Pardey & Co.
Pluqueri, H.
Rosa, F. Perez.
Senior, B. T.
Senior, Jacobo.
Senior, De Sola & Co.
Senior & Co., S. P. de.
Stacey, Federico.
Struntchal, H.
Strunz, August.
Vengoechea & Co.
Vicente, Lafaurie.
Villar, Bell & Co.
Voigt, Aristides.
Wehdeking, Focke & Co.
Whelpley, Samuel M.
Wolff & Co., A.

Wine merchants.
Sala y Ca., M. E.

BOCAS DEL TORO.

Importer and exporter.
Williams, Geo. F.

Merchants.
Frike, J. H. D.
Hein, L. H.

BOGOTA.

Banks.
Banco de Bogota.

BOGOTA—Continued.

Banks—Continued.
Banco de Colombia.
Banco Internacional.
Banco Nacional.
London Bank of Mexico and South
limited.

Commercial agents.
Perez ó Hijo, L. M.
Restrepo & Arteaga.
Silva & Co.
Suarez, Domingo.
Vergara, F. Javier.
Zapata, Dámaso.

Commission merchants.
Almanzar, R. Rafael.
Angel, Uscategui & Co.
Arbelaez, Eliseo.
Bayon, Santiago.
Camacho, Roldan & Tamayo.
Cortes, José, M. & E.
Curriols, F. N.
Espinoza, G. Rafael.
Fajardo & Janaut.
Gasbrols, José T.
Gonzalez Bros., Benito.
Groot, Francisco.
Gutierrez, Rufino.
Jaramillo, Luis Palmo.
Lorenzana & Montoya.
Mercado, O. Ramon.
Montijo, Isaac.
Patiño, Federico.
Paz, José Miguel.
Pedro, L. Guerrero.
Perez ó Hijo.
Pombo & Montijo.
Posada, Benito.
Rafael, Baltazar C.
Rasch, Cárlos.
Restrepo & Arteaga.
Silva ó Hijo, R.
Ueros Bros.

Merchants, general.
Alvarez, I. de D.
Billy, Paulina.
Bonnet & Co.
Boshell, W. G.
Buendia & Herrera.
Bustamente, R. Gonzalez.
Camacho & Co., Cárlos.
Camargo & Co.
Carrizosa Hermanos.
Casas, Nicolas.
Castellanos & Corral.
Castello, Cárlos A.

BOGOTA—Continued.

Merchants, general—Continued.
Castrellon, Camilo H.
Cubillos, J. German.
Delgadillo & Co.
Dordelly, Cardenas & Rocha.
Duarte, Juan de M.
Duque, Francisco.
Durana, Guillérmo.
Escobar, Guillermo.
Ester, Mariano.
Fanco, Cárlos.
Fanco, Mariano.
Fergusson, Noguera & Co.
Fonnegra, Juan M.
Freese, George.
Garay & Guarin.
Garcin Hermanos.
Gomez. Calderon M.
Gonzalez, Benedicto.
Gonzalez Hermanos, Benito.
Guevara, Leopoldo.
Gutierrez & Escobar.
Guzman, Rufino.
Jaramillo & Hijos, V.
Koppel & Co., A.
Koppel & Schloss.
Lambardi & Fernandez.
Lorenzana & Montoya.
Manuel, M.
Medina Hermanos,
Mejia & Hijos, José M.
Molano, Primitivo.
Montoya & Ortega.
Montoya, Sr., Juan A.
Murcia, José Maria.
Nieto, Augustin.
Orrantia, Luis Patino.
Padilla, Demetrio.
Padilla, G. Rafael.
Pardo & Hijo.
Pena, Manuel H.
Perez & Hijo, L. M.
Plata Hermanos.
Posade, G. Leonidas.
Price, Jorge W.
Pulecio, Antonio.
Quesada, Manuel.
Restrepo Hijos, Gomez.
Restrepo, Sr., & Co., José M.
Reyers, Rafael.
Robles, Luis Maria.
Salgar & Leon.
Samper & Co., Antonio.
Samper & Hijos, Manuel.
Samper & Hijo, Miguel.
Santiago, Guarin & Co.

BOGOTA—Continued.

Merchants, general—Continued.
Silva & Hijos, E.
Tanco, Leopoldo.
Terlese & Co., Julian.
Thorin Hermanos.
Trujillo, Vargas & Co.
Urdaneta, Alejandro.
Urdaneta, General Cárlos.
Uribe & Montealegre.
Uribe, R. Luciano.
Uribe, Toro Manuel.
Vargas & Hermanos, Francisco.
Vargas, Belisario.
Vargas & Co., Luis.
Velez, Antonio.
Wieto Hermanos.
Zapata, Cárlos.

BUCARAMAUGA.

Merchants.
Gomez, Juan de la C.
Keller, Charles.

BUENAVENTURA.

Merchants.
Baguamento, F.
Baltan, J. F.
Benitez, J. F.
Bergonzali, Luis F.
Bonilla, Manuel J.
Capurro, Bern.
Frigeni & Paguamento.
Harra, Hilario.
Lopez & Co., B.
Malfitana, J.
Menotti, Francisco.
Otero & Co.
Otero, Jaime.
Puente, Juan de G.
Saavedra, Ant.
Torres, C.
Vallego, Antonio.
Videla, Ant.

BUGA.

Merchants.
Salcedo & Co.
Sinistena, Bowen & Co.

CALI.

Merchants.
Argaez y Carbajal.

CALI—Continued.

*Merchants—*Continued.
Echeverria Hermanos.
Gaviria & Co., E.
Menotti, Alfonso.
Restrepo & Uricoechea.
Simmonds, C. H.
Uricoechea, Dr.Luis J.

CARTAGENA.

Banks.
Banco de Bolivar.
Banco de Cartagena.
Banco Union Popular.

Commission merchants.
Alandete Hermanos.
Araújo, Joaquin.
Benedeti & Co., R.
Bossio, Bme. Martz.
Espiella, H.
Gomez & Co., Manuel.
Jaspe, Amaranto.
Lecompt, A.
Leon, Blas de.
Marcia, Pedro.
Myers & Daniels.
Perdomo, Luis Manuel.
Pombo Hermanos.
Zubiria, N. de.

Importers and exporters.
Alandete Hermanos, importers general merchandise.
Araújo, Joaquin, importer general merchandise.
Bossio, Bme. Martz.
Delgado Bros., importers drugs.
Franco, F. & A., exporters produce, importers drugs and hardware.
Gomez y Ca., Manuel, importers wines and general merchandise.
Jaspe, Amaranto, importer glassware, hardware, and machinery.
Jaspe, Jeneroso, importer stationery and fine arts in general.
Lecompt, A., exporter and importer of general merchandise.
Lemaitre, Ernesto D., importer groceries, wines, exporter rubber.
Leon, Blas de, exporter and importer of general merchandise.
Myers & Daniels, importers dry goods.
Perdomo, Luis Manuel, importer general merchandise.
Pombo Hermanos.
Vasquez, Manuel J., importer drugs.
Zubiria, N. de, importer general merchandise, exporter rum.

CARTAGENA—Continued.

Merchants, general.
Alandete Hermanos.
Alandete, Simon.
Amaranto, Jaspe.
Araújo, Antonio L.
Araújo, Jonquim.
Araújo, José Dionisio.
Araújo, Santiago.
Arrazola, J. M.
Castillo, R.
Ferrer, Hortensio.
Franco, F. & A.
Gastelbondo, Dr. Juan S.
Gomez & Co., Manuel.
Hanobergh, A. F.
Lemaitre, E. D.
Leon, Blas de.
Lopez, Navarro & Jaspe.
Martinez, B.
Mathieu & Hanobergh.
Mayer & Daniel.
McMaster, William B.
Merlano & Co.
Merlano, C. A.
Nuñez, Dr. Rafael.
Pombo Hermanos.
Pombo, Ignacio.
Romero, Viuda de Tedo.
Sagrera, F.
Valentine, Lincoln.
Vega, José Maria de la.
Velez, Danies & Co.
Velez, Pedro.
Velez, F. F.
Zubiria, Francisco de.

COLON (ASPINWALL).

Druggists.
Haffeman, W.
Preciado & Bros.

Electric Light.
Panama Electric Light Co.

Merchants, general.
Boston Ice Co.
Brandon & Bros. I., commission dry goods.
Cespedes, José A.
De Leon & Co., M. A.
De Leon, U. G.
Dieterich, H.
Dolphy, A.
Ehrman, D. L.
Isaacs & Asch, dry good, liquor, and provisions.
James & C.o, A.
Joseph, S.

COLON (ASPINWALL)—Continued.

Merchants, general—Continued.
Lam Sang.
Maduro, Isaac L.
Maal & Hermano, W. P.
Monteverde, A. B.
Pasos, J. M., dry goods.
Perbett.
Rathbun & Hirschberg, exporters of produce and timber.
Soracco, S., provisions.
St. Domingo, J. & R., commission.
Toledano, S. L.
Waldron, G. G. H., general commission agent.
Wells, Fargo & Co., agent.
Wing Hing Lee.

CÚCUTA.

Merchants.
Andresen-Möller & Co.
Berti Hermanos.
Blanco & Barroso.
Estrada Hijos.
Faber & Estrada.
Ferrero, Trinidad.
Lagomaggiore & Co.
Minlos, Breuer & Co.
Möller, Christian A.
Reyes Gonzalez & Hermanos.
Soto & Benöhr.
Soto, Ardila & Co.
Vale, Julio.
Vale, Montana & Co.
Van Dissel, Thies & Co.

HONDA.

Commission agents.
Hallam, Henry.
Leon, Joaquin H.
Martinez & Co., B.
Paz, Miguel.
Perez & Co., Anselmo.
Perez & Rodriguez.
Restrepo, José M.
Richoux & Co., Paul.
Vengoechea, Francisco.

Druggists.
Escobar, Restrepo & Co.
Garcia, Francisco B.
Lozano, Miguel.
Richoux & Co., Paul.

Grain merchants.
Amado, Dionisio.
Barrera, José P.
Braun, Nicolas.
Castellon, Martin.

HONDA—Continued.

Grain merchants—Continued.
Castro Rada, J. M.
Conde, Martin.
Gutierrez, Antonio.
Gutierrez, Manuel.
Guzman, Clemente.
Mora, Gregorio.

Merchants.
Cardona & Urrutia.
Castellon, Gregorio.
Garcia & Co., Cesar.
Gonzalez & Gallego.
Hallam, Henry.
Leon, Joaquin H.
Martinez & Co., B.
Navarro, Bernardo.
Paz, Miguel.
Perez & Rodriguez.
Richoux & Co., Paul.
Samper & Hijos, Miguel.
Torres, Julio.
Vargas & Hermanos, Francisco.
Vengoechea, Francisco.

Merchants, importers, and exporters.
Cardona & Urrutia.
Castellon, Gregorio.
Garcia & Co., Cesar.
Hallam, Henry.
Martinez & Co., B.
Navarro, Bernardo.
Perez & Co., Anselmo.
Perez & Rodriguez.
Richoux & Co., Paul
Samper & Hijos, Miguel.
Torres, B. Julio.
Vargas & Hermanos, Francisco.
Vengoechea, Francisco.

Provision merchants.
Perez & Co., Anselmo.

IBAGUE.

Merchants.
Restrepo, Juan de Dios.
Sicard, Mirtiliano.

LORICA.

Merchant.
Mendez, M. M.

MEDELLIN.

Banks and bankers.
Banco de Antioquia.
Banco de Medellin.
Banco Popular de Medellin.

MEDELLIN—Continued.

Banks and bankers—Continued.
  Banco del Progreso.
  Banco del Zancudo.
  Botero Arango ó Hijos.
  Restrepo, Marcelius & Co.
  Restrepo & Co.
  Vicente Villa é Hijos.

Exporters of coffee.
  Angel, Alonso.
  Echavarría, Juan José.
. Lalinde & Hermano, Gabriel; also rubber an
    hides.
  Ospina Hermanos.
  Perez & Hijos, Bartolomé; also rubber and
    hides.
  Uribe & Munoz.
  Vasquez, E. & J.

Gold-mining companies.
  Compañia del Zancudo.
  Compañia de Chorros y Sitioviejo.
  Compañia Inglesa Fontino y Bolivia.
  Compañia de las Colonias.
  Cortada de San Antonio.

Gold-smelters.
  Ospina Hermanos.
  Restrepo & Escobar.

Merchants, general.
  Alvarez, Manuel J.
  Amador, José María.
  Angel, Alonso.
  Araújo, Leocadio Maria.
  Corral & Toro.
  Echevarria, Rudesindo é Hijos.
  Garcia Hermanos.
  Heiniger & Bachman.
  Isaza & Escobar.
  Jaramillo, Tomás M.
  Lalinde & Hermanos, Gabriel.
  Lalinde & S. Mejia.
  Martinez, Juan de S.
  Melguizo, A. M.
  Melguizo, Pablo E.
  Montoya & Hijos.
  Moreno, Juvenal & Luis.
  Olarte, Luis.
  Pardo, José María Botero.
  Perez & Hijos, Bartolomé.
  Perez Hermanos.
  Perez & Hijos.
  Piedrahita & Co., Gutierrez.
  Restrepo & Hijos, Fernando.
  Restrepo & Co., M.
  Restrepo, Pastor & Co.
  Restrepo & Pelaez.
  Restrepos Hermanos.

MEDELLIN—Continued.

Merchants, general—Continued.
  Santamaria & Martinez.
  Toro, Alonzo & Daniel.
  Uribe & Escobar.
  Uribe & Co., Gomez.
  Uribe, M. A. & J.
  Uribe & Hijos, Mariano.
  Uribe, Lisandro M.
  Uribe, Rafael U.
  Uribe, S. Tomás.
  Vasquez, E. & J.
  Vasquez, Federico.
  Velez & Bravo.
  Velez, Marceliano.
  Velez & Co., M. M.
  Villa & Hernandez.
  Villa & Toro.
  Zapata, Jaramillo & Hijo.

OCAÑA.

Merchants.
  Jocome & Hermanos, José D.
  Lobo, Gervasio J.
  Rincon, Manuel Roca.
  Rizo, Rafael M.
  Trespalacios, José R.

PALMIRA.

Merchant.
  Dominguez & Co., José M.

PANAMA.

Bankers.
  Ehrman, Henry.
  Piza, Lindo & Co.

Chemists and druggists.
  Coralles, M.
  Espinosa, M.
  Köhpcke & Co.
  Mora, Manual A.
  Preciado & Co., Y.

Importers and exporters.
  Alfaro Hermanos, importers boots
    exporters rubber, hides, skins
    paiba, sarsaparilla.
  Arias, F. Ramon, importer hardwi
    furnishing goods, provisions, a
    variety.
  Arosemena, Florencio, importer gr
    provisions.
  Arosemena Hermanos, importers
    dlery, provisions, kerosene, etc.
    pearls, woods, etc.

PANAMA—Continued.

Importers and exporters—Continued.

Ascoli Hermanos, importers dry goods, clothing, wines, etc.

Boston Ice Co., importers timber, etc.

Boyd, Frederico, importer pine lumber.

Brandon & Bros., Isaac, importers groceries and provisions, wines; exporters hides.

Calvo, Juan N., importer groceries and provisions; exporter rubber, hides, skins, balsam copaiba, coffee, etc.

Cardoze, J. H., importer dry goods.

Corvalles, M., importer drugs.

Ehrman, Henry, importer cigars; exporter hides.

Fernandez y Hermano, L. A., importers housefurnishing goods, provisions, etc.

Guardia & Quelquejeu, importers crockery, glassware, lamps, hardware, house-furnishing goods, provisions, etc.

Herbruger, Leona de Leon de, importer dry goods and small wares.

Herrera, Gustavo, importer dry goods and small wares; exporter balsam copaiba.

Heurtematte & Co., M., importer dry goods, clothing, small wares, boots and shoes, liquors.

Isaacs & Asch, S. L., importers clothing, house-furnishing goods, hardware, and building materials.

Köbpcke & Co., importers drugs.

Lewis & Co., G., importers ship chandlery, provisions, wines, building materials.

Lindo & Co., Alfred, importer dry goods, clothing, small wares, ironmongery, wines.

Lindo, Mauricio, importer dry goods and small wares.

Lunau, Herman, importer dry goods.

Lyons & Co., E., importers hardware, crockery, glassware.

Maduro y Hijos, importers dry goods, haberdashery, wines; exporters pearls, hard woods.

Manent & Co., Jaime, importers dry goods and small wares.

Manuel & Co., Espinosa B., importers of drugs.

Marchand & Verdan, importers watches and jewelry.

Mora, Manuel A., importer drugs.

Müller, Luis, exporter rubber only.

Orillac, Alfredo, importer provisions, wines, spirits.

Osorio, M., importer groceries, provisions, liquors; exporter hides, rubber, sarsaparilla.

Pinel, Prospero, importer firearms, sewing machines, stoves, hardware, agricultural implements; exporter pearls.

PANAMA—Continued.

Importers and exporters—Continued.

Piza, Lindo & Co., importers provisions, liquors, dry goods; exporters hides, rubber.

Piza, Piza & Co., importers dry goods.

Preciado & Co., Y., importers drugs; exporters medicinal herbs, as copaiba, sarsaparilla, etc.

Recuero, J. N., importer ship chandlery, provisions, hardware.

Remon, Nicolás, importer stationery.

Salmon & Co., importers dry goods.

Sasso & Sons, importers dry goods and small wares.

Sun, Hop Wo, importer provisions, teas, liquors, etc.

Toledano, A., importer dry goods, provisions, liquors.

Toledano, S., importer dry goods and small wares.

Wing Wo Chong & Co., importers provisions, Chinese silks, and Chinese fancy goods and curios.

Ironmongers.

Lyons & Co., E.

Merchants.

Henriquez, Manuel D.

Henriquez, Moses D.

Menotti Hermanos.

Obarrio & Co., N.

The Bijou, cigars, cutlery, stationery, and toilet articles.

Vasquez, M. de la A.

Ycaza, J. J.

Opium dealer.

Yip, Can Hing.

Printing office.

Panama Star and Herald Co.

PASTO.

Merchant.

Segura, Dositeo.

POPAYAN.

Merchants.

Castro, Cesar.

Pardo & Hurtado.

Plata, Federico.

Rafael & Diego Caicedo.

Valasco, Polidoro Hermanos.

QUIBAO.

Merchants.

Baldrich, Dario.

Ferrer, Eladio.

Lozano, Indalecio.

RIO HACHA.

Merchants.
Camazo, José Guecco.
Christoffel, Juan D.
Dugand, Reyes Guecco de.
Henriquez, T. V.
Pereira, Joaquin.
Pinedo, Morris.
Pinedo, Samuel.
Weber Hermanos.

RIO SUCIO.

Merchant.
Rosa, Salvador de la.

SABANILLA.

Merchants, general.
Dasnille & Wenels.
Meir, J. A.
Pardo & Doval.
Vengoeche & Gonzalez.

SAN GIL.

Merchants.
Galvis, Santiago.
Rueda y Barrera.

SAN PEDRO.

Merchant.
Sanchez, P. Pablo.

SANTA MARTA.

Merchants, general.
Alzamora, H. José.
Andreis, José.
Angulo, Manuel G.
Angulo, Pedro.
Avendaño, Salcedo Manuel.
Castro, Antonio F. de.
Ceballos, Severo F.
Dávila, Francisco E.
Echeverria, Juan B.
Echeverria, Ricardo E.

SANTA MARTA—Continued.

Merchants, general—Continued.
Fergusson, Noguera & Co., commercial agents.
Granados, José Ignacio D.
Hernandez, Indalecio.
Hernandez, Santiago.
Herrara, E. Joaquin.
Infante, Pedro Antonio.
Joaquin, José R.
Mier, Manuel J. de.
Perez, Apolinar C.
Robles, José Francisco.
Salis, Pedro de.
Sanchez, Juan.

SANTIAGO DE VERAGUAS.

Merchants.
Fabrega, Dalixto.
Fabrega, José Manuel.

SINCELEJO.

Merchant.
Casseres, N. Gomes.

TUMACO.

Merchants.
Benitez, Francisco.
Benitez, Miguel.
Castillo, é Hijos, P. D. del.
Clark, Thomas.
Costillo, M. A. de.
Delgado, Delio.
Ganimara & Leeder.
Nicolas, Arias.

TUNJA.

Merchant.
Jimenez, Adolfo M.

ZAPATECAS (DEPARTMENT SANTANDER).

Merchant.
Gomes, F. G.

Costa Rica.

ALAJUELA.

Banks and bankers.
Banco de Costa Rica.
Caja de Ahorros.
Caja de Descuentos.
Sucursal del Banco Anglo.

Coffee growers and exporters.
Alfaro, Pedro.
Cananza, Is. de.
González, Deodono.
Montealegre & Co.
Montenegro, Florentino.
Sandoval, Manuel.
Soto, Jesus.
Soto, José M.
Soto, Mauriltio.
Tournon & Co.
Vasco, José L.

Druggists.
Cortez & Padilla.
Ocampo, Gabriel José.
Ruiz, Pompilio.
Silva Octavio.

Groceries and provisions.
Alvarez, Magdaleno.
Arana, Procopio.
Ardon, Apolina.
Cagigal, Cayetano.
Calvo & Sobrino.
Calvo, Alfredo.
Calvo, Juan.
Calvo, M. Santiago.
Frutos, José D.
Moya & hermanos.
Paz, Manuel de la.
Rozabal, Bartolomé.
Sandoval, José María.
Sibaja, S. & Fernández.
Sibaja, Martinez Joaq.
Soto, Maurilio.

ALAJUELA—Continued.

Groceries and provisions—Continued.
Vargas, J. M.
Villegas, Arturo.

Importers of dry goods.
Alfaro, Pedro.
Ardon, Rodolfo.
Barquero, Ignacio.
Blanco, Martin.
Calvo & Sobrino.
Jinesta, Soto Francisco.
Lopez, Miguel.
Sandoval, Manuel.
Soto & Sibaja.

Retail general merchants.
Acosta, Paulino.
Alfaro & Co.
Barquero, Ignacio.
Blanco, Martin.
Bonilla, Ricardo.
Calvo, Anselmo.
Cagigal, Cayetano.
Frutos, José Dolores.
González, José.
Gómez, Luis.
Güell, Santiago.
Herrera, Vicente.
López, Liguel.
Odubert, F.
Ruiz, Espíritu Santo.
Umaña, José C.
Vargas, Eugenio.
Vargas, J. M.

Wholesale import and export merchants.
Arana, Procopio.
Montenegro, Florentino.
Sandoval, Manuel.
Soto, Francisco J.
Soto, José Manuel.

ASERRI.

Druggist.
Badilla, Joaquin.

ATENAS.

Druggist.
Esquival, Guillermo.
Importer.
Rojas, Geronimo.
Retail general merchants.
Arias, Pedro B.
Yenkis, Juan.

CARTAGO.

Banks and bankers.
Banco Anglo Costarricense.
Guzmán. Simeón.
Jimenez, Manuel J.
Druggists.
Escoto, Juan A.
Guier, E. A.
Saenz, Ezequiel.
Importers and exporters.
Aguilar, Ramón.
Blanco, Manuel V.
Carranza, J.
Casasola, Nicolás.
Garcia, J.
Garcia, M.
Garcia, Pedro.
Guzmán, Simeon.
Jegel, Guillermo.
Jimenez, M. D.
Jimenez, F. &. N.
Jimenez, J. M.
Morales, Rafael.
Pachero, J.
Peralta, Bernardino.
Peralta & Co., Mestre.
Pinto, J. F.
Rodriguez, Juan.
Rojas, Mercedes J.
Troyo, Ramón.
Troyo & Co.
Retail general merchants.
Alvarado, Prudencio.
Avendaño, Juan.
Casasola, Nicolás.
Centeno, Rigoberto.
Coto, Valerio.
Li, Allan.
Pacheco, Eufrasio.
Rodriguez, Juan.
Zúñiga, Tobias.

DESAMPARADCS.

Druggist.
Ureña, Isidro.
Retail general merchants.
Cruz, Antonio.
Flores, Antonio.
Garcia, Joaquin.

GRECIA.

Coffee growers and exporters.
Esclante, M.
Fernandez, P. D.
Quezada, Ramón.
Merchants, exporters.
Maroto, Esteban.
Maroto & Co.
Quezada, Ramón.
Vega, D.
Merchants, importers.
Ellinger & hermanos, Luis.
Fernandez, Pio J.

HEREDIA.

Cloth manufacturers.
Troyo, J. Ramón.
Velarde, Federico.
Coffee growers and exporters.
Carazo, F.
Lizano hermanos.
Lizano, Joaquin.
Mora, M.
Morales, Bráulio.
Ortiz, Paulino.
Trejos hermanos.
Druggists.
Flores, M. J.
Flores, Juan F.
Zamora, Julián.
Importers and exporters and wholesale merchants
Chaverria, Manuel.
Chaverri, Mariano.
Flores & Morales.
Lizano, Joaquin.
Morales, Bráulio.
Moya, F. J.
Ortiz y hijo, Paulino.
Pacheco y hermano.
Pasapera, Salvador.
Rivera, Manuel.
Rosabal, Amado.
Torres, Juan M.
Trejos hermanos.
Ulloa & Zamora.
Zamora, José Maria.
Zamora, Manuel.

HEREDIA—Continued.

Retail general merchants.
Arguedas, Ramón.
Fernández, Fernando.
Ortiz, Paulino.
Pérez, Francisco.

LIBERIA.

Druggist.
Acuña, Juan.
Alvarado, Rodolfo.
Rojas, Toribio.

Retail general merchants.
Bolivar, Matias.
Rivera, Rafael.
Santos, Salvador.
Vallejos, Matilde.

LIMÓN.

Commission merchants.
Brown, Agencia.
Taylor, T. L.
Wichman, Luis.

Importers and exporters and wholesale merchants.
Brown, A. K.
Compañia de Agencias.
Keith, Minor C.
Laprade, Leon S.
Lindo, Aug. A.
Taylor, W.
Unckles, V.

Retail general merchants.
Aguay, Sara.
Amado, Elisa.
Dohaney, Sofia.
Miller, A. C.
Silbano, Elisa.

NARANJO.

Druggists and retail general merchants
Chinchía, Antonio.
Hidalgo, José.
Sanchez, José María.

NICOYA.

Druggists and retail general merchants.
Ramos, Guadalupe.
Sanchez, Manuel G.

PUNTARENAS.

Banks.
Banco Nacional.
Banco Anglo Costarricense.

PUNTARENAS—Continued.

Commission merchants.
Brenez, Miguel.
Esquivel, Arturo.
Esquivel & Co., F.
Gil Mayorga, Francisco.
Romagosa, Juan E.
Rohrmoser, Francisco.
Zúñiga, Darío.

Druggists.
Brenes, Miguel.
Sarmiento, Ignacio.
Toledo, Nazario.

Grocers.
Alvarez, Petra.
Castillo, Martin.
Cortés, José.
Darce, Silvestre.
McAdam, J.
Mora, Dolores C. de.
Nuñez, Encarnación.
Sanchez, Narcisa.

Importers and exporters and wholesale merchants.
Brackett, Eugene A.
Brenes, Miguel.
Bustos, Antonio.
Clavera, Francisco.
Compañia de Agencias.
Cruz, Francisco.
Dent, Rafael.
Duprat, J.
Esquivel y Vega.
Harley, Peter.
Herrero & Co., G.
Jenkins, Juan.
Lizano y Hno.
McAdam, John.
Man, Chong, Sing & Co.
Mata, Juan Bta.
Mencia, Inés Sra.
Peña & Co., N.
Rios, Juan.
Rohrmoser, F.
Rohrmoser & Revelo.
Suñol, Juan.
Walle, S. De.
Wing, Chong, Sing & Co.

Retail general merchants.
Baldonado, Ramón.
Darce, Silvestre.
Diaz, José.
Ellis, Janny.
Figueroa, Anibal.

Silversmiths.
Barrueta, Francisco.
Marroquin, Manuel.

PUNTARENAS—Continued.

Special manufacturers.
Angulo, José, tortoise-shell goods.
Anduray, Manuel, tortoise-shell goods.
Castro, Mercedes, salt.
Conde, José A.
Flores, José, salt.
Guevara, Juan, salt.
Marroquin, Manuel, tortoise-shell goods.
Mora, Petronila, salt.
Obando, Roque, salt.
Ramirez, Jorge, salt.
Rodriguez, Rafael, salt.
Salas, Melchor, salt.
Villalobos, Feliciano, salt.

SAN JOSÉ.

Banks and bankers.
Banco Anglo-Costarricense.
Banco de Costa Rica.
Banco de la Unión.
Banco Nacional.
Collado, A.
Cruz, Antonio.
Esquivel, Aniceto.
Harrison, Percy G.
Hernández, Juan.
Le Lacheur, Dent & Co.
Mora & Co., Juan C.
Ortuño, Gaspar.
Peralta, Francisco.
Rohrmoser, Ernest.
Rojas, Juan.
Tinoco & Co.

Breweries.
Deugo, Manuel V.
Richmond, Gregorio.

Booksellers and stationers.
Lines, Vicente.
Molina, Guillermo.
Montero, Joaquin.
Morrel y Ca.
Ureña, Sixto A.

Commission merchants.
Bennett, Jaime.
Calvo, Rafael Fonseca.
Echeverria, Francisco.
Echeverria, Santiago Q.
Field, W. J.
Lujan & Montealegre.
Mendez, Jenaro Castro.
Pisa, Benjamin.
Price, D. C.
Ross, J. Jaime.
Sharpe, Cecil.
Villafranca hermanos.

SAN JOSÉ—Continued.

Druggists.
Bansen, Maximiliano.
Botica de San José.
Carballo, Florentino.
Calderón, Manuel.
Carranza, Bruno.
Durán & Nuñez.
Hermann & Zeledon.
Iglesias, Pedro.
Jiménez, Mariano.
Macis, Nicolás.
Nuñez Jiménez, Francisco.
Quezada, Francisco.
Rojas, Elías.
Rojas y Soto.
Rucabado, Jenaro.
Saso, Mauricio.
Salazar, Miguel.
Silva, Carlos J. de.
Valverde, P. J.
Zeledón, José C.

Engravers and sculptors.
Baldomero, Llela.
Blanco, Cruz.
Mérida, Rafael.
Sanchez, Rafael.

Exporters of coffee.
Alfaro, J.
Alvarado, Santiago.
Bennett, Jaime G.
Calsamiglia, B.
Coronado, José Andres.
Cubero & Echandi.
Dent, Teresa.
Duran, José.
Echeverria, Juana A. de.
Ellinger & Hno.
Esquivel, A.
Esquivel, Fabian.
Esquivel, M. N.
Gallardo, A. & F.
Garcia, José M.
González, Alberto.
Herran & Hno.
Hernandez, Juan.
Jiménez, A. E.
Jiménez, Leemes.
Keith & Tinoco.
Luján, Manuel.
Mata, Juan R.
Millet, F. N.
Montealegre, M. L.
Péralta, F.
Piza, Julio.
Santiago, Federici.
Schroeter & Co., O. von.

SAN JOSÉ—Continued.

Exporters of coffee—Continued.
Sharpe, Cecil.
Tournon & Co., Hto.
Vargas, M. José.

Foundries.
Deugo, Manuel V.
Fundición de San José.
Ross & Morales.

Grocers.
Almuella, Agustín.
Alvarado, Eleodoro.
Alvarado, Julio.
Andrés, Marcelino.
Arana, Telésforo.
Ardón, Paulino.
Artavia, José.
Azcona, Bibiana.
Cagigal, Francisco.
Calvo, María Manuela.
Carvajal Jiménez, Teodoro.
Casasola, Rafael.
Castro, Bartolo.
Escalante y Hno.
Flores, Francisco.
Frías, José.
Fuentes, Gregorio.
Garbanzo, Salvador.
Guillén, Rafael.
Gutierrez, Concepción C. de.
Gutierrez, Yanuario.
Hidalgo, José.
Hurtado, Pedro.
Incera, Isidro.
Lara, Fermina.
Leiva, Apolonio.
Liquidano, Laureano.
López, Felix.
López, Rosendo.
Martín, Alejo.
Marquez, Abraham.
Millet, Miguel.
Monje, Gregorio.
Mora, José.
Mora, Ignacio.
Mora, J. M.
Moya, León.
Muñoz, Ramón.
Navarro, Ciro.
Odio, Ismael.
Pagés, Cañas & Co.
Palacios, José.
Paniagua, Miguel.
Pérez, Sebastián.
Perasa, José.
Price, David C.
Prada y Gonzáles.

SAN JOSÉ—Continued.

Grocers—Continued.
Salazar, Filadelfo.
Solano, Agustín.
Solas, Agustín.
Soborio, Napoleón.
Solano, José María.
Subaldia, Carlos.
Vals, Pedro.
Vicente, Eusebio.
Villavicencio, Rodolfo.

Hatters.
Antillón, Francisco.
Esquivel, José.
Esquivel, Alberto.
Veiga López, M.

Hardware and tools.
Argüello, M.
Carazo, Manuel.
Cubero, Jesus.
Dent y Ca.
Lahmann, Fedo.
Morell y Ca.
Muñoz, José.

Importers of drugs.
Bansen, Dr. Max.
Duran & Nuñez.
Hermann & Zeledon.
Soto & Giustiniani.
Rojas, Elías.
Valverde, Dr. Panfilo.

Importers of dry goods.
Alfaro, J.
Calsamiglia, B.
Castro, Teodosio.
Coronado & Hno.
Cubero & Echandi.
Ellinger & Hno., Luis.
Goicochea & Co., F.
Hernández, Juan.
Herrero & Co., G.
Knöhr, Juan.
Levskowicz & hijo.
Muñoz & Acostas.
Schroeter & Co., O. von.
Steinworth & Co., W.
Troyo & Co., J. R. R.
Weidel & Veiga.

Importers of hardware.
Bradway, Wm.
Lahmann, F. H.
Macaya & Rodriguez.
Morrell & Co.

Importers of provisions.
Atmuella, Agustín.

SAN JOSÉ—Continued.

Importers of provisions—Continued.
Benedictis, G.
Bradway & Co.
Escalante & Hermo.
Esquivel & Cañas.
Esquivel & Garvanzo.
Morrell & Co., Arthur.
Pagés & Cañas.
Perez & Co., S.
— Ortuno & Co.
Rodriguez & Macaya.
Soley, Antonio.
Terrés, Pedro.
Trejos & Co.

Import and export and wholesale merchants.
Adiego, Miguel.
Alandete & Pradilla.
Alfaro & Co.
Bansen, M.
Benedictis, G. de.
Berry, James.
Bradway, G.
Calsamiglia, Bartolomé.
Calvo, Manuel M.
Castro, Teodosio.
Carranza, Bruno.
Collado, Adrián.
Cubero é hijos.
Dent, Le Lacheur & Co.
Dent & Co., R. W.
Denne, H. A.
Durán, José.
Duprat & Co., F.
Echeverría, Juan F.
Ellinger & hermano, Luis.
Esquivel, Narciso.
Esquivel & Cañas.
Facio, Justo A.
Fernández y Tristan.
Field & Co., W. J.
Fonseca, Mariano.
Goicochea & Co.
Gutierrez, Ezequiel.
Hernández, Juan.
Herrera y Ca., G.
Jager, J.
Jiménez, A. E.
Jiménez, Roberto.
Journon & Co., H. J.
Keith, M. C.
Knöhr, Juan.
Lahmann, F.
Lara, Salvador.
Levakowicz, Isidro.
Levakowicz & Son, J.
Lizano y hermano.

SAN JOSÉ—Continued.

Import and export and wholesale merhants—Cont d
Lujan & Montealegre.
Macaya y Rodrigues.
Mata, Juan R.
Mata & Lujan.
Melgarejo, Antonio G.
Menendez, C.
Millet, J. Napoleón.
Monastel, Cleto.
Montealegre, Francisco.
Montealegre, Mariano.
Morrell & Co.
Montealegle & hermano. J. U.
Muñoz & Acosta.
Nauté Mauricio.
Ortuño, Gaspar.
Pagés, Cañas & Co.
Peralta, Francisco.
Piza & Co.
Robles, M. A.
Rohrmoser, Francisco.
Rohrmoser & Co., E.
Ross, Robert.
Rudd, Harrison N.
Sacripanti, José.
Schroeter & Co., Otto von.
Steinworth & Co., W.
Terrés, Pedro.
Tournon & Co., H.
Thompson & Co., Gmo.
Trejos y Aquilar.
Troyo & Co., J. R. R.
Uribe & Batalla.
Vella & Co., Felice.
Victor y Hoey.
Villafranca, Francisco.
Villafranca hermanos.
Villafranca, Rafael B.
Wenceslao de la Guardia.
Wingfield, Richard.
Witting, Gmo.

Photographers.
Calderón, Prospero.
Rudd, H. N.
Valiente y Marichal.
Zamora, Fernando.

Retail general merchants.
Alfaro & Co., T.
Atmella, Augustin.
Audrain, Constant.
Audrain, Leoncio.
Bradway, Guillermo.
Cabello, Francisco.
Carazo, Señorita.
Chavarria, Lucas.
Carranza, Manuel J

SAN JOSÉ—Continued.

ail general merchants—Continued.
Carrasco, Rodrigo.
Carrasco, Tomás.
Cagigal, Francisco.
Cardona & hermano, A.
Cerlain, C.
Cepa, Abelardo.
Coronado y hermano.
Cubero é hijos, J. J.
Day, Carlos.
Durán, José.
Elizondo, Procopio.
Esquivel, José.
Esquivel, Arturo.
Esquivel, Narciso.
Esquivel, Roberto.
Esquivel, Alberto.
Escalante y hermano.
Flores, Francisco.
Goicoechea & Co., F.
González, Pedro.
Gutierrez, Rosario.
Herrera & Co., Gorgonio.
Hurtado, Pedro.
Incera, Isidro.
Lahmann, Federico.
Landerer, Pablo.
Leiva, Apolonio.
Levskowicz é hijo, J.
Marquez, Abraham.
Monstel, Cleto.
Mascuel, Manuel.
Mena y hermano, Miguel.
Millet, Miguel.
Moya, León.
Montealegre y Carazo.
Odio, Ismael.
Quezada, Francisco.
Quiroz, J. Tedorico.
Rawson, Dolores Q. de.

SAN JOSÉ—Continued.

Retail general merchants—Continued.
Uribe y Batalla.
Villavicencio, Rodolfo.
Vicente, Estanislao.
Veiga, Manuel.

Silversmiths.
Córdova, José.
Jardín, Arencio.
Sojo, Santana.
Valle, Andréz del.

Watchmakers and jewelers.
Antillon, Sotero.
García, Venancio A.
Siebe, Luis.
Saenz, Adolfo.
Sojo, Santa Ana.
Soto y Ramirez.

SAN RAMÓN.

Druggists and retail general merchants.
Guerrero, Manuel Maria.
Jurado, R. B.
Miranda, Valeriano.
Lobos, Rudecindo.
Rodriguez, Luis.
Urrutia, Pedro.

SANTO DOMINGO.

Druggists and retail general merchants.
Chacón, José B.
Flores, Juan.

TRES RIOS.

Druggists and retail general merchants.
García, Pedro A.
Mora, Juan A.
Pacheco, Eufracio,
Rojas, Alejandro.
Zúñiga, Tobias.

ECUADOR.

AMBATO.

Importers and exporters.
Barona Hermanos, general merchandise.
Chacon Hermanos, druggists.
Costales, Vicente A., general merchandise.
Puyal, Ramon, general merchandise.
Sevilla, Aquilino, general merchandise.

BABAHOYO.

Merchants, cotton and woolen stuffs.
Barrera, Benigno.
Barrola, Francisco.
Espinosa & Barreto.
Flores, Maria.
Guerrero, José.
Guzman & Co., Paulino.
Lama, Antonio.
Verdereti, Ramon.

Provision merchants.
Acevedo, Catalina.
Avendano, Pedro.
Bueñano, M.
Camacho, Adelaida.
Cardona, José B.
Castillo, Fidel.
Cornejo & Co.
Escandon, Amador R.
Fileur, Pablo.
Iturralde, Aurora.
Orozeo, J.
Torres, Dolores.
Vega, Nicolas.
Villaus, Belisario.
Vivas, Julio.

Woven goods.
Barzola, Francisco.
Barreto & Espinosa.
Guerrero, J.
Marino, Manuel.
Saona, Antonio.
Vazquez, César A.
Verdesoto, Ramon.

BAHIA DE CARAQUEZ.

Importers and exporters.
Ceperat, Juan.
Constantini, Z.
Goddard, E. I.
Gostalle, Josefa V. de.
Polit, Juan.
Santos & Co.
Santos, Alejandro.
Santos, Elio A.
Seperak, I.
Uscocovich, G.
Villacis, G.

BALLENITA.

Merchant.
Millett, Alberto.

CALZETA.

Merchants.
Alarcón, J. J.
Alban, Floracio.
Villavicencio, G. L.

CANOA.

Importers and exporters.
Lozano, F.
Santos, J. A.

CHONE.

Importers and exporters.
Bowen, Oliva.
Constantini, Zéfiro.
Hidalgo, Jacinto.
Hidalgo, Miguel.
Olea, José.
Santos, Elio A.
Uscocovich, G.
Villavicencio, S.

CUENCA.

Bank.
Sucursal del Banco del Ecuador.

CUENCA—Continued.

Merchants.
Aguilar, Antonio.
Aguilar, Vicente.
Diaz, Dolores.
Diaz, Vicente.
Izquierdo, Eloy.
Jonroe, Juan.
Ochoa. Ignacio.
Ordonez Bros.
Regalado, Andrés.
Valéncia, J. F.

Quinquina, sulphur.
Flores & Carlo, L.
Vivar, Victor.

ESMERALDAS.

Cigar manufacturers.
Aba, José.
Figuero, José.
Figura, José.
Molina, N.
Molina, Vicente.

Merchants.
Arroyo, Teodomiro.
Bueno, Elias.
Calderon, Antonio.
Conchas, Julio.
Diaz, Téoflio.
Guerra, Facundo.
Guerrero, M.
Guerrero, Mariano.
Gunes, Pedro.
Martinez, Ramon.
Meneses, Juana.
Palacios, Miguel M.
Piloro, Antonio.
Portes, Adriano.

Merchants, importers and exporters.
Calderon, Manuel A.
Canduti, David.
Gasteln, M.
Gomez, Pedro G.
Lopez, José.
Manaño, Rogelio.
Prias & Co.
Quintero, Ladislao.
Quiteria, Miguel A.
Racines, Firso.
Solari, Benito.
Triarte, Telesforo.
Trujillo, Placencio
Villasis, Ramon.
Yamijselli, Ant.
Zuñiga, Rosalie.

GUAYAQUIL.

Banks and bankers.
Banco de Credito Hipotecario.
Banco del Ecuador.
Banco Internacional.
Banco Territorial.
London Bank of Mexico and South America, limited.
Coronel, Francisco J.
Lopez, Daniel.
Reinberg, Martin, & Co.
Seminario Hnos.
Stagg, L. C.

Commission merchants.
Alvardo y Befarauo.
Arroyo, Manuel M.
Bravo Hnos.
Caamaño y Roblés.
Calderón, Benigno S.
Carbo, Pedro Mariño.
Castillo & Co.
Castro, Velázquez y Co.
Coronel, Francisco J.
Franco, Juan de D.
Gálvez, Francisco J.
Leon, Ricardo.
Lopez, Daniel.
Pavia, Eduardo.
Pazmiño Hnos.
Peña, Velarmino.
Ponce, Luis M.
Reinberg, Martin, & Co.
Requena, Enrique
Reyna, Leonardo.
Serrano, Leandor & Co.
Seminario Hnos.
Stagg, L. C.
Suarez, Manuel M.
Tarry, Eduardo.
Tolá, Agustin.
Villavicencio, J. F.
Zevallos Hnos.

Exporters.
Arroyo, Manuel M.
Aviles, Thomas E.
Bruno, Rigoberto Sanchez.
Caamaño & Robles.
Coronel, J.
Hijos de Luzarraga.
Kaiser, Oldenburg & Co.
Madrid, Fernandez.
Maro. Oneteria & Co.
Reinberg, Martin, & Co.
Reyre linos.
Roca & Henriques.
Saenz, Montjoy & Pavia.

GUAYAQUIL—Continued.

Exporters—Continued.
Urgelles, J. M.
Zevallos Hnos.

Importers of Chinese goods.
Almacen de Té y Sedería.
Con San Cui & Co.
Ni Sing & Co.
On Chong & Co.
On Long & Co.
San Lee & Co.
San Long & Co.
Sin Ni Wo & Co.
Sun Chong Wo & Co.
Vo San Long.
Woon & Co.
Wo Sing & Co.

Importers of general merchandise.
Abadie Hnos.
Arroyo, Manuel Maria.
Bunge & Co.
Chambers, Geo.
Duran & Levrey.
Goldschmidt, Alfredo.
Grosberger.
Guillamet, José.
Henriques, E. H., succ.
Hurtado, M. G.
Jones, R. B., & Co.
Koppel, Karl, & Co.
Kruger & Co.
Lopez, Daniel.
Mejia, Manuel & Co.
Marin y Ollague.
Murillo, G. E.
Norero, N., & Co.
Orrantio, M.
Osa, Noverto & Co.
Pena, Oscar.
Reinberg, Martin, & Co.
Rhode, E., & Co.
Saenz, Montjoy & Pavia.
Seminario Hnos.
Stagg, L. C.
Vignola & Costa.
Ycaza, Francisco J.
Zevallos Hermanos.

Importers of groceries.
Alarcón, Frazmo.
Barretta, Gerónimo.
Biggio, Luis.
Bottaro, Juan.
Calvo, Carreras.
Campodónica, César.
Campodónico, Miguel.

GUAYAQUIL—Continued.

Importers of groceries—Continued.
Canepa, Manuel.
Carbo, Manuel José.
Castagneto & Co.
Castillo & Co.
Chinga, Toribio.
Cussianovich, José.
Dupplere, Roberto.
Forsa & Podesta.
Frugone, Pio G.
Game, F. M.
Guzman, Gumercindo.
Inzua, Ramon.
Juanola & Co.
Kruger & Co.
Madinyá & Co.
Mearfá & Co.
Mórtola, Juan.
Mortula, Fortunato.
Murillo y Vargas Machuca.
Mejia & Co.
Parodi, Agustini.
Parodi Hnos.
Parodi, Luis.
Plaza, Almiro.
Puig, Verdequez, Jaime.
Puig, Verdequez, T.
Ribera, Joaquin.
Rodriguez & Co.
Sanchez, Carlo M.
Segala, Lértora.
Sercovich, Jorge.
Sonino, José.
Tramontana, Lucas.

Importers of hardware.
Alverado y Bejo.
Chevasco & Co.
Duran & Co.
Garrier, Maurice.
Gamez, J. Prio, successor of.
Icaza, Francisco J.
Icaza, Oldenburg & Co.
Kaiser, Guillermo.
Kruger & Co.
Medida, Damián J.

Importers of linen goods and haberdashery.
Aguirre, Pedro A.
Azevado y Wagner.
Baluarte, Manuel.
Bianchi, José.
Cabazes Hnos.
Castellano, Domingo.
Cucalón, Roberto.
Drouet, Obdulio.
Flores, Vicente, y Hnos.

S. Ex. 8, pt. 11——8

GUAYAQUIL—Continued.

Importers of linen goods, etc.—Continued.
Gainsborg, S. H.
Grimaldo, Antonio.
Grosberger, S. C.
Hurtado, Miguel.
Icaza.
Kaiser, Guillermo.
Madinyá & Co.
Mateus, Manuel A.
Nobva y Macias, Tlfno.
Raimond, C.
Renella, Antonio.
Roggiero e Hijo, Enrique.
Saona, Armando.
Sanchez, Vergára & Co.
Feran Hnos
Zevallos, Francisco A.

Importers, miscellaneous.
Banqueriso, Feó Juan, office furniture.
Barboto & Co., drugs.
Botica Comercio, drugs.
Bunge & Co., dry goods.
Carbo, Manuel José, glass and earthenware.
Cevallos, Francisco, dry goods.
Chevasco & Co., naval supplies.
Druet, Obdulio, dry goods.
Empresa de Carros Urbanos, street railway supplies.
Guayaquil Lager-Beer Brewing Association, brewers' supplies.
Heredia & Co., drugs.
"Ingenio Valdez," succ., importer of machinery and exporter of sugar.
Janer, Fedro, drugs.
Koppel, Karl & Co., dry goods.
Larreta, Juan A., undertakers' supplies.
Lopez, Lescano. Carlos, drugs.
Martiz, E. C., sole leather.
Maulme Hermanos, jewelry.
Morla Hermanos, importers of machinery and exporters of sugar.
Moscoso & Co., stationery.
Norero & Co., dry goods.
Offner, Alberto, jewelry.
Papaseit, R., & Co., stationery.
Pavia, Eduardo.
Payeze & Co., drugs.
Poppe, Frederico, hats.
Puig, Jaime, y Mir, importers of machinery and exporters of sugar.
Rasch, Augusto, & Co., drugs.
Rigail, Aquiles, ready-made clothing.
Tyler, E. A., lamps and lamp goods.
Vinelli y Persico, jewelry.
Yeaza, Eduardo, dry goods.
Yeaza, Francisco, dry goods.
Zanatta, Luis, ready-made clothing.

IOSAGUA.

Merchant.
Velasquez, Francisco.

JIPIJAPA.

Importers and exporters.
Andrade, Camilo.
Campozano, A. H.
Gonzales, José Joaquin.
Lopez, Daniel.
Lopez Hermanos.
Lourido, C.
San Lucas, M., & Co,
Villacreses, Sebastian.
Zuluaga, Juan D.

LA COCA.

Merchant.
Moran, Javier.

MACHALILLA.

Merchants.
Alban, Alfredo.
Vallejo, P.

MANTA.

Commission merchants.
Delgado, Ricardo, & Co.
Miranda, J. F.
Moreira, Pedro A.
Paz, J. E.
Rodriguez, Cordova & Co.
Rodriguez, F.
Ruperti, Emilio.

Importer and exporter, general merchandise.
Ruperte, Emilio.

Merchants.
Azua, J.
Bermúdez, J. Ma.
Chavez, M. J.
Chavez, Nicolás.
Delgado, J. R.
Freyre, Augusto.
Gallo, Juan.
Loor, J. J.
Lopez, J. F.
Moreira, Nicanor.

MONTECRISTI.

Importer and exporter, general merchandise.
Azua, Juan.

Merchants.
Acevedo, J. D.
Arcentales, Ezequiel.
Arcentales, M. J.
Anchundia, Manuel S.
Anchundia, Pedro.

MONTECRISTI—Continued.

Merchants—Continued.
Anchundia, Ramon.
Ceballos, Fernando.
Cedeño, Pedro.
Chaves, Nicolas.
Chavez, Juan & Co.
Delgado, J. F.
Delgado, Manuel Ma.
Delgado, Maximino.
Reyes, J. C.
Robles, Manuel.

PORTOVIEJO.

Importers and exporters.
Chiriboga, Hector.
Loor, J. J.
Sabando, Daniel.

Merchants.
Aguilera, B. R.
Avila, J. H.
Bowen, Oliver.
Mora, Virgilio.
Saavedra, Angel.
Sabando, Zenon.
Santana, Celso.
Santana, Celso.
Segovia, Antonio.
Robles, Manuel.
Veles, I. S.
Yepes, Enrique.

QUITO.

Banks.
Banco de la Unión.
International Bank.

Importers.
Alonia, Antonio, exporter hides.
Baca, Ignacio, y Hermanos, dry goods.
Calvo, Ramon, hardware, groceries, wines.
Carbo, Esteban, hardware, groceries, wines.
Espinosa & Co., stationery supplies.
Freyle, N., dry goods.
Gachet, Agusto, general merchandise.
German, M., & Co., general hardware.
German, R., hardware.
Gouln, Luis, dry goods.
Heredia, Ignacio, general merchandise.

QUITO—Continued.

Importers—Continued.
Hermann, A., brewer.
Herrera, Manuel.
Koppel, Karl & Co., dry goods.
Laffite, Lucien, dry goods.
Larrea, Manuel Jijon, manufacturer of woolen cloth.
Madrid, Carlos, hardware, groceries, wines.
Mora, Miguel, dry goods.
Moscoso, Mateo, dry goods.
Narvaez, José, hardware, groceries, wines.
Ordonez, Salvador, y Hermanos, manufacturers of cotton cloth.
Ortiz, Vidal, dry goods.
Patino, R., dry goods.
Pazmino, L. R., dry goods.
Proano, Ignacio, dry goods.
Puente, Wencesloa, general merchandise.
Salvador Hermanos, general merchandise.
Schibbye, Alejandro, drugs.
Silva & Paredes, fancy goods.
Stahlschmidt & Kistormacher, drugs.
Urutia, Julio, general merchandise.
Vascones, José, tailors' goods.

RIO CHICO.

Importers and exporters.
Alcivar V., Miguel.
Josa, Juan.

ROCAFUERTE.

Merchants.
Arcentales, Fco. J.
Cedeño, J. J.
Cedeño, J. R.
Loor, Ricardo.

SANTA ANA.

Merchants.
Ceteño, Pedro A.
Mendaza, J. A.
Pico, Ma. Antonio.
Reyes, I. E.

SANTA ELENA.

Merchants.
Panchana, Liborio, general merchandise.
Pena, Leopold, exporter.
Velez, Manuel, exporter.

Guatemala.

AMATITLAN.

Wholesale import and export merchants.
Barillas, M.
Catalant & Co.
Monterrosa, M. R.

ANTIGUA.

Imports.
Arango, José M.
Redondo, José y Alvarez.

CHIQUIMULA.

Retail general merchants.
Cruz, Juana.
Lobos, Antonio.
Peralta, Juan B.
Portillo, Dolores R.
Sagastume, Pablo.

Wholesale import and export merchants.
Aldana, P.
Herbruger, Francisco.
Nuño, A.
Ortega, Fernando.
Porta, Pío.
Portal, R.
Siguí, Jorge.
Terracena, Daniel.

COBAN (Alta Vera Paz.)

Wholesale import and export merchants.
Boyer & Co., R.
Champney & Bird.
Constant, C.
Cordona, Lino.
Dieseldorff & Co., H. R.
Dieseldorff, W. A.
Domadien, A.
Leger, Jorge.
Linares, S. V. J.
Moulds, W. R.
Planas, Juan.
Sarg Hermanos.
Sierra, M.
Trabanino, Vicente C.

ESCUINTLA.

Retail general merchants.
Alvarado, Manuel.
Amado, Paula.
Aparicio, Francisco.
Azurdia, J.
Bolaños, J.
Castro, Felisa.
Guevara, María.
Hurtado, María.
Quintanillá, Dolores.
Zúñiga, Aparicio.

Wholesale import and export merchants.
Baur, Juan.
Gomar, Bernabe.
Ruckwardt, Manuel.

ESQUIPULAS.

Hatter.
Toledo, Francisco.

Photographer.
Recinos, Abel.

Wholesale import and export merchants.
Benavides, Socorro de.
Palencia, Francisco.
Sagastume, Tránsito.
Villeja, Antonio.

GUATEMALA.

Banks and bankers.
Angulo & Co., Dámaso.
Angulo, Manuel.
Angulo, Rafael.
Banco Columbiano.
Banco de Guatemala.
Banco de Occidente.
Banco Internacional.
Calvo, Carlos.
Echeverría Valdés, Manuel.
Eyssen & Co.
Fisher & Co.
Ibargüen, Rufino.
Jaramillo, Cárlos.

GUATEMALA—Continued.

Banks and bankers—Continued.
London Bank of Mexico and South America,
  Limited.
Martin, R. H.
Muydan & Prinz.
Urruela, Manuel.
Villa, Ricaredo de.

Booksellers and stationers.
Capella, Juan.
Cariñez, Mariano.
Goubaud, E.
Ortiz Urruela, Juan Francisco.
Partegas, Antonio.

Boots and shoes.
Aguirre & Co.
Brau, Victor.
Cabrera, Simeón.
Córdova, Mariano.
Franco, Simeón.
Granados y Hermanos.
Guzmán, Manuel.
Marroquín, Juan.
Mendoza, Eugenio.
Milán, José María.
Ramirez y Hermano, Vicente.
Rosales y Hermano, Ignacio.
Salazar, Saturnino.
Vásquez, Santos.

Commission merchants.
Alvarado, Alfredo F.
Aréyalo, Guillermo.
Asturias, Eleázaro.
Balcarcel, J. Tomás.
Carrillo, Miguel.
Castejón, Javier.
Castillo é Hijo, Domingo.
Cobos, Nicolás.
Cruz, Salvador.
Fernández, Francisco.
García, Feliciano.
García, Ignacio.
Gimes, Eduardo.
Larreynaga, Manuel.
López, Ricardo.
Morales, Servando.
Ozaeta, Julián.
Palacios, Victor.
Palomo, Tomás.
Polanco, Francisco.
Rivas, Valentin.
Ruiz, Benjamin.
Samayoa, Francisco.
Sandoval, Gregoria.
Schmid, Rodolfo.

Commission merchants—Continued.
Vivás, Eduardo.
Zúñiga, Félipe.

Druggists.
Arévalo, Federico.
Asturias, Rodrigo.
Castellanos, Prudencio.
Castillo Hermanos.
Dardón, Félix.
Escobar, José María.
Gallardo, Rafael.
Gálvez, José María.
Gandara, Isidro.
González, José L.
González, Miguel.
González Mora, Rafael.
Madriz, Francisco.
Mancilla, Leopoldo.
Monge, Manuel.
Montiel, Joaquín.
Montenegro, Mariano.
Morales, Federico.
Moreno, Juan B.
Orantes, Fernando.
Ortiz, Manuel.
Rodriguez, Manuel C.
Saravia, José C.
Saravia, Salvador.
Sierra, Isaac.
Solares, Joaquin.
Sosa, Francisco.
Zelaya, José María.
Zúñiga, & Co.

Engravers.
Ayala, Matéo.
Chávez, José Angel.
España, Apolinario.
Herrera, Próspero.

Founders.
Artes y Oficios, Escuela de.
Carranza, Emilio.
Chinchilla, Rafael.
Escobar, Angel.
Garibaldi, José.
Klee, Juan.
Rivera, Nazario.

Hatters.
Bátres, Francisco.
Bedoya, Fernando.
Bedoya, Jorge G.
Flores, José.
Franco, Juan.
Leal, J. Francisco.
Luna, Manuel E.
Morales, Máximo.

GUATEMALA—Continued.

Hatters—Continued.
Ortega & Co., Tomás A.
Sánchez, Francisco.

Lithographers.
Castro, Pedro.
Cruz, Ernesto.
Salvatierra, Viviano.

Photographers.
Cano, F. y Muñiz.
Frener, Camilo E.
Herbruger, E.
Jas, Juan J.
Kildare, E. J.

Retail general merchants.
Acain, Joaquín.
Aguilar, Salvador.
Aguirre, Ramón.
Arellana, Nicolás.
Asturias, Eduardo.
Asturias, Rubio Miguel.
Ayado, Manuel.
Ayau, Rafael.
Azpuru, Francisco.
Barrios, Pedro J.
Bermejo, José.
Bolaños Hnos.
Broks, Josefa.
Castañeda, Martin.
Castillo, Joaquín.
Cerna, Ismael.
Cervantes, Manuel.
Diaz, Joaquín.
Donovan, Maria.
Durán, Teodora.
Echeverría Valdés, Juan.
Echeverría Valdés, Manuel.
Estrada, Eduardo.
Fernández, J.
Gaegauf, Hugo.
García, José.
García, Ramón.
García Moreno, Juan.
Geering, Eduardo.
González, Angel.
González, Pablo.
González Valdés, José.
Granados, Guillermo.
Herbruger, Alfredo.
Herran, Emilio.
Herrera, Julio.
Irigoyena, Cárlos F.
Kauffmann, J. A. C.
Klissmann, Ludolfo.
Kock, Sofus.
Labin, Manuel.

GUATEMALA—Continued.

Retail general merchants—Continued.
Larreynaga, Alejo.
López, Dolores.
Lowenthal.
Maegli, Juan.
Magee, Juan & Alfredo.
Machuca Vargas, Antonio.
Maria, Francisco.
Mazorra, Miguel & Jacinto.
Medina, Juan.
Monterrosa, Rodolfo.
Muttini, Enrique.
Nájera, Fernando y Manuel.
Novella, Julio.
Novi, Antonio.
Ortiz, Guillermo.
Penado, Manuel.
Petrilli, Emilia.
Piñol, Cármen.
Prinz, Herman.
Quiñonez é Hijo, Rafael.
Rheiner, Juan.
Ricasens, Manuel.
Romero, Maria.
Roque, José Maria.
Sarg, Francisco C.
Schaeffer, Pablo.
Schewer, Gustavo.
Sosa, Francisco.
Stampf, Otto.
Tielemans, Cárlos.
Valdcavellano, Narciso.
Valenzuela, José.
Valle, Emeterio.
Vargas Machuca, Antonio.
Vázquez, Manuel.
Wyld, Ernesto.
Wyld, Jorge.

Special manufacturers.
Azurdia, Ramón, mattresses.
Barillas, Guadalupe, chocolate.
Barreda, Antonio, wicks and fuses.
Castillo, David, furniture.
Castillo, Dorotea, chocolate.
Castillo, Joaquín, shirts.
Campo, Manuel, wicks and fuses.
Campo, Manuel, rubber stamps.
Castellanos, Prudencio, sulphuric acid.
Chávez & Hno., Luis, wooden combs.
Cruz, Dolores, mattresses.
Diez, Domingo, shirts.
Fahsen, Pascasio, furniture.
Falla, Dolores, white lead.
Frener, Camilo, rubber stamps.
Garrido, Pedro, violins.

GUATEMALA—Continued.

Special manufacturers—Continued.
Garcia, Joaquin.
Gil, Venancia, mattresses.
Giovannetti, Antonio, shirts.
Gutierrez, Wenceslao, furniture.
Hernández, Clementa, furniture.
Herrera, Belisario, furniture.
Irungaray, Dolores, chocolate.
Izaguirre, Gertrudio, mattresses.
Matheu, Manuel, mattresses.
Mayorga, Luz, mattresses.
Pinagel, Agusto, furniture.
Romero, Pedro, chairs.
Ruiseco, Félix, shirts.
Vasseaux, Javier, carriages.
Zapatal, Isidro G., umbrellas.

Special merchants.
Aguiere, Juana M. de, sugar.
Aguilar, Angela, boots and shoes.
Alfredo, Rosa, sugar.
Anguiano, Manuel, china and glassware.
Anzueta, Rafael. furniture.
Asturias, Luis, boots and shoes.
Bátres, Dolores, gunpowder.
Bátres, Julián, sugar.
Bátres, Palomo Miguel, sugar.
Bazar, Sociedad de Artesanos, furniture.
Beauchêne, Pedro, gunpowder.
Beltramena, Bernardo, china and glassware.
Beteta, Carmen A., china and glassware.
Bravaix. Cárlos, china and glassware.
Castro, José Maria, artificial flowers.
Córdova, Mariano, boots and shoes.
Crocker, Concepción, boots and shoes.
David, Josefina de, perfumes.
Escobar, Victoriano, boots and shoes.
Estrada, Victoriano, sugar.
Estrada, Luisa, boots and shoes.
Fernández, Dionisio, sugar.
Figueroa, Carmen F. de, woods.
Galán, Manuel, tobacco.
Galán, Brigido, tobacco.
Garza, Carmen, florist.
Girón, Isabel M., woods.
González, Bailón, woolen goods.
González, Basilio, sugar.
González, Miguel, china and glassware.
González Piñola, Ricardo, furniture.
Grima Dolores, L. de, china and glassware.
Guerra, Cruz G. de, sugar.
Gutierrez, Wenceslao, furniture.
Guzmán, Maria, boots and shoes.
Herrera, Patrocinio, woolen goods.
Izquierdo, Juan, gunpowder.
Laguardia, Dolores, sugar.

GUATEMALA—Continued.

Special merchants—Continued.
Landero, Luz, gunpowder.
Lara, Maria, boots and shoes.
Machado, Manuel, sugar.
Mántara, Juana, florist.
Mazarugos, Inés, boots and shoes.
Mencos, Francisco, woods.
Molina, Manuel, woods.
Morales, Máximo, woolen goods
Murga, Ramón, sugar.
Nannini, Aurelio, pianos.
Orellana, Isabel de, woolen goods.
Ortiz, Juan, woods.
Ortiz, Miguel, church ornaments.
Padilla, Ramón, woods.
Paz, Julián, fancy articles.
Peralta, Vicente, sugar.
Pineda, Marcelino, woods.
Piñol, Carmen, boots and shoes.
Polanco, Antolina, boots and shoes.
Porras, Manuel C. de, boots and shoes.
Recinos, Ramón, coffins.
Reyes, J., furniture.
Rodas, Francisco, furniture.
Rodriguez, Guillermo, sugar.
Samayoa, Doroteo, sugar.
Samayoa, José Maria, sugar.
Storm & Whitney, gunpowder.
Teil, Javier Du, sugar.
Urrutia, Christina, florist.
Valle, Josefa, sugar.
Valle, Miguel, coffins.
Vásquez, Lucila, furniture.
Vásquez, Manuel, woods.
Vásquez, PilorR. de, salt.
Villagrán, Magdalena.

Watchmakers and jewelers.
Arriola, Francisco.
Bravaix, Cárlos.
Castro, J. M.
Durán, Ramón.
Gauvin, Enrique.
Guerrero, Salvador.
Motlet, Marcelino.
Nájera, Diego B.
Rodeman, Jorge.
Rosemberg, Emilio.
Widmer, Federico.

Wholesale import and export merchants.
Abrahamson & Co., Rosenthal.
Aguiero & Co.
Alfaro & Co.
Arenzana & Llarena.
Arrechea, José Rafael.
Arrechea, Luis.

GUATEMALA—Continued.

Wholesale import and export merchants—Cont'd.
Ascoli & Co., E.
Baltramena, Bernardo.
Bauer & Co.
Becker & Eyssen.
Beltromena, Manuel.
Benito & Co., J. B.
Bertrand & Co.
Blenler & Co., Otto.
Boyd, Gustavo.
Camacho, Francisco.
Carrera, Antonio.
Colama, Miguel.
Compañia de Teléfonos de Guatemala.
Descalzi & Co.
Descamp, Eduardo.
Estrada, V. M.
Eyssen & Co., Lorenzo.
Fisher & Hnos.
Ganadara, Urruella & Co.
Godoy, A.
Grote, German.
Grotewald & Co.
Guillarel, Casimiro.
Herrera & Co.
Hockmeyer & Co.
Jaramillo, Juan N.
Jump, Thomas.
Kriemler & Co., Juan.
Kuhsick, Guillermo.
Lambert, Walter C.
Llarena, Antonio.
Maegli, Gaegauf & Co.
McIlwaine, José.
McNiver, Stanley.
Mathew & Co., Federico.
Mathew & Co., Victor.
Meyer & Hnos.
Meyer & Co., Luis Da Costa.
Minondo & Co., Joaquin.
Nanne, Guillermo.
Newman & Co., J.
Ortega & Co., L.
Paul & Co.
Payens, Shulitz.
Petrelli, E.
Pierri, Juan.
Pineda & Grotta.
Ponciano, J. F.
Prado, Miguel.
Prinz & Co., Enrique.
Rivero & Co., Manuel.
Rivero & Hnos., S.
Rosenberg, Emilio.
Rosenthal & Sons, A.

GUATEMALA—Continued.

Wholesale import and export merchants—Cont'd.
Rottman, Eduardo.
Ruiz & Co., J. & M.
Sacripanti, José.
Samayoa, José M.
Sanchez & Co., Pedro.
Schwartz & Co.
Silva, Vasconcelos.
Sinibaldi, Alejandro M.
Sinibaldi, Rafael C.
Smyth, E. R.
Sosa, Francisco.
Steinborth & Co., W. S.
Telégrafos Nacionales de Guatemala.
Torriello, Coronel Enrique.
Ugarte & Co., R.
Urruela, Gandaaa & Co.
Urruela & Co., M.
Valdeavellano, A. G.
Valdés, Manuel Echeverría.
Van Der Henst, J. E.
Van Der Pute & Tertzwell.
Vásquez, Manuel J.
Villa, Enrique V.
Whilnes, Stoun S. V.
Whitney & Co.
Wolf, Jacobo.
Zadik & Co., A.

HUEHUETENANGO.

Boots and shoes.
Argüeta, Martin.
Chávez, Valeriano.
Sosa, Antonio.
Druggists.
Aguilar, Porfirio.
Hernández, Celestino.
Hatter.
Herrera, Pedro.
Retail general merchant.
Galindo, J.
Special merchants.
Cardón, Apolinario, wagons and carts.
Jirón, Manuel, manufacturer of hammocks.
Wholesale import and export merchant.
Arriola, J.

IZABEL.

Wholesale import and export merchants.
Ferguson, Samuel.
González, Cristobal.
Guttmann, R. S.
Javalois & Co., S.
Knight & Potts.
Pott, T. J.

JALAPA.

Boots and shoes.
Guzmán, Vicente.
Montenegro, Mariano.
Druggist.
Cifuentes, Francisco.
Retail general merchants.
Argueta, Ignacio.
Bonilla, José Antonio.
Sandoval, Juan.

JUTIAPA.

Wholesale import and export merchants.
Castell, J.
Champney & Bird.
Gudiel, F.

LA ANTIGUA.

Wholesale import and export merchants.
Mathew & Co.
Palomo, M.
Vargas, M.
Vivas, E.

LIVINGSTON.

Wholesale import and export merchants.
Clarck, Joseph.
González y Porta.
Martínez & Ferguson.
Rich, Isidro.
Tisne, Laveryant.
Wardland, S. Henry.

MATAQUESCUINTLA.

Boots and shoes.
Florín, Eulogio.
Retail general merchant.
Aquino, Cecilio.

MAZATENANGO.

Druggist.
Monzan, Gabriel F.
Wholesale import and export merchants.
Alvarado, D. F.
Barras & Hermanos.
De León, J. M.
García, F.
Martínez, E.

QUEZALTENANGO.

Bank.
Banco de Occidente.

QUEZALTENANGO—Continued.

Druggists.
Debaus, Oscar.
Galver & Co.
Ligorria, Macario.
Saeur, León.
Saller de M., Pablo.
Sarda & Mora.
Photographer.
Soler. Genaro.
Printing establishment.
Tipografía de la Industria.
Wholesale import and export merchants.
Ariz hijo, Vicente.
Ascoli & Co., E.
Diebold, L. N.
Gutierrez, Doroteo.
Hockmeyer & Co.
Keller & Linse.
Koch Hnos. & Co.
Mackenney & Martinez.
Martinez, Gerónimo.
Meyer & Co., Adolph.
Ortega & Co., Luis.
Pacheco, Quirino.
Paganini Hnos.
Pierri, David.
Stahl & Co., Julio.
Zadik & Co., A.
Zadik & Cheesman.

RETALHULEU.

Commission houses.
Compañía de Agencias é Industrias de Occidente, Limitada.
Indalecio, Lifontes.
Juan, Zoller.
Drugs.
Chever & Co., T.
Molina & Galver.
Ruíz, Ernesto.
Ugarte & Co., M.
Jeweler.
Fuchard, Otto.
Photographers.
Anaya, Carlos.
Ugarti, Rafael.
Wholesale merchants.
Alvarado, Guillermo.
Ascoli & Co.
Bertrand & Co.
Bruni, Hector.
Carrera, Antonio.

RETALHULEU—Continued.

Wholesale merchants—Continued.
Laeisz & Co.
Obstaele, Adolfo.
Palacios, Teotilo.
Suarez & Co., A. E.
Zadick & Co.

SALAMÁ.

Boots and shoes.
Asención, Hermenegildo.
Leal, Narciso.
Rodriguez, José María.

Hatters.
Jiménez, Francisco.
Mendozo, Rafael.
Belloso, Juan S.
, Chavarría, Rosa.

Retail general merchants.
Coronado Hno., Leandra.
García Hno., Braulia.
Leal, Adelida.
Marcales, Margarita de.
Narciso, Sebastian.

Watchmaker and jeweler.
Presa, Francisco.

Wholesale import and export merchant.
Callmeyer, David.

SAN MARCOS.

Wholesale import and export merchants.
Barrios, Juan.
Coronado, Manuel.
Corzo, Miguel.
León, F. de.
Maldonado, F.
Rivas, Rafael,
Sanches, F.
Tenorio, Juan.
Vázquez, Padre J.

SANTA CRUZ.

Wholesale import and export merchant.
Leiva, Samuel.

TECPÁN.

Wholesale import and export merchants.
Acuña, José.
Aguirre & Co.

TOTONICAPÁN.

Boots and shoes.
Arriola, J. M.
Coutiño, Fruto.
León, Mariano de.
Pereira, Julián.

TOTONICAPÁN—Continued.

Druggist.
Gutierrez, José C.

Engravers.
Avila, Valentin.
Herrera, Próspero

Hatter.
Culebro, Leopoldo.

Special manufacturers.
Aypajá, Manuel, galloons.
Chuc, Manuel, galloons.

Watchmaker and jeweler.
Córdova, Delfino.

Wholesale import and export merchants.
Carney, David.
Coronado, Angel B.
Enriquez, Lúcas.
Estrada, F.
Sánchez, Petrona.

TUMBADOR.

Wholesale import and export merchant.
Soliz, Francisco.

ZACAPA.

Boots and shoes.
Huezo, Francisco.
López, Agapito.
Navas, Ezequiel.

Druggists.
Klee, Rosendo J.
Nájera, Salvador.

Hatters.
Coto, Manuel.
Esquivel, Abelino.
Gómez & Hno., Cayetano.
Molina, Manuel.

Special manufacturer of spirits of turpentine.
Pérez, Santos.

Special merchants.
Antony, Horacio, boots and shoes.
Barrientos, Domingo, tobacco.
Castañeda, Eduardo, sugar.
Castañeda, Federico, sugar.
Peralta, Antonio, tobacco.
Salguerro, Juan B., tobacco.

Wholesale import and export merchants.
Castañeda & Co.
Cruz, María.
García, Juan.
Nuflo, José.
Palacios, José María.
Sosa, Vicente.
Windelberg & Co.

Haiti.

AQUIN.

Importers.
Durand & Co., J. B.

AUX CAYES.

Merchants.
Blanchet & Co., H.
Condé fils & Co., D.
Jacobsen, Johs.
Mundmeyer & Co., H.
Roberts, Dutton & Co., agents Banque Nationale d'Haïti.

CAPE HAYTIEN.

Bank.
Branch of the Banque Nationale d'Haïti.
Banker.
Nolting & Co.
Importers of dry goods.
Arnaud, Phileas.
Chitarin, A.
Elie & Co., F.
Laroche, Robert.
Terlonge, A.
Importers of dry goods, lumber, and provisions.
Czaykowski & Co., C.
Durand, P. F.
Dévé, Reine & Co.
Etienne & Co., H.
Irvin, François.
Lyon & Co., Edw.
Mompoint jeune & Co.
Importers of dry goods and provisions.
Acacia, J. J.
Altiéry, Leroy & Co.
Auguste, Raoul.
Auguste, Seymour.
Blain, J. R.
Blot frères.
Clérié, Thomas.
Deetjen, R. E., & Vᵉ Castaing.
Desroches, Edouard.
Desroches, Fabre.

CAPE HAYTIEN—Continued.

Importers of dry goods and provisions—Cont'd.
Dugué, Périclès.
Hector & Mackenzie.
Jimenes & Co.
Kampmann, Edward.
Laratte fils.
Laroche, T. L.
Latortue, A. Julian.
Lenoir, Isaac.
Leveille, Béris.
Martin, Edouard.
Mary, Volney.
Montreuil, Josias.
Montreuil & Co., Edouard
Penette & Co., C.
Schomberg & Co., R.
Schütt & Co., Otto.
Trott, Ezekiel.
Westen, Jules.
Importers of French goods.
Albaret, Vᵉ A.
Auguste, Danmer.
Dupuy, M de. M. R.
Fabre, Albert.
Gaspard & Co., A.
Laroche, E. T.
Laroche, Vᵉ Jh.
Laroche, Robert.
Martin, Ed.
Terlonge, A.
Importers of hardware, glass, etc.
Auguste, J. D.
Pierre, F. W.

GONAÏVES.

Banks and bankers.
McGuffie & Co., James M.
National Bank of Haiti.
Osler, J.
Riboul & fils, Vᵉ D.
Merchants.
Coën fils, C., exporter of logwood.
Entwisle, V.

GONAIVES—Continued.

Merchants—Continued.

Etienne & Co., G. A.
Hurmann & Co., F., importers of dry goods and exporters of produce.
Keitel & Co., importers and exporters of general merchandise and produce.
Kelly Bros., importers of provisions.
Krause & Co., P.
Lancelot & Co., Vᵉ P., importers of dry goods.
McGuffie, E. J.
McGuffie & Co., J. B.
Osler, John H.
Sterlin, L. and C., importers of dry goods.
Wulff & Co.

JACMEL.

Bank.

Branch of National Bank of Haiti.

Merchants, importers and exporters.

Bernier, G. F.
Denis, M.
Feron, F.
Laloubère. A. C.
Mundineyer, Nephew & Co.
Poux, M.
Simmonds Brothers.
Vital, J. B.
Watty & May.
Wöltge & Cie , L.

JEREMIE.

Bank.

Branch of the Banque Nationale d'Haiti.

Importers and exporters.

Acluehe, L. P.
Besson, Thomas.
Blanchet, A. A.
Blanchet, F. C.
Gaveau, L.
Gostalle & Co., V.
Laraque, Depaix.
Lavaud & Co., A.
Lavaud & Gaveau.
Laville, Jules.
Mainvielle fils.
Margron, G.
Petit & Co., E.
Rouzier, Arthur.
Rouzier, Cuvier.
Rouzier, L. T.
Sansaricq, C.
Touchard, Martineau & Co.
Villedrouin, K.
Villedrouin, V.

MIRAGOANE.

Merchants. general.

Merentie & Co., J.
Mitchell, F. W., exporter.

PETIT GOAVE.

Merchants, general.

Ewald, C.
Merentie, H.
Merentie & Co., F.

PORT AU PRINCE.

Banks and bankers.

Ahrendts, Aug.
Bieber & Co., Otto.
D'Aubigny & Co.
Dejardin, Luders & Co.
Elie & Co., F. ;
Hermann & Co., F.
Keitel & Co., G.
Miot frères & Co.
Miot, Scott & Co.
National Bank of Haiti.
Simmonds frères.
Vieux & Laraque.
Weber & Co.
Weymann, Ch.
Woolley & Co., F.

Exporters.

Bieber & Co., Otto.
Boutin & Co., N.
D'Aubigny & Co.
Dejardin, Luders & Co.
Désiré, Lefebre & Co.
Gaëtjens & Riboul.
Herman & Co., F.
Keitel & Co., G.
Miot, Scott & Co.
Simmonds frères.
Weber & Co.
Weymann, Ch.

Importer of crockery and chinaware.

Brun, J. C.

Importer of drugs.

Pohlmaun & Co.

Importers of dry goods.

Auguste, Tancrède.
Arnaud, Phiteas.
Baptiste, Raoul J.
Bertoni & Co., J.
Boutin & Co., N.
Carré & Co., N.
Gaëtjens & Riboul.
Giordani, J. P.
Hodelin, L., merchant tailor.
Jaeger, E.
Lahens & Co., Th.
Lalew, C. de.
Lüdecke, Fred.
McGuffie, R.
Mevs & Co., H. S.

PORT AU PRINCE—Continued.

Importers of dry goods—Continued.
 Miot, Anníbal.
 Pratelli, Copello & Co.
 Prézeau, B.
 Revest, G.
 Rivière, Pétion.
 Sylvain, M., clothier.
 Schickhardts & Co., Aug.
 Vorbe, C.
 Weymann, Ch.

Importers of French goods.
 Brisson, Th.
 Carvalho, C. F.
 Castera, Ernest.
 Castera & Co., F.
 Caze, J. C.
 Coles, F. B.
 Fères & Co.
 Guérin, A. L.
 Guyot, A.
 Laroche, E. P.
 Menos & Co., G.
 Roy, Herard.
 Roy, Pétion.
 Weil & Co., Simon, French clothing.

Importer of furniture.
 Stark, Wm.

Importers of general merchandise.
 Audain, J. J.
 Fères & Co.
 Green, Kenaebel & Co.
 Mevs & Co., H. S.

Importer of German goods.
 Rodewalt & Co.

Importers of hardware.
 Flambert, M.
 Green, Kenaebel & Co.
 Mevs & Co., H. S.
 Mevs, Sierig & Co.
 Pratelli, Copello & Co.
 Rodewalt & Co.
 Stark, Wm.
 Stecker & Co., R.

Importers of lumber.
 Flambert, M.
 Green, Kenaebel & Co.
 Péloux & Co., L.

Importers of provisions.
 Auguste, Tancrède.
 Barthe & Co., Ed.
 Bigaud & Co., E.
 Bourjolly, A.
 Bosselmann, M.
 Célestin, Roselva.

PORT AU PRINCE—Continued.

Importers of provisions—Continued.
 Chefdrue & Co., E.
 Cínéas fils & Co.
 Cuths & Co., Oliver.
 Demeuran & Co., E.
 Etienne fils.
 Guercy & Co., Albert.
 Guercy & Co., Aug.
 Huttinot, L. G.
 Jeansème, J. A.
 Leroy, L.
 Lota & Co., N.
 Marcelin & Co., Ed.
 Martelly & Co., A.
 Menos & Co., G.
 Merentie & Co., F.
 Mermantin, D.
 Miot & Co., M.
 Paillière, Painson & Co.
 Paillière fils.
 Painson & Co.
 Péloux & Co., L.
 Phillips, Thos. A.
 Roux & Delinois.
 Rigaud, Cand.
 Rigaud & Co., E.
 St. Macary, Eug.
 St. Rome, A.
 Sergile & Co., A. J.
 Viljoint & Co., A.

Importer of rum, paint, etc.
 Barbancourt & Co.

Importer of stationery.
 Guyot, A.

Importer of matches, clocks, etc.
 Milke & Co.

PORT DU PAIX.

Importer.
 Elizee, E. & A.

Merchants, general.
 Kainer & Co., G.
 Poiterien & Co.

ST. MARC.

Banks and bankers.
 Boutin & Co., N.
 Grullon, Adriano, & Co.
 Herrmann & Co., F.
 Miot fils & Co.
 National Bank of Haiti.

Importers and exporters.
 Acoune, Juene.
 Boutin & Co., N.

ST. MARC—Continued.

Importers and exporters—Continued.
Charles & Co., Ch.
Dalencour, A.
Grullon, Adriano, & Co
Herrmann & Co., F.
Miot fils & Co.

ST. MARC—Continued.

Importers and exporters—Continued.
Philippon & Co., A.
Pinard & Co., R.
Sterlin, L. N. C.
Thorby, V., & Co.
Woolley & Co., C.

Honduras.

AMAPALA.

Bank.
Banco de Honduras.
Commission merchants.
Dubón, Agustín.
Kohncke, Teodoro.
Rossner, José.
Druggist.
Dubón, Agustín.
Hatter.
Flores, Manuel.
Retail general merchants.
Abadie & Co., P.
Dubón, Agustín.
Rossner, José.
Sosa, A.
Wholesale import and export merchants.
Abadie & Co., Pedro.
Bardales, General Santos.
Dubón, Agustín.
Gattorno é hijos, J. B.
Guzmán, F.
Heyliger, Cornelio.
Kohncke, Teodoro.
Moncada, S.
Rossner & Co., J.
Rudolph, C.

BONACCA.

Importer.
Bayly, William.

CHOLUTECA.

Boots and shoes.
Sanchez, Fausto.
Wholesale import and export merchants.
Gattorno, J. B.
Guillén, J. B.
Midence, Antonio.
Rodriguez hnos.

S. Ex. 8, pt. 11——9

COMAYAGUA.

Boots and shoes.
Alvarado, Leandro.
Morales, Cruz.
Drugs.
Munth, Julio.
Reina, Toribio.
Retail general merchants.
Aguirre, Adán.
Araque, Maria.
Castillo & hnos., Matías.
Mendoza, Teodoro.
Ucles, Encarnación.
Ulloa, Tomasa.
Wholesale import and export merchants.
Aguirre, Adán.
Arias, Celio.
Berlios, Victorino.
Castillo é hijos, M.
Delpech & Co., M.
Dubón, Tiburcio.
Fiallos, Juan Francisco.
Fiallos, J. M.
Henden, Santiago.
Mundt, Julius.
Recarte, Feliciana.
Reina, Toribio.
Valenzuela, Alonzo.
Valenzuela & Co., R.
Velásquez, Ochoa.

DANLI.

Wholesale import and export merchants.
Castillo, Jacobo.
Gamero, M.
Verda, Matilde.

ERANDIQUE.

Wholesale import and export merchant.
Muñoz, E.

129

GRACIAS.

Wholesale import and export merchants.
Cisneros, José María.
Hernández, G.
Muñoz, Rosa.
Pineda, Nazario.
Trejos, Eulogio.
Villela, Belisario.

GUANAJA.

Wholesale import and export merchants.
Sinclair, John.
Torres, Dionisio.

GUINOPE.

Importers and exporters.
Barradalles & Co., general merchandise.
Torres, Francisco, general merchandise.

JUTICALPA.

Boots and shoes.
Becerra, Rafael.
Rivas, Fernando.
Silversmith.
Mercadad, Marcos.
Wholesale import and export merchants.
Bertrand, P.
Cáliz, F.
Fortin, Castro.
Fortin, Carlos F.
Gardela, G.
Morales, Florencio.
Rosales, A.
Zelaya, J. M.
Zelaya, I.

LA ESPERANZA.

Wholesale import and export merchants.
Alvarez Castro, J. A.
López, A.
Mejía, V.

LA PAZ.

Wholesale import and export merchants.
Alvarado, Casimiro.
Colindres, Manuel.
Salinas, Martin.
Suarez, B.
Vasquez, Toribio.

MARCALA.

Wholesale import and export merchant.
Ramirez, C.

NACAOME.

Wholesale import and export merchant.
Cisne, José.

OCOTEPEQUE.

Boots and shoes.
Buezo, Ramon.
Coto, Salvador.
Díaz, Samuel.
Erazo, Luciano.
Flores, Marcelino.
Morataya, Manuel.
Sandoval, Braulio.
Salguero, Lino.
Torres, Leandro.
Druggists.
Bocanegra, Juan.
Duque, Jorge.
Soliz, Marcial.
Umaña, Manuel.
Grocers.
Ardón, J.
López, Francisco.
Retail general merchants.
Ardón, J.
Carranza, Francisco.
Chinchilla, Victor.
Fuentes, Pedro.
Hernández, Francisco.
Madrid, Juan.
Morales, Sixto.
Ortiz, Juana V. de.
Rodriguez, Maximo.
Solís, Carlos.
Umaña, Francisco.
Umaña, Florencio.
Umaña, Dolores.
Valle, Gertrudis.
Vidal, Juana.
Wholesale import and export merchant.
Villela, Juan J.

OLANCHITO.

Wholesale import and export merchants.
Arriaga, Cristóbal.
Castro, Tomás.

OMOA.

Boots and shoes.
Rodriguez, Andrés.
Wholesale import and export merchants.
Cosales, Pedro.
Cabus, José María.
Estapé, Luis.
Estapé & Casaula.
Lee, Maiselmo.
Rivera, José Angel.

PERSPIRE.

Importers.
Molina, Marcial.
Jivon & Medina.

PUERTO CORTÉS.

Commission merchants.
Alger & De León.
Merilees, J. W.

Druggist.
Panting, Jorge.

Silversmith.
Rosales, Juan.

Wholesale import and export merchants.
Belisle, J. J.
Brown, Huberto.
Castro, Praxedes.
Debrot hnos.
De León & Alger.
De León, Reginaldo.
Harman, León Wm.
Kraft, Eduardo.
Leiva, Florencio.
Merreilles, John.
Prince, Pedro C.
Seymour, Henry.
Stain, Samuel.
Ugarte hnos.
Vidaurrete, Próspero.

ROATAN.

Druggist.
Gaumer, Geo. F.

Wholesale import and export merchants.
Aguirre, Federico.
Burchard, W. C.
Flynn, E. H.
Izaguirre, David.
Rivera, J.
Suarez, B.

SAN JUANCINTO.

Importer.
Jacoby, E. A.

SAN PEDRO SULA.

Commission merchants.
Carraccioli, Joaquin.
Martinez, León.
Reynard, José Maria.
Rich, Jaime.

Druggist.
Guild, W.

Retail general merchants.
Mejía, Abraham.
Ramos, Francisco.

Special manufacturer.
Arnoux & Co., sugar.

Wholesale import and export merchants.
Arnoux & Co.
Arn aud &Co., P., general merchandise.

SAN PEDRO SULA—Continued.

Wholesale import and export merchants—Cont'd.
Bähr, Jorge.
Cabus, Martin.
Colliers, Guillermo.
España, Lorenzo.
Fiallos & Co., Francisco.
Funes, Caesar, general merchandise.
Girbal, Federico.
Gost & Mahler, general merchandise.
Hernández & Co., Simeón.
Ingles, Lorenzo.
López, W. L.
Maradiaga y Garcia.
Martinez, León.
Meza, Rafael.
Mitchell, Dr. J. M., drugs.
Panting & Co., general merchandise.
Pedroza, Carlos.
Prince, Pedro C.
Ramos, Francisco.
Valenzuela, José Maria.

SANTA BARBARA.

Boots and shoes.
Aguilar, José Maria.
Flores, Adolfo.
Muñoz, Manuel.

Hatters.
Baide, Luis.
Barahona, José Maria.

Photographer.
Veroy, Francisco.

Retail general merchants.
Fletes, Evaristo.
Guzmán, Ignacio.
Inglés, Lorenzo.
Laurent y Alfredo.
Paredes, Andrés.
Paredes, Salvador.
Paz, Onofre.
Paz, Fidel.
Rivera, Lucio.
Rodriguez, Gregorio.
Romero, Paz.

Silversmith.
Ortega, Albino.

Wholesale import and export merchants.
Aguilar, Vicente.
Fajardo, Julian.
Pineda Mejía, José Maria.

SANTA ROSA.

Boots and shoes.
Caledonio, J.
Contreras, Alonzo.

132 HONDURAS.

SANTA ROSA—Continued.

Boots and shoes—Continued.
Orellana, Antonio.
San Martin, Rodolfo.

Druggist.
Arias, Juan A.

Retail general merchants.
Buezo, Julio.
Coboa, Indalecio.
Erazo, David.
Esquivel, Florencio.
Henríquez, Macedonio.
Henríquez, Trinidad.
López, Fulgencio.
Madrid, Tomás.
Madrid, Agustin.
Madrid, Rafael.
Macedonio, Antonio.
Medina, Antonio.
Meliton, Cordova.
Penado, Rosendo.
Portillo, Teodoro.
Rios, Leoncio.
Toledo, Manuel.

Wholesale import and export merchants.
Castellanos, Victoriano.
Cáliz, Justo.
Fiallos, Francisco.
Guist, Constantino.
Meliton, Cordova.
Milla y hnos.
Rich, Jaime.
Rosendo, Agustin.
Tenorio, Miguel.
Villa, José Maria.

TEGUCIGALPA.

Bank.
Banco de Honduras.

Books and stationery.
Vigil, José L.

Boots and shoes.
Andino, Benjamin.
Irias, Mariano.
Zúñiga, Florencio.

Commission merchants.
Grau, Julio F.
Streber, Ricardo.

Druggists.
Aguelera y Ca., J.
Angulo, M.
Arias, Pedro.
Bernhard, Albert.
Diaz, Joaquin.
Botica del Hospital.
Midence y hno., Ramón.

TEGUCIGALPA—Continued.

Druggists—Continued.
Streber, M.
Ucles, J.

Grocer.
Reyes, Gervacia de.

Hardware and tools.
Balette, Julio.
Reyna, José Maria.
Sotero, José Lazo.
Zelaya hermanos.

Photographer.
Aguirre, Francisco.

Printing establishment.
Tipografía Nacional.

Retail general merchants.
Cubas, Dionisio.
Guardiola, Gonzálea.
Molina, Cipriano.
Retes, Tomasa.

Silversmiths.
Aguilar, Antonio.
Ordoñez, Timoteo.

Watchmaker and jeweler.
Bohlander, Juan.

Wholesale import and export merchants.
Agurcia & Soto, general merchandise.
Aguirre, J. T., photographer.
Ayestas, Vicente.
Ariza, Francisco.
Baker, Alden H.
Bernhard, Albert, drugs.
Bernhard, George, commission.
Beyer & Backer, A. H.
Bogran, Don Luis.
Bohlander, Juan.
Castillo é hijos.
Diaz, Joaquin, drugs.
Diaz hnos.
Estrada, J., general merchandise.
Estrada, Jacobo, general merchandise.
Fernández, Benito, general merchandise.
Fernández, Ramiro, general merchandise.
Fiallos, Rafael, drugs.
Fontecha, Dr. R., wines, liquors, etc.
Fritzgartner, Dr. R.
Gamero & Co.
Gutierrez, José Maria.
Gutierrez & Co., López.
Hilder, F. F.
Jirón, Quintin.
Laines, Samuel, general merchandise.
López, Antonio, general merchandise.
Lagos & Co.
López, Antonio, general merchandise.
López, Rafael.

TEGUCIGALPA—Continued.

Wholesale import and export merchants—Cont'd.
Lozano, Julio, general merchandise.
Martinez, Florencio.
Matute, T.
Medina, Juan Antonio.
Meza, S.
Midence, E.
Midence, Ramón, general merchandise, drugs, liquors, paints.
Molina, M.
Morlan, Alberto E., jewelry, clocks, and musical instruments.
Planas, Francisco, general merchandise.
Planas, Ledo. Ponciano.
Pinetta, José, wines, etc.
Robles, D.
Streber, Ricardo, general merchandise and liquors.
Sevilla, Leopoldo, general merchandise.
Streber & Zurcher.
Traviesa, Federico, general merchandise.
Toledo, Eusebio.
Ucles, Alberto, general merchandise.
Ugarte, Tomasa de, general merchandise.
Valentine, W. S.
Vigil, Manuel.
Vigil, Ramón, general merchandise.
Vigil, Marcial, general merchandise.
Vigil, José L.
Villafranca & Sons, general merchandise.
Wüchner, Henry.
Zelaya, Abelardo, general merchandise.
Zúñiga, Miguel, general merchandise.
Zúñiga, Alberto.
Zúñiga, Diego.

TRINIDAD.

Wholesale import and export merchant.
Fajardo, Julián.

TRUJILLO.

Banks and bankers.
Aguan Nav. & Imp. Co.
Hurley, Thomas H.

TRUJILLO—Continued.

Banks and bankers—Continued.
Ord, Joseph.
Velásquez, Cipriano.

Drugs.
Dillet, Alfonso.

Wholesale import and export merchants.
Betancourt, Fernando.
Binney, Melhado & Co.
Castillo, J.
Castillo, Prospero.
Castillo hnos.
Debrot, Federico.
Dillet, Motute.
Dillet & Ruis.
Font, J.
Glynn, C. & J.
Izaguirre & Co., D. M. J.
Julia, D. José.
Lafitte, Juan.
Melhado, W. M.
Ord, Joseph G.
Sosa, Donaldo.
Tristá, Carlos L.

UTILLA.

Wholesale import and export merchants.
Phipps & Co.
Rivera, Blas.
Torres, Serafio.
Woodville, R.

YUSCARÁN.

Wholesale import and export merchants.
Barrantes, Rafael.
Castillo, Matilde.
Córdova, Mónico.
Gradiz, Trinidad.

YORO.

Wholesale import and export merchants.
Quiroz, J.
Urmeneta, Tomás.

Mexico.

ACAPULCO, GUERRERO.

Arms and ammunition merchants.
Alzuyeta Hnos. y Ca.
Fernandez y Ca., B.

Banks and bankers.
London Bank of Mexico and South America.
Alzuyeta Hnos. y Ca.
Fernandez y Ca., B.
Uruñuela y Ca., P.

Books and stationery.
Alzuyeta Hnos. y Ca.
Fernandez y Ca., B.
Pintos, Antonio.
Rodriguez, Ignacio.
Uruñuela y Ca., P.

Commission merchants.
Alzuyeta Hnos. y Ca.
Bello Hnos.
Caamaño, Eduardo M.
Fernandez y Ca., B.
Kastan, Pedro.
Lobato, Aristeo.
Mediola, José.
Stoll, German.
Uruñuela y Ca., P.

Drugs.
Butron, Antonio.
Link, Sucr.
Posado, Roberto S.

Dry goods.
Alzuyeta Hnos. y Ca.
Fernandez y Ca., B.
Bello Hnos.
Caamaño, Eduardo M.
Córdova, Ramon C.
Mendiola, José.
Rodriguez, Ignacio.
Uruñuela y Ca., P.

Fancy goods.
Alzuyeta Hnos. y Ca.
Fernandez y Ca., B.
Rodriguez, Ignacio.
Uruñuela y Ca., P.

ACAPULCO, GUERRERO—Continued.

Glassware.
Alzuyeta Hnos. y Ca.
Fernandez y Ca., B.
Uruñuela y Ca., P.

Groceries.
Bello Hnos.
Bustos, Antonio.
Caamaño, Eduardo M.
Célis, Ernesto G.
Córdova, Ramon C.
Cuevas, Joaquin.
Liquidano, Faustino.
Liquidano, Herlindo O.
Maresco, José.
Olvera, Luis.
Payno, Isabel G. de.
Pintos, Antonio.
Rodriguez, Ignacio.
Rivera, Marcial.
Villamar, Francisco.
Valeriano, Juan.
Vizcaino, Aureliano.

Hardware.
Alzuyeta Hnos. y Ca.
Fernandez y Ca., B.
Uruñuela y Ca., P.

Importers of groceries.
Alzuyeta y Ca.
Fernandez y Ca., B.
Mendiola, José.
Uruñuela y Ca., P.

Importers and exporters.
Alzuyeta y Ca.
Fernandez y Ca., B.
Uruñuela y Ca., P.

Ironware, dealers and manufacturers.
Fernandez y Ca., B.
Pacific Mail Steamship Company.

Jewelers.
Bermudez, Pablo C.
Martinez, Pánfilo.

ACAPULCO, GUERRERO—Continued.

Jewelers—Continued.
Ramírez, Gumesindo.
Tellechea, Ignacio.

Manufacturers and dealers in boots and shoes.
Arévalo, Enrique.
Cardona, J. Encarnación.

Manufacturers, brick.
Canales, Francisco.
Martinez, Francisco.
Villamar, Francisco.

Manufacturer, cotton goods.
Fernandez y Ca., B.

Manufacturers, cotton, linen, and woolen goods.
Bello Hnos.
Fernandez y Ca., B.

Manufacturer, soap.
Pintos, Antonio.

Sewing machines.
Mazzini, Angel.

Tailors.
Elias y Tavares.
Piza, Victor.

Tobacco dealers
Alzuyeta Hnos. y Ca.
Fernandez y Ca., B.
Uruñuela y Ca., P.
Villamar, F.

Unclassified merchants.
Loughery, W. Robert.
Oetling, Gericke y Ca.

Watchmakers and silversmiths.
Bermudez, Eraclio.
Bermudez, Pablo C.
Garcia, G. P.
Luz, Daniel H.
Martinez, Pánfilo.
Mazzini, Angel.
Ramírez, Gumesindo.

AGUAS CALIENTES, AGUAS CALIENTES.

Agricultural implements.
Aguilar Hermanos.
Barkly, A.
Berber, Vicente.

Banks and bankers.
Banco Nacional.
Guinchard, J. Rufujio.
Antonio Vda. de Chavez é Hijos.

Books and stationery.
Aguilar Hermanos.
Camino, M.

AGUAS CALIENTES, AGUAS CALIENTES—
Continued.

Boots and shoes.
Alvarez, Cruz.
Nuñez, Marciano.

Carriage manufacturers and dealers.
Chevas, Gil.
Santoyo, Pedro.

China, glassware, etc.
Bernal, Andrés.
Castañeda, Margarito S.
Elizondo y Ca., Valera.
Espino, Francisco.
Iturbide, Bonifacio.
Palacio, Emetrio.
Sagredo, Cárlos.
Valdés, Pedro.

Commission merchants.
Aguilar Hermanos.
Berber, Vicente.
Gomez, Juana D.

Drugs.
Gonzalez, Alubiade.
Marin, Francisco.
Rosa, Luis de la.
Sandoval, Miguel.

Dry goods.
Aguilar Hermanos.
Cazón, Agustin.
Corpu, Pedro (wholesale).
Davila, Cleto Maria.
Diaz, Leon.
Duron, Reyes (wholesale).
Elizondo y Ca., Valera.
Gilly, Juan.
Gonzalez, Marin.
Leautaud Hermanos.
Martinez, Manuel.
Martinez, Severino.
Romero, Manuel.
Vazquez, Ignacio.
Zuluaga, Manuel.

Fancy goods.
Aguilar, Edmundo.
Chavez, Rafael.
Chavez, Trifonio.
Leal, Alberto.
Sagredo, Cárlos.

Groceries and provisions.
Aguilar Hermanos (importers).
Berber, Vicente.
Castañeda, Margarito.
Cruz, Fernando.
Dávalos, Suc.

AGUAS CALIENTES, AGUAS CALIENTES—
Continued.

Groceries and provisions—Continued.
  Espino, Francisco.
  Gonzalez, Espiridion.
  Leal, Alberto.
  Morfin Vargas Hermanos.
  Ocampo, Epifanio.
  Ortiz y Vallejo.
  Pedroza, Francisco.
  Valdez, Pedro.

Hardware.
  Berber, Vicente.
  Bernal, Andrés.
  Castañeda, Margarito S.
  Espino, Francisco.
  Gonzalez, Esperidion.
  Herrera, Florentino.
  Palacio, Emetrio.
  Perez, Esteban.
  Sagredo, Cárlos.
  Valdés, Pedro.
  Ventura, Nicanor.

Hat manufacturers and dealers.
  Alemán, Santos G.
  Parra, Felipe.
  Parra, Juan.

Ironware merchant and manufacturer.
  Berber, Vicente.

Jewelry, watches, and silver.
  Iturbide.
  Robles, Victor.
  Romo, Ricardo.
  Sagredo, Cárlos.
  Sancedo, Juan.
  Von Faber, Ricardo.

Lithographers.
  Davalos, Nestor.
  Pedrosa, Trinidad.

Manufacturers of brass and iron bedsteads.
  Arteaga, Juan.
  Hernandez, Valentin.

Paints, colors, and varnishes.
  Carrasco, J.
  Irigoyen, Adalberto.
  Vargas, Anastasio.
  Vargas, José.

Pianos and organs.
  Inostrosa, Gregorio.
  Perchez, José.

Saddlery and harness.
  Diaz, Juan.
  Sandoval, Miguel.
  Sandoval, Pascual.

AGUAS CALIENTES, AGUAS CALIENTES—
Continued.

Sewing machines.
  Normann, Alberto.

Unclassified merchants.
  Aguilar, Edmundo.
  Aguilar, Luis.
  Bernal, Francisco M.
  Chavez, F. Ruiz.
  Davalos, Enrique.
  Gonzalez, Marin.
  Leal, Arturo N.
  Lopez, Fernando.
  Morfin y Ca, Antonio.
  Ocampo, Tomas.
  Quinchard y Vallego.
  Romero, Miguel.
  Vargas Hermanos.
  Zuloaga, José María.

ALAMOS, SONORA.

Commission merchants.
  Ocharan y Ca., Oscar.
  Robinson, Tomás.
  Salazar, Pedro L.

ALLENDE, CHIHUAHUA.

Commission merchant.
  Benitez, Cayetano.

Boots and shoes.
  Chavez, José G.

Dry goods, groceries, and provisions.
  Benitez, Cayetano.
  Chabre, Martin.
  Maynez, Miguel H.
  Ochoa, José D.
  Russek y Hno., Marcos.

AMECA, JALISCO.

Drugs.
  Del Rio, Antonio S.
  Fernandez, Aurelio M.

Groceries and provisions.
  Martinez, Adolfo de J.
  Uribe, Salvador.

ATLIXCO, PUEBLA.

Arms and ammunition.
  Leichtlein, Felipe.

Carriage manufacturer and dealer.
  Salazar, José María.

China and glassware.
  Leichtlein, Felipe.

ATLIXCO, PUEBLA—Continued.

Dry goods.
Avalos, Ignacio.
Cabrera, Antonio.
Morales, Tomás.
Ramirez, Lorenzo.

Fancy goods.
Leichtlein, Felipe.

Groceries and provisions.
Carbajal, Antonio.
Carbajal, Manuel.
Cardoso, Febronio.
Hernandez, Luis.
Mendieta, Agustin.
Otero, Pedro.
Rivera, Ignacio.
Rocha, Bernardo.
Rosales, Pedro.
Ruiz, Manuel.
Soto, Angel.

Hardware.
Lechtlein, Felipe.

Paints and oils.
Barcenas, Gabriel.
Leichtlein, Felipe.

AUTLAN, JALISCO.

Merchants.
Araiza, Francisco.
Barragan, Ireneo R.
Corona, Juan.
Espinosa, Gregorio.
Gomez, Wulfrano.
Michel, Gregorio.
Santana, Agapito.

BRAVO, NUEVO LEON.

General merchants.
Benavides, Espiridon.
Cantu, Wenceslao.
Garza, Casimiro.
Gonzalez, F. E.
Rodriguez, Agapito.
Salinas, Manuel.

BUSTAMANTE, NUEVO LEON.

Flour mill.
Santos, Herederos de D. Mauricio de los.

General merchants.
Garza, Cruz.
Garza y Hno., Eduardo.
Menchaca, Lazaro.
Santos y Serna, Jesus.
Santos, Luis S.
Santos, Rafael.

CADEREYTA, NUEVO LEON.

General merchants.
Cantu, Guadalupe.
Cantu, Lázaro.
Cantu, Mateo.
Cantu, Rafael C.
Fox, Eduardo.
Gracia y Hijo, Platon.
Guitierrez, Policarpo.
Jamez, Buenaventura.
Leal, Bartolo de J.
Leal, Felicitas.
Lozano, José M.
Margain, Alfonso.
Palacias y Ca., Miguel.
Rodriguez, Romolu.
Serrano, Eugenio.

CAMARGO, TAMAULIPAS.

Exporters of hides and skins.
Garcia, Donaciano G.
Peña, Juan Garcia.

Importers.
Garcia, Donaciano G. (general merchandise).
Gutierrez y Hno., José Angel.
Madrigal, Santos Valle.
Peña, Juan Garcia.
Tames y Hno., Donaciano.

CAMPECHE, CAMPECHE.

Agricultural implements.
Berron, Fernando.
Castellot Hermanos.

Bankers.
Cano Diego, Fernando J.
Castellot Hermanos.

Boots and shoes.
Leon, Gualter.
Medina, José J.
Ortiz, Antonio.
Ortiz, Cárlos.
Quijano, Felipe.

Carriage manufacturers and dealers.
Mendoza, Pilar.
Perez, Lorenzo.
Rodriguez, Ignacio.

China and glassware.
Estrada, A. Mendez.

Commission merchants.
Garcia, Juan Garcia.
Oliver y Ca., A.

CAMPECHE, CAMPECHE—Continued.

Drugs.
Del Rio, Joaquin.
Espinola, Manuel.
Gala, Joaquin R.
Lauz, Manuel A.
Lavalle, Eduardo.
Leon, Agustin.
Oliver, Manuel Lopez.

Dry goods.
Castellot Hermanos.
Castillo, José M.
Lopez, José T.
MacGregor, José F. Estrada.
Oliver y Ca., A.

Fancy goods.
Araoz, Pablo J.
Baeza, Julio.
Estrada, A. Mendez.

Furniture dealer.
Campos, Juan de la Cabada.

Groceries and provisions.
Berron, Fernando.
Boldo, Narciso (importer).
Cano y Cano, Francisco.
Cano y Diego, Fernando J.
Castellot Hermanos.
Diego, Ignacio Cano.
Llovera, Antonio.
Mena, Ricardo.
Oliver y Ca., A.

Hardware.
Berron, Fernando.
Berron Hermanos.
Zuloaga, José.

Hats.
Rodriguez, José.

Paper.
Araos, Pablo J.

Sewing machines.
Oliver y Ca., A.
Ramirez, Antonio I.

CARMEN, CAMPECHE.

Dry goods.
Goyta, Garcia y Ca.
Pallas, Francisco.

Drugs.
Arcué, Venancio S.
Ibarra, A.
Lagunera, Manuel.

General merchants.
Aniza, Benito.
Burgos Hermanos.
Colarelo y Ca., B. F.

CARMEN, CAMPECHE—Continued.

General merchants—Continued.
Domingo, Perez y Field.
Escribano, José Poveda.
Ferrer, Felipe.
Ferrer, José Otero.
Guliana, Numa (books).
Hernandez, Quirino.
Martinez, Antonio.
Manjarrez Hermanos.
Nieves y Ca.
Pallas, Francisco (dry goods).
Paullaada, Esteban.
Quintana, Joaquin (commission merchant).
Ropeto, Juan Luis (groceries and provisions).
Saeno, Policarpo.
Slovero, Juan.
Williams y Ca. (importers).
Zaldivar, Antonio.

CATORCE, SAN LUIS POTOSI.

Banker.
Marza, Gregorio de la.

Druggists.
Barba, José M.
Kaufmann, Valentin.
Urista, G.
Villa, G.

General merchants.
Almaza, Tomás.
Baranda, Joaquin.
Barando, Pablo.
Dominguez, Juan.
Echavarria, Lázaro.
Egone, Joaquin A.
Gomez, Higinio.
Menzibal, Juan M. de.
Quadra, Agapito.
Saurez, José.

Mining companies, names and managers.
Ameztoy y Aguinaga, Miguel Ameztoy.
Compañía Concepcion y Annexas, Joaquin M. Ramos.
Del Penasco, Higinio Gomez.
Gregorio de la Marza, Pedro de la Marza.
La Cruz, Melchor Romano.
La Filosofal y Candelaria, Leonidas Coronado.
La Purisima, Pedro de la Marza.
San Elias, Higinio Gomez.
San José Pauza Plomo, Gustavo Dressel.
Santa Lucia, Higinio Gomez.
Socavon de Boqueiro, Juan Dominguez.
Socavon de Dolores y Annexas, Melchor, Romano.
Socavon del Refugio y Annexas, Luis Flores Alatorre.
Union Catorcena, Vicente Irizar.
Union Potosina, Luis Flores Alatorre.

CEDRAL, SAN LUIS POTOSI.

Druggists.
Delgado, Abrahan.
Pozas, José.

General merchants.
Licea, Victoria.
Melendez, Ignacio.
Morano, Anastacio.
Padilla, Refugio.
Trueba, Pedro Barcena.
Urisarri, Martin.

Mining companies.
Merla, Martin.
Miranda, Gabriel.

Reduction works.
Jesus María.
La Concepcion.
Ia Luz.
San Gabriel.

CERRALVO, NEUVO LEON.

Agricultural and mining machinery.
Garza, Rafael V.

Factory.
Martinez, Juan.

Fancy goods.
Garza, Luis.
Salinas, Gregorio.

Furniture.
Garza, Z. de la.
Viscaya, D.

General merchants.
Guerra, Fructuosa.
Garza y Mendez.
Tijerina, Domingo.
Vela, Jesus M.
Viscaya, Domingo.

Hardware and arms.
Gonzales, Rafael.

Hat factory.
Vela, R.

Mining companies.
Colorado.
La Blanca.
La Exploradora.
Parisima Refugio.
Union Minera.

Tannery.
Berlanza, Mendoza.

Trunk maker.
Marichalar y Ca.

CHALCHICOMULA, PUEBLA.

Drugs.
Altamirano, J. M.
Amador, M.
Castillo, Francisco.
Morales, S. L.

Dry goods merchants.
Reynaud, Camilo.
Rivera, G.
Urichi y Sobs, Otaolo.

Fancy goods.
Bocanegra, J. Maria.
Maldonado y Rousset.

General merchandise.
Campos, M.
Cordero, Viuda de R.
Delgado, F.
Gomez, Juan N.
Martinez, E. L.
Rodriguez, A. J. M.
Rodriguez, José de J.

Hats.
Martinez, Guadalupe.

Hardware.
Meza, Alejo.

Stationery.
Mellado, José M.

CHALCHIHUITES, ZACATECAS.

General merchants.
Escoban, Jesus Gonzalez.
Gonzalez, Filandro.
Mandoza, Pedro.
Muguiro, Luis.
Ochoa, Jesus G.
Olagaray, Cornelio F.
Pena, Manuel.
Perez y Hno., Gregorio.
Rios, Buenaventura.
Rubelcava, Wenceslao.
Ubillos, Agustin.
Valdez, José Ma.

CHARCOS, SAN LUIS POTOSI.

Mining companies.
Compañia del Tiro General.
Compañia Mina de Santa Inez.
Mina de San Sebastian.

Reduction works.
Sr. Diaz de Leon.

CHIAPAS, CHIAPAS.

General merchants.
Farrera, Vicente.
Flores, Romualdo.
Guirao, Narciso.
Lazos, Augusto.
Parriagua, Wenceslao.
Ramos, Benedicto.
Solorzano, Refugio.

CHIHUAHUA, CHIHUAHUA.

Agricultural implements and hardware.
Amendari, Ramon.
Balderran, Narciso.
Brittinghaus, J. M.
Fandoe Succ., Luis.
Fraser & Chalmers.
Ketelsen y Degetau.
Lerma, José.
Lynch y Ca.
Norwald, Enrique.
Reinhardt, H. O.
Rembez & Bezaury.
Serraga, Juan.
Taseira, Felix F.

Banks and bankers.
Sucursal del "Banco Nacional."
"Banco Minero Chihuahuense."
Banco de Santa Eulalia.
Banco Mexicano.
Banco de Chihuahua.
Ketelsen y Degetau.
Maceyra, Felix F.
Macmanus, é hijos, F.
Solas, Miguel.

Booksellers and stationers.
Maceyra, Félix.
Miramontes, Donato.
Villar, Antonio.

Boots and shoes.
Coriche, Dario.
Larrang, J. A.
Martinez, José.
Molina, J. J.
Ortegon, Policarpo.
Perchoz, José.
Vidal, Matías.
Williams, J.

Carriages.
Carroceria de Lamm.
Carroceria de Lerma.
Lerma, Juan.

China and glassware.
Armendariz, R.
Creel, Enrique.

CHIHUAHUA, CHIHUAHUA—Continued.

China and glassware—Continued.
Rutiaga, Eduardo.
Vidal, Matías.

Commission merchants.
Arguelles, Ganuto.
Armendariz, R.
Castro, Trinidad.
Cuevas, Santiago.
Ketelsen y Degetau.
Madrid, J.
Navarro, E.
Reinhardt, H. O.
Sanchez.
Terrazas, Juan.
Vega, Anastasio.
Villa, Antonio.

Drugs.
Botica del Aguila.
Botica de Carlos Cueley.
Botica de Evaristo Ordaz.
Botica Mexicana.
Botica Universal.
Dávila, Cleto M.
Elizondo, Valéra.
Gonzales, Alcibiades.
Lafon, Emilio.
Marin, Juan.
Rosa, Luis de la.
Sandoval, Miguel.

Dry goods.
Corpu, Pedro.
Duron, Reyes.
Ketelsen y Degetau.
La Fábrica de Francia.
La Francia Maritima.
La Sorpresa.
Maceyra, J. F.
Macmanus é hijos, F.
Nordwald, H.
Rubin y Ca., J.
Sanchez, José María.

Fancy goods.
Ketelsen y Degetau.
Nordwald, H.
Rembez y Bezaury.

Furniture dealers.
Armendariz, Ramon.
Ketelsen y Degetau.
Lynch y Ca.
Nordwald, Enrique.
Rembez y Bezaury.
West, Ch.

CHIHUAHUA, CHIHUAHUA—Continued.

Groceries and provisions.
Aldana y Hnos.
Armendariz, Ramon.
Dale Bros.
Ketelsen y Degetau.
Maceyra, Félix F.
Molinar y Sánchez.
Nordwald, H.
Padilla y Ca., Albino.

Hat stores.
El Sombrero Rojo.
Sombrerería Mexicana.

Iron and steel workers.
Compañía Industrial Mexicana, Tomás Fletcher, President.

Ironware dealers and manufacturers.
Ketelsen y Degetau.
Nordwald, H.
Reinhardt, H. O.

Jewelers and watchmakers.
Alguin, Antonio.
Arellano y Ca., Serriano.
Hogland, Enrique.
Gautier, N
Zavalza y Pina.
Zavalza, C.
Zavalza, Felipe.

Musical instruments.
Inostrosa, Gregorio.
Miramontes, D.
Perchez, José.

Merchants, general.
Aldana, R. S.
Altamirano, Manuel M.
Armendario, Ramon.
Azrinzulo, Antonio.
Azumolo, Juan M.
Bessauri, Felix.
Chaves, Genaro J.
Creel, Enrique C.
Fandoa, Luis.
Ketelsen y Degetau.
Lequinázaval, Domingo.
Loya, Cárlos.
Maceyra, Felix F.
Macmanus y hijos, F.
Maye, Gustavo.
Miñagoren, Pedro.
Munoz, Silvino.
Navarro, Benigno.
Navarro Hermapos.
Norwald y Ca.
Partida Hermanos.
Puig y Domingo.
Salas, Miguel.

CHIHUAHUA, CHIHUAHUA—Continued.

Merchants, general—Continued.
Sanchez, José María.
Schusster, B.
Stalfordt, J.
Tejeda, Refugio.
Terraza, Juan.
Treviño Hermanos, Gonzales.
Venmehren, Guillermo.

Paints, oils, and varnishes.
Carrasco, J.
Irigoyen, Adalberto.
Newton & Andrew.
Vargas Anastasio.
Vargas, José.

Sewing machines.
Adler, M.
Ketelsen y Dejetau.
Macmanus, Franc°.
Norwald, Enrique.
Reinhardt, H. O.

CHILPANCINGO, GUERRERO.

Bankers.
Fuente, Egidio de la (Banquero de "La Mútua").
de Celis, Gabriel F. (Agente del "Banco Nacional").

Drugs.
Manjarrez, Juan Cruz.
Parra, Miguel.
Rodriguez, Alberto.

Principal merchants.
Cabañas, José M.
Calvo, Ignacio (general merchandise).
Campos, Rafael A.
de Celis, Gabriel F.
Enriques, Lucas (general merchaudise).
Ferreyro, Francisco I. (books and stationery).
Gavito, Juan (general merchandise).
Godinez, Sabás y Vicente.
Guevara, Donaciano (general merchandise).
Morlet, A.
Patino, Manuel.
Reyes y Hermano, A.
Rodriguez, Agustin (general merchandise).
Rodriguez, Alberto.
Rodriguez, Tomás.

CIUDAD GUERRERO, TAMAULIPAS.

Boots and shoes.
Mejía, Tomás.
Siller, Manuel.
Vergard, Agustin.

Commission merchants.
Ramirez, Manuel.
Soltero, Crescencio.
Yañez, Lorenzo.

CIUDAD GUERRERO, TAMAULIPAS—Continued.

Drugs.
Fernandez, Antonio M.
Gonzalez, Martin.
Winslow, Cárlos.

Dry goods.
Ruiloba, José.
Ruiz, Vicente.
Sanchez, Francisco.
Volpe Hermanos.

General stores.
Canales, G.
Flores, Juan Manuel.
Flores, Joaquin.
Garza, E. Gutierrez.
Garza, Guillermo.
Garza, Porfirio C.
Gonzalez, Emetrio.
Gutierrez, Anastacio.
Gutierrez, Cadena.
Gutierrez, Encarnacion.
Gutierrez, Juan de Dios.
Sada, Justino.
Salazar, Victor.
Saldaña, I.
Vela, Manuel Ramirez.
Villa, Erasmo.

Hardware and house-furnishing goods.
Chavez, Marcelo. .
Gutierrez, Juan de D.
Hughes, D. M.
Saldaña, I.

Jewelers.
Gonzalez, Agustin.
Garzo, Guillermo.

CIUDAD JEREZ, ZACATECAS.

Banker.
Castellanos y Ca., Antonio R.

Carriage dealer.
Castellanos y Ca., Antonio R.

Drugs.
Escobedo, J. Villalobos.
Ortiz y Ca., José María.
Roman y Ca., Tomas C. de.

Dry goods.
Berumen, J. Antonio.
Brilanti, Rafael.
Escobedo, Higinio.
Escobedo, Juan P.
Hoyo, Eugenio del.
Sanchez, Francisco de B.
Silva, Francisco Escobedo.

Fancy goods.
Arellano, Luis.

CIUDAD JEREZ, ZACATECAS—Continued.

Furniture.
Castellanos y Ca., Antonio R.

General goods.
Carrillo, Castellanos y Damas.

Hardware.
Arellano y Ca., Luis.
Cabrera, José Felix.
Escobedo, Juan de D.

Sewing machines.
Gutierrez, Manuel Macía.

CIUDAD JUAREZ, CHIHUAHUA.

Arms and ammunition.
Ketelsen y Degetau.

Banks and bankers.
Banco Chihuahuense.
Banco Minero.
Sucursal del Banco Nacional del Paso, Texas.
Sucursal del Banco Minero Chihuahuense.
Bronson, E. B.
Ochoa, Inocente.

Boots and shoes.
Alarcon, G.
Echeverria, J. L. de.
Goodman, José.
Kahn Bros.
Ketelsen y Degetau.
Ortuzar Hermanos.
Trueba, Domingo.
Trueba, G.

Carriage dealer.
Riebeling, Maximiliano.

China and glassware.
Loeb Hermanos.

Commission merchants.
Alvarez, Joaquin A.
Arguelles, Camilo.
Barroso, Cliserio.
Ketelsen y Degetau.
Paso, Luis del.
Woodside, T. J.

Drugs.
Cuadra, J. Garcia.
Hernandez, H.
Lewis y Ortega.

Dry goods.
Alarcon, G.
Blumenthal, Sam.
Echeverria, J. L. de.
Flores, J. María.
Flores, Nicolas.
Goodman, José.
Kahn Bros.
Ketelsen y Degetau.

CIUDAD JUAREZ, CHIHUAHUA—Cont'd.
Dry goods—Continued.
Ochoa, I.
Ortuzar Hnos.
Trueba, Domingo.
Trueba, Isidoro.
Groceries and provisions.
Barroso, Genaro.
Ortuzar Hnos.
Paso, Luis del.
Sanchez Hnos.
Trueba, D.
Hardware.
Krakauer, Zork y Moye.
Jeweler.
Kahn Hermanos.
Millers.
Augerstein & Schuster.
Augulo, Alfonso.
Music store.
Walz, W. G.
Sewing machines.
Ketelsen y Degetau.

CIUDAD MIER, TAMAULIPAS.
General merchants.
Bavnet y Ca., C.
Canales ó hijo, Albina.
Guerra y Ca., Jesus.
Viscaya, Enrique.

CIUDAD PARRAS, COAHUILA.
Agricultural implements.
König, Guillermo (viuda de).
Sieber y Ca., C.
Bankers.
Behr, Juan.
Madero y Ca., Manuel.
Misa, Gonzalez.
Yarto, José.
Boots and shoes.
Charles y Hermano, M.
Garcia, Anastacio.
Talavera, Juan.
Carriage dealer.
Olvera y Hermano.
Commission merchant.
Behr, Juan.
Drugs.
Aguirre, Pedro.
Martinez, Alfonso.
Maynes, Eduardo.
König, Guillermo (viuda de).
Dry goods.
Adame, Porfirio.
Chapman, Fernando.
Martinez, Martin.
Misa, José Gonzalez.

CIUDAD PARRAS, COAHUILA—Cont'd.
Fancy goods.
Behr, Juan.
König, Guillermo (viuda de).
Maynez y Ca.
Sieber y Ca., C.
Furniture.
Sieber y Ca., C.
Groceries and provisions.
Behr, Juan.
Chapman, Fernando.
Martinez, Martin.
Misa, José Gonzalez.
Rojo, Remigio.
Ruiz, Ernesto.
Joint stock company.
de Valasco y Ca., Ruiz.
Hatters.
Behr, Juan.
Misa, José Gonzalez.
Martinez, Martin.
Hardware.
Behr, Juan.
König, Guillermo (viuda de).
Sieber y Ca., C.
Music stores.
Behr, Juan.
Prince de Maynez, Margarita.
Sewing machines.
Behr, Juan.
König, Guillermo (viuda de).

CIUDAD PORFIRIO DIAZ, PIEDRAS NEGRAS.
Commission merchants.
Cordeuas, Vicente.
Farias Hermanos.
Holck & Co., C.
Jimenez Hermanos.
Musquiz, Rafael.
Riddle, I. W.
Sasno & Co., M.
Shofter, I. N., customs agent, Mex. Int. R. R.
Co.
Druggist.
Cooper, E. H.
General merchandise.
Arnaiz, Juan.
Palacio Hermanos.
Washington, A.
Hardware.
Ladner Bros.
Mecke, Juan L.
Seiber & Co., C.

CIUDAD PORFIRIO DIAZ, PIEDRAS NEGRAS—Continued.

Merchants, miscellaneous.
Barreda & Samana, dry goods.
Bowman & Titus, groceries.
Joseph, A., furniture.
Lechonger, L., jewelry and fancy goods.
Oppenheimer, M. L., dry goods.

CIUDAD SAYULA, JALISCO.

Agricultural implements.
Preciado, Paulino.
Vizcayno y Larios.

Arms and ammunition.
Vazquez, Pablo.

Boots and shoes.
Cortez, Silvestre.
Ramos, Policarpo.

Carriage dealer.
Larios, Benigno.

Drugs.
Cisneros, José.
Duran, Alberto.
Mourett, Juan O.

Furniture dealers and manufacturers.
Alcarez, Epitacio.
Figueroa, Pascual.

Groceries and provisions.
Aguilar, Clemente.
Aguilar, Graciano.
Aguilar, José L.
Cisneros y Hermano.
Cisneros, José Antonio.
Fuente, Francisco de la.
Fuente, Miguel W. de la.
Fuentes, Pablo.
Gil, Manuel Robles.
Juan y Torre, A.
Preciado, Paulino.
Torres y Ca., Rafael.
Vazquez, Vicente N.
Vizcayno y Larios.

Ironware dealers and manufacturers.
Preciado, Paulino.
Vizcayno y Larios.

CIUDAD VICTORIA, TAMAULIPAS.

Drugs.
Garza, Juan.

Dry and fancy goods.
Bustamante, M.
Hinojosa, R.

CIUDAD VICTORIA, TAMAULIPAS—Cont'd.

Grocers, liquors, tobacco, general merchandise.
Barreda, Manuel.
Bulnes y Albite.
Bustamante, Manuel.
Collado, A. S.
Diez y Hnos.
Escandon, Blas.
Fernandez, Antonio.
Guevara, José M.
Hinojoso, Rafael.
Lavin, Casimiro.
Prieto, Fco. S.
Ruiz, Ruperto N.
Tapia, Pascual.
Teran y Hnos., Juan.

Hardware and paints.
Hinojosa, R.

Mining company.
King y Ca.

COLIMA, COLIMA.

Agricultural implements, arms, and ammunition.
Oldenbourg, Jorge.

Bankers.
Alcarez, José M.
Barreto, Gregorio.
Flor, Christian.
Flor y Kofani.
Guizar y Ca.
Medina, Agustin.
Oetling y Ca., Alejandro, Suc.
Vargas, Agustin.

Banks.
Banco de Londres, Méjico y Sud América, Ltd. (agency).
Banco Nacional (agents, Arnoldo Vogel y Ca.)

Books and stationery.
Campero, Severo.
Schmidt, J. F. A.
Urzua, Juana.
Urzua, Silvestre D.

Boots and shoes.
Chanona, Antera.
Ruiz, José.

Cardboard manufacturer.
Guerrero, Luis.

Carriage dealers.
Cosio, Tiburcio.
Dorantes, Eduardo.

Commission merchants.
Flor, Christian.

COLIMA, COLIMA—Continued.

Commission merchants—Continued.
Oetling y Ca., Alejandro, Suc.
Ruiz, Porciano.
Vega, Ramon J. de la.

Drugs.
Cuera, Francisco C.
Fuentes, Ignacio.
Mendoza, José L.
Moni, Agustin.
Morril hijo, Augusto.
Orozco, Crescencio.
Suarez, Cosmo.

Dry goods.
Bazan, Ramon.
Diaz, Epifanio.
Oetling y Ca., Alejandro, Suc.
Rodriguez y Ca., Guzman.
Rosas, Luisa García.
Silva, Porfirio.
Silva, Roberto.
Urzua, Juana (silks).

Fancy goods.
Oldenbourg, Jorge M.
Rendon, José María.

Furniture dealers and manufacturers.
Benitez, Justo.
Bustos, Othon.
Quiñones, Marcelino.

Groceries and provisions.
Alvarez, Gregorio.
Barreto, Isidoro.
Bazan, Ramon.
Calleja, Antonio de la.
Diaz, Epifanio.
Flor, Christian.
Flor y Kofani.
Garcia, Esteban.
Gomez, S.
Guizar y Ca., Dolores.
Gutierrez, Ignacio D.
Oetling y Ca., Alejandro. Suc.
Oetling Hermanos y Ca.
Oldenbourg, Jorge.
Plaza, Alberta de la.
Plaza, Francisco de la.
Rodriguez y Ca., Guzman.
Rodriguez, Manuel.
Rosas, Luis García.
Vargas, Francisco.
Vega, Ramon J. de la.
Vogel y Ca., Arnoldo.

Hardware.
Ceja, José María.
Eschacht, Agustin.

COLIMA, COLIMA—Continued.

Hardware—Continued.
Oldenbourg, Jorge.
Rendon, José María.
Rodriguez, Manuel.
Smith y Madrid.

Hat stores and manufacturers.
Gudiño, Roque.
Parra, Aurelio.
Perez, José María.

Importers and exporters.
Flor, Christian.
Guisar, Dolores.
Madrid, Zenobio.
Oetling y Ca., Alejandro, Suc.
Oldenbourg, Jorge.
Plaza, Enrique de la.
Rodriguez, Manuel.
Ruiz, Ponciano.
Vanderlinden, Vogel y Ca.

Ironware dealers and manufacturers.
Barreto, Isidoro.
Barreto, Miguel.
Flor, Christian.

Jewelers.
Oldenbourg, Jorge.
Rodriguez y Ca., Guzman.

Lithographer.
Rivera, Rosendo R.

Sewing machines.
Gutierrez, Ignacio D.
Ibarra, Eliezer M.
Morril ó hijo, Augusto.
Oldenbourg, Jorge.

COLOTLAN, JALISCO.

Bankers.
Muro, Ramon del.
Real, Miguel S. del.

Drugs.
Castillo, Ramon Mora.
Trujillo, Celedonio.

Dry goods.
Lopez y Ca., Cipriano.
Moreno, Adolfo.
Rodriguez, Sóstenes.
Saldaña, Miguel.
Zulueta, Juan.

General merchandise.
Barragan, Rosendo.
Cardenas, Manuel.
Escobedo, J.
Casas, José María Rodriguez.

COLOTLAN, JALISCO—Continued.

General merchandise—Continued.
Castañeda é hijos (viuda de).
Lopez y Ca., Cipriano.
Mayorga, José María.
Moreno, Adolfo.
- Real, Damien del.
Saldaña, Miguel.
Sandoval, J.
Zulueta, Juan.

CÓRDOBA, VERACRUZ.

Bankers.
Diaz, José Fernandez.
Valdez, Mariano R. (agent Banco de Londres y México).

Booksellers.
Baturoni, Ana Antª Roy de.
Leal, Alvino A.
Ortega, Antonio.

Commission merchants.
Carbajal, Luis Mª.
Diaz, José Fernandez.
Gomez, José Diaz.
Gonzalez, Luis F.
Hernandez y Hernandez.
Izquierdo, Victor.
Leal, Alvino A.
Lopez, Luis.
Martinez, Antonio Loredo.
Mateos, Manuel.
Mingo, Cirilo.

Drugs.
Arenas, Francisco de P.
Limon, Daniel.
Roiz, Cárlos.
Vazquez y Ca., Severo.
Villegas, Mariano.

Dry goods.
Aragon, Rafael Benito.
Bonilla, Lauro.
Carretero, Raymundo.
Izaolo, Basilio.
Izaola y Hno., Silvestre.
Jimenez, Francisco.
Lopez, Camilo.
Leal, Antonio.
Marquez y Ca., Torcuato.
Victorero, Francisco Sanchez.

General stores.
Aspray, Noriega.
Bauper y Ca.
Calima, Tranquilino.
Cordova, Lucas.
Costafreda, Pedro.
Diaz, Pedro.

CÓRDOBA, VERACRUZ—Continued.

General stores—Continued.
Fernandez, José Camacho.
Fernandez, José Diaz.
Galan, Enrique.
Garay, Ramon.
Hernandez, Rafael.
Herrero y Ca.
Jimenez, Francisco.
Junque y Isidorio.
Lopez, Anselmo.
Lopez, Gregorio.
Louistalot, Victor.
Moral y Portilla.
Natali, Francisco.
Quevedo, Francisco Cordova.
Rodriguez, Antonio.
Rodriguez, Ramon.
Tapia, Moises.
Tavares, Ramon.
Valdez, Mariano R.

Groceries and provisions.
Andrade, Santiago.
Camacho, J. Fernandez.
Caudaudop, Pedro.
Diaz, Pedro.
Espinosa, J. de J.
Galan, Enrique.
García, Ramon.
Hernandez, Ricardo.
Huerta, Ricardo.
Izquierdo, Victor.
Lanza, Enrique de la.
Leal, Albino A.
Martinez, Antonio Loredo.
Natoli, Francisco.
Posada Hermanos.
Quevedo, Francisco.
Roman, Eulalio.
Sains, Juan.
Torre, Rufino de la.
Valdez, Mariano R.
Vique, Angel Hernandez.

Hardware and house furnishing.
Abascal, Manuel.
Calleja y Ca.
Cortes Hermanos.
Hernandez, Guadaloupe.
Salamanca, José María.
Tresgallo, José.
Vargas, Rafael.

Hats.
Lopez y Ca., Camilo.
Muñoz, Alberto.
Ruiz, Francisco.

148 MEXICO.

COSALA, SINALOA.

Merchants.
  Aragon, Manuel.
  Basoco, Antonio.
  Beltran, José M.
  Cota, Francisco.
  Padilla, Cesareo.
  Rodriguez, Facundo.
  Ruiz, Leoncio.

CUATRO CIENEGAS, COAHUILA.

Druggists.
  Garza, L. De la.
  Zambrano, Fructosa.

Flour mills.
  Castro, Manuel.
  Ferrino, Miguel.

Furniture.
  Zepeda y Hno., Isaac.

General merchants.
  Arredondo, Martin.
  Bruno, D.
  Fenerro, Miguel.
  Zambrano, Niceforo.
  Zepeda, Bartolo.
  Zepeda, F. Arredondo.

Manufacturers of liquors.
  Arredondo, Martin.
  Castro, Salomon.
  Ferrino y Ca., Miguel.
  Garza, Fco. Arredondo.

Mining companies.
  Compañía Minera de Santa Elena.
  Compañía Minera El Barril.
  Purisima Mining Company.
  San Marcos Mining Company.
  Zona Minera de Buena Vista.

Sawmill.
  Hartmann y Ca., Ed.

CUENCAME, DURAGNO.

General merchants.
  Aleman, Antonio.
  Montalvo, Rafael.
  Montalvo, W.
  Ortiz, Cruz, Sucs.

Mining companies.
  Godfrey, W. S., Mgr.
  Mathews, Jas. F., Mgr.
  Verlardena.

CUERNAVACA, MORELOS.

Agricultural implements, hardware, and iron-ware.
  Diez, Miguel M.

CUERNAVACA, MORELOS—Continued.

Agricultural implements, hardware, and iron-ware—Continued.
  Pagaza, Juan.
  Pino, Luis.
  Rico, Leandro.
  Rios, Francisco.

Bankers.
  Portillo y Gomez, Ramon (agente Banco Nacional).

Booksellers and stationers.
  Elias, Bernabé L. de.
  Flores, Rosendo.
  Jimenez, Hesiquio.
  Pagaza, Juan.
  Reyes, Francisco de P.

Boots and shoes.
  Diaz, Manuel.
  Diaz, Santiago.
  Rodriguez, José M.
  Sanchez, Lorenzo.

China and glassware.
  Rico, Leandro.
  Rios, Francisco.

Commission merchants.
  Elias, Francisco de.
  Pagaza, Juan.
  Rico, Leandro.
  Ruiz, Rafael A.

Drugs.
  Argandar, Ricardo.
  Escalante, José M.
  Florez, Felipe García.
  Gutierrez, Miguel.

Dry goods and clothing.
  Fiz, Manuel.
  Gonzalez, Tomás (hats).
  Hernandez, Ramon.
  Martinez, Alejo.
  Marsan Hermanos (silks).
  Naudin, Señorita (silks).
  Rico, Leandro (dry and fancy goods).
  Tallabas, Francisco (silks and dry goods).

Fancy goods.
  Mejía, Romualdo.
  Rico, Leandro.
  Sanchez, Romualdo.
  Tinoco, Camilo.

Furniture.
  Manjarrez, Ignacio.
  Pino, Luis.

Groceries and provisions.
  Azcarate, Francisco.

CUERNAVACA, MORELOS—Continued.

Groceries and provisions—Continued.
  Azcarate, Viuda de.
  Elguera, José.
  Flores, Rosendo.
  Orihuela, Agustin.
  Pagaza, Juan.
  Rios, Lino.
  Rios, Francisco.
  Robles, Ignacio.
  Rodriguez, José M.

Jewelers.
  Ramirez, Delfino.
  Rosales, Manuel.

Lithographer.
  Gobierno, La del.

Merchants, general merchandise.
  Azcarte, Viuda de F.
  Barquin, José.
  Bustamente, Luis Rios.
  Francisco Sobrinho.
  Hermande, Aramburo.
  Muñoz, Agustin.
  Pagaza, Juan.
  Sol, Felipe del.

Sewing machines.
  Castañeda, Dionisio.
  Diaz, Miguel M.
  Ruiz, Rafael A.

Sugar-planters.
  Amor, Escandon Ignacio.
  Araoz, Joaquin.
  Arena, Alejandro.
  Barron, Guillermo.
  Bautista, Alaman Juan.
  Carmona, Jorge.
  Célis, Viuda e Hijos de.
  Torre, Isidor de la.
  Escandon Hermanos.
  Flores, José.
  Garcia, Icazbalrela Joaquin.
  Goriba, Faustino.
  Guerra, José T.
  Monterde y Adalia, Agustin.
  Reina, Crescencio.
  Romero y Vargas, Ignacio.
  Rovalo, Agustin.
  Villegas de Peña Guadalupe.

CULIACAN, SINALOA.

Agricultural implements, hardware, and iron-ware.
  Salmon y Hermano, L.
  Tamayo, Severiano.

CULIACAN, SINALOA—Continued.

Bankers.
  Cifra, Enrique.
  Castro Hermanos, Martinez de.
  Castro, Pomposo Martinez de.
  Haas, Agustin.
  Izabel, Ignacio.
  Izaguirre, Baltazar.
  Salmon y Hermano, L.
  Uriarte, Domingo.

Booksellers and stationers.
  Diaz y Ca., Ramirez.
  Paredes, Miguel R.
  Ramirez y Moreno.
  Tamayo, Severiano.

Boots and shoes.
  Beltran, Marcelino.
  Gonzalez, J.
  Gutierrez, Gil.
  Juarez, Antonio.
  Vidoles, Rafael.

Carriage dealers.
  Cuadros, Aniceto.
  Robles, Antonio.

Commission merchants.
  Cifra, Enrique.
  Haas, Agustin.
  Kördell, Eduardo.
  Faredes, Miguel R.
  Ramirez y Moreno.
  Salmon Hno., L.
  Velasco, Ildefonso.

Drugs.
  Batiz, Conrado.
  Kördell, Eduardo.
  Villareal, Ignacio.

Dry goods.
  Almada, J. Marcelino.
  Almada y Ca., Ponciano.
  Astorga Hermanos.
  Clouthier, Manuel.
  Escudero y Ca., Manuel.
  Ituarte, Luis de.
  Izurieta, Manuel.
  Martinez, Juan.
  Murillo, José María.
  Salmon, José María.
  Salmon y Hermano, L.
  Urrea, Angel.
  Vega, José de la.
  Vega, Luciano de la.

Fancy goods.
  Tamayo, Severiano.

Furniture.
  Granados, Cárlos M.

150   MEXICO.

CULIACAN, SINALOA—Continued.

Groceries and provisions.
Almada y Ca., Ponciano.
Amador, Trinidad.
Amezcua, Luis.
Escudero y Ca., M.
Martinez, Juan.
Salmon y Hermano, L.
Vega, José de la.
Vega, Luciano de la.
Jeweler.
Garcia, Santos.
Hat stores.
Espinosa, Cenovio.
Noriz, J.
Sewing machines.
Escudero, Manuel.
Salmon, José María.
Salmon y Hermano, L.
Urrea, Angel.

DURANGO, DURANGO.

Agricultural implements.
Alvarez, Francisco.
Boker y Ca., R.
Hildebrand, Julio, Suc.
Stahlknecht y Ca.

Banks and bankers.
Banco Nacional de México (agentes: Hildebrand, Julio, Suc.).
Damm, Maximiliano.
Hildebrand, Julio, Suc.
Juanbelz Hnos.
Stahlknecht y Ca.

Booksellers and stationers.
Barrera, Rafael.
Gurza, Luis.
Torre, Ignacio de la.

Boots and shoes.
Candia, Tomás Hernandez.
Gomez, Arturo.
Hernandez, Natividad.
Hody, Juan.
La Bota Roja.
Olagaray, Juan B.
Perez, Tomás.
Romo, Manuel.
Carriage dealers.
Ball, Juan W.
Castro, Jacinto.
Flores, Epifanio.
Flores, J.
Flores, Luciano.
China and glassware.
Böse, Luis.
Wilmanns, Francisco.

DURANGO, DURANGO—Continued.

Commission merchants.
Alvarez y Ca., Francisco.
Alvarez, Ramon.
Avalos, J. de D.
Damm, Maximiliano.
Doorman y Ca., Julio.
Grenaldo, Viuda y Hijos de.
Gurza Hermanos y Ca.
Hildebrand, Julio, Suc.
Juanbelz Hermanos.
Loweree Hnos., Suc.
Moller, Guillermo.
Rio y Ca., Pedro del.
Prendis, Santiago.
Rodriguez, Cristobal.
Salcido Hermanos.
Ugarte, Simon.
Drugs.
Avila, Manuel de.
Botica Central.
Botica del Carmen.
Botica del Hospital.
Cobos, F.
Herrera, Justino.
Ostoloza, Eusebio de.
Peña, Cárlos Leon de la.
Tavizon, Arcadio.
Torres, Viuda de.
Dry goods.
Borelly y Crez.
Castañeda, Juan N.
Damm, Maximiliano.
Gurza Hnos. y Ca.
Herrera y Ca.
Hildebrand, Julio, Suc.
Jaquez, J.
Juanbelz Hnos.
Tessier y Bourillon.
Uranga, Antonio.
Dry goods and groceries.
Alvarez, Juan.
Bastera, Andres.
Bose y Schmidt.
Brancho, Toribio.
Castillo, J.
Clarke, C.
Damm, M.
Doorman y Ca.
Hengeler y Deras.
Hildebrand, Julio, Suc.
Juanbelz Hnos.
Loweree Hermano.
Olagaray, Juan B.
Rodriguez, C.
Stahlknecht y Ca.

DURANGO, DURANGO—Continued.

Fancy goods.
   Ciudad de Roma.
   La Bonanza.
   La Palma.
   La Suiza.
   Mercería Alemana.
   Mercería Mexicana.
Furniture.
   Rios, Fernando.
   Valdez, Luis.
   Vazquez, José M.
Groceries and provisions.
   Castillo Hermanos.
   Damm, Maximiliano.
   Duran, Manuel.
   Duran y Ca.
   Falfan, Alejandro.
   Herrera, Antonio.
   Herrera, Epifanio.
   Hildebrand, Julio, Suc.
   Loweree Hnos., Suc.
   Medina, Julian.
   Parra, Cárlos.
   Páura, Juan F.
   Portillo y Ca., Rosario.
   Ramirez, Leandro.
   Rio, Pedro del.
   Salcido Hnos. y Ca.
   Tubet, Joaquin.
   Ugarte, Simon.
   Vazquez, Agustin.
Hardware.
   Barrera, Rafael.
   Böse, Luis.
   Ciudad de Roma.
   La Palma.
   La Suiza.
   Marini, Miguel.
   Schwartz, Cárlos E.
   Stierlin y Ca.
   Wilmanns, Francisco.
Hatters.
   Cervantes, Donaciano.
   Simbeck, Ramon.
Ironware, dealers and manufacturers.
   Fundicion del Cerro, Mercado.
   Isón, Márcos.
   Piedras, Azules.
   Rodríguez, Cristobal.
   Stahlknecht y Ca.
Iron and steel.
   Durango Steel and Iron Co.
   Flores, Rosa.
Jewelers.
   Ibargüen, Desiderio.
   Ibargüen, Luciano.
   Rodriguez, Martin.

DURANGO, DURANGO—Continued.

Joint stock companies.
   Compañía Limitada de Tranvias de Durango.
   Compañía Manufacturera del Tunal.
   Compañía Manufacturera de la Montaña de Fierro.
Lithographers.
   Flores, Francisco.
   Gómez, Miguel.
Sewing machines.
   Hildebrand, Julio, Suc.
   Swain, Cárlos.

ENSENADA DE TODOS SANTOS. LOWER CALIFORNIA.

Bankers.
   Godbee, Antonio.
   Irnison y Ca.
Carriage dealers.
   Beamer, P. W.
   Lidy, S. B.
Furniture.
   Clark, J.
Groceries and provisions.
   Andonaegui y Ormart.
   Cabezuz y Ca.
   Carrillo y Hnos., M.
   Ibs y Ca., Jorge.
   Merkens y Ca., James.
   Rivera, G., Suc.
Sewing machines.
   Bello José Lugo.

FRESNILLO, ZACATECAS.

Merchants.
   Aguilar, Alejandro (drugs).
   Berronet, Juan B. (dry goods).
   Campuzano, Antonio (dry goods, groceries, and provisions).
   "Compañía Restauradora de Proaño" (joint stock).
   "El Portal" (drugs).
   "El Ferrocarril" (drugs).
   "El Fenix" (drugs).
   Esnaurrizar, Ricardo (general merchandise).
   Flores y Ca., Pedro (commission merchants).
   Laredo, Teodoro (fancy goods).
   Ortega ó hijo, M. (dry goods).
   Ortega, Esteban (groceries and provisions).
   Ramirez, Florencio (dry goods).
   Ramos, José (sewing machines).
   Real, Ignacio del (dry goods).
   Vargas y Ca., J. Suc., (commission merchants).
   Zamora, Refugio (carriages).

GARCIA, NUEVO LEON.

General merchants.
   Buentello, Cárlos.
   Buentello, Rafael.
   Fernandez, Teodoro.

GARCIA, NUEVO LEON—Continued.

General merchants—Continued.
Garcia, M.
Garcia, Pedro.
Garza, Candelario.
Garza, Inez.
Garza, Maura.
Gaxa, Felipe.
Gonzales, Juan.
Gouzales, Porfirio.
Guerra, J. C.
Ramirez. Fabian.
Ramirez, Julian C.
Robles, Jesus.

GUADALAJARA, JALISCO.

Arms and ammunition.
Arrington, W. B.
Lacroix Hermanos.
Ruiz, Donaciano.
Banks.
"Banco Nacional de México," Sucursal. Director: Juan Camba.
"Banco de Lóndres y México," Sucursal. Director: Luis Rosas.
Bankers.
Collignon y Ca., Ed.
Corcuera Viuda e Hijos.
Valle Hermanos Fernandez del.
Somellera Hermanos Fernandez.
Kunhardt, Teodoro.
Martinez Negrete, Francisco.
Rumus, Hijos de.
Somellera Hermanos.
Booksellers.
Ancira y Hermano.
Librera del Arzobispado Agencia.
Moya, Cárlos.
Pais, Pedro.
Romero, Cárlos Z.
Sanchez y Ca., Eusebio.
Vila y Escobedo.
Boots and shoes, wholesale.
Arias, José María.
Arrieta, Espiridion.
Castro, Silvestre.
Castellanos, Silvestre.
Córdova e Hijo, Ramon.
Dávalos, Benigno.
García, Roman.
Gomez, J.
Guardado, Modesto.
Gutierrez, Clemente C.
Gutierrez y Ca., Matias B.
Hernandez, Félix.
Hermosillo, Arnulfo.
Martinez, Fermin.
Mercado, Eliodoro Z.

GUADALAJARA, JALISCO—Continued.

Boots and shoes, wholesale—Continued.
Murillo, José María.
Murillo, Julian.
Nava, Alberto.
Nuñez, Sabas.
Orozco, Luis.
Ortega, Pablo.
Otero, Ricardo.
Pedroza, Evaristo.
Ramos, J.
Rodriguez, Sucesores.
Saldaña, Esteban.
Villavicencio, Pedro.
Zepeda, Antonio.
Boots and shoes, retail.
Alvarado, Félix.
Asencio, María.
Barrajas, Felipa.
Barrajas, J.
Bermudez, Ramon.
Bernal, Francisca.
Berrueco, Dolores.
Charles, Francisca.
Chavez, Josefa.
Cornejo, Viviano.
Curiel, Guadalupe.
García, Antonia.
García, Maximiana.
Garibay, Leonilde.
Gonzalez, Dolores.
Hernandez, Bernardo.
Hernandez, Juana.
Hernandez, Margarita.
Mercado, Calixta.
Miramontes, Teresa.
Padilla, Luciana.
Pedroza, Evaristo.
Prieto, Guadalupe.
Rodrigo, Catalina.
Rodriguez, Maura.
Silva, Eduarda.
Silva, Eugenia.
Sondoval, Magdalena.
Vargas, Alberto.
Carriage dealers.
Alvarez, Leonardo.
Cano, José María.
Chavez, Victor.
García, Genaro A.
Gomez, Arcadio.
Haro, Sebastian.
Lauro de Anda.
Perez, Gabriel.
Suerez, Lino.
Chemicals and acids.
Agraz, Félix.
Escamilla, Librado.

GUADALAJARA, JALISCO—Continued.

China and glassware.

Amberg y Velad.
Bartholly, Agustin, Sucr. (Guillermo Brandt).
Behn, Cárlos.
Castillo y Zúñiga.
Garibay, Ramon.
Gonzalez, Palomary y Ca.
Romero, Antonio.
Vallarta, Francisco.
Zavala y Ca., Juan.

Commission merchants.

Agraz, Salvador J.
Agraz, Bazan y Ca.
Arce y Arias.
Ascher, Emilio.
Aguilú y Ortiz.
Barroso, Renito.
Basave, Cárlos.
Benares, C.
Blume y Ca.
Brandt, Guillermo.
Camarena, Julian.
Castañeda Palomar, Ramon.
Castillo, J. Alvarez.
Campo, Loreto Martinez del.
Chavez y Guido.
Ciuana & Co.
Collingnon & Co., Ed.
Córdova ó Hijo, Ramon.
Cortina, José.
Sombrera Hnos Fernandez.
Flores, Pascual I..
Galindez, Daniel.
Galvan, Juan.
García, Sancho Cárlos.
Garcia, Paulino.
Gonzalez, Olivares y Hermano.
Gravenhorst, Gustavo.
Guerrero, Placido.
Heymann, Alfonso, Succ.
Infante, Francisco.
Infante, José M.
Infante, Luis.
Iniquez, Evaristo.
Iturbide, Eduardo.
Lopez, Rafael.
Maconzet, Salvadore.
Martinez, Pablo.
Mead, Dionisio.
Mier, Atansio.
Montano, Manuel.
Mora ó Hijos, Ramon de la.
Moreno y Palomar.
Navarro y Ca., T. I.
Navarrete, Pablo.
Negrete, Francisco.
Ornelas, Manuel S.

GUADALAJARA, JALISCO—Continued.

Commission merchants—Continued.

Oseguera, Epifanio.
Oseguera, Gabino.
Otero y Aguiar.
Peña, Enrique de la.
Peña y Hermano, Fernando de la.
Quevedo, Luis de García.
Ramirez, Ramon.
Retana, José J.
Romero de Parra y Ca., E.
Romero, Cárlos Z.
Salcedo, Joaquim.
Sancho, Cárlos.
Silva y Michel, Francisco.
Solorzan, Ignacio.
Stampa, Manuel.
Torres, Pablo.
Ugarte, Francisco.
Vallejo Hermanos.
Vallejo, Juan.
Vazquez, Francisco.
Villalobos, Emilio.
Villareal, Ramon.
Vudriffed Hermanos.

Cordage.

Alvino, Martin del C.
Camacho, Juan.
Cremieur, Merced.
Fuentes, J.
Garcia, Tomasa.
Monico, Atilano.
Padilla, Luciano.
Padilla, Soledad.
Rubio, Alejandro.
Rubio, J.
Verber, Rosario.

Druggists.

"San Vicente de Paul," Acosta, Pedro.
"Sagrado Corazon," Ayala, Ramon.
Asencio, J.
"La Purísima," Bernal, Francisco.
"La Independencia," García, Conte Alejo.
"Del Auxilio," Gonzalez, Tomás.
Droguería Universal.
Gutierrez Estevez, Antonio.
"Botica Alemana," Jaacks, Juan.
"De Medrano," Jaacks, Juan.
"La Soledad," Mancilla, Manuel.
"Las Mercedes," Montaño, Jacinto.
"San José," Montaño, J.
"Santísima Trinidad," Ocampo, Cortes.
"San Agustin," Ornelas, Antonio.
"Del Refugio," Ornelas, Lorenzo.
"Santa Teresa," Padilla, Valazquez Mariano.
Perez, Lázaro.
Perez, Cárlos.
Puga, Nicolas.
"La Cruz Verde," Romo, José María.

154 MEXICO.

GUADALAJARA, JALISCO—Continued.

Druggists—Continued.
"Nuestra Señora de Lourdes," Servin, Camilo.
"De la Compañía," Torres, Vidal.
"De Santo Domingo," Ulloa, Aurelio.
"Nuestra Señora del Rosario," Villa Gordoa y Guzman.
"Jesus María," Zuloaga, Cárlos.

Dry goods, imported and domestic.
Alvarez Tostado, Eusebio.
Arias Trinidad, Merced.
Audiffret y Garcin.
Brihuega y Ca., Manuel.
Caire y Tirán.
Fortoul y Chapuy.
Fortoul, Bellon y Agorreca, T.
Franco, Celso.
Gas y Cogórdan.
Gómez, Prisciliano.
Gómez y Hno., Matías.
Garibi, José.
Gonzalez, Andrés.
Gonzalez, Amado.
Gonzalez, Romero Vicente.
Kunhardt y Rose.
Lebre, Barréire y Ca.
Navarro, Nestor.
Romero, Eduardo.
Tangassi, Guillermo.
Toro, Angel.
Zuloaga, J.

Dry goods, silks, laces, and millinery (imported).
Audiffred y Gacin.
Caire y Tiran.
Fortoul, Chapuy.
Fortoul, Bellon y Agorreca, T.
Franck y Ca., M., Sucursal de México.
Gas y Gogordan.
Kunhardt y Rose.
Lebre, Barriere y Ca.

Electric light companies.
Public Electrical Light Co., Hutchinson, E. A., director.
Incandescent Light Co., Sanchez, Rafael, director.
Public Incandescent Light Co., Schiaffino, M. L., director.

Flour dealers.
Basave y Ca., Cárlos.
Canedo y Valdivieso.
Cortina, José.
Galindez, Daniel.
García, Apolonio.
García, Paulino.

GUADALAJARA, JALISCO—Continued.

Flour dealers—Continued.
García Sancho, Cárlos.
Gomez, Matias.
Gonzalez, José.
Llano, F. Simon del.
Martinez, Pablo.
Mora é Hijos, Ramon de la.
Navarro y Compa, T. I.
Peña y Hno, Fernando de la.
Torres Morfin, José María.
Valdovinos, Maximiano.
Vazquez, Francisco.

Furniture, imported and domestic.
Amberg y Velad.
Arrington, W. B.
Behn, Carlos.
Gonzalez y Echeverria, Bazar de Mueblería.
Hernandez, Arcadio.
Jiminez, Trinidad.
Navarro y Ca., T. I.
Orozco Gonzalez, Antonio.
Ruiz, Donaciano.
Vallarta, Francisco.

General merchandise.
"Bazar Universal", Gonzaloz y Gutierrez.

Glass and glassware.
Alvarez y Gutierrez.
Bartholly, Sucesor, Agustin.
Behn, Cárlos.
Castillo y Zúñiga.
Escamilla Librado.
Romero, Antonio.
Romero, Felipe.

Groceries and provisions (imported).
Alvarez y Gutierrez.
Alvarez, Santiago.
Badial, Florentino.
Badial, Juan.
Barron, Lucas.
Bosque, Manuel.
Cardenas é hijo, José.
Castillo y Zúñiga.
Cedeño, Apolonio.
Corona, José María, y Hermano.
Cortes, Avelino.
Covarrubias, Antonio.
Chavez, J. T.
Davila y Matute.
De Anda, Anastasio.
Diaz, Ambrosio.
Dominguez, Ignacio.
Fernandez, José G.
Flores, Esquez y Compañía.
García, Margarito.

GUADALAJARA, JALISCO—Continued.

Groceries and provisions—Continued.
Garibay, Ramon.
Garibay, Francisco.
Gomez, José María.
Gonzalez Arias, Miguel.
Haro, Bárbaro.
Hernandez, H.
Hernandez, Prisciliano.
Izquierdo, Albino.
Martinez, Pedro.
Martinez Cubeiro, Salvador.
Mora, Hilario de la.
Muñoz, Ignacio.
Navarro, Ignacio.
Navarro, Eulogio.
Navarro, Rafael T.
Nuñez, Valeriano.
Nuñez, Ignacio.
Nuño, Manuel.
Oceguera, Abraham
Oceguera, Rosendo y Hno.
Ornelas, Mariano.
País, Pedro.
Pérez, Dominga G. de.
Rico, Adolfo.
Rios, Rafael.
Rodriguez, Encarnación.
Rodriguez, Mauro.
Rodriguez, Baltazar.
Romero, Antonio.
Romero, Felipe.
Romero, Francisco.
Romero, José Maria E.
Ruiz, Ponciano.
Ruiz, Rosalio D.
Ruiz, Natalio.
Saucedo, Abundio.
Servín, Camilo.
Silva y Ca., Hilario.
Velasco, Luis G.
Zalazar, Manuel.
Zavala y Ca., Juan.

Groceries and provisions, imported and domestic.
Alvarez y Gutierrez.
Castillo y Zuñiga.
Garibay, Ramon.
Gomez, José María.
Romero, Antonio.
Zavala y Compañía, Juan.

Hardware and machinery.
Amberg y Velad.
Bartholly, Agustin, Suc.
Behn, Cárlos.

Hardware, general.
Amberg y Velad.
Arce, J.

GUADALAJARA, JALISCO—Continued.

Hardware, general—Continued.
Bartholly, Sucesor, Agustin.
Behn, Cárlos.
Gonzalez, Palomar y Compañía, Benito.
Vallarta, Francisco.
Zuloaga, Juan M.

Hardware (iron and copper).
Alvarez del Castillo, Sucesores.
Behn, Cárlos.
Camerena, Julian.
Corcuera, Viuda ó Hijos.
Gonzalez, Olivarez y Hno.
Martinez, Pablo.

Hatters.
Alvarez, Maximino.
Anaya, Francisco J.
Chavez, Florencio.
Gutierrez, Celerino.
Hernandez, Praxedis.
Ibarra, Vicente.
Navarro, Francisco.
Norwald, Luis.
Perez, Petra.
Placencia, Lino.
Placencia, Anastasio.
Quirarte, Leonides.
Ramirez, Pedro.
Reyes, Herlindo.
Rufino, Juan.
Ruiz, Andrés.
Torres, Longinos.
Zölly Hermanos.

Importers (direct).
Collignon y Ca., Ed.
Navarro y Compañía, T. J.
Somellera Hermanos Fernandez.

Jewelers.
Aguilar, Sabino.
Diaz, Cárlos.
Salmeron, Daniel.
Torres, Heliodoro.
Ulloa, Eustacio.

Jewelers and watchmakers.
Arrington, W. B.
Castañeda, José A.
Castro, Antonio.
Martinez, Ramon.
Ruiz, Donaciano.
Torres, Juan B.
Torres, Jacinto.
Vallarta, Francisco.
Winterhalder, Antonio.

Lime and brick.
Avilia, Trinidad.
Camarena, Fermin.

156

MEXICO.

GUADALAJARA, JALISCO—Continued.

Lime and brick—Continued.
Casillas, Albino.
Hernandez, Trinidad.
Luna de San Sebastian.
Piedra, Trinidad.
Placencia, Ireneo.

Lithographers.
Ancira y Hermano.
Dieguez, Trinidad.
Iguinez, José María.
Isaguirre, José A.
Rodriguez, Alberto.

Lumber dealers.
Camarena, Fernin.
Casilla, José.
Cortés, Ramon.
Gonzales, Ambrosia.
Iguinez, Evaristo.
Orozco, Gonzalez Antonio.
Ramirez, José.
Romero, Bonifacio.
Solis, Viuda de.
Vargas, Francisco.
Villegas, Nicolás.
Villaseñor, Enrique.

Machinery and agricultural implements.
Behn, Cárlos.
Castañeda, Palomar.
Collignon y Compª.
Kipp, Juan H.
Stettner, Mauricio.

Mineral waters.
Asencio, J.
Branca, Albino.
Ocampo, Manuel y Hermano.
Ornelas, Antonio J.
Perez, Lázaro.
Perez, Cárlos.

Musical instruments.
Arce, J.
Castro, Silvestre.
Collignon y Compa., Eduardo.
Corvera, Miguel.
Durán, José María.
Gomez, Luis.
Gonzalez, Palomar y Compañía, Benito.
Heymann, Sucesor, Alfonso.
Navarro y Compª., T, I.
Navarrete, Pablo.
Rojas Vertiz, José María.
Ruiz, Donaciano.
Sanchez y Compañía, Eusebio.
Sausa, Martin.

GUADALAJARA, JALISCO—Continued.

Musical instruments—Continued.
Torres, Juan B.
Valenzuela, Alejandro.
Vila y Escobedo.

Notions.
Aguilar, Zenona.
Andrade, Margarita.
Carrillo, Ignacia.
Corona de Arévalo, Feliciana.
Estrada, Petra.
Estrada, María.
Flores, J.
Flores, Felipa.
Jimenez, Refugio.
Landa, Francisco.
Larios, Crescencia.
Macías, Ricarda.
Parra, Eusebia.
Parra, Juana.
Ramirez, Refugio.
Valle, Antonio.
Villalobos Ruiz, Amado.

Paints and oils.
Agraz, Félix.
Betancourt, Roque.
Elizalde, Familia de.
Escamilla, Librado.
Hidalgo, Rafael.
Lupercio, José María.
Navarro, Ignacio.

Paper—Blank books.
Ancira, Hermanos.
Cabrera, José.
Guevara, Ricardo.
Iguinez, José María.
Ma tinez Suarez, Margarito.
Perez Lete, Sucesores.
Robles, José María.
Sanchez, Eusebio.

Cardboard.
Vazquez, Pedro.
Villavicencio, Santos.

Printing paper.
Ancira y Hno., Modesto.
Castillo y Zúñiga.
Collignon y Compa, Eduardo.
Corcuera é Hijos, Viuda.
Castañeda, Palomar.
Zavala y Compa, Juan.

Wall paper.
Gonzalez, Palomar y Ca., Benito.
Sanchez y Compa., Eusebio.

Perfumery.
Asencio, J.

GUADALAJARA, JALISCO—Continued.

Perfumery—Continued.
Corona de Arévalo, Feliciana.
Fortoul, Bellon y Agorreca, T.
Gonzalez, Palomar y Ca., Benito.
Jaacks, Juan.
La Croix Hermanos.
Pérez, Lázaro ó Hijo.

Petroleum depots.
Alvarez y Gutierrez.
Castillo y Zúñiga.
Guerrero, Cirilo.
Oltzen, J.
Sanchez, Rafael.
Valencio, Francisco.

Pharmacists.
Acosta, Pedro.
Adame, Francisco.
Ayala, Ramon.
Alvarado, Ignacio.
Arce, Julio G.
Arreola, Manuel.
Asencio, J.
Bernal, Francisco.
González, Tomás.
Gonzalez, E.
Gutierrez, Estevez.
Guzman, Manuel.
Jaacks, Juan.
Mancilla, Manuel.
Montaño, Jacinto.
Murillo, Eutiquio.
Navarro, Luis.
Ocampo, Cortes.
Oliva, Adolfo.
Oliva, Juan.
Ornelas, Antonio J.
Ornelas, Lorenzo.
Orozco, Agustin.
Pacheco, Leal.
Perez, Arce.
Perez, Cárlos.
Perez, Lázaro.
Perez, Manuel.
Puga, Adrian.
Puga, Nicolas.
Romo, José María.
Rubalcava, Martin.
Suarez, Cenobio.
Tortolero, Nicolas.
Ulloa, Aurelio.
Uribe, Abel.
Vargas, Francisco.
Villa Gordoa.

Porcelain.
Saavedra, Gregorio (general).
Gonzalez, Francisco.

GUADALAJARA, JALISCO—Continued.

Pottery.
Coblan, Juana.
Corona, María.
Lopez, J.
Lopez, Petra.
Lozano, Refugio.
Lowerre, Manuel.
Navarro de Rasura, Anatasia.
Quirarde, Merced.
Quirarde, Trinidad.
Rodriguez, Esteban.
Ruiz Velasco, Salvador.
Ruiz, Dolores.
Sanchez, Inocencio.
Verrea, Luisa.

Printers' supplies.
Guevara, L. Ciro.
Kipp, Juan H.
Ocampo y Cortés y Hnos., Manuel.
Puga, Nicola.

Salt pork importers.
Diaz, Guadalupe.
Espinosa, Perfecto.
Nuñez, Valeriano.
Oceguera, Abraham.
Perez, J. Merced.
Reynoso, Martin.
Reynoso, Pablo.
Sanchez, Ignacia.
Silva, German.
Valadez, Ignacio.

Sewing machines.
Amberg y Velad, ("White").
Arrigton, W. B., ("Naumann").
Behn, Carlos, ("New Home").
Espinosa, José María, ("Wheeler y Wilson").
Hermosillo, Arnulfo, ("Singer").

Silk goods.
Corona, Antonio.
Corona de Arrevalo, Feliciana.
Fortoul, Bellon y Agorreca, T.
Gaudinot y Banoni.
Muro, Rafaela del.
Paez, Luz M. de.
Rendon, Guadalupe.

Sporting goods.
Agraz, Félix.
Castillo y Zúñiga.
Chavez, Plutarco.
Escamilla, Librado.
Lacroix Hno*.
Luna, Secundino.
Navarro, Ignacio.
Rodriguez, Feliciano B.
Ruiz, Donaciano.

GUADALAJARA, JALISCO—Continued.

Stationery.
  Ancira y Hermano.
  Gonzalez, Palomar y Compañía, Benito.
  Iguinez, José María.
  Moya, Cárlos.
  Paez, Pedro.
  Romero, Cárlos Z.
  Sanchez y Ca, Eusebio.
  Vila y Escobedo.

Sugar merchants.
  Blume y Compañía.
  Castañeda, Palomar.
  Carcuera, Viuda ó Hijos.
  Gonzalez, Olivarez y Hno.
  Mora e Hijos, Ramon de la.
  Peña y Hno., Fernando de la.
  Remus, Hijas de.
  Ugarte, Francisco.

Tinware and brassware.
  Alatorre (viuda de).
  Alvarado, Encarnacion.
  Arzate, Francisco.
  Bárcena, J.
  Camacho ó Hijo, Celso.
  Camacho, Canuto.
  Camacho, Florencio.
  Gallegos, Lucio.
  Gallegos, Severiano.
  Gonzalez, Modesto.
  Gutierrez Hermanos.
  Mendoza, Máximo.
  Olea, Lauro.
  Pelez, Anacleto.
  Perez, Quirino.
  Suarez, Plácido.

Toys.
  Arce, J.
  Armeria, Refugio.
  Aumada, Petra.
  Bartholly, Sucr, Agustin.
  Bautista, Agapita.
  Behn, Cárlos.
  Carranda, Pomposa.
  Corona de Arrevalo, Feliciano.
  Enciso, Soledad.
  Espinosa, Dolores.
  Fortoul, Bellon y Agoreca, T.
  Franck y Ca., M.
  Gonzalez, Palomar y Compañía, Benito
  Luna, Secundino.
  Manriquez, María L.
  Mondragon, Longinos.
  Paez, Luz.
  Ramirez, J. R.
  Ramirez, Francisco.
  Roveles, Josefa.

GUADALAJARA, JALISCO—Continued.

Toys—Continued.
  Salazar, Cleofas.
  Valdivia, Lucas.
  Vallarta, Francisco.
  Villaseñor, Espiridiona.
  Zuloaga, Juan.

Undertakers.
  Alatorre, Salvador.
  Cana, José María.
  Hernandez, Arcadio.
  Jimenez, Trinidad.
  Orozco, Gonzalez.

Varnish and axle grease.
  Agrez, Félix.
  Escamilla, Librado.

Wines, imported.
  Castillo y Zúñiga.
  Collignon y Compañía, Eduardo.
  Fortoul, Belon y Agorreca.
  Garibay, Ramon.
  Galindez, Daniel.
  Huber, Victor.
  Lions, Remigio.
  Martinez, Negrete, Francisco.
  Pais, Pedro.
  Quevedo, Luis G.
  Rolleri y Compañía, José.
  Romero, Antonio.
  Romero, Carlos Z.
  Sanchez y Compañía, Eusebio.
  Tiran, Julio.
  Vila y Escobedo.
  Zavala y Compañía, Juan.

Wood and coal.
  Casilla, Albino.
  García, Isabel.
  Gómez, Sóstenes.
  Hernandez Cortés, Teresa.
  Huerta, Zenon.
  Lara, Francisco.
  Luevalo, Magdalena.
  Lares, Trinidad.
  Padilla, J.
  Pérez, Féliz.
  Prieto, Gerónimo.
  Pulido, Gregorio.
  Reynoso, Juan.
  Rios, Juan.
  Reyes Calixto, D.
  Travares, José María.

Wool merchants
  Agraz, Félix.
  Escamilla, Librado.
  Gonzalez, Olivarez y Hno.
  Morfin, Marcelino.

GUADALCAZAR, SAN LUIS POTOSI.

General merchants.
Campean, Braulio.
Cordova, Jesus.
Garcia, Macario.
Garcia, Prisciliano.
Posado, Florencio.
Rubalcava, Santos.

Mining companies.
Guadalcazar Quick-Silver Mfg. Co.
Guzman, Lorenzo T.
Revilla y Ca., Tomás.
Sherman y Ca., A.

GUANAJUATO, GUANAJUATO.

Agricultural implements.
Castañeda, Francisco de P.
Ederra, Francisco X.
Palassou, Enrique.
Stallforth, Alcazar y Ca.

Arms and ammunition.
Manriquez, Francisco.
Moya, Mauro.
Nunes, Narciso.
Palassou, Enrique.
Villegas, Castulo.

Bankers.
Alcazar, Ramon.
Arce, Genaro.
Castañeda, Francisco de P.
Ederra, Francisco.
Jimenez, Gregorio.
Markassousa, Cárlos.
Stallforth, Alcazar y Ca.

Banks.
Sucursal del "Banco Agrícola."
Sucursal del "Banco de Lóndres y México."
Sucursal del Banco Nacional Mexicano.

Booksellers and stationers.
Alvarez, Alejandro.
Bouret, Cárlos.
Castan y Camps, Celestino.
Fuente, Pedro de la.
Gallardo, Abrahan.
Obregon, Claudio.
Pallassou, Enrique.
Vaol, Emilio Lopez.
Verdayes y Ca., F.

Boots and shoes.
Alvarado, J.
Arias, Margarito.
Bernard, Enrique.
Duarte, Emetrio.
Heredia, Francisco.

Boots and shoes—Continued.
Machuca, J. M.
Madrid, Felipe.
Pedroza, Ceferino.
Rodriguez, Francisco.
Rodriguez, Caterino.
Soria, Concepción.
Soria, José E.
Soria, N.
Villanuev Francisco.

Carriages.
Valtierra, Nabor.

China and glassware.
Abascal, Diego.
Acostas, Santos.
Caloca y Ca.
Caudra, Luis.
Fuentes, J.
Gomez, Felipe.
Obregon Hermanos.
Obregon, Claudio.
Ortego, Monico.
Palassou, Enrique.
Pedrosa, Francisco de P.

Commission merchants.
Baca Hno., J. B.
Castorena, Gaudel.
Dominguez, Magdaleno.
Fuentes y Romero.
Gutierrez, Antonio.
Guzman, Feliciano.
Hernandez Hnos.
Langenscheidt, Enrique.
Manrique, Florentino.
Martinez, Antonio.
Meyerberg, Enrique.
Nuñez, Narciso.
Osante Hnos.
Reinoso, Manuel.
Rodriguez y Ca., C.
Stallforth, Alcazar y Ca

Copper goods.
Alvarez, Ramon.
Bonifacio, Antonio.

Drugs.
Aragon, Felipe.
Arreguin, B.
Casillas, Tomás.
Fonseca, Tomás.
Gasca y Ca.
Gazca, J.
Leal y Ca.
Lopez, Francisco.
Maicote, Sirio.

GUANAJUATO, GUANAJUATO—Continued.

Drugs—Continued.
Marquez y Ca.
Obregon y Marquez.
Ruoda, José.
Salcedo, Vicente.
Soto, Emilio.
Sotura, Cárlos.
Vazquez Suc.
Vazquez, Ignacio.
Villafuerte, Elías.
Villanueva y Ca.

Dry goods.
Baca Hno., J. B.
Barquin y Espinosa.
Beraud Hnos.
Bolivar y Puebla.
Brun y Jame.
Caguen, Maximo.
Caire y Audriffed.
Erquicia, P., Suc.
Garcia y Hno, Enrique.
Goerne, Luis.
Gonzalez y Villaseñor.
Heran, Cayetano, Suc.
Hernandez Hnos.
Langenscheidt, Enrique.
Lozano y Espinosa.
Osacar Hnos.
Osante Hnos.
Romaña, Mariano.
Rongecillo, Antonio.

Fancy goods.
Alferez, Florencio.
David, Emilio.
Esperon y Ca., Victor,
Fuentes y Piña, Wenceslao.
Gallardo, Abrahan.
Obregon, Claudio.
Ortega, Monica.
Palassou, Enrique.

Furniture.
Aguirre, J.
Bonifacio, Antonio.
Jouannaud, Leonardo.
Obregon, Claudio.
Porras, Anastasio.
Segura, Adrian.
Segura, Alejandro.

Groceries and provisions.
Abascal, Diego.
Acosta, Santos.
Arteaga, Florencio.
Bolaños, Mateo.
Caloca, Tomás.
Castro, Margarito.

GUANAJUATO, GUANAJUATO—Continued.

Groceries and provisions—Continued.
Cervantes y Ca.
Cueller, Antonio.
Erquicia, P., Suc.
Estrayer y Ca., A.
Garcia, Felix.
Goerne Hnos., Guillermo.
Mañon, Ruperto.
Obregon, Claudio.
Robles, Roman.
Sabino, Iza.
Rojas y Hno., Eusebio.
Torres, Pedro.
Trueba, Mateo.
Valadez, Manuel.
Zarrate, Francisco.

Hardware.
Abascal, Diego.
Alcazar y Ca.
Bonifacio, Antonio.
Denné, Alfonso.
Gallardo, Abran.
Goerne, Luis.
Langenscheidt, Enrique.
Osante Hermanos.
Palassou, Enrique.
Rodriguez y Ca.

Hatters.
Barriga y Ca., Francisco.
Bordier, Isidoro.
Solorzano y Ca., Antonio.

House-furnishing goods and tinware.
Alvarez, Bruno.
Damen, Alfonso.
Delgado, Tiburcio.
Duran, Pablo.
Flores, Hilario.
Flores, Narciso.
Frias, Modesto.
Moron, Antonio.
Reina, Ricardo.
Vasquez, Ignacio.

Importers and exporters.
Abascal, Diego.
Acevedo, Alejo.
Ajuria, M.
Alcazar y Ca.
Alferez, Florencio.
Berniga, F.
Brune & James.
Buand Hermanos & Ca., Enrique.
Caire, Andriffed & Co.
Caloca & Co.
Castro, Margarito.
Cuellar, Antonio.

GUANAJUATO, GUANAJUATO—Continued.

Importers and exporters—Continued.
Delgado, Amado.
Errecalde, Guillerme.
Fernandez, Ignacio.
Flebe, Joaquin.
Gallardo, Abrahan.
Garcia de Leon, Domingo.
Gerilant, Federico.
Goerne, Luis.
Gonzalez & Villaseñor.
Gutierrez, Lino.
Hernandez y Hijo.
Hernandez, Alejandro.
Herrera, J.
Infante, Anastasio.
Issa, Sabino.
Lara, Gregorio.
Mármol, Pascual.
Obregon, Claudio.
Ossante Hermanos.
Palassou Hermanos.
Perez, Antonio.
Reynoso, Luis.
Robles, Roman.
Rojas, Eusebio.
Solorzano, Antonio.
Trueba, Mateo.
Velazquez, José.

Ironware dealers.
Denné, Alfonso.
Gallardo, Abrahan.
Palassou, Enrique.
Stallforth, Alcazar y Ca.

Jewelers.
Galacion, Gabellon.
Gerilant, Federico.
Hernandez, Alejandro.
Hernandez y Hijo.
Laux, Luis.
Perez, Antonio.
Vallalpando, Antonio.
Wieland, Federico.

Lithographers.
García, Emilio.
Loreto, Faustino.

Lumber merchants.
Anda, J. M.
Alvarado, Rafael.
Herrera, Benito, Suc.
Lopez, Trinidad.

Music store.
Fuente, Pedro de la.

Paints and varnishes.
Arteaga, Florencio.
David, Emilio.

S. Ex. 8, pt. 11——11

GUANAJUATO, GUANAJUATO—Continued.

Paints and varnishes—Continued.
Hijar, Geronimo.
Palassou, Fernando
Santoyo, Antonio.
Valdez, Manuel.
Zorate, Francisco.

Perfumery.
Hermano y Obregon.

Photographers.
Contreras, Vicente.
Iñigo y Ramirez.

Pianos and organs.
Langenscheidt, Enrique.
Meyerberg, Enrique.
Villapando, Antonio.

Sewing machines.
Castro, Margarito.
Herrera, J.
Palassou, Enrique.
Portillo, Cleofas.
Williams, Eduardo.
Wineburgh, David.

Ship chandlers' goods.
Castro, Manuel.
Cepeda, Santos.
Morales, Refugio.
Rodriguez, Lorenzo.

GUERRERO, TAMAULIPAS.

Banker.
Ruiloba, José.

Druggists.
Fernandez, A. M.
Gutierrez, M. Gonzalez.
Winslow, Cárlos.

Dry and fancy goods.
Chavez, Marcelo.
Garza, Ventura.
Gongora, Rafael.
Gutierrez, Juan de D.
O'Connor, Tomás.
Ruiloba, José.
Saldana y Hnos., I. I.
Volpe y Hnos., M.
Zapata, Juan.

General merchants.
Garza, Blas.
Garza. Guillermo.
Gutierrez, Anastasio.
Gutierrez, Diego.
Zapato, Federico.

GUAYMAS, SONORA.

Agricultural implements.
Aguilar, F. A., Suc.
Baston, Donaciano.

GUAYMAS, SONORA—Continued.

Agricultural implements—Continued.
Cosca y García.
Lund y Ca., William.
Seldner y von Borstel.

Arms and ammunition.
Baston, D.
Seldner y von Borstel.

Bankers.
Aguayo Hnos.
Aguilar, F. A., Suc.
Möller y Ca., G.
Willard, A.

Banks.
Banco Nacional.
London Bank of Mexico and South America.

Booksellers and stationers.
Baston, D.
Markert, F. A.
Seldner y von Borstel.

Boots and shoes.
Oun Choy Chan.
Tung Chung Lung.

Carriage dealer.
Hale, Charles E.

China and glassware.
Baston, D.
Seldner y von Borstel.

Commission merchants.
Iberry, W.
Martinez, Luis A.
Willard, A.

Drugs.
Dávila, Luis G.
Gayon, R.
Wallace, Alejandro.

Dry goods.
Aguilar, F. A., Suc.
Basazabal, Juan.
Cosca y García.
Hernandez y Lopez.
Möller y Ca., G.
Möller, J. R.
Seldner y von Borstel.
Wolf, H.
Zenizo, Juan.

Furniture.
Baston, G.
Lund y Ca., William.
Moran, Antonio.

Groceries and provisions.
Aguilar, F. A., Suc.
Baston, Donaciano.
Camou, Juan.

GUAYMAS, SONORA—Continued.

Groceries and provisions—Continued.
Cosca y García.
Escobosa y Ca., Rafael.
Iberry, Wenceslao.
Iberry y Huerta.
Jáuregui, Luis.
Möller y Ca., G.
Seldner y von Borstel.
Zenizo y Hno., Juan.
Zuniga, Ramon.

Hardware.
Baston, D.
Seldner y von Borstel.

Iron and ironware.
Aguilar, F. A., Suc.
Baston, D.
Cosca y García.
Möller y Ca., G.
Seldner y von Borstel.

Jewelers.
Brückelmeyer, C.
Dueñas, Ramon V.

Printers.
Avilés, L.
Gaxiola y Ca., Eduardo.

Sewing machines.
Canale, Aurelio.
Cohn, Max W.
Cosca y García.
Lund y Ca., William.
Seldner y von Borstel.
Singer Manufacturing Co., agency.

HAUALAHUISES, NEUVO LEON.

General merchants.
Benitez, Antonio.
Cuellar, Bernardino.
Leal, Esteban.
Martinez, Fortino C.
Martinez, Yndelacio S.
Noyolu, Pablo.
Pedraza, Adolfo.

HERMOSILLO, SONORA.

Agricultural implements.
Calderon, Antonio.
Castro, Juan D.

Bankers.
Calderon, A.
Ruiz, Rafael.

Booksellers and stationers.
Calderon, Antonio.
Castro, Manuel F.
Possehl y Ca., Luis.

HERMOSILLO, SONORA—Continued.

Boots and shoes.
Assun y Ca., Wong.
Chanjon, Santiago.
Lara, Donaciano.
Loug y Ca., Cong.
Sainz, Silviano.
Yepiz, José I.

Carriage dealers.
Grijalva, Manuel.
Moreno, Juan.
Ruiz, Librado.

China and glassware.
Horvilleur, Leon.
Ruiz, R.
Seldner y von Borstel.

Commission merchants.
Calderon, Antonio.
Dauelsberg, German.
Rodriguez, A. A.
Serrano, Cristobal.

Drugs.
Avila, J. M.
Botica Nueva.
Davila y Ca., L. G.

Dry goods.
Calderon, Antonio.
Camon y Hermanos, L.
Echevarría, Camilo.
Escalante, Vicente V.
Horvilleur, Leon.
Loaiza, Filomeno.
Rodriguez, Francisco E.
Rodriguez, Rodolfo.
Ruiz, R.
Possehl y Ca., Luis.

Fancy goods.
Calderon, Antonio.
Horvilleur y Ca., Leon.
Possehl y Ca., Luis.
Ruiz, R.
Seldner y von Borstel.

Furniture.
Teran, Arturo.
Seldner y von Borstel.

General agents.
Castañeda, Eduardo.
Encisas, José M.
Enciso, Leonardo.
Escalante, Manuel.
Rodriguez, Luis.
Serrano, Cristobal.
Velasco, Florencio.

HERMOSILLO, SONORA—Continued.

Groceries and provisions.
Arvizu y Ca., J. J.
Calderon, Antonio.
Camou y Hermanos, L.
Castro, J. D.
Echevarría, Camilo.
Fereira y Ca., Manuel.
Gonzalez, Dionisio.
Horvilleur, Leon.
Loaiza, Filomeno.
Ruiz, Rafael.
Seldner y von Borstel.

Hardware.
Ruiz, Rafael.
Seldner y von Borstel.

Hatters.
Felix, Alberto.
Horvilleur y Ca., Leon.

Ironware dealers and manufacturers.
Calderon, Antonio.
Castro, J. D.
Ruiz, R.
Seldner y von Borstel.

Jeweler.
Kroft, Samuel H.

Joint stock companies.
"El Progreso."
"La Sonorense."

Lithographer.
Ramirez, Aniceto.

Music store.
Possehl y Ca., Luis.

Sewing machines.
Maddonado, J. M.
Singer Manufacturing Company.

HIDALGO DEL PARRAL, CHIHUAHUA.

Bankers.
Erquicia, Pedro, Suc. (agente "El Nacional").
Gomez, Francisco (agente "El Banco Mexicano").
Hinojar, Juan.
Moya, Mauro (agente "Banco Nacional").
Palacios, A. (agente "El Minero").
Roncon, Antonio.
Stallforth Hnos.

Booksellers and stationers.
Norberto, Aizpuru.
Pablo, Ortiz.

Boots and shoes.
Ramirez, Telésforo.
Rivas, Tomás.
Saenz, Laureano.
Torres, Felipe.
Torres, Felix.

HIDALGO DEL PARRAL, CHIHUAHUA—
Continued.

Carriage dealer.
Perez, Luis.

Commission merchants.
Behr, Juan.
Hernandez Hnos.
Nuñez, Gabriel.
Stallforth Hnos.

Drugs.
Arellano, Alejandro del.
Mena, A., Suc.
Rivera, Vicente.
Soto, Emilio.

Dry goods.
Bolivar, Canuto.
Corral y Gonzalez.
Erquicía, Pedro. Suc.
Esperon y Ca., Pedro.
Flores é Hijo, Victor.
Hagen y Ca., Maxo.
Hernandez Hnos.
Mula, Maximo.
Ronquillo, Antonio.
Vaca y Hno., Juan B.

Fancy goods.
Esperon y Ca., Victor.
Fuentes y Piña.
Hagen y Ca., Maxo.

Furniture.
Fuentes y Piña.
Knigge, Cárlos.
Murillo, Bernardino.
Stallforth Hnos.

Groceries and provisions.
Erquicia, Pedro, Suc.
Esperon, Victor.
Fuentes y Peña.
Hernandez y Hnos.
Knigge, Cárlos.
Roncon, Antonio.
Ronquillo, Antonio.
Stallforth Hnos.
Torres Hnos., Pedro.

Hardware.
Esperon, Victor.
Fuentes y Piña.

Lithographer.
Ortiz, Pablo.

Paints, oils, and varnishes.
Rentería, José M.

Sewing machines.
Cushing y Walpuk.
Moreau, Arnaldo.

Silks.
Guerrero, Ramon.

HUAMANTLA, TLAXCALA.

Agricultural implements, ironware, and hardware.
Hernandez, Miguel.
Ortega, Miguel.
Ruiz, Enrique.

Banker.
Ruiz, Enrique.

Commission merchants.
Mellado, Nicolas.
Ortega, Miguel.
Ruiz, Enrique.

Drugs.
Covarrubias, Gregorio.
Covarrubias, Mariano.
Crespo, José M.
Ramires, Agustin.

Dry goods.
Cairo, Desiderio.
Cairo, José.
Corona, Juan.
Crespo, Luis G.
Fabre, Amador.
Paredes, Julian.
Robert y Ca., S.
Ruiz, Manuel.

Fancy goods.
Hernandez, Miguel.
Ortega, Miguel.
Torreblanca, Miguel.

Groceries and provisions.
Barrera, Fermin.
Corona, Filomeno.
Corona, Manuel.
Cortes, José M.
Cortes, Miguel.
Machuca, Sacramento F. de.
Carbajal, Viuda de.
Estrella, Gabino.
Garcia, Manuel.
Heredia, Miguel.
Hernandez, Antonio.
Lozano, Filomeno.
Machuca, Angel.
Machuca, Angel Vargas.
Mantilla, Cárlos.
Maraver, Demetrio.
Maraver, Sabino.
Marquez, J. de J.
Moreda, Francisco.
Ortega, Adelaide.
Ortega, José M.
Romero, Miguel.
Ruiz y Hermano, Bernardo.

HUAMANTLA, TLAXCALA—Continued.

Fancy goods.
Hernandez, Miguel.
Ortega, Miguel.
Torreblanca, Miguel.

Lithographer.
Jordan, Manuel.

Paints, oils, and varnishes.
Covarrubias, Gregorio.
Ortega, Miguel.

IRAPUATO, GUANAJUATO.

Agricultural implements.
Aguilera, José Refugio.
La Nacional Irapuatense.
Vargas y Hermanos, Juan.

Booksellers.
Aguirre, Franco.
Hernandez, Nicolas.
"La Soledad."

Boots and shoes.
Barbosa, Genaro.
Cervantes, Pablo.
Juarez, Agustin.

Carriages.
Aguilera, José Refugio.

China and glassware.
Flores y Ca., Antonio.

Commission merchants.
Aguilera, Vicente.
Bocanegra, Manuel.
Lopez, Librado.
Peredo, J. M.

Drugs.
Aguirre, Francisco.
Canal, Ignacio.
Cruz, Luis.
Galvan, S.
Gondalez, Aguirre.
Moral, Manuel M. de.
Orozco, Miguel.
Reynoso, Enrique.
Rico, Ampelio F.
Rivera, Apolinar.

Dry goods.
Armand, Napoleon.
Diaz, Vicente.
Flores, Antonio.
Hernandez, Nicolas.
Vargas, Nicolas.
Vallas, Angel.
Vega, Gabriel.
Velasco y Ca., José.

Fancy goods.
Martinez, Susano.
Vega, Gabriel.

IRAPUATO, GUANAJUATO—Continued.

Groceries and provisions.
Vargas, Nicolas.
Velasco y Ca., José.

Hardware.
Acosta, Genaro.
Cerda y Ca., Roman.

Hardware and house furnishings.
Acosta, Genaro.
Alvarado, Guadalupe.
Rangel, Antonio.
Vega, Gabriel.

Hats.
Zepeda, J.

Iron and ironware.
Acosta, Genaro.
Vargas, Nicolas.
Villaseñor, Trinidad.

Music.
Conejo, J.
Gonzalez, Simon.
Marmolejo, Jacobo.

Paints and varnishes.
Acosta, Genaro.
Aguilera y Ca., Guadalupe.
Cerda y Ca., Roman.

Pianos and musical instruments.
Cosio, A.
Gonzalez, Simon.

IXTLAN DEL RIO, TERRITORIO DE TEPIC.

Agricultural implements and ironware.
Cosio, Emilio.
Ortiz, Miguel C.

Commission merchants.
Cosio, Emilio.
Lounegon, Alfredo.
Menchaca, Enrique.
Ortiz, Pablo.

Drugs.
Arriola, Agustin V.
Ortiz, Miguel C.
Parra, José María.

Fancy goods.
Otiz, Miguel C.

Groceries and provisions.
Cosio, Emilio.
Menchaca, Enrique.
Ortiz, Miguel C.

General merchandise.
Aguirre, José María.
Cosio, Emilio.
Espinosa, Guillermo.
Figueroa y Ca., José María.
Menchaca, Enrique.

IXTLAN DEL RIO, TERRITORIO DE TE-PIC—Continued.

General merchandise—Continued.
Monroy y Hermano, Francisco.
Ortiz, Miguel C.
Ortiz, Pablo.
Ortiz, Prisciliano.
Partida y Ca., Flavio.
Pimienta, Manuel.

Hats.
Ortiz, Marcelina Ocegueda de.

Sewing machines.
Ortiz, Prisciliano.

JALAPA, VERACRUZ.

Bankers.
Cerdán, Agustín.
Pasquel, F. de P.

Booksellers and stationers.
Escribano, Manuel.
Luelmo, Pedro M.
Rocha, Manuel M.

China and glassware.
Escribano, Manuel.

Commission merchants.
Casas, Vicente R.
Hoyos Hermanos.
Pastrana, Guillermo.

Drugs.
Cambas, José Rivera.
Casas, Rodolfo.
Crespo, Antonio.
Gutierrez, Manuel Lozada.
Martinez, Señoritas.
Pastrana, Virginia.
Pozo, Juan.
Quiroz, Manuel.
Redondo, Juan Perez.
Trigos, Ildefonso.

Dry goods.
Bouchez, Cárlos.
Cordera, Angel.
Cordero, Luis.
Garcia, Antonio.
Juano y Nieto.
Manuel, Viuda de Emilio.
Oncins y Ca.
Rivera, Antonio Perez.
Rodriguez, J. A.
Sáyago, Mariana.
Teruel, Cárlos García.

Fancy goods.
Bouchez, Cárlos.
Cordero, Luis.
Escribano, Manuel.

JALAPA, VERACRUZ—Continued.

Fancy goods—Continued.
Loaiza, Tomás.
Luelmo, Pedro M.
Rodriguez, José A.

Furniture.
Luelmo, Pedro M.

Groceries and provisions.
Acosta, Cárlos.
Aparicio ó Hijos, Luis.
Barrientos, Emilio.
Dominguez, Basilio.
Escribano, Manuel.
Guevara, Francisco Javier.
Hernandez, Manuel.
Herrera, Joaquin Gomez.
Jimenez, Vicente.
Ramirez, Juan.
Rodriguez, Faustino.
Romero, Mariano.
Sanchez, Manuel Leon.
Terán, Roman.
Valle, Micaela del.
Vela, José M.
Zárate, Francisco.
Zárate, Tomás.

General stores.
Aragon y Martinez.
Cordera, Angel.
Escribano y Ca.
Escobar Hermanos.
Franchechi, Viuda de J.
Guevara, Francisco.
Juarez y Nieto.
Pastorisa.
Romero, Mariano.
Sulueta, Ramon.
Teran, José María.
Zubieta, Ramon.

Hardware.
Bouchez, Cárlos.
Cordero, Luis.
Luelmo, Pedro.
Loaiza, Tomás.

Hatter.
Malpica, Luis.

Jeweler.
Sänger, Emilio.

Sewing machines.
Bouchez, Cárlos.
Garcia, Antonio.
Martines, Antonio.
Oncins y Ca.
Romero, Albino.

JAUMAVE, TAMAULIPAS.

General merchants, grocers, etc.
Garcia, Manuel C.
Gordon, Vicente.
Martinez, Aniseto.
Rivero, Jesus.
Rivero, Sotero.
Trejo, Zeferino.
Vertiz, Romulo S.
Villanueva, Bandel.

JIMENEZ, CHIHUAHUA.

Forwarding and commission agents.
Harmon y Rollins.

General merchants.
Aguilar, T. S.
Alcola, C.
Baca Hnos., A. J.
Bunley, C.
Gonzalez, C.
Nunes, Gabriel.
Pratt, B.
Russak y Ca., Marcus.

JIMENEZ, TAMAULIPAS.

General merchants.
Betancourt, F.
Caballero y Hno., Santos.
De le Fuente, E.
Lazo, Celso.
San Romain, Justo.
Saldivar e Hijo, Benito.

LA BARCA, JALISCO.

Bankers.
Acuña, Inocencio.

Boots and shoes.
Acuña, Inocencio.
Mora, Miguel.
Nuñez, Pomposo.

Carriages.
Santiago, Gregorio.

Commission merchants.
Aceves, Pedro.
Villaseñor, J.

Drugs.
Mendoza, Luis G.
Rio, María Refugio del.

Dry goods.
Acuña, Inocencio.
Castellanos, Fructuoso.
Hernandez, Francisco.
Jimenez, Mariano.
Lara, Ruperto.
Mora, Miguel.
Otero, Alberto Gil
Tamayo, Marino.

Sewing machines.
Mora, Miguel.

LAGOS, JALISCO.

Booksellers.
Gonzalez, Refugio.
Larios, Gerónimo.
Larios, Margarito.

Boots and shoes.
Galvan, F.
Gonzalez, J. B.
Jordan, I.

China and glassware.
Cabrera y Ca., R.
Rodriguez, D.

Commission merchants.
Bocanegra, A. Suc.
Kegel, Augusto.
Rodriguez, Félix.

Drugs.
Aguirre, David Gonzalez.
Bocanegra, J.
Lanuza, F.
Leon, F. G.

Dry goods.
Lozano, A.
Valle y Ca., F. del.
Vega, Pedro.

Fancy goods.
Larios, G.
Larios, M.
Lopez, Pedro, Suc.
Rodriguez, D.

Groceries and provisions.
Cabrera y Ca., R.
Hernandez Hnos.
Larios y Ca., H.
Manriquez, F.
Zuñiga ó Hijo, J. M.

Hardware, iron, and ironware.
Cabrera y Ca.. R.
Gonzalez, Refugio.
Rodriguez, D.

Hatter.
Gonzalez, R.

Lithographer.
Reyna, B.

Paints, oils, and varnishes.
Rodriguez, D.

LAMPAZOS, NUEVO LEON.

Groceries, tobacco, and liquors.
Allen, Juan.
Castano Hermanos, V.
Elizondo, Juan B.
Gonzales, Mauricio.
Gonzales, Roque.
Tovar, José María.

Commission merchants.
Bortoni y Ca., G.
Castano Herms., V.

LA PAZ, LOWER CALIFORNIA.

Boots and shoes.
Cruz, Cresencio.
Chacón, Carmen.
Hong Chong Tai.
Quinteros, Francisco.
Quon Yuen Ley.

Commission merchants.
Cabezud, F.
Moreno, Guillermo.
Silver, William.
Valdovinos, Maximiano.
Viosca, James, jr.

Drugs.
Hidalgo, M. M.
Landero, José.
Santana, Ochoa.

Importers.
Arriola, Agustin.
Cabezud y Ca.
Cota y Pelaez.
Gonzalez é Hijos., M.
Hidalgo y Ca.
Moreno & Alvarado.
Ramirez, Lantaro.
Rivera, G., Suc.
Ruffo, A.
The Pearl Shell Company of Lower California.

Sewing machines.
Canalizo, G.
Cohn, Max W., agent Singer Sewing Machine Co.
Romero, Ignacio M.

LEON, GUANAJUATO.

Agricultural implements.
Alvarado, Luz.
Dávalos y Ca.
Fisch y Ca.
Gonzalez, M.
Heyser, Jorge.
Nuñez, Nestor.

Arms and ammunition.
Beruman, Eufemio.
Olmo, R. del, Suc.
Rembez, B.

Bankers.
Morales, Benigno.
Pöhls y Guedea, Suc.
Rembez y Bezaury.
Servin, Ramon.

Banks.
Sucursal del Banco de Lóndres y México.
Sucursal del Banco Nacional.

LEON, GUANAJUATO—Continued.

Booksellers and stationers.
Campos, Juan N.
Izquierdo, J.
Olmo, R. del, Suc.
Portillo y Guemes.
Villalobos, Rafael.

Boots and shoes.
Barbara, Valente.
Jaqueres, Agustin.
Maldonado, Juan.
Ruiz, Teodoro.
Segura, Lauro.

China and glassware.
Bittrolff y Niemeyer.
Campos, Juan M.
Munguia, Serapio.
Martinez y Hermano, Fernando.
Olmo, Ramon del, Suc.
Perez, José.
Perez, J. A.
Rico, Juan P.
Salas, Fernando Puento.

Clothing.
Barbier, Santiago.
Bessonart y Apesteguy.
Bustamante, Angel.
Echeagaray y Ca.
Garcia, A. de Leon.
Gonzalez y Ca.
Mena, Sabino.
Muñatones, José.
Obregon, Cárlos.
Thommé, Lorenzo.

Clothing, hats, etc.
Aldana, Pablo.
Avila, Sebastian.
Carpio, Cárlos.
Chavez, José.
Delgado, Amado.
Flebe, Joaquin.
Gonzalez, Baltasar.
Hagelstein, Luis.
Hernandez, C.
Lopez y Hermano.
Lopez, Ildefonso.
Malacara, Manuel.
Manguia, Serapio.
Manrique, Santiago.
Muñoz, E.
Ramirez, Victoriano.
Salas, Fernando Puento.
Salgago, Pascual.
Segura, J.
Trueba, Norberto.

LEON, GUANAJUATO—Continued.

Commission merchants.
Alatorre y Araujo.
Alfaro, J. de la Luz.
Alvarado, Luz.
Fisch y Bischoff.
Fuentes y Piña.
Garza, Francisco C.
Gonzalez, Juan M.
Hernandez y Alvarez.
Lopez, Juan S.
Luna, Miguel Luna.
Martinez y Hermano, F.
Mena, Cleto.
Munguia, S.
Pöhls y Guedea, Suc.
Segura, Miguel F.
Torres, Wenceslao.
Zimenez, Salvador.

Dealers in native produce.
Echeagaray y Ca., Suc.
Fuentes y Piña.
Madrazo, Manuel.
Manrique, Santiago.
Rembez y Bezaury.
Valazquez, J.

Drugs.
Acosta, Pedro.
Castro, Juan N.
España, Antonio.
España, Miguel.
Gonzalez, Francisco Aguerro.
Gonzalez, Luis.
Leal y Ca.
Ortiz, José.
Ruiz, Petronilo.

Dry goods.
Barbier, Santiago.
Bessonart.
Brune y James.
De Nava y Ca., Lopez.
Echeagaray y Ca., Suc.
Fisch y Bischoff.
García, Aparicio.
Jamé, Mariano.
Martinez y Hermano, Fernando.
Munatoes, José María.
Obregon, Cárlos.
Pöhls y Guedea.
Portilla y Guemes.
Rico, Juan P.
Salas, Fernando Puento.
Thomé, Lorenzo.
Villalobos, Rafael.

Fancy goods, laces, etc.
Bittrolff y Niemeyer.

LEON, GUANAJUATO—Continued.

Fancy goods, laces, etc.—Continued.
Campos, Juan N.
De Nava y Ca., Lopez.
Echeagaray y Ca.
Fuentes y Piña.
Hermosillo, Amada.
Izquierdo, Zenon.
Oller, Antonio.
Olmo, Ramon del, Suc.
Perez, José A.
Pöhls y Guedea, Suc.
Portillo y Hayser.
Robles, Felipe.

Flour merchants.
Gonzalez, J. M.
Manrique, Santiago.
Raynaud, Julio.
Sierra, Manuel.
Torres, Eulalio.

Furniture dealers.
Bittrolff y Niemeyer.
Fuentes y Piña.
Olmo, Ramon del, Suc.
Pöhls y Guedea, Suc.
Rembez y Bezaury.

Groceries and provisions.
Fernandez, Manuel.
Fisch y Ca.
Gaona, Luis.
Hernandez, Librado.
Manrique, Santiago.
Torres, Wenceslao.

Hardware.
Bittrolff y Niemeyer.
Campos, Juan N.
Martinez y Ca., Fernando.
Olmo, Ramon del, Suc.
Perez, José A.
Rembez y Bezaury.
Robles, Felipe.

Hatters.
Aldama, Pablo.
Aldana, Manuel.
Flebbe, Joaquin.

Iron and ironware.
Gaona, Luis.
Manrique, Santiago.
Rembez y Bezaury.

Lithographer.
Gomez Hermanos.

Pianos and musical instruments.
Bittrolff y Niemeyer.
Cortez, Estanislao.
Olmo, Ramon del, Suc.

LEON, GUANAJUATO—Continued.

Pianos and musical instruments—Continued.
Pöhls y Guedea.
Rico, Juan P.

Sewing machines.
García, Agustin.
Nuñez, Nestor.

Watches and jewelry.
Arnold, Cárlos.
Barroso, Pascual.
Gray, Francisco.
Long, Luis.
Rembez y Bezaury.

Wool exporters.
Garza, Francisco Cortina.
Manrique, Diego.
Muñoz, E.
Muñoz, Ramon.
Oller, Antonio.

LINARES, NUEVO LEON.

Booksellers.
Infante, Modesto.
Perez, Ramon García.

Commission merchant.
Tamez y Tomaseo.

Drugs.
"Aguila."
"Leon."
"Serna."
"Wells."

Dry goods.
Adame, Mariano.
Barrera, Presiliano.
Fuente, Francisco de la.
Garza, J. García.
García, Mariano.
Lozano, Donaciano.
Pequeño, Pantaleon.
Sepúlveda, Genaro.
Sepúlveda, Isaac Garza.
Tamez y Tomaseo.
Vivanco, Manuel.

Fancy goods.
Melendez, José María.
Perez, Ramon García.
Rodriguez, Ramon.
Vidales, Viuda de.

Groceries and provisions.
García, Mariano.
Pequeño, Pantaleon.
Sepúlveda, Genaro.
Sepúlveda, Isaac Garza.
Vivanco, Manuel.

LINARES, NUEVO LEON—Continued.

Hardware.
Fouga, Bernardo.
Tamez y Tomaseo.

Hatters.
Arreaga, Joaquin.
Garza, J. Garcia.
Quijano, Apolinar.
Sepúlveda, Genaro.

Sewing machines.
Larrumbe, Ismael.

MAPIMI, DURANGO.

General merchants.
Darnaud y Hijo.
McMoon, Cosme.
Valadez, Indelacio.
Villareal, Sotero.
Valles, Anto.
Velasco, C.

Mining companies.
Compañía Minera de Penoles. Mining, Smelting, and Refining Company.
Theo. Hoffay, Mgr.
Trowe, Paul G.

MATAMOROS, COAHUILA.

Flour mill.
Rodriguez, Tomás.

General merchants.
Chavez, Dionicio.
Fuente, M. B.
Perez, C. M.
Rodriguez, L.
Vega, G. de la.
Vega, Cristobel.

MATAMOROS, TAMAULIPAS.

Arms and ammunition.
Bielenberg, Jorge.

Bankers.
Iturria y Ca., N.
Nielsen, Enrique.

Banks.
Agencia del "Banco Nacional."
Bank of London, Mexico and South America, limited.
Mexican Railway Bank.

Booksellers and stationers.
Bennevendo, Emilio.
Boesch, J. P.
Cardenas, J. A.
Martinez, Miguel García.
Purdié, Samuel.

MATAMOROS, TAMAULIPAS—Continued.

Carriage dealers.
Chassignet, E.
García, Andrés.
Miranda, Agustin.
Schultz, Federico.

China and glassware.
Muñoz, L.

Commission merchants.
Cavazos, Antonio.
Cross, Meliton.
Gazano, G.
Iturria, Francisco.
Muguerza, Francisco G.
Passement, Alfredo.

Drugs.
Barragan, Miguel.
Brayda, C.
Brayda, Victor.
Bremer, Eduardo.
Calderon, José.

Dry goods.
Arredondo, Manuel.
Bernheim, J.
Boesch, J. P.
Burchard y Hermano.
Cardenas, J. A.
Cross, Meliton H.
Fernandez, Francisco.
Garibay, Lorenzo.
Guinea y Ca., B.
Laviolette, Viuda de.
Longoria, Policarpo.
Miller, Rafael M.
Petitpain, Luis M.
Urtusastegui, B.

Exporters of hides, skins, and domestic produce.
Armendaiz, F.
Cross, J. S. & M.H.
Follain, G.
Neilsen, H.
Yturria, Bernardo.
Yturria y Ca., F.

Fancy goods.
Bennevendo, Emilio.
Boesch, J. P.
Jacques, Levy.

Furniture.
Cross, M. H.
Muñoz, L.
Scherck, Francisco.
Sorbert, Enrique H.

Groceries and provisions.
Arredondo, Manuel.
Cross, M. H.

MATAMOROS, TAMAULIPAS—Continued.

Groceries and provisions—Continued.
Dávila, Francisco.
Gonzalez, José R.
Iturria, Francisco.
Iturria y Ca., F.
Levy, J.
Muguerza, Francisco García.
Muñoz, L.
Portillo, Inocencio.
Raphael & Bloomberg.
Rougier y Ca., Marcelino.

Hardware.
Boesch, J. P.
Doulet, A.
Madrazo, Miguel.
Márquez, Felipe.
Rougier y Ca., Marcelino.
Sansat, Juan.

Importers.
Barragan, M. (drugs).
Bennevendo, M. (cutlery, hardware, and notions).
Bielenberg, G. (arms, ammunition, jewelry, and sewing machines).
Brayda, V. (drugs).
Brown, W. (undertakers' supplies).
Cross, J. S. & M. H. (general merchandise).
Darrouzel, J. (liquors).
Guinea & Co., B. (dry goods).
Laviolette, Viuda de (dry goods).
Levy, J. (groceries and notions).
Madrazo, M. (hardware).
McMillan, John (tinware).
Miller, R. M. (dry goods).
Muñoz, L., Suc. (general merchandise).
Muguerza, F. Garcia (general merchandise).
Petitpain, L. N. (dry goods).
Rougier y Ca., M. (general merchandise).
Raphael & Bloomberg (general merchandise).
Urtuzastegui, B. (dry goods).

Jewelers.
Bielenberg, Jorge.
Belemberg y Quast.
Hinojosa, José A.

Sewing machines.
Bielenberg, Jorge.
Cardenas, Manuel.

MATEHUALA, SAN LUIS POTOSI.

Druggists.
Baigen, José.
Canal, José.

MATEHUALA, SAN LUIS POTOSI—Cont'd.

General merchants.
Arrieta, Nemesio.
Barrenechea Hermanos.
Caezo y Ca., I.
Garza y Ca., José A.
Herrera y Inquanzo.
Moreno, Anastasio.
Soriano y Ca., Jesus.
Trevino Hermanos.
Vargas, Concepcion.
Viadero. Hilario.

Woolen mill.
Romano, Adriano.

MAZATLAN, SINALOA.

Agricultural implements.
Charpentier, Reynaud y Ca.
De Leon Hnos., Diaz.
Heymann, Suc.
Loubet y Ca.

Arms and ammunition.
Alexandre y Gaskin, J. J.
De Leon Hnos., Diaz.

Bank.
National Bank of Mexico (branch).

Bankers.
Bartning, Suc.
Echeguren Hnos. y Sobrinos.
Escobar, J.
Melchers, Suc.
Somollera Hnos.

Booksellers and stationers.
Charpentier, Reynaud y Ca.
De Leon Hnos., Diaz.
Heymann, Suc.
Paez, Donaciano.

Boots and shoes.
Coppel Hnos.
Dantoja, Hijo y Ca., José C.

Carriage dealers.
Moneda, José.
Montiel, J.

China and glassware.
Charpentier, Reynaud y Ca.
De Leon Hnos., Diaz.
Heymann, Suc.

Commission merchants.
Cruz, Joaquin Santa.
Echeguren, Francisco.
Farber, Juan C.
García, Genaro.
Gonzalez, Guillermo.
Guzman y Varela.
Haas y Ca., Guillermo.

MAZATLAN, SINALOA—Continued.

Commission merchants—Continued.
Hecht, Enrique.
Kelton, E. G.
Pantoja, Pijo y Ca., José C.
Retes y Ca., Peiro.
Reynaud, Suc.
Romero, Desiderio.
Schmidt, Enrique.
Schober, Leopoldo.
Zeiss, Rodolfo.

Drugs.
Canoblo Angel.
Espinosa, Luis C.
Kördell, Federico.
Nuño, Angel.
Valadez, J. J.
Zúñiga y Ca., M.

Dry goods.
Bartning, Suc.
Beltran, Lucas.
Escobar, José.
Haas y Ca., G.
Herrerías, Marcelino.
Izaguirre y Esquerra.
Maldonado, Juana R. de.
Melchers, Suc.
Mendia y Ca., Hernandez.
Paez, Donaciano.
Rios, Juana.
Somellera Hnos.
Tapia, Librado A.
Vega Hnos.
Vega, Manuel de la.

Fancy goods.
Charpentier, Reynau y Ca.
Dávalos, Abrahan.
De Leon Hnos., Diaz.
Escobar, J.
Escobar, José.
Heymann, Suc.
Maldonado, Juana R. de.
Maxemin, J.
Melchers, Suc.
Mendez y Ca., Hernandéz.
Nuñez, Francisco.
Tapia, Librado Andrés.

Furniture.
Leon, Santiago.
Loubet y Ca.
Rea, Luis.

Groceries and provisions.
Andrew, R.
Bartning, Suc.
Beltran, M., Suc

MAZATLAN, SINALOA—Continued.

Groceries and provisions—Continued.
Campos, Santiago.
Canobio, Angel.
Cardinault, Edmundo.
Charpentier, Reynaud y Ca.
De Leon Hnos., Diaz.
Elorza y Ca., Tamés, Suc.
Goldschmidt y Ca., Suc.
Gutierrez, Antonio.
Heymann, Suc.
Hidalgo, Careaga y Ca.
Longavay, Gregorio.
Loubet y Ca.
Magaynes, Gumesindo.
Maxemin, J.
Melchers, Suc.
Peña, Antonio de la.
Rey, Viuda de.
Sotomayor, L. M.
Vargas, Rafael.

Hardware, iron, and ironware.
Ayala, Catarino.
Charpentier, Reynaud y Ca.
De Leon Hnos., Diaz.
Heymann, Suc.
Hidalgo, Careaga y Ca.
Loubert y Ca.

Hatters.
Carrion, Francisco.
Flores, Juan.
Hernandez, Trinidàd.
Muro Hnos.
Schober, L.

Importers.
Bartning, Suc.
Charpentier, Reynaud y Ca.
De Leon Hnos., Diaz.
Goldschmidt y Ca., Suc.
Haas y Ca., G.
Heymann. Suc.
Mendia y Ca., Hernandez.
Peña, Antonio de la.
Tapia, Andrés L.

Jewelers.
Escudero, Ignacio.
Marshall, Juan L.

Lithographer.
Retés, Miguel.

Manufacturers.
Felton Bros., ice, brooms, and matches.
Retés, Miguel, cardboard.

Paints, oils, etc.
Rea, L.

MAZATLAN, SINALOA—Continued.

Sewing machines.
Haas y Ca., G.
Melchers, Suc.
Mendia y Ca., Hernandez.

Silk goods.
Mendia y Ca., Hernandez.
Yuen y Ca., Kwong Yue.

MERIDA, YUCATAN.

Agricultural implements, arms, etc.
Albertos, Leopoldo.
Alvarez y Ca.
Ayroa, Gregorio Diégo.
Crasemann, Suc.
Dondé y Ca., M.
Escalante, E.
Esenat, Antonio.
Gutierrez y Ca.
Gutierrez, L.
Gutierrez, Ricardo.
Haro y Ca., B.
Juanes, Ramon P.
Molina y Ca., O.
Nicolin Hermanos.
Ponce y Ca., José M.
Ravensburg, German.

Bankers.
Crasemann, Succ.
Dondé y Ca., M.
Escalante, E.
Haro y Ca.
Molina y Ca.
Perez y Ca., B. Azner.

Banks.
Banco Mercantil de Yucatan.
Banco Yucateco.
Bank of London, Mexico and South America, Ltd.
National Bank of Mexico.

Booksellers and stationers.
Baqueiro Hnos., Gomez.
Canto, Gil.
Canton, Eraclio G.
Diaz, Gustavo.
Luis Bros.
Martin y Espinosa, José.
Solis y Ca., Aznar.

Boots and shoes.
Aresiequi, E.
Cámara, Pedro.
Darrillo y Ca., Basilio.
Carvajal, Juan Gonzalez.
Carrillo, Benito.

MERIDA, YUCATAN—Continued.

Boots and shoes—Continued.
Ciriaco, Espejo.
Cayoe, Eulalio.
Hernandez, Juan de D.
Hernandez, Mateo.
Hernandez, Molina J.
Mendoza, Guadalupe.
Mendoza, José G.
Pren, J. G.
Rubio, Lucas.
Ruiz, Castillo.
Ruiz, Domingo.
Ruiz, Viuda de.
Salazar, Martin.
Villamil, P.

China and glassware.
Carranca, Camilo.
Cervera, V.
Sosa, F.

Commission merchants.
Cervera y Ca., Venancio.
Cicero Hermanos y Ca.
Conton, Rodolfo G.
Contreras y Ca., P. Peon.
Diégo y Ca., A. Cano.
Dondé y Ca., M.
Escalante, E.
Escuder, Diego Hernandez.
Escudero, Rafael Hernandez.
Gonzalez y Ca., Luis G.
Haro y Ca.
Laviada, Miguel.
Lisarraga y Ca., J.
Luis Bros.
Molina, Felipe.
Molina, O.
Perez, B. Aznar.
Regil y Vales.
Torre é Hijos, G.

Druggists.
Aguilar, Santiago.
Andrade, Rafael.
Avila, Cruz.
Casares, Eduardo.
Castillo, Gerado.
Font, José.
García, Francisco López.
Negron, Francisco.
Pacheco, Lorenzo.
Perez, Pinto.
Pinto, Pablo.
Ponce, Abelardo.
Ponce, W.
Reguera, Pedro.
Rivera y Ca.

MERIDA, YUCATAN—Continued.

Druggists—Continued.
Rubis, Francisco.
Trancoso, Pedro.
Villamil, Miguel.

Dry goods.
Alpuche y Ca., Tomás.
Alvarez y Ca.
Cano y Ca., B.
Canton Frexas.
Capetillo y Arce.
Cáseres L., Isaac.
Castillo, Rivas y Ca.
Dondé y Ca., M.
García. Fajardo, A.
Gonzalez, Pablo.
Herrera, Nemesio.
Hübbe, E.
Padron, Sergio.
Patron, Loza y Ca.
Pinel, Manuel.
Ponce y Ca., M. y A.
Toledo y Ca., Viuda de.
Vales y Ca.

Fancy goods.
Crasemann, Suc.
Laviada y Ca.
Ravensburg y Ca., German.
Tenorio y Ca.
Vales y Ca., C.

Furniture.
Castillo y Ca., G. A.
Crasemann, Suc.
Leopoldo, Alberto.
Perez y Ca., Delfin.
Ponce y Ca., R.
Tenorio y Ca., C.
Zavala, Lorenzo.

Groceries and provisions.
Almeyda, Manuel.
Alonso y Ca., E.
Aragon, Juan.
Aragona, Daniel.
Atocha y Ca., R.
Avila, Faustino.
Bolio, Adolfo.
Bolio Hermanos.
Calp, Jaime.
Cámara é Hijos, C.
Campo, Joaquin.
Cano y Ca., A. Diego.
Cano y Ca., B.
Canto, G.

MERIDA, YUCATAN—Continued.

Groceries and provisions—Continued.
Canton, R. Gregorio.
Canton, Rogerio G.
Carrillo, José C.
Carrillo, Magdaleno.
Castillo, Juan B.
Castillo, Pedro.
Cervera y Ca.
Cevera, Venancio.
Cicero Hermanos y Ca.
Concha, Miguel.
Contreras y Ca., Peon.
Espinosa y Ca.
Ferraes y Ca., N.
Fuentes, Bartolomé.
Fuentes y Ca.
Fuentes, Francisco.
Gallareta, Manuel J.
Gonzalez y Ca.
Gonzalez, Francisco.
Haro y Ca.
Hidalgo, José de.
Hübbe, José Millet.
Lopez, E. Franco.
Lujon, Gabriel.
Mena, Melquiades.
Mendicuto, Isidro.
Milan y Ca., Ramon E.
Milon, Gregorio.
Molina y Ca., O.
Mota, Tiburcio.
Ortiz y Ca.
Ortiz, Viuda de.
Palma Hermanos, Suc.
Ramos, Domingo P.
Rojas, Felipe R.
Vales y Ca.
Villamil y Ca.
Zapata y Ca., J.

Hardware, tools, etc.
Alvarez y Ca.
Ayroa, Gregorio Diego.
Crasemann, Suc.
Dondé, Manuel.
Esenat, A.
Gutierrez y Ca., R.
Gutierrez, L., Suc.
Juanes, Ramon P.
Laviala y Ca.
Leopoldo, Alberto.
Ravensberg y Ca., G.
Nicolin Hermanos.
Villamil Hnos. y Ca.

Hatters.
Encalada, C.
Medina, Pedro.

MERIDA, YUCATAN—Continued.

Hatters—Continued.
Sansores, E.
Serrano, L.

House furnishing goods.
Burgos, José D.
Rivas, Bosénito.
Sanchez, José Ruz.
Valencia, Domingo.

Importers, exporters, and commission merchants.
Alcina, Agustin.
Alvarez y Ca. (importers dry goods).
Ancona, Nicanor (exporters, hemp).
Aznar, Benito.
Aznar, Perez y Ca.
Bolio, Eduardo.
Cámara, Camilo (exporters, hemp).
Cámara y Ca., P.
Cámara, Manuel Dondé.
Cano y Ca., B. (importers, groceries and provisions).
Canton, Amado.
Cicero, Hermanos y Ca. (importers, groceries and provisions).
Cicero, Pedro.
Contreras y Ca., P. Peon (importers, groceries and provisions).
Crasemann y Ca., S. (importers, fancy goods and notions).
Diego y Ca., A. Cano (importers, groceries and provisions).
Dondé y Ca., M. (exporters, hemp).
Escalante y Bates, E. (exporters, hemp).
Frexas y Ca., J. Canton (importers, dry goods).
Galera, Dario.
Gardarillas, Marcelino.
Gonzalez, Pablo (exporters, hemp).
Gonzalez, Pedro.
Gutierrez y Ca., L. (importers, fancy goods and notions).
Gutierrez y Ca., R. (importers, fancy goods and notions).
Gutierrez, Eduardo Gonzalez (exporter, hemp).
Haro y Ca.
Haro y Concha.
Haro y Pena.
Hernandez, Rafael (exporter, hemp).
Hoffman y Dominguez.
Hoyo, Celestino Ruis del.
Hoyo, Francisco Ruis del.
Ibarra y Ca.
Laviada, Miguel.
Laviado y Ca. (importers, fancy goods and notions).
Lizarraga y Ca., F.
Loza y Ca., Patron (importers, dry goods).
Luis Bros.

MERIDA, YUCATAN—Continued.

Importers, exporters, and commission merchants—Continued.

Milan, Gregorio.
Milina, Felipe.
Molina y Ca., O. (exporters, hemp).
Ortiz y Ca., Viuda de (importers, groceries and provisions).
Padron, Sergio (importer, dry goods).
Palma Hnos., Suc. (importers, groceries and provisions).
Peon, Augusto (exporters, hemp).
Perez y Ca.
Pinelo, Manuel (importer, dry goods).
Ponce y Ca., J. M. (exporters, hemp).
Ravensburg y Ca., G. (exporters, hemp and importers fancy goods).
Regil, Viuda ó Hijo de.
Rivas y Ca., Castillo (importers, dry goods).
Rotger y Ca., Pedro.
Rucio, Manuel.
Seal, Pedro.
Toledo y Ca., Viuda de.
Vales y Ca. (importers, dry goods).
Zapata y Ca., J. (importers, groceries and provisions).

Jewelers.

Aragon, Paulino.
Barcelo y Mateo.
Basulto, Joaquin.
Basulto, Juan E.
Cabrera, Eulalio.
Carranca, Camilo.
Carrillo, Loreto.
Claudon, Luis.
Dellenberg, Enrique.
Dominguez, Cárlos.
Flores, Tiburcio.
Monforte, Juan C.
Quen, Figio.
Ramirez, José D.
Rodriguez, Francisco.
Rodriguez, Saturnio.
Rosel, Policarpo.
Sanchez, Mateo.

Lithographers.

Caballero, Ricardo B.
Cuevas, J. D.
Gamboa, José.
Quijano, Santiago Bolio.

Music stores.

Cuevas, Juan de.
Gasque, Ramon.
Luis Bros.
Ortis y Ca., Viuda de.

MERIDA, YUCATAN—Continued.

Sewing machines.

Caballero y Ca., A.
Crasemann, Suc.
Gutiérrez, L., Suc.

MEXICO CITY, MEXICO.

Acids and chemicals.

Delgado, Rafael.
Droguería Universal.
Eguía Lis, José María.
Félix y Ca., Cárlos.
Garduño, Gabriel.
Laigle, Ernesto.
Marin, Crescencio.

Agencies for foreign goods (sale by sample).

Alcántara, F. de P.
Alfaro, Ignacio F. de.
Argüelles, Ed.
Astorquiza y Vivanco.
Bannister, Juan.
Benitez, Landa y Ca.
Biquard y Ca.
Borel, Luis.
Bossler y Ca., Germán.
Cavaroc, L.
Carrillo, Ruiz y Rivera.
Castelló, Gutiérrez y Ca.
Commageré y Peon.
"Compañía Commercial Austriaca Transatlántica."
Dahlhaus, Edmundo.
Daus, Federico O.
Dunbar, Diego S.
Düring y Ca., M.
Echeverría, Pedro.
Franco y Santaella.
Gastón y Ca., José M.
García, Cuervo y Menendez.
Gendroy, M.
Goetschel y Ca.
Gonzalez Hnos.
Gutiérrez, Miguel N.
Ibarra, Vicente.
Irigoyen, Martin de.
Jacques P. y J.
Jacques y Eyssantier.
Morlet, Teófilo.
Merino Hnos. y Ca.
Navarro y Ca., F.
Nieto, Juan N.
Pfeiffer, Federico (represents American wines and liquors).
Perez y Ca., P.
Reboulet, Louis.
Reppeto, Juan.
Rico, Gil.

MEXICO CITY, MEXICO—Continued.

Agencies for foreign goods (sale by sample)—Continued.

Ritter y Ca., Federico.
Ruiz, Ballesteros y Ca.
Ruth y Ca.
Salcido, Rafael.
Scheibe, G.
Samuel Hermanos.
Seeger, Guernsey y Ca.
Stankiewicz, G. M.
Torre, Rodolfo de la.
Viadero, J.
Villarroel, Jesus M.
Woodrow, Guillermo B.
Zaccarini y Ca., A.

Agencies for American manufacturers only (sale by sample).

Meyer, J. H.
Sriber, Cárlos.

Agricultural implements.

Adams, F., Suc.
Arce, J.
Badoin y Ca., E.
Becerer, Cárlos.
Boker y Ca., Roberto.
Bowes, Scott, Read, Campbell & Co.
Charreton Hnos.
Dorn y Ca., Guillermo.
Garth, German.
Guthiel, A.
Hoffmann Hermanos.
Hulvershorn y Ca.
Jacot, Alejandro.
Leffmann é Hijos.
Lhose y Ca., Guillermo.
Lhose, S.
New York Plow Co.
Malo y Ca., Alberto.
Rio, José María del.
Sommer y Ca., Rapp.
Ulrick y Ca., D.
Wexel y Degress.
White, Juan.

Arms and ammunition.

Aizpuru, Patricio.
Alva, Ramon.
Alvarado, Joaquin.
Alvarez, Modesto.
Andrade, Antonio.
Anzoutegal, José.
Aranzubla, Manuel.
Arena, Joaquin.
Argandar, Alejandro.
Boche, Alfredo.
Carrion, C.
Combaluzier, A.
Mendiola y Ca., M.

MEXICO CITY, MEXICO—Continued.

Arms and ammunition—Continued.

Morel, C.
Pagliri, Fernando.
Quintana Hnos.
Sanchez, D.
Urbarrena y Quintana.
Wexel y De Gress.

Army contractors, for arms, ammunition, clothing, shoes, etc. .

García, T. L.
Llamedo, Juan.
Pombo, Ignacio.

Artificial flowers.

Albert y Ca., J., Suc.
Deuchler y Kern.
Hulvershorn y Ca., G.
Priani, Antonio M.

Banks and bankers.

"Banco Nacional de México."
"Banco de Lóndres y México."
"Banco Internacional ó Hipotecario de México."
Barron, Forbes y Ca.
Benecke, Est., Suc.
Bermejillo Hnos.
Cardeña y Ca., Suc.
García Teruel, Luis.
Gargollo, José.
Gross & Co.
Ibañez, Manuel.
Jacobowicz, Fabian de.
Lavie y Ca.
Llamedo, Juan.
Martín y Ca., P.
Martinez y Ca.
Mijares y Ca., A.
Ortiz de la Huerta, R.
Pelaez, Pedro.
Rio, F. de P. del.
Samuel Hermanos.
Sanchez, Delfin.
Scherer y Ca., H.
Sommer, Herrmann y Ca.
Struck y Ca., Gustavo.
Teresa, Nicolás de.
Watson, Phillips y Ca.

Blast furnaces.

Honey, Richard, San Juan de Latran, No. 12, City of Mexico, proprietor of :
   Apulco Furnace, Apulco, Hidalgo.
   Comanja Furnace, Comanja, Jalisco.
   Encarnacion and Guadalupe Furnaces, Encarnacion and Guadalupe, Hidalgo.
   La Trinidad Furnace, La Trinidad, Hidalgo (post-office, Tulancingo).
   Los Reyes Furnace, Los Reyes, Hidalgo post-office. Telancingo).)
   San Miguel Furnace, Zacualtipan, Hidalgo.

MEXICO CITY, MEXICO—Continued.

Booksellers and stationers.
Abadiano, Viuda é Hijos de.
Aguilar é Hijos.
Aguilar y Ortiz.
Andrade y Morales, Suc.
Andrade y Soriano.
Arnaldo, Luis G.
Ballescá y Ca., J.
Bernard, A.
Bouret, Cárlos.
Budin, N., Suc.
Buxó y Ca., J.
Cambeses, M.
Canols, Juan.
Cueva, Ramon.
Chavez, N.
Diaz de Leon, Francisco.
Dorn, Guillermo.
Dublau y Ca.
Fernandez y Ca., M.
Fuente Párres, J. de la.
Gallegos, Hermanos.
Garay, Adrian de.
Griffin y Campbell.
Hamilton, H. P.
Herrara, J.
Herrera y Benavides.
Hoeck, F. P.
Jens, J. F.
Kauser y Martin.
Lions y Ca., H. y V.
Lüdert, Federico A.
Martin, Luis.
Martinez, Vicente.
Maza y Ca.
Montauriol, Cárlos.
Murguía, Eduardo.
Nichols, Benito. Suc.
Nicolau, Joaquin.
Ortega, J.
Ortega y Vazquez.
Parres y Ca., F., Suc.
Portu, E.
Remirez y Ca., J.
Rivera y Rico, Edmundo.
Rivera y Rio, José.
Sainz, Ricardo.
Sanchez, C.
Spaulding, D. S.
Tamborrel, Cárlos.
Treuber Hermanos.
Urias, J.
Urrea, Antonio R.
Valdes y Cueva.
Vaugier, Federico.
Vincourt, Cárlos.

MEXICO CITY, MEXICO—Continued.

Boots and shoes.
Abarca, Ausencio.
Aceves, Juan A.
Alegre, Julian.
Alfaro, Juan.
Almonte, Francisco.
Araujo, Jorge.
Arellano, Arcadio.
Arévalo, Juan.
Arpide y Ca., U.
Ascoitia, Catalina.
Ataide, Prisciliano.
Barranco, Vicente.
Becherel, Josefa.
Benitez, B. G.
Bermeo, Antonio.
Bernal, Marcelino.
Bernal, Ramos, Angel.
Briseño, Juan.
Briseño, Manuel.
Bucardo, Trinidad.
Buenrostro, José.
Camacho, Jacinto.
Carmona, Cárlos.
Carmona, Esther.
Carillo, Pablo.
Casillas, Rafael.
Castillo, Fermin del.
Cazadero, Angela.
Celada, Teófilo.
Cervantes, Enrique.
Chacon y Ca., Gabriel.
Dávalos, Faustino.
Dávalos y Hno., F.
Davó, Francisco.
Daza, Jacinto.
Delgado, Agustin.
Díaz, J.
Diosdado, F. C.
Dominguez Hnos.
Espinoza, Eulogio.
Espinoza, Ildefonso.
Esteva, Sabino.
Fernandez y Ca., B.
Flores, J.
Fournier, Joseph.
García, Loreto.
García, Luis G.
García, Paulino.
Gomez, Antonio.
Gomez, L. G.
Gonzalez, Catalina.
Gonzalez, German.
Gonzalez, J.
Gonzalez, Juan.
Gonzalez, M.

MEXICO CITY, MEXICO—Continued.

Boots and shoes—Continued.

Gonzalez, Muñoz M.
Gorostiaga, J. M.
Guadarrama, Salvador.
Gutiérrez y Hnos., José D.
Guzman, Marcos.
Halsey, Cristina.
Hormigo, Manuel.
Hurtado, Atanasio.
Islas, Guadalupe.
Iturriaga, E.
Izunza, Ignacio.
Jaramillo, Braulio.
Juarez, Hilario.
Lara, Daniel.
Leite, J.
Leon, Diégo.
Lopez, José María.
López, Juan.
Lopez, Juan C.
Lopez, Geogorio.
Martinez, Adolfo.
Martinez, Concepción.
Martinez, Evaristo.
Martinez, Jacinto.
Mayorga, Justo.
Mejia, Luis.
Mena, Rosa.
Mendez, Antonio.
Mendoza, J. M.
Migoni, Luis.
Molina, Hilario.
Monroy, G.
Monroy, Guadalupe.
Montaño. Angel.
Montes de Oca, Antonio.
Montes de Oca, Lázaro.
Morales, Angel.
Morales, Lucas.
Moreno, Ana María.
Muñoz, Abrahan.
Muñoz, Juan.
Muñoz, Mariano.
Muriel, Pedro.
Nava, Agustina.
Nava, Juana.
Nogueron, Apolonio.
Núñez, S.
Núñez, Sabino.
Ocampo, Jacobo.
Ordoñez, Pedro.
Ortiz, J.
Ortiz, Ramon.
Ortiz, Teodoro.
Pascal, M.
Peñaflor, Marcos.

MEXICO CITY, MEXICO—Continued.

Boots and shoes—Continued.

Perea, Petrea A. de.
Perez, Juan.
Perez, Petra.
Pichardo y Ca., R. A.
Pietra Santa, A.
Pietra Santa, Edo.
Portacarrero, Agustin.
Portron, Luis.
Pozo, Badillo Juan.
Ramirez, Eusebio.
Ramirez, Santillana A.
Reyes, Apolonio.
Rivero, Paz.
Robles, Porfirio.
Rodríguez, E.
Rodríguez, Pedro.
Rojas, Casimiro.
Rojas, Soledad.
Romano, Conpn.
Rosas, José.
Ruiz, Manl.
Saldaña, Migl.
Saladaña Hijo, T.
Salgado, Pedro Ma.
Santa María, Feliciana.
Santa María y Ca., L.
Sarmiento, Marco.
Segura, G.
Segura, M.
Sevilla y Villagrán.
Sigales, Canuto.
Sobrino, Ramón.
Solachi, Romualda.
Somera, Albino.
Soto, José Ma.
Soto, María.
Suarez, María Refugio.
Tapia, Francisco.
Tapia, Luis G.
Telles, Gumesindo.
Tesorero, Atanasio.
Tinoco, Luciano.
Torres, Antonio.
Torres, Ma. de J.
Trejo, Francisco.
Troncoso, Anselmo.
Trueba, Enrique.
Urosa, Angel.
Valencia, Miguel.
Valle, J. A. del.
Vara, Mauro.
Varas de Valdez, J.
Vargas, Pedro.
Vega, Atanasio.
Victorio, José.

180

MEXICO.

MEXICO CITY, MEXICO—Continued.

Boots and shoes—Continued.
Zariñana y Ca., J. L.
Zetina y Ca., C. B.
Zetina, J.

Brick, lime, and cement.
Aduna, Sabina.
Alva, Manuel.
Alvarez, Cipriano.
Alvarez, J.
Alvarez, Márcos.
Alvarez, Teodoro.
Arizcorreta y Ca., Lauro.
Cabrera, Guadalupe.
Cárdenas, A.
Cardona, Juan.
Córdova, Luis F.
Castillo, Antonio.
Compañía Manufacturera de Cal Hidráulica.
Fernandez, Simona.
Flores, Manuel M.
Forey, Juan.
Galicia, Cayetano.
García, Leon.
Garnica, José.
Hähener, Pablo.
Idrac, Cárlos.
Lama, Angel de la.
López, Simon.
Lozano, Soledad.
Luengas, Luis A.
Mijares, R.
Montes de Oca.
Negrete, Benito.
Núñez Juana.
Olguín Silvo.
Olvera, Dolores.
Omaña, Fernando.
Omaña, Gregorio.
Omaña, María de J.
Pacheo, C.
Perez, Cecilio.
Priani, A.
Rangel, Francisco.
Rangel y Uribe.
Rey, José.
Reyes, Teodoro.
Rio, M. del.
Rodriguez, E.
Romo, Salvador.
Rosa y Rangel, Ma.
Rosas, Manuel.
Rosellon, Domingo.
Rubalra, Francisco.
Sanchez, Isaac.

MEXICO CITY, MEXICO—Continued.

Brick, lime, and cement—Continued.
Sanchez, Joaquin.
Sil, Jacinto.
Silva, Jesus.
Talonio, Lorenzo.
Tapia, Juan.
Unda, Gabriel.
Vargas, Benigna.
Vargas, Ladislao.
Vargas, Luisa.
Vasquez, Albino de.
Vasquez, Ambrosio.
Velasquez, Antonio O.
Velazquez, Manuel.
Vera, Cirilo.
Viñas, Edo.
Violante, Juan.
Zamora, Miguel.
Zúñiga, Francisco.

Carriages.
Balderes, Avineda.
Boker y Ca., Roberto.
Ceaser, Joaquin.
Ducastaing y Ca., E.
Elcoro y Ca., Valentín.
Maza, José.
Moricard, J.
Nava, Felipe.
Olaez, Agustin.
Orozco, Victor E.
Pascal, M.
Ramirez, Juan.
Risser, Adolfo.
Sanchez, F. G.
Seres y Ca., Blas.
Suarez, Gabriel Martinez.
Vent, Andrés.
Wexel y De Gress.
Wilson y Ca., T. H., Suc.
Wilson Hijos y Ca., Hugo.

Carriageware.
Boker y Ca., Roberto.
Combaluzier, A.
Rio, José María del.

China and glassware.
Aguirre y Hnos., I.
Albear, Miguel.
Aranjo, Mariano.
Avalos, Camilo.
Becerril de Corneja, A.
Bravo y Blumenkorn.
Calsseller, Alberto.
Calvet, Victor.

MEXICO CITY, MEXICO—Continued.

China and glassware—Continued.

Cornejo Hno., Aurelio.
Dorn y Ca., Guillermo.
Derflinger, Antonio.
Dupont, Juan M.
Durruty, D.
Espejel M.
Guerrero y Tangassi.
Gutierrez, Nestor.
Hildebrand y Ca., F.
Lohse y Ca., G., Suc.
Mendez, Francisco.
Ocampo, Agustin.
Olea, Mariano.
Pino, Tomás del.
Priani, Antonio M.
Rigal, Lubet y Ca.
Rio, J. M. del.
Rufo y Ca.
Sarraille, J.
Septien y Serrano,
Sommer, Hermann y Ca.
Troncoso y Cilveti.
Uriarte, M. del Rio.
Wilson, Thomas H., Suc.

Commission merchants.

Astorquiza y Vivanco.
Bannister, Juan.
Barral y Loréa.
Biquard y Ca., Av.
Bischoff, Emilio.
Borda, Ignacio.
Borel, Luis.
Borrell, Justiniano.
Bossier y Ca., German.
Campos, Manuel S.
Castelló Gutierrez y Ca.
Cosio, Victorio.
Coussirat y Costés.
Diaz Barreiro, Ramon.
Dosal y Hno., José.
Duran, Gabriel.
Ebner y Borneman.
Escurdía Hermanos.
Esteinon y Roumagnère.
Eyssautier, Melchor.
Figueroa, Isauro.
Franco, Santaella y Ca.
Gándara y Ca., J.
García Hnos. y Ca.
Gaston y Ca., J. M.
Gilly, Juan.
Gonzales Guera, A.
Graef, Federico.
Gutierrez, Miguel N.

MEXICO CITY, MEXICO—Continued.

Commission merchants—Continued.

Haro, Agustin.
Heredia, Guillermo.
Jacques, P. y J.
Knight, Bruce.
Lohse, Santiago C.
López y Teresa.
Malgor, Martin.
Manuel, Clemente.
Mijares y Ca., A.
Monroy y Morales.
Mora y Ca., Casto de la.
Morlet, Ituart y Cea.
Moyano y Bermudez.
Muñiz, Félix.
Ortega, Paulino.
Payró, Leandro.
Pfeiffer y Ca.
Prado, C.
Puga, Max.
Reboulet, Louis.
Revuelta, Valentin.
Ritter y Ca., Fedo.
Rojas, Luis.
Rovalo, Agustin.
Ruiz, Ballesteros y Ca.
Rul, Manuel P.
Sainz, Justiniano.
Salcido, Rafael.
Samuel, Lionel.
Santiago. Ag de.
Santa Marina é Hijos.
Scheibe, Gust.
Schultze y Ca., Suc.
Sobrino y Barreneche.
Suarez, Mac.
Uhink y Ca.
Villarroel y Gutierrez.
Watson, Phillips y Ca.
Walker y Borda.

Contractors (mines and railways).

Adam, F., Suc.
Anciaux y Ca.
Arce y Co., J.
Arozarena, Rafael M. de.
Bannister, Juan.
Boker y Ca., Roberto.
Brinckman y Turnbull.
Catera, Francisco.
Gore, T. S.
Hoas, G.
Hamson, J. H.
Prez y Ca.
Read y Campbell, Sn. J.
Seeger, Guernsey y Ca.

MEXICO CITY, MEXICO—Continued.

Coopers.
Buzon, Francisco.
Camiragua, José.
Campos, Eduardo.
Enriquez, Ciriaco.
Flores, J.
Medina, Francisco.
Osorio de Vazquez, G.
Soriano, Paulino.
Villegas, Guadalupe.
Villareal, Juan B.

Cordage.
Albiso, Sabino.
Basurto, Manuel.
Baez, Felipa.
Buenrestro, F.
Campos, J.
Chavez, Albino.
Enciso, M.
Galván, Ignacio.
Gonzalez, B.
Hernandez, J. S.
Hernandez, J. M.
Lozado, Santos.
Lozano, José Ma.
Lozano, J. G.
Oviedo, M. Dolores.
Pimentel, Rafael.
Pinto y Leon Miguel.
Prado, Andrés del.
Soto, José M.
Sotres y Carbajal M.
Vazquez, Mariano.

Drugs (homeopathic).
Gonzalez é Hijo, J.

Drugs, retail.
Aguilera y Ca.; E.
Artigas y Ortega.
Almaráz, Andrés.
Alonso, Ed. M.
Altamirano, Fern.
Amelio, Blas.
Arellano, Manuel.
Arteaga, Ramon.
Arrillaga y Patiño.
Aveleyra Hnos.
Avila, Miguel.
Barradas, Francisco.
Bautista, Rafael.
Becerril, Manuel.
Beguerisse, A.
Beguerisse y Ca.
Bermejo, Rafael B.
Bermudez, Antonio.
Bernal, Francisco.
Bustillos, J. F.
Cañas de Iturralde, Juan.

MEXICO CITY, MEXICO—Continued.

Drugs, retail—Continued.
Carmona y Valle, J. M.
Cervantes, Silva A.
Chabolla, Francisco.
Chavez, J.
Cienfuegos, Francisco.
Coronado, Agustin.
Dominguez, E.
Dominguez, Enr.
Flores, Francisco A.
Franco, Bolañ, s A.
Frey, Eugenio.
Gaona, Juan B.
Geray, Adrian de.
García, Colin N.
Gomez Tagle, Isidorio.
Gonzalez, Luis.
Gonzalez, Ignacio.
Conzalez, J. D.
Gordillo, Francisco B.
Grisi, Vda. de.
Guerrero, Agust.n.
Guerrero, Florentino.
• Hernandez, Agustin.
Huguenin, Cárlos.
Iriarte, Manuel.
Jáuregui, M. J.
Kaska, Dr. Francisco.
Kentzler, F. Emil.
Larrea, F L. de.
Larrea, Lelo de.
Lazo de la Vega, J. M.
Licea, Vicente.
Liz, Benjamin.
Lucio, Victor.
Luna y Drusina.
Lozano y Hno. Mar.
Llamas, Francisco.
Marin, C.
Marin, Hidalgo N.
Marin y Ca., N.
Márquez, Miguel M.
Martinez, Agustin.
Mena, A.
Moncayo, J. A.
Montaño, Ramon.
Montes de Oca, Fr.
Morales, Enrique.
Morales, José D.
Navarrete, R. M.
Oñate, J.
Orihuela de G.
Oropeza, Felipe S.
Oropeza, Marcial.
Ortega, Lorenzo A.
Patiño, Cárlos M.
Patiño, Francisco.
Patiño, Guadalupe.

MEXICO CITY, MEXICO—Continued.

Drugs, retail—Continued.
Payró, A.
Peña, Manuel.
Perez, Severiano.
Portilla, Guillermo.
Prado, R. N.
Ramirez, Juan.
Reyes, Julio.
Rio de la Loza, Francisco.
Rio de la Loza, Max.
Rio de la Loza, Rafael.
Salazar, Manuel A.
Sanchez, M.
Sanchez, Manuel.
Sanders, Bernardo.
Schmitz, A.
Schmitz y Ca., A.
Senisson. Gmo.
Tajona, J.
Torres, Manuel.
Tricio, Salvador.
Urbina, Manuel.
Uribe, Alejandro.
Urueta, Bernardo.
Vargas, J. H.
Vazquez, Miguel.
Vera, Julio D.
Verdugo P.
Villagran, S.
Villaseña, Luis R.
Vidales, Nestor.
Zúñiga, Miguel.

Drugs, wholesale.
Andrea y Soriano.
Bachiller.
Bennet y Ca., Suc.
Biester, Enrique.
Brito, Alfonso.
Bustillo, José E.
Carman, Henry B.
Carmona y Aparicio.
Chorne, Agustin.
Daumy, Serafina C.
Droguería Universal.
Falero, J.
Farine y Sanders.
Felix y Ca., Cárlos.
Gallardo, Ignacio.
Gudiño, Justo Z.
Hinojosa, Pedro.
Labadie y Ca., J., Suc.
Leiter, Miguel E.
Perez, Z. M.
Spyer, Joseph.
Tejera, Luis.
Uihlein, José Suc.
Vargas y Ca.

MEXICO CITY, MEXICO—Continued.

Dry goods :
Clothing. wholesale (imported goods)—
Bellon y Ca., M.
Brehm y Ca., Suc.
Chauvet y Ca., Max.
Donnadieu y Ca., F.
Ebrard y Ca.
Lambert, Reynaud y Ca.
Levy y Martin, A.
Meyran Hermanos.
Ollivier y Ca., J.
Reynaud y Ca., A.
Richaud, Aubert y Ca.
Robert y Ca., S.
Rovés y Ca., B. Suc.
Schmidt y Bourjau.
Schultze y Ca., Suc.
Signoret Honnorat y Ca.
Struck y Ca., Gustavo.
Tron y Ca., J.
Weil y Ca., Simon.

Clothing, retail (imported goods)—
Alvarez, Tostado M.
Barquin y Ca., Felipe.
Gomez y Ca., M.
Haure, Mirande Juan.
Macías, Gaspar.
Mirande, Eduardo.
Migoya, Manuel.
Rivera Hermanos.
Santaolalla y Ca., D.
Valdes, Antonio.

Clothing, retail (domestic and imported goods)—
Alvarez y Ca., V.
Allemand, Victoriano.
Andrade, Luis G.
Arróyave, Francisco V.
Blancas, Juana.
Castillo Ruperto, A. del.
Castro, Luz.
Cervantes, Sixto.
Chavez ó Hijos, Viuda de.
Cuellar y Ca., C.
Gomez, Jacinto.
Hurtado, Espinosa y Ca., L.
Mirande, Ed.
Monroy, Rafael.
Muñoz, Trinidad.
Mondragon, Benita A. de.
Moll, Juan.
Olvera, Anastasio.
Piedras, Antonio.
Pérez, Petronila.
Pérez, Rosa.
Pérez, Sixto.
Preaut, Pablo.

MEXICO CITY, MEXICO—Continued.

Dry goods—Continued.

Clothing, retail (domestic and imported goods)
—Continued.

Rangel, Margarita.
Rocha, Plácido.
Rocha, Tranquilino.
Rubio, José María.
Sanchez, Felipe.
Vazquez, Antonio.
Zaldivar, Felipe.

Clothing for men and boys—

Adalid, Ceron ó Hijo, J.
Carmona, Ildefonso.
Carmona y Velazquez, J. M.
Carmona y Vilchis, V.
Franck y Ca., M.
Garcia, Benitez y Ca.
Montes de Oca, A.
Quiroga y Ca., José.
Tovar, José María.

Clothing for women and children—

Bayonne, E.
Chauvet y Ca., Max.
Coblentz, Benito.
Deuchler y Kern.
Fourcade y Ca., A.
Laborde, Wartenweiler y Ca.

Cloths, imported—

Brehm y Ca., Suc.
Gendrop, Th.
Levy y Martin, A.
Struck y Ca., Gustavo.
Weil y Ca., Simon.

Millinery—

Burgaud, F.
Carballeda y Fougerat.
Carrilles y Ca., M.
Coblentz, Benito.
Coblentz, Silvano.
Flores, Gonzales y Ca., J.
Guérin y Ca.
Hoppenstedt y Ca., T.
Lagrave, Pablo.
Larrea y Cordero, J.
Levy y Ca., A.
Levy y Martin, A.
Maurel, F.
Morales y Ca., Edo.
Polack, Hipo.
Prado, Godoy y Ca.
Prado y Ca., M. del.
Rodrigo, L.
Rodriguez y Ca., S.
Schweitzer, Vda. ó Hijos de.
Vega y Ca., Eur. S.

MEXICO CITY, MEXICO—Continued.

Dry goods—Continued.

Passementerie and lace goods—

Biquard y Ca.'
Deuchler y Kern.
López, Demetrio.
López de Bárcena, Magdna.
Martinez, Lucas.
Pujol, Antonio.
Valdez, Estanislao.
Velasco, Melchora.

Silk goods, wholesale—

Albert y Ca., Julio, Suc.
Brehm y Ca., Suc.
Horn y Ca., A.

Silk goods, wholesale and retail—

Albert y Ca., Julio. Suc.,
Deuchler y Kern.
Hulvershorn y Ca., G.
Laborde, Wartenweiler y Ca.

Silk goods, retail—

Aguirre, Soledad.
Albert y Ca., Julio, Suc,
Alvarez, Severa.
Andrade, María de J.
Angon, Dolores.
Anguiano, Simona.
Azcárate, Abrahan.
Baez, Isabel.
Ballestreros, Serápia.
Barrera, Benita.
Barros, Ignacia.
Basurto, Cayetano.
Berthier, Carmen.
Besserer, Sofía.
Blanc y Hnos., J.
Blanco, Ano.
Blanco y Ca., Luis G.
Bonilla, Juliana.
Calderon, Adelaida.
Camacho, Dolores.
Cañizo, Loreto.
Cásares, Refugio.
Cohen, F.
Contreras y Ca., Franco.
Corisola, Adela.
Cornejó, María.
Crespo, Concn.
Cruz, Efrén.
Cuervo, Juan.
Cueva, Ramon.
Diaz, Felicitas.
Echeverria, Teresa L. de.
Elizaga de Huici.
Escobar, Refugio.
Escudero, Luz.
España, Rosa.

MEXICO CITY, MEXICO—Continued.
Dry goods—Continued.
Silk goods, retail—Continued.
  Espejel, Clementina.
  Espinosa, Romana.
  Estrada, Refugio.
  Fernandez, Merced.
  Garcia, Dolores.
  Godoi, Concepción.
  Góngora, Angel.
  Gonzales, Agn.
  Gonzales, Juana.
  Gonzales, Justa. .
  Guadalajará y Ca., R.
  Guerrero, Teresa.
  Gutierrez, Cecilia.
  Hermann, Matilde.
  Izaquirre de Meriuo.
  Jayme, María de J.
  Larrea, M. L. de.
  Lascano, Loreto Ch. de.
  Lavillette, A.
  Lefebvre, A.
  Legorreta, Josefina.
  Lujo, Francisco.
  Martel y Sanchez.
  Mendoza, Concepción B. de.
  Merino, Soledad.
  Migoni, Carmen.
  Momo y Miguel.
  Morquecho, Petra R.
  Muñoz, Rosario.
  Olmos, Soledad.
  Omaña, Cárlos.
  Ornelas, Elena.
  O'Farrell, Rómulo.
  Pacheco. Romero M.
  Pampillon, Piedad.
  Pimentel, Guadalupe.
  Pineda, J.
  Poza, Dionisia.
  Pruneda, Matilde.
  Ramirez, Angela V. de.
  Reyes, Luz.
  Ricard, A. de.
  Romero, Antonio.
  Romero, Cenobio.
  Romero, María.
  Rosales, María A.
  Rosello de Beltran, I.
  Salazar de Mulcelo. D.
  Salazar, Francisco.
  Sandoval, Miguel.
  Santiesteban, María.
  Sencie de Morales.
  Sequeyro, F.
  Serano, Dolores.
  Signoret. Honorat y.
  Solis, Loreto.

MEXICO CITY, MEXICO—Continued.
Dry goods—Continued.
Silk goods, retail—Continued.
  Sotomayor, L.
  Terroba, Manuel M.
  Torres, Guadalupe.
  Trejo de Vega.
  Valle, Rafael G. del.
  Varela, Luis.
  Varela, Refugio A. de.
  Vargas, Guadalupe.
  Vilchis, Francisca.
  Vidaurrázuga, Mariana.
  Zuvizar, María Refugio.

Silk, linen, and hosiery importers.
  Albet y Ca., Suc.
  Bellon y Ca.
  Brehm y Ca.
  Burgaud, F.
  Chauvet y Ca., Max.
  Deuchler y Kern.
  Donnadieu y Ca., F.
  Ebrard y Ca.
  Frank, M.
  Fourcade y Ca., A.
  Garcin, Faudon y Ca.
  Guérin y Ca.
  Horn y Ca., A.
  Laborde, Wartenweiler y Ca.
  Levy y Martin.
  Meyran Hermanos.
  Ollivier y Ca., J.
  Reynaud y Ca., A.
  Richaud, Aubert y Ca.
  Robert y Ca., S.
  Rovés y Ca., B., Suc.
  Schultz y Ca., Suc.
  Schmidt y Bourjeau.
  Signoret, Honorat y Ca.
  Struck, Gustavo.
  Tron y Ca.
  Weil, Simon y Ca.

Tapestries, draperies, and carpetings.
  Albert y Ca., Julio, Suc.
  Boysen y Wintermantel.
  Compañía Comercial Austriaca-Trasatlántica.
  Fontaine, Pedro.
  Hoffmann y Urquía, A.
  Huhn. Edo. M.
  Nieto, Vicente.
  Urrutia, Lázaro.
  Velasco, Cárlos L.

Electrotypers.
  Bustamante, Muguía.
  Cordoba, Pedro.
  Llagostera, Pedro.
  Mata, Filomeno.

MEXICO CITY, MEXICO—Continued.

Engravers.
Bouligny y Ca.(limitada).
Dalmau, F. de P.
Diener y Rothacker.
Galaviz, Anto. H.
Gutiérrez, Lucio.
Mosser, Luis.
Pagaza, V.
Pastrana, G. R.
Peña, Tomás de la.

Fancy goods (wholesale and retail).
Billonneau, Cassou y Ca.
Bravo y Blumenkron.
Delarue, Eugenio.
Diehl y Ca., M.
Düring y Ca.
Elcoro, López y Ca.
Gahrtz, German.
Gutiérrez, Miguel.
Hulvershorn y Ca.
Lefèbvre, Alfredo.
Lohse y Ca., G., Succ.
Pezaña, Marcial.
Philipp y Ca., Max A.
Río, José Maria del.
Sommer, Herrmann y Ca.
Uriarte y del Río, M.
Zivy y Ca., D.

Fancy goods (retail).
Albert y Ca., J., Suc.
Argudin, Juan S.
Arnaldo, Luis G.
Barrera, Josefa.
Bayonne, E.
Billonneau, Cassou y Ca.
Björklund y Joransson, C. A.
Bonnerue y Ca.
Calvert, Victor.
Candil, Gonzalo.
Coblentz, Benito.
Deuchler y Kern.
Deverdun, C.
Escalante, Zeferino.
Garcia, Cuervo y Menendez.
Garibay, Agustin.
Gonzalez, Bonifacio.
Granados, Julio.
Guerrero y Tangassi.
Gutiérrez, Miguel.
Hillebrand y Ca., E.
Iglesias, Miguel.
Laborde, Wartenweiler y Ca.
Lefebvre A., Refugio.
Lohse y Ca., G., Succ.
Morel, Camilo.
Pastor, Santo.
Pivardière, Adolfo.
Quintana Hnos.

MEXICO CITY, MEXICO—Continued.

Fancy goods (retail)—Continued.
Raynaud, Eugenio.
Rigal, Lubet y Ca.
Sommer, Herrmann y Ca.
Spaulding, D. S.
Tellez y Ca., T.
Troncoso y Silveti.

Fireworks dealers.
Guardiola, Valentin.
Mata, E.
Pereira Máximo.
Pereyda, Máximo.
Torres, Dario.

Flour and feed.
Alvarez, M.
Barron, José J.
Bracho, Alberto A.
Casso, Manuel.
Castro, Vicente de P.
Ceballos, J.
Cejudo, Abel.
Charreton Hermanos.
Diffonty, Enrique.
Galnares, G.
Llamedo, Juan.
Monasterio, Bernardo.
Pacheco, Miguel.
Piña, Pedro.

Foundries.
Bandoin y Ca.
Brandi, J.
Bustamante, José E.
Charreton Hnos.
Dantan, Luis.
Duchatesu. C.
Finanmore y Ca.
Fusco, Antonio.
Iglesias y Valezzi.
Malo y Ca., Alberto.
Marshall y Ca.
Munguía é Hijos, P.
Neveu Hermanos.
Pascuali, J. M.

Furniture, imported.
Benac, B.
Boker y Ca., Roberto.
Boysen y Wintermantel.
Bravo y Blumenkron.
Combaluzier, A.
Compañía Comercial Austriaca Trasatlántica.
Fortuño, Manuel.
Hillebrand y Ca., E.
Hoffman y Urquia, A.
Kuhn, E. M.
Laborde, Wartenweiler y Ca.
Lohse y Ca., G., Suc.
Río, José Maria del.

MEXICO CITY, MEXICO—Continued.

Furniture, imported—Continued.
Sommer, Herrmann y Ca.
Urrutia, Lázaro.
Velasco, Cárlos L.
Furniture, imported and domestic.
Aldana, Victor.
Arteaga, Francisco.
Ayllón, Fernando.
Barrera y Cd., José.
Barezynski Hnos.
Benag, B., Pte.
Boysen y Wintermantel.
Calderon, Manuel.
Carrillo, Cornelio.
Chávarri, Juan J. de.
Chavarría, Juan B.
Delgado, Eusebio.
Fontaine, Pedro.
Garnica, María L. de.
Garnica, José M.
Garrido, J. M.
Gutierrez, Manuela.
Herrera, Gabriel.
Herrera, Juan.
Hoffmann y Urquia, A.
Ingolsbee y Furbish.
Kuhn, E. M.
Lara, Adrian.
Martinez, Gonzalo.
Martinez Miguel.
Mondragón, Porfiria.
Olvera, Antonio.
Padilla, Epifanio.
Palacio, Mariano.
Quintana Hnos.
Rico, Lorenzo.
Rodriguez, Blas C.
Ruiz de Garrido.
Sanchez, Enrique.
Sota y Ca., P. de la.
Urrutía, Lázaro.
Velasco, Cárlos L.
Villaverde, Inés.
Wienery y Ca., Robt. J. F.
Zendejas, Plácido.
Gas fixtures, lamps, etc.
Aguirre y Hnos., I.
Bennet, Juan A., Suc.
Boker y Ca., Roberto.
Cejudo, Felipe.
Compañía Comercial Austriaca Trasatlántica.
Dorn, Guillermo.
Finlay y Ca., J. J.
Fortuño, Manuel.
Gabrtz, German.
Hillebrand y Ca., E.
Izquierdo y Garibay.

MEXICO CITY, MEXICO—Continued.

Gas fixtures, lamps, etc.—Continued.
Leffman é Hijos, Martin.
Lohse y Ca., G., Suc.
Lopez y Ca., Elcoso.
Max, A. Philip.
Rio, J. M. del.
Roa, Eduardo.
Sommer y Ca., Hermann.
Valdes y Rufo.
General merchandise.
Aburto, Isidoro.
Aldama, Victor.
Alfaro y Piña, Manuel.
Altuna Hnos.
Alonso, Ramón.
Alvarez y García.
Alvarez, Salvador.
Arenal, Luis.
Ballesteros, Antonia.
Bárcena, Manuel.
Becerril, Angela.
Becerril, Estéban A.
Berruecos, José Ma.
Bustillos, Santos.
Butrón, R.
Calderón, M. Manuel.
Calderón, M. Francisco.
Campillo Rafael.
Contreras, Angela S. de.
Cortez, Fidencio.
Diaz de Thompson, G.
Dozal, S.
Elzaurdia, Domingo V.
Espinosa, Vicente.
Espinosa, Francisco.
Fernández, Gregorio.
Franco, Ricardo.
García, Diego.
García, José.
Garrido, Dionisio.
Gonzalez y Ca., A.
Goñi, Vicente.
Gutierrez, Juan.
Gutierrez, Julian.
Guzmán, José.
Hermosa Hnos.
Irastorza Hnos.
Junco, Angel.
Lopez y Ca., A.
Llamas, Porfiria.
Llop, Franco.
Manilla, Vicente.
Mejía, Matéa.
Milla, G.
Milla, Mariano.
Molleda y Ca., Manl.
Ocharán, Félix.

MEXICO CITY, MEXICO—Continued.

General merchandise—Continued.

Orea, Constanzo.
Ortiz, Juan R.
Pedregal, Manuel.
Perez, Gomez Manuel.
Perez, José.
Purón, Francisco.
Ramirez, Gumesindo.
Rivera, Antonio.
Rivera, María.
Rodrigo, N.
Rodriguez y Ca.
Saenz, Rafael.
Sanchez, Angel.
Sastrias, Juan.
Sordo, Vicente.
Soto, Juan Pablo.
Torno. José del.
Uribe, José.
Urrutia, Juan.
Varela, Amado.
Via y Sobrada, Pedro.
Villar, Alejo.
Zapata, José B.
Zaldivar, Sostenes.
Zaválburo, José.

Glass plate and mirror.

Aguirre, Ignacio.
Araujo, Mariano.
Arnaldo, Luis G.
Azcona, José.
Castro, Bern.
Derflinger y Ca., A.
Dorn y Ca., G.
Jimenez, Miguel.
Hildebrand y Ca.
Martinez, Agustin.
Martinez y Ca.
Maya, Flor M.
Sarraillé, Juan.
Septien y Serrano.
Wissel, N.

Groceries and provisions:

Groceries and provisions (imported)—

Abascal y Perez.
Alonso, Vicente.
Baranda Hnos.
Barreneche y Ca., S.
Basagoiti y Posada.
Gutierrez y Ca., Quintin.
Lavie y Ca.
Martinez del Cerro y Ca.
Noriega, A., Suc.
Noriega, Ignacio de.
Ortiz Hnos., Antonio.
Ponton Hnos.
Ponton, Ramón.
Rico, Gil.

MEXICO CITY, MEXICO—Continued.

Groceries and provisions—Continued.

Groceries and provisions (imported)—Contin'd.

Rolla y Ca., A.
Rovalo, Agustin.
Sanchez, Ambrosio.
Solano, Claudio.
Sauto, Muñúzuri y Ca.
Toriello, Guerra José.
Torre Hnos.
Trueba Hnos.
Uhink Hnos. y Zahn.
Uhink y Ca.
Zepeda, Francisco.

Preserved food (imported).

Bazax, Justino.
Coqui y Ca., F.
Genin, Viuda de A.
Gutierrez y Ca., Quintin.
Mason y Fernandez.
Sanchez, Ambrosio.
Silvani y Ca., Enrique.
Uhink Hnos. y Zahn.
Zepeda, Francisco.

Groceries and provisions (stores).

Aceves, José María.
Aceves, Guadalupe.
Acha, Saturnino de.
Aguirre, Antonio.
Aja, Rosendo.
Alanis, Manuel.
Alexandre y Cisneros.
Alfaro, Rafael.
Alonso, Romano.
Alonso, José Simon.
Alonso y Salvadores.
Alvarado, Santiago.
Alvarez, Antonio.
Alvarez y Gonzalez.
Alvarez, Santiago.
Amaro, Santos C.
Amaya, Luis G.
Amezcua, Pedro.
Aparicio, Enrique.
Aparicio y Hermano.
Arce y Ca., M.
Arce, Maximino.
Areño, Hermanos, F.
Arena, Venancio Z.
Arroyo, Manuel.
Badillo, Eulalia.
Bahena, Irenea.
Bárcena, Manuel.
Bárcena, Victor.
Barragan, Gregorio.
Barreda, Manuel.
Barro, Juan.
Benet, José.
Benet y Ca.

MEXICO CITY, MEXICO—Continued.
Groceries and provisions—Continued.
Groceries and provisions, stores—Continued.

Bobadilla, Arcadio.
Borel, Urbano G. de.
Bravo, José María.
Bustamante, Robustiano.
Cabrera, Maximino.
Camacho, Ricardo.
Campo, José.
Campos, Francisco.
Camus, Ramon.
Cañas, Cayetano.
Cañas, Juan.
Cárdenas, Antonio.
Carrandi, Pedro.
Carrera, Lizardo.
Caso, Juan.
Castellanos, Cristina.
Castillo y Acevedo Hno.
Castro, José María.
Castro, Juan M.
Celada Hermano.
Celcrio, Benito.
Celorio, Rufino.
Celorio y Diaz.
Cobian, José.
Cofiño, Lúcas.
Crespo, Francisco.
Crespo, Manuel.
Crespo, Nicanor.
Cué, Fernando.
Cué y Ca., Tomás.
Diaz, Catarina.
Diaz, Epifanio.
Diaz, Manuel S.
Diégo y Suarez.
Donesteve, Jacinto.
Espinosa y Ca., F.
Fernandez, D.
Fernandez, Campillo.
Fernandez, Santiago.
Fernandez, Serafin.
Ferrer y Ca., Angel.
Flores, Leopoldo.
Flores, Telesfora.
Fuente y Gutierrez.
Gainza, Romualdo.
Galarza, Maximo.
Galvan, Ignacio L.
Gallegos, Antonia.
Gamedo, Francisco.
Gamez, Hesiquio.
Garay Hermano.
Garces y Hno.
García, Alejandro.
García, Alonso José.
García, Angel.
García, Antonio.

MEXICO CITY, MEXICO—Continued.
Groceries and provisions—Continued.
Groceries and provisions, stores—Continued.

García y Hno., Francisco.
García, Leopoldo.
García, Manuel.
García y Cué.
García, H.
García, Sordo, M.
Garrido, Dionisio.
Gavito y Ca., Victor.
Giles, Francisco.
Gomez, Alfredo.
Gomez Hermano.
Gomez, Tomás.
Gonzalez y Ca., M.
Gonzalez, Atilano.
Gonzalez, Costales y Solares.
Gonzalez, Felix.
Gonzalez, Fernando.
Gonzalez, José.
Gonzalez, Lope.
Gonzalez, Mariano.
Gonzalez, Máximo.
Gonzalez, Portillo José.
Gonzalez, Sanchez B.
Gonzalez, Timoteo.
Gorostiago Hnos.
Granada, Manuel.
Granada, Pedro de.
Gutierrez, Antonio.
Gutierrez, Diego.
Gutierrez, Jacinto.
Gutierrez Pelaez, Juan.
Gutierrez, Severiano.
Gutierrez, Severino.
Gutierrez y Sierra.
Helguera, José Ma.
Hermosilla, Eduardo.
Hernandez, Antonio.
Hernandez, Juana.
Hernandez y Rodriguez.
Herrera, Cristóbal.
Herrera, Juan.
Herrera, Rogelio.
Herrero, Manuel.
Hevia, Juan.
Huerta, Emilio.
Huerta, Rafael.
Huerta y Prieto.
Ibarra, Juan.
Iturriaga, Enrique.
Jimenez, Miguel.
Junco y Sobrino.
Lamadrid, Gabriel.
Lechuga, Miguel.
Llano, Pedro del.
Loidi, Gabino.
López, Arturo.

MEXICO CITY, MEXICO—Continued.

Groceries and provisions—Continued.
Groceries and provisions, stores—Continued.

López, Froilan.
López, Saturnino.
López, Telésforo.
López y Sanchez.
Lozano, Donato M.
Machin, Santiago.
Madariaga y Paralez.
Márquez, Francisco.
Márquez, Juan.
Martinez, Enrique.
Martinez, Felipe.
Martinez, Francisco de P.
Martinez, Isidra.
Martinez, Manuel.
Martinez, Ponciano.
Martinez y Ca.
Mazon y Fernandez.
Melgosa, Angel.
Mendoza, Francisco H.
Mendoza, Sobrino José.
Mijares, Juan.
Mijares, Vicente.
Mondragon, Jacinto José.
Montiel, Antonio.
Morales, Ignacio.
Morales, Lorenzo.
Nareda, Antonio.
Navarro, T.
Noceda y Hermano.
Noriega, Joaquin.
Noriega, Pablo.
Noriega y Alonso.
Noriega y Barrial.
Novoa, Domingo.
Novoa Hermanos.
Olmos, Tiburcio.
Oropeza, Demetrio.
Oropeza y García.
Orraca José.
Ortiz, Alberto.
Ortiz, Faustino.
Oruó y Hermano, Angel.
Pacheco, Tomás.
Pagaza, Angel.
Palau, Ramón.
Pedregal, Gumesd. N.
Pedregal, Noriega M.
Pedregal, Sanchez Pedro.
Perales, Juan.
Perez y Hermano, Ed.
Perez, Fernandez A.
Perez, Facundo.
Perez, Fernandez.
Perez, José.

MEXICO CITY, MEXICO—Continued.

Groceries and provisions—Continued.
Groceries and provisions, stores—Continued.

Perez y Echenique.
Perez y Martinez.
Pesquera, Ramón.
Portilla, Ramón.
Posada Hnos. y Ca.
Posada, Juan.
Posada y Osorio.
Posada y Pardo.
Posada y Ca., José.
Prado, Isaac.
Prieto, Juan.
Prieto, Ramón.
Puertas, Joaquin.
Puertas, Pedro.
Puertas y Hermano, Pedro.
Quintana, Benigno.
Ramirez, Aristeo.
Ramirez, Maximiano.
Rendon, Eligio.
Reyes, Anselmo.
Reyes, Perez F.
Reyes, Simon.
Riancho, Francisco.
Riego y España.
Riego y Sainz.
Rio del Ramón y Man.
Rivera, Gaspar.
Rivero, José María.
Rivero y Perez.
Robina y Arenas.
Robina y Ca., J.
Rodriguez, Dionisio.
Rodriguez, Francisco.
Rodriguez, Rafael.
Rojo, Andrés.
Romano y Ca., M.
Rosado, M.
Rosado, Pedro.
Rosales, Ausencio.
Rosales, Javier.
Rosales y Ramos, A.
Rozado, Pedro.
Ruenes, Basilio.
Ruiz, Hernandez.
Ruiz, Ignacio.
Ruiz, Luis G.
Ruiz, Romana R. de.
Ruiz, Rafael.
Ruiz y Ca.
Sainz, Julian.
Sainz, M.
Sainz y Hnos.
San Cristobal, Lúcas.
San Martin, Francisco.

MEXICO CITY, MEXICO—Continued.

Groceries and provisions—Continued.
Groceries and provisions, stores—Continued.
Sanchez, J.
Sanchez, Julian.
Sanchez, Leopoldo.
Sanchez, Valentin.
Sanchez Hnos. y Ca.
Sanchez y Ca.
Sanchez y del Villar.
Sanchez y Fernandez.
Sanchez y Ortega.
Serrano, Antonio.
Sicilia, J.
Silva, Gerardo.
Silva, J. María.
Sisniega, Fernando.
Sobrino, S.
Sordo, Isidro.
Sordo, José.
Sordo, Juan.
Sordo, Juan S.
Sordo, Noriega Isidro.
Sordo Hnos.
Sordo y Ca., H.
Sordo, Ramón H.
Sordo, Tomás.
Sosa, Leonardo.
Sosa, Santiago.
Soto, Vicente G.
Sotomayor, José G.
Sotres y Hnos, Cosme.
Sotres, José.
Tamés, Miguel.
Tapia, Mariano.
Tapia, Vicente G.
Tores, J.
Torno, Francisco del.
Torno, Guillermo del.
Trueba. Andrés.
Trueba y Calleja.
Ugalde y Ca., F. R.
Urquijo y Ruiz.
Urriza y Berraonda.
Valdéz, Trid.
Valle y Ca., F.
Valle y Velar.
Vazquez y Ca., M. M.
Vazquez, Urbana.
Vega, Balvino de la.
Vega y Fuentes.
Vega y Gutierrez.
Vegas, Juan Gutierrez.
Vela y Ruisanchez.
Verdeja Hnos.
Vergara, Galdo M.
Vidal y Ca., M.

MEXICO CITY, MEXICO—Continued.

Groceries and provisions—Continued.
Groceries and provisions, stores—Continued.
Villar, Emilio.
Villar, Ignacio.
Villeda, A.
Yarto, Isidro.
Zayas de Valasco, M.
Zepeda, Franco.
Zorrilla, J. Fausto.
Sugar, wholesale.
Compañía en Participación de Frutos Nacionales.
Torre Hnos., Isidoro de la.
Sugar and liquors.
Rovalo A.
Gunpowder.
Boche, Alfredo.
Boker y Ca., Roberto.
Düring y Ca., M.
Philipp y Ca., Max A.
Hardware.
Brass bedsteads.
Bernal, Angel.
Boker y Ca., Roberto.
Filardi, Nicolás.
Fortuño, Manuel.
Inastrillas, F.
Linet, Luis.
Lopez Mata, Antonio.
Mestas y Garro.
Rio, José Ma. del.
Salazar, Bernardino.
Sommer, Herrmann y Ca.
Brassware.
Boker y Ca., Roberto.
Fortuño, Manuel.
Lohse y Ca., Suc., G.
Philipp y Ca., Max A.
Sommer, Herrmann y Ca.
Hardware, wholesale and retail.
Aguirre Hnos., Ignacio.
Boker y Ca., Roberto.
Castañeda, Telésforo.
Combaluzier, A.
Delarue, Eugenio.
Düring y Ca., M.
Elcoro, López y Ca.
Gahrtz, German.
Guerrero y Tangassi.
Lohse y Ca., Suc., G.
Rio, José M. del.
Sommer, Herrmann y Ca.
Hardware, retail.
Agis, Alfredo.
Alvarez, José.

MEXICO CITY, MEXICO—Continued.

Hardware—Continued.
Hardware, retail—Continued.
  Amador, C. J.
  Angulo, Luis.
  Aranda, Trinidad.
  Bernal, Antonio.
  Coria de Cerezo, R.
  Díaz, Gonzalez.
  Fernández, Bartola.
  Gamper, Guillermo.
  Garza, Manuel.
  García, Pedro.
  García, R.
  Gonzalez, Eduardo.
  Gonzalez, Paulina.
  Gonzalez, Rosa L.
  Granados, Rodrigo.
  Herrera, Catalina.
  Hijar, Francisco.
  Jimenez, Felipe.
  Jimenez, Sebástian.
  Leite, J., Guadalupe.
  Lopez, Manuel.
  Marmolejo, Ruperto.
  Navarro, Agustin.
  Olivera, J.
  Ortinez, F.
  Paredes, J.
  Patiño, Cecilio.
  Pezaña, Marcial.
  Posadas, Luis.
  Ramos, Luisa.
  Rangel, Lucio.
  Reyes, Nicolasa.
  Rodríguez, J. M.
  Rojas, Lauro.
  Rosales, Pedro.
  Sandoval Guillermo.
  Soriano, J. R.
  Vazquez, Cármen.
  Vergara, Anastacio.
  Zamora, Enriqueta.
Iron and ironware.
  Elcoro y Ca., Valentin.
  Charreton, Hermanos.
  Honey, Ricardo.
  Rio, José María del.
Hats, wholesale.
  Albert y Ca., Julio, Suc.
  Borel, Luis.
  Compañía Comercial Austriaca-Trasatlántica.
  Horn y Ca., A.
  Zölly Hermanos.
Hats, wholesale and retail.
  Dallet y Ca.
  Landwher y Medina Suc.

MEXICO CITY, MEXICO—Continued.

Hats, wholesale and retail—Continued.
  Marquez, Modesto.
  Pellotier y Ca., Tho.
  Warnholtz y Ca. Suc.
  Zölly Hermanos.
Hats for ladies.
  Anciaux, Teresa.
  Bayonne, E.
  Chesneau, Anna.
  Delafontaine, Paulina.
  Deuchler y Kern.
  Fourcade y Ca., A.
  Laborde, Wartenweiler y Ca.
  Landwehr y Medina Suc.
  Martel y Sanche.
  Warnholtz y Ca. Suc.
  Zölly Hermanos.
Hats, retail.
  Alanís Franco.
  Alfaro, Ausencio.
  Alfaro, Pantaleon.
  Aparicio, Franco. S.
  Beltran, Josefa.
  Bermúdez, J. C.
  Blanco y Ca., Manl. B.
  Buendia, Trinidad.
  Cacho, Camilo.
  Calo, Donaciano.
  Castillo, Joaquin.
  Castillo, Luis F.
  Dávalos, J. L.
  Dávalos, Agustin.
  Garduño, Felipe.
  Gómez y Ca., Anto.
  Gómez, Gabriel.
  Gonzalez, Agapito.
  Gonzalez, Victor.
  Hernandez, Zeferino.
  Herrera y Ca., A.
  Idrac y Ca., T. F.
  Jollinez, Henrique.
  Lobato, Enrique.
  López, Amado.
  Mateos. Ignacio.
  Molino, Pablo.
  Perez, Francisco.
  Perez, Trinidad.
  Portocarrero, Agustin.
  Rangel, Abraham.
  Rangel, José Asuncion.
  Rodriguez, Isaac.
  Romero, José.
  Sanchez y Ca., V.
  Serrano, Crispin.
  Talavera, Tomás.

MEXICO CITY, MEXICO—Continued.

Hats, retail—Continued.
Talavera, Francisco.
Torres, Anasta.io.
Torres, Valeriano.
Trejo y Nava.
Trujillo, Francisco.
Urbina, Mánuel.
Yurén, Luis.
Zaldivar, Francisco.
Zúñiga. Severo.

House furnishing goods and tinware.
Aburto, H.
Aschart, N.
Ballesteros, J.
Bonilla, Gil.
Escanden, Antonio.
Forre, M. de la.
García, J.
Martinez, Juan.
Pinto, Manuel.
Sanchez, V.
Vazquez, Victoriano.

Iron merchants.
Bizet Hermanos.
Bourlou, Alfredo.
Charreton Hermanos.
Gutheil, A.
Leffman 6 Hijos, M.
Lhose, S.
Lhose y Ca., G.
Lopez y Ca., Elcoro.
Petherie, Juan.
Rio, J. M. del.
Spaulding, Cadenas.
Togno y Ca.

Jewelry, watches, and silverware:
Dealers in jewelry.
Arana, Manuel.
Bittrolff, Hugo.
Diener y Rothacker.
Jacot, Alejandro.
Klein, Ricardo.
Lagarrigue, Luis, Suc.
Lagarrigue, Luis.
Laue, German.
Landa, Miguel R.
Llop, J.
Muiron y Ca.
Perret, Enrique.
Rodriguez, E.
Schäfer, Martin.
Schreiber y Ca.
Sommer, E.
Van Rooten y Debroé, Suc.
White, A.
Zivy y Hauser, Suc.

MEXICO CITY, MEXICO—Continued.

Dealers in watches and clocks.
Duhart, Vicente H.
Hernandez Aguirre, Tomas.
Prolongo, Federico.
Vazquez, Francisco.
Villareal, Bernardo.

Dealers in watches, clocks, and jewelry.
Arana, Manuel.
Bittrolff, Hugo,
Diener y Rothacker.
Jacot, Alejandro.
Klein, Ricardo.
Lagarrigue, Luis.
Lagarrigue, Suc.
Landa, Miguel R.
Laue, German.
Llop, J.
Muiron y Ca.
Perret, Enrique.
Schäfer, Martin.
Schreiber y Ca.
Sommer, E.
Valverde, J.
Zivy y Hauser, Suc.

Manufacturing jewelers.
Diener y Rothacker.
Klein, Ricardo.
Montiel, Luis.
Muiron y Ca.
Schäfer, Martin.
Sommer. E.
Van Rooten y Debroé, Suc.

Silversmiths.
Diener y Rothacker.
Muiron y Ca.
Sommer, E.
Zivy y Hauser, Suc.

Silverware.
Acosta, Félix.
Alvarez, Andrés.
Arteaga, Cirilo,
Arteaga, Juan.
Avila, Silviano.
Cacho, Benigno.
Camacho, Albino.
Carrillo, Antonio.
Carrillo, J.
Carrillo, Guadalupe.
Collado, Enr.
Cosío, Alejandro.
Cosío, Anselmo.
Diener y Rothacker.
Esparza, J.
Gaitan. Juan.
Gonzalez, Paulino.

MEXICO CITY, MEXICO—Continued.

Silverware—Continued.
Guevara, Rafael.
Hernandez, Felipa.
Ilizaliturri, Josefa.
López, José.
Llop, Francisco.
Marchena, José F.
Martinez, Francisco,
Martinez, Vicente.
Montell, Luis.
Morales, J. José.
Neyra, Víctor.
Orduña, Baltazar.
Ponton, Antonio.
Rocha, Luis.
Romano, Estanislao.
Rodriguez, J.
Rodriguez, Estanislao.
Rodriguez, Matéo.
Rosellon, Nicolas.
Sanchez, Juan.
Soto, J. F.
Tagliabure, Pedro.
Torre, Amado D. de la.
Tovar, Nicanor.
Vega, Severo.
Velasco, José.
Villavicencio, Joaquin.
Zambrano, Rosalío.

Watch and clock makers.
Arredondo, Florencio.
Camargo, Alberto.
Cárdenas, J.
Celis, Mauricio R. de.
Corchado, Luis.
Dávalos, Juan M.
Delgado, Evaristo.
Diaz, Agustin C.
Diener y Rothacker.
Duhart, Vicente H.
Esquivel, Cárlos.
Farell, Enrique.
Gonzalez, Patricio.
Klein, Ricardo.
Laue, German.
López, Daniel.
Marin, Vicente.
Martin, Juan.
Martinez, Francisco.
Medina, Manuel.
Montaña, Angel.
Moreno, Juan.
Muiron y Ca.
Pagaza, Vicente.
Peña y Ca., F. de la.

MEXICO CITY, MEXICO—Continued.

Watch and clock makers—Continued.
Plata, Pedro G.
Ramirez ó Hijos José.
Rios, Manuel.
Rodriguez, Estanislao.
Romero, Florencio.
Romero, Francisco de P.
Sandoval, Francisco.
Sandoval, José.
Schäfer, Martin.
Silva, Marcial.
Sommer, E.
Soto, Rafael.
Valverde, J.
Van Rooten y De Broé, Suc.
Vecino, Manuel.
Villanueva, Juan B.
Walker, José.

Lithographers.
Fernandez, Cárlos.
Flores, Juan.
Gómez, Merino y Ca.
Guerra y Valle, J.
Iriarte, Hesiquio.
Montauriol, Cárlos.
Moreau y Hno., Emilio.
Murguía, Eduardo.
Revuelta, José L.
Sainz, Ricardo.
Salazar, Hipólito.

Lumber dealers.
Baez, Anastasio.
Cantero, M.
Cobo, Manuel.
Cobo y Ca., C.
Espinosa y Ca. L.
Fabre, Maurilio.
Franco, José.
Galindez, D.
Gonzalez, Manuel.
Guerrero, Gerónimo.
Hidalgo, Trinidad.
Huerta del Valle, Antonio.
Jimenez, Adolfo J.
Meca, Nicolás de.
Monterde, Luis.
Ondarza y de la Torre.
Orozco, Toribio.
Palacios y Ca., Ignacio.
Pinal, Julio.
Ponce de Leon, Gil.
Romero, Francisco.
Sancha, Juan de la.
Sanchez, Barquera L.
Trejo, Martiniana.

MEXICO CITY, MEXICO—Continued.

Lumber dealers—Continued.
Velazquez, Gayol y Ca.
Villar, Mariano.
Zetina y Ca., R.

Machinery:
Machinery importers.
Adam Suc., F.
Arce y Ca., J.
Arosarena, Rafael M. de.
Besserer, Carlos.
Boker y Ca., Roberto.
Charreton Hnos.
Combaluzier, A.
Lohse, Santiago C.
Lohse y Ca. G., Suc.
Malo y Ca., Alberto.
Marshall y Ca.
Philipp y Ca., Max. A.
Read y Campbell.
Rio, José María del.
Seeger, Guernsey y Ca.
Sommer, Herrmann y Ca.
Stankiewicz, G. M.
White, Juan.

Sewing machines.
Alarcon, Francisco.
Bacmeister, Julio.
Boker y Ca., Roberto.
Bush y Ca., C. M.
Compañía Manufacturera de "Singer."
Hulvershorn y Ca., G.
Jacot, A.
José María del Río.
Lohse y Ca., G., Suc.
Patton, C. F.
Sommer, Hermann y Ca.
Uhink y Ca.

Sugar machinery.
Arce y Ca.
Gahrtz, German

Meats, salted and smoked.
Aceves. J. A.
Aguilar, T.
Acalá, G.
Aldrete, Angel.
Arceo, P.
Arcinas, J.
Arco, R.
Becerril. G.
Bobadill i, A.
.Botilla, P.
Carmona, T.
Castelan, Enr.
Castelan, Ignacio.

MEXICO CITY, MEXICO—Continued.

Meats, salted and smoked—Continued.
Castellanos, A.
Castellanos, D.
Castillo, C.
Castillo, J.
Castillo, N.
Cerrano y Castillo.
Coronado, R.
Escamilla, J.
Exiga, Luis.
Galvan y Cárdenas, Ignacio.
Gómez, R.
Gonzalez, F.
Gomar, F.
Granados, D. de Herrera.
Haro, C.
Hernandez, Dolores G.
Hernandez, F.
Hernandez, J.
Hernandez y Zepeda.
Higareda, A.
Jaime, Josefa.
López, M.
Marmolejo, T.
Martinez, A.
Mejía, A.
Mejía, Luis.
Mejía, V.
Merino, R.
Moncayo, M.
Montes de Oca J.
Navarro, M.
Ocampo, J.
Omaya, C.
Perez, J.
Perez, P.
Pineda, J.
Pineda, R.
Quintanilla, G.
Quiroz, F.
Ramirez, Procopio.
Ramirez, P.
Reyes, J.
Rivero, V.
Rodriguez, A.
Robin, M.
Rojas, S.
Sanchez, S.
Serrano, Pedro.
Torres, Enrique.
Urbina, J.
Valadez, S.
Valdéz, S.
Velis, J.
Victor, R.
Villavicencio, N.

MEXICO CITY, MEXICO—Continued.

Meats, salted and smoked—Continued.
   Zepeda, B.
   Zepeda, J.

Merchant tailors.

   Adalid, Ceron ó hijos.
   Argumosa Hermanos.
   Bertezenne y Ca., E.
   Best y Hernandez.
   Carmona, Ildefonso.
   Carmona y Velazquez, J. M.
   Carmona y Vilchis, V.
   Cerezo y Ca.
   Chauveau, Juan.
   Cuellar, Lamberto.
   Dávalos, Ramon.
   Delbouis, J. P.
   Dreinhofer, J. F.
   Dubernard, Eugenio.
   Dufour y Cassasús.
   Echeverría, F.
   Franck, Amando.
   Franck y Ca., M.
   García Benitez, Félix.
   García Benitez, B.
   García Benitez, Tiburcio.
   Garibay y Ca., Ignacio.
   Gasca, Maximiliano.
   Gonzalez, Enrique.
   Hernandez, Fernando.
   Hernandez, Norberto J.
   Jamin, Alberto.
   Jimenez, Pablo.
   Kips, Alexix F.
   Lafage, Fernando.
   Macin, J. R.
   Maire, E.
   Mariaca, Santos.
   Maurel, F.
   Merino y Ca.
   Mivielle, E.
   Montes de Oca, A.
   Morales, Higinio.
   Navarro, Juan de M.
   Peralta, Antonio.
   Polack, Hipolito.
   Ramirez, C.
   Salin, Rafael.
   Sarre, Luis.
   Sevilla, Ignacio.
   Tovar, José María.
   Urreiztieta, Arturo.

xican curiosities.

   Spaulding, D. S.
   St. Hill, C. M.

MEXICO CITY, MEXICO—Continued.

Mills:
  Corn mills.
    Aguilar, Fortino.
    Aguilar, Miguel.
    Arroyo, Sixto.
    Astiz, Antonio.
    Bracho, Alberto A.
    Caballero, J. M.
    Clotas, Gervasio.
    Dettmer, Cárlos.
    Garibay, José María.
    Martinez, Serafin.
    Villa de Moros y Ca.

  Oil mills.
    Brun, Desiderio.
    Cortes ó Herigaray.
    Frank, Guillermo.
    Garibay y Gay.
    Gómez, Agustin.
    Gonzales y Ca., Angel.
    Vazquez, Braulio.
    Ziehl y Tellitú.

  Wheat mills.
    Albaitero y Arrache.
    Castro, Francisco de P.
    Charreton Hnos.
    Echenique, José Ma.

Mineral waters.
   Bazar, Justino.
   Bourlón, Alfredo.
   Lastinère, B.
   Gourgues, Désormes y Ca.

Mining articles.
   Gahrtz, German.
   Lohse y Ca., G., Suc.
   Philipp y Ca., Max. A.

Musical instruments.
   Bush y Ca., C. M.
   Espinosa, José Inés.
   Fernandez, Mariano.
   Hidalgo, Manuel.
   Hernandez, Tomás.
   Nagel, H., Suc.
   Sanchez, Barquera ó Hijo, J.
   Oñate, Jesús.
   Solano, Rómulo.
   Wagner y Levien, A.

Objects of art.
   Hillebrand y Ca., E.
   Lohse y Ca., G. Suc.
   Pellandini, Claudio.
   Philipp y Ca., Max A.
   Zivy y Hauser, Suc.

MEXICO CITY, MEXICO—Continued.

Opticians.
Calpini Suc.
White, A.

Paints, oils, etc.
Anaya, Félix.
Arévalo, Francisco.
Barrera, Arcadio,
Barroso, Francisco,
Barroso, Ismael.
Boufet, Javier.
Candil, Gonzalo.
Canseco, Hilario.
Cruz, José.
Dolzelet, Leopoldo.
Espínola, Antonio.
Estarrona, Juana.
García, Gonzalo.
Gomez, La Madrid.
Guzman, Angel.
Hernandez, Estéban M.
Martorano y Ca., Antonio,
Morales, Ismael.
Montes de Oca, D.
Navarro, J.
Pastén, Ignacio,
Pezaña, Marcial.
Piedra y Hnos., Marcos E.
Rangel, Maximino.
Rio de la Loza y Miranda.
Rivas, Jacinto.
Rojas, R.
Rosa, Manuela de la.
Rosell, Antonio.
Rosell, Joaquin,
Ruiz, Francisco E.
Ruiz, Agustin.
Serna, Juana.
Urrutia y Leon.
Urrutia, Miguel.
Vallejo, P.
Velez, Bibiano.
Vigueras, Agustin.
Vilchez, Francisco.
Yañez, Ref.
Zetina, Rafael R.

Paper:
Blank books.
Arquero, Ricardo.
Fuente, Parres, Suc.
Lions y Ca., H. y V.
Lüdert, Federico.
Martin, Luis.
Maza y Ca.
Quintero y Ca., A.
Saniz, Ricardo.

MEXICO CITY, MEXICO—Continued.

Paper—Continued.
Cardboard.
Alvarez, Rul y Ca.
Valdés y Cueva J.
Villa ó hijos, G.
Villa y Villanueva.

Importers of paper.
Seeger, Guernsey y Ca.
Trueba, Fernando de.
Trueba, Hermanos.

Paper boxes.
Barroso, Amado,
Orellana y Esteva.
Baez, Rafael

Paper manufacturers.
Benfield, Juan M.
Orozco, Marcelino.
Rémirez y Ca., I.
Sanchez Navarro, Carlos.

Wall paper.
Arnaldo, Luis G.
Brillanti y Ca.
Delarue, E.
Droguería Universal.
Huguenin, C.
Rio, José María del.
Trueba Hermanos.

Perfumery and toilet articles.
Beltran y Hermano.
Claverie, P.
Farine y Sanders.
Labadie, J. Suc. y Ca.
Malavear, Inocencio.
Saint Marc, P.
Tellez y Ca., F.

Petroleum.
Aguirre Hermanos, Ignacio.
Anzurez, Est. R.
Avila, María.
Brun, Desiderio.
Candás, Manuel.
Cejudo, Felipe.
Cervantes, Ponciano.
Diaz, Guadalupe.
Diaz de Parra, Guadalupe.
Durán, Angela J. V. de la.
Frank, Guillermo.
Gomez, Agustin.
Gonzalez, C.
La Compañía de Petróleo.
Lopez, Manuela.
Martinez, Gúadalupe.
Perez, Cecilio M.
Ramirez, Ricardo.

MEXICO CITY, MEXICO—Continued.

Petroleum—Continued.
Riva, Rafael.
Rovelo, María.
Rubaira, Pedro.
Sanchez de Suarez, Inés.
Solís, Loreto.
Urquieta, Josefina.
Waters Pierce Oil Co.

Photographers.
Alvarez, J.
Calderon y Ca., Antonio.
Carriedo, J.
Cruces, Antonio.
Figuerea, Agustin Campa.
Gomez y Flores, J.
González, Macario.
Gove y North.
Guerra y Ca.
Guzmán, J.
Iglesias, Francisco.
Manero, Luis.
Martinez, Andrés.
Maya, José M.
Nieto y Ca.
North Suc. (Emilio Osbahr).
Sanchez, Concepción.
Suarez, Guadalupe.
Valleto y Ca.
Veraza, Luis.
Wolfenstein Suc. (N. Winther).

Playing cards.
Mungula é Hijos, P.

Printing offices and printing materials:
  Printing offices.
Abadiano, Viuda é hijos de.
Aguilar é hijos.
Agüeros, Victoriano.
Barbedillo, José J.
Bouligny y Ca. (Limitada).
Butler, Juan W.
Cabrera, Daniel.
Casas y Ca.
Castillo, J. V.
Corona, M.
Correa, José.
Cortina, Vald. M.
Cumplido, I., Suc.
Díaz de Leon, Francisco.
Dublan y Ca., E.
Dufez, E.
Escalante, Ignacio.
Esteva, Gonzalo A.
Fusco, Federico M.
García, Torres V.
Gonzalez Murúa, P.

MEXICO CITY, MEXICO—Continued.

Printing offices and printing materials—Cont'd.
  Printing offices—Continued.
Guerra y Valle Joaquin.
Gutierrez y Ca., S.
Haegell, Emilio.
Hargrove, R. K.
Imprenta del Gobierno Federal.
Imprenta de "El Combate."
Imprenta del "Círculo Católico."
Imprenta de "La Escuela Correccional de Artes y Oficios."
Imprenta del Diario "Trait d'Union."
Imprenta de "El Partido Liberal."
Jens, J. F.
Lagarza, Juan.
Lars, Mariano.
López y Ca., A.
López y Ca., Alfonso E.
López, José.
Lugo, Francisco.
Mata, Filomeno.
Murguía, Ed.
Murguía, L.
Nava, L.
Nichols Suc.
Oficina tipográfica de la Secretaría de Fomento.
Orozco, Epifanio D.
Ortiz, Monasterio Angel
Párres y Ca., F. Suc.
Paz, Cárlos.
Paz, Ireneo.
Salazar, Daniel R.
Sanchez, Santos T.
Smith, David C.
Soné, F. A.
Soto, Gabriel.
Steelman, A. J.
Terrazas, José J.
Trigueros, C.
Vanegas y Arroyo, Antonio.
Veraza, Guillermo.
Villagran, Francisco.
Villanueva, Atanasio.
Velasco, J. Reyes
Zúñiga, Petra.

Printing and lithographic inks—
Diaz de Leon, Francisco.
Seeger, Guernsey y Ca.
Trueba Hermanos.
Zaccarini y Ca., A

Type, presses, etc.—
Bustamente, José E.
Lohse y Ca., G., Suc.
Munguía é Hijos, P.

MEXICO CITY, MEXICO—Continued.

Printing offices and printing materials—Cont'd.
Type, presses, etc.—Continued.
Seeger, Guernsey y Ca.
Sommer, Herrmann y Ca.

Rubber stamps.
Dael, Federico.
Fouard, Juan.
Galaviz, Antonio H.
Mosser, Luis.
Pastrana, Guillermo R.
Robertson, F. E.

Saddlers.
Aguilar, Mariano.
Alvarado, Santiago.
Alveraz, Mariano.
Avíla, José.
Ballesteros, Juan.
Castro, Antonio.
Dominguez, Marciano.
Garay, Vicente.
Gonzalez, J. T.
Gros, Emile.
Guerrero, Ramon.
Jimenez, Estéban.
Lessance, A.
Lozano, David.
Ortiz, Clemente.
Ortiz, Juan R.
Perez, Casimiro.
Reyes, Pedro.
Ruiz, Manuel.
Vazquez, Luis.

Scientific and surgical instruments.
Andrade y Soriano.
Biörklund y Joransson, A.
Bustillos, Evaristo.
Calpini Suc.
Felix, Cárlos.
Henning, Jorge.
Joransson, Cárlos.
Leiter, C., Suc.
Lohse y Ca., G., Suc.
Philips, Max.
Taussaint y Ca.

Ship chandlery.
Enriquez, J.
Lozano, Vicente.
Villagra, Theodosio.

Shoemakers' supplies.
Brehm y Ca., Suc.
"Compañía Comercial Austriaca-Trasatlántica."
Horn y Ca., A.
Schmidt y Bourjau.
Schultze y Ca., Suc.

MEXICO CITY, MEXICO—Continued.

Tinware.
Aburto, Félix.
Alvarez, J.
Anaya, Trinidad.
Ayala, Juan.
Badillo, Domo.
Barros, Lauro.
Belmont, Ignacio.
Bernal, Angel.
Blancas, Manuel.
Caballero, Manuel.
Castillo, José.
Chavez, Antonio.
Chavez, Antonio.
Cherlin, Luis.
Clavel, Leandro.
Córdoba, Margarito.
Díaz, Mariano.
Dominguez, Nic.
Espinosa, Est.
Espinosa, Ponciano.
Flores, Agustín.
Flores, Pedro.
Fuentes, Pedro.
García, Abraham.
García, Macario.
Garduño, J. M.
Garduño, Manuel.
Gomez, Pablo.
Gomez, Tomás.
Hidalgo, Faustino.
Iglesias, Manuel.
Iglesias, Miguel.
Jimenez, Lúcas.
Jimenez, Felipe.
Legorreta, Blas.
Lozano, Andrés.
Magariño, Manuel,
Márquez, Mariano.
Morales, Sixto.
Muro, Domingo.
Novoa, Micaela.
Nuñez, Vicente.
Olarte, Pedro.
Ortiz, Francisco.
Parra, Eduardo.
Quesadas, Antonio.
Quesadas, Juan.
Revilla, Arcadio.
Ruiz, Bartolo.
Rujano, J. A.
Salgado, Silverio.
Sanchez, Vidal.
Santa María, Manuel.
Silva, Julián.
Sotelo, Trinidad.

MEXICO CITY, MEXICO—Continued.

Tinware—Continued.
Torre, Román de la.
Torre, José R. de la.
Torres, Juan.
Valdéz, Franciso.
Vazquez, Adalberto.
Velasco, Florencío.

Tombstones.
Backus, Brisbin y Ca.
Cherubini, Angel.
Marcili, C. S.
Masselin, A.
Tangassi, Francisco.
Urrutia, L.

Toys.
Calvet, Victor.
Córdova, Agustín.
Cosío, Juan.
Cotera, Merced.
Cuellar, Antonia.
Deverdun, C.
Enriquez, Guadalupe.
Gómez, Isabel.
Jurado de Acalá, Elena.
Larré, Pedro.
Pivadière Adolfo.
Raynaud, E.
Rivero, Luis.
Sandoval, Miguel.
Velazquez de Leon, Margarita.
Vidriería Nacional de Apizaco.

Travellers' outfits.
Boker y Ca., Roberto.
Combaluzier, A.
Franck y Ca., M.
Lohse y Ca., G., Suc.
Philipp y Ca., Max A.

Umbrellas.
Bouras, Pablo.
Gambú, Adolfo.
Guerin y Ca.
Hoppenstedt y Ca., T.
Lagrave, P.
Lefèbvre, A.
Logero, G.

Undertakers.
Ascorbe y Ca.
Carmona y Ca., J.
Gayosso y Ca.
Moctezuma, G.
Trevino, M.

Wine merchants, importers.
Castelló, Gutierrez y Ca.
Consonno, Julio.

MEXICO CITY, MEXICO—Continued.

Wine merchants, importers—Continued.
Genin, Viuda de A.
Gutierrez y Ca., Quintín.
Mancina Hnos.
Morales Manso, Alberto.
Repetto, Juan.
Rigal, Lubet y Ca.
Rolla y Ca., A.
Sanchez, Ambrosio.
Sauto, Muñúzuri y Ca.
Uhink y Ca.
Uhink Hnos y Zahn.
Zepeda, Francisco.

Wine and liquor distillers.
Alegre, Julián.
Boeuf, Francisco.
Durant, Joaquin.
Fonts, Martín.
García, Alejo.
Garduño, Miguel.
Gaviño, Salvador.
Gutiérrez y Ca., Prudencio.
Laville, J. P.
Leriche, Cárlos.
Rafols, Fernando.
Tardos y Ca., Julio.
Vidal y Ca., Pablo.
Xicluna, Jorge.

Wood and coal.
Ayala, Perez, Viuda é Hijos de.
Campollo, Márcos.
Espinosa, Eust.
Guerra, Antonio.
Guerrero y Arechavala.
Lomas, Domingo.
Mora de Arroyo, Ignacia.
Noriega, R.
Ortiz, Diégo.
Rodriguez, José.
Roldan, A. José.
Silva y Ca., José.

Woods, hardwoods and mahogany.
Baez, Anastasio.
Cantero, M.
Cobo, Cesáreo y Ca.
Cobos, Manuel.
Fabre, Mauriléo.
Franco, José.
Galindez, Diógo.
González, Manuel.
Guerrero, Gerónimo.
Hidalgo, Trinidad.
Huerta, Antonio.
Jimenez, Adolfo J.
Meca, Nicolás.

MEXICO CITY, MEXICO—Continued.

Woods, hard woods, and mahogany—Continued.
Monterde, Luis.
Ondarza y de la Torre.
Orozco, Toribio.
Palacios y Ca., Ignacio.
Pinal, Julio.
Ponce de León, Gil.
Romero, Francisco.
Sancha, Juan de la.
Sanchez, Barquera E.
Trejo, Martiniana.
Villar, Mariano.
Zetina, R.

Wool dealers.
Dehesa, Estéban.
Fuentes, Guillermo.
López, Isidro.
Picazo, Petronilo.

MINERAL PENOLES, DURANGO.
General merchants.
Aguilera, Natividad.
Barcena, Marciano.
Dezas, Domingo.
Escobar, Nepomuceno.
Helguers, Julio.
Lazo, Gmo.
Manriquez, Porfirio.
Parra, Rafael.
Ruiz, Concepcion D.
Sumaran, Ignacio.
Tinoco, Pablo.
Villareal, Juan B.

MONCLOVA, COAHUILA.
Agricultural implements and hardware.
Castenada, Ramon Musquiz.
Cuellar y Ca., Fco. P.
Gonzales y Ca., H.G.

Cotton factory.
Degetau y Garza.

Druggist.
Fernandez, Juan C.

Flour mills.
Gutierrez, Romualdo.
Prince, Roberto.
Rios, José M.

Furniture and carriages.
Blackaller, Alberto.

General merchandise.
Aldrete y Ca., Amado.
Ballestero, Indelacio.
Castenada, Ramon Musquiz.
Cuellar y Ca., F. P.

MONCLOVA, COAHUILA—Continued.
General merchandise—Continued.
Flores y Hno., Cruz.
Fuentes, Andrés A.
Fuente, Teófilo.
Gonzales y Ca., H. G.
Paez, Cecilio.
Villareal, José V.

MONTEMORELOS, NUEVO LEON.
Dry and fancy goods.
Diaz, Manuel.
Peña, José L. de la.

General merchants.
Adame, R.
Arena, M. de la.
Ballesteros, J.
Ballesteros, P.
Barocio, J. N.
Barocio, V.
Becerra, M.
Berlanga, B.
Berlanga Hermanos.
Berlanga, Luis.
Bronde, J. P.
Cantu, A. P.
Daren, M.
Garcia y Ca., L.
Garza, B. de la.
Garza, E. de la.
Gomez, F.
Leal, E.
Martinez, N.
Martinez, R. M.
Ordonez, C.
Padillo, F.
Paras, Antonio.
Perez, E.
Rocha, F.
Trevino, A.
Trevino, H.
Vensameye, A.

Hardware.
Barocio, Elías.
Parras, Alberto.

MONTEREY, NUEVO LEON.
Agents for imported goods (sale by sample).
García, Ignacio.
Guerra, David.
Palacio, Federico.
Piazzini, Cárlos.

Agricultural implements.
Dressel, Rodolfo.
Langstroh, Suc.
Piazzini, Cárlos.

MONTEREY, NUEVO LEON—Continued.

Arms and ammunition.
Dressel, Rodolfo.
Freese, Luis K.
Langstroh, Suc.

Bankers.
Armendais, Francisco.
Holck y Ca., C.
Maiz y Ca., Pedro.
Martinez, Francisco.
Milmo, Patricio.
Rivero, Valentin.
Wells, Fargo & Co.

Banks.
London Bank of Mexico and South America, Ltd.
Sucursal del Banco Nacional.

Booksellers and stationers.
Elizondo, Manuel Lozano.
García, Leopoldo.
Grim, Francisco.
Langrange y Ca., Desiderio.
Langstroh, Suc.
Martinez, Francisco A.

Boots and shoes.
Allegro y Ca.
Franco, José María.
Gonzalez, Juan B.
Leon, Vicente de.
Menchuca, Tomás.
Nuñez, Estanislao.
Ortiz, Tomás.
Ramos, Merced.
Rosas, Fidel.
Treviño, Francisco Z.

China and glassware.
Ancira Hermanos.
Dressel y Ca.
Langstroh, Suc.
Rico, Leandro.
Rios, Francisco.

Commission merchants.
Elias, Francisco de.
Oliver, Francisco.
Pagaza, Juan.
Rico, Leandro.
Ruiz, Rafael A.

Clothing, hats, etc.
Armendais, Francisco.
Arvele y Olivier.
Barrios, Roque.
Calderon, José.
Cardenas, Martinez.
Digatan y García.

MONTEREY, NUEVO LEON—Continued.

Clothing, hats, etc.—Continued.
Doud y Ca., Patricio.
Elizonda y Ca.
Fiz, Manuel.
Galindo, Jacinto.
García, Bernardino.
García, Mariano.
García, Praxedes.
Garza, Fernando.
Gonzalez, Juan B.
Gonzalez, Lorenzo.
Gutierrez, José.
Hernandez y Hermanos.
Holke, Cárlos.
Jamie, S.
Jimenez, Desiderio.
Lozano y Ca.
Maiz, Pedro.
Martinez, Alejo.
Martinez y Hermanos, Cardenas.
Martinez y Hermanos, Fernando.
Milmo, Patricio.
Oliver, Francisco.
Palacios, Federico.
Pautrier, Emilio.
Rivero, Valentin.
Rodriguez, Hila io.
Roel, Estéban.
Treveño y Ca, Silvestre.
Tallabas, Francisco.
Treviño, Francisco.

Druggists.
Argandar, Ricardo.
Bello, Francisco.
Breiner y Ca., Eduardo.
Bremer y Ca.
Cantú, Agustin.
Cortazar, Joaquin.
Escalante, José M.
Flores, Felipe García.
García, Antonio.
Gonzalez, Felipe G.
Gutierrez, Miguel.
Hinojoso, Tomás.
Lafon, Antonio.
Lafont, Emilio.
Lazcano y Ca.
Margain, José O.
Martinez y Echartea.
Mean y Hermanos.
Mears, Juan H.
Mearts, José.
Perez, Ramon G.
Rodriguez, Eusebio.
Saldaña, Ignacio.

MONTEREY, NUEVO LEON—Continued.

Druggists—Continued.
Sanchez, J.
Sepulveda, Vicente.
Dry goods and notions.
Ayala y Ca., Cárlos.
Brainerd y Ca.
Drenel, Rudolfo.
Lozano, Inocencio.
Pautrier, E.
Reyes, Juan.
Rios, David.
Fancy goods.
Mejía, Romualdo.
Rico, Leandro.
Sanchez, Romualdo.
Tinoco, Camilo.
Furniture.
Pino, Luís.
Groceries and provisions.
Azcárate, Francisco.
Azcárate, Viuda de.
Elguera, José.
Flores, Rosendo.
Orihuela, Agustin.
Rios, Francisco.
Robles, Ignacio.
Rodriguez, José M.
Hardware.
Ancira Hermanos.
Dressel y Ca.
Rios, Francisco.
House-furnishing goods.
Ancira y Ca.
Trujillo, Prudencio.
Jewelers.
Ayala, Cárlos M.
Barrios, Roque.
Martinez y Hermanos.
Ramirez, Delfino.
Rivero, Valentin.
Lithographer.
La Litografía del Gobierno.
Lumber.
Martinez y Hermano, Fernandez.
Portillo y Gomez, R.
Merchants, general, wholesale.
Calderon, José.
Castro, Victoriano.
Clausen y Ca.
Coindran, L. G.
Degetau y Dose.
Farnava y Ca., Viuda de.

MONTEREY, NUEVO LEON—Continued.

Merchants, general, wholesale—Continued.
García, Bernardino.
Guera, David.
Holck y Ca.
Jarie, Salvador.
Madera y Ca.
Maíz y Ca., P.
Milmo, Patricio.
Morrell, José.
Oliver, Francisco.
Oliver y Hermanos.
Palacio Arguelles.
Rivero y Ca.
Rivera, Valentin.
Schonian y Dressel.
Weber y Ulrick.
Zambriano y Hijo.
Merchants, wholesale commission, general.
Artichi, Francisco.
Ayala, Bruno.
Bernardi, Reynoldo.
Cantu, Adolfo.
Elizondo y Ca.
Maiz y Ca., Pedro.
Martinez y Hermanos.
Photographers.
Lagrange Hermanos.
Rendon, Nicolás.
Yañes, Rafael.
Pianos, organs, etc.
Zambrana Hermanos y Ca.
Sewing machines.
Daudet y Ca., Patricio O.
Fox, Joaquin.
Galindo, Elías.

MORELIA, MICHOACAN.

Agricultural implements.
Seeger, Guernsey y Ca.
Wolburg, Gerardo S.
Arms and ammunition.
Aguirre y Achótegui.
Bankers.
Basagoiti y Ca..J.
Gravenhorst, Gustavo J.
Solorzano, M. M.
Banks.
Bank of London and Mexico (agency).
National Bank (agency).
Booksellers and stationers.
Aguirre y Achótegui.
Guerrero, Plácido.
Velasquez, J.

MORELIA, MICHOACAN—Continued.

Boots and shoes.
Cornejo, Miguel.
Huarte, Joaquin.
Oseguera, Francisco.

China, crockery, and glassware.
Morera, Victor J.
Oseguera, Epifanio.

Commission merchants.
Carbonel, Antonio.
Elizarraras, Rafael.
Guerrero, L. Cámpuzano.
Lozano, Manuel.
Ruiz, Nemesio.
Sámano, Luis G.
Seeger, Guernsey y Ca.
Vega, Ramon.
Velasquez, J.
Velez, José.

Drugs.
Arrega, Teodora.
Angondar, Ricardo.
Burgos, Merando.
Cervantes, Andrés.
Elizarraras, Rafael.
Franco, Ignacio.
Gonzalez, Antonio.
Gonzalez, Ciraco.
Gutierrez, Miguel.
Huacuja, Lamberto.
Lopez, Ezequiel.
Martinez, Silviano.
Mier, Atanasio.
Montaño, Manuel.
Muñoz Hermanos.
Montenegro, Manuel Oviedo.
Ortiz, Nicanor.
Otiz y Cano, Miguel.
Padilla, Genaro.
Harra, Enrique.
Vallejo, Juan.

Dry goods, notions, etc.
Alba, F. G.
Audiffred Hnos.
Bose, Garcin y Hermanos.
Carbonel, Antonio.
Castaneda y Ca.
Cortes y Ca., T.
Infante, José M.
Infante, Pelot y Ca.
Quiros, Pedros.
Ramirez, Ramon.
Ruiz, Nemesio.
Sauve Hnos., Francart.
Villagomez, M.

MORELIA, MICHOACAN—Continued.

Fancy goods.
Burgos, Antonio.
Calderon, Sacramento S.
Guerrero, P.
Vega, Nicolás.
Wolburg, Gerardo S.

Furniture.
Gutierrez, Evaristo.
Velez, Juan.

Groceries and provisions.
Basagoite y Ca., J.
Flores, Juan.
Gonzalez, Manuel.
Izquierdo.
Martinez, Ignacio.
Oseguera, Epifanio.
Ramirez, Ramon.
Torres y Gil.

Hardware, cutlery, and tools.
Aguirre y Achótegui.
Burgo y Ca.
Guerrero, Plácido.
Martinez, Loreto.
Oseguera, Epifanio.
Ponce de Leon, J.
Rangel, Juan.
Wolburg, Gerardo S.

Hatters.
Diaz, Francisco.
Monge y Rodriguez.
Pellotier y Ca., T.

Hides and leathers.
Breña, Ausencio.
Garcia, Antonio.
Ibarrola, José M.
Ortiz, Nicolás.
Sachez, Agustin.
Topio, Ignacio.

Jewelry, watches, and silverware.
Goyzueta.
Goyzueta, Felix.
Humbert, Onesimo.
Marquez, Antonio.
Ramirez, Mariano.
Trautz, Federico.

Lithographer.
Imprenta de la Escuela de Artes.

Paints, oils, etc.
Mier, A.

Photographers.
Bocanegra, Rodolfo.
Gutierrez y Ca.
Manríquez, R.
Torres Huos.

MORELIA, MICHOACAN—Continued.

Pianos and organs.
Alba, Felix.
Cardenas, Manuel.
Espinosa, Mucio.
Estrado, Joaquin.
Gomez, Alberto.
Lozano, Manuel.
Novoa, José María.
Ramirez, Ramon.
Reynoso, Ignacio.

Saddlery and harness.
Navarete, Francisco.
Rivera, Apolonio.

Sewing machines.
Alzua, Manuel Oviedo.

Undertaker.
Velez, Juan.

NIEVES, ZACATECAS.

General merchants.
Alcala, Dolores C. de.
Arellano, José.
Ballardo, Pablo.
Barca, Joaquin Calderon de la.
Calderon y Ca., Jorge.
Fernandez, Pioquinto.
García, J. P.
Pinera, Lauro G.
Ramirez, Miguel.
Real, Pedro del.
Torres, Juan.
Ugalde, Eugenio.
Villanueva, José.
Zapata, Refugio.

NOMBRE DE DIOS, DURANGO.

General merchants.
Bonilla, José.
Fiscal, Cárlos.
Mijares, Jesus Vasquez.
Pedroza, Antonio.
Ramirez, Vicente.
Soto, Hijino.
Vargas, Isaac.
Vasquez, Eduardo.

NUEVO LAREDO, TAMAULIPAS.

Banks and bankers.
Belden Hnos.
Holck y Ca., C.
O'Conor, Tomás.

Booksellers and stationers.
Cárdenas, Santiago.
Cueva y Hermano, A.

NUEVO LAREDO, TAMAULIPAS—Cont'd.

Commission merchants.
Belden Hermanos.
Erhard, Antonio M.
García, Agapito A.
Hernandez, Juan.
Holck y Ca., C.
Mendiríchaga, Tomás.
O'Conor, Tomás.
Rodriguez, Manuel.
Serna, Rafael.

Drugs.
Dupoyet, Teodoro.
Theriot, A. F.
Treviño, Sebastian.

Dry goods.
Bruni y Hermano, A. M.
Daimend, Miguel.
Hirsch, Mauricio.
Joseph, Alberto.
Larralde Hermanos y Ca.
Mendiríc Laga, Tomás.
Morris y Ca., E.
O'Conor, Tomás.

Groceries and provisions.
Ancira, Jacobo.
Ancira, Julio.
Baez, J. E.
Bruni y Hermano, A. M.
Flores, Marcos Garza.
García, Agapito A.
Lozano, Eduardo.
Montegui, W.
O'Conor, Tomás.
Rigal, Pedro.
Rosenthal y Hermano.

Hardware, etc.
Montegui, W.
O'Conor, Tomás.

Hats.
Ancira, Jacobo.

Printers.
Cueva y Hermano, A.
Vara, Indalesio.

Sewing machines.
Cárdenas, Santiago.
Cueva y Hermano, A.
Joseph, Julio.
O'Conor, Tomás.
Theriot, A. F.

OAXACA, OAXACA.

Agricultural implements.
Philipp y Ca., Max. A.
Stein y Ca., Gustavo.

OAXACA, OAXACA—Continued.

Banks and bankers.
Barrenquy, P. L.
Richards, Constantino.
Sucursal del Banco Nacional.
Stein y Ca., Gustavo.
Zorrilla y Ca., José.

Blast furnaces.
La Reforma Furnace (Francisco, Quijano, proprietor).

Booksellers and stationers.
Campo, L. F. del.
Peralta, M.
San German, Lorenzo.

Boots and shoes.
Cuervo y Ca.
Nuñez, Manuel.
Ruiz Hermanos.

Carriages.
Almovejo, A.
Rivera, M.

Commission merchants.
Barrenquy, L.
Barriga, Francisco.
Bravo, Juan T.
Castro, José M.
Cruz, Santiago.
Falcon, Antonio.
Guerrero, José.
Mateos, M.
Müller, Eduardo.
Prado, Antonio.
Stein y Ca., Gustavo.
Zorrilla y Ca., José.

China and glassware.
Frieben Hermanos, Suc.
Heinrichs y Ca., Enrique.
Philipp y Ca., Max. A.

Drugs.
Alvarez, J. A.
Bolaños, Ramon.
Bustamante, Pedro.
Carbo, Antigua de.
Eresarte, M.
Peña, G.
Ruiz, Pomposo.
Santaella, Amado.
Tolis y Renero.

Dry goods.
Contreras, M. T.
Gay, G.
Heinrichs y Ca., Enrique.
Larrañaga, José.
Laugier, L.

OAXACA, OAXACA—Continued.

Dry goods—Continued.
Peralta, Manuel.
Quijano y Ca., F.
Reguera, L. P.

Fancy goods.
Heinrichs y Ca., Enrique.
Frieben Hermanos, Suc.
Philipp y Ca., Max. A.
San German, Lorenzo.

Groceries and provisions.
Allende y Sobrino, Manuel.
Quijano, Francisco G.
Stein y Ca., Gustavo.

Hardware.
Esperon, M.
Frieben Hermanos, Suc.
Heinrichs y Ca., Enrique.
Philipp y Ca., Max. A.
San German, Lorenzo.

Importers and exporters.
Allende y Sobrino.
Barriga ó Hijo.
Esperon, Gabriel.
Figueroa, Ignacio.
Moya, Luis.
Quijano y Ca.
Peña, Juan Cobo de la.
Richards, C.
Stein y Ca., Gustavo.
Trapaga, Juan.
Uriarte, Francisco.
Weicher y Ca.
Zorrilla y Ca., José.

Iron and ironware.
Barriga, Francisco.
Quijano y Ca.

Jewelry.
Serivante, Luis.

Lithographer.
Santa Ana, J.

Manufacturer of brass and iron bedsteads.
Mellado, Cueto J.

Music store.
Heinrichs y Ca., Enrique.

Paints and oils.
San German, Lorenzo.
Zolis, Camilo.

Sewing machines.
Trieben Hermanos, Suc.

Silk goods
Gallardo, V.
Ibanez y Ca., R

ORIZABA, VERA CRUZ.

Agricultural implements.
Carrillo, Borrego y Ca.
Vivanco, Angel.

Arms and ammunition.
Espinosa. José.
Limos, Primitivo.
Lopez, Justo.
Rufier, Juan B.

Banks and bankers.
Mazon Hnos. (agents "Banco Nacional").
Torre y Ca., Suc. (agents "Banco de Lóndres y México").

Booksellers.
Aguilar, Mendoza y Ca.

Boots and shoes.
Camiro, Anastasio.
Cruz, Francisco.
Gaetan, Cipriano.
Gaston, Francisco.
Jimenez, Crescencio.
Muñoz. Francisco.
Ramirez, Vicente.
Ramos, Guadalupe.
Saldaño, José de J.

Chemicals and acids.
Trujillo, Samuel.

China and glassware.
Carrillo, Borregos y Ca.
Lignon y Ca.

Commission merchants (sale by sample).
Bermudez, Conrado.
Cuadra, J. Guadalupe.
Lopez, Sebastian.
Marquez, Blas.
Torres, José M.
Soto, Facundo.

Commission merchants.
Berea Hermanos.
Espinosa, Diego.
Eulogio, V.
Gomez, Tiburico.
Laredo, José M.
Lastre, José Mena.
Llera, Justino.
Minvielle, Juan.
Peralta y Guevara.
Regoyos, Julian.
Roman, Vicente.
Segura, Ricardo.
Soto, Facundo.
Verea, Adolfo.

Dealers in hides.
Brando, Juan.

ORIZABA, VERA CRUZ—Continued.

Dealers in hides—Continued.
Cerilla, E.
Mercadante, Juan.
Teilhe, Francisco.

Drugs.
Anaud, Viuda de.
Bustamante, A.
Bustamante, José M.
Bustillos, J. E.
Carrillo, Cartabuena Joaquin.
Diaz, Juan.
Eizaguirre, J. Manuel.
Espinosa y Ca., José.
Mendizabal y Cabresto, Miguel.
Portas, Rafael.
Rincon. José.
Sanchez, Lorenzo.
Talavera, Ismael.
Valverde, J. Manuel.

Dry goods and notions.
Alonso, Felipe.
Amada, Pedro.
Bustillo, S.
Cuesta, Fernandez.
Cuesta, José Fernandez.
Escudero, Enrique.
Foudevila y Ca., José.
Garragori, P.
Gomez, Luz.
Gross, Teófilo.
Islas, Rafael.
Mazon Hnos.
Rogna, Ricardo.
Sigori y Ca.
Sota, Gomez.
Ureta, Marcos.
Ureta, Rufino.
Villa y Aresti, Sotero.
Vivance, Estevas.
Vivanco, Dionisio.

Engravers.
Morgado, Vicente.
Zenon, J.

Fancy goods.
Alonso, Felipe.
Bello y Ca., F. J.
Carrillo Hnos.
Fernandez, Casto.
Guerrero, Josefa Acosta de.
Liguori y Ca., Francisco.
Rojina y Ca.

Flour mills.
Flores, Francisco.
Guevara, Luis.
Guevara, N.

208 MEXICO.

ORIZABA, VERA CRUZ—Continued.

Flour mills—Continued.
Mesa, Luis.
Sanz, José.
Sota, Francisco.
Sota, Dolores S. de
Sota, Isidoro.
Sota, Severino de la.
Torre y Ca., Suc.

Furniture.
Grosse, Teófilo.
Lienert, Eduardo.

General merchandise.
Argumedo, Cárlos.
Baturoni, Ramon.
Bravo, José.
Cross y Ca., Castillo.
Espinosa, Diego.
Mendizabal, N.
Morillo, Agustin.
Naredo, José M.
Pimentel, Ramon.
Penasco, J. M.
Rodriguez, Manuel.
Sota, Facundo.
Tejada, Ambrosio.
Valverde, Ramon.
Victorino, Eulogio.

Groceries and provisions.
Aguerrela, José.
Aguilar, Pascual.
Alvarado, Tomás.
Alvarez, Agustin.
Andrade, José.
Arreguin, Primitivo.
Baldivia, Ignacio.
Campos, Francisco.
Castillo, Timoteo.
Dominguez, José.
Espinola, Máximo.
Garces, José M.
García, Ramon.
Giminez, Antonio.
Gomez, Cortes Ismael.
Hernandez, Lucio.
Hernandez, Prudencio
Hernandez, Tiburcio.
Ibarra, Joaquin.
Lopez, Pedro.
Merodio, Pedro Diaz.
Peralta, A.
Porras, Julian.
Riquelme, Pedro.
Rivera, Basilio.
Rivera, Sabino.
Rojino y Ca., Arcadio.

ORIZABA, VERA CRUZ—Continued.

Groceries and provisions –Continued.
Rojino y Ca., Ricardo.
Rodriguez, Plutarco.
Romero, Joaquin.
Saldaña, Joaquin.
Tejeda, Manuel.
Tentones y Ca.
Toledano, Angel.
Valdivia, Ignacio.
Vivanco, Antonio.
Zello, Francisco T.

Hardware.
Avila, José M.
Bello y Ca., Fr. J.
Blanco, Bonifacio.
Brando, Juan.
Carmona, Patricio.
Carrillo Hnos.
Islas, Rafael.
Liguori y Ca., Francisco.
Lopez, Epitacio.
Mercadanti, Juan.
Merino, Rafael.
Miuchaque, Juan.
Ojeda, Encarnacion.
Perez, Felipe.
Teilhe, Francisco.
Vega, José Sanchez.

Hatters.
Beltran, José.
Camarillo, Francisco.

House-furnishing goods.
Buendia, Luis.
Mañon, Abrahan.
Rosette, Amadeo.

Iron and ironware.
Cravillo, Borrego y Ca.
Liguori y Ca., Francisco.

Lithographer.
Gonzalez, Juan O.

Lumber dealers.
Castillo, Antonio.
Cortez, María Guadalupe.
Mármol, Fabian del.

Machinery.
Fougeras, Pedro.
Grosse, Teófilo.
Hernandez, Miguel.
Liguori y Ca., F.
Pimentel, L.
Vivanco y Estevez.

Merchants, wholesale (general merchandise).
Aguilar, Juan.

ORIZABA, VERA CRUZ—Continued

Merchandise, wholesale (general merchandise)—
Continued.
Bárranco, Gabriel.
Camarillo y Teller.
Fernandez, Castro.
Jaramillo, Ismael.
Mazon Hermanos.
Sota, Isidoro.
Vitorero, E.

Music store.
Oropeza, Alfredo.

Paper.
Escandon é Hijos, Guadalupe A. de.

Photographers.
Castillo, Manuel.
Diaz, Lucio.

Printing offices.
Aguilar, Juan C.
Franck, Pablo.
Gonzalez, Juan.
Rosete, Margarita.

Saddlery and harness.
Cerrillo, Miguel.
Cueto, Ignacio. •
Martinez, Antonio.
Perez, Manuel.
Solis, Anastasio.

Sewing machines.
Islas, Ruperto.

Sugar merchants.
Bringas, José María.
Gargollo y Parra.
Guevara, M.

Undertaker.
Grosse, Teófilo.

Watches and jewelry.
Arenjo, Andrés A.
Mayo, José María.
Palacios, Felix.

PACHUCA, HIDALGO.

Agricultural implements.
Alvarez, José Reyes.
"El Bazar."
Guridi y Giese.
"La Ciudad de México."
Maquivar y Ca.

Bankers.
Aguirre, Trinidad.
Duarte y Ca., Julian Pérez.
Gomez, Adelberto.
Jari, Jaime.

PACHUCA, HIDALGO—Continued.

*Bankers—*Continued.
Landero y Ca., J. de.
Wells, Fargo & Co.

Booksellers.
Pastrana, Evaristo.
El Instituto Literario.
Zuverano, José.

Boots and shoes.
Badillo Carmona de.
Castelazo, Conrado.
Corchado, Gumesindo.
García, Lorenzo.
García, Vicente.
Guzman, Gertrudis.
Hermosillo, Crisanta de.
Hidalgo, Soteral.
Maldonado, Antonio.
Maldonado, Pablo.
Mugés, Trinidad.
Ponce, Vicente.
Rodrigues, Antonio.
Soto, Librado.
Zendejas, Pedro.
Zepeda, Sostenes.

China and glassware.
Kahn y Hermanos, Felix.

Commission merchants.
Duarte y Ca., J. Perez.
Hernandez, Alejandro (sale by sample).

Drug stores.
"Botica Martinez Elizondo."
"Botica Mexicana."
Conteras, Angel.
Corral y Navarro.
"De Dolores," Felipe Guerrero.
"De la Providencia."
"El Refugio," Felipe Guerrero.
"Farmacia Moderna."
Lescalle, Fernando.
Moreno, Norberto.
Montenegro, José.

Dry goods and notions.
Alfaro, Ramon.
Bloch, Maurice.
Bonavit Hermanos.
"Cajon Mexicano."
"El Puerto de Liverpool."
"El Importador."
Escudero, Fernando.
Escudero Hijo y Ca., Fernando.
García, Alejandro.
Gutierrez, Francisco.
Julien Hermanos.
"La Reforma del Comercio."

S. Ex. 8, pt. 11——14

PACHUCA, HIDALGO—Continued.

Dry goods and notions—Continued.
"La Francia Marítima."
Lambert y Garnier.
Mercheyer Hermanos.
Sangier y Ca.

Dry goods (cloths and tailoring).
Aguilar, Mariano.
Castro, José Martinez.
Chavarria, Valentin.
Escudero, Fernando.
Gonzalez, Antonio.
Imbert y Mauriso.
Langier, Juan.
Mecheyer Hermanos.

Fancy goods.
Bonavit Hermanos.
Cacho y Ca.
"El Bazar."
Guridi y Giese.
"La Ciudad de México."
Marquivar y Ca.

Flour merchants.
Gareia, Albino.
Hernandez, Albino.
Leon, Refugio.

Furniture.
Guerrero, J.
Hernandez, Felix L.
Herrera, Felix.
Rivera, Gregorio.

Groceries and provisions.
Alvarez, Reyes.
Boule, Viuda de Antonio.
Cacho y Ca., Francisco.
Cravioto, Manuel.
"El Navío Mercante."
Estrada, Felipe.
Gonzalez, Angel.
Gonzalez y Ca., J., Suc.
"La Antigua Sevillana."
Maquivar y Ca.
Tafolla, Antonio.
Urquijo, Gabriel.

Hardware.
"El Bazar."
Guridi y Giese.
Islas, Vicente Ignacio.
"La Abeja."
"La Ciudad de México."
Maquivar y Ca.

Hatters.
Jara, Miguel.
Vargas, Juan.

PACHUCA, HIDALGO—Continued.

Jewelers and watchmakers.
Andrade, Arelia.
Bonavit Hermanos.
Cervantes, Luis.
Gonzalez, Fernandez.
Kahn Hermanos, Felix.
"La Ciudad de Paris."
Peña, Francisco.
Reina, Vidal.
Soria, Julian.

Lithographer.
Camacho, Refugio.

Lumber merchants.
Diaz, Rodriguez.
Hidalgo, Mateo.
Rozales, Francisco.

Paints and oils.
"El Bazar."
Garnica, Cárlos P.
Islas, Ignacio.
Nava, Justo Pastor.
Robles, Antonio.
Seguri, Luis.

Pianos, organs, etc.
Aguilar, I.
Montenegro, I.
Rodriguez, M.

Printing offices.
Camacho, Refugio.
"El Explorador."
"Del Progreso."
Imprenta del Gobierno.
"Imprenta Económica."
Pasco, Guillermo.

Saddlery and harness.
Carpintero, Roman.
Espinola, Refugio.
Lopez, Luis.

Sewing machines.
Kahn Hermanos, Felix.

PARRAL, CHIHUAHUA.

General merchants.
Bolivar, Canuto.
Corral y Gonzalez.
Erquicia, Suc.
Espiron y Ca.
Espiron, Victor.
Flores y Hijo, Victor.
Fuentes y Pena.
Hagen y Ca., Max.

PARRAL, CHIHUAHUA—Continued.

General merchants—Continued.
Knigge, Cárlos.
Mula, Maximo.
Ronquillo, Anto.
Stallforth Hnos.
Torres Hnos., Pedro.
Vaca y Hno., Juan B.

PARRAS, COAHUILA.

Agricultural and mining machinery.
Koenig, Viuda de Gmo.
Seiber y Ca., C.

Bankers.
Behr y Rojo.
Madero y Ca.
Misa, J. G.

Druggists.
Aguirre, Pedro.
Koenig, Viuda de Guillermo.
Martinez, Alfonso.
Maynes, Ed.

Dry goods.
Adame, Porfiro.
Chapman, Fernando.
Lajous, Rene, Suc.
Maynez y Ca.
Misa, José Gonzalez.

Flour mills.
Lajous, J. Rene, Suc.
Madero y Ca.
Morales, Pedro.
Navarro, Luis M.

General merchants—groceries, liquors, and tobaccos.
Aguirre, Rafael.
Lajous, Rene, Suc.
Misa, José Gonzalez.
Rojo y Behr.
Ruiz, Ernesto.

Hardware.
Behr, Juan.
Hagen y Ca., Max.
Koenig, Viuda de Gmo.
Seiber y Ca., C.

Manufacturers of liquors.
Aguirre, Rafael.
Lajous, Rene, Suc.
Madero y Ca.

PARRAS, COAHUILA—Continued.

Manufacturers of liquors—Continued.
Navarro Hnos.
Rojo, Remigio.
Ruiz y Ca., de Velasco.

Mining companies.
La Parrena.
Penoles.

PATOS, COAHUILA.

Brickmakers.
Fransto, Anastasio.

Flour mills.
Garcia, Bernardino.
Trevino, Manuel C.
Salas, Dr. Ismael.

General merchants.
Narro, Marino.
Rodriguez, Pablo.

PENJAMO, GUANAJUATO.

Banks and bankers.
Agencia del "Banco Nacional."
Agencia del "Banco de Lóndres y México."
Villaseñor Hermanos.

Commission merchant.
Magaña, Julio.

Drugs.
Covarrubias, Gregorio N.
Garcidueñas, Gregorio N.

Dry goods.
Alvarez, Ramon.
Echeveria y Cestan, Sinforiano.
Ocejo y Ca., Adolfo.

Groceries and provisions.
Alvarez, Ramon.
Arredondo, Federico.
Bardomiano, Navarro y Ca.
Herrera, Juan.
Orijel, Tiburcio.
Prado, Buenaventura.
Rios, Mariano.

Printing office.
Magaña, Julio.

Sewing machines.
Magaña, Julio.

PEÑON BLANCO.

Cotton factories.
Belen.
Bracho Hnos.
Flores y Dufar, Juan N.
Guadalupe.
La Concha.
Nafarrate Hnos.

Flour mills.
Flores, Juan J.

General merchants.
Benites, Francisco
Pesquera, José.

PINOS, ZACATECAS.

Carriages.
Garza, Genaro.
Zapata, Alejandro.

Drug stores.
" Botica del Comercio."
" Botica de San Luis."

Groceries and provisions and general merchandise.
Arellano, Isabel.
Arellano, Pioquinta.
Delgado, Antonio.
Garza, Genaro.
Martinez y Hermano, Camilo.
Navarro, José E.
Santillanes, Florencio.
Villaseñor, Francisco de P.
Villaseñor, Narciso.
Villaseñor y Hno., Antonio.

Printing office.
Villaseñor, Francisco de P.

Saddlery and harness.
Ruiz, Clemente.

Sewing machines.
Rojas, Simon G.

Silk goods.
Serna, Angel.

PROGRESO, YUCATAN.

Banker.
Haro y Ca.

Boots and shoes.
Aguilar, Donato.

Commission merchants.
Acevedo, J.
Ancona, N.

PROGRESO, YUCATAN—Continued.

Commission merchants—Continued.
Barrera y Sandoval.
Canton, Francisco.
Diégo y Ca., A. Cano.
Luis, F.
Marin, Nicoli, y Ca.
.   Mena, Daniel P.
Novelo y Ca.
Regil y Vales.

Drugs.
Capetillo, Pedro.
Marin, Rafael Perez.

Groceries and provisions.
Acevedo, Justo.
Barrera, Alejandro.
Barrera y Sandoval.
Marin, Nicoli, y Ca.
Molina y Ca., O.
Novelo y Ca., Luis F.
Ramos, Leon.
Rivos Hnos.
Sabido, Ignacio.
Sierra, Clemente.

Importer of fancy goods, furniture, etc.
Crasemann, J., Suc.

Printing office.
Moreno, Domingo Canton.

PUEBLA, PUEBLA.

Acids and chemicals.
Ibañez y Lamarque.
Manuel, Mena.

Agricultural implements.
Acedo é Hijos.
Sommer, Herrmann, y C.
Sumner y Ca., John M.
Valdez, Dario.

Arms and ammunition.
Centurion, Manuel.
Donaciano, Leon.
Donaciano, Ruiz.
Dorenberg y Ca., J.
Glockner y Ca.
Morroquin, Manuel.
Sommer, Herrmann, y Ca.

Banks and bankers.
Sucursal del Banco Nacional.
Sucursal del Banco de Lóndres y México.
Bauer y Ca.

PUEBLA, PUEBLA—Continued.

*Banks and bankers—*Continued.
Berkembuch Hnos.
Conde, Manuel.
Contollen y Ca.
Fernachon, E.
Galindo y Galindo.
Gavito é Hijo, F.
Gutierrez Palacios, Vicente.
Hernandez, A.
Hidalga, Vicente.
Pacheco, Joaquin.
Perez, Felix.
Saldivar, José Maria.
Teruel, Manuel.

Booksellers and stationers.
Angulo, Alberto.
Aspuru, Bernardino de.
Barros, Manuel Espino.
Baslois, Nacriso.
Báur, Cárlos.
Beguerisse, Enrique.
Eizaguirre, Lorenzo.
Galindo y Bezarez, Manuel.
Gallegos, Antonio.
Lainé, Ramon.
Lara, Pantaleon.
Paz y Puente, Francisco.
Senties, Francisco.
Tagle, Carlos.
Tagle, Matéo.
Villegas, José Maria.

Boots and shoes.
Arce, Dorotéo.
Arnaud y Saller.
Bello, Manuel.
Baes, Guadalupe.
Bueno, Angel R.
Corro, Isidro.
Diaz, José de J.
Domerq, Pedro.
Franco, Alejandro.
Gomez, Alberto.
Gomez, Nicolás.
Gonzaga, Luis Ramirez.
Lozano, Lúcio.
Manzano, Hilario.
Mateos, Luis C.
Ochoa, Rafael.
Perez y Ca.
Perez, José Maria.
Vieja, Aduana.

Carriages.
Angulo, José de J.
Brito, J. M.
Camacho, Cecelio.

PUEBLA, PUEBLA—Continued.

*Carriages—*Continued.
Delgado, Mariano.
Golzarri, Elenterio.
Gutierrez, José M.
Pastor, Manuel.
Rodriguez, Antonio.
Valenzuela, Reyes.

China and glassware.
Banuelos, Miguel.
Colombres, Eduardo.
Dorenberg y Ca., J.
Fernandez, Mariano.
Fernandez y Ca., Cenobria.
Lopez, Francisco.
Oropeza, José Maria.
Palacios, Antonio.
Peredo, Suarez.
Rojos, Manuel.
Romero, Hilario.
Toguera, Miguel.

Church furnishings.
Cardoso, Vicente de P.
Haller y Glawatz.

Commission agents (sale by sample).
Peemans y Marron.
Salles, Arnaud.
Sumner y Ca., John M.
Vazquez. Dorotéo.

Commission merchants.
Arrioja, Adolfo.
Arrioja, Gustavo.
Baur, Cárlos.
Blanco, José.
Calderon, Adolfo.
Calderon, M. M.
Daza, Manuel G.
Fernandez y Ca., Mariano.
Franco, Zeperino.
García, Luis Tesnel.
Gollado, José María.
Garrido, Miguel.
Gomez, J. María.
Larrasilla, Rafael.
Machorro, José de J.
Maldonado, Manuel.
Manzano, Eduardo.
Meza, Luis Bernado.
Mier, Antonio S.
Montiel, Miguel.
Morales, Bernabé.
Molina, Teófilo.
Olavarietta, J. M.
Ortíz, Barbollu.
Perez, Salazar.
Pineda, Andrés.

PUEBLA, PUEBLA—Continued.

Commission merchants—Continued.
Quintana, Carlos.
Ramirez, Enrique.
Rangel, Pablo.
Rojano, Rafael.
Rosales, José Librador.
Sanchez, José María.
San Martin, Marcelo.
Serrano, Francisco.
Thomas, Manuel.
Thomas y Teran, M.
Turnbull, Guillermo.
Vasquez, Dorotéo.
Von der Beck y Ca.
Zambrano, José María.
Zamora, Miguel.
Zuñiga, Cárlos.

Druggists.
Andifred, Maúa de J.
Arrioja, Delfino.
Arrioja, Joaquin.
Barrios, José M.
Barros, Cárlos E.
Bautista y Ca., Paulino.
Bequerisse, Pedro.
Bequerisse, Santiago.
Botello y Ca.
Botica de San Francisco.
Botica de Santa María.
Cal, Marcus.
Campus, Luis.
Carrasco, Vibriano.
Castillo, Rómulo.
Coriche, Guadalupe.
Crespo, Luis.
Diaz, Plácido B.
"Droguería Universal."
Encinas, Gregrorio.
Fernandez, Antonio.
Gil, Antonio.
Gomez, R,
Gonzalez, Pascual.
Hanez, J.
Ibanez y Lamarque, Joaquin.
Inchaguaregui, Luis.
Inchaurregui, V.
Lamarque, G.
Maldona, Manuel M.
Mariscal y Ca.
Moreno, M.
Rangel, Angel.
Reinal José.
Rodriguez, Rafael.
Rojano, Agulles.
Rojano, Nicolas.

PUEBLA, PUEBLA—Continued.

Druggists—Continued.
San Martin, M.
Suarez, Deodora.
Torquero, J.

Dry goods.
Avendaño, P. A.
Ballo y Cabrero.
Benitez y Hermanos.
Benito y Ca., C.
Chaix, Pedro.
Charles, Cárlos.
Conde, Manuel.
Dichel y Ca.
"El Puerto de Liverpool."
Garcia, P.
Gavito e Hijo.
Guthiel, y Ca.
Gutiérrez y Palacios.
Haller y Glawatz.
"La Independencia."
"Las Fábricas Universales."
Lions Hnos.
Lopez, A.
Lopez, Santos L.
Matienzo, Juan.
Mora, Rafael.
Ortiz y Hnos., Borpillo.
Peon, Manuel.
Perenz y Ca., Hernando.
Perez, Felix.
Quijano, Alberto.
Rivero, Ignacio.
Rosales, Antonio.
Serrano, Francisco L.
Sevilla é Hijos, J. N.
Teruel, Manuel.
Velasco Hnos.
Villaret y Duttner.
Watermeyer, German.

Engravers.
Herrera, Manuel.
Nevé, Tomas.

Fancy goods and notions.
Arce, M.
Arrioja, J. de.
Arrioja y Valverde, E.
Azla, B.
Benitez, Ricardo.
Cardoso Hnos.
Chaiz Hnos.
Diehl y Ca.
Dorenberg y Ca., J.
Lyons y Ca.
Moreno y Ca.

PUEBLA, PUEBLA—Continued.

Flour and Corn mills.
Amaniscar, Francisco.
Avalos. Aurelio.
Baez y Ca., Cárlos.
Benitez, Miguel.
Benitez, Emilio.
Conde, Francisco.
Diaz, Francisco.
Furlong, Tomas.
Gavito ó Hijo, Florencio.
Gil, Hernandez.
Gonzalez, P. M.
Haquét, Juan.
Islas, Laureano.
Larre, Tomas.
Latorre, Tomas.
Leblanc, A.
Lopez, Clemente.
Mauret Hnos.
Miez, Sebastian.
Montiel, A.
Pardo, S.
Perez, Juan.
Rofray, José.
Rosa, Francisco de la.
Teruel, M. García.
Tuta, José de J.
Vellegas, P.
Villegas. Eduardo.
Zúñiga, Berges de.

Flour merchants.
Beyes, Trinidad.
Calderon, Becerra Manuel.
Calderon, Manuel Macias.
Charles, Mariano.
Diaz, Francisco.
Lara, Pascual.
Toquero, Miguel.
Torija, Luis.

Foundries.
Acedo, Fausto.
Esparragoza, Miguel.
Lopez, Francisco.
Marshall, Tomas.
Rivera, José Diaz.
Toquero, J.

Furniture.
Aguilar Hnos., J.
Aguilar, José M.
Alvarado, Gabriel.
Arana, M. de la Luz.
Arraiga, Joaquin.
Baces, J. de L.
Baez, José.
Bueno, José.

PUEBLA, PUEBLA—Continued.

Furniture—Continued.
Cano, Vicente.
Castillo, Juan.
Costo, José.
Denetro, Francisco.
Domingo, Anastasio.
Dorenberg y Ca., J.
Fajardo, Miguel.
Fernandez, Francisco.
Gomez, Andrés.
Gonzalez, Andrés.
Guevara, Francisco.
Guevara, J.
Guevara, J. de J.
Gutierrez, Santiago.
Huesca, J.
Lara, Francisco.
Leroux, Juan.
Lopez, Albino.
Manzano, José María.
Martinez, A.
Medina, Guadalupe.
Mendez, José M.
Pacheco, Claro.
Pavon, Miguel.
Ramos, Juan.
Reyes, Francisco.
Rio, Juan Pablo del.
Rosano, Jorge.
Rosano, Luis.
Rosario, Jorge.
Sanchez, Francisco.
Sanchez, Ignacio.
Sanchez, Rafael.
Sommer, Herrmann y Ca.
Valdes, Claudio.

Gas fixtures, lamps, etc.
Bueno, José.
Castillo, Juan.
Fajardo, Miguel.
Fernandez, Francisco.
Lopez, Albino.
Martinez, A.
Medina, Guadalupe.
Mendez, José M.
Ramos, Juan.
Reyes, Francisco.

Glass and crockery.
Banuelos, Miguel.
Fernandez, Cenob.o.
Fuentes, G. de M.
Oropeza, Mariano.
Palacios, Miguel.
Paluisee, Javier.
Rojas, Manuel.

216 MEXICO.

PUEBLA, PUEBLA—Continued.

Glass and crockery—Continued.
Santillana, José de J.
Toquero. Miguel.
Vanden Bussche y Ca.

Groceries and provisions.
Acevedo, Bernardo.
Conde y Cosío.
Diaz, Manuel Pérez.
García Hnos.
Hernandez, Viuda de.
Linage, Pedro.
Mendoza, Guillermo.
Moreno y Hno., Rafael.
Paz y Puente, Joaquín.
Pereda, Casto.
Ponce, José de J.
Quevedo Hnos.
Quintana, E.
Rubin, Eugenio Micr.
Rubin, José Diaz.
Rugerio, Rafael.
Sanchez y Hno., F.
Valdez, Tomás.
Valverde, Eduardo.

Hardware, cutlery, and tools.
Blumenkron y Bravo.
Charles, Cárlos.
García, Paz.
Glockaer y Ca.
Guthiel y Ca.
Lopez, Antonio.
Lopez, Francisco.
Martinez, Manuel.
Paz y Puente, Francisco.
Rosales, Antonio.
Ruiz, Miguel.
Sommer Herrmann y Ca.
Traslosheros, Francisco.

Hatters.
Carcaño, Margarito.
Esmenjaud y Couttolenc.
Gonzalez, José Pellon.
Gonzalez, José Ma. C.

Hides, wholesale.
Acho, R.
Arrioja, Francisco.
Barriga, Leonardo.
Beiran, García.
Domerge, Teresa.
Gomez y Ca., Nicolas.
Martinez, Bernabe.
Montiel, José Maria.
Turnbull, Strybos y Mora.

House furnishing goods.
Careaga, José Maria.
Cisneros, Agustin.

House furnishing goods—Continued.
Cisneros, Rafael.
Cueto, Manuel.
Medina, J.
Reyes, Francisco.

Importers.
Baur, Carlos (books, stationery, scientific apparatus).
Beguerisse, Enrique (books and stationery).
Benito y Ca., C. (clothing, especially knitted goods and cassimeres).
Dorenberg y Ca., J. (fancy goods, furniture, chinaware, musical instruments).
Droguería Universal (drugs).
Faure y Ca., Augustin (conserves and comestibles).
Haller y Glawatz (dry goods, articles of luxury, church furnishings).
Ibañez y Lamarque (drugs).
Iñigo Hermanos (groceries and liquors).
Sommer, Herrmann y Ca. (machinery, hardware, fancy goods, paints and oils, pianos).
Sumner & Co., John M. (agricultural implements and machinery).

Iron and ironware.
Lopez, Francisco.
Rivera, José D.

Jewelers and watchmakers.
Anzures, Rafael.
Berestain.
Blumenkron, Bravo.
Carretero, Francisco.
Espinosa, Manuel.
Gauthier, Julio.
Glackner y Ca.
Guerrero é Hijo, Felix.
Guerrero, J.
Herchman, Cárlos.
Jacobi, Rodolfo.
"La Ciudad de Paris."
Liar, José M.
Marroquin, Mauuel.
Mendívil y Ca.
Mora, José.
Ochoa, José.
Ochoa, Juan.
Otañes, Rafael.
Palacios, Miguel,
Patiño, Eduardo.
Pedraza y Hno.
Perret, Federico.
Ramirez, Cárlos.
Rangel, Nestor,
Ruiz, Feliciano.
Ruiz, J.

PUEBLA, PUEBLA—Continued.

Jewelers and watchmakers—Continued.
 Shiverer, Andrés.
 Soriano, Ignacio.

Joint stock company.
 Compañía de Alumbrado eléctrico.

Lithographers.
 Campomanes y Ca.
 Gonzalez, Juan.
 Osorio, José M.

Lumber merchants.
 Berkemburchs, Jorgo.
 Fernandez, Francisco.
 Ferrer, Gabriel.
 Freyría, Enrique.
 Friera, Eduardo.
 García, Eduardo.
 Ibarra, Fernandez.
 Leon, Justo.
 Palafox, Teodóro.
 Pastor, Manuel.
 Traslosheros, Francisco.

Machinery.
 Alatorre, Cárlos B.
 Guthell y Ca.
 Rosales y Doremberl.
 Valdes, Domingo.

Music stores.
 Bueno, Benjamin R.
 Dorenberg y Ca., J.
 "El Camino de Hierro."
 Sommer, Herrmann y Ca.

Paints, oils, etc.
 Bueno, Benjamin R.
 "El Vesubio."
 García, Paz.
 Hernandez, Francisco J.
 Huerta, José M.
 "La Esperanza."
 "La Industria."
 Lopez, José Andrés.
 Lozado, Luis del Carmen.
 Mayorga, Mariano.
 Morales, Francisco.
 Olivares, Cárlos M.
 Padilla, Castulo.
 Padilla, Cayetano.
 Pavon ó Hijos, A.
 Paz y Puente, Francisco.
 Peralta, Ignacio.
 Sommer, Herrmann y Ca.

Paper.
 Lara, Manuel.

PUEBLA, PUEBLA—Continued.

Photographers.
 Barreal, José.
 Becerril, Lorenzo.
 Cabrera, Abraham.
 Del Monte Hnos.
 Gercíu, Benito.
 Lobato, Emilio G.
 Martinez, Joaquin.
 Pacheco, J.

Pianos and organs.
 Cuevas, José.
 Espinosa, D.
 Gracidas, Felipe.
 Olmedo, Felix.
 Polo, Agustin.
 Romero, José M.
 Velazquez, Francisco.

Printing offices.
 Alarcon, Pedro.
 Angulo, Alberto.
 Bochler, Isidoro.
 Boctar, M.
 Campomanes y Ca.
 Corona, Miguel.
 Franco, José de J.
 Gonzalez, J.
 Imprenta del Colegio.
 Imprenta del Gobierno.
 Impr nta del Hospicio.
 Imprenta y'Litografía.
 Lara, Benjamin.
 Macias, Ismael.
 Martinez, Joaquin.
 Moneda, Ignacio.
 Neve, Tomás.
 Ortiz, Dario.
 Osorio, José M.
 Pastor, Miguel.
 Pita, Joaquin.
 Romero, Isidro.
 Ruiz, Francisco.

Saddlery and harness.
 Coeto, Manuel.
 Dovantes, Antonio.
 Franco, Herlindo.
 Juarez, Juan José.
 Lopez, Estéban.
 Medina, José M.
 Sanchez, Ignacio.
 Tellez y Hno., Enr.
 Turnbull, Alberto M.

Sewing machines.
 Anzures, Rafael.
 Clokner y Centurion.

218

PUEBLA, PUEBLA—Continued.

Sewing machines—Continued.
Corn y Ca., Guillermo.
Guthell y Ca., Agustin.
Lopez, Antonio.
Marroquin, Manuel.
Rosales, Antonio.
Sommer, Herrmann y Ca.
Voiers y Ca., S. H.

Silk goods.
"El Hilo de Oro."
"La Parisiense."
"La Violeta."
Luna, J. M. Ramos.
"Paraguería Francesca."
Reyes, Eugenio.

Silversmiths.
Antigua Platería Alvarcz.
Guerrero, Felix.
Guerrero, J.
Patiño, A.
Patiño, Eduardo.
Ruiz, Agustin.

Tailoring establishments.
"Bella Jardinera."
Cortez, Vicente.
"El Surtidor."
Lara, José.
Marquez y Hno., P.
Pinero, Manuel.

Sugar merchants.
Colosia, M.
Illescas, Rafael.
Marron y Ca.
Ramora, R.

Undertaker.
Rio, Juan Pablo del.

Upholstery, carpets, etc.
Guevara, José de J.
Pacheco, Claro.

PUERTO DE MANZANILLO, COLIMA.

Agricultural implements
Ruiz, Ponciano.

Boots and shoes.
Ruelas, Serapio.

Commission merchants.
Ruiz, Ponciano.
Seuthe, Othon.

Drugs.
Ochoa, A.
Ruiz, P.

PUNTO DE MANZANILLO, COLIMA—Cont'd.

Dry goods.
Padilla, Teodóro.
Ruiz, Ponciano.
Solorzano, Fernando.

Furniture.
Cardenas, O.

Groceries and provisions.
Padilla, Teodóro.
Ruiz, Ponciano.
Seuthe, Othon.

Merchants.
Corona, Agustin (paper).
Gregor, Vicente (watchmaker).
Ochoa, Adalberto (acids and chemicals).
Ochoa, Luis (cloths).
Ruiz, Ponciano (stationery, general merchandise.)
Solorzano, Juan (saddlery and harness).

PUERTO MULEGÉ, LOWER CALIFORNIA.

Banker.
Navarro, Francisco.

Boots and shoes.
Alvarez, Miguel.
Gonzalez, Gabriel.
Rojas, Margarito.

Carriages.
Gonzalez. Antonio.

Drugs.
Rodriguez, Vidal.
Nuño, J. E.

Dry goods.
Benson, Oton.
Fierro, Cruz.
Fierro, Mauricio.
Gamez, Genova.
Gorosave, Vicente.
Irigoyen, Ramon.
Nuño, J. E.
Ozuna, Estéban.

Fancy goods.
Fierro, Mauricio.
Gamez, Genovevo.
Gorosave, Vincente.
Nuño, Cárlos J.

Furniture.
Félix, Hijinio.

Groceries and provisions.
Benson, Oton.
Gamez, G.
Fierro, Mauricio.
Gorosave, Vicinte.
Irigoyen, Ramon.

PUERTO MULEGÉ, LOWER CALIFORNIA—
Continued.

Hatter.
Villavicencio, Guadalupo.

Jewelry.
Gamez, Genovevo.

Saddlery and harness.
Jordan, Fernando.
Rosas, Francisco.

Sewing machines.
Gamez, G.

QUERÉTARO, QUERÉTARO.

Agricultural implements.
Gonzalez y Ca.
Plagemann, Ricardo J.

Arms and ammunition.
Plagemann, Ricardo J.
Viuda é hijos de Solorio.

Banks and bankers.
Agencia del "Banco Nacional."
Arias, Andrés G.
MacGregor, L. R.
Monfort, Sinecio.
Sucursal del "Banco de Lóndres y México."
Ugalde, Baltasar R.

Booksellers and stationers.
Chavez Suc.
Gonzalez y Ca.
Gonzalez, José.
Ibarra, Guadalupe.
Parres, José.
Plagemann, Ricardo J.

Boots and shoes.
Balandra, Ignacio.
Diaz, Hilarion.
Dominguez, Alberto.
Galan, Cenobio.
Gomez, Eulalio.
Moreno, Casimiro.
Muñoz, Manuel.
Saldaña, Antonio.

Carriages.
Leon, Benito.
Leon, Eulalio D.
Ramos, Benigno.
Trejo, Alejandro.

China and glassware.
Alday, Manuel.
Arias, Andrés G.
Gonzalo, Antonio.
Desidero y Ca., Rosendis.
Loyola, Antonio.

QUERÉTARO, QUERÉTARO.—Continued.

China and glassware—Continued.
Loyola, Ramon.
Mendez, José M.
Rivera, José M.

Clothing.
Arnaud y Martel.
Irdrac, Teófilo.
Marcel, Dionisio.
Mayrant y Richaud.
Mendez 6 Hijos.

Commission merchants.
Arias, Andrés G.
Arnaud, Agustin.
Contreras, Luis G.
Rivera, José M.
Trejo, Pablo.
Ugalde, Baltasar R.

Drugs.
Aguirre, José.
Arnulfo, Miguel.
Carmona, Juan.
Carrillo, Gabriel.
Cobo, Manuel.
Diaz, Aurelio.
Gonzalez y Ca.
Guerrero y Hno., Alberto.
Jauregui, F. de.
"La Verónica."
Makomilk, Pedro.
Marroquin, F.
Rodriguez, Francisco.
Rodriguez, Ramon.
Ruiz, Aurelio.
Septien y Montaño.
Velasco, José.
Vera, Esteban.

Dry goods.
Arnaud, Agustin.
Balbos, Francisco.
Córdova y Hno., J.
Maciel, Dionisio.
Martin y Ca., Arturo V.
Ruiz y Campos.

Engravers.
Balvanera, Teodoro.
Espinosa, José M.
Lámbarri y Ca., M.
Lira, Silvestre.

Fancy goods.
Aguilar, Demetrio.
Olvera, Fernando.
Plagemann, Ricardo J.
Rivera, José M.
Rosas, Antonio.

QUERÉTARO, QUERETARO—Continued.

Fancy goods—Continued.
  Vargas, Gregorio.
  Viuda é hijos de Solorio.
  Viuda de Rea.

Flour mills.
  Molino Colorado.
  Molino de Guadalupe.

Furniture.
  Arias, Andrés G.
  Carmona, Santiago.
  Gonzalez, José.
  Plagemann, Ricardo J.

Groceries and provisions.
  Arias, Andrés G.
, Camacho, Benito.
  Galeana, Ignacio.
  Gorraes, Ventura.
  Loyola, Antonio.
  Resendez y Ca., Desiderio.

Hardware.
  Aguilar, Demetrio.
  Gonzalez y Ca., José.
  Plagemann, Ricardo J.

Hatters.
  Corona, Francisco.
  Corona, Pedro.
  Franco, Juan.
  Vazquez, Feliciano.

Iron and ironware.
  Arias, Andrés G.
  Plagemann, Ricardo J.
  Ugalde, Baltasar R.

Jewelers.
  Borja, Adolfo.
  Monfort, Sinecio.
  Sinrob, Emiliano.

Jewelers and watchmakers.
  Altamirano.
  Esparza, Cárlos.
  Manilla, Nemesio.
  Monfort, Sinecio.
  Pereira, Pedro.
  Richarte, Julian.
  Sinrob, Emiliano.
  Vasquez, Rafael.

Joint stock company.
  Ferrocarril Urbano de Querétaro.

Lithographers.
  Lambarri y Ca., Miguel M.

Music stores.
  Gonzales y Ca.
  Rivera, José M.

QUERÉTARO, QUARÉTARO—Continued.

Paints, oils, etc.
  Aguilar, Demetrio.
  Gonzalez y Ca.
  Plagemann, Ricardo J.
  Reyes, Sevilla.

Paper.
  Bremer, Cárlos.

Perfumery.
  Alday, Manuel.
  Arnaud y Eartel.
  Bastida, Vicente.
  Mendez, José M.
  Olivera, Melchor.
  Rivera, José M.
  Torres, Nicolas.

Photographers.
  Balvanero, Teodoro.
  Flores, Ignacio Muñoz.
  Gomez, Benigno.
  Ruiz, Antonio.

Printing offices.
  Frias y Soto, Luciano.
  Gonzalez y Ca.
  Lambarri y Ca., Miguel M.

Pianos and organs.
  Arcos, M.
  Mendoza, Trinidad.
  Mosquera, Manuel.
  Romillo, Miguel.

Saddlery and harness.)
  García, Felipe.
  Hernandez, S.
  Molino, Manuel del.
  Perez, Antonio D.

Silk goods.
  Monfort, Dolores F. de.
  Rea, Porfiria.

Silversmiths.
  Alfaro, J.
  Barbosa y Hno., Agustin.
  Barrera, Evaristo.
  Gonzalez, J.
  Muñoz, Hermenegildo.
  Ojeda, Juan.
  Serrano, J.
  Vega, José.

Upholstery, carpets, etc.
  Gonzalez, J.
  Sartundo, Manuel.

ROSARIO, SINALOA.

Merchants.
  Arellano, Lorenzo (carriages).
  Campa, Francisco B. (carriages).
  Chaides, Fortino (hardware).

ROSARIO, SINALOA—Continued.

Merchants—Continued.
Espinosa, Antonio (drugs).
Gomez, Catalina M. de (fancy goods).
Güemez, Pomposo (dry goods).
Ibarra, Cárlos (drugs).
Imaña, Federico (hats and notions).
Navarrette, Angel (groceries).
Nuñez, Pedro P. (groceries).
Regenstein, Juan (dry goods).
Ribers, Cárlos S (drugs).
Rodriguez, Francisco de A. (furniture, dry goods, groceries).
Tellería, Francisco (dry goods).
Valadez, Vicente (photographer, bookseller, and commission merchant).
Valadez y Ca. (printing office).
Valdez, J. O. (groceries).
Zasusta, Angel P. (dry goods).

SABINAS, COAHUILA.

Coal dealers.
Alamo Coal Company.
Coahuila Coal Company.

General merchandise.
Fuentes, Dionisio.
Plant, C. T.
Valdez, Jesus Flores.

SALAMANCA, GUANAJUATO.

Bankers.
Calzada, Altagracia.
Martinez, Asuncion.

Boots and shoes.
Hernandez, German.
Mares, Juan.
Nuñes, Serapio.
Ramirez, Serapio.
Rivera, Atanasio.

Clothing and tailoring.
García, Marcos.
Rangel, Anecedo.
Santana y Medina.

Commission merchants.
Domezain, Ismael.
Flores, E.
García, J.
Ochoa, S.
Portusae, Manuel.

Drugs.
"Botica de Guadalupe."
"Botica de la Salud."
"Botica de la Union."
"Botica de San José."
Lopez, Florentino.

Dry goods.
Casillas, Valentin.
Flores, Eduardo.

SALAMANCA, GUANAJUATO—Continued.

Flour mills.
Alvarez, J.
Garcidueñas, Apolonio.

Groceries and provisions.
Domenzain y Ca., Ismael.
Zarandona, Domingo.

Hatter.
Oviedo, Valentin.

Kid glove factories.
Aboites, Manuel.
Andaluz, José M.
Campos, Miguel.
Freyre, Luis.
Gomez, Modesto.
Vidal, Antonio.

Manufacturers of brass bedsteads.
Penitentiaría.
Vargas, Mauro.

Photographers.
Roa, Luciano.
Villanueva, Refugio.

Printing offices.
Aboites, Manuel.
Domenzain y Ca., Ismael.
Penitenciaría.

Sewing machines.
Romano, J. Alva.
Stecately, Francisco.

Silversmiths.
Blanco, J.
García, Julio.
Olivarez, Cirilo.

SALTILLO, COAHUILA.

Agricultural implements.
Hayes, Juan.
Sieber y Ca., Clemente.

Arms and ammunition.
Sieber y Ca., Clemente.

Banks and bankers.
Banco Comercial.
Purcell, Guillermo.
Sota, Bernardo.

Booksellers and stationers.
Bouret, C.
Farga, Antonio.
Fuente, Antonio de la.
Sieber y Ca., Clemente.

Boots and shoes.
Aguirre, Antonio.
García, Juan.
Martinez y Ca., Ramon.
Molina, Ascencio.
Regalado, Toribio.
Salinas, Felix.
Sanchez, Juan.

SALTILLO, COAHUILA—Continued.

Boots and shoes—Continued.
Valdes, Florencio.
Valdez, Porfirio.
Valle, Antonio del.

Commission merchants.
Lopez Hnos.
Martinez & Woessner.
Sieber y Ca., C.

Drugs.
Barreda, Mauricio G.
Carothers, J. D.
Figueroa, José I.
Fuente, Sostenes de la.
Hernandez, Hilario.
Pena, F. de.
Rodriguez, J.
Warremosch, M.

Dry goods.
Mazo Hnos.
Negrete, José.
Signoret y Groués.
Soto, Bernardo.
Volpe, Donato.

Fancy goods.
Hayes, Juan.
Sieber y Ca., C.

Flour merchants.
Arispe y Ramos, Francisco.
Flores, Gabriel.
Paurcell, Guillermo.
Valdes, Juan.

Flour mills.
Arispe y Ramos, Francisco.
Barousse, Lezin.
Flores, Gabriel.
Leon y Aragon, Ramon de.

Furniture.
Blumenthal y Cordt.
Sieber y Ca., C.

Groceries and provisions.
Aguirre, Cárlos.
Calzada, Eusebio.
Desommes y Ca., H. V.
Garza, Marcelino.
Martinez, Anastasio.
Negrete, José.
Purcell, Guillermo.
Ramos, Ma.
Rodriguez, Dámaso.
Sota, Bernardo.

Hardware and tools.
Bertanga, A.
Cardenas, José.
Hayes, Juan.
Hernandez, Timoteo.
Moya, Eusebio.

SALTILLO, COAHUILA—Continued.

Hardware and tools—Continued.
Muarras, Francisco.
Myjica, Manuel.
Ortiz, Tranquilino.
Sieber y Ca., C.
Valverde, Antonio.

Hatters.
Hesselbart, Cárlos.
Palafox, Angel.
Signoret y Groués.

House-furnishing goods.
Aguirre, J.
Alvardo, Juan.
Cenicero, Gerónimo.
Charles, Simon.
Ortiz, Felipe.
Rodriguez, Damosa.
Salinas, Felix María.

Iron and ironware.
Hayes, J.
Sieber y Ca., C.

Jewelers and watchmakers.
Camacho, Cárlos.
Castillo, Juan.
Flores, Cárlos.
Pena, Rosa.
Sieber y Ca., C.
Urbina, Venturo.

Lithographer.
La Litografía del Gobierno.

Lumber dealers.
Ancira, J. M. Martinez.
García, Marcellino.
Lopez, Pablo A.

Paints, oils, etc.
Martinez ó Hijos, Anjel.
Sieber y Ca., C.

Paper.
Compañía Manufacturera de Papel del Saltillo.

Photographers.
Vazquez Hnos.
Zertuche, Rubén.

Pianos and organs.
Medrano, Casimiro.
Villanueva y Francescoui.

Printing offices.
Cardenas, Mariano.
Fernandez, Severo.
Fuentes, Francisco G.
Peña, Simon de la.

Sewing machines.
Blumenthal, E.
Hayes, Juan.
Mazo Hnos.

SALTILLO, COAHUILA—Continued.

Tailoring establishments.
Dávila, Juan.
Lopez, Antonio.
Martinez, Luciano.

Woods.
Martinez y Woessner.

SALVATIERRA, GUANAJUATO.

Booksellers and stationers.
Fuente, Juan de la.
Rivera, Francisco L.
Martinez, Zacarías.

Boots and shoes.
Barajas, J.
Gonzalez, Francisco.
Hernandez, Ignacio.

Carriages.
Coria, J.

Clothing, hats, etc.
Bolaños, J.
Carrera, Hilario H.
Escobedo, Leandro.
Fabre, Adolfo.
Lira, Lucas.
Miranda, Máximo.
Nieto, Rafaél.

Commission merchants.
Arias, J.
Capetillo, Casildo.
Estrada, Primitivo.
Mendez, Luis G.
Ramirez, Encarnacion.
Saldaña y Ca., J.

Drugs.
Anaya, Luis.
Ceballos, Antonio.
Espinosa, Manuel.
Gomez, Alberto.
Martinez, Ismael.
Moreno y Ca., José Leal.
Ruiz, Ramon.
Sanchez, Trinidad.
Teliberto, Benito S.

Dry goods.
Carrera y Hnos., Hilario.
Fabre, Adolfo.
Múgica, German.

Flour merchants.
Argomedo, Juan D.
Scanlan, Santiago.

Flour mills.
Argomedo, Juan D.
Llamaso, Francisco.

SALVATIERRA, GUANAJUATO—Continued.

Groceries and provisions.
Gomez, Alberto.
Guzman, Francisco.
Martinez, Zacarías.
Nieto, Rafaél.
Páramo, Francisco.
Rodriguez, Francisco.
Sancen, Remigio.
Soto, J.

Hardware and house furnishing goods.
Avilés, José.
Balandra, Eugenio.
Biskamp, Ernesto.
Guisa, José M.
Vargas, Bernabe.

Hatter.
Reyes, Pedro.

Jewelry.
Coria, Penasal.
Guisa, Pasenal.
Reyes, Antonio.

Lumber dealers.
Aragon, Vicente.
Espanza, Juliano.
Miranda, Máximo.

Manufacturer brass bedsteads.
Figueroa, J.

Mills.
Argumede, Juan D.
Ayala, Luis.
Campos, Francisco.
Maldonado, Manuel.
Scanlan, Santiago.
Soriano, Aniceto.
Soto, J.

Printing offices.
Balandra, Francisco.
Ruiz, Temoteo.

Sewing machines.
Morens y Ca., J. Leal.
Rivera, G. M.
Romano, Alva.

SAN BLAS, TERRITORIO DE TEPIC.

Bankers.
Barron, Forbes & Co.
Delius y Ca.
Lanzagorta Hnos.

Boots and shoes.
Casillas, Modesto.
Hernandez, José García.

Commission merchants.
Delius y Ca.
Garrido, Liborio.

SAN BLAS, TERRITORIO DE TEPIC—Cont'd.

Commission merchants—Continued.
Horsten, Otto von.
Lanzagorta Hnos.

Drugs.
Flores, B. H.
Martinez, B. L.
Romo, José M.

Dry goods.
Horsten, Otto von.
Lanzagorta Hnos.

Fancy goods.
Horsten, Otto von.

Groceries and provisions.
Aguirre, Manuel.
Bejarano, Juan.
Delius y Ca.
Fierros, B.
Lanzagorta Hnos.
Lorenzano, E.
Najar, A.
Ortiz, P.
Uribe, F.
Velazquez, B.

Importers and exporters.
Barron, Forbes & Co.
Delius y Ca.
Menchaca Bros.

Saddlery and harness.
Rios, Felix J.

Sewing machines.
Delius y Ca.
Horsten, Otto von.
Lanzagorta Hnos.

Tailor (merchant).
García, Zacarías.

SAN BUENAVENTURA, COAHUILA.

Druggists.
Still, Enrique M.
Villareal, A. L.

Flour mill.
Thomas y Hermanos.

General merchants.
Cerna, Felix.
Gutierrez, Enrique.
Kessler, Cárlos.
Morales y Hno., Wenceslao.
Sanchez, Margil.

SAN CRISTOBAL LAS CASAS, CHIAPAS.

Bank.
Banco Nacional (agente: W. Paniagua).

Boots and shoes.
Kramsky, Vicente.

SAN CRISTOBAL LAS CASAS, CHIAPAS—Continued.

Boots and shoes—Continued.
Mendez, Tránsito.
Tobilla, Secundino.

Commission merchants (sale by sample).
Dorantes, Jimenez y Ca.
López, Emerenciano.

Drugs.
Paniagua, Wenceslao.
Pineda y Rodriguez.
Ramos, Teófilo.

Dry goods.
Balboa, Angel.
Bonifaz, Fernanda.
Farrera, Vicente.
Lazos, Augusto.
Molinari, Angel.
Paniagua, Wenceslao.
Ruiz, José M.
Ruiz, Tirso.
Zapata, Francisco.
Zavaleta, Ezequiel.

Engraver.
Ruiz, Mariano N.

Fancy goods.
Trujillo, Celso.

Flour mills.
"Albarrada."
"Chamula."
"La Isla."
"Los Arcos."
"Santo Domingo."

Groceries and provisions.
Bolaños, Francisco Ortiz.
Dominguez, Adolfo.
Farrera, Vicente.
Paniagua, Wenceslao.

Photographer.
Zepeda, Buenaventura.

Printing offices.
Flores, Novato.
Imprenta del Gobierno.
Pineda, Vicente.
Salazar, Cárlos.
Sociedad Católica.

Saddlery and harness.
Roman, J.
Ruiz, Fernando.

Silversmiths.
Molina, Celso.
Ruiz, Abrahan.
Ruiz, Nicasio.

Tailors (merchant).
Aguilar, Manuel.

SAN CRISTOBAL LAS CASAS, CHIAPAS—
Continued.

Tailors (merchants)—Continued.
Ramos, Hermelindo.
Ramos, Primitivo.

Watchmaker.
Ruiz, Mariano.

SAN DIMAS, DURANGO.

General merchants.
Escobosa y Burns.
Laveaga y Ca.

Mining companies.
Laveaga y Ca.
Mineria de Candelaria.
Negociacion Ventana.
Negociacion Villa Corona.

SAN JUAN BAUTISTA, TABASCO.

Arms and ammunition.
Cahero, Manuel.

Bankers.
Berreteaga y Ca., M.
Bulnes Hnos.
Jarnet y Sastre.
Lamadrid, Tomás G.
Serralta, Salvador.

Books and stationery.
Graham, José M.

Commission merchants.
Bulnes Hnos.
Merino, José M.
Rosas, Justo.
Suarez Hnos.

Drugs.
Ponz, Manuel.
Serralta, Salvador.

Dry goods.
Arteach y Peral.
Azuela, Manuel.
Benito y Ca., G.
Berreteaga y Ca., M.
Bueno, Victor.
Heeres, José Fernandez.
Hermógenes, Cué.
Forteza y Ca.
Lamadrid, Tomás G.
Lopez, Becerra y Ca.
Madrazo, Felipe.
Pastor y Rodriguez.
Ripoll y Ca., M.
Romano y Ca., Suc.
Trueba, José G.
Villaveitia, Ramon.

S. Ex. 8, pt. 11——15

SAN JUAN BAUTISTA, TABASCO—Cont'd.

Engraver.
Diaz, José Sanchez.

Fancy goods.
Diaz, Isidoro M.

Furniture.
Merino, Froilán.

Groceries and provisions.
Benito y Ca., G.
Berreteaga y Ca., M.
Knapp y Ca., E.
Lopez, Becerra y Ca.
Pastor y Rodriguez.
Repoll y Ca., M.
Roman y Ca., Suc.

Hardware.
Diez, Isidoro M.

Hatters.
Galindo, Antonio.
Nieto, Francisco Morgado.

Music store.
Kildsen, Guillo.

Photographs.
Flor, Manuel de la.

Printing offices.
Avalos, José M.
Castillo, Amado Hernandez.
"Imprenta del Gobierno."
Trujillo, Juan S.

Watchmakers.
Hunter, David.
Sanchez, Eulogio.
Serrano, A.

SAN JUAN DE GUADALUPE, DURANGO.

Agricultural implements.
Rodriguez, Felipe.
Saldaña, Bernardo.

Boots and shoes.
Aguayo, Atilano.
Martinez, Florentino.

Commission merchant.
Puga, Francisco E.

Drugs.
Aspilcueta, Guillermo.
Goitia, José B.

Dry goods.
Aguayo, Atilano.
Botello, Buenaventura.
Delgadillo Hermanos.
García, Nicanor.
Mireles, Eduardo.
Ortiz, Agustin.

SAN JUAN DE GUADALUPE, DURANGO— Continued.

Dry goods—Continued.
  Puga, Francisco E.
  Ramirez, Gerónimo.
  Rodarte, Cástulo.
  Rodriguez, Felipe.
  Saldaña, Bernardo.

Fancy goods.
  Rodarte, Cástulo.

Flour mills.
  Rodriguez, Felipe.
  Saldaña, Bernardo.

Groceries and provisions.
  Puga, Francisco E.
  Rodriguez, Felipe.
  Saldaña, Bernardo.

Merchant tailors.
  Agüero, Bonifacio.
  Esquivel, Deciderio.
  Gonzalez, Apolonio.
  Martinez, Florentino.

Music store.
  "El Municipal."

Sewing machines.
  Puga, Francisco E.

Silversmith.
  Velazquez, Severiano.

SAN JUAN DE LOS LAGOS, JALISCO.

Agricultural implements.
  Perez, Francisco Jiménez.

Books and stationery.
  Gonzalez, Francisco de P.
  Romo, Rosa.

Boots and shoes.
  Alba, J. de.
  Perez, Pablo.
  Ruiz, Ascencio.
  Torre, R. de la.

Carriage dealers.
  Jiménez, Modesto.
  Martin, Fidel.

Commission merchants.
  Galindo, Espiridion.
  Gonzalez, Tirso.
  Martin, José (sale by sample).
  Torre, Cecilio de la (sale by sample).

Drugs.
  Gallardo, Eligio.
  Montero, Cosmé.

Engraver.
  Segoviano, Isabel.

SAN JUAN DE LOS LAGOS, JALISCO— Continued.

Fancy goods.
  Martin, Juan N.

Furniture.
  Torre, Felix de la.
  Torre, Ramon de la.

Groceries and provisions.
  Ornelas, Domingo.

Hatters.
  Sanchez, Arcadio.
  Segoviano, Martin.

Lithographer.
  Martin, José.

Manufacturers of brass bedsteads.
  Anda, Ignacio de.
  Rodriguez, Antonio.
  Rodriguez, Juan.

Merchant tailors.
  Alba, Rutilo de.
  Flores, Miguel.
  Gonzalez, Manuel.
  Martin, Melquíades.
  Ramos, Pragedio.
  Reynoso, Eliséo G.

Music stores.
  Leon, Manuel de.
  Rodriguez, Isidoro.

Photographers.
  Gonzalez, Francisco de P.
  Hermosillo, Francisco.

Printing offices.
  Martin, José.
  Tortelero, José.

Saddlery and harness.
  Diaz, Eutimio.
  Perez, Pastor.

Sewing machines.
  Martin, José.

Silversmiths.
  Alba, Eduardo de.
  Avila, Reyes.
  Flores, Severo.
  Gonzalez, Cruz.
  Leon, Benjamin de.
  Sanchez, Eduardo.

SAN JUAN DEL RIO, QUERÉTARO.

China and glassware.
  Basurto, Pascual.

Commission merchants.
  Fernandez y Gutiérrez (sale by sample).
  Sanchez, Felipe (sale by sample).
  Ugalde, A.
  Ugalde, Ignacio V.

SAN JUAN DEL RIO, QUERÉTARO—
Continued.

Drugs.
Covarrubias, Léon.
Macias, Juan.
Olloqui, Agustin R.
Ugalde, Amador E.

Dry goods.
Escobar, J. Hurtado.
Hurtado, Juan.
Ugalde, Alberto.
Ugalde, Ignacio V.

Fancy goods.
Hernandez, Pablo.
Hurtado, Juan.

Flour mills.
Cañizo, Manuel.
Dorantes, Teófilo.
Torre, Manuel de la.

Groceries and provisions.
Guadarrama, Guadalupe,
Ruiz, Joaquin.
Ugalde, Bernabé.

Hatter.
Contreras, Manuel.

Iron and ironware.
Ugalde, Bernabé.

Merchant tailor.
Garrido, Ignacio.

Paints and oils.
Ugalde, Bernabé.

Printing office.
Ugalde, Bernabé.

Sewing machines.
Garrido, Ignacio.

SAN LUIS DE LA PAZ, GUANAJUATO.

Merchants.
Arellano, Reyes (merchant tailor).
" Beneficiadora de Metales " (joint-stock company).
Bustamante, J. (merchant tailor).
Garbari, Fabian (dry goods).
Huerta, Antonio (flour mill).
López, Roberto (sewing machines).
Martinez, Eleno (drugs).
Martinez, Juan (merchant tailor).
Olivares, Francisco (fancy goods).
Paulín, Juan Flores (drugs).
Ponce, Santos (silversmith).
Rangel, Miguel (merchant tailor).
Salazar, Pedro (merchant tailor).

SAN LUIS POTOSÍ, SAN LUIS POTOSÍ.

Agricultural implements, arms and ammunition.
Clemente, Hermosillo.

SAN LUIS POTOSÍ, SAN LUIS POTOSÍ—
Continued.

Agricultural implements, arms and ammunition—Continued.
Philipp y Ca., Max A.
Saenger, Fernando.
Silva, Nemesio.
Storck y Grumbrecht.
Torres, Juan.

Banks.
Sucursal del " Banco de Lóndres y México."
Sucursal del " Banco Nacional."

Bankers.
Bahnsen y Ca., J. H.
Larrache y Ca., Suc.
Meadi y Hnos., Federico J.
Soberon, Matías Hernandez.

Booksellers.
Cabrera, Antonio.
Esquivel y Ca., M.
Kaiser, Juan.
Parres, Ramon F.
Vazquez, Francisco.

Boots and shoes.
Arochi, Eduardo.
Borrego, Viuda de.
Coca, Luis.
Córdova, Juan.
Esparza, Francisco.
Izquierdo, Felipe.
Lopez, José G.
Reyes, Manuel.
Romero, Pomposo.
Santillana, A.

Carriage dealers.
Rios, Casimiro de los.
Tena, Hilario.

China and glassware.
Aguirre y Ca., Luis.
Deliz, Santiago.
Gedovius, German.
Gonzalez, Felipe.
Gutheil y Ca., Agustin.
Manrique, H. de Lara.
Philipp y Ca., Max A.
Reyes, Antonion.
Storck y Grumbrecht.

Commission merchants.
Camacho, Francisco.
Cerda, Margarito Lopez de la.
Gómez, Macedonio.
Lasker, Julio.
Meade y Hnos., Federico J.
Pitman y Ca.
Rodriguez y Rodriguez.

SAN LUIS POTOSÍ, SAN LUIS POTOSÍ—Continued.

Copper goods.
Bueno, Domingo.
Mejía, Juan.
Vazquez, Ramon.

Drugs.
Alcocer, Anastasio.
Baquero y Ca.
Crespo, Luis G.
" Droguería Universal."
Goribar, Juan I. Garcia.
Hermosillo, Mariano.
Limon, Francisco.
Lopez, Antonio.
Muñoz y Fonegra.
Olmedo, Estéban.
Outanon, N.
Paez, Rafael.
Rodriguez y Ca.
Valdez, José.
Villaseñor, J. M.

Dry goods.
Abascal y Ca., Pedro.
Anda y Villalobos.
Caire, Michel y Ca.
Cassanueva y Ca.
Dias de Leon, José.
Franck y Ca., M.
Gregorio, Brieva.
Lozano, Antonio.
Muriedas y Ca.
Rivero y Liaño.
Signoret y Ca.
Valle, Garcia y Ca.

Engravers.
Cenachillo, Pedro.
Hidalgo, Juan.
Muñoz, Ramon.

Fancy goods.
Aguirre y Ca., Luis.
Amado, Molino.
Gedovius y Unna.
Gonzalez, Felipe N.
Gonzalez, Nestor.
Pedroza, Francisco.
Philipp y Ca., Max A.
Puente, Homobono.
Saenger, Fernando.
Salinas, Andrés.
Storck y Grumbrecht.

Flour merchants.
Alcocer, Anastasio.
Bustamante, Domingo.
Davila, Julio.
Goribar, Francisco.

SAN LUIS POTOSÍ, SAN LUIS POTOSÍ—Continued.

Flour merchants—Continued.
Meade y Hermano, G.
Otahegui, José M.
Othon, Manuel.
Parra, Cayetano.

Flour mills.
Farias, Agustin.
Goribar, Juan.
Muriedas y Ca.
Villalba y Narezo.

Furniture.
Aguirre y Ca., Luis.
Geodovius y Unna.
Heredia, Manuel.
Philipp y Ca., Max A.
Schrader é Hijo, J. H.
Storck y Grumbrecht.
Weber, Pedro.

Foundries.
Schrader é Hijo, J. M.
Villalba y Narezo.

Groceries and provisions.
Alba, Celedonio.
Arrieta, Tranquilino.
Cantolla y Ca.
Cerda, Margarito Lopez de la.
Chavez, Juan.
Delgado, Feliciano.
Diliz, Santiago, Suc.
Felipe, Vicente.
Galindo, José.
Galvan, Onofre.
Hermosillo, José.
Herrera y Ca.
Higinio, Alonso.
Lara, H. Manrique de, Suc.
Lazcoz y Ca., Francisco.
Llaca y Ca., Enrique.
Márquez y Ca.
Mora, Juan.
Nieto, Hilario.
Olavarría y Ca.
Pedroza, Valentin.
Rangel, Apolonio.
Reyes, Antonio J.
Reyes, L.
Salas, Joaquin B.
Socesa y Ca.

Hardware.
Aguirre y Ca., Luis.
Elcoro y Ca., Valentin.
Gedovius y Unna.
Philipp y Ca., Max A.
Sänger, Fernando.
Storck y Grumbrecht.

SAN LUIS POTOSÍ, SAN LUIS POTOSÍ—Continued.

Hatters.
Campos, J. Lorenzo.
Gomez, Manuel.
Lozano, Antonio.
Marquez, Guadalupe.
Noriega y Tejo.
Quintas, Benito.
Sanchez y Ca.

Importers.
Aguirre y Ca., Luis (fancy goods, hardware, furniture, musical instruments, wines, liquors, and toys).
Bahnsen y Ca., J. H. (dry goods, importers and exporters).
Caire, Michel y Ca. (dry goods).
Droguería Universal (drugs, surgical instruments, etc.).
Facon, Constant, Suc. (cloths).
Frank y Ca., M. (dry goods).
Muriedas y Ca. (dry goods, hats).
Norwood, José.
Philipp y Ca., Max A. (fancy goods, hardware, chinaware, perfumery, paper, furniture, pianos, lamps, arms, and ammunition).
Rodriguez y Ca., Rafael (drugs).
Sanchez y Ca. (hats).
Signoret y Ca. (dry goods).
Storck y Grumbrecht (machinery, hardware, chinaware, fancy goods, mirrors, etc.).
Valle, García y Ca. (dry goods).

Iron and ironware.
Aguirre y Ca., Luis.
Elcoro y Ca., Valentin.
Meade y Hnos., Federico J.
Saenger, Fernando.
Storck y Grumbrecht.
Valladolid, Francisco.

Jewelers and watchmakers.
Guerrero, Demetrio.
Herfter, Ernesto.
Landereche, Juan.
Martinez, Ramon.
Philipp y Ca., Max A.
Storck y Grumbrecht.
Tosgobbi, Francisco.
Vildósola, Francisco.

Lithographers.
Cabrera, Antonio.
Esquivel y Ca.
Kaiser, Juan.
Parres, Ramon F.
Vazquez, Francisco.

Merchandise, imported and domestic.
Alcocer, Anastasio.
Aresti y Ca.

SAN LUIS POTOSÍ, SAN LUIS POTOSÍ—Continued.

Merchandise, imported and domestic—Continued.
Bahnsen y Ca., J. H.
Barrenechea Hnos.
Cabrera, Emigidio.
Caire, Michel y Ca.
Campos, Agapito.
Cerda, Margarito Lopez de la.
Cervantes, Antonio E.
Dosal, Ramon.
García, J.
Gonzalez, Dario.
Goribar, Juan I. García.
Hermosillo, Clemente.
Ipiña, Encarnacion.
Lavin, Emetrio.
Meade y Hnos., Federico J.
Othon, Ramon.
Pitman y Ca.
Soberon, Matías H.
Varona y Ca.

Merchant tailors.
Dávila, M.
Facon, Constant, Suc.
Franck y Ca., M.
García, Pascual.
Guerrero, Francisco.
Perez, Julian.

Music stores.
Aguirre y Ca., Luis.
Kaiser, Juan.
Philipp y Ca., Max A.

Opticians.
Grunstein, F.

Paints and oils.
Montante, Arilleta.
Montante y Nieto.

Petroleum.
Meade y Hnos., Federico J.
"Waters Pierce Oil Co."

Photographers.
Barraza A.
Clausnitzer, Cárlos.
Pedroza, Eugenio.
Serratos y Ca., A.

Printing offices.
Barbosa, Ricardo.
Dávalos, Cárlos.
Esquivel y Ca.
Faustino, Leija.
"Imprenta de la Escuela Industrial Militar."
"Imprenta de El Estandarte."

Sewing machines.
Bush y Ca., C. M.
Sänger, Fernando.
Weinburg, D.

SAN LUIS, POTOSÍ, SAN LUIS POTOSÍ—
Continued.

Tinware.
Alanis, Silvestre.
Arzueta, Angel.
Castañeda, Dumas.

Upholstery and carpets.
Gedovius y Unna.

SAN PEDRO DE COLONIA, COAHUILA.

Bankers.
Horner, Justin.
Madero y Hernandez.
Purcell, Gmo.

Druggist.
Garza, Miguel.

Flour mill.
Horner, Justin.

General merchants.
Acosta, Jesus.
Buenavidas Hnos.
Cerda y Hernandez.
Galvan, Onofre.
Gonzalez, Mauro.
Purcell, Gmo.
Quijano y Hns., M.
Rivas, Lucas.
Rodriguez, Marcello.
Taffinder, Santiago.

Hardware and agricultural implements, china and glassware.
Nancke, Rudolfo.
Purcell, Gmo.

Soap and cotton-seed oils.
Belden, Fco.
La Esperanza.
La Favorita.
Stephens y Ca.

SANTA CATARINA, NUEVO LEON.

Dry goods.
Rodriguez, Ansencio.

Factories, cotton.
Andrew, Samuel.

Factories, hat.
Hesselbart, Cárlos G.

Mining companies.
Humbert, J. E.
Lopez, Eutemio.
Sanchez, Anastasio.

SANTA ROSA, COAHUILA.

Druggists.
Berchelman, A. G.
Chapa, P.

SANTA ROSA, COAHUILA—Continued.

Flour mills.
Bunsen, Conrado.
Mangel, Ambrosio.

General merchandise, groceries, tabacco.
Davilla, Miguel Musquiz.
Elizondo y Hijo., E.
Elizondo, Rafael.
Galan, Juan José.
Galan, Roman.
Long, Jacobo.
Quiroz, Rafael A.
Rodriguez, Miguel.
Rodriguez, Trinidad.
Urista, Leandro.

Hardware.
Castellano, Estanislao.
Elizondo y Hijo.

Mining companies.
Cedral.
La Bonita.
La Fronteriza.
La Luz.
San Juan.
Gertrudio, Santa.

SANTA ROSALIA, CHIHUAHUA.

General merchants.
Acres, W.
Ameraga, Rafael Mazo.
Bezanilla y Ca.
Cordero, Vicente.
Gonzalez, José Guadalupe.
Guevara, Miguel.
Palacio, Vicente.
Prieto, Marco.
Sarli, Vicente.
Stoppelli Visconti y Ca.

Mining and agricultural machinery and hard. ware.
Cordero, Vicente.

SIERRA MOJADA, COAHUILA.

General merchants.
Guzman, Anto Trevino.
Pena, Juan Garcia.

Mining companies.
Constancia Compañia.
La Esmeralda.
La Parrena.

SINALOA, SINALOA.

Agricultural implements, mining machinery, and hardware.
Alcalde, Octaviano.
Felix, Cárlos.

SINALOA, SINALOA—Continued.

General merchants.
Alcalde, Octaviano.
Felix, Cárlos.
Laura, Tomás.
Mendez, Miguel.
Monge, Jesus.
Nuvez, Juan N.
Rojo, Pedro C.
Pena y Saracho.
Valdez, Cárlos.

SOMBRERETE, ZACATECAS.

Carriage builders.
Castrillon, Fernando.
Rodriguez, Ricardo.
Flour mills.
Barrios, Manuel.
Rodarte, Jesus.
General merchants.
Amezaga, Joaquin.
Bracho, Manuel.
Diaz, Juan N.
Lazalde Hnos.
Martinez, Francisco.
Moqui, Jesus V.
Parra, Cárlos.
Parra, Enrique.
Parra, Juan B.
Perez y Hno., Gregorio.
Sanchez, Leandro.
Sierra, Lovenno.

TAMPICO, TAMAULIPAS.

Banker.
Schutz, Federico F.
Carriage dealers.
Aretia, Antonio.
Morales, Manuel.
Commission merchants.
Basadre, Gregorio Cortina.
Cruz y Amorevieta.
Dominguez y Ca.
Jolly y Ca., Eduardo L.
Lastra y Ca., Diégo de la.
Madraza, Juan.
Prom, Juan.
Schutz, Federico F.
Stussy, F.
Trópaza Hnos.
Ugarte Hnos.
Drugs.
Gonzalez, Felipe.
Omar, Herederos de P. G.
Solórzano, Juan B.

TAMPICO, TAMAULIPAS—Continued.

Dry goods.
Caloca y Ca., S.
Cruz y Amorevieta.
Lastra y Ca., D. de la.
Lopez y Rodriguez.
Reynaud Hermanos.
Ugarte Hermanos.
Fancy goods.
Borde Hermanos.
Borde, J. F.
Dauban, Eugenio.
Peredo, Francisco.
Groceries and provisions.
Barrios, Pantaleon.
Castillo, Macario.
Dominguez y Ca., A.
Grillo, Simon Torres.
Madrazo, Juan.
Rodriguez y Ca., Bartolo.
Saunders, Santiago.
Stussy, Federico.
Tessada, Enrique.
Trueba, Domingo.
Velez, Miguel.
Hardware.
Borde Hermanos.
Borde, J. F.
Dauban, Eugenio.
Peredo, Francisco.
Hatters.
Cruzado, Eduardo.
Najera, Luis G.
Printing offices.
García, Francisco G.
Garza, J. de la.
Segura, Cárlos B.
Silversmiths.
Gauban, Cárlos.
Gauban, N. B.
Rojas, Cliserio.
Vargas, Miguel.
Watchmakers.
Cabieres, Ismael.
Rojas, Cliserio.
Woods.
Cambo, Nicolas del.
Saunders, Santiago.

TEHUACAN, PUEBLA.

Boots and shoes.
Gonzalez, Perfecto.
Navarro, José de la Luz.
Carriage dealers.
Castañon, Juventino.
Rosete, Joaquin.

TEHUACAN, PUEBLA—Continued.

China and glassware.
Cacho, Samuel.
Maillé, Emilio.

Commission merchants.
Aldama, Leandro.
Gamez, Severiano.
Loyo, Gerónimo Arandia.
Puente, Ignacio de la.

Drugs.
Amezcua y Orduña.
Ariza, Vicente.
Lince, Antonio E.
Montano, Juan B.

Dry goods.
García, Vicente P.
Gaymard y Spitatur.
Martinez, J. de J.
Pastor, José.
Puente, Ramon de la.

Engraver.
Gonzalez, Miguel.

Fancy goods.
Cacho, Samuel.
Heres, Cárlos G.
Maillé Ca., Emilio.

Flour mills.
Cacho, Agustin.
Ceballos, Juan Diaz.
Gonzalez, Daniel.
Rocamoro, Viuda de.

Groceries and provisions.
Espinosa Hnos., L. M.
Martinez y Ca., R
Mazay Hnos., R.
Puente, Fernando de la.
Rocamoro, Viuda de.

Hardware.
Bermudez é Hijo, José.
Heras, Cárlos G.

Hatter.
Martinez, José de J.

Joint-stock company.
Compañía de Transportes y Comisiones.

Photographer.
Vidal, Manuel.

Printing office.
Nolasco, Agustin.

Sewing machines.
Gutiérrez, Miguel.

Silversmiths.
Olivier, Próspero.
Solis, José de J.

TEHUANTEPEC, OAXACA.

Banker.
Larrañaga, M.

TEHUANTEPEC OAXACA—Continued.

Boots and shoes.
Cruz, Bruno.
Guzman, Emilio.
Jacinto, Mariano.
Jimenez, Pedro.
Mendez, Francisco.
Orozco, Isidro.
Sanchez, Francisco.
Trinidad, Mariano.
Valdivieso, Mateo.
Villalobos, Francisco.

Commission merchant.
Koch, C. R.

Drugs.
Gonzalez, Amador.
Huacuya, José M.
Solana Hnos.

Dry goods.
Echazarreta, F.
Langner y Arrillaga.
Larrañaga, M.
Romero, Juan C.
Santibañez, Antonio.
Solana Hnos.
Toledo, Arnulfo.
Toledo, Juan.

Groceries and provisions.
Bustillo, Santiago.
Echazarreta, F.
Guzman, Francisco.
Langner y Arrillaga.
Larrañaga M.
Santibañez, Antonio.
Solana Hnos.

Hatter.
Pacheco, José.

Merchant tailors.
Espinosa, Mariano.
Marquez, Enrique.
Sibaja, Feliciano.
Sibaja, Zenon.

Photographer.
Palacios, Conrado.

Printing offices.
"Imprenta del Istmo."
Medardo y Zabulon Hnos.

Saddlery and harness.
Chinar, Juan M.
Jacinto, Justo.
Jacinto, Luciano.
Reyna, Laureano.
Sierra, Homobono.
Valdiviejo, Damien.

Sewing machines.
Langner y Arrillaga.

TENANCINGO, MEXICO.

Acids and chemicals.
Valero, Marcos.

Arms and ammunition.
Hernandez, Donaciano,

Bankers.
Pacheco, Rómulo.
Zepeda, Cárlos.

China and glassware.
Hernandez, Donaciano.

Commission merchants.
García, Atenógenes.

Drugs.
Guzman, Ignacio
Jonguitud, Leonidas.
Valero, Marcos.

Dry goods.
Izquierdo, Miguel.
Pando, Bernardo de.

Engraver.
Nuñez, Everado.

Fancy goods.
Hernandez, Donaciano.
Jimenez, Rafael.

Flour mills.
" Chalchihuapa. "
" El Salto. "
" Santa Ana. "

Furniture.
Garibay, Crescencio.
Rivera, Cástulo.

Groceries and provisions.
Pacheco, Cruz.
Pacheco, Rómulo.
Pacheco, Severo

Hardware.
Alvarez, Francisco.
Hernandez, Donaciano,

Hatter.
Valero, Francisco.

Lithographers.
Rodriguez, Galacion.
Rójas, Efren.

Merchant tailors.
Garibay, Antonio.
Gordillo, Vicente.

Paints and colors.
Alvarez, Francisco.
Hernandez, Donaciano.

Photographer.
Villegos, Plácido.

Printing offices.
Estrada, Francisco.
Herrera, Juan.

TENANCINGO, MEXICO—Continued.

Saddlery and harness.
Rivera, Isidoro.

Sewing machines.
Villegas, Jacinto.

Silk goods.
Pando, Bernardo de.

Silversmiths.
Nuñez, Everardo.
Penaloza, Manuel.
Reynoso, José.

Watchmakers.
. Nuñez, Everardo.
Reynoso, José.

TENANGO DEL VALLE, MEXICO.

Boots and shoes.
Rodriguez, Calixto.
Santana, Benigno.
Talavera, Luis.
Tejedo, Saturnino.
Valez, Severo.

Carriages.
Pichardo, Celedonio.

Drugs.
Azoños, Crisefon Garduño.
Duran, Agustin.
Moral, Julio P. del.
Sanchez, Margarito.

Fancy goods.
Azoños, Francisco Duran.

Flour mills.
" Molino de Santa Rosa."
Sanchez, Cosme.

Furniture.
Arellano, Juan.
Arellano, Pedro.

Groceries and provisions.
Algani, Alvaro G.
Bustamante, Francisco D.
Cervantes, J.
Lopez, Preciliano.

Hardware, iron, and ironware.
Azoños, Francisco Duran.

Joint-stock company.
Compañía Union Mercantil

Merchant tailors.
Diaz, Luz.
Gutiérrez, Fernando.
Juarez, Eulogio.
Morales, Dionisio.
Velazquez, Adrian.

Music store.
Azoños, Francisco Duran.

Paints and oils.
Azoños, Francisco Duran.

TENANGO DEL VALLE, MEXICO—Cont'd.

Photographers.
Arellano, Gumesindo.
Moral, Julio P. del.

Printing office.
Diaz, Manuel Estrada.

Saddlery and harness.
Gonzalez, Gabino.
Martinez, Merced.

Sewing machines.
Arellano, Gumesindo.

Silk goods.
Ochoa, Margarita.
Ortiz, Merced Maya de.

Silversmiths.
Abrego, Sotero.
Rosales, Máximo.
Veucis, José María.

TEPIC, TERRITORIO DE TEPIC.

Bankers.
Aguirre y Ca., Juan A. de.
Barron, Forbes y Ca.
Delius y Meyer.
Menchaca Hnos.

Booksellers and stationers.
Bouret, Suc.
Ocegueda, J. Emilio.
Retes, J. M.

Commission merchants.
Andrade, J.
Delius y Meyer.
Herrera, José Luis (sale by sample).
Menchaca Hnos.
Sierra, Manuel.

Drugs.
Fenelon y Ca., Cárlos.
Gonzalez, Gerónimo, Suc.
Guzman, Francisco.
Retes, Benjamin D.
Virgen, Fernando Gomez.

Dry goods.
Anaya, Francisco.
Andrade, J.
Anguiano, Daniel M.
Beyer Hnos.
Chaurand y Ca., Jacques.
Mardueño, Juan.
Menchaca Hnos.
Retes, José M.
Retes, N. y V.
Sierra, Manuel.

Fancy goods.
Gebers, Viuda de.
Maldonado, Manuel.

TEPIC, TERRITORIO DE TEPIC—Cont'd.

Groceries and provisions.
Altimirano, Miguel.
Borboa, J.
Brambila, Manuel Perez.
Castillo, Vicente.
Corona, J. Cruz.
Delius y Meyer.
Flores, Máximo G.
Hernandez, Trinidad.
Leal, Viuda de.
Ocegueda, Ireneo.
Perez, Nicolás.
Rodriguez. Nicolás.
Somellera, Rivas y Ca.

Hardware.
Gebero, Viuda de.
Maldonado, Manuel.

Hatter.
Landwehr, Guillermo.

Iron and ironware.
Aguirre y Ca., Juan A. de.
Retes, José M.
Zuazo, J. Antonio de.

Jeweler.
Castañeda, José E.

Oil mills.
Corona, José C.
Hernandez, Trinidad.

Photographers.
Guerra, José M.
Rivero, Mariano.
Trejo, Cruz.
Muñoz, José M.

Printing offices.
Herrera Hermanos.
Imprenta de la Escuela de Artes.
Imprenta del Gobierno.
Legaspi, Viuda de.
Ocegueda y Ca., J. Ireneo.
Ocegueda, J. Emilio.
Retes, José M.

Saddlery and harness.
Gongora, Cristófero F.

Sewing machines.
Beyer Hnos.
Leal, Viuda de.

Silversmiths.
Gonzalez, Marcial.
Lopez, Pedro.
Quintero, Roberto.
Soto, Filomeno.

Watchmakers.
Castañeda, José.
Gonzalez, Pedro.

TEZIUTLAN, PUEBLA.

Agricultural implements.
Zorrilla, Manuel.

Arms and ammunition.
Alvarez, Antonio.
García, Gumesindo.

Commission merchants.
Lapuente Hermanos y Ca.
Molino, Luis Cabada.

Drugs.
Azcue, Juan Garces.
Casas, Federico M.
Mayaudon, Amado.

Dry goods.
Diaz Hermanos.
Ramos, Isidro.
Rodriguez y Ca., García.
Solano, Eulogio.
Viñalez ó Hijo, Pedro.
Zorrilla, Manuel.

Fancy goods.
Klinof, Trinidad M. de.
Ramos, Isidro.

Groceries and provisions.
Ramos, Isidro.
Rodriguez y Ca., García.
Viñalez ó Hijo, Pedro.
Zorrilla, Manuel.

Hardware.
Klinof, Trinidad M. de.
Ramos, Isidro.

Hatter.
Sanchez, Ramon.

Iron and ironware.
Zorrilla, Manuel.

Merchant tailors.
Eizaguirre, Vicente.
Murrieta, Ignacio.

Paints and oils.
Calderon, Benigno.

Photographers.
Hernandez, Francisco.
Saavedra, Enrique.
Vargas, Alfredo.

Printing offices.
Amable, Agustin.
Cuesta, Jacinto.

Saddlery.
Moctezuma, Desiderio.
Villegas, Joaquin.

Silversmith.
Jimenez, Mauricio.

Upholstery and carpets.
Rosano, Luis.

TIXTLA GUERRERO, GUERRERO.

Watchmaker.
Ortega, Gilberto.

Banker.
Bello, Vicente.

Boots and shoes.
Aburto, Paulino.
Damien, José.
Encarnacion, Ramon.
Muñiz, Rafael.
Rodriguez, Domitilo.
Rodriguez, Rafael.

Drugs.
Muñoz, Pascuela.

Dry goods.
Godines, Sebás.

Merchant tailors.
Gonzalez, J.
Navarrete, Nazario.
Vargas, Julio.

Printing office.
Muñiz, Margarito.

Saddlery and harness.
Osorio, José.
Valadez, Juan.
Vargas, Mariano.

Silversmiths.
Cervantes, Luis.
Navarreta, Manuel J.

TLACOTALPAM, VERACRUZ.

Agricultural implements.
Cházaro ó Hijos, Francisco.
Cházaro, J. A., Suc.
Perez, José L.
Schleske, Mauricio.

Bankers.
Cházaro ó Hijos, Francisco.
Cházaro, J. A., Suc.

Books and stationery.
Hernandez, José J.

Commission merchants.
Cházaro ó Hijo, Francisco.
Cházaro, J. A., Suc.
Perez, José L.
Schleske, Mauricio.

Drugs.
Murillo, M.
Reyes, Miguel Marquez.
"San Jose."
"Tlacotalpeña."

Dry goods.
Crespo, Ignacio.
García y Ca., Benito.
Martinez, José Albino.
Pons, Francisco.

TLACOTALPAM, VERACRUZ—Continued.

Furniture.
Fontan, Manuel.
Lipp, Jacob.
Reyes, Luis Felipe.

Fancy goods.
Morteo, Encarnacion.
Perez, Cesareo.
Villar Hermanos.

Groceries and provisions.
Carlin Hnos.
Cházaro é Hijos, Francisco.
Cházaro, J. A., Suc.
Fernandez, Francisco.
Lopez, Ramon A.
Perez, José L.
Roca, Ramon.
Schleske, Mauricio.
Villar Hnos.

Hardware.
Morteo, Encarnacion.
Schleske, Mauricio.

Hatters.
Beirana, Juan.
Claudio, Angel.
Herrera, Antonio.
Ortiz, Antonio.

Printing office.
" La Reforma. "

Silversmiths.
Beirana, Luis.
Peralta, Juan.

TLAXCALA, TLAXCALA.

Banker.
Viñas, J. de J.

Carriage dealer.
Santillana, Cayetano.

Drugs.
Amad, José.
Atamoros, Francisco.
Escudero, J.

Engravers.
Chumacero, Manuel.
Raso, Tiburcio del.

Fancy goods.
Barrera, Ignacio.

Flour mills.
Aquiles de Pain.
Gavito, Francisco G.
Hernandez, Cárlos L.
Rivera Hnos., Feliciano.

Groceries and provisions.
Gavito, Francisco Gonzalez.
Manriquez, Donaciano.

TLAXCALA, TLAXCALA—Continued.

Groceries and provisions—Continued.
Mendoza, Manuel.
Ramos, J.
Vazquez, Juan.

Iron and ironware.
Picazo Hnos.

Oil mill.
Rivera, Rafael.

Photographer.
Heredia, Miguel.

Printing office.
Calderon, Joaquin Diaz.

Saddlery and harness.
Carrasco, José M.
Carvajal, Pedro.
Prieto, Cecilio.

Sewing machines.
Corona, Agustin G.
Rio, Joaquin del.

Silversmiths.
Alvarez, Nicolás.
Garibay, Manuel.
Olivares, Bartolo.
Robles, José M.
Trujillo, Filomeno.

TOLUCA, MEXICO.

Banker.
Cortina, Tomás.

Booksellers.
Gordillo, Pascual Gonzalez.
" Librería de la Juventud."
Velazquez, José.

Boots and shoes.
Barbabosa y Gomez, J.
Hernandez, Ausencio.
Legorreta, Vicente.
Quiroz, Teófilo.

Carriage dealer.
Betancourt, Abundio.

Commission merchants.
Gonzalez y Benavides.
Medina Garduño, Manuel.

Commission merchants (sale by sample).
Barenque, Demetrio.
Gomez, Antonio Vilches.
Medina y Cruz, Manuel.

Drugs.
Araujo, Rafael.
Fernandez, Fernando.
Gutiérrez, Felix.
Hernandez, Mariano.
Rodriguez, Juan.

TOLUCA MEXICO—Continued.

Dry goods.
Ballina, Ramon.
Prichardo, Francisco.
Rojas, Juan Gonzalez.
Valdez, Angel.

Engraver.
Sanchez, José M.

Flour mills.
Henkel ó Hijos, Viuda de.
Hinajosa, Carlota.

Groceries and provisions.
Barrera, J.
Cortina y Hnos., Joaquin.
Lopez, José.
Valdez, Darío.

Hardware.
Gallegos, José.
Gonzalez y Benavides.
Lopéz, José.
Vazquez, Lorenzo J.

Hatters.
Alcocer, Manuel.
Lopez, J.
Torres, Luz.
Zölly Hermanos.

Lithographers.
Martinez, Pedro.
Rentería, Felipe.

Merchant tailors.
Flores, Ismael.
Quintana, Ildefonso.
Vaez, J.

Notions.
Gallegos, José.
Gonzalez y Benavides.
Lopez, José.
Vazquez, Lorenzo J.

Paints and oils.
Solalindo, J.

Photographers.
Alba, Daniel.
Torres Hermanos.

Printing offices.
Imprenta de la Escuela de Artes y Oficios.
Manon Hermanos.
Quijano, Atanasio.

Sewing machines.
Lopez, José.

Silk goods.
Alconeda, Josefa Valdez de.
Santillan, Nicolás.

TOLUCA MÉXICO—Continued.

Silversmiths.
Almazan, J.
Quiróz, Mariano.

Upholstery and carpets.
Arellano, J.

Watchmakers.
Avila, Enrique.
Olmedo, Juan.

TORREON, COAHUILA.

Merchants.
Clefford y Arellano (groceries and provisions.)
De Coster, E. (commission merchant).
Díaz, M. (merchant tailor).
Moore, L. A. (notions, provisions, dry goods).
Sanchez, Luis (mills).
Treviño, J. M. G. (commission merchant).

TULA, TAMAULIPAS.

General merchants.
Cretanos, Juan J.
García, Salvador.
Otero, Ramon.
Rodriguez, Gerónimo.
Saldana Hnos.

TUXPAM.

Bankers and lumber.
Johannsen, G.
Stussy, F.

Drugs and chemicals.
Boyd, R. L.
Garmendia, E.

Dry goods and commission merchants.
Achao & Co.
Bosanez, Pedro.
Cerverio, Gutierres y Ca.
Chas, F. M.
Gregorio, Sanchez y Ca.
Johannsen, G.
Morales, J. M.
Nontoto Hermanos.
Portus y Chao, R.
Sedano & Bosanez.

Iron and glass ware.
Eckard, Justo.
Lafarey, J.

Notions and fancy goods.
Eckard, Justo.

Paints, oils, etc.
Eckard, Justo.
Johannsen, G.
Stussy, F.

TUXPAM—Continued.

Printing office.
Loso, Miguel.

Shoes, notions, etc.
Dechamp, Julio.

TUXTLA GUTIERREZ, CHIAPAS.

Boots and shoes.
Chanona, Antero.
Ruiz, José.

Commission merchant.
Thomas, Augusto.

Drugs.
Chanona, Domingo.

Engraver.
Yañes, Nabor.

Groceries and provisions.
Cano Hnos.
Cueto y Ca.
Farrera, Vicente.
Gout y Ca., L.
Zorrilla y Ca.

Hatter.
Bustamante, Estéban.

Merchant tailors.
Cruz, Rafael.
Culebro, J.
Culebro, Vidal.

Saddlery and harness.
Cleus. Pedro.
Diaz, Santos.

Silversmiths.
Marcelin, Mariano.
Muñiz, Vicenti.
Yañes, Nabor.

VENTANAS, DURANGO.

General merchants.
Carrol y Ca., Gmo.
Morones, Martin.

Mining companies.
Ventanas Consolidated Mill and Mining Company.

VERACRUZ, VERACRUZ.

Agricultural implements.
Bello y Ca., F.J.
Düring y Ca., M.
Prado, Pepin y Ca., A.S. del.
Sommer, Herrmann y Ca.
Varela y Ca., R.

Bankers.
Galainena y Ca., J., Suc.
Martinez Hnos.

VERACRUZ, VERACRUZ—Continued.

Bankers—Continued.
Sommer, Herrmann y Ca.
Struck y Ca., Gustavo.
Villa Hnos., Suc.
Zaldo Hnos. y Ca.

Banks.
Sucursal del Banco de Lóndres y México (agent: Federico Howes).
Sucursal del Banco Nacional de México (agent: Teodoro Chobat).

Booksellers and stationers.
Cabrera, Manuel.
Carredano, Viuda de.
Jimenez, R. Rodriguez.
Paso y Troncosa, J. del.

Boots and shoes.
Aguero, Serapio.
Carbonell, Paulino.
Cuneo, Juan.
Diaz, Julian.
Font, Francisco.
Gonzalez, José D.
Horro, Bernardo.
Lopez, Juan.
Mantecon, Pedro D.
Moll, J.M.
Ramos, Blas.
Roque, Basilio.
Sanchez, Alejandro.
Valdes, Guadalupe.

China, glassware, lamps, etc.
Izazola, José I.
Palomo, J.
Ribera, Francisco.
Ritrer y Ca., R.C.
Segundo, Alonso.

Commission merchants.
Aladro y Ca.
Ascorve y Ca., P.J.
Benito y Ca., G.
Busing y Ca., Guillermo, Suc.
D'Oleire y Ca., Suc.
Galainena y Ca., J., Suc.
García, Rafael.
Hoyos, Braulio.
Ibargüen, Bernabé.
Ituarte, Parres y Ca.
Lama y Ca., García de la.
Loustan y Ca., D.
Markoe y Ca., M.C. de.
Mendez y Ca., P.G
Muñoz y Ca., F.J.
Olózaga, José d', Suc.
Pagés, José Gonzalez.
Pardo, Juan M.

VERACRUZ, VERACRUZ—Continued.

Commission merchants—Continued.
Tejeda y Ca., S.
Temprana, C., Suc.
Torres, Vicente Reyes.
Torre, Antonio H. de la.
Valdez, Manuel Pastor.
Varela, R.
Villa Hnos., Suc.
Zaldo Hnos. y Ca.

Drugs.
Barrillo, A.
Carrillo y Ca.
Lomonaco, A.
Luis, H., y Hoyos.
Mariscal, Cárlos.
Müller, G., Suc.
Rio, Arturo del.
Rodriguez, Antonio S.
Serralta y Ca., S.

Dry goods.
Aparicio y Ca.
Aragon y Hno., Julian.
Benito y Ca., C.
Busing y Ca., Guillermo, Suc.
Juano, Francisco de.
Ollivier y Ca., J.
Ramos y Ca., R.
Sanchez y Fernandez.
Struck y Ca., Gustavo.
Stürcke, García., Suc.
Ulibarrí, S.
Zaldo Hnos. y Ca.

Exporters.
Aragon y Hno., Julian.
Busing y Ca., Guillermo, Suc.
Düring y Ca., M.
Franchi, Ochoa y Ca.
Galainena y Ca., J.
Ituarte y Ca., F. J.
Markoe y Ca., M. C. de.
Martinez Hnos.
Rivas y Meyenn.
Struck y Ca., Gustavo.
Valdéz, Mariano R.
Valdéz, Manuel Castro.
Zaldo Hnos. y Ca.

Furniture.
Arrieta, Teófilo.
Izazola, José I.
Zárate, J. de J.

Groceries and provisions.
Calleja Hnos. y Ca.
Franchi, Ochoa y Ca.
Galainena y Ca., J., Suc.

VERACRUZ, VERACRUZ—Continued.

Groceries and provisions—Continued.
Gomez y Ca.
Guillaron y Ca.
Ituarte y Ca., F. J.
Landero, Pasquel y Ca.
Leycequi y Ca., L. C.
Markoe y Ca., M. C. de.
Martin, García y Ca.
Martinez Hnos.
Martinez, Rivera y Ca.
Oliver, Manuel.
Rasines, Perez y Ca.
Rivas y Meyenn.
Rolla, Gentini y Ca.
Sierra y Hno., R.
Tejeda y Ca., S.
Villa Hnos., Suc.
Wittenez, Vila y Ca.

Hardware.
Bello y Ca., F. J.
Düring y Ca., M.
Escandon, Alberto.
Gonzalez, Cipriano.
Nicolas, Eulogio de.
Prado, Pepin y Ca., A. S. del.
Sommer, Herrmann y Ca.
Varela y Ca., R.

Hatters.
Avila, José de J.
Barros y Murillo.
Valdés y Ca., M.

Importers.
Aragon y Hno., Julian.
Bello y Ca., F. J.
Benito y Ca., C.
Busing y Ca., Guillermo, Suc.
Cuesta, Cornejo y Ca.
Düring y Ca., M.
Franchi, Ochoa y Ca.
Galainena y Ca., J. S.
Izazola, José I.
Müller, G., Suc.
Olivier y Ca., J.
Prado, A. S. del.
Ramo y Ca., R.
Rivas y Meyenn.
Sierra y Hno., R.
Sommer, Herrmann y Ca.
Struck y Ca., Gustavo.
Stürcke, García., Suc.
Ulibarri, S.
Varela y Ca., R.
Wittenez, Vila y Ca.
Zaldo Hnos. y Ca.

VERACRUZ, VERACRUZ—Continued.

Iron and ironware.
Sommer, Herrmann y Ca.
Varela, R.

Jewelers.
Luengo, L.
Melendez, Luis.

Music stores.
Bello y Ca., F. J.
Carredano, Viuda de.

Notions.
Bello y Ca., F. J.
Düring y Ca., M.
Escandon, Alberto.
Gonzalez, Cipriano.
Nicolas, Eulogio de.
Prado, Pepin y Ca., A. F. del.
Rivera, Francisco.
Sommer, Herrmann y Ca.
Varela y Ça., R.

Paints and oils.
Torres, Vicente Reyes.

Photographers.
Hijos de Ritcher.
Ibañez ó Hijo.

Printing offices.
Ledesma, J.
Menvielle, Miguel.
Rossel ó Hijo, J.
Zayas, Enrique R.

Saddlery and harness.
Avila, José de J.

Sewing machines.
Cuesta, Cornejo y Ca.
Mantecon y Ca., G.
Sommer, Herrmann y Ca.

Silk goods.
Aragon y Hno., Julian.
Benito y Ca., C.
Stürcke, García, Suc.
Zaldo Hnos. y Ca.

Watchmakers.
Huguenin, C.
Naspleda, José.

Woods.
Tejeda y Ca., S.

VIESCA, COAHUILA.

Agricultural implements and hardware.
Lazous, Luis.
Narro, Antonio,

Brick manufacturers.
Murrillo Hnos.

Drugs.
Leon, Daniel de.
Murrillo Hnos.

VIESCA, COAHUILA—Continued.

Flour mills.
Hernandez, Felicitas.
Lazous, René, Sucs.
Murrillo Hnos.

General merchants.
Lazous, Luis.
Lobo, Leon.
Murrillo, Estanislao.
Murrillo Hnos.
Narro, Antonio.

Mining company.
Rafael de la Fuente y Ca.

Salt wells.
Lazous, Luis.
Mier, José.
Narro, A.

VILLA CANATLAN, DURANGO.

General merchants.
Calderon, Onesinao.
Juambelz, Angel J.
Morales, Francisco.
Morales, Marcos.
Valenzuela, Pablo.

VILLA GUAZAPARES, CHIHUAHUA.

General merchants.
Albeztegui y García.
Contreras, Manuel.
Daniel, Ignacio.
Grajeda, Casario.
Gutierrez, Pedro J.
Loya, Francisco.
Loya, Manuel.
Loya y Sanchez.
Navarez, Roman E.
Oscaran y Ca.
Ramos Hnos.
Rodriguez, Feliciano.
Rodriguez, Luis.
Salido, Martino.
Zarinana, Franco.

Mining companies.
Compañía Minera del Carmen.
Compañía Minera de Palmarejo.
Compañía Minera de Santa Rita.
Compañía Minera de Yoricarichi.
Guadalupe y Calvo.
Hurnapa.
Septenarion.

VILLALDAMA, NUEVO LEON.

Druggists.
Argueta, J. M.
Zombrano, E. S.

Groceries, tobacco and liquors.
Botello, Salome.
Guerrero, Amado.

VILLALDAMA, NUEVO LEON—Continued.

*Groceries, tobacco, and liquors—*Continued.
Santos, Nicolás.
Solis y Hno., V.
Villareal, Antonio.
Villareal, José M. S.

Mining companies.
Exploring Mining Company.
Guadalupe Mining Company.
Iguano Smelting and Mining Company.
Villaldama Developing Company.

VILLA LERDO, DURANGO.

Bankers.
Hernandez Hnos., Sucs.
Ritter, Federico.

Cotton mills.
Prince, Torres y Prince.

Cotton seed oil mills.
Belden, Fco.
Francke, Hugo.

Druggist.
Bruciaga, Aug.Reyes.

Dry and fancy goods.
Calderon, Alberto.
Calderon, Pedro.
Hernandez Hnos., Sucs.
Leal, Pedro.
Mestres, Sixto.
Quijano y Ca., M. D.
Ritter, Federico.

Flour mills.
Douglas Hnos.
Navarro, Pedro.
Sanchez, Enrique.

General merchants.
Aguilar y Ca., E. J.
Alvarez, Francisco.
Ballesteros, M. S.
Bermudez, R.
Chaves, D.
Elizidondo y Ca., P.
Gamboa, Canuto.
Guerra, T. G.
Jiminez, F.
Lujan, A.
Quiros Hnos.
Ruiz Hermanos.
Terjuel, Francisco R.
Trevino, J. M. Gonzalez.
Villalobos, P.
Villareal, S.
Ybarra, I. M.

S. Ex. 8, pt. 11——16

VILLA LERDO, DURANGO—Continued.

Hardware, agricultural implements, mining machinery, crockery.
Balsiger y Francke.
Fuchs, Ernesto.
Fuentes y Pena.
Mengdehl, Federico.
Ritter, Federico.
Tajan, J., Sucs.

Jeweler.
Sterling, Henry.

Wholesale grocers.
Balsiger y Francke.
Hernandez Hnos., Sucs.
Lajous y Ca., Rene.
Ritter, Federico.

ZAMORA, MICHOACAN.

Bankers.
Agencia del Banco de Lóndres y México.
Epifanio, Jimenez.

Booksellers and stationers.
Calderon, J.
Hernandez, Luis G.
Mora, Nicolás T.

Boots and shoes.
Cavadas, Estanislao.
Leon, J.
Mora, Felipe.
Morales, Mariano.
Morales, Ruperto.
Pimentel, Prisciliano.
Valadez, Federico.

China and glassware.
Cano, Francisco.
"La Luz."

Commission merchants.
Calderon, J. (sale by sample).
Peña, Fernando.

Drugs.
"La Providencia."
Maldonado, José M. Torres.

Dry goods.
"Arco-Iris."
Bustamante, J. M.
"Ciudad de México."
"Ciudad de Paris."
"El Cambio."
"El Mundo de Colon."
García, Francisco C.
"La Reforma del Comercio."
Meillan, Francisco.
Monterde y Ca., Tomás.
Ramirez, Prisciliano.

ZAMORA, MICHOACAN—Continued.

Flour mills.

De Chaparaco.
De la Guardia.
De la Estanzuela.
De Yartún.
En Jacona.
La Concepcion.
La Purísima.
San Pedro.

Groceries and provisions.

Alcaráz, Mariano.
Benitez, Francisco.
Cabrera, Estanislao.
Calderon, J.
Castellanos, Aniceto.
Fernandez, Rafael Marquez.
García, Epifanio.
García, Francisco C.
Garibay, J.
Hurtado, Luis.
Isarrarás, J.
Isarrarás, J. Natividad.
Madrigal, Francisco A.
Madrigal, J. Refugio.
Meillan y Fabier.
Mendoza, Manuel García.
Mendoza, Ma. García.
Mora, Rafael Marquez de la.
Orozco, Arcadio H.
Padilla, Ramon.
Peña, Fernando.
Rio, Diégo V. del.
Verduzco, Diégo.

Hardware.

Ortiz, J. M. del Rio.

Hatters.

Hurtado, J. Nabor.
Lopez, Antonio.
Perez y Ca., Francisco.

Iron and ironware.

Peña, Fernando.

Manufacturer of brass and iron bedsteads.

Mendoza, Genaro.
Saavedra, J.

Merchant tailors.

Amezcua, José M.
Leon, Francisco.
Mendez, Narciso.
Ochoa, Francisco.
Osio, Arcadio.
Ramos, Trinidad.

ZAMORA, MICHOACAN—Continued.

Notions.

Orozco, Manuel.
Rio, J. M. del.

Photographers.

Gutiérrez, Celerino.
Mares, Santiago.
Verduzco, J. M. Torres.

Printing offices.

Madrigal, J. M.
Maldonado, J. M. Torres.
Viuda é Hijos de Silva Romero.

Saddlery and harness.

Rio, Rodriguez del.
Sanchez, Ruperto.
Victorio, Fernando.

Sewing machines.

Orozco, Arcadio H.

Silversmiths.

Manriquez, Vicente.
Padilla, José M.

Watchmakers.

Mendez, Manuel.
Orozco, Miguel.
Verduzco, José M. Torres.

ZACATECAS, ZACATECAS.

Agricultural implements.

Camacho, Francisco.
Ibargüengoytia, J. & M.
Karbe, Fernando.
Ortiz, Ramon.
Petit, Juan A.

Bankers.

Ibargüengoytia, J. & M.
Ortiz, Ramou C.
Portilla, Ildefonso.
Samper, José.

Booksellers and stationers.

Bouret, Cárlos.
Medina, A.

Boots and shoes.

Acevedo, Andrés.
Carbajal Hnos.
Dominguez, José M.
Luna, Guadalupe R.
Oyharçabal, O

Carriage dealers.

Escuela de Artes y Oficios.
Hospicio de Niños, en la villa de Guadalupe.
Serapio Galvan, en la villa de Guadalupe,

ZACATECAS, ZACATECAS—Continued.

Commission merchants.

Arbaiza, José.
Camacho, Francisco.
Dorigo, Arturo L.
Gallardo, Manuel Ortiz (sale by sample).
Gonzalez y Hno., F. Gomez.
Gordoa, Benjamin G.
Ibargüengoytia, J. & M.
Leon y Ca., Cruz Diaz de.
Ortiz, Ramon C.
Pacheco, Manuel.
Palmer Hnos.
Petit, Juan A.
Solorzano, José E.
Velasco, Juan.
Yermo Hnos.

Drugs.

Alvarez, Agustin.
Calderon, Antonio.
Delgado, J. Correa.
Duran, R.
Gonzalez, Luis G.
Hubert y Ca., C.
Moreno, Basilio.
Ponce, Juan P.
Rodriguez, Margarito.
Torres, José.
Valadez, Gumesindo.
Valle, Gerónimo de.

Dry goods.

Aubert, Enrique.
Bellon y Ca., M.
Cairé y Garnier.
Cazon y Ca., Antonio.
Dokhelar, Juan.
Franck y Ca., M.
Haramboure y Ca., J.
Olavarria, Luis.
Pellat y Jean.
Perez, Francisco.
Rougón Hnos.
Teillery y Ca., Suc.
Viadero y Ca.

Engraver.

Villegas, Vicente F.

Flour mills.

Escobedo, Anacleto.
Tumoine, Victor.

Groceries and provisions.

Corvera, Pascual.
Etchart y Segura.

ZACATECAS, ZACATECAS—Continued.

Groceries and provisions—Continued.

Gonzalez y Hno., F. Gomez.
Hatchandy y Ferran.
Ledesma, Atanasio.
Macías, Luis.
Martinez, Mónica.

Hardware.

Bittrolff y Niemeyer.
Karbe, Fernando, Suc.
Neubert, Gustavo.
Rodriguez Hnos.
Schroeder, Gustavo.
Schwartz, Cárlos.

Hatters.

Doering, Federico.
Flebbe, Joaquin.
Langmack, Guillermo, Suc.
Zölly Hnos.

Iron and ironware.

Camacho, Francisco.
Gordoa, Benjamin Gomez.
Ibargüengoytia, J. & M.
Petit, Juan A.

Jewelers and watchmakers.

Brüchner, Guillermo.
Dorian, Cárlos.
Gonzalez, Tomás M.

Lithographer.

Espinoza, Nazario.

Merchant tailors.

Franck y Ca., M.
Lopez, Simon.
Rios, J. F.
Rios, Leonardo.
Ruiz, Alberto.
Trujillo, Tranquilino.
Valdez, Marcos.

Notions.

Baurraud, Guillermo.
Bittrolf y Niemeyer.
Heheren, Edmundo.
Ferran, Roman.
Ferran, Tomás.
Karbe, Fernando, Suc.
Neubert, Gustavo.
Rodriguez Hnos.
Senisson, Amado.
Schroeder, Gustavo.
Schwartz, Cárlos.

ZACATECAS, ZACATECAS—Continued.

Photographers.
 Barraza, Agustin.
 Hierro y Bonilla.
 Orozco, Manuel.

Printing offices.
 Alvarez, Manuel Rodriguez.
 Ceniceros y Villarreal, Manuel.
 Esparza, Mariano R.
 Espinoza, Nazario.
 Hospicio de Niños, Guadalupe.
 Imprenta de la Escuela de Artes y Oficios.
 Lorck, Tomás.

Saddlery and harness.
 Martinez, Juan Pablo.
 Rodriguez, Pablo.

ZACATECAS, ZACATECAS—Continued.

Sewing machines.
 Swain, Cárlos.
 Velazquez, S. J.

Silk goods.
 Caraza, Viuda de.

Silversmiths.
 Arteaga, Tirso.
 Ortega, Lino.
 Salazar, Exiquio.

Watchmakers.
 Brüchner, Guillermo.
 Dorian, C.
 Lebre, D.
 Romo, Pedro.

Nicaragua.

ACOYAPA.

Wholesale import and export merchant.
Sevilla, Cirilo.

BLUEFIELDS.

Importers.
Brown & Harris.
Levy & Levis.
Sargent, J. I. *
Simmons, John H.

Merchants, general merchandise.
Clerici, A.
Ebensperger & Co.
Friedlander, J.
Ingram, H. Clay.
Sing, C. M.
Thomas & Nephew, J. O.
Weil & Co., S.
Wilson & Belanger.

BUENOS AYRES.

Retail general merchants.
Chamorro, Doroteo J.
Salamanca, Gregorio.

CHICHIGALPA.

Machinery.
Deshon & Pineda.

CHINANDEGA.

Bankers.
Callejas & Baca.
Druggists.
Baca, Francisco.
Granera, Inocente.
Navarro, Angel.
Tijerino, Toribio.
Retail general merchants.
Navarrete hnos., Ignacio.
Navarrete hno.. Sinforosa.

CHINANDEGA—Continued.

Retail general merchants—Continued.
Navarro, Cruz.
Reyes, José.
Salinas, Juan.
Sanson, Gertrudis y Estefania.
Tijerino hnos.
Silversmith.
Meza, Enrique.
Machinery.
Baca, Manuel Antonio.
Wholesale import and export merchants.
Callejas, Santiago.
Callejas, Juan F.
Gasteozoro, T. M.
Gorlero, Juan.
Gorlero é hijo.

CHOLUTECA.

Wholesale import and export merchant.
Lagos, César.

CORINTO.

Commission merchants.
Brenes, Pedro.
Monterey y Co., José.
Palazio, L.
Commission merchants and exporters.
Palazio & Co., E.
Wasmer & Lutzner.
Retail general merchants.
Valle, Salvador.
Wholesale import and export merchants.
Jericho, Guillermo.
Palazio, Henry.
Palazio & Co., E.
Valle, Narciso.
Vargas, Francisco.
Wasmer & Von Lutzow.

245

GRANADA.

Banks and bankers.
Arana, Salvador.
Chamorro y Zabala.
Morales, Santiago.
Urbine, Manuel.
Vargas, Juan.
Banco de Nicaragua.

Boots and shoes.
Romero, Miguel.

Commission merchants.
Espinoza, G.
Garcia & Co., José Maria.
Martinez, Abraham.
Traña, J. Luis.

Druggists.
Alvarez, F.
Barrios, Teófilo.
Guerrero, Alfonso.
Guzmán, Horacio.
Guzmán, V.
Lacayo, Alberto.
Morales, José Maria.
Pasos, Agustin.
Urtecho, Juan Ignacio.
Vargas, Pedro R.

Exporters coffee, hides, and dye woods.
Arguello, Luis.
Arguello, Manuel.
Arguello, Mariam.
Barillas, Benjamin.
Barillas, Carlos.
Castrillo, David.
Cesar & Chamorro.
Chamorro & Bro., Fernando.
Cuadra & Sons, Virginia.
Derbyshire, Fred.
Espinoza, Gonzales.
Gomez & Sons, Josefa.
Lacayo, Alberto.
Lacayo, Delfino.
Lacayo, Fernando and Manuel.
Lacayo, Panfilo.
Lacayo & Bro., Alfredo.
Morales, Santiago.
Pellas, A. E.
Sandoval, Benjamin.
Vargas, Juan.
Vaughn Bros.

Hatter.
Palacio, Casimiro del C.

Importers drugs and chemicals.
Alvarez, F.
Barberna, Narciso.
Chamorro, Filadelfo.

GRANADA—Continued.

Importers drugs and chemicals—Continued.
Guzman, Virgilio.
Henriques, Maximiliano.
Lacayo, Alberto.
Lejarez, Señor Don.
Martiney, Señor Don.
Monteil, Luis.
Morales, José Maria.
Pasos, Agustin.
Urtecho, Juan Ignacio.
Vargas, Pedro R.

Importers general merchandise.
Arguello, Luis.
Arguello, Mariano.
Cesar & Chamorro.
Chamorro & Co., Salvador.
Chamorro & Bro., Fernando.
Coronel, Manuel A.
Lacayo, Fernando and Manuel.
Quadraé Hijos, Virginia de.
Pasos & Co., P.
Peter & Co., Alberto.
Wolff & Co., S.
Ximenes & Bro., Salvador.

Photographers.
Alfaro Bernardo.
Cassinelli, Antonio.
Sanson & Co., Fernando.

Planters, general.
Arellano, Faustino.
Baez, Rito.
Berard, Agustin G.
Costigliolo y Zalala.
Guzmán, Fernando.
Lacayo, Daniel.
Lacayo, Fernando.
Quadra, Vicente y Joaquin.
Zelaya, Leandro.

Planters, sugar.
Costigliolo y Zabbala.
Espinola y Ca.

Planters, cocoa.
Arguello, José.
Chamorro hermanos.
Menier, E.
Quadra, U. y J.

Planters of coffee.
Aviles, A.
Bermudez, José T.
Brown hnos.
Espinola, Francisco.
Lacayo, Daniel.
Lacayo, F. y M.
Lacayo, Tomás.
Roman, Desiderio.

GRANADA—Continued.

Planters of coffee—Continued.
Vagnan y hermanos.
Vega, Juan.

Printers.
Cuadra, J. de J.
Rivas, Anselmo II.
Romero, Miguel.

Retail general merchant.
Bendaña, Fernando.

Silversmith.
Ruiz, Alberto.

Special manufacturers.
Barcenas, J. J., coffee machinery.
Lacayo, Lisimaco, castor oil.

Special merchants.
Blen, Adolfo, wines and liquors.
Downing & hnos., cigars.
Guzmán, Enrique, sugar.
Lacayo, Roberto, woods.
Ortega, Salvador, flour.

Watchmakers and jewelers.
Chamorro, Martín.
Lacayo, José.
Lacayo, Roberto.
Palavacini, Vicente.
Ramirez y Ca., P.
Ryos, Felipe.

Wholesale import and export merchants.
Arguello, Luis.
Arguello, Mariano.
Avilés & Co.
Avilés, Mercedes.
Bermudes, J. Ignacio.
César & Chamorro.
Chamorro, Fernando.
Chamorro, R. & F.
Chamorro, Dionisio.
Chamorro, Alejandro.
Chamorro, Adela.
Chamorro, Pedro J.
Chamorro, Salvador & Co.
Chamorro & Zavala.
Chesnay, Emilio.
Collado, Guillermo.
Coronel, Manuel Antonio.
Costigliolo, J. S.
Cuadra, E. & S.
Cuadra é hijos, Virginia de.
Downing, A. A.
Espinoza, Sebastián.
Fiallos, Mariano.
Gousain, Hilario.
Lacayo, Fernando & Manuel.
Lacayo, Carlos A.
Lacayo & Co., Manuel.

GRANADA—Continued.

Wholesale import and export merchants—Cont'd.
Lacayo & Co., Roberto.
Lacayo & hno., Alfredo.
Lacayo, Pastora V. de.
Lacayo, Lisimaco F.
Lacayo, Saturnino.
Lanuza & Co.
Lugo, Alberto.
Marenco, Constantino.
Martínez, Bernardo.
Martínez, Dr. J. J.
Martínez é hijos, Esmeralda de.
Mejia hijo, Luis.
Morales, Santiago.
Morales, Celedonio.
Morales, Tránsito.
Morales, Herculano.
Morenco, Federico.
Ocón, Trinidad.
Pasos & Co., P.
Quadra é hijos, V. de.
Quadra é hnos., Manuel.
Quadra, Ezequiel y Salvador.
Quadra, Vicente.
Rivas, Asunción P.
Rocha & Co.
Rutishauser & Co., Antonio.
Sequeira, Narciso.
Selva, Hilario.
Tefel, Teodoro.
Ubago hnos.
Vargas, Juan.
Vargas, Justiniano.
Vaughan hnos.
Vela, Serapio.
Vivas hijo, Rosario.
Ximenez & Co., Torres.
Zavala, Joaquin.
Zelaya & Co., Victor.

GREYTOWN.

Banks and bankers.
Banco de Nicaragua.
Hoadley, Ingalls & Co.

Commission merchants.
Nicaragua Navigation and Trading Co.
Pellas, J. A.
Saenz & Co.
Scott & Co., C. D.

Merchants, general merchandise.
Bergmann, C. F.
Cohen, S.
D'Souza & Co., E. L.
Enriquez & Smith.
Gosdensk, J.
Hatch & Brown.

GREYTOWN—Continued.

*Merchants, general merchandise—*Continued.
Nicaragua Navigation and Trading Co.
Saenz, L. E.
Solomon & Harris.

Wholesale import and export merchants.
Bergmann, J. J.
Hatch & Brown.
Mongrio y Aragun.
Pellas, F. A.
Saenz & Co.
D'Sousa & Co., E. L.

IMOTEGA.

Importers.
Chavez & Noguero.

JINOTEGA.

Importer.
Cardenal, Cruz.

JINOTEPE.

Druggist.
Zúñiga, L.
Importer of general merchandise, exporter of hides and coffee.
Roman & Co., José Leon.

JUIGALPA.

Druggist.
Gutierrez, Eliseo.
Retail general merchant.
Baez, David.

LEON.

Banks and bankers.
Banco Agricola Mercantil.
Banco de Nicaragua.
Aguero Coronado de Marin.
Lacayo, Leonardo.
Lacayo, Narciso & Co.
Midence, Justo.
Orosco, Espiridion.
Perez, Manuel.
Boots and shoes.
Agüero, Federico.
Bustos, Antonio.
Delgado, Cipriano.
González, Trinidad.
Grijalva, Tomás.
Montalvan, Francisco.
Saavedra, Isaac.
Saenz, Antonio.
Salmerón, Atanacio.
Sequeiro, Alejandro.
Soto y hno., Rafael.
Zapata, Manuel.
Commission merchants.
Agustin, John S.
Fiallos, Mariano.
Druggists.
Argüello, David.
Barrios, Eleodoro.

LEON—Continued.

*Druggists—*Continued.
Castro, Julio.
Herdocia, Rodolfo F.
Hospital, Botica del.
Icaza, Alejo J.
Marin, Basilio.
Midence & Co., importers.
Pallais, Desiderio.
Telleria, Tomás.
Engraver.
Rodas, Rosendo.
Foundries.
Lindo, Pastor.
Osorno, Vicenta.
Rocha é hijo, Josefa.
Hardware and tools.
Ardila, Benito.
Banegas, Gregorio.
Calderon, Trinidad.
Cisne, Leopoldo.
Leon, Luciano. •
Mungua, Salvado.
Hatters.
Cartin, Luis.
Sanabria, Angel.
Santell, José.
Sequeira, Bernardo.
Toruno, Ramon.
Hides and leather.
Balladares, Paula.
Baneto, Desiderio.
Escorcia, Sebastian E.
Granera, Felipe.
Gutierrez, Salvador.
Mayorga, Coronado.
Montalban, Venancio.
Osepo, Vicente.
Valle, Sinforoso.
Paints and varnishes.
Molina, Demetrio.
Zapata, Manuel.
Photographers.
Godoy, Manuel.
Lazarenco, Alejandro.
Perez, Roman.
Sedilez, Samuel.
Printers.
Gross, Constantine.
Gurdian, J. Cástulo.
Hernandez, Benito.
Orue, Antonio.
Ruiz, Joaquin.
Retail general merchants.
Alemán, P. E.
Barrios, M.
Boquin, Francisco.

LEON—Continued.

Retail general merchants—Continued.
Granera, Miguel G.
Gutierrez, Camilo.
Herdocia, Francisco L. de.
Mayorga, Cleto.
Peter, Alberto, y Ca.
Robelo, Luis S.
Saenz, Jenson.
Sarria, José.
Torres, Aurora.

Silversmiths.
Argeñal, Francisco.
Quiñonez, Andrés.
Zamora, José.
Zapata, Gregorio.

Special manufacturers.
Bayle, Luis de, machinery.
Chesnay, dyes.
Salgado, Carmen, oil.

Tinware and house-furnishing goods.
Breneo, Antonio.
Robelo, Sinforiana.
Soliz, Nazario.

Wholesale import and export merchants.
Alvarado, Federico.
Alvarado hijo, Pedro J.
Arana, Eleodoro.
Argüello & Prado.
Balladares, F. & L.
Balladares, Manuel.
Blume, Lotto.
Boyes, P. R.
Cardenal, Salvador.
Chica, Ramon.
Eisensteick & Co., P.
Dreyfus, Jorge.
Florke & Co., Emilio.
Guerrero & Montenegro.
Gutierrez & Co., Marín, S. B.
Hausen, B.
Lacayo é hijos, Gabriel.
Lacayo & Co., N.
Lacayo, Narciso.
Marín, Coronado A. de.
Mayorga, Fulgencio.
Morris, G. A. K.
Montalvana, V.
Motter, Floerck & Co.
Navas, Vicente.
Pérez, Juan.
Poten, Schubert & Co.
Reyes, Salvador.
Roquin, Francisco.
Sacasa, Antioco.
Salamanca, Paulino.
Salinas, Rafael & Alejandro.

LEON—Continued.

Wholesale import and export merchants—Cont'd.
Salinas & Co., Domingo.
Salinas, Norbeto.
Schneegans & Co., Federico.
Soto hnos., Rafael.
Telleria, Tomás.
Teran, Justo.
Thomas, James.

MANAGUA.
Banks and bankers.
Banco de Nicaragua.
Hirchen y Ca.
Rivas, Francisco Gomez.

Booksellers and stationers.
Barcenas, Joaquín.
Mejía, J.

Boots and shoes.
Contreras, J.
Guerrero, Francisco.
Robleto, J. Angel.
Robleto, Narciso.

Commission merchants.
Campo, Francisco.
Denegri, Remotti A.
Navarro, Tiburcio.
Olivares, Juan Florencio.
Olivares, Francisco.
Silva, Silvestre.
Solórzano, Federico.
Zavala, Luis.

Druggists.
Bengoechea, J. C.
Bravo, Jorge.
Bustamante, L.
Cabrera, Rafael.
Cárdenas, Adán.
Gomez, Luciano.
Groumeyer, P.
Medrano, Mauro.
Ramirez, Gerónimo.
Vega, Francisco.
Velásquez, Márcos E.

Engraver.
Montes de Oca, J.

Exporters coffee, hides, dye woods, etc.
Arguello, P. P.
Bengoechea, J. C.
Bermudez, Salvador.
Blume, Otto.
Burlet, Pedro.
Cardenas, Adán.
Chamorro & Co., Salvador.
Elizondo & Son, Joaquín.
Frixione, Daniel.
Gomez, Luciano.
Groumeyer & Co., P.

MANAGUA—Continued.

Exporters coffee, hides, dye woods, etc.—Continued.
Guisto, Pablo.
Hyden & Co., Morris.
Jericho, Guillermo.
Lopez, Luis E.
Martinez, Tomas.
Mejia, Bernabe.
Mejia & Marenco.
Ortiz, Pedro.
Paez, Ignacio.
Peter & Co., Alberto.
Raminez, Alberto.
Raminez, Pedro R.
Remotti, Alessandro.
Rivas, R. A.
Rivas, Rodolfo.
Robleto, José A.
Rodriquez, J. D.
Saballos, Hipolito.
Saenz & Co., Adan.
Saenz, Ramon.
Solorzano, Antonio.
Solorzano, Carlos.
Solorzano, Francisco.
Suhr, Adolfo.

Grocers.
Aranda, Teresa.
Bone, María J.
Diaz, Felipa.
Fonseca, Gabriela.

Importers of drugs and chemicals.
Bengoechea, Señor Don.
Bravo, Dr.
Cajina, Cleto.
Gomez, Luciano.
Guerro, Benito.
Guerro, Pastor.
Lembke & Co., Gustavo C.
Mayorga, José Dolores.
Murillo, Carlos A.
Obando, Pablo J.
Ortega, Luciano.
Velasquez & Ca.

Importers of general merchandise.
Blume & Co., Otto.
Chamorro & Co., Salvador.
Elizondo é Hijo, Joaquin.
Garcia é Hijo, Remigio.
Gronmeyer & Co., P.
Hernandez, Zacarias.
Hyden & Co., Morris.
Jericho & Co., Guillermo.
Low & Co., H. E.
Martinez, Tomas.
Mejia, B.
Mejia & Marenco.

MANAGUA—Continued.

Importers of general merchandise—Continued.
Nuñez, J. A.
Ortiz & Co., Pedro.
Peter & Co., A.
Robleto & Co., José A.
Saenz, Adan.
Schnegans & Co., Federico.

Photographer.
Maritano, Fernando.

Planters of coffee.
Bancki, Julio.
Bermudez, Francisco.
Bermudez, Salvador.
Cabréra, Rafael.
Castrillo, Salvador.
Cuadra, Asunción.
Cuadra, José de la Paz.
Chamon, Salvador.
Garmendia, Isabel.
Friccione, Daniel.
Gómez, Luciano.
Lacayo, Fernando.
Lacayo, Lisimaco.
Lacayo, Pánfilo.
Navas, Vicente.
Portocarrero, Bernabé.
Portocarrero, Fernando.
Saenz, Luis & Ramon.
Savallos, Hipólito.
Solórzano, Antonio.
Solórzano, Ramon.
Tritione, Daniel.
Vega, Juan.
Vigil, Vicente.
Zelaya, Santos Francisco.

Printers.
Arias, Juan P.
Burgos, Guadalupe.
Castillo, Justo J.
Garcia, Manuel M., Pio M. T., Félix y F.
González, B.
Hernández, J.
Silva, R. Ramon.
Vargas, Concepción.
Zelaya, Félix P.

Retail general merchants.
Bárcenas, Joaquin.
Calderón, Manuel.
Cárdenas, Adán.
Cuadra, J. de la Paz.
Chamorro, Rodolfo.
Chamorro, Salvador.
Chamorro, Emilio.
Chesnay, Emilio.
Elisondo, Joaquin.
Elisondo, Benjamin.

MANAGUA—Continued.

Retail general merchants—Continued.
Espinoza, Miguel.
Florke Emil.
Gronmeyer, Pablo.
Jansen, Carlos.
Lacayo, Lisimaco.
Low, Enrique.
Martinez, Tomás.
Morales, Francisco.
Portocarrero, Fernando.
Rivas, Rafael A.
Robleto, J. Angel.
Saenz, Adán.
Sivan, Juan R.
Wells, Dolores S. de.

Silversmiths.
Silva, Silvestre.
Soliz, Bruno.

Watchmakers and jewelers.
Bárcenas, Joaquín.
Portugués, Juan J.
Robleto, T. A.

Wholesale export and import merchants.
Adam, José.
Bahlike, Julio C.
Bárcenas, Joaquín.
Calderón, hijo & Co., Manuel.
Chamorro, Salvador.
Cuandra, J. de la Paz.
Estrada, Dionisio.
Gabarrete, Máximo.
Gabarrete, Agapito.
Giusto, Pablo.
Jansen, Carlos.
Jericho & Co., Guillermo.
Lacayo, Lisimaco F.
Larios, Gilberto.
Low, H. E.
Macauley, D. Bernard.
Morales, Francisco B.
Murray, D. L.
Ortiz & Co., Pedro.
Peter & Co., Alberto.
Robleto, José Angel.
Saenz, Adán.
Solórzano, Z. Francisco.

Wood merchant.
Moreira, E.

MASAYA.

Boots and shoes.
Abaunza, Justo.

Commission merchant.
Carrión, Fernando Z.

MASAYA—Continued.

Druggist.
Argüello, L.

Exporters, coffee, hides, and dye woods.
Cardoze Bros., Ignatius.
Oquel, Luis.
Ortega, Luis.
Pimentel, Gil.
Ramirez, Mercedes.
Rosalez, Claudio.
Ximenes Bros., P.
Zelaya, Benito.

Importers of drugs and chemicals.
Baca, José A.
Bolaños, Alejandro.
Cesar, Julio.
Ruis, Pedro J.
Sequeira, Anselmo.
Wasner, Francisco.

Importers of general merchandise.
Arceyut, P. Joaquin.
Abaunza, Benjamin.
Brenes, Fernando.
Carrion, Alejandro.
Carrion, Fernando Z.
Castrillo, Petrona.
Lopez, Blas.
Luna, Audato.
Martinez & Co., Dolores.
Martinez, Maria de J.
Nuñez, Carmen.
Prado, Jacobo.
Solorzano, Enrique.
Zuniga, Francisco.

Wholesale import and export merchants.
Cardoza hnos., J.
Lacayo, Mariano.
Martinez, Tomás.
Cesar, Octaviano.
Climie, Wm.
Nuñez, Filadelfo.
Nuñez, J. A.
Oreamuno & César.
Pimentel, Gil.
Rosales, Leandro.
Solórzano, Cárlos.
Solórzano, Federico
Vega, Antonio.
Zurita, Rafael.

MATAGALPA.

Druggist.
Alanis, L.

Importer.
- Chavez & hijo, Ignacio.

MOMOTOMBO.

Merchant and manufacturer.
Argüello & Co., Peñalva.

OCOTAL

Boots and shoes.
Gutierrez, Manuel.
Morazán, Juan.

Retail general merchants.
Paguaga, José Maria.
Irias, Benito.
Calderón, Francisco.

Silversmith.
Villacorta, Juan V.

Wholesale merchant and importer.
Lovo, Pastor.

POTOSI

Retail general merchants.
Abarca, Apolinar.
Lemus, José.

REALEJO.

Merchants.
Brennes, Pedro.
Garcia & Deshon.
Montealegre, M.
Monterey & Co.
Navarro, Pantaleón.
Thompson.
Van Muller & Co.

RIO GRANDE.

Wholesale import and export merchants.
Pictora, Alcine.
Smith, Enrique.

RIVAS.

Banker.
Maliaño ó hijos, Maria V. de.

Boots and shoes.
Galarza, Leandro.
Hurtado, Gerónimo.
López, Saturnino.

Druggists.
Barrios, M. J.
Flint, Earl.
Maliaño, Donoso.
Velásquez, Zacarias.

Grocers.
Carmona, Juana.
Leiva, Mercedes.
Pineda, Josepha.
Sandino, Pantaleona.
Talavera, Modesta Ana.

RIVAS—Continued.

Importers of drugs and chemicals.
Canton & Guerra.
Central Botica.

Retail general merchants.
Aguilar, Manuel A.
Bendaña, José.
Chamorro, Marquezo.
Gallegos, Filadelfo.
Guerra, Leonidas.
Llanes, Elias.
Martinez, Francisco.

Silversmiths.
Ferrer, Joaquin.
Rios, Ignacio.
Abaunza, Pastor.
Alvarez, Lino.

Watchmaker and jeweler.
Serra, Juan B.

Wholesale import and export merchants.
Carazo, Mannel A.
Fuentes, Virginia Torres de.
Goodman, H.
Jiménez & Co., Torres.
López & Maliaño.
Maliaño ó hijos, Maria D. de.
Maliaño, Dr Donoso.
Martinez, Nemesio y Luis.
Padilla, Francisco.
Sacasa, Simona H. de.
Urcuyo, Vicente.
Urcuyo, Macario.

SAN JORGE

Importer.
Marin, Felipe.

Retail general merchant.
Arcia, Juan C.

SAN JUAN DEL SUR.

Commission merchants.
Chrisman, C. A. R.
Murray, D. L.
Sacasa, Daniel.

Wholesale import and export merchants.
Hoffman, Ferdinand.
Holman, Carlos.
Pizzi & Co., Carlos.

TIPITAPA.

Commission merchant.
Chamorro, Damaso.

Paraguay.

Banks.
Banco Agricola.
Banco de Comercio.
Banco del Paraguay y Rio de la Plata.
Banco Hipotecario.
Banco Nacional.
Banco Territorial.

Booksellers.
Fisher y Quell.
Gradin, E.
Kraus, H.

Carriage-maker.
Fiori, A.

Coal merchant.
Manzoni Hnos.

Commission merchants.
Artaza y Frontanilla.
Borge, Francisco.
Canstatt, S.
Cristofanini.
Domaniscki.
Fassoli y Casartelli.
Feartherston.
Flores, Facundo.
Flores, T.
Fuster, José.
García, Aquiles.
Heiman, Simon & Co.
Lamas, Vicente.
Lavatier, D.
Manzoni Hnos.
Marrero, Gregorio.
Risso, Franciscŏ.
Taboada, Antonio.
Uriarte, Eduardo.
Vierci y Tiscornia.

Cutlery.
Hocquard, Alfredo.
Rosch, Víctor.

Dry goods.
Battilana, T.
Cano, Silforiano.

Dry goods—Continued.
da Costa, M.
Ferran, Angel.
Ferriol, Bernardo.
Fernandez, Eleuterio.
Gaona & Co.
García y Fernandez.
Gaspar, Manuel.
Gonzalez, Guillermo.
Gonzalez, José.
Martinez, Lopez.
Montero, Francisco.
Muñoz y Aranda.
Ros y Alvarez.
Schufini, J. B.
Solalinde, M.
Talavella, A.
Yuzzi, P.

Fireworks.
Gomez, Avelino.

Flour merchants.
La Palma de Quaranta.
Molino Nacional, Saguier, Vargas & Co.

Fruit merchants.
Anchar, Nicasio.
Bajac & Co.
Delmes, J.
Diaz, Pastor.
Figueroa.
Franco, Fern.
Goviño, Juan A.
Jacobo.
Molas, Basilio.
Narvaez, D.
Pancracio & Co.
Perazzo, Ant.
Ramirez, J.
Ramos, V.
Recentini, Pedro.
Santander, Faustino.
Troche, T.
Urdulez, J.
Valiente, Rafael.

253

ASUNCION—Continued.
General merchants.

Acosta, Nicasio.
Alarcon, Bernardo.
Alberto, Juan C.
Amarilla, Maria.
Angel, Pascual.
Azareto, Blas.
Baez Hnos.
Balan, Franqui.
Barbosa, Maria.
Basili, José.
Bastrebi, S.
Batteyro & Echeguren.
Battilana, Teodoro.
Beatier, Juan.
Bello, José.
Benitez, Bernardino.
Berdejo, Feliciano.
Bernaza, Ambrosio.
Borian, M.
Caballero, Miguel.
Cabezasi, Antonio.
Cabrera, Gerónimo.
Calvo, Ramon.
Candia, Manuel.
Capurro, Juan.
Caravia, Spiro.
Carballo, Antonio.
Careaga, Juana.
Careaga, Rafael.
Caroso, Ambrosio.
Casalito, Domingo.
Castellani, A.
Castro, Emilio.
Cellario Hnos.
Centurion, Agustin.
Céspedes, Irene.
Chaves, F. P.
Colman, T.
Cotuiro, J.
Cristofanini, A.
Crosas, A.
Dalio, José.
Decoud, Silverio.
Delgado, Francisco.
Delvalle, José.
Diaz, Felipe.
Diaz, Filomena.
Diaz, Gregorio.
Diaz, Juana.
Doldan, José.
Domeque, Pedro.
Elizeche, Juan.
Erico, Pablo.
Falco y Hnos.
Fernandez, Eleuterio.

ASUNCION—Continued.
General merchants—Continued.

Ferrara, Francisco.
Ferrari, Angel.
Fischer, Eduardo.
Fleitas, Modesto.
Flores, Guillermo.
Fondicala, Lorenzo.
Fracchia, Francisco.
Fretes, Asuncion.
Fretes, Matias.
Gadea, Martin.
Galeano, Valentin.
Gilleo, Pedro.
Gaona & Co., Francisco.
Garayano, Domingo.
García & Co., Fernandez.
García, A.
García, Juan.
Garrido, Gabriel.
Gimenez, S.
Gomez, Antonio.
Gomez, Tomasa.
Gonzalez, Emiliano.
Gonzalez, Gabino.
Gonzalez, Gregorio.
Gonzalez, José.
Gonzalez, Zacarias.
Grenzi, Antonio.
Guerreros, Eusebio.
Gutierrez, Mariano.
Hill, Frank D.
Ibarra, Josefa.
Ibarra, Rufino.
Irrazabal, Isabel.
Juzzi, P.
Klug, César.
Laflor, Ceferino de.
Lassere Hermanos.
Leal, Felipe.
Liviéres, Lorenzo.
Lopez, Magdalena.
Machain Hermanos.
Magrini, Luis.
Maldonado, Eleuterio.
Mantero, Pedro.
Manzan, Francisco.
Marinelli, Juan.
Martinez, Juan de M.
Martinez, Silvano.
Matto, César A.
Mazzi, Antonio.
Mendez, Francisco.
Mereles, Tomasa.
Mieres y Rodriguez.
Min, Reyes.
Montero, Francisco.

ASUNCION—Continued.

General merchants—Continued.

Moreira, Manuel.
Munoz & Aguinaga.
Nardi y Bartolo.
Navarro y Andruez.
Nega, Claudio.
Negri, Juan B.
Oliveira, Alberto.
Oliveira, D.
Oliveira, Joaquin.
Ortellado de la Cruz.
Ortellado, José María.
Ortiz, Bernardo.
Pandi, L.
Pani, Salvador.
Parodi, Lorenzo.
Parodi, Pablo.
Parra R. B.
Patiño, Manuel.
Paula, Francisco de.
Pellegrini, Domingo.
Pereira, José.
Picasso, Luis.
Pinho, Ernesto.
Pittari, Antonio.
Pizurno, Ezequiel.
Polanich, Santi- go.
Poletti, Domingo.
Prato, Emilio.
Ramirez, F.
Ramirez, Juan B.
Reinter, Bernardino.
Richard, Alfredo.
Riquelme, Pedro A.
Riquelme, Tomasa.
Riveros. A.
Rodriguez, Miguel.
Romero, V.
Rosa, Albino de.
Rosa, Rufino.
Ruiz, E.
Ruiz, Juan.
Saguier, Carlos R.
Saguier Hermanos.
Salcano, Valentin.
Salinas, S.
Salvione, José.
Scherenio, Fdo.
Silva, C.
Sosa, Faustina.
Stanch, Lucas.
Suani, Agustin.
Taboada, P.
Talabella, Antonio.
Talico, M.
Trajan, Manuel.

ASUNCION—Continued.

General merchants—Continued.

Turró, Antonio.
Turró, Francisco.
Ucedo, José.
Valdez, Cármen.
Valdez, Lucio.
Valdez, Tomasa.
Valdovinos, Emiliano.
Valdovinos, Pedro.
Valentin, Manuel.
Valenzuela, Miguel G.
Valiente, Daniel.
Vasquez, Pedro A.
Ventre, Gerónimo.
Ventre, S.
Ventura, Antonio.
Vieini, Tomás.
Vila, Manuel.
Villarica, José.

Hardware.

Crovato, Rodi & Co.
Pirovano & Co., G.
Prats, E.
Rius y Jorba.

Importers.

Almandoz y Zorazabal.
Angulo & Co.
Augusti, Rafael.
Bajac & Co., Miguel W.
Bello, Enrique.
Bibolini Hnos.
Billordo y Ca.
Boettner & Co., Alfredo.
Casaccia, Jorge.
Casartelli Hnos.
Crovato, Rodi & Co.
Esmeriz & Co., Francisco.
Fernandez Hnos.
Fernandez y García.
Fisher y Quell.
Frachua & Tiscornia.
Gaona & Co.
Garcia & Fernandez.
Gomez & Co.
Gonçalves, Ricardo Mendez.
Heidske, Chr.
Heisecke, Cristian G.
Manzoni Hnos.
Monte & Co.
Pin, F.
Pirovano & Co., G.
Ribeiro & Co., Cazal.
Rius y Jorba.
Ros y Alvarez.
Solalinde, Manuel.
Uribe & Co.

ASUNCION—Continued.

Jewelers and watchmakers.
  Cabrera & Co., P.
  Lopez & Klunge.
  Martinez, J. M.
  Otaegui, P.
  Perret, Martin.

Liquor merchants.
  Brégains, Luis.
  Duval.
  Evali, Luis.
  Parini.
  Pecci Hnos.
  Rabéry & Co., Luis.
  Riquelme, Sábas.
  Sciolle, P.
  Servian, T.
  Van Strate, Luis.

Lithographers.
  Casaús, Placido.
  Godel & Co., A.

Produce merchants.
  Angulo & Co.
  Casnedi, Felipe.
  Corpa, Juan.
  Gaona & Co., Francisco.
  Risso, Francisco.
  Patri, Luis.
  Ruiz, T.
  Uribe & Co.

CARAGUATAY.

General stores.
  Bergara, Ignacio.
  Dacosta, Francisco G.
  Diaz, Nicasio.
  Escurra, Daniel.
  Fraix, Anselmo.
  Fretes, Anastasio.
  Gonzalez, Froilan.
  Miranda, Francisco.

CARAGUATAY—Continued.

General stores—Continued.
  Nuñez, Hipol.
  Perez, Valentin.
  Samaniego, Candido.
  Villano, Cayetano.
  Villati, Diego.
  Zapata, Victor.

Silversmiths.
  Insaurralde, José Maria.
  Villasanti, Juan.

Spirit manufacturers.
  Campo, Ventura.
  Dacosta, Francisco G.
  Diaz, Nic.
  Oveido, Juan M.
  Recalde, Josefa.
  Vera, Doroteo.

Sugar growers.
  Antunez, Laureano.
  Medina, Dionisio.
  Samaniego, Castor.
  Villagró, Pilar.

VILLA DEL PILAR.

Commission merchants.
  Centurion, Adriano.
  Granada, Ignacio.

Merchants, wholesale.
  Dos Santos, Antonio.
  Rébori, Venturi.

Shipbuilders.
  Altgelt & Co.
  Bouzante, Esteban.

Wood exporters.
  Altgelt & Co.
  Benza, Lorenzo.
  Dos Santos, Ant.
  Rébori, Venturi.

Peru.

AREQUIPA.

Bankers.
Reimers, Alvino.
Branch of the Bank of Callao.

Hardware merchants.
Bize & Escomel.
Vidaurrazaga & Co., V.

Merchants, importers and exporters.
Albareda, Ramon, books, stationery, etc.
Barron, Enrique L., hides.
Bebin Hermanos.
Belannde, Mariano A.
Bize & Escomel.
Braillard Bros. & Co., wool and cascarilla.
Bustamente, Juan & F.
Castillo, José S.
Cavallero, Angel.
Chabanaise, Gustavo, drugs, perfumery.
Chabaneise, Viuda de, hats and fancy goods.
Cornejo, Pedro Gomez, cocoa and coffee.
Espinosa, Leandro.
Eumel Bros. & Co., cocoa.
Farpán, José M.
Folga é Hijos, M.
Gibson, Henry W., wool and hides.
Gibson, Patrick & Co., wool and coffee.
Guinaud, Julio, jewelry, etc.
Heusser, Juan.
Irriberry, Harrison & Co., wool and cascarilla.
Juste & Co.
Moron, José D., drugs, perfumery.
Muniz, A. M., jewelry, etc.
Paulson Bros., coffee.
Pena, José M., wool and hides.
Portugal, José F., drugs, perfumery.
Reimers, Alvino, wool and hides.
Reinecke, Robert & Co., wool and cascarilla.
Revera, José V.
Sprinckmöller & Co., C.
Stafford & Co., hides, cattle, and sheep.
Torres, Mariano de P.
Vidaurrazaga, V., hardware, paints, etc.

Woolen goods, wholesale.
Reimers, Alvino.
Reinecke & Co.
Stafford & Co.

ASCOPE.

Merchant.
Ludoweig & Co.

BARRANCA.

Merchant.
Rosas, C.

CALLAO.

Bank.
Banco del Callao.

Commission agents.
Albarracin & Freundt.
Alzamora, Sabino.
Anderson & Maravoto.
Balbuena, José C.
Berninzon, Enrique.
Bueaño, J. C.
Canessa, M.
Cavalic, S.
Conroy & Co.
Dañino, J.
Elizaldo, S.
Ferrande, P.
Flores, Guerra J.
Gore, Teofilo.
Grace Bros. & Co.
Lacharrière & Co.
Landi, Canessa & Co.
Merel, José.
Muelle, Miguel.
Newton, J.
Ondereyck & Co.
Pallete y Hermano.
Peraₜₐ & Co., J. C.
Rossell & Co., R.
Salinas, Juan.
Thornley & Co.
Voss, Juan.
Weiss & Co., Carlos.
Weisu, Roberto.

Merchants, general, import and export.
Aicardi, importer dry goods.
Asti, A., importer Chilian produce.
Backus & Johnston, importers articles for brewery.

S. Ex. 8, pt. 11——17

257

CALLAO—Continued.

Merchants, general, import and export—Cont'd.

Barabino Hermanos.
Berninzone & Co., E.
Brent, H. M.
Canessa, M., importer tobacco.
Carnicich, S., importer dry goods.
Delande, Lorenzo, importer, general,
Delaude, L., importer, general merchandise.
Delepiane Bros., importers dry goods.
Grace Bros. & Co., importers general merchandise and ship chandlery.
Keiffner, A., importer articles for brewery.
Landi & Canessa, importers, mining utensils, and exporters of minerals.
MacKay & Co., importers, hardware and sewing machines.
Mackehenine, C.
Martensen, A., importer, hats.
Milne & Co., A., importer, wheat, rice, etc.
Molfino & Co., D., importers, general.
Morea, A., importer, Chilian produce.
Muller, M., importer, medicines and drugs.
Newton, J., importer, stationery.
Nosiglia Bros., importers, general merchandise.
Ostoja, B., importer, hardware.
Paul, Julio, lumber.
Peralta, Juan C., opium.
Perez & Co., P., importers, general merchandise and ship chandlery.
Piaggio, F. G., importer, general merchandise.
Pinasco, J., importer, dry goods.
Rossell & Co., importers, general merchandise.
Schroder & Co., C. M., importers, general merchandise and mining utensils.
Serra & Casanova, importers, drugs.
Shute & Co., Thomas, importers, ship chandlery and coal.
Simpson Bros., importers, general merchandise.
Solimano Hnos., importers, Chilian produce.
Schultz, Adolpho, importer, general.
Tiscornia, importer, Italian produce.
Toso & Sanchez, importers, wheat and flour.
Trisano, S., importer, drugs.
Vidaurrazaga, A., importer, hardware.
Weiss, Charles & Co., importers, general merchandise and mining utensils.

CAÑETE.

Merchant.

Esparte, Leandro.

CATACAOS.

Merchants.

Allison, Enrique, exporter.
Cabredo, Justo, groceries.
Feijou, Miguel, importer.

CATACAOS—Continued.

Merchants—Continued.

Garcia, Manuel E., importer.
Leon, Ernesto, importer.
Plateros, Ramon, groceries.

CERRO DE PASCO.

Merchants.

McNulty. M. C.
Valle, Angel.

CHANCAY.

Merchant.

Garmendia, Francisco.

CHICLAYO.

Bankers.

Branch of the Bank of Callao.

Importers and exporters.

Campodonico, Eug.
Campodonico y Scaperlenda.
Chow Sing Lou boki Ca.
Clarke y Ca.
Curriel, F. G.
Dall' Orso, V.
Dall' Orso & Descalzi.
Fry, G. E.
Gorbitz y Cia.
Klinge, H.
Wing On Tay y Ca.

Merchants.

Boggio, Pablo.
Branchi, Cesar.
Casanova e Hijos, Viuda de.
Cuglievan y Ca.
Curriel, Felix German.
Dall' Orso & Descalzi.
Rourdan, Juan.
Russo, José.
Tassara, Juan.
Valle, Pablo.

CHIMBOTE.

Merchant.

Pezet, Victor.

CHINCHA.

Merchants.

Sanguinetti Hermanos.

ETEN.

Merchants.

Curriel, F. G.
Lopez, Luis.
Maurtua, P.
Solf, Alfredo.

FERREÑAFE.

Merchant.

Curriel, Felix German.

HUACHO.

Alcantara, Manuel, cotton dealer.
Andres, Allen, cotton dealer.
Dulanto, Manuel, cotton dealer.
Flores Fermin Bros., cotton dealers.
Laos, Domingo A., cotton dealer.
Luna Hermanos.
Romero, Manuel I., cotton dealer.
Saco, Alejo, cotton dealer.

ICA.

Merchants.
Bosa, D. Raul, cotton dealer.
Divizia, Francisco.
Picaso & Bros., cotton dealers.

JAUJA.

Merchant.
Valle, Angel.

LAMBAYEQUE.

Merchants.
Curriel, Felix German.
Descalzi, Luis.
Maltesse, N. O.
Ruiz, Aurelio.
Importers and exporters.
Fry, Wm. V.
Schaefer, Carlos.

LIMA.

Banks.
Banco del Callao.
Banco de Londres, Méjico y Sur-América.
Banco Italiano.
Brokers.
Ascher, Paul.
Finnie, A. S.
Godoy, Joaquin.
Gomez.
Jacoby, Fernando.
Jacoby, Sigmundo.
Loayza, Ildefonso.
Lopez, Gerardo.
López, J. B.
Rosemberg, Rodolfo.
Exporters.
Anselmo & Co., J. B., cotton and coffee.
Ayulo & Co., Enrique, wool, cotton, and sugar.
Bates, Stokes & Co., cotton and metals.
Beausire, Mathison & Co.. wool, cotton, and sugar.
Bryson & Co., J. B., metals.
Duncan, Fox & Co., wool, cotton, and sugar.
Ferrari, Peschiera & Cosso, wool and coffee.
Gildemeister, J., metals.
Grace Bros. & Co., wool, cotton, and sugar.
Graham, Rowe, & Co., wool, cotton, and sugar.

LIMA—Continued.

Exporters—Continued.
Haines & Co., E., cotton and sugar.
Kitz & Co., A., cocoaine.
Ludoweigh & Co., sugar and metals.
Otto & Co., Ph., silver.
Schroeder, C. M., cocoa, cocoaine, cascarilla.
Weiss & Co., cocoa, cocoaine, cascarilla.
Furniture merchants.
Bernasconi, Angel.
Bertrix, José.
Chelle, Nedro.
Dubois, Eugenio.
Garcia, Gregorio.
Giesman, Juan.
Hoch, Koppler & Co.
Lapiere, Jorge.
Leon, Manuel.
Malherbe.
Orbegozo, Diego.
Quiros, Manuel.
Scolari & Co., Juan.
Zavalaga, Vicente.
Merchants in general.
Abele, Eugenio, lithographer.
Abrahamson, Herman.
Accini, Agustin.
Adriansen, Luis F.
Aguallo, Francisco B.
Alban, José.
Albarracin, José.
Albertis, Francisco M. de.
Aliaga.
Alibert, Agustin, wines and liquors.
Alonso, José.
Alty, Thomas William.
Alvan, José Ignacio, jeweler.
Alvarado, José Zenon.
Alvarez, Juan Antonio.
Alzamora, Manual, drugs.
Amoretti, Lorenzo.
Anaya, Juan M., drugs.
Anderson, Carlos G.
Anselmi Hermanos, coal merchants.
Anselmo, J. B.
Anzardo y Garcia.
Aramburn, Pedro D.
Arana, Angel.
Aranda y Reyes, Manuel.
Araos, Antenor, merchant.
Araos, Antonio T.
Araoz, Federico.
Argote, Domingo Felipe.
Arguedas, José Antonio.
Arimborgo, Angel.
Arnaes, Juan Francisco, printer.

PERU.

LIMA—Continued.

Merchants in general—Continued.
Ascenso y Ca.
Ascher, Pablo.
Aservi, Arturo.
Aservi, Eleodoro.
Aspitarte Hermanos.
Astengo, Angel.
Avalos, Belisario.
Ayala, Felipe S., printer.
Azaldegui, Manuel.
Babot, B. D.
Bacigalupi, Pedro.
Backus y Johnston, brewers.
Badiere, A.
Balarezo, Ezequiel.
Balarezo, Urbano.
Balarezo, Urbano.
Balbuena. Eduardo.
Balbuena, José de la Cruz.
Bambaren, A.
Bances, coal merchant.
Bar, Carlos.
Barbagelatta, Clemente.
Barbe, Juan.
Barcelli, Marcelo, jewelry.
Barreda, Eduardo.
Barreto, Alberto.
Barrios, F.
Barrios, Lucio E.
Bartet, Juan.
Basombrio, Juan Climaco.
Bassadre, Modesto.
Bayly, Santiago A.
Becher, Oscar.
Becker, Adolfo E.
Beltran, José Miguel.
Bermasconi y Ca., A.
Bernaola, Eduardo Ramon.
Bernos, Alfonso.
Bernizon, Enrique S.
Berninzon y Ca., Enrique.
Bert, Clemente.
Betini, José.
Beza, José.
Bisso, Tomas.
Blum, Moises.
Boeschel, Carlos.
Boggiano & Co., M. G., jewelers.
Boggiano, Aquiles, drugs.
Boggio, Bartolome.
Bolarte, Baltazar, jeweler.
Bolezzi, Juan B.
Bolognini, Domingo.
Bonani, Arturo.
Bonino, J. J.

LIMA—Continued.

Merchants in general—Continued.
Bonnaffe, Eduardo.
Botto, Juan.
Boursot, Victor.
Bower y Bodero.
Bravo, Pedro José.
Brenner, Christian.
Brenner, David.
Bresani, J. y F.
Bresciani, C.
Bresciani, Juan.
Bresciani, Tomas.
Brillman, Jacobo.
Broggi Hermanos, merchants.
Broggi, Jorge.
Bromberg, Max.
Bronley, Ernesto.
Brown, Roberto.
Brutton, Tomas.
Bryce, Enrique.
Buepaño, Diego.
Buepaño, Juan S.
Bufet, J. A.
Buse, Diedrich.
Bustamante, Jesus, drugs.
Cabello, Gustavo.
Caceres, J. D.
Cadamartori, Jose.
Calderoni, Enrique.
Calderoni, Fidel.
Calderoni, Juan J.
Calmet, Luis V.
Calvy, Sebastian, drugs.
Camogli, Luis Felipe.
Campodonico Hermanos.
Campodonico, Federico, groceries.
Campodonico, Juan.
Campos, Fuentes José Maria.
Campoverde, printer.
Canepa, Juan Bautista.
Canesa, Nicolas.
Cantuarias, José Manuel.
Canedo, José G. de.
Canevaro Hijos, José.
Capella, Miguel.
Carbone, Bartolomé.
Carbone, Juan.
Cárdenas, Domingo.
Carlin, Leopoldo.
Carré, Miguel.
Carrere, Eduardo
Carrillo, Mariano.
Casareto, Pedro.
Casas y Cuello, José
Castagnino.

LIMA—Continued.

Merchants in general—Continued.

Castagnino, Lazari.
Castaños, Eugenio P.
Casterot.
Castillo, Antonio.
Castillo, Isaac.
Castro, Osete Juan.
Cazaretto, Antonio.
Cebrian, José.
Cenarro, Enrique, merchant.
Cervantes, Pedro H.
Chapellier, B.
Chaves, Mariano, drugs.
Chepotel, Santiago.
Chiappi, Luis.
Chiciliere, Boracio y Ca.
Chiurliza, Lorenzo.
Cobian, Ismael.
Collado, Maximiliano.
Colom, Francisco.
Coloma, Gustavo E.
Colvide and Co., booksellers.
Combe, Pedro.
Compan, Valentin.
Concha, Manuel.
Conroy, Cárlos L.
Conti, Segundo, drugs.
Copello, Juan Bautista, drugs.
Copello, Luis, drugs.
Cordova, Antonio F. de.
Corocker, Henry, plumber.
Correa, Manuel Antonio.
Cortes, Juan.
Corveto, José.
Corzo, Cipriano.
Cossu y Schiaffidi, Juan.
Costa, Angel F.
Costa, Ernesto.
Costes, Enrique.
Courret & Co., photographers.
Cox, Carlos.
Crens, Juan.
Crevani, M.
Crosby, Francisco L.
Crosby Hermanos.
Croveto.
Cueva, Martin.
Cuneo, Juan C.
Cuneo y Ca.
Daly, Pedro.
Dammerst, José Luis.
Dancourt, Arturo.
Dans & Co.
Darner, Lorenzo.
Dartnell, Ricardo P.
Davis Bros.

LIMA—Continued.

Merchants in general—Continued.

Dawson, Thomas.
De Albertis, Mario.
De Bernardi Hermanos.
Delaude, groceries.
Delfin, Luis.
Delgado, Enrique.
Delgado, Miguel.
Delgado, Ruperto.
Delgado, Vicente G.
Deluchi y Ca., F. N.
Dellepiani, Francisco.
Demartini Hermanos, hosiery.
Denegri, Americo.
Denegri, Aurelio.
Denegri Hermanos, hardware.
Denegri, José A., drugs.
Denegri, Manuel.
Denegri, Miguel.
Derteano, Manuel D.
Devoto, Fortunato, groceries and wines.
Diaz, Calleja Juan.
Dobrich, Juan.
Dockendorff y Ca.
Dora, Luis.
Dora, Nicolas.
Drago y Lertora, groceries.
Duany y Ca., Juan, manufacturer of cigars.
Dubois, Eugenio.
Dubois, Juan Luis.
Ducla, Juan.
Dugenne, Edmundo.
Dupuy, Federico.
Dühring, Gaspar.
Duthil, Faustino.
Echenique, Rufino P.
Eckstein, A.
Ego, Aguirre Federico E.
Egoavil, Pedro.
Eicken, lace merchant.
Engelbrech, H.
Escobar, Aurelio.
Escobar, José Pablo.
Escoubes, J.
Escribene, Tomas P.
Espantoso, Eduardo.
Espinosa, José R.
Espinosa, Justo P.
Estke, Guillermo.
Etchebaster, Adolfo.
Fabra, Juan.
Fabrica de Escobas.
Falco Hermanos, merchants.
Falco, Teodoro.
Falcone, Nicolas.
Farfan, Manuel.

LIMA—Continued.

Merchants in general—Continued.
Febrero, B. G., cigars.
Fernand y Hermanos, P.
Fernandez, José Maria.
Fernandini, Francisco.
Ferrando, Pedro, earthenware.
Ferraro, Agustin F.
Ferrer, Juan P., drugs.
Ferrer, José Antonio.
Ferreyra, Joaquin.
Field y Ca., Arturo.
Figari é Hijos, Juan.
Figari, Adolfo L.
Figari, Bartolome.
Figari, Juan J
Figari, Luis.
Figari, Luis L.
Figari, Manuel M.
Figueroa, Juan B.
Figueroa y Parra, Eusebio.
Finnie y Ca.
Flores, Guerra José.
Flores, José Toribio Gigua.
Flores, Manuel D.
Foissard, Luis.
Fontanes, Eugenio.
Forgues, Alexis.
Fort, Julio.
Fournier, Talledo Juan.
Frachia, Domingo, drugs.
Franck y Ca., clothing.
Frassinetti, Juan, boots and shoes.
Freundt, Carlos E.
Freund, Luis, pianos.
Fry, Guillermo.
Fuentes, Eloy.
Fuentes, Patricio Nicolas.
Fuller, Jorge B. Enrique.
Gagliardo Hermanos, hosiery.
Gallour y Ca.
Gallese, Federico, drugs.
Gallo Hermanos.
Galves, Agustin.
Galves, Mariano.
Gamarra y Cordova, José M.
Gamero y Ca., J. S.
Garagori, Juan Francisco.
García, Domingo.
García, Federico.
García, José del C.
García, José Gregorio.
García, Luis and Sacio, cotton.
García y Zapata, Guillermo.
Gardini, Federico.
Garibay, Jacinto.
Garibotto, José A.

LIMA—Continued.

Merchants in general—Continued.
Garland, Guillermo.
Garragorri, Juan.
Garragorri, J. G.
Gatti, Señora.
Gaye, Hilario.
Genit, Nicolás.
Gerbolini é Izola.
Gestro, Luis.
Giacometti, Flavio.
Gianelli y Ca., groceries.
Giani, J. B., jewelers.
Giatti, Clara, types and printing materials.
Giese, Francisco José.
Gimeno, Joaquín.
Ginffre, José.
Ginochio, E.
Godoy, Joaquín.
Godoy y Riera, José Antonio
Gogelein, Emilio.
Gomez, Muriano.
Gongora, César.
Gottuzzo, Bartolome.
Govea, Tomás.
Goyeheneix, Francisco.
Goybenne, Armando.
Grana, Santiago.
Grec, Emilio J., drugs.
Grelland, Enrique.
Grundell, Coca.
Grundell, S., hardware.
Guembes, Agusto.
Guerin, Agusto.
Guerra, José.
Gulda, Federico.
Gutierrez, Roberto G., cigars.
Gutman, Luis.
Gutman, Santiago.
Guyllen, Isidro, printer.
Guzman, Juan Antonio.
Guzman, Manuel.
Hachmeister, Agusto, tailor.
Hague, Juan P.
Hague y Castagnini, drugs.
Hardt, Ernesto.
Hart, Juan.
Hart Bros., plumbers.
Harten y Ca.
Hartley, Ricardo A.
Helguero, Pedro A.
Helms, Alberto H. F.
Hermosa, Nicolas B., drugs.
Hernandez, Santiago A.
Herouard, P., hardware.
Hertle y Tello.
Higginson, Enrique E.

LIMA—Continued.

Merchants in general—Continued.

Hinojosa, César.
Hinojosa, José Nicanor.
Hochkoppler José.
Hoefken, Hugo,
Holcombe, Jorge E. R.
Holder, Alberto.
Holguin, Vicente.
Humphreys and Co., E., hardware.
Hurtado, Agustin, dry goods.
Idiaquez, José Manuel.
Ingunza, Francisco.
Ingunza, Francisco R.
Inzira, C. Manuel.
Iparraguirre, José.
Iparraguirre, José Marcos.
Iriarte, Julio F.
Iriarte, Mariano E.
Ismodes, J. F., drugs.
Jacobs, Guillermo.
Jacoby, Fernando, jewelry.
Jacoby, Sigmundo, jewelry.
Jauregui, Manuel.
Jimeno, J.
Jochamovitz, Julio.
Johnson, Juan M.
Jordan, Manuel.
Jurgens, Cárlos U.
Jurgens, Juan.
Kast, Federico Guillermo.
Kemish, plumber.
Kidd, Santiago.
Kitz, Arnaldo.
Kitz y Ca., A.
Klinge, F.
Kollmann, Gustavo.
König, Cárlos, sewing machines.
Lamarca, Cárlos M.
Larco, Antonio M.
Larco, José Alberto.
Larrabure, Michel.
Larrañaga, Pedro F.
Larti.ue, Grat.
Lartirigoyen Hermanos, tanners.
Lasagnac, crockery.
Lauper, Alberto, confectioner.
Laura, Marius, groceries.
Lawezzan, Alejandro.
Le Bihan, Cárlos.
Lee, Masson Cárlos.
Leith, Samuel E.
Lembecke, Guillermo.
Leonard, Félix, mineral waters.
León, Lucas.
Lepiani, Melchor.
Lerch, Federico.

Merchants in general—Continued.

Loli, Pedro.
López, Goytozolo.
Loredo, German.
Loredo, José, cloth.
Loredo, José J.
Ludoweig, Julio.
Macdonald.
Mache, Enrique.
Machiavello, Agustin.
Madariaga, Alejandro de.
Maggiole é Hijos.
Maggiole, Simon.
Malatesta, Juan.
Malherbe, Juan B.
Malmborg, Nicolás, shoes.
Maravoto, Enrique.
Maravoto, Federico.
Marini, J. V.
Marquezado, Eugenio.
Marriott, Enrique.
Marsano, Nicolás.
Marscoff, Guillermo.
Martens, Adolfo.
Masias, Baquijano, printer.
Masias, Federico I., printer.
Masias, Francisco.
Masias, Juan, printer.
Mata, Domingo, liquors.
Mata y Galindo, José, druggist.
Matheus, Manuel A.
Matheos, Manuel L.
Mathison, J.
Matos, Nicanor.
Mazzoli, Benito.
Mejia y Morales, Hilario, druggist.
Mendez y Ca.
Mendiburu, Genaro.
Mendiola.
Mendoza, J. M.
Mercier, Edmundo.
Merel, José.
Merello, Agustin.
Merello, José.
Merlo, J.
Meyans, Santiago.
Meyer, Victor, beer.
Mezzano, José.
Michael, Mauricio.
Michel, Camilo.
Michieii, Pedro.
Mignolli, Juan.
Migoni, wines.
Milne and Co., rice and flour.
Minolli, José.
Mignolli, Juan.

LIMA—Continued.

Merchants in general—Continued.

Minuche, Faustino, drugs.
Mitchel, Carreras Juan.
Mojovich, Jorge.
Mola y Sanchez, Gregorio.
Molfino & Co., D., hardware, etc.
Molfino, F.
Molfino, Francisco C.
Mombello y Ca., Cárlos.
Monzante, Miguel.
Morales, José de los Santos.
Morelli, Lorenzo.
Moreno, Manuel J.
Moreno, Miguel S.
Morison, Alejandro.
Morla, Manuel.
Morla, Manuel S.
Moses y Ca.
Moulinié, F., wines and spirits.
Muelle, Juan.
Muhlig, Ricardo.
Mujica, Elias.
Musante, Eugenio.
Mustiga y Tassara.
Nagaro, Geraldo.
Naranjo, Elciario.
Neumann, Emilio.
Niemeyer, C. F., music store.
Noel, Diego, commercial agent.
Noriega, Gerardo, watches.
Noriega, Pedro.
Nosiglia, Adolfo.
Nosiglia Hermanos.
Nosiglia, Juan.
Novack, Pablo.
Odriozola, Enrique.
Olcese, Juan.
Oliveres, Manuel.
Ophelan, Fernando.
Orellana, Alonso.
Orellana, Pedro.
Orezzoli, Valerga y Ca.
Ortíz, José Félix.
Osorio, Pedro José.
Ostoja, Baltazar.
Ostoja Hermanos.
Otayza, Luis.
Otero, Eusebio.
Otero, Juan L.
Ottenheim, Mauricio.
Oviedo, Juan de Dios.
Oviedo, Vega Manuel.
Oyague, Arturo.
Oyague, José Lucas.
Paganini, Juan.

LIMA—Continued.

Merchants in general—Continued.

Pagano, Mateo.
Palacio, Samuel S.
Palerano & Rebozo.
Pallete, Pedro José.
Pardí, Juan.
Pardo, Eulogio.
Pardo, ó., Arco, shoes.
Pasaperes, Juan.
Pazos, Cárlos.
Pedemonte, Augusto.
Peirano, Tomás, wines.
Pellegrini, Modesto.
Pellerano, Gabriel.
Pellerano, Pilotto y Ca.
Peña, Caigas Francisco de la.
Peña y Coronel, Gregorio.
Peña y Costas, Juan Manuel.
Peña y Prado Hermanos.
Pendola, merchant.
Perez, Dámaso.
Perez, Gil.
Perez, Manuel, hardware.
Pernot, merchant.
Petersen, Teodoro.
Pezet, Mercaderes.
Pflucker & Hermanos, C. M.
Pflucker, Guillermo.
Piedra, Salvador.
Piedra, Víctor de la.
Piérola, Manuel A.
Pina, Domingo de la.
Pinna, Luis.
Plaza, Lascano Antonio.
Polis, A. H.
Ponte, Ribeiro Juan da.
Poppe, Santiago.
Porras, Domingo.
Porta, Federico.
Portaro, Vicente.
Pow Fon y Ca.
Pow Lung y Ca.
Prefumo, Lorenzo.
Prevost, Enrique S.
Price, Enrique.
Prince, Cárlos, printer.
Pruge, Cárlos.
Puccio & Co., Ernesto.
Puccio, José Ernesto.
Puente, Florencio.
Puente, José Fernandez.
Puig, Pedro.
Pujó y Clori.
Puyo, Enrique.
Quincot, Juan.

LIMA—Continued.

Merchants in general—Continued
Quiroga, Evaristo.
Quistorf, merchant.
Racatagliata, José.
Radavero, José.
Raffo, Domingo.
Raffo, Félix.
Rainoso, Mateo.
Ramirez, José del Carmen.
Rehder, Constantino.
Remy, Felix, drugs.
Remy, Juan Felix, drugs.
Révora, Francisco.
Rey, Luis.
Reyes y Montano, commission merchants.
Rezzo, Manuel.
Ribot & Comas, wines.
Rigan, Joaquin.
Rios, Ricardo R.
Risi, José.
Ritter, Enrique Adolfo.
Rivarola, Francisco.
Rivarola, Juan B.
Rivarola, Nicolás.
Rivas, Manuel.
Rivera, Luis G.
Rivera, Manuel F.
Robert, José A.
Rodriguez, Loyola Manuel.
Rodriguez, Manuel, drugs.
Rodriguez, Teodoro.
Roggero, Lorenzo, watches.
Roggero, Pedro F.
Roggero y Ca.
Roggero y Raffo, glass.
Rojas, Guillermo R.
Roldan y Ca., cigarettes.
Rollet, Alejandro, coach manufacturer.
Romero, Andrés Avelino.
Roselló, Pedro.
Rosenthal, Cárlos.
Rossel, C.
Rouillon, Leonardo N.
Rubini, M.
Rudini, Marsiglio, machinery.
Ruiz, Martin, drugs.
Rullier, Alfredo.
Rutte & Ritter.
Rutte, Rodolfo de.
Saco, Flores.
Saco, Gabriel.
Saget, Agustín.
Sanchez, Márcos Aurelio.
Sanchez y Gaffron.
San Cristoval, Evaristo.
Sanmartí, Primitivo.

LIMA—Continued.

Merchants in general—Continued.
Sañudo, Nestor.
Saravia, Enrique.
Sarria, Juan Francisco.
Sass, Cárlos.
Sass, Gulda y Ca.
Sassoni, Egidio.
Satler, merchant.
Scamarone, Amadeo, coal.
Schlæfli, watches.
Schattini, Diego.
Schofield, Thomas.
Schröder, Cristian M.
Schröder y Ca., importers.
Schwalb Hermanos, opticians.
Schwarz, Wilhelm.
Scotland, Santiago.
Seer, Lotario.
Sesarego, Manuel.
Signone y Velasquez, drugs.
Silva, Porfirio.
Solar, Enrique del.
Solar, Hermanos.
Soldevila, Juan.
Solf, Jorge Edmundo.
Soria, Fernando (hijo).
Sormani, Alexander, musical instruments.
Sotomayor, Federico.
Stàgno, Antonio S.
Stahl, W.
Stanshi, Luis.
Steiger, Francisco.
Stewart, David M.
Stokes, Juan S.
Strömsdörer, Juan.
Suero, Octavio.
Swayne, Enrique.
Swayne, Guillermo.
Taboada, Miguel R.
Talleri, Angel.
Talleri, Francisco.
Tasara, Luis.
Tealdo Hermanos.
Tealdo y Ca., N. B.
Tello, Manuel, drugs.
Terré, Juan.
Thol, E.
Thompson, Enrique.
Thorne, Teodoro E.
Tode, Roberto.
Toro, Federico de la Rosa.
Torres, Cárlos A.
Torres, Leonidas A.
Traverso, Santiago.
Trefogli y Talleri, wall paper, picture frames.
Truell Hermanos.

266 PERU.

LIMA—Continued.

Merchants in general—Continued.

Trujilo, E.
Ugarriza, Fernando E.
Uribe, Bartolomé.   .
Valdeavellano, Benito.
Velez, Ricardo A.
Venegas, Wenceslao.
Verneuil, Alfredo de.
Vidal, Tomás.
Vidaurrazaga, Vicenta.
Vieytes, Eduardo.
Vigors, Jorge.
Villanueva, Julio.
Villanueva, Manuel N.
Valdez, Eduardo.
Valega, Tomás.
Valle, Andrés G. del.
Valle, Tomás.
Vallebuona Hermanos.
Valle-Riestra, Alfredo.
Vallejos, José.
Vance, R.
Vasquez, Daniel.
Vasquez de Velazco, Daniel.
Veintimilla, José Ignacio.
Velaochaga, Emilio J.
Velarde, Alejandro.
Velarde, Federico.
Vochon and Co., Chinese store.
Wakeham, Federico M.
Welles, Martin B.
Wing Tong Hin y Ca.
Wing Wong Chong y Ca.
Zagal, Manuel T.
Zafiudo, Nestor.
Zapata, Manuel.
Zavala, Pedro José.
Zegarra, Hector Coronel.
Zevallos, Lizardo.
Zevallos Velasquez, Manuel, druga.

Merchants, importers.

Abrahamson & Co.
Abrahamson Hermanos.
Anselmo & Co.
Ayulo & Co., E.
Bar, Cárlos, clothing.
Bates, Stokes & Co.
Barton, R., manufacturer.
Bayle & Co., E. W.
Bonini, J. J.
Bower, Guillermo, pianos.
Bowes, Scott & Western, engineers.
Brandes, Guillermo, pianos.
Bresciano, Tomás.

LIMA—Continued.

Merchants, importers—Continued.

Bretoneche, Santiago, manufacturer of wagons.
Broggi Hermanos, fancy goods.
Bufet, J. A.
Caballero, Eduardo.
Canevaro ó Hijos.
Chapelier, B., draper.
Cherner, H. and R.
Chioino, J. J.
Clayssen, Luis.
Cluzon, B., tobacco.
Collamp Hermanos.
Collamp, F.
Davis Bros.
De Albertis & Co., F.
Dhores & Co., Pierre, hairdressers and perfumers.
Duncan, Fox & Co.
Eckstein, A.
Farina, Francisco.
Ferrando & Co.
Figarié Hijos., J.
Fourcade & Combe.
Frank, A. M., draper.
Gagliardo Hermanos.
Gaimer, J.
Gallese & Co.
Garcia, José del C.
Guttmann, Luis.
Hague & Castagnini, wholesale druggists.
Haines & Co.
Hardt, E. & W.
Hardt Hermanos.
Hardt, T.
Herourard, Pedro, hardware.
Heyneman, E.
Heynemann & Co.
Humphreys y Ca., hardware.
Hurtado, R. O.
Jauregui, Pedro.
Kitz, Heck & Co.
Klinge & Co.
Knauer & Co.
Lafon Hermanos.
Lanezzari, Kenger & Co.
Ledenty y Ca., Viuda de.
Loredo, German.
Loredo, José J.
Ludowieg.
Ludwig, Grim & Co,
Menchaca & Co., G., hardware.
Mathison, Beausire y Ca.
Milne y Ca.
Molfino & Co., D., hardware.
More, Pedro.

LIMA—Continued.

Merchants, importers—Continued.

Moses & Co.
Normand, Julio.
Newton, J., bookseller.
Ott & Co., Ph.
Otero, Eusebio.
Ottenheim Hermanos.
Palma, Nuñez.
Perret, Julio.
Peschiera, Ferrari & Cosso.
Pie & Depleage.
Pié, Pablo.
Plenge, Cárlos.
Polis & Co.
Raoul, Nicoli.
Rehder, Constantino.
Remy, J. F., wholesale druggist.
Rivari, Luis.
Romero, Calixto.
Ruté, Ritter y Ca.
Sass, Gulda & Co.
Scotto & Co.
Schmidt Hermanos.
Schmitt, J. H.
Schroder, S. A.
Stahl, Eugenio.
Stahl, W.
Sueyras & Co., Augustin, tobacco.
Thol, Enrique.
Trefogli & Talleri.
Weir & Co., grocers.
Weiss & Co., Cárlos.
Welch & Co., jewelers.
Wing, On Chong & Co.
Wo Chong & Co.
Zender, Simon.

Sugar planters.

Aspilaga Bros.
Beltram, Pedro.
Bryce Bros., Luis.
Canevaro & Sons, José.
Dreyfus, Augusto,
Ferreyros, Guillermo.
Figari Bros.
Gutierrez, Vicente.
Derteano Herederos de Dionisio.
Larco Bros.
Larco & Co., Viuda de.
Montero, Juan Manuel.
Pardo, Mariano B. de.
Pfucker & Madalengottia.
Rodriguez, Nicolas.
Sociedad Agricola Casa Grande, Limitida.

LIMA—Continued.

Sugar Planters—Continued.

Swayne, H.
Tenaud, Julio.
Valdeavellano, Benito.
Valle, Tomás.

Wood merchants.

Averdieck, Federico.
Chiulizza, Lorenzo.
Deposito de Maderas.
Ginochio, Enrique.
Haines y Ca., E.
Paul, Julio.
Razuri, Antonio.

MOLLENDO.

Merchants.

Braillard Bros.
Calderon & Gutierrez.
Carzola Hermanos.
Danelsberg, Schubering & Co.
Golding, J.
Jefferson & Trochan.
Meier, Enrique.
Rada & Co.
Ramos & Co.
Reiniche & Co., Robert.
Robilliard, J. F.
Stafford & Co.
Visscher & Co., Alejandro.

MOQUEGUA.

Merchant.

Minuto, Agustin.

NASKA.

Merchant.

Divizia, Francisco.

PACASMAYO.

Merchant.

Montenegro y Ca., J.

PALPA.

Merchant.

Divizia, Francisco.

PATIVILCA.

Merchant.

Rosas, C.

PAITA.

Merchants, import, export and commission.
Artadi & Co.
Blacker & Co.
Cabredo Hermanos.
Canepa Hermanos.
Duncan, Fox & Co.
France, J. E.
Garcia, M.
Gerbrich, Walter.
Giudino, Romolo L.
Hilbe & Co.
Hilbeck & Co., F.
Hopkins, John F., jr.
Leon, Dario.
Lopez, F. P. & Co.
Machuca y Vega Fred.
Pallete, Baltazar.
Perez & Co.
Raygada & Co.
Talman, N.
Tweddle, H. J.

PIMENTAL.

Merchant.
Dall' Orso y Descalze.
Tallaque, Ric.

PISCO.

Merchant.
Divizia, Francisco.

PIURIA.

Bankers.
Branch of the Bank of Callao.
Merchants.
Blacker & Co., importers dry goods.
Bregante, Lazaro, groceries.
Campos, Genaro, dry goods.
Canals, Jaime, dry goods.
Candara, Francisco, dry goods.
Chiriboga, José Maria, exporter goatskins.
Clark, Emilio, importer.
Duncan, Fox & Co., importers and exporters
Galvez-Matta Hermogenes, dry goods.
Guzman, Luis, dry goods.
Helguero, Francisco E., groceries.
Hilbek & Co., importers.
Leigh, H. H., importer.
Mendoza, Ricardo, importer.
Mujica, José Antonio S., dry goods.
Mova, Eugenio, groceries.
Mova, Serapio, dry goods.
Navarro, Baltazar, dry goods.
Palacios, Miguel, groceries.
Pales, Jacinto, groceries.
Perroni y Vallebuona, groceries.

PIURIA—Continued.

Merchants—Continued.
Perez, Manuel, drugs.
Plata, Clodoveo, candle manufacturer.
Puente, José M., dry goods.
Rodriguez, Nicanor, dry goods.
Raidias, Ramon, dry goods.
Schaefer, Cálos, importer.
Serra, Manuel J., drugs.
Vegas y Hijos, Fernando, dry goods.
Zapata Hnos., dry goods.

SALAVERRY.

Merchants.
Gottfried y Hermanos, E.
Orrezole, S. S.

SAN JOSE LAMBAYEQUE.

Leather dressers.
Moya, Julian.
Pichini, Juan.
Vasenies, José.
Merchants.
Branchi, César.
Casanova, Manuel.
Curriel, Felix G.
Chong, Sing Long.
Dallorso, Virgilio.
Dallorso & Descalzi.
Hilk & Co., F.
Klin, G.
Muga, José Maria.
Otero, Eliodoro.
Quiñones, Juan.
Romero, F.
Rondan & Russo.
Tassara, Juan.
Torres & Castro.
Valle, Pablo.
Wigon, Tay & Co.
Rice mills.
Dallorso, Virgilio.
Lopoint, Alfredo.
Sugar growers.
Aspillaga Herm.
Carbulú, Carmen V. de.
Gonzales, Abalardo.
Gutierrez, Vicente.
Navarrete & Ramon, Pedro.
Pardo, Felipe.
Polo, Hermanos.
Rodriguez, Manuel.
Romero, José F.
Salazar, Sebastian.

SULLANA.

Merchants.
Arens, José, importer and exporter.
Arroyo, Miguel, importer and exporter.
Barreto, Roberto, commission.
Cruz, Buenaventura, dry goods.
Figallo, José, distiller.
Garcia, Hnos., dry goods and groceries.
Merino, José E., drugs.
Pempel, Federico E, commission.
Zavallos, Vicente, dry goods.

TAMBO.

Merchants.
Sanguinetti Hermanos.

TARMA.

Merchant.
Valle, Angel.

TERRENAFE.

Merchants and exporters.
Castillo, Hermanos.
Castre y Eggart.

TERRENAFE—Continued.

Merchants and exporters—Continued.
Leon y Noya.
Muro, Fresco.
Torres, Agustin.

TRUJILLO.

Merchants.
Gottfried, E., y Hermanos.
Ludoweig & Co.
Vasquez, Julio & Federico.

Sugar planters.
Barua, Fortunato.
Chopitea, José Ignacio.
Garcia & Garcia.

TUMBEZ

Merchant.
Baldine, William.
Gervaise, Cereace.
Lawler, Tomas.
Piaggie, F. G.
Silva, Antonio.
Zaput, Mateo.

Republic of Salvador.

ACAJUTLA.

Importers.
Compañía de Agencias.
Mitchel, W. J.

Merchants.
Compañía General del Pacifico.
Blanco & Trigueros.
Carazo & Ramirez.
Dorantes & Ojeda.
Compañía del Muelle, Drevon & Co.
Gomar, Joaquin.
Melendez, Manuel.
Mejia, Encarnación.
Peralta, José Maria.
Parraza & Prado.
Ruano, Emeterio.
Valle & Co., Andrés.

AHUACHAPÁN.

Boots and shoes.
Gonzalez, Margarito.
Garrido, Isidro.

Druggists.
Carballo, Valentín.
Magaña, Simeón.

Grocers.
Alfaro, Margarito.
Chavez y hno., Claudia.
Durán, Luisa G. de.
Flores, Andrea.
Guerra, Dionisio.
Guerra, Virginia.
Linares, J.
Melgar, Eulalia.
Mendoza, Rafaela.
Romero, Mercedes.

Hatters.
Garcia, Estanislao.
Velarde, Federico.

Retail general merchants.
Arriaze, Dolores.
Cadenas, Eusebio.

AHUACHAPÁN—Continued.

Retail general merchants—Continued.
Contreras, Romualdo.
Gómez, Juana.
Guerra, Maria.
Herrera, Nicanor.
Herrera, Isabel.
Llanos, Mariana M. de.
Mena, Leonor M. de.
Moscoso, Luisa.
Rivas, Mercedes.
Vasquez, Aparicio.

Silversmiths.
Canjura, J.
Duarte, Onofre.

Wholesale import and export merchants.
Durán, Onofre.
Morán, Fabio & Co.
Müller, Federico.
Samayoa, Ana.
Valdivieso, Samuel.

ANAMORÓS.

Merchant.
Zepeda, Felipe.

ARMENIA.

Grocer.
Romillo, José.

Retail general merchants.
Garcia, David.
Molina, Arcadia.
Torres, Juan.

Wholesale import and export merchant.
Mayer, Zeferino.

CHALATENANGO.

Boots and shoes.
Cortés, Claro.
Torres, Lorenzo.

SALVADOR.

CHALATENANGO—Continued.

Druggists.
García, José J.
Morales, José María.
Peña, Miguel.
Tobías, Ismael.

Grocer.
Ortíz, Balbina.

Silversmiths.
Barrerra, Modesto.
Obando, Esteban.

Wholesale import and export merchant.
Alvergue, Fernando.

CHALCHUAPA.

Boots and shoes.
López, Manuel.
Novoa, Albino.
Pineda, José P.

Photographer.
Baxter, Enrique.

Retail general merchants.
Ahuja hnos.
Goetzchull, Solomón.
Hidalgo, Cruz.
Lizarralde, Eduardo de.
Martino. José María.
Peñate, Eleodoro.
Trajo, Francisco.

COATEPEQUE.

Boots and shoes.
Cienfuegos, Petronilo.

Grocers.
Arbizú, Pilar.
Cardona, Mercedes.
Cardona, Paula.
Castrillo, Eleodoro.
Cienfuegos, Adelaida.
Delgado, Sofía.
Menéndez, Socoro.
Ruano, Anastacio.

Retail general merchant.
Barrientos, Balbino.

COJUTEPEQUE.

Banker.
Díaz, Narciso.

Druggists.
Castellanos, Crescencio.
Escobar, Camilo.
Palma, Apolonio.
Revelo, Joaquín.

Grocers.
Amaya, Maximo.
Cáceres, Adela.

COJUTEPEQUE—Continued.

Grocers—Continued.
Díaz, Josefa.
Díaz, Sara.
Figueroa, Josefa Antonia.
Inglés, Mercedes.
Mineros, Lugarda.
Muñoz, Josefa

Hatters.
Anzueta, Anton.
Hernández, Salvador.
Martínez, Esteban.
Pleités, Esteban.

Silversmiths.
Maltéz, José María.
Obando, Carlos.

Watchmaker and jeweler.
Castellanos, Alberto.

Wholesale import and export merchants.
Amaya, Miximo.
Bazán, Albino.
Bustamante, Guadalupe.
Contreras, Juan.
Díaz, Narciso.
Nuila, Ventura.
Vila & Sigüenza.

COMASAGUA (La Libertad).

Manufacturer of coffee machinery.
Körner, Felipe.

DOLORES (Cabañas).

Boots and shoes.
Colocho, Pedro.

GOTERA.

Druggist.
Rovelo, Norberto.

Grocers.
Cruz, Amelia.
Gómez, Esteban.
Mendoza, Lazaro.
Molina, Anita.
Rosa, Francisco.
Rosa, Paz.
Romera, Leandra.

GUAYABAL.

Wholesale import and export merchant.
Panameño, Eusebio.

ILOBASCO.

Boots and shoes.
Rodas, Juan.

ILOBASCO—Continued.

Grocers.
Castellanos, Ramón.
Elena, Simeón H.
Portillo, Dolores.

Retail general merchants.
Barbón, José G.
Choto, Rafael.
Córdova, Francisco.
González, Margarito.
López, Manuel.
Orellana, Encarnación.
Peña, José María.
Romero, Ana I.

Silversmith.
Alvarenga, Daniel.

Wholesale import and export merchant.
Rosas, Leandro.

IZALCO.

Boots and shoes.
Herrera, Víctor.

Druggist.
Liévano, José María.

Grocers.
Alvarez, Rosa.
Menéndez, Lauriano.
Ramos, Juana.

Retail general merchants.
Barrientos y hermano, Tránsito.
Craik, Mercedes de.
Ramos y hermano, Josefa.
Vega, Joaquina.

Wholesale import and export merchant.
Velásquez, Felipe.

JAYAQUÉ.

Manufacturer of coffee machinery.
Meléndez, Manuela.

JACUAPA.

Banker.
Durán, Macedonio.

Boots and shoes.
Castillo, Manuel.
Cruz, Manuel.
Cruz, Guillermo.
Monica, Teodosio.
Rosales, Pedro.

Commission merchants.
Durán, Macedonio.
Escobar, Tiberio.

Druggist.
Burgos, Rafael.

S. Ex. 8, pt. 11——18

JACUAPA—Continued.

Grocers.
Castillo, Margarita de.
Castillo, Ramona.
Jurado, Angela.
Sandoval, Nicolasa.

Retail general merchants.
Arawjo, María.
Bautista, María de.
Castro, José María.
Galvez, Inés.
Gutierrez, Josefa.
Gutierrez, Carlos.
Gutierrez, Manuel.
Mora, Miguel.
Montoya, Mercedes.
Rosales, Damiana.

Silversmith.
Orantes, Máximo.

LA LIBERTAD.

Commission merchant.
Blanco, Trigueros.

Druggists.
Marcenaro, Nicolás.
Velis, Felipe J. de.

Grocers.
Calderón, C.
Guzmán, Eloisa G. de.
Prieto, Gertrudio.

Hatter.
Torres, Gregorio.

Wholesale import and export merchants.
Courtade, Emilio.
Flamenco, María.
Marcenaro, Nicolás.
Huezo, Vicente.
Vargas hnos., Diego.

LA UNIÓN.

Boots and shoes.
Palada, E. Gutierrez.
Ramirez, Benito.

Commission merchant.
Marcenaro & Co., Juan Bautista.

Grocers.
Andino, Leonarda P. de.
Courtade, Carmen P. de.
Huezo, Santos P. de.
Huezo, Mercedes.
López, Salvador.
Perry, Elena.
Rosales, J. G. de.
Zaldivar, Hortensia P. de.

LA UNIÓN—Continued.

Manufacturers of tortoise-shell goods.
Amaya, Ignacio.
Echeverría, Abel.
López, Dolores.
Sanchez, Federico.

Retail general merchants.
Huezo, Gregorio.
Padilla, Isabel V. de.
Salazar, Manuela.
Sosa, Rosa V. de.

Silversmith.
García, Salvador.

Wholesale import and export merchants.
Marcenars & Co., J. B.
Padilla, Remigio.
Rodríguez, Pablo.
Vicente y Ca.
Vila, Francisco.

METAPAN.

Grocers.
Aguilar, J.
Castro, Domingo.
Duarte, Paulina de.
Hernández, Bibiano.
Leiva, José.
Lemus, Manuel.
Montoya, Felipe.
Ruiz, Juan.

Retail general merchants.
Quintana, Rafael.

Wholesale import and export merchants.
Lima hermanos.
Sosa, Bonifacio.

NEJAPA.

Manufacturer of coffee machinery.
Andrade, Manuel.

OLOCUILTA.

Wholesale import and export merchant.
González, Octavio.

QUEZALTEPEQUE.

Grocers.
Borjas, Estebana.
Castro, Benigna de.
Cáceres, Santos C. de.

Hatter.
Urrutia, Salvador.

Manufacturer.
Cortéz y hno., Cornelio.

S. JULIÁN (Sonsonate).

Merchant.
Romero, Víctor.

SAN ANDRÉS.

Wholesale import and export merchant.
Muñoz, Eduardo.

SAN MIGUEL.

Banker.
Padilla, Remigio.

Boots and shoes.
Arias, Juan.
Bustillos, José María.
Colindres, Vicente.
Lara, Juan.
Mayorga, Guillermo.
Morales, David.

Druggists.
Cano, J.
Celarié, José María.
Holtmeyer hnos.
Hegg, Manuel.
Meardi, Mauricio.
Muñoz, Brígido.
Rosales, Enrique R.

Grocers.
Aguirre, Felipa.
Araya, Ana Josefa.
Avila, Anita B. de.
Balmaceda, Miguel.
Barreyro, Isabel de.
Bado, Mauricia de.
Cabrera, Señorita.
Fernández, Adela.
Flores, Agustín.
Guzmán, Virginia.
Herrera, Pastor.
Hernández, Dolores B. de.
Hernández, Máximo.
Mena, Simón.
Medina, Apolonio.
Molina, Victoria.
Morales, David.
Peraza, Josefa.
Reyes, Beatriz.
Rosales, Mercedes P. de.
Suay, Cipriano.
Suárez, Francisco.
Valenzuela, Ercilia F. de.

Hatters.
Abendano, Ramón.
Aguado, José María.
Carías, Baltazar.

SAN MIGUEL—Continued.

Hatters—Continued.
López, Gregorio.
Reyes, Esteban.

Photographers.
Guerrero, Vicente.
Mena, Ramon.
Sol, Eloy.

Printers.
Arias, Timoteo.
Herrera, Pedro P. y Rito.
Imprenta del Instituto de Occidente.

Retail general merchants.
Alvarez, Francisco B.
Avila, Carmen.
Cuadra, Carmen R. de.
Díaz, Antonio.
Dinarte, Simeón J. de.
Gómez, Dolores.
Hernández, Carlos.
Lastra, Ramón.
Meardi, Mauricio.
Rosales, Enrique R.
Schönenberg, Juan.
Viñerta, Josefa G. de.
Zelaya, León.

Silversmiths.
Anduray, Aureliano.
Ávila, Daniel.
Osorio, Modesto.
Rosales, Manuel.
Salmerón, Gregorio.
Salmerón, Agustin.
Tebes, Tomás.
Vargas, Leonidas.

Special manufacturers.
Gómez, César, tortoise-shell goods.
Paz, Martin, tortoise-shell goods.
Paz, Santos, tortoise-shell goods.
Huezo, Ireneo M. de, tortoise-shell goods.
Rosales & Alvares, mineral waters.

Wholesale import and export merchants.
Alvarez, Francisco V.
Argüello, José.
Argüello, Ramón.
Argüello, Marcelino.
Briqueto y Charlaix.
Canessa, Antonio & Co.
Canessa, Cayetano.
Canessa y Ca., Ambrosio.
Calvo, Manuel.
Dardano, Pedro.
Demutti, Antonio.
Días, Antonio.
Fernández, Antonio J.
Haltmeyer, Emilio.

SAN MIGUEL—Continued.

Wholesale import and export merchants—Cont'd.
Hungentobler & Haltmeyer.
Mazzini, Miguel.
Mirino & Manent.
Mendoza, Anselmo.
Mendoza, Jacinto.
Miardi & De Mutti.
Muñoz & Co., B.
Muñoz, Brigido.
Padilla, Remigio.
Palacios & Co., Francisco.
Pöhll, Alfonso.
Prieto, Carlos G.
Quiros hermanos.
Rivera, Ruano.
Romero, Carmen.
Schönenberg, Juan.
Snay, Cipriano.
Vila & Vila.

SAN SALVADOR.

Banks and bankers.
Banco Internacional.
Banco Occidental.
Banco Particular.
Blanco & Trigueros.
Blanco y Lozano.
Duke é hijo, J. M.
Lagos, Miguel.
Lagos, Pilar.
Rosales, José.

Booksellers and stationers.
Cousin, Anselmo.
Anguelo, M.
Goubaud, Emilio.
Herrera & Co., Manuel.
Mathias hnos.
Pozo & Gutierrez.
Prado & Co., Federico.
Rivera, Desiderio.

Boots and shoes.
Aguilar y Serrano.
Cirino, Morales.
Sagrera y Ca., José.
Preto hnos. y Ca.

Druggists.
Aranjo & Co.
Aranjo & Bustamente.
Avalos, F. Pablo.
Cáceres & Vaquero.
Liévano, Juan.
Luna, David.
Niebecker, Otto von.
Palomo & Co., M.
Rivera, Carlos.
Rivera hermanos.

SAN SALVADOR—Continued.

Grocers.
Aguilar, Josefa.
Alfaro, Diego.
Arévalo, Anastacia.
Castellanos, Dolores.
Cisneros, Manuela.
Monterroso. Regina.
Palacios, Magdalena.
Palacios, Asunción.
Peña, Emilia.
Quijano, Jacinta.
Quiteño, Mercedes.
Ramos, Anita.
Reales, Ramona.
Serrano, Bernabé.
Valencia, Francisca.
Vega, Leocadia.

Hardware, cutlery, and tools.
Anguilar, Francisco.
Ralette, Sullo.
Aubuisson y Ca., D.
Dorantes y Ojeda.

Hatters.
Avila, Clemente.
Blanco, Miguel.
Bonilla, Luis.
Moreno, Rafael.
Molina, Domingo.
Murillo, Elias.
Ruiz & Co., J. M.
Ruiz, Luis A.

Lithographer.
Guevara, Teódulo.

Photographers.
Imery hermanos.
Somelian, Agustin.

Planters, general.
Aguilar, Manuel.
Alvarez, Emilio.
Boguen, Francisco.
Borgia, Bustamente.
Cellier, A.
Dárdano, Felix.
Dorantes y Ojeda.
Lozano, Cruz.
Ruano, Emetrio S.
Ulloa, Cruz.
Zaldivar, Rafael.

Printing offices.
Grande, Pedro.
Imprenta del Comercio.
Imprenta de la Juventad.
Imprenta Nacional.
Mirón, Francisco y Alejandro.
Vaquero, Francisco.

SAN SALVADOR—Continued.

Silversmiths.
Camacho, Leoncio.
Campos, Marcelino.
Campos, Gregorio.
Campos, Crescencio.
Cruz, Nicolás.
Flamenco, Joaquin.
Garcia, Vicente.
Platero, Fernando.
Rivas, Anastacio D.
Sanchez, Carmen.
Solórzano, Justo.
Villarán, Manuel.
Zamora, Rafael.

Special manufacturers.
Ellis, Benito, phosphorus.
Góngora & Co., Manuel, phosphorus.
Kreitz, Teodora, coffee machinery.

Special merchants.
Arrazola, Concepción, woods.
Carrera, Pablo, woods.
Cousin, Anselmo, church ornaments.
Cuon, Vallon, silks.
De León, Venancio, woods.
Gómez, Cecilio, woods.
Solis, Francisco, woods.
Tonfo-Chón, silks.
Tan-Hinlon, silks.

Watchmakers and jewelers.
Casati, Carlos B.
Dreyfus & Cohen.
Escamilla. Manuel.
Escamilla, Rómulo.
Glasser & Co., Marcus.
Imeri, Narciso.

Wholesale import and export merchants.
Aguilar, J. F.
Alvarez, Emilio.
Ambrogi, Constantino.
Arrazola, M.
Balette & Goens.
Blanco y Trigueros.
Blanco & Lozano.
Bloom, Baruch & Co.
Bouineau, A.
Bousquet, Pablo.
Bustamante y hermano, Mariano.
Castro, Emigdio.
Cohen & Dreyfus.
Courtade, Emilio.
Cousin, Anselmo.
Cronmeyer, A.
D'Aubuisson, G.
D'Aubuisson, Carlos.
Durtour, Jorge.

SAN SALVADOR—Continued.

Wholesale import and export merchants—Cont'd.
Dominguez y hermano, D.
Dorantes & Ojeda.
Duke & Son, J. Mauricio.
Ellis hijo & Co.
Glaser, C. & M.
Gouband, E.
González, José Antonio.
Gonzáles y Ca., J. O.
Haas & Co., B.
Hoephl, O.
Lagos & hermanos.
Levy, G.
Madrid & Co., B.
Manning, Moffatt & Co.
Mata, Juan.
Mejia, Escobar & Co.
Melendez, Carlos.
Melendez y Perez.
Mena, Eduardo.
Mendoza, Dionisio.
Merlos, Dionisio.
Moffatt & Blair.
Moffat; John.
Niebecker, A.
Paloma & Co., M.
Pawski, L. W.
Perez, Párraga & Co.
Prado & Co., F.
Peralta, Antonio.
Perez, Alonzo.
Prieto hermanos.
Revelo, A. J.
Rivera hermanos.
Rivas & Soler.
Ruiz & Co., J. Manuel.
Sagrera hermanos.
Salinas, Alberto.
Salazar, Emeterio.
Selva, Julian.
Serrano, Pedro.
Schönenberg, Roberto.
Soundy, A. I.
Tunstall, Thomas T.
Ungo, M.
Yúdice & Co
Zaldivar, R.
Zaldivar, Mariano.

'SAN VINCENT.

Boots and shoes.
Barrera, José Maria.
Guerrero, Matias.
López, J. Manuel.
Druggists.
Amaya, Nicolás.

SAN VINCENT—Continued.

Druggists—Continued.
Gálvez, Vicente.
Miranda, Luis.
Retail general merchants.
Lagos, Mannela.
Mejia, Leona.
Mineros, Sebastián.
Ramirez, Vicente.
Revelo, Abelina.
Samayoa, Vicente.
Valencia, Ignacia.
Silversmiths.
Pinel, Rodrigo.
Pino, José.
Saragoza, Antonio.
Salinas, Ciriaco.
Sosa, Manuel.
Watchmaker and jeweler.
Miranda, Guadalupe.
Wholesale import and export merchants.
Angulo, Nicolás.
Carranza, Camilo.
Figueroa, Josefa.
Gálvez, Vicente.
Miranda, Octavio.

SANTA ANA.

Banker.
Alvarez, Francisco.
Boots and shoes.
Aguirre, José.
Calderón, Esteban.
Erazo, Simón.
Francisco, Antonio.
Rivas, Carlos.
Rosales, Salvador.
Sanabria, Ramón.
Taboada, José.
Commission merchant.
Alstchul, Emilio.
Druggists.
Carballo, Miguel.
Guillén, Francisco.
Haecker, Francisco E.
Interiano, Julio.
Lara, Manuel L.
Rodriguez, Anastacio.
Trabanino, Tadeo.
Vides, José Maria.
Engravers.
Aguilar, Lario.
Alfaro, Rosalio.
Lecree, Andrés.
Roca, Antonio B.

SANTA ANA—Continued.

Hatters.
Durán, Asunción.
Morales, Máximo.
Torre, Juan V. de la.

Photographers.
Guerrero, Salvador.
Recinos, Abel.
Shevlin, Santiago.

Printing office.
Martónez, Alberto.

Watchmaker and jeweler.
Guerrero, Salvador.

Wholesale import and export merchants.
Aepli & Gross.
Agacio, A. B.
Agacio, Antonio.
Altschul, Emilio.
Alvarez de Viscara, María.
Alvarez hermanos.
Argeta, V.
Augsburg, A. W.
Belismelis, E.
Berkfeld & Rhode.
Bloom, Baruch & Co.
Carazo y Ramirez.
Casanova, Eduardo.
Casin, M.
Cichero, Sebastián.
Cienfuegos, Elias.
Cohen & Dreyfus.
Dellipiane & Daglio.
Díaz, Santiago.
Escobar, José.
Garma, L.
Goldtree, Liebes & Co.
Haas & Co., B.
Liberti & Co., Angel.
Maten, P.
Mathies & Co., C. G.
Matheu, P.
Matheu hermanos.
Martinez & Co., José María.
Martinez, Macario.
Mena, E.
Méndez, Alberto.
Montalvo, Manuel.
Párraga, Manuel A.
Pena y Ca., Francisco.
Rodriguez, Brigido.
Rodriguez, Isidoro.
Rodriguez, J. & S.
Sichero, S.
Subia, Daniel.
Valle, Andrés.
Valle, José.

SANTA ELENA (Usulután).

Engraver.
Munguia, Saturnino.

SANTA TECLA.

Boots and shoes.
Barahona, Tomás.
Coto, Mariano.
Méndez, Leoncio.
Merino, Francisco.

Druggists.
Nuñez, J. F.
Sol, Manuel.
Tijerino, Nicolás.

Engraver.
Hernández, Daniel.

Founder.
Luner, Valeria.

Grocers.
López, Bernardino.
Meléndez, Adela de.
Olivares, Ignacia de.
Olivares, Dolores.
Ulloa, Adela de.
Villalta y hno., S.

Retail general merchants.
Ambrosio, Evaristo.
Angulo, Roman.
Arrieta, Reyes.
García, Asunsión.
Molina, Ismael G.
Molina, José G.
Rugama, Elias.

Silversmiths.
Burgos, Miguel.
González, Andrés.

Special manufacturers.
Alcaine, Matias, machinery.
Fernández, José María, machinery.
Flamenco, Rufino, rubber stamps.
Mason, James, machinery.
Orellana, Pablo, machinery.
Ulloa, Cruz, machinery.

Wholesale import and export merchants.
González, José.
Lemus & Sanchez.
Mason, Phillips & Co.
Meléndez, Manuel.
Orozco, Benito.
Rivas, Tomás.
Soto, Enrique.

SANTIAGO DE MARÍA (Usulután).

Merchant.
Flores, J.

SENSUNTEPEQUE.

Boots and shoes.
Ayala, Patricio.
Blanco, Cipriano.
Cruz, Marcos.
Fuentes, Carlos.
Henriquez, Pedro.
Lara, Fernando.
Lacayo, Samuel.
Navarrete,.Máximo.
Rivas, Hermógenes.
Romero, Jacinto.
Druggists.
Dawson, José.
Hernández, Joaquín.
Novoa, Serafín.
Velasco, Dionisio.
Engraver.
Peralta, David.
Grocers.
Amaya, Gregorio.
Ayala, J.
Ayala, Margarita.
Echeverría, Pio.
Echeverría, José María.
Ircheta, Victor.
López, Nicolasa.
Méndez, Miguel.
Novoa, Adolfo.
Parra, Gertrudis.
Parra Moreno, José D.
Pérez, Damián.
Rodriguez, Serafio.
Hatters.
Albayero, Agapito.
Fernández, Bernardo.
Sanchez, Eustaquio.
Photographers.
Letona hermanos.
Retail general merchants.
Bonilla, Martina.
Castro, Pascual.
Hernández, Ester.
Hernández, Céfora.
Lacayo, Justo.
Lacayo, Rosa.
Mayorga, Dolores.
Parra, Gertrudis.
Silversmith.
Hernández, Daniel.
Wholesale import and export merchant.
Hernández, Joaquín.

SONSONATE.

Boots and shoes.
Alpinez, Eusebio.
Beltrán, Manuel.
Choto, Daniel.
Montes, Marcelino.
Druggists.
García, Francisco A.
Llevano, Ciriaco.
Rivera, Abraham.
Engravers.
Castaneda, Mariano.
Castaneda, José María.
Grocers.
Calderón, María.
Cea, Carlos.
Cea, Petrona.
Printing office.
Velásquez, José María.
Retail general merchants.
Calderón, María.
Mencía, Victoriano.
Rodríguez, Jacoba.
Vega, Ambrosio de la.
Wholesale import and export merchants.
Agacio, Antonio B.
Ahuja & hermanos.
Casin, M.
Cea, Francisco Orantes.
Claude, A.
Dardano, Guillermo.
Demorro, Rafael.
Montis, Rafael.
Ramagoza é hijo.
Ruiz & Co., J. & M.
Rivero hermanos.
Rodriguez, Isidoro.
Sosa, Martin F.
Soria, Juan.
Spies & Müller.
Vega, Ambrosio de la.
Vilanova, V.

SUCHITOTO.

Boots and shoes.
Bonillo, Bartolo.
Durán, León.
Padilla, Rafael.
Umaña, Ramón.
Druggist.
Martel, José María Peña.

SUCHITOTO—Continued.

Grocers.
Aguirre, Dolores P. de.
Martel, Gerónima A. de.
Peña, Juana M. de.

Hatters.
Peña, Ignacio.
Rivera, Ruperto.

Photographer.
Solórzano, Guillermo.

Retail general merchants.
Aranjo, Gerardo.
Arrazola, Mercedes V. de.
Prieto, Carlos.
Vaquero, Nicolás.

Silversmith.
Ramos, Nemesio.

Wholesale import and export merchants.
Aguilar, Francisco.
Vaquero, Nicolás.

TECOPA.

General merchant.
Bautista, Clara.

TEOTEPEQUE.

General merchant.
Cienfuegos, Ceferino.

Wholesale import and export merchants.
Corleto, José Antonio.

TONACOTEPEQUE.

Boots and shoes.
Mármol, Dolores.

Druggist.
Bennett, Francisco.

Grain merchant.
Cortéz, Joaquín.

Grocers.
Calderón, Santos.
Estrada, Refugio de.

Manufacturers of drums.
González e hijos, Manuel

USULUTÁN.

Boots and shoes.
Avalos, Alejandro.
Sanches, Pío.

Druggist.
Gómez, Felipe.

Retail general merchants.
Angulo, Rita de.
Aparicio, Josefa.
Chavez, J. de.
Civallero, Luis.
Coto, Ramona.
Flores y hermanos, Anita.
Ochoa & Co., Rosa.
Penado, Guadalupe.
Rosales, Marcelina de.

Silversmith.
Funes, Venancio.

Wholesale import and export merchant
Munguía, Ricardo.

ZACATECOLUCA.

Boots and shoes.
Zaldaña, Rodolfo.

Druggists.
Carrillo, Manuel.
Carrillo, Rafael.
Rodriguez, J.
Rodriguez, Adrian.

Retail general merchants.
Molino, Francisco.
Molino, Mariana A.
Rodriguez, J.
Rodriguez, Adrian.
Villacorta, Serafina.

Silversmiths.
Mena, Gerófilmo.
Villagrán, Mariano.

ZARAGOZA.

Wholesale import and export merchant
Péres, Alonzo.

Santo Domingo.

AZUA.

Importers and exporters.
Echenique & Co., T. B.
Freites, Andres.
Freites, Prospero.
Garcia & Co., H.
Gomez, Pascual.
Iturla & Co., T. B.
Oca, Francisco Montede.
Ortez, Daniel.
Vicini, T. B.

MONTE CRISTI.

General import and export merchants.
Bauduy, Enrique.
Espin, Antonio.
Jimenes & Co., J. G.

PUERTO PLATA.

Agricultural implements.
Heinsen & Co.

Ale and beer.
Batlle. Cosme.
Chiodi & Co., G.
Cocco, Manuel.
Ginebra y Ca., José.
Klüsener & Co., C.
Loinaz, Diego.

Banks.
Banco Nacional de Santo Domingo.
El Banco de la Compañía de Crédito.

Bookseller and stationer.
Castellano. Manuel.

Boots and shoes.
Amabile, M. G.
Chiodi & Co., G.
Ginebra y Ca., José.
Puyans, B. R.
Simpson, C.
Vives & Caballero.

Dentists.
Barranco, Virgilio.
Jones, G. W.

PUERTO PLATA—Continued,

Druggists.
Botica del Mercado.
Botica San José.
Fraser, C. A.
Levy, T. G.

Dry goods.
Amabile, M. G.
Barrera Hermanos.
Batlle, Cosme.
Chiodi & Co., G.
Ginebra y Ca., José.
Klüsener & Co., C.
Puyans, B. R.
· Vives & Caballero.

General merchants.
Batlle, Cosme.
Chiodi & Co.. G.
Cocco, Manuel.
Ginebra y Ca., José.
Klüsener & Co., C.

Groceries and provisions.
Amabile, M. G.
Barrero, Antonio.
Batlle, Cosme.
Canto, J. M. del.
Chiodi & Co., G.
Colson, J. H.
Cocco, Manuel.
Ginebra y Ca., José.
Klüsener & Co., C.
Loinaz, Diego.
Mir, Felipe.
Piola & Co., E.
Piola & Co., M.
Puyans, B. R.
Vives & Caballero.

Hardware and tools.
Chiodi & Co., G.
Ginebra y Ca., José.
Heinsen & Co.
Vives & Caballero.

PUERTO PLATA—Continued.

Importers, exporters, and commission merchants.
Amabile, M. G., provisions and dry goods.
Arzeno, José.
Barrera, A., provisions and dry goods.
Batlle, Cosme, general.
Botica San José, drugs.
Chemin de Fer Central Dominicalu, railroad building.
Chiodi & Co., G., provisions, dry goods, hardware, and lumber.
Fraser, C. A., drugs and medicines.
Ginebra & Co., José, general.
Heinsen & Co., W., provisions and hardware.
Klüsener & Co., C., provisions and hardware.
Levy, T. G., drugs and medicines.
Lithgow, Washington.
Loinaz, Diego, provisions and lumber.
Manecke, H. J., provisions.
Mella y Brea, Y.
Pimentel, Aguilar & Co., provisions.
Piola & Co., D., provisions and dry goods.
Puyans, B. R., provisions and dry goods.
Senior, W., jr., provisions and dry goods.
Vives & Caballero, provisions and dry goods.

Physicians.
Garrido, P. M.
Lellundi, U.

Planters.
Barranco, F.
Boltel, Manuel.
Ginebra y Ca., José.
Lithgow Bros.
Shultz, H.

Printing offices.
Castellano, Manuel.
Journal of Commerce.
Porvenir.
Taylor, H. A.

Sewing machines.
Amabile, M. G.
Batlle, Cosme.
Chiodi & Co., G.
Ginebra y Ca., José.
Klüsener & Co., C.
Puyans, B. R.
Vives & Caballero.

Soap manufacturer.
Compart, J. L.

Telegraph company.
Compañía Telegráfica de las Antillas, M. Rousell, agent.

SAMANA.

Merchants, import and export.
Baucalari, Gisbert.
Boiman, P.
Carravelli, Antonio.
Cernuda, Canuto.
Mella y Brea, Y.
Sturla, A.

SANCHEZ.

Merchants, import and export.
Batlle, Cosme.
Baucalari, Gisbert.
Boiman, P.
Caravelli, Antonio.
Castillo, Manuel.
Cernuda, Canuto.
Garcia, Fuilo.
Ginebra & Co., José.
McLelland, Thomas.
Morrilo, Matthew.
Shultz, W.
Sturla, A.

SAN PEDRO DE MACORÍS.

Importers.
Bass, Wm. L.
Castro, Juan F. de.
Ferrero, Bartolomeo.
Friedheim, Ehlers & Co.
Mellor, Santiago W.
Leyba, R. M.
Pardo, Julio.
Santonel, J. M.

SANTO DOMINGO CITY.

Exporters.
Hoblt, F.
Lemos, J. de.
Leyba & Co., J. M.
Pou & Co., M.
Ratto Hermanos.
Vicini, T. B.

Importers of American, English, French, and German goods and provisions.
Abreu y Ca., E.
Aguasvivas, M.
Alfonseca & Co., T.
Alvarez, R.
Aybar y Ca., Andrea.
Aybar Hermanos.
Baez, Felix.
Bass, A.
Bazile, Isadoro.
Blome, Lajara y Ca.

SANTO DOMINGO CITY—Continued.

*Importers of American, English, French, and
German goods and provisions—Continued.*

Cambaso Hermanos.
Curiel & Co., Samuel.
Damiron & Co., A.
Delgado, Angel.
Delgado, R., drugs.
De Lemos, J.
De Marchena, Elias.
De Marchena, Eugenio.
Dominguez, Alonia.
Enriquez, Salvador.
Eshler, Friedheim & Co.
Farrand & Co., J. W.
Galvan, Rafael, drugs.
Garcia & Co., H., stationery and printing.
Goussard, B., drugs.
Henriquez & Co., S. C.
Herrera, Alejandro.
Hohlt, Federico.
Lamarche, drugs.
Lebron y Ca., J.
Lebron, Sanchez M.
Leyba & Co., J. M.
Lopez y Dominques.

SANTO DOMINGO CITY—Continued.

*Importers of American, English, French, and
German goods and provisions—Continued.*

Mamias & Co.
Mansfield, George.
Marchena & Co.
Marchena, Eugenio.
Marchena Hermanos.
Mastrerzi, Antonio.
Michelena ó Hijos, S.
Meses y Ca., José.
Penha, E. L.
Pitaluga, Salvador.
Pinedo & Co., Enrique.
Pinedo, Rodolfo.
Pon. Hijos y Ca., I.
Pon & Co., Miguel.
Pozo y Ca., Luis.
Ricart, Enrique A.
Rocha & Co.
Rodriguez, Cristobal.
Rodriguez, Fernando M.
Roquez, José R.
Sanchez, Juan P.
Ventura, Giovanni.
Vicini, T. B.

Uruguay.

INDEPENDENCIA.

Bank.

Banco Nacional.

Storekeepers.

Bullo, Nicolas, commission, wool, dry hides, produce.
Casaretto, Miguel.
Cardonnet & Co., A.T.
Chichizola, A.S.
Corvetto, José.
Fourodono & Co., Francisco.
Nadal & Co., Jaime.

Exporter.

Liebig's Extract of Meat Co., limited.

MALDONADO.

Retail merchants, general stores.

Alegre & Co.
Booth, Juan.
Bordas, Casimiro.
Camino, José M.
Devicenzi, José.
Hurbin, Hes.
Lagistra, J.
Mantaras, Eufrasio.
Martinotti, I.
Mier, Francisco.
Pintos, Saturnino.
Pou, Jaime.
Tassano, Domingo.

MONTEVIDEO.

Bankers.

Bastos & Co.
Carrau & Co.
Ferrés, Salvador.

Banks.

Banco Comercial.
Banco Constructor Oriental.
Banco Constructor Uruguayo.
Banco Crédito Real Uruguayo.
Banco de Crédito Auxiliar.

MONTEVIDEO—Continued.

Banks—Continued.

Banco de España y Rio de la Plata.
Banco Español Uruguayo.
Banco Francés.
Banco de Lóndres y Rio de la Plata.
Banco Lloyd del Plata.
Banco Nacional.
Banco Mercantil del Rio de la Plata.
English Bank of the River Plate, limited.
English Bank of Rio de Janeiro, limited.
London and Brazilian Bank, limited.
Sociedad de Crédito Hypotecario.
Sociedad General de Crédito.

Booksellers and stationers.

Adsarias, R.
Arandi, F.
Arroyo, Francisco.
Barreiro & Ramos.
Berot, Andrés.
Caccia, Emilio.
Cores, Vazquez.
Cuspinera, Teix & Co.
Gadea & Co., J.
Galli & Co.
Ibarra, Francisco.
Jacobson & Co.
Pittaluga & Co.
Radici, Alejandro.
Rius, Andrés.
Schmit, J.J.
Seiger, A.E.
Teix & Co.
Toloza, Z.
Valle, Marcelino.
Vieites, Manuel.

Furniture merchants.

Acquarone & Co.
Acquarone, F.
Ballestreri & Co.
Bascain, Juan.
Bovidier & Treglia.

MONTEVIDEO—Continued.

Furniture merchants—Continued.

Brelier ó Hijo, P.
Calvo, B.
Canepa & Franco.
Caviglia Hermanos.
Ceitan, J.
Cerri & Morfino.
Dubine, Luis.
Durandean, J.
Elena, J.
Esquenole, J.
Ferier, C.
Ferro, A. L.
Fontana, C.
Gargallo, Francisco.
Giorello Hermanos.
Introini, E.
Irgio, T.
Jens & Co.
Junio, A.
Lanza, Francisco.
Licor, J.
Livio, J.
Martino, A.
Mezzera, Virginio.
Mollese, J. B.
Monteverde, F. L.
Monti, Casal.
Morelli & Siandra.
Nacino & Elena.
Paladino, M.
Pisante, D.
Revello, J.
Sueca & Hermano.
Taboada, Ricardo.
Talasco, J.
Tassistro, A. J.
Toscano & Co., V.
Urtado, B.
Zignago, J.

Grain merchants.

Badetto, C.
Baffo & Hermanos, J.
Bonaldi, E.
Carbonelli, J.
Coll & Co., I.
Durán, José.
Fita, M.
Giude, Leon.
Gomez & Co., M.
Lascazes, Victor.
Levrero & Co.
Riera, Pedro.
Roquetta, Gaspar.
Rosses, Joaquin.
Tuvio, B.

MONTEVIDEO—Continued.

Importers, exporters, and commission merchants.

Aguiar y Braga, importers, wines.
Alarcon y Brito, commission merchants.
Aliseris, C., importers.
Alvarez y Iglesias, importers arms, hardware, machinery, etc.
Alvarez Hnos., importers hardware.
Alvariza y Cia., importers dry goods.
Ameglio y Hijos, importers wines.
Amezaga, Diez y Ca., importers dry goods.
Ashworth y Ca., importers general merchandise.
Ayerbe y Ca., importers cloth.
Ballefin, P. C., commission merchant.
Bally, C. F., importer shoes, leather, etc.
Barclay, Mackintosh y Ca., importers dry goods.
Barberouse y Perez, importers dry goods.
Barreiro y Brunengo, importers printing presses and paper.
Barrére, Grassie & Co., importers kerosene, lard, and general merchandise.
Barreta y Mesquita, commission merchants.
Bates, Stokes & Co., general importers and exporters.
Beduchaud, A., commission merchant.
Behrens, C., importer saddlery, harness, and belting.
Bell, Towers & Co., importers hardware and agricultural implements.
Benvenuto, L. M., commission merchant.
Bonomi y Ca., Juan, importers hardware and agricultural implements.
Bonomi, Morelli y Ca., L., importers hardware and agricultural implements.
Bottini y Ca., M., ship chandlery.
Broqua, Scholberg y Ca., arms, etc.
Casal, Maeso y Ca., commission merchants.
Casaravilla, Sieura y Ca., importers fancy goods, electroplate, statuary, bric-à-brac, paintings, etc.
Citterio y Ca., importers general merchandise.
Conti, José, importers dry goods.
Costa, F. D., importers.
Costa y Crovetto Hnos., importers.
Dauree, E., importer wines, liquors, preserved fruits, etc.
Delsarte, D., importer wines and liquors.
Diaz y Carrico, importers wines, liquors, sapolio, etc.
Elliot, Maccio y Ca., general importers and exporters.
Farriols, N., importer and wholesale grocer.
Farini y Hijos, general importers, kerosene, lard, starch, etc.

MONTEVIDEO—Continued.

Importers, exporters, and commission merchants—Continued.

Ferber y Thode, importers dry goods.
Ferrer, Galeano, Guani y Ca., general importers.
Fidauza, Pianavia y Ca., importers dry goods.
Franchi, A., importer arms.
Fribolini, C., exporter.
Frugoni Hnos.; importers dry goods.
Furest y Ca., importers dry goods.
Galibert, J., exporter fruit.
Galli y Ca., importers paper, stationery, etc.
Gaminara, L., importer.
Garabelli é Hijo, A., importers dry goods.
Garavagno Hnos. y Ca., importers dry goods.
Gerson Hnos., A., importers jewelry.
Goldaracena y Ca., importers dry goods.
Gonzalez, Francisco, general importers.
Garostiza, E., importers and wholesale grocers.
Granara y Ca., J., general importers.
Groscurth, H., importer machinery.
Harley, Viuda de, importer machinery, boilers, etc.
Helguera, F. B., importer and wholesale grocer.
Howard y Ca., T. W., exporters.
Humphreys y Ca., F. L., commission merchants.
Irisari y Otero, general importers.
Kock Jeune, importer jewelry and diamonds.
Laimann y Reimer, general importers.
Lamaison, Juan, ship chandlery and hardware.
Lamp, Th., general importer.
Lansac, Julio, importer tapestries and upholstery.
Latorre, D., commission merchant.
Lena y Recalde, commission merchants.
Leuhda Hnos., importers Spanish wines.
Libert Frères, general importers and exporters.
Lozano, E., importer dry goods.
Machado y Ca., F., importers and wholesale grocers.
MacLennan, C. E., importer and exporter.
Mailhos, J. M., importer arms.
Mallmann y Ca., importers and exporters.
Manito y Ca., M. J., importers wines.
Martinez y Ca., M., importers.
Martinez y Barras, L., commission merchants.
Mas, V., importer wines.
Masañes y Ca., importer wines.
Masurel Fils, exporters.
Mendoza y Duval, C., commission merchants.

MONTEVIDEO—Continued.

Importers, exporters, and commission merchants—Continued.

Menet y Ca., importers dry goods.
Minelli, Gonzalez y Ca., importers and wholesale grocers.
Mir, García y Ca., importers dry goods.
Monte y Ca., importers and exporters.
Moratorio, A., importer dry goods.
Moreau, Julian, commission merchant.
Musante y Cía., J., importers and wholesale grocers.
Noboa y Lafarge, commission merchants.
Noguera y Ca., S., importers wines.
Ohrt, Adolfo, importer wines, beer, etc.
Otero, P. S., commission merchant.
Otto, Feller R., importer jewelry.
Oyenard, Etchebarne y Ca., importers and wholesale grocers.
Pagés y Rosés, general importers.
Palma, Juan A., importer dry goods.
Peiramale Hnos., importers dry goods.
Peixoto, Morales y Ca., importers wines.
Petit, Seré, Bolondo y Ca., importers, exporters, and commission merchants.
Pietracoprina, importer dry goods.
Poteuze y Ca., L. M., importers and exporters.
Poujade, P., importer.
Primo Liendo, importer dry goods.
Quierolo, F. G., importer.
Quierolo, E., importer.
Quierolo Hijo, Mateo, importer.
Quierolo y Ca., E., importers.
Quincke, E., importer agricultural machinery.
Rabe, Adolph, importer agricultural machinery.
Ramos, Pereira y Ca., importers agricultural machinery.
Recalde y Lena, commission merchants.
Rein y Ca., importers dry goods.
Repetto, I. Lacaste, importers dry goods.
Ricart y Rosasco, importers.
Rivara y Milans, importers dry goods.
Rodriguez y Ca., J. M., importers dry goods.
Rolando y Ca., importers dry goods.
Rossi y Ca., importers and wholesale grocers.
Rueté, F. L., general importer and exporter.
Russi, Crosignani y Leira, commission merchants.
Salvo y Ca., Solari, importers dry goods.
Sanguinetti Hnos., importers dry goods.
Saralabós, commission merchant.
Saunders, R. P., commission merchant.
Serejo y Etchepare, commission merchants.

288

URUGUAY.

MONTEVIDEO—Continued.

Importers, exporters, and commission merchants—Continued.

Shaw, J., general importer and exporter.
Stephano Risso Hijo, importer.
Steinhauser y Ca., J., importers jewelry.
Stünz, Ernesto, commission merchant.
The Central Agency, importers sewing machines, thread, etc.
Theobald y Ca., J. K., importers and exporters agricultural implements.
Tornquist y Ca., importers.
Trabucati y Ca., importers hardware.
Vazquez y Ca., importers.
Verninck y Desteves, importers arms.
Vleati Cayetano. importer.
Viana, Canale y Ca., importers dry goods.
Vidiella y Ca., importers dry goods.
Vieira, R. Manuel, importer wines.
Vilaró y Ca., F., general importers.
Villamil y Ca., importers wines.
Vivo y Ca., importers wines.
Wattinere, Bossut, exporter.
Weisse & Evans, importers coal.
Westerich, R., importer.
Williams & Co., exporters.

Leather manufacturers and merchants.

Aguilera, Juan.*
Ball, C. F.†
Cambiaso, C.*
Frarcara Hermanos.†
Lauza Herm. & Prat.
Marexiano Hermanos.†
Sartori, R.†
Sartori, Trillo T.†
Veiga, Ant.†
Zanoletti & Co.†

Merchants, general, wholesale.

Adami, C.
Aguerre, J. L.
Aguiar, Braga & Co.
Alixeris, Cárlos.
Alvarez Hermano.
Alvarez ó Iglesias.
Alvirira & Co.
Amezaga, Diez & Co.
Arostegui, M.
Ayerbe & Co., A.
Balparda, José P.
Bally, C. F.
Barberousse, Perez & Co.
Barclay, Campbell.
Barrat, N.
Barrere, Grassie & Co.

* Manufacturers.

MONTEVIDEO—Continued.

Merchants, general, wholesale—Continued.

Barrero & Brunego.
Baroso & Co.
Bastos & Co.
Bayolo, Massa & Co.
Beduchaut, A.
Bolondo & Co.
Bompet Hermanos & Co.
Bonatti, Martinez.
Bonifacio & Co.
Braga & Co., A.
Brandao & Lopez.
Broglia, P. Giacobino.
Bulla, Fernando.
Cardoso & Co.
Carlisle, Smit & Co.
Carrau & Co.
Casabal & Co., D.
Casal, Riveiro & Co.
Casal, Eusebio.
Casaravilla, Sienra & Co.
Caseaux, R.
Castillo. Grela & Co.
Cavales, Carrillo & Co.
Ceresola & Finochetti.
Charlet & Co.
Chide & Philipot.
Chlaepfer, Ferber & Co.
Citerio & Co.
Conti, José.
Corbacho Hermanos.
Correa, F.
Costa di Gio Batta.
Costa, F. D.
Danieri, G.
Danrée, E.
Delorenzi, José.
Del Ré & Co.
Delsarte, D.
Del Aqua & Hus, E.
Deville & Co., A.
Diaz & Carricó.
Dufrechou, Hijo & Co.
Duplesis, L.
Engelbrecht & Koh.
Escaderoso, P.
Falcone, C.
Farriols, Narciso.
Ferber & Thode, F.
Ferrere, J. B.
Ferres, Pedro.
Furest & Rivera.
Gallardo & Co., C.
Galli & Co.

† Merchants.

MONTEVIDEO—Continued.

Merchants, general, wholesale—Continued.
Gaminara, L.
Gandos, Leoncio.
Garabelli é Hijo.
Garavagno Hermanos & Co.
Garcia & Carbonell.
Gasparini, J. M.
Gerson Hermanos, A.
Guilani Hermanos.
Goldaracena & Co.
Galerons, C. B.
Gomez, P. E.
Gonzalez & Soñora.
Gonzalez, Francisco.
Gonzalez & Co.
Gorostiza, E.
Granara, J.
Guerin & Co.
Guido, S.
Helguera & Co.
Helguera, F. B.
Horse, J. I.
Howard & Co., F.
Huxan & Co., R.
Imbert Hermanos.
Imenes & Co.
Irrisari, J. A.
Laens, Sagori.
Laimaun & Reynier.
Lamberte & Co., Levi.
Lanieri, G.
Lanza & Prat.
Leunda Hermanos.
Liebet Frères.
Linck, Augusto C.
Llaguno Hermanos.
Lopez, Abella & Co.
Lozano, E.
MacGregor, Aitken & Co.
MacLemaman, C. E.
Mallmann & Co.
Manito & Co.
Marini & Co.
Martins & Co.
Mascinas & Co.
Marurel Fils.
Matthew, Piresent & Co.
Mihomenes & Co.
Mir, Garcia & Co.
Miralles, V. D.
Musente & Co.
Muxi, J.
Olarte, Requena & Co.
Orepuela & Co., J. F.
Ortuno, Francisco.
Osorio, Azpiazu & Co.

MONTEVIDEO—Continued.

Merchants, general, wholesale—Continued.
Oyenard, Etchevarne.
Pagés & Roses.
Palet & Co., P.
Palma, Feijoo & Co.
Payse, J. M.
Peiramale Hermanos.
Peirano Hermanos.
Peixoto, Morales & Co.
Primo, Liendo.
Queirolo Hermanos.
Queirolo, E.
Queirolo, J. G.
Queirolo Hijo, Mateo.
Quineque, E.
Quintella, Angel.
Rabe, Adolph.
Repetto, J.
Reyes, Anaut & Co.
Rios & Co.
Rissig, T.
Risso & Co., E.
Rivara & Millano.
Rivera & Co., R.
Rodriguez, Puig & Co.
Rodriguez & Co., J. M.
Rolando & Co.
Rosciano, Valdés & Co.
Rosell Hermanos.
Roses, Rius.
Roure & Co., J.
Rubio, Hijos de A.
Rubio & Garcia, M.
Saigado & Co., L.
Seijo & Co.
Shaw, J.
Sienza, R.
Sienra & Co., Rafael.
Silva, Irmão.
Soñora, C.
Spangemberg & Co.
Stefano Riso, Hijo de.
Storace Hermanos, Nicolas.
Sugasti é Hijos.
Tocarent, José.
Toruquist & Co., E.
Trabucati & Co.
Tremoleras é Hijos.
Varci & Co., V. de.
Vecino, José.
Viana, Canale & Co.
Vidiella & Co.
Vignale, Parma & Co.
Vilaro Hijo.
Villamil & Co.
Vivo & Co., A.

MONTEVIDEO—Continued.

Merchants, general, wholesale—Continued.
Wattiné, Bossout & fils.
Wedekind, Feher & Co.
Wielle, H. B.

Steel merchants.
Espino, A.
Etchevetz & Munyo.
Halty, M.
Munyo & Co., J.
Reventós, José A.

Tobacco manufacturers.
Abal, Juan.
Bossio, L. M.
Cavadini, Pascual.
Crespo, Antonio.
Gamba, E.
Lois, A.
Mailhos, Julio.
Mandarano, N.
Medina, B. de.
Poretti, J. B.
Rodriguez, A. M.
Triay, B.
Triay, Onofre.

Wine merchants.
Aguiar, Braga & Co.
Almar, Marti & Co.
Bastos & Co., Manuel.
Dávila & Co.
Martins & Co.
Mas, Vicente.
Matarredona & Ozomi.
Noguera & Co.
Pino & Mora.
Sociedad Central de Consumos.
Villamil & Co.

Wood merchants.
Aguerre, Bartolo.
Aguerre, Bernardo.
Bonomi Hermanos.
Bonomi é Hijos.
Carrére & Fynn.
Chiappi, Juan.
Deambrosi, J.
Etchepareborda & Co.
Favaro & Co., Alejandro.
Matto, Pijuan & Co.
Monge, Leoncio.
Montero, Wentuiscs F.
Otaegui & Narizano.
Panario, Ponce & Co.
Pastorino, José.
Quartino & Lapuente.
Queirolo é Hijos.

MONTEVIDEO—Continued.

Wood merchants—Continued.
Ravera Hermanos.
Spangemberg & Scaglia.
Sucenua, Antonio.

PAYSANDÚ.

Banks.
English Bank of River Plate, limited.
National Bank of the Republic Uruguay.

Exporters of preserved meats, dried meats, and extract of meat.
Argentó, V.
Elizondo, Sebastian.
McCall & Co., William.
Santamaria & Co.
Zorrilla & Co., Garcia.

Exporters of wool.
Carzolio, Juan.
Corbet, Eugenio.
Etchemendy, Pedro.
Fontano, José.
Hufnagel, Plottier & Co.
Iraburú Hermanos.

Importers of hardware.
Bernasconi, José.
Colombo Hermanos.
Pedoja, Santiago.
Pedoja, Veracundo.

Merchants, exporters of hides, tallow, and other animal products.
Argento, Vicente.
Carzolio, Juan.
Corbet, Eugenio.
Elizondo, Sebastian.
Etchemendy, Pedro.
Fontaus, José.
Hufnagel, Plottier & Co.
McCall & Co., Wm.
Santamaria & Co., A.
Iraburú Hermanos.
Zorrilla & Co., Garcia.

Merchants, importers of general merchandise.
Chaplin & Taylor.
Horta & Hermano, Miguel.
Hufnagel, Plottier & Co.

Merchants, importers of furniture.
Branca, L.
Civelli, B.
Piaggio, S.

Merchants, importers of boots and shoes.
Ferrero, Francisco.
Marro & Co., Pedro.
Podesta, Leonardo.

ROSARIO DE STA. FÉ.

Merchants.
Machado & Co., J.
Recaguo, Olcese & Cazeneure.
Sabathie é Hijos, J.

SALTO.

Banks.
Banco Comercial.
Banco Inglés del Río de la Plata.
Banco Nacional.
Caja de Ahorros.

Cutlery merchants.
Fabier, Francisco.
Studler, Emilio.

Merchant, commission.
Noguerra, Ventura.

Merchants, general.
Abascal, Ramon.
Avellanal & Co.
Comas, José.
Fernandez, Domingo.
Fernandez, Hermanos.
Gallino, Luis.
Lluveras, José.
Orcasitas & Arteta.
Scarella, Nicolas.
Solari Hijos, Pedro.
Víacava, Nicolas.

SAN JOSÉ.

Bankers.
Abelé & Co.
Galan & Co.
García Hermanos.
Illa & Co.
Martinez, Bacza.
Perez, N.

SAN JOSÉ—Continued.

Hardware and iron ware.
Maglia & Co.
Prata, Agustin.
Roverti, P.
Villamil Bros.

Storekeepers.
Arenas, A.
Arismendi, M.
Altonoga, R.
Cabrera, F.
Calzada Hermanos.
Canet, Manuel.
Clavel, J.
Corbacho, J.
Diaz, Pedro.
Egusquiza, M.
Fariña, M.
Fernandez, A.
Ferret, J.
Freire, F.
Galan, Pedro.
Garcia, S.
Garrido, C.
Lamaison, José.
Lopez, C.
Menendez, J.
Menendez & Gonzalez.
Munichon, L.
Pastoriza, A.
Perez, Adolfo.
Perez, I. M.
Quesada, G.
Saiuz, S.
Seijas, I. M.
Seijas, J. R.
Seijas, M.
Seijas, P.
Tireno & Co.

Venezuela.

BARCELONA.

Bank agency.
Banco Comercial.
Commission merchants.
Grundo, Nicolas.
Salazar, Hernandez.
Importers, exporters, and commission merchants.
Caro y Ca., Daniel de.
Dominici é Hijos, S.
Baiz, Ignacio H.
Gomez, H. G. D. C.
Hernandez, M. Salazar.
Rolando, Andres (Succ.).
Rolando, Aquiles.
Rolando, Armado.
Valencia, Julio J.

BARQUISIMETO.

Merchants.
Garcia Hermanos & Co.

BETIJOQUE.

Coffee and commission merchants.
Sanz, J.
Sanz, J. R.

BOCONO.

Commission and coffee merchants.
Berti, Vicente.
Castillo Hermanos.
Segovia, Pacifico.
Urdaneta, L. M.
Villasmil, I. M.
General stores.
Briceño Hermanos.
Castillo, Lisimaco.
Cazorla, Leon.
Leon, Crisanto.
Madrid, Manue
Saavedra, Max.

BOCONO—Continued.

General stores—Continued.
Saavedra, Santana.
Urdaneta, Luis Maria
Uzcátegui, Francisco de P.
Villasmil, Juan N.
Importer.
Caracciolo Parra Picón.
Iron merchant.
Briceño Abad.
Merchants.
Berti, Vicente.
Briceño Hermanos.
Castillo Hermanos, coffee and commission.
Galbaldon, Fabricio.
Gonzalo, Pablo Maria.
Henriquez, Eliseo.
Madrid, Manuel.
Riera, Domingo.
Saavedra, Santana.
Segovia, Pacifico.
Villasmil, Juan N.

CARÁCAS.

Banks.
Banco de Venezuela.
Banco de Carácas.
London Bank of Mexico and South America, limited.
Blank book manufacturers.
Herrera, Irigoyen y Ca.
Rothe, Alfredo.
Books.
Carranza Hnos.
Cedillo, Juan C.
Graells Hermanos.
Planchart y Velutini.
Puig Ros y Hermano, L.
Rothe, Alfredo.
Silva, Antonio J.

CARÁCAS—Continued.

Bookbinders.
Gonzalez, Pedro Jacinto.
Jimeno, Julian.
León, José Cruz.
Martinez, Daniel.
Rothe, Alfredo.
Sadó. Joaquin. ,

Brass ware.
Aagaard, Torvaldo.
Bolland, Tomás.
Falkenhagen, Juan.
Friede, Adolfo.
Fuenmayor, Fco. de Borja.
Marquez, Pedro.
Nordmann, Julio.
Rodriguez Amaral, Felipe.

Coffee mills.
Calderin, Eliodoro.
Castro, Matias.
Chenel & Co.
Daviot, Gral. Vicente.
Franco, Agusto.
Gallegos, Rómulo.
Márquez, Juan.
Ochoa y Ca.
Payares, Juan José.
Salas, José.
Yépez, Dr. Antonio E.

Commission merchants.
Raasch, Ed. y Oscar.
Brignone. Delfino y Ca.
Cabana y Tirado.
Cadenas y Ca.
Delfino y Echenique.
Diaz, Pedro Antonio.
Diaz y Echezuria.
Dominguez & Ca.
Egaña, Juan Bautista.
Francia y Ca., Felipe.
Franklin y Echeverria.
Hellmund y Ca., C.
Larrazábal Hermanos.
Lugo, Manuel Felipe.
Machado, I. B.
Martí Moragas, J.
Martinez, Alvarez y Ca.
Martinez Espino, A.
Mayz, Francisco.
Molina y Ca.
Orta, Aquilino.
Pérez Hermanos.
Quiroba. Juan.
Rodriguez, Juan Maria.
Sanchez y Ca., J. A.

CARÁCAS—Continued.

Commission merchants—Continued.
Santana Hermanos y Ca.
Sebastian, Delfino R.
Sosa y Ca., Santiago.
Trujillo, Luis A.
Volcán y Madriz.

Corn mills.
Carreño, Juan Bta.
Conde y Ca.
Correa, Emilio.

Crockery.
Benitez Hermanos.
Flores, Simón.
Spírito, Santiago.
Tovar y Galindo.

Drugs.
Acosto, Rodriguez & Co.
Albrand, Eduardo.
Alcántara Hermanos.
Alvarez de Lugo y Ca.
Arteaga Revenga y Ca., M.
Braun y Ca.
Dominguez y Ca.
Eskildsen, Julio.
Garcia, Esteban S.
Gathmann, Eduardo.
Gaudens, Francisco.
González, Rafael.
González, Wadskier, J.
Heyden, Cárlos.
Jahnke, Cárlos E.
Jelambi, J. Angel.
Lerzundi y Ca., M.
Lessman & Co., R.
Martinez y Martinez.
Marvéz y Ca.
Marvéz, A. B.
Mossello y Ca.
Ochoa, Elias.
Rodriguez, Teodocio.
Schütte, Guillermo.
Stürup y Ca., G.
Tejera, Rafael.

Dry goods, wholesale.
Arón Daniel & Fils, y F. Walts.
Becker & Co.
Benatar, Bendelac & Co.
Blohm, Valentiner & Co.
Boggio, Yanes & Co.
Brandt, Luis.
Corrales & Co.
Delfino, Báez & Co.
Dohrn & Co.
Eickhörn, Eduardo.

CARÁCAS—Continued.

Dry goods, wholesale—Continued.
Eraso Hnos. & Co.
Jacobson & Co.
Lassère & Co.
Leseur, Römer & Co.
Matos & Co., M. A.
Nuñéz & Co.
Pérez, Diaz & Co
Pérez & Co., José Antonio.
Pérez, Juan Pablo.
Pérez, Santiago.
Ramírez, José F.
Rivero, Travieso & Co.
Röhl & Co., J.
Ruiz, Jaime & Co.
Santana Hnos. & Co.
Seijns & Co.
Sota, Herrera & Co.
Sucre & Co.

Electric and galvanic apparatus.
Borges & Co., G. M.

Furniture.
Charles, Ageno.
León, Jorge.
Llaca, J. M.
Martinez Egaña, Simón.
Merentes, Miguel.
Müller, Cárlos.
Palacio Abreu, Antonio.
Rivero Escudero & Hno.
Ruiz, Juan Antonio.
Rus, Eloy.
Ruz, Leopoldo.
Sahmkow, G.
Suarez Hnos.
Yanes y Ca., Pedro.

Groceries and provisions, wholesale.
Báez y Ca.
Boulton y Ca., H. L.
Brignone, Delfino y Ca.
Cabana y Tirado.
Cabrera y Landaeta.
Cardenas y Ca.
Castillo, Casaux & Co.
Chapellin y Ca., M.
Dominguez y Ca., J. O.
Egaña, Juan Bautista.
Forsythe, Gorrondona y Ca.
Francia y Ca., F.
Franklin y Echeverría.
Franklin, Agusto.
Garcia, Seijas y Ca.
Gutierrez, Samuel.
Hellmund y Ca., C.
Herrera, Sucre & Co.

CARÁCAS—Continued.

Groceries and provisions, wholesale—Continued.
Invernizio y Ca.
Jiménez, Rodriguez y Ca.
Larrazábal Hermanos.
Linares, J. E.
Lugo, Manuel Felipe.
Machado J. M.
Marti Moragas.
Martinez Alvarez, E.
Martinez Espino, Antonio.
Molina y Ca.
Montemayor, Lorenzo de.
Moser & Co.
Pérez Hermanos.
Rodriguez, Juan Maria.
Sánchez y Ca., J. A.
Sosa y Ca.
Suárez, Gregorio.
Trujillo, Luis A.
Volcán y Madriz.
Zárraga, José Antonio.

Hardware.
Becker, Brun y Ca.
Jaireu y Ca.
Neuville Hermanos.
Róo y Ca., H.
Santana & Co.

Hardware, small.
Aguado, Simeón.
Arón Daniel & Fils, y F. Waltz.
Basalo Hermanos.
Basalomena, Emilio.
Becker, Brun y Ca.
Bourgoet, Leoner de.
Cohen y Ca.
Corrales y Ca.
Dohrn y Ca., Max.
Dupuy, Miguel.
Eickhorn, Eduardo.
Ettedgui, H.
Garcia Hermanos.
Gonzalez Seijas, Eleuterio.
Guinand Frères.
Hass, Adolfo.
Jarrën y Ca., L.
Lassère y Ca.
Möller y Ca.
Muñoz & Co.
Olivo y Ca.
Perrault y Ca., A.
Roche, Emilio.
Rodriguez Diaz, Enrique.
Róo y Ca., H.
Ruiz, Manuel.
Santana y Ca.

CARÁCAS—Continued.

Hardware, small—Continued.
Saúmel y Ca., C.
Urios & Baz.
Vera León, Juliáu.
Hatters.
Arévalo y Ca., José Antonio.
Arón Daniel & Fils, y F. Waltz.
Dohrn y Ca., Max.
Dubbers y Wiese.
Guánchez, Dionicio G.
Hernández Silva, Adolfo.
Jacobson y Ca.
Pardo, Ritz & Aporta.
Pérez y Paul.
Pérez y Ca., M. F.
Roche y Ca., E.
Roche, Emilio.
Rodríguez Díaz, H.
Importers and exporters.
Arón Daniel y Fils, y F. Waltz, importers.
Baasch, Eduardo y Oscar, importers and exporters.
Becker y Ca., Otto, importers and exporters.
Becker, Brun y Ca., importers.
Benatar, Bendelac & Co.
Blohm, Valentiner y Ca., importers and exporters.
Boggio, Yanes y Ca., importers.
Boulton y Ca., H. L., importers and exporters.
Brandt, Luis, importer.
Brignone, Deltíno y Ca., importers.
Cadenas y Ca., R., importers.
Chaumer y Ca., importers.
Chenel y Ca., importers.
Corrales y Ca., importers.
Delfino, Baez y Ca., importers.
Eickhorn, Eduardo.
Eraso Hermanos y Ca., importers and exporters.
Eraso, Domingo, exporter.
Forsyth, Gorrondona & Co., importers.
Hellmund y Ca., C., importers and exporters.
Hermanos Casas y Ca., importers.
Herrera, Yrigoyen y Ca., J. M., importers.
Hurtado, Teófilo, importer.
Invernizio & Co., importers.
Jacobson y Ca., importers.
Jarren y Cn., L., importers.
Jiménez, Rodríguez & Ca., importers.
Lassère y Ca., importers.
Léicibabaza y Ca., importers.
Lescur, Römer y Ca., importers and exporters.
Linares, J. E., importer and exporter.
Matos y Ca., M. A., importers and exporters.
Mendoza y Ca., Lopez, importers.

CARÁCAS—Continued.

Importers and exporters—Continued.
Montaubán, Augé y Ca., importers and exporters.
Ochoa & Co., Guillermo, importers.
Olivo y Ca., G.
Pérez y Diaz, importers.
Pérez, Díaz & Co., importers.
Pérez y Ca., importers.
Pérez & Co., J. A., importers.
Pérez, Juan Pablo, importer.
Pérez, Santiago, importer.
Ponte y Ca., R., importer.
Porras E., Herman, importer.
Rauber, E., importer.
Rivero, Travieso y Ca., importers.
Roche, Emilio, importer.
Röhl y Ca., J., importers.
Róo y Ca., H., importers.
Ruiz, Jaime y Ca., S., importers.
Santana Hermanos y Ca., importers and exporters.
Santana y Ca., importers.
Seijas & Co., R., importers.
Sosa, Santiago, importer.
Sucre y Ca., importers.
Zuloaga, Carlos, importer.
Jewelry stores.
Ammé y Ca., J. G.
Beiner, Emilio.
Böttger y Ca., A.
Bosque, Luis.
Buono, L.
Cachazo, Antonio.
Ely Hermanos.
Gathmann Hermanos.
Lemoine, E. D.
López, J. M.
Luisi, Antonio.
Marrero, Camilo.
Picard y Ca., S.
Vilardebó, Pedro.
Joint stock companies.
Agencia Funeraria.
Compañia del American Telephone Consolidated.
Compañia del Ferrocarril de la Guaira á Carácas.
Compañia del Ferrocarril Central de Carácas á Valencia.
Compañia del Ferrocarril del Carácas al Valle.
Compañia del Gran Ferrocarril de Venezuela.
Compañia del Teléfono Intercontinental.
Compañia de Navegación y Ferrocarril de Carenero. limitada.

CARÁCAS—Continued.

Joint stock companies—Continued.

Compañia de Pastas Italianas, Escobas y Velas.

Compañia de Minas de Petróleo en los Estados los Andes y Falcon Zulia, "Constancia Dacowich."

Compañia "Nueva Constructora."

Compañia Proveedora de Maderas del País, Aserradas al Vapor.

Compañia Ytalo Venezolana, "El Ramio."

Lithographers.

Bérghaenel, Max.

Linares Hermanos, Succ.

Neun, Henrique.

Remstedt, Juan.

Office stationery and furniture.

Arredondo, Betancourt y Ca., T. de.

Carranza Hnos.

Cedillo, Juan C.

Herrera Irigoyen y Ca., J. M.

Jagenberg Hermanos y Cia.

Llamozas y Ca., S. N.

Planchart y Velutini.

Porras E., Herman.

Rojas Hermanos,

Silva, Antonio J.

Photographers.

Arismendi y Manrique.

Fernández y González.

Lessman, Federico.

Navarro, Martinez J. J.

Pinottini, Juan Bautista.

Salas E.

Piano manufacturers.

Arismendi, Pedro P.

Montoya, Manuel.

Montoya, Victor Manuel.

Rodriguez Colina, Lorenzo.

Thriemmer, Hugo.

Pianos.

Arredondo, Betancourt y Ca., T. de.

Heny, E.

Sanme, C. M., Succ.

Saumell y Ca.

Printing offices.

Aldrey Jiménez, Succ., Teófilo.

Antero Hermanos.

Arambúru Hermanos.

Arredondo, Betancourt y Cia., T. de.

Borges & Co., José R.

Calcaño, Francisco de P.

Castillo, Licdo., Luis Felipe, director.

Castro & Co.

Coll Otero, Pedro.

CARÁCAS—Continued.

Printing offices—Continued.

Damirón, A.

Espinal ó Hijos.

Figueredo, Carlos B.

Herrera, Irigoyen y Ca., J. M.

Michelena, Tomás.

Monasterios Velasquez, J. M.

Pierre, Guillermo F.

Porras, Emilio.

Porras, E. Herman.

Pumar, Cárlos.

Quintero, Domingo.

Rothe, Alfredo.

Soriano, Succ., J. M.

Urdaneta B., Enrique.

Saddlery and harness.

Daumen, A.

Díaz, Marcos.

Fajardo, Pedro J.

Fajardo, Rafael.

Mellior, Alejo.

Muñoz, Angel Maria.

Muñoz, Vicente.

Osio, Vicente.

Pérez, Pablo Vicente.

Ponte, Andrés Avelino.

Sarmiento, José de J.

Schmale, H. C.

Sewing machines.

Heny, E.

Pérez y Díaz.

Silversmiths.

Bosque, Luis.

Buono, L.

Caballero Caballero, Andrés.

Castro, Leopoldo.

Esparragoza, Manuel.

Fuenmayor, J. M.

López, J. M.

Marrero, Camilo.

Martinez, Eladio.

Moreno, Rafael.

Polanco, Domingo.

Soriano López, Pedro Vicente.

Thompson, Vicente.

Vázquez, Félix.

Vázquez Hermanos.

Soap and candles.

Díaz, Pedro Antonio.

Mendoza y Ca.

Porras E., Hermán.

Quiroba, Juan.

Zarraga, José Antonio.

Tailoring establishments.
Agudelo, J. M.
Argote, Ventura.
Argouet ó Hijo.
Arias, Santiago.
Berra, Eusebio A.
Blanco Ojeda, Juan.
Blanco Silvestre, V.
Blomontt, Antonio.
Boom, Luis.
Calafell Hnos.
Chaumer y Ca.
Cruz & Co., L.
Díaz, Francisco de P.
Díaz Matos, Luis María.
Duprat y Ca., T. A.
Echezuría y Ca.
Fajardo, J. M.
Fourastié, Pablo.
García, J. Demetrio.
Greil, José.
Guerrero, Inocencio.
Ibarra, Luis.
Kleinkow, Luis.
Kühnhold, C. J.
Lovera, Félix María.
Martínez, Antonio Lino.
Mendoza y Ca.
Monasterios, Isidoro.
Ortega, Mariano.
Padrón, J. Bta.
Palma, Juan.
Pardo, Eduardo Luis.
Pérez & Co., Manuel Felipe.
Porras, Manuel.
Pulgar, Domingo.
Quintero, Noriega y Ca.
Roche, Emilio.
Roche y Ca., E.
Rodríguez & Co.
Sanz, Anacleto.
Sanz, Simón.
Toro, Eduardo.
Valdez Ernesto.

Tinware.
Bosque, Eduardo Vicente.
Díaz, Félipe.
Engelbrecht, Guillermo.
Ibarra Villareal, Pedro.
Mejías, Fidel.
Planas, Francisco de Paula.

Underclothing.
Cubria y Ca., Fermin.
Oropeza y Feo.

Underclothing—Continued.
Pérez, Manuel Félipe.
Pérez, Miguel G.
Romero y Fernández.

Undertakers.
Agencia Funeraria.
"La Equitativa"
"La Nacional."

Wax articles.
Agencia Funeraria.
Fernández y Ca.
González Lovera, Marcelino.

Wholesale merchandise.
Arón Daniel & Fils, & F. Walz.
Becker y Ca., Otto.
Bentato y Ca.
Blohm, Valentiner y Ca.
Boggio, Yanes y Ca.
Brandt, Luis.
Corrales y Ca.
Delfino, Báez y Ca.
Dohrn y Ca., Max.
Eraso Hermanos y Ca.
Ghio y Eikhorn.
Jacobson y Ca.
Lassère y Ca.
Leseur, Römer y Ca.
Lundt, C. Fred.
Matos y Ca., M. A.
Morales, Pérez y Ca.
Pérez, Juan Pablo.
Pérez, Santiago.
Ramírez, José F.
Rivero, Travieso y Ca.
Röbl y Ca., J.
Ruiz, Jaime y Ca.
Santana Hermanos y Ca.
Seijas y Ca., R.
Sucro y Ca.

Wines and liquors.
Aguilar y Ca., E. M.
Delfino & Co., R.
Palacios, Pedro.

CARUPANO.

Banks.
Banco de Carácas, Agents A. Lucca & Co.
Banco de Venezuela.

Commission merchants.
Alvarado, Carlos Pío.
Orsini ó Hijos, J.

CARUPANO—Continued.

Importers and exporters (general merchandise).
Cova, R. Silva.
Figuera & Co., Julio.
Franceschi & Co., José.
Jouclá & Co.
Lucca & Co., A.
Massiani & Co., F.
Navarro, José M.
Raffalli Hnos.
Requena, Francisco.
Vicentelli & Santelli.

Pharmacies.
Alvarado, Buenaventura.
Maiz, Luis Carrera.
Perez, José Pablo.
Silva, Luis José.

Soap and candle manufacturers.
Silva, Marcos.
Vallanilla & Marcano.
Vasquez & Rodriguez.

Wines and liquors.
Angel Mattei & Co.

CIUDAD BOLIVAR.

Bank agency.
Banco de Venezuela.

Commission merchants.
Afanador, Ramón & José.
Bermudez hijo, Ricardo.
Bigott & Co., Manuel.
Machado, Tomás.
Machado Siegert, José Tomás.
Mantilla, Alejandro.
Michelangeli & Figarella.
Guaderrama, Mateo.
Plessmann, Cuno.
Rodriguez & Co., M. A.

Drugs.
Agosto, J. B.
Kühn & Co., William.
Morreno, Ygnacio.
Scherling, Conrado.

Hatters.
Aldag & Co., Theo.

Importers and exporters.
Aldag & Co., Theo.
Battistini & Co., A.
Battistini, D. M.
Blohm & Co.
Frustuck Hermanos.
Gardes & Co.
Mathison Hermanos.

CIUDAD BOLIVAR—Continued.

Importers and exporters—Continued.
Mosch, Kraft & Co.
Palazzi & Co.
Pietrantoni Hermanos.
Sprick, Luis & Co.
Tomassi & Co., B.
Vicentini & Co., C.
Wulff, Juan.

Jewelers.
Buren, Antonio von.
Crapulli & Barletta.
Huth, Ernesto.

Machinery and brass goods, plumbers' supplies, iron ware, etc.
Underhill, Geo. F. (water works).

Printing offices.
El Bolivariense.
Machado, Julio S.
Ortega R., J. M.

Saddlers.
Kahler & Durcksmeier.

Tobacco manufacturers.
Guaderrama, Mateo.
Simonpatrí, Tomás.

Undertakers.
Araujo, Natalio.
Ulloa, J. M.

CORO.

Merchants.
Capriles, J. A.
Capriles, M., exporter, commission, and importer.
Cook ó Hijos, G., exporters, importers, and commission.
Correa, R. A., importer, exporter, and commission.
Curiel, Elias, exporter, commission, and importer.
Henriquez, Isaac C.
Senior ó Hijo, J. A., exporters, commission, and importers.

CUMANA.

Drugs.
Madriz, Otero, F.
Mayz, P. Lúcas.
Rivas ó Hijos, J. A.

Furniture.
Concheiro, José.

CUMANA—Continued.

Importers, exporters, and commission merchants, general.
Berrizbeitia y Hermanos, E.
Henriquez, J. López.
Himiob, Andres.
Mattei, Miguel.
Pietri, Luis.
Rivas ó Hijos, J. A.
Rojas Hermanos, Badaracco.

Merchants, commission.
García Nuñez, F.
Madrid, J. J.
Mattei, Miguel.

Merchants, general merchandise.
Aristeguieta, F.
Bermudez, J. C.
Blanco, Pedro.
Bossio & Co., N. G.
Bruno, A.
Bruzual & Sobrino, M.
Bruzual é Hijos, C.
Bruzual, J. Alejandro.
Bruzual, Ramón.
Castaño, Miguel.
Castro, Mario.
Cebollero, Manuel.
Guevara, M. M.
Henriquez, J. López.
Himiob, Andrés.
Ibarra, Surga R.
Isaba, Justo.
López, J. D.
Madrid, J. J.
Martinez, A. G.
Martinez, Diomedes.
Mayz Calzadilla, J.
Mitá, Márcas.
Nuñez, J. F.
Rivas ó Hijos, J. A.
Rivero, J. J.
Rojas P. y Hermanos.
Santos, José.
Sucre, Salvador.
Traverso, D.

Printing offices.
Martinez, M. A.
Milá de la Roca, B.
Serra Rius, F.

Rum manufacturers.
Arias, F.
Benuperthuy. P. D.
Martinez, Jacinto.
Pérez, Bernardo.
Ramos, M.

CUMANA—Continued.

Rum manufacturers—Continued.
Rosa, P. Luis de la.
Serra R., F.
Vallanilla, L.

Tailoring establishments.
Fernández, B.
Soto, J. D.

Undertakers.
Boisellier, Ch.
Himiob, A.
Vallanilla, J. J.

DUACA.

General merchants.
Bell, J. D.
Colman, A. A.

ESCUQUE.

Commission and coffee merchants.
Muchacho, R.
Muñoz, Emilio.

LA GUAIRA.

Banks.
Banco Comercial de Carácas.
Banco de Venezuela.

Importers, exporters, and commission merchants.
Almenar y Ca., A., general merchandise.
Aquino, E.
Arteaga, R. T., general merchandise.
Ayala, Leopoldo, general merchandise.
Badillo hijo, L., general merchandise.
Baiz, A., drugs.
Becker, Brun & Co., general.
Blohm, Valentiner y Ca., general.
Bonetin, H. L., general.
Boulton y Ca., H. L., general merchandise.
Chapellin y Ca., R., general merchandise.
Cortes, Federico G., hardware.
Dominguez y Ca., E., general merchandise.
Dupouy y Ca., A., general merchandise.
Escobar hijo, R., general merchandise.
Galan y Ca., Cárlos, general merchandise.
Galindo, Juan F., general merchandise.
García, Anselmi & Co.
García, Correa y Ca., L. F., general merchandise.
Gentil, A. Perret, general merchandise.
Guardia & Co., Juan Antonio, general merchandise.
Hellmund y Ca., C., general merchandise.

LA GUAIRA—Continued.

Importers, exporters, and commission merchants—
Continued.

Leseur, Römer y Ca.. general merchandise.
Mallory y Ca., G., general merchandise.
Marturet y Ca., E., general merchandise.
Massone y Gasperi, liquors.
Mayora & Co., Adolfo, general merchandise.
Miranda y Ca., R., general merchandise.
Moreau, O. F.
Moreau y Ca., Chirinos, general merchandise.
Padron, Juan B., general merchandise.
Pérez y Morales, general merchandise.
Pérez y Ca., W. Carias, general merchandise.
Rivas, M. Castillo, general merchandise.
Ruíz, R. M., general merchandise.
Salas y Montemayor, general merchandise.
Scholtz, J. C., general merchandise.
Stürup, G., drugs.
Velises, Anselmo P., general merchandise.
Vidal, Ignacio, general merchandise.
Winckelmann & Co., O., general merchandise.

MARACAIBO.

Banks.
Banco del Comercio.
Banco de Maracaibo.

Merchants, import, export, and commission.
Ampire & Co., D.
Beckmann & Andresen, importers hardware.
Blohm & Co., importers and exporters.*
Boscan & Zabala.
Boulton, jr., & Co., H. L., importers and exporters.*†
Bozo y Ca., Eduardo, importers, exporters, and commission.
Bustamente & Co., A., importers, exporters, and commission.†
Cabrera & Luciani, importers, exporters, and commission.*
Christern & Co., importers.*
Cooke é Hijos, G.
Dagnino & Co., M., importers, exporters, and commission.
De Lima & Co., jr.
Eduardo & McGregor, importers.
Gomez, J. & H. D. C., importers.*
Henriquez & Co., dry goods, bakeries; exporters of dividivi and fustic.
Lagomaggiore & Co., importers, exporters, and commission.
Minlos, Breuer & Co.
Parra, Pocaterra & Co.
Pinedo, G. G., exporter, fustic and dividivi.
Pons, Ramon, exporter and commission.†

MARACAIBO—Continued.

*Merchants, import, export, and commission—*Ctd.
Rivas y Garbiras.
Sariol, José, exporters and commission.
Soto, Focion & Co., exporters and commission.
Troconis & Co., Curiel, importers, exporters, and commission.
Urdaneta & Co., Angel.
Van Dissel, Thies & Co., importers, exporters, and commission.

MERIDA.

Coffee merchants.
Briceño, Abelino.
Lares, Prisco.

Drugs.
Bourgoin & Co.
Parra Picón, Dr. Ramón, importer.

Flour manufacturer.
Salas, Luis Ma.

General merchandise.
Arria, José T.
Caraconli, Victor.
Parra Picón, Caraciolo, importer.
Picón, Obdulio.
Ruíz, Cárlos.
Salas Hermanos & Co.
Salas é Hijo, Federico.

Printing offices.
Baralt, Ignacio.
Cordero, Julio F.
Picón Grillet, Pablo A.

MIRANDA.

Merchant.
Rios, Félix Antonio.

NIRGUA.

Merchants.
Llanos & Co., M.

PUERTO CABELLO.

Commission merchants.
Albornoz & Burguillos.
Baasch, E. & O.
Berrisbeitia, E.
Brandt, Cárlos.
Capriles, B.
Dominguez & Co., A.
Guruceaga, J. J. de.

* Dry goods and provisions and a general business in hardware.   † Principally provisions.

PUERTO CABELLO—Continued.

Commission merchants—Continued.
Jesurum, M.
Polly & Co.
Rivas, Fensohn & Co.
Salas, D. H.

Dry-goods merchants.
Ascher & Co.
Baasch, Mauss & Co.
Blohm & Co.
Braschi ó Hijos.
Leseur, Römer & Co.

Foundry.
Wittstein & Co.

Hardware merchants.
Mestern & Co.
Redler & Co., O.
Reinboth & Co., M.
Seidel & Co., L.

Merchants, general.
Alegrette & Co., S. Martí.
Baasch, Mauss & Co.
Bannelos, Manuel y Luis Martinez.
Beselin & Co.
Betancourt, A.
Braschi ó Hijos, A.
Ermen, A.
Escarra, F. C.
Garces & Aune.
Guruceaga, J. J. de.
Puncel, Luis.
Rodriguez, Cárlos.
Volkmar, William H.

Merchants, importers, exporters of dry goods and produce.
Ascher & Co., H.
Blohm & Co.
Braschi ó Hijos, A.
Leseur, Römer & Co.

Merchants, importers of provisions, exporters of produce.
Beselin & Co.
Boulton & Co.
Ermen, A.
Frey, M.

Merchants, importers, and exporters.
Ascher & Co., Hn.
Baasch, Eduardo & Oscar.
Berrisbeitia, Eduardo.
Beselin & Co.
Blohm & Co.
Boulton & Co.
Brandt, Cárlos.
Braschi ó Hijos, A.

PUERTO CABELLO—Continued.

Merchants, importers, and exporters—Continued.
Frey, Matias.
Leseur, Römer & Co.
Lowenbehn & Co.
Rivas, Baasch & Fensohn.

Provision merchants.
Diaz, Antonio Rodriguez.
Rivero, Roberto.
Rodriguez & Marim.

Sawmills and timber business.
Hill, R. S.
Reuter, T. & M.

Soap manufacturers.
Frey, T.
Hill, R. S.

Tanneries.
Dachary, T. P.
Picher, M.

RUBIO.

Planters and exporters.
Cordero Hermanos.
Zerez Hermanos.

SAN CRISTOBAL.

Merchants.
Andersen, Möller & Co., importers and exporters.
Berti Hermanos, commission merchants.
Branger Hermanos, importers and exporters.
Cardenas C., Rafael, importer and exporter.
Flores Hermanos, importers and exporters.
González Bona Hermanos, exporters and importers.
Lagomaggiore & Co., importers and exporters.
Minlos, Breuer & Co., importers and exporters.
Rivera, Encarnación, commission merchant.
Sánchez Hermanos, importers and exporters.
Sánchez, Nepomuceno, exporter.
Sánchez & Co., T. W., importers and exporters.
Somedey Hermanos, importers and exporters.
Van Dissel, Thies & Co., importers and exporters.

TARIBA.

Importers and exporters.
Cardenas, Gabriel, importer and exporter.
Sanchez, Cruz, exporter.

TINAQUILLO.

Merchant.
Landaeta, Tomás.

VENEZUELA.

303

TOCUYO.

Merchant.
Pérez, Tamayo Hermanos.

TOVAR.

Flour mill (American system).
Burguera, Elias.

General merchandise and coffee merchants.
Berti, Domingo F.
Citraro, Angel Ma.
Garcia, Ramón C.
González, Felipe, provision.
Mendez Hermanos, provision.
Mendoza, Codina.
Orsolani Hermanos.

Importers.
Burguera & Co., Elias, importers, exporters, and commission.
Citraro, Angel Ma.
Garcia, Ramón C.

Printing office.
Jesus, Vicente de.

TRUJILLO.

Commission and coffee merchants.
Briceño Hermanos.
González, Sienforiano.
Guerra, Juan B. C.
Marquéz, Martin.

VALENCIA.

Bank.
"Banco de Venezuela, Sucursal de Carabobo."
Booksellers.
Bethencourt é Hijos, A.
González, José.
Marvéz, Pacifico y Leopoldo.
Méndez, Hermanos.

Boots and shoes.
Bosque, Santiago.
Calcayno, Manuel.
Castillo, Pedro.
Chantereuil, Luis.
Cureau, Hortencia B.
Fernández, Joaquin R.
Gomes Calafat, T.
Guevara, Juana C. de.
Hulman & Cureau.
Jaen, Vicente.
Rulmann, A.
Sánchez, Andrés.
Commission merchants.
Berrizbeitia Hermanos.

VALENCIA—Continued.

Commission merchants- Continued.
Burgos, León.
Lienero, Luis.
Ortega Martinez Hnos.
Sánchez, Damián W.

Drugs.
Alezones, G. A.
Blanco, Espinoza A.
Blaubach, Alejandro O.
Brandt y Cisneros.
Feo Hermanos.
Feo & Co., Francisco.
Feo, Federico G.
Feo, José Antonio.
Feo & Co.
Feo é hijo.
Feo y Alvarado.
López, Eudoro.
Olivares, José R.
Paz Cortez, Rafael.
Romero, Francisco I.
Utrero, Francisco J.
Verano, Francisco.

Dry goods, wholesale.
Abadie y Anglade.
Becker, Gossewisch & Co.
Blohm & Co.
Boggio, Yanes y Monteverde.
Calafat & Co.
Leseur, Römer & Co.
Nuñez & Co., Juan.
Sandoval, Luis.
Tarbes & Co., B.
Foundries.
Albert é hijos, C.
Winckelmann Hermanos & Co.
Groceries and provisions, wholesale.
Albornoz, A. J.
Antich, M. F.
Baasch, Paz & Co.
Betancourt & Co., M. A.
Boulton, Kolster & Co.
Cedeño, Gregorio.
Garcia, Leonardo.
González & Co., Leopoldo.
Joly Hermanos.
Mendoza & Co., E.
Ortega Martinez Hnos
Palau & Co., Juan.
Sánchez G., Cárlos.
Salvatierra & Co., T.
Hardware.
Brendel & Co., F.
González & Co., H.

VALENCIA—Continued.

Hardware—Continued.
  Letteron, A.
  Mestern & Co.
  Seidel & Co.
  Winckelmann Hnos. & Co.

Hatters.
  Aigster, J. C.
  Frohlke, Eduardo.
  Hamann & Co.
  Ravillard, A.
  Ruiz, Santos.
  Rulmann, Eloy.

Iron and brass ware.
  Agreda, Emilio.
  Berdú. Franquínes.
  Cabreca & Co., Eliseo.
  Váez Olivero, Eduardo.

Lithographer.
  Castro, Julio.

Photographers.
  Rey hijo, Prospero.
  Rotundo, Cárlos J.

Saddlery.
  Bosque, Santiago.
  Ceballos. I.
  Castro, Francisco J.
  Gómez Calafat, Francisco.
  Hulmandy, Curean.
  Pancini, Emilio.

Sewing machines.
  Heny, E.

Small hardware.
  Arévalo y Corao.
  Feo, J. J.
  Herrera & Co. Ramón E.
  Marvez, Pacifico y Leopoldo.

VALENCIA—Continued.

Small hardware—Continued.
  Mendez Hermanos.
  Tarves & Co.

Tailoring establishments.
  Acosta, Ladislao.
  Alvarado, Genaro.
  Betancourt, T. M. V.
  Blanco, José Luis.
  Chirinos, T.
  Lezama, José G.
  Linares, Manuel Ma.
  Romero, Luis F.
  Sanz, Jacinto.
  Sirot, Camile.

Tobacco.
  Escorihuila, Ramón.
  Fancite, Olegario.
  Garcia, Carlos Maria.
  Peréz Meléndez, Antonio.
  Soler, José.

Undertakers.
  Guerra, J. de J.
  Lamas, Francisco.

VALERA.

Merchants.
  Carradini, Andrés, commission and coffee merchant.
  Gentini, Eduardo, commission and coffee merchant.
  Giaccopini, Domingo, commission and coffee merchant.
  Meyer, Karl, importer and exporter.
  Murzi, Constantino, commission and offcee merchant.

Antigua.

Agricultural implements.
Bennett & Co., Geo. M.
Comache & Co., A. J.
Davis, Geo.
Gomes, Manuel.
McDonald & Co.
McDonald, James.
Ranier & Co., D. W.

Ale and beer dealers.
Bennett & Co., Geo. W.
Comache & Co., A. J.
Forrest, Wm.
Gomes, Manuel.
McDonald & Co.
McDonald, James.
Moore, Wm. H.
Murdoch & Co.

Bank.
Colonial Bank.

Booksellers and stationers.
Bridger, John.
Malone, W. W.

Boot and shoe dealers.
Bridger, John.
Forrest Bros.
Galbraith, S.
Gardner Bros.
McAdam, A.
Madswick & Co.
Martine, Delos.
Moore, W. H.
Murdoch & Co.
Pigott, Robert.
Pigott, Thomas.
Thibon, Louisa.
Warnford & Co.

Carriage and wagon manufacturers and dealers.
Bennett & Co., Geo. W. (dealers).
McDonald & Co. (dealers).
St. Luce, C. P. (manufacturer).
White, Henry (manufacturer).

Coal merchants.
Bennett & Co., Geo. W.
Comache & Co., A. J.
Gomes, Manuel.

Druggists.
Bridger, John.
Taylor, Samuel.

Dry-goods dealers.
Forrest, Wm.
Galbraith, S.
McAdam, A.
Madswick & Co.
Martin, D. I.
Martine, Delos.
Moore, Wm. H.
Murdoch & Co.
Pigott, Robert.
Pigott, Thomas.
Thibon, Louisa.
Warnford & Co.

Furniture dealers.
McAdam, A.
Moore, Wm. H.
Murdoch & Co.

General merchants, wholesale and import.
Archer & Co.
Bennett & Co., Geo. W.
Comache & Co., A. J.
Gomes, Manuel.
Gonsalves, Jeremiah.

General merchants, wholesale and import—
Continued.

Jardine Bros., DeLusa.
McDonald, James.
McDonald & Co.
Mendes, A. R.

Groceries and provisions.

Bennett & Co., G. W.
Bridger, John.
Comache & Co.
Faussett, Thos.
Forrest, Wm.
Gomes & Co., M.
McAdam, A.
McDonald & Co.
Malone, W.
Martin, D. J.
Martine, Delos.
Moore, Wm. H.
Murdoch & Co.
Rannie & Co.
Scotland, Lucas & Co.
Thibon, Louisa.
Thibon, Mrs. T.

Hardware and tool dealers.

Bennett & Co., Geo. W.
Comache & Co., A. J.
Davis, Geo.
Forrest, Wm.
Gomes, Manuel.
McAdam, A.
Martine, Delos.
Murdoch & Co.
Ramier & Co., D. N.
Scotland, Lucas & Co.

Importers.

Archer & Co.
Baynes, Thos.
Beard, C. H.
Bennett & Co., G. W.
Burns, Jas.
Comache & Co., A. J.
Court, A. H. A.
Foote, J. F.
Foote, T. D.
Freeland, John.
Galbraith, Samuel.

*Importers—*Continued.

Gomes, M.
Goodwin, Wm.
Goodwin, Rob't.
Gonsalves, Jeremiah.
Guffroy, V.
Holberon, George.
Jackson, Chester E.
Lane, E. H.
Lucas & Co., Scotland.
McAdam, A.
McDonald & Co., M.
Maginley, John.
Maginley, James.
Mendes, A. R.
Nugent, Oliver.
Nugent, Oliver, jr.
Rannie & Co., D. N.
Sedgwick, Samuel.
Shand, C. A.

Iron merchants.

Bennett & Co., Geo. W.
Comache & Co., A. J.
Gomes, Manuel.

Jewelry and watches.

Bridger, John.
Forrest, Wm.
Galbraith, S.

Lumber merchants.

Bennett & Co., Geo. W.
Comache & Co., A. J.
Davis, Geo.
Gomes, Manuel.
McDonald & Co.
Ramier & Co., D. N.
Scotland, Lucas & Co.

Machinery dealers.

Bennett & Co., Geo. W.
Comache & Co., A. J.

Musical instruments.

Bridger, John.
Forrest, Wm.
Galbraith, S.
Warnford & Co.

Photographer.

Faussett, Thos.

ANTIGUA—Continued.

Saddlery and harness.
Bennett & C., Geo. W.
Forrest, Wm.
Gomes, Manuel.
McAdam, G.
Murdock & Co.
Ramier & Co., D. N..

Sewing-machine dealers.
Forrest, Wm.
Galbraith, S.
Martin, Delos.

Sugar-estate stores, dealers in
Bennett & Co., Geo. W.
Comache & Co.
Davis, Geo.
Gomes, Manuel.

ANTIGUA—Continued.

Sugar-estate stores, dealers in—Continued.
Ramier & Co., D. N.
Scotland, Lucas & Co.
Trunks and travelers' outfits.
Forrest, Wm.
McAdam, A.
Martine, Delos.
Moore, W. H.
Murdoch & Co.
Undertaker.
James, John.
Wall-paper dealers.
Bridger, John.
Forrest, Wm.
McAdam, A.
Moore, Wm.
Murdoch & Co.

Bahamas.

NASSAU.

Bank.
Bank of Nassau.

Booksellers and stationers.
Methodist Book Depot.
Morseley, Percy J.
Stationery and book store.

Boots and shoes.
Globe boot store.
Holmes, A. T.
Russell, Thos.

China and glassware.
Brice, D. A.
Farrington & Co.
Hilton, W.
Lofthouse, T.

Coal merchants.
Darling & Co., T.
Rahming, H. T.

Commission merchants.
Adderley, Geo. B.
Albury & Co., R. W. D.
Armbrister & Co., W. E.
Brice, D. A.
Bullard, F.
Culmer & Russell.
Curry, W. H.
Darling & Co., T.
Farrington, R. W.
Fitzgerald, F. A.
George & Co., J. S.
Johnson & Bro.
Johnson, J. S.
Menendez Bros.
Pyfrom, W. R.

Commission merchants—Continued.
Rahming, Henry T.
Sands, C. T.
Sands & Bros., J. P.
Saunders, Pembroke.
Saunders & Son, S. P.
Sawyer & Co., R. H.
Weech & Son, W. J.
Young & Higgs.

Contractors and builders.
Aranha.
Bascom, N. J.
Cox, John A.
Dorsett, Thomas.
Dupuch, Jos. E.
Johnson, Enoch.
Styles, Thomas.

Drugs.
Albury, Joseph B.
Bahamas Dispensary.
Holmes, F. A.
Lightbourn, R. M.
Nassau Dispensary.
New Providence Dispensary.

Dry and fancy goods, importers.
Armbrister & Co., W. E.
Brice, D. A.
Brice, Lorenzo.
Bullard, Francis.
Burnside, Geo.
Culmer & Russell.
Curry & Sons, W. H.
Depot General Merchandise.
Hall, E. S.

NASSAU—Continued.

Dry and fancy goods, importers—Cont'd.

Harris, Benj.
Henry, A. M.
Higgs & Bro.
Higgs & Co., Geo. R.
Holmes & Son.
Holmes, A. T.
Jones, Emeline A.
Kemp, Edward C.
Kemp, M. E.
Knowles, J. R.
Knowles, M. C.
Knowles, Theo.
Lightbourn, J. H.
Lofthouse, T. H. T.
Lofthouse, Mrs. E. J.
McDonald, D. J.
McDonald, D.
Maura, W. J.
Menendez Bros.
Menendez & Son.
Menendez, W. J
Metropole, The.
Moore, A. F.
Moore, T. P.
Musgrove, R. N.
Perpall, C. R.
Pyfrom, W. R.
Russell, Thomas.
Sands, C. T.
Sands, R. H.
Sands, W. P.
Saunders, H. R.
Saunders, P.
Sturrup & Bro.
The Globe.
Thompson & Co., J. A.
Turtle, J. F. W.
Turtle & Sands.
Volunteer & Thistle.
Weech & Son, W. J.
Whitehead, P. M.
Young & Higgs.

Exporters.

Adderley, G. B. (woods, bark, cotton, sponge, and fruit).

NASSAU—Continued.

Exporters—Continued.

Culmer & Russel (woods, bark, cotton, sponge, and fruit).
Johnson, J. H. (woods, bark, cotton, sponge, and fruit).
Johnson & Bro. (woods, bark, cotton, sponge, and fruit).
Nassau Sponge Exchange Co., Ltd. (sponge).
Sands, C. T. (woods, bark, cotton, sponge, and fruit).
Saunders & Son, S. P. (woods, bark, cotton, sponge, and fruit).
Sawyer & Co., R. H. (woods, bark, cotton, sponge, and fruit).
Young & Higgs (woods, bark, cotton, sponge, and fruit).

Groceries and provisions.

Adderley, Geo. B.
Alfred, John.
Albury, H. C.
Bosfield & Bros., G. A.
Brown, J. H.
Culmer & Russell.
Curry & Sons, W. H.
General Merchandise Depot.
Henry, Cope S.
Henry, W. J.
Johnson, Jos. S.
Industrial & Coöperative Society.
Knowles, M. C.
Pyfrom, W. R.
Pritchard & Bro.
Rae, S. H. C.
Rahming, Henry T.
Roker, Joseph.
Sands & Bros., J. P.
Sturrup & Bro.
Young & Higgs.

Hardware.

Bahamas Ironmongery Co.
General Hardware Co., C. S. Rae, manager.
George & Co., J. S.
Weech & Son, W. J.

NASSAU—Continued.

Ice merchants.
Nassau ice house, J. H. Brown, proprietor.
Pritchard Bros.
Sands & Bros., Jas. P.

Jewelers.
Brown & Musgrove.
Demerett, John.
Minus, A. C. J.
Minus, A. T. S.
Thompson, H. J.

Liquors.
Alfred, John.
Brown, J. H.
George & Co., J. S.
Henry, Cope S.
Henry, W. J.
Roker, Joseph.
Sands & Bros., J. P.

Lumber.
Dupuch, J. E.
Hall, Edwin S.
Sands & Bros., J. P.
Sawyer & Co., R. H.
Rohming, H. T.

Photographer.
Sweeting, Richard.

Planters.
Brown, John.
Burnside, Alfred.
Fitzgerald, Chas. T.
French, N. J.
Johnson, Joseph S.
Lightbourn, Henry C.
Nicolls, J. W. B.
Roker, Joseph.
Sands, Charles T.

Preservers and packers.
Culmer, J. W.
Johnson, J. S.
Sands, C. T.

NASSAU—Continued.

Printers and publishers.
Kemp, C. H.
Meseley, P. J.
Smith, S. Theus.

Shell dealers and manufacturers.
Camplejohn, G. C., jr.
Edgar, E.
Evans, R. H.
Florance, G.
Saunders & Son, S. P.
Thompson, H. J.
Thompson, Thomas H.

Shipbuilders.
Aranha, Francis J.
Bethel, Albert J.
Brown, J. R.
Cooper, S. A.
Evans, G.
Fernandes, Philip.
Higgs, G. W., proprietor of Marine Railway.
Ramsay, John.
Rodgers, J. A.

Sponge dealers.
Adderley, G. B.
Brown, J. B.
Dupuch, Joseph E.
Hall, E. S.
Higgs, Geo. W.
Johnson & Bro.
Lightbourn, H. W.
Saunders & Son, S. P.
Sawyer & Co., Robert H.
Treco, P. A.
Young & Higgs.

Undertakers.
Bascom, N. J.
Bridgewater, J. A.
Elliott, N. S.
Hall, W. L.
Johnson, W. E.
Lightbourn, Wm.
Pearce, R. A.

Barbados.

BRIDGETOWN.

Agricultural implements.
Carter & Co.
Harrison & Co., C. F.
Hutchinson & Co., G. W.

Arms and ammunition.
Carter & Co.
Harrison & Co., C. F.
Hutchinson & Co., G. W.
Waterman & Co., C. A.

Banks.
Barbados Savings Bank.
Colonial Bank.

Booksellers and stationers.
Barrow, A.
Bowen & Sons.
Bowen, I. Sinderby.
Fraser, Jas.
Shepherd, W. A.
Slim, B. T.

Boots and shoes.
Bowen, E. A.
Cumberbatch, J. S.
Da Costa & Co.
Lawlor & Co., T.
Ramsey, Elder & Co.
Taylor, C. F.
Whitfield & Co., Geo.

Carriage importers and dealers.
Bayne, A. T.
Cotton & Co., D. P.
Davis, E. W.
Harrison & Co., C. F.
Trowbridge & Co.

Coal dealers.
Cavan & Co., M.
Daniel & Co., Limited.
Thorne, H. E.

BRIDGETOWN—Continued.

Commission merchants.
Carter & Co.
Cavan & Co., M.
Challenor & Co.
Clairmónte & Co.
Cotton & Co., D. P.
Da Costa & Co.
Daniel & Co., F.
Fleurot & Co., J.
Garraway, T. S.
Giles, N.
Gill & Co., John.
Hanschell & Co.
Harrison & Co.
Harrison & Co., C. F.
Hutchinson & Co., G. W.
Laurie & Co.
Leach & Co., B.
Leacock & Co., W. P.
Lynch & Co., J. A.
Musson, Son & Co., S. P.
Sealy & Co., Joseph S.
Trowbridge & Co.

Drugs.
Browne, J. A.
Chandler & Co., J. W.
Croney, C. F.
Gill & Co., John.
Grogan & Co., W. R.
Knight & Co.
Leach & Co., Benony.
Mann, L. H. W.
Moore, G. P.
Rogers & Co., John.

Dry goods.
Brown, S.
Chaderton, E. M.
Da Costa & Co.

BRIDGETOWN—Continued.

Dry goods—Continued.

     Edwards, R. H.
     Goodridge, C. M.
     Goodridge, D. G.
     Harrison & Co., C. F.
     Inniss, E. C.
     Lawless, L. W.
     Lawlor & Co., Thomas.
     Mosely, Mrs.
     Poulson, Mrs.
     Quirk & Co.
     Ramsey, Elder & Co.
     Rogers, E N.
     Sampson, L. W.
     Sealy & Co., J. S.
     Sinclair, J. E.
     Warton, J.
     Whitfield & Co., Geo.

Exporters.

     Cavan & Co., M.
     Challen & Co., R.
     Da Costa & Co.
     Daniel & Co., F.
     Laurie & Co.
     Leacock & Co., W. P.
     Lynch, Jas. A.
     Musson, Son & Co., S. P.

Furniture dealers.

     Carter & Co.
     Carter, A. Percy.
     Cotton & Co., D. P.
     Da Costa & Co.
     Eckstein, B. M.
     Harrison & Co., C. F.
     Haynes, J. O.
     Hutchinson.
     Roberts, Thomas.
     Seifert & Co., J. R. H.

Groceries and provisions.

     Alleyne & Arthur.
     Alleyne & Son, B.
     Allder Bros.
     Barrow & Co., J. B.
     Carter & Co. (coöperative store).
     Clinckett & Co.
     Cotton & Co., D. P.
     Da Costa & Co.

BRIDGETOWN—Continued.

Groceries and provisions—Continued.

     Hoad & Co., John.
     Ince & Co., C. W.
     Inniss. B.
     Inniss, James H.
     Inniss & Co.
     Johnson & Co.
     King & Co., T. E.
     Mayers, John.
     Skeete, Edward.
     Waterman & Co., C. A.
     Whitfield & Co , George.

Hardware.

     Carter & Co.
     Cotton & Co., D. P.
     Croney, James W. (plumbers' supplies).
     Gill Bros. (iron and brass founders)
     Harrison & Co.
     Herbert, Thomas.
     Hutchinson & Co., G. W.
     King, P. R.
     Roberts, Thomas.
     Simpson & Co., D. M. (importers of machinery).

Importers.

     Bayne, Alexander T. (paints, oils, etc.).
     Chandler & Co., J. W. (teas).
     Clarke, W. C. (lumber, coal, and general stores).
     Collymore & Wright (lumber, coal, and general stores).
     Cotton & Co., D. P. (hardware and general stores).
     Daniel & Co., F. (lumber, coal, and general stores).
     Gill & Co., John (tea).
     Hood & Co., John (liquor).
     Hutchinson & Co., Geo. W. (general goods).
     Inniss, J. H. (lumber, coal, and general stores).
     Leach & Co., Benony (tea).
     Manning, T. (lumber, coal, and general stores).

BRIDGETOWN—Continued.

Importers—Continued.

Plinner, Thomas (jewelry and fancy articles).
Sealy & Co.,Joseph S.(general stores).
Simpson & Co., D. M. (machinery).
Smith & Co., J. (lumber, coal, and general stores).
Thorne, H. E. (lumber, coal, and general stores).

Jewelers.

Bayley & Co., Alex.
Gibbons, G. R.
Plimmer, Thomas.
Seifert & Co., J. R. H.

Liquors.

Barrow & Co., Joseph B.
Carter & Co.
Cavan & Co., Michael
Cotton & Co., D. P.
Da Costa & Co.
Giles, N.
Hood & Co., John.
Hutchinson & Co., Geo W.
Inniss, Benjamin.
Whitfield & Co., Geo.

Merchants, general.

Barrow, Alfred (books and stationery, spectacles).
Bowen, I. Sinderby (toilet articles, stationery).
Burton, John (funeral furnishings).
Carter & Co. (house-furnishing goods, plantation stores).

BRIDGETOWN—Continued.

Merchants, general—Continued.

Chandler & Co. (fancy goods, drugs).
Cotton & Co., D. P. (general goods).
Da Costa & Co. (universal supplies).
Harrison & Co., C. F. (furniture).
Hutchinson & Co., Geo. F. (universal supplies).
Johnson & Co., W. L. (fertilizers, carriages).
Seifert & Co., J. R. H. (sewing machines, trunks, toilet articles).
Waterman & Co., C. A. (explosives).
Whitfield & Co., George (household goods).

Ship chandlers.

Cotton & Co., D. P.
Da Costa & Co.
Harrison & Co., C. F.
Herbert, John.
Hunte, J. T.
Hoad & Co., John.
Inniss, James H.
Johnson & Co., W. D.
Whitfield & Co., Geo.

Tailors and outfitters.

Branker, John D.
Clairmonte, F. N. A.
Clarke, Joshua.
Davis, John.
Dyal, J. E.
Dyal, W. E.
Wright & Co., T. A.

Bermuda.

CRAWL.

Importer.
Hollis, Dudley.

DEVONSHIRE.

Importer.
Wilson, J. F.

HAMILTON,

Importers.
Barritt, John.
Berg, John E.
Chiappa, J. P.
Duerden, R. H.
Friswell, J. J.
Harnett, J. W.
Heyl, J. B.
Ingham, S. S.
James, S. S.
James, W. T.
Meyer, E. A.
Masters, J. E.
Miles, T.
O'Neil, C. G.
Outerbridge, F. K.
Paschal, A.
Recht, H. G.
Robinson, R. L.
Robinson, S. D.
Wingwood, A.
Wolff, E. W.

Merchants.
Burrows & Co., J. F.
Conyers, J. A.

HAMILTON—Continued.

*Merchants—*Continued.
Jackson, J. H.
James, W. T.
Lockwood & Ingham.
Martin, S. A.
Outerbridge, H. C.
Pitt, T. H.
Trott & Cox.
Trunington Bros.
Wadson.
Walker & Co.

SHELLY BAY.

Importers.
Davis, T. H.
Pearman, T. J.

ST. GEORGES.

Importers.
Inglis, Albert.
McCallan & Co.

SOMERSET BRIDGE.

Importers.
Brown, James.
Robinson, L. J.
Somerset Coöperative Association.

THE FLATTS.

Importers.
Darrell, Clarence.
Trott, Reid.

British Guiana.

AMSTERDAM.

AMSTERDAM.

Bookbinder.
    Macdonald, W.

Chemists and druggists.
    Apothecaries' Hall.
    Clements, R. P.
    Downer & Co.
    Hughes & Co.
    Isaacson & Co.

Commission merchants.
    Davson & Co., S.
    Ingall, Wm.
    McKinnon, David W. A.

Dry goods.
    Ashurst, C. P.
    Davson & Co., S.

General merchandise.
    Davson, & Co., S.
    Ingall, Wm.
    Lade & Co., James.
    Patoir & Co., J. E.
    Perot & Co., James E.
    Wreford & Co., S.

Gold and silver smiths.
    Elliot, E. B.
    McInnis, I.
    Mendonça, M. N.
    Tucker, T.
    Yearwood, W. R.
    Young, J.

Hardware.
    Davson & Co., S.
    Gomes, Diogo.
    Wreford & Co., S.

AMSTERDAM—Continued.

Importers.
    Ashurst, C. P. (dry goods).
    Collier & Son (general merchandise).
    Davson & Co., S. (general merchandise).
    Hughes & Co. (groceries, wines, and liquors, drugs, cigars, etc.).
    Isaacson & Co. (surgical instruments, drugs, etc.).
    Lade & Co., James (general merchandise).
    Perot & Co., James E. (breadstuffs, provisions, wines, etc.).
    Wreford & Co., S. (dry goods, liquors, groceries, etc.).

Liquor merchants.
    De Freitas, Julio.
    De Mendonça, jr., & Co., M.
    Gaskin, C. P.
    Hughes & Co.
    Perot & Co., James E.
    Soares, Antonio.
    Wreford & Co., S.

Printer and publisher.
    Macdonald, Wm.

Provisions.
    Camacho, Antonio Fernandes.
    Collier & Son.
    Davson & Co., S.
    De Mendonça, jr., & Co., Manoel.
    Gomes, Diogo.
    Ho-a-Hing.
    Hughes & Co.
    Ingall, Wm.

AMSTERDAM—Continued.

Provisions—Continued.
Lade & Co., James.
Patoir & Co., J. E.
Perot & Co., James E.
Wreford & Co., S.

Saddlers.
Ferrel, John.
Fraser, H.
Jones, James E.
Wreford & Co., S. ·
Yard, T.

Tailors.
Ashurst, C. P.
Brown, E.
Crouch, J.
Davson & Co., S.
Elliott, T.
Hartley, T.
King, E. T. N.
Lade & Co.
Leisseur, L. J.
McGee, E. T.
Miller, Charles.
Patoir & Co.
Sealy, J.
Weithers, G.
Wreford & Co., S.

Timber.
Berbice Steam Sawmill.

Watchmakers and jewelers.
Clements, R. P.
Elliott, E. B.
King, J. A.
McInniss, W.
Sargent, T. M.
Yearwood, W. R.

GEORGETOWN.

Account-book manufacturers.
Baldwin & Co.
Jardine, C. K.
Thomson, J.

Banks.
British Guiana Bank.
Colonial Bank, London.

GEORGETOWN—Continued.

Boiler-makers.
Barnwell, Nathan A.
Buchanan & Co., Robert.
Daw, Richard.
Sproston Dock & Foundry Co.
Warren, James.

Bookbinders, booksellers, and stationers.
Baldwin & Co.
Jardine, C. K.
Thomson, J.

Boot and shoe makers.
Applewhite, H.
Bash, W. A.
Bunyan, John.
Campbell, J. N.
Couse, P. E.
Daw, W.
Denny, Jno. E.
Dottin, W. C.
Ferreira, Pedro.
Gomes, John.
Hall, J.
Holder, Wm.
Inniss, Thomas.
Jones, F.
Jones, J.
Maxwell, E.
Norton, A.
Oliver, J. J.
Paragraph, J.
Richardson, G. D.
Richardson, W. R.
Rodgers, Wm.
Rufino, John.
Sargent, B. T.
Voltaire & Co., R. D.
Waterman & Co., R. J.
Wood, D. J.
Young & Bros., S. A.

Building contractors.
Bollass, G. W.
Bradshaw, J. R.
Bugle & Co., A. P.
Edey, George.
Evelyn, R.
Franker, B.

GEORGETOWN—Continued.

Building contractors—Continued.
Hannays, G.
Hope, J. G.
Job, Solomon A.
La Pénitence Woodworking Company.
McDavid, W. A.
Mussenden, H. C.
Norville, Y. N. G. A.
Pooler, Alexander.
Quail, Emanuel.
Shareles, J. B.

Cabinet-makers and upholsterers.
Blackuey, John.
Blenman, J.
Collet, G.
Coward, M. T.
Cowes, Thomas.
Cummings & Co., S. A.
Delph, J. F.
Delph, J. T.
George, Simeon Benjamin.
Goddard, H.
Goddard, Joseph.
Greaves, J.
Hodge, Benj.
Hyndman, J.
Jordan, jr., J. T.
King, J. T.
Lam-a-Sue.
Mehler & Co.
Park & Cunningham.
Powers, J. F.
Rodgers, Henry.
Small, Alfred.
Straghan, R. T.
Wong-Yeo-Wing & Co.

Chemists, agricultural and analytical.
Douglas, William.
Franck, Joseph.
Fuller, W. J.
Harrison, John B.
Millar, William M.
Pfeiffer, Herr.
Pontifex, S. R.
Scard, F. I.
Von Ziegesar, Heinrick.

GEORGETOWN—Continued.

Chemists, etc.—Continued.
Wegò, Herr.
Wilson, John.

Chemists and druggists.
Alty & Co., J. D.
Amson, H.
Austin, J. E.
Alleyne, J. R. A.
Belmey, L. J.
Brodie & Rainer.
Bunbury, Nathan.
Cendrecourt & Co., H. M.
Cendrecourt, C.
Coronel & Co.
Croker, Isaac.
Daly, E. A. B.
Davis, H.
De Souza, J. L.
Edghill, P. E.
Fonseca, E. G.
Green, G. H.
Haynes, Leopold.
Isaacson & Co., H.
Johnson, J. H.
Jordan, Josephus & Co.
Kerr, W. B.
Klien & Co., Joseph.
Leal, R. S.
Lobo, Isaac.
Lord, A. M.
Main Street Dispensing Co., prop., E. T. White.
Mall, M.
Max & Co., E. L.
Pitta, M. G.
Roberts, Alex.
Scott & Co.
Steman, B.
Stewart, Ezekiel.
Tross, D.
Van Nooten & Co.
Virtue & Co.
Wharton, W. H.
Wilson, J.

Chinese merchants.
Chong & Co., S.
Hing Cheong & Co.
Kwong Tai Lung & Co.

GEORGETOWN—Continued.

Chinese merchants—Continued.
Low-A-Yan & Co.
Wo-Lee & Co.
Wong-A-Choy.

Commission merchants.
Baptista, João.
Birch & Co.
Conrad & Co., Herman.
Conrad, Wakefield & Co.
Currie & Co., Donald.
Daniel & Co., Thomas.
Da Silva, Abel María.
Dawson Bros. & Co.
Farnum & Co.
Garnett & Co.
Ledoux & Co., Henri.
MacGowan & Co., D. H.
Perot & Co., A. W.
Sandbach, Parker & Co.
Smith, Wm.
White, E. T.
Wieting & Richter.

Dry goods.
Abraham, B. V.
Bettencourt & Co., Geo.
Booker Bros. & Co.
Colonial Co., Limited.
Crawford & Co., R.
Currie & Co., Donald.
Da Silva & Gonsalves, Abel.
Davis & Co., J. Wood.
De Cairos Bros. & Co.
De Jonge & Smith.
D'Oliveyra Co., E.
Flett, Smith & McGregor.
Fogarty, William.
Garnett & Co.
Goldsmith, F. E.
Hing Cheong & Co.
Humphrey, John H.
Italian Warehouse, M. A. French, manager.
Kwong-Tai-Lung Co.
Ledoux & Co., Henri.
Little & Co., Geo.
Low-A-Yan & Co.
McLeod & Co., Edwin.

GEORGETOWN—Continued.

Dry goods—Continued.
Oldfield, A. W.
Playfair & Co.
Reed, T. B.
Reick's Establishment, D. Ouckama, manager.
Rodriguez, A. G.
Smith Bros. & Co.
Smith & Oldfield.

Exporters.
Barr, Alex.
Booker Bros. & Co.
Bugle & Co., A. P.
Farnum & Co.
Ferreira & Co.
McLeod & Co., Edwin.
Wieting & Richter.

Foundries.
Buchanan & Co., Robert.
Leandro Bros. & Co.
Railway Foundry.
Sproston Dock and Foundry Co.

General merchandise.
Abraham, B. V.
Bettencourt & Co., Geo.
Booker Bros. & Co.
Colonial Co., Limited.
Currie & Co., Donald.
Da Silva & Gonsalves, Abel.
De Jonge & Smith.
D'Oliveyra & Co., E.
Garnett & Co.
Little & Co., Geo.
Low-A-Yan & Co.
McLeod & Co., Edwin.
Oldfield, A. W.
Smith Bros. & Co.
Smith & Oldfield.

Gold and silver smiths.
Abraham, B. V., jr.
Archer, R. M.
Cosson, M.
Feelin, James.
Fraser, G. A.
Gale, C. H.
Green, L. G.
Isaacson, W. A.

GEORGETOWN—Continued.

Gold and silver smiths—Continued.

Jacelon, C. F.
Martin, José.
Pakeman, W. A.
Peppietto, C. W.
Pickering, E.
Punch, Thos.
Sargent & Co., T. M.
Schüler, Chas.
Schüler, Hubert.
Schüler & Sons, J. A. W.
Smith, Samuel A.
Wagner, E. C.

Hardware.

Barr, Alex.
Bettencourt, G.
Booker Bros. & Co.
Da Silva, Abel María.
Da Silva & Gonsalves, Abel.
Forbes & Co.
Rodriguez, A. G.
Sharples, jr., J. B.

Hatters.

De Freitas, Fonseca.
Gomes, J. B. N.
Reick's Establishment, D. Ouckama, manager.

Importers.

Abraham, B. V., jr. (jewelry and notions).
Alty & Co., J. D. (drugs and chemicals).
Bettencourt & Co., Geo. (general merchandise).
Birch & Co. (American food products, ice, and live stock).
Booker Bros. & Co. (general merchandise and ship chandlery).
Camp Street Dispensary, H. Davis, proprietor (drugs, wines, liquors, groceries, cigars, tobacco, etc.).
Cedancourt, Charles (drugs, wines, liquors, groceries, cigars, tobacco, etc.).
Colbeck, W. R. (pianos).
Collier & Son (teas, wines, dry goods, groceries, etc.).

GEORGETOWN—Continued.

Importers—Continued.

Colonial Co. Ltd. (estates' supplies, machinery, etc.).
Conrad & Co., Herman (wines, dry goods, liquors, etc.).
Conrad, Son & Co. (chemicals).
Conrad, Wakefield & Co. (general merchandise).
Currie & Co., Donald (general merchandise).
Davis & Co., J. Wood (general merchandise).
De Cairos Bros. & Co. (general merchandise).
De Jorge & Smith (wines and liquors).
Demerara Crushed Feed and Grocery Company (general merchandise).
Demerara Ice House and Aërated Waters Factory.
D'Oliveyra & Co., E. (dry goods, jewelry, musical instruments, etc.).
Farnum & Co. (general merchandise).
Hing Cheong & Co. (general merchandise).
Isaacson & Co., H. (drugs, chemicals, perfumes, toilet articles, cigars, tobacco, groceries, wines, etc.).
Italian warehouse, M. A. French, manager (general merchandise).
Kaufman & Co., R. T. (drapery, millinery, and fancy goods).
Kwong-Tai-Lung & Co. (Chinese goods).
Macquarrie, Charles J. (wines, liquors, cigars, and mineral waters).
Park & Cunningham (general merchandise).
Perot & Co., A. W. (American merchandise).
Playfair & Co. (general merchandise).
Scott & Co. (general merchandise).
Smith Bros. & Co. (general merchandise).
Smith & Oldfield (general merchandise).

GEORGETOWN—Continued.

Importers—Continued.

Strong, H. (pianos and musical instruments).

Virtue & Co. (chemical, electrical, and photographic apparatus).

Wharton, W. Hewley (general merchandise).

White, E. T. (American lumber, feed, provisions, and wines).

Wieting & Richter (American flour).

Liquor merchants.

Baptista, João.

Bayley, B. S.

Birch & Co.

Booker Bros. & Co.

Brazão, José Antonio.

Chapman, J. I.

Colonial Company, Limited.

Conrad & Co., Herman.

Conrad & Son.

Correiro, M.

Crosby & Forbes.

Currie & Co., Donald.

Da Costa, J. S.

D'Aguiar, Claudino B. R.

D'Aguiar, José Gomes.

Da Mattos, T. A.

D'Andrade, A. A.

D'Andrade, Joaquin.

De Freitas & Co., J. G.

De Paiva, Manoel.

De Souza, F. F.

D'Gouveia, M. Gomes.

D'Oliveira, P.

Dos Santos, J. P.

Dos Santos, Silvestre.

Faria, José De Franca.

Farinha & Co.

Ferreira, Antonio.

Ferreira, Remigio.

Ferreira, T. A.

Ferreira & Co.

Garnett & Co.

Gomes, Antonio.

Gomes, José Soares.

Gonsalves, Jacintho.

Gonsalves & Co.

GEORGETOWN—Continued.

Liquor merchants—Continued.

Henriques, J. J.

Jardin & Co.

Jardin, José Gomes.

Jonge & Smith.

Ledoux & Co., Henri.

Lee Kang.

Little & Co., Geo.

Macquarrie, C. J.

Psaila, L.

Ramsay, Hill & Co.

Rodrigues, Maria R.

Roza, J. S. F.

Silvano, J. & María.

Silvano, J. & J. G.

Smith Bros.

Teixeira, María B.

Viera, J. Baptista.

White, E. T.

Music stores.

Baldwin & Co.

Colbeck, W. R.

D'Oliveyra & Co., E.

Gale, C. H.

Strong, H.

Thomson, James.

Paints, oils, varnishes, etc.

Da Silva, Abel María.

Da Silva & Gonsalves, Abel.

Rodgers, A.

Smith & Co., James.

Photographers.

Siza, Julio A.

Stevens, Prof. W. H.

Plumbers.

Barry, Richard.

Burgess, J. H.

Ford, Earnest.

Forte, H. A.

Gaskin, Samuel.

Harris, Jas. H.

Prescod, H.

Price, Robt.

Printers and publishers.

Applewhaite, Jas.

"A União Portugueza" office.

GEORGETOWN—Continued.

Printers and publishers—Continued.

Baldwin & Co.
Hinds, W. H.
Jardine, C. K.
"Nugget" office.
Semple, D. M., manager Government printing office.
Thomson, James.
Valladares & Co.

Provisions.

Baptista, João.
Chong & Co., C. S.
Collier & Son.
Conrad & Co., Herman.
De Faria, Augusto Caesar.
Demerara Crushed Feed and Grocery Company.
Ferreira & Co.
Forbes & Co.
Hing Cheong & Co.
Isaacson & Co., H.
Klein & Co., Joseph.
Main Street Dispensary, E. T. White, manager.
Scott & Co.
Van Nooten & Co.

Saddlers.

Austin, Jos.
De Rooy & Co., J. W.
Drayton, John C.
Edghill & Co., P. E.
Emerson, Albert.
Estwick, John D.
Fernandes Bros.
Grainger, Wm.
Knox & Co.
Ouckama, D.
Young, S. H.

Soda-water manufacturers.

Alty & Co., J. D.
Birch & Co.
Macquarrie, C. J.
Virtue & Co.

Steam sawmills.

Bugle's Sawmill.
Charlestown Sawmill.

GEORGETOWN—Continued.

Steam sawmills—Continued.

D'Andrade Bros. Sawmill.
Georgetown Sawmill.
Kingston Woodworking Factory.
La Pénitence Woodworking Company.

Tailoring establishments.

Applewhaite, P. H.
Brathwaite & Smyth.
Carew, S. A.
Estwick, Jos.
Ford, W.
Keizar, T.
Lord, G. N.
Mapp, Wm. F. T.
Moe, W. A.
Ouckama, D.
Parris, L. E.
Parris, Wm.
Quenteon, Wm. M.
Robinson, J. L.
Seales, J.
Smith, Isaac T.
Thompson, Samuel.
Wallace & Co.
Yearwood, D. D.

Timber merchants.

Birch & Co.
Bugle, M.
D'Andrade Bros.
Fernandes, Manoel.
Georgetown Sawmill.
Gonsalves, Antonio, sr.
Gonsalves, José, and Wm. Shields.
Huthersall, W. H.
La Pénitence Woodworking Company.
Lopes, M. J.

Umbrellas.

Da Silva, A.
Da Silva, Manoel.

Watchmakers and jewelers.

Abraham, jr., B. V.
Kaufman & Co., R. T.
Peppiette & Co., C. W.
Sargent & Co., T. M.
Schüler & Sons, J. A. W.

S. Ex. 8, pt. 11——21

322 BRITISH COLONIES.

British Honduras.

BELIZE.

Bootmakers.
  Bain, A.
  Bogle, James.
  Butcher.
  Ewers, J. C.
  Heusner, Jacob.
  Lind, Henry.
  M'Lachlan, James.
  Selgado, Francis.
  Williams, K. H.

Builders.
  Andueza, Francisco.
  Arnold, James C.
  Cattouse, E.
  Coffin, J.
  Elliot, John.
  Escolastico, Cancino.
  Fairweather, Benjamin.
  Genoris.
  Horn, Henry.
  Kevlin, Henry.
  M'Donald, John.
  Munnings, John.
  Myvett, C.
  Ottley, Charles B.
  Percival, George.
  Reneau, Benjamin.
  Reneau, James Wesley.
  Shield, George.
  Stain, St. Clair.
  Trapp, James.
  Wagner, John K.

Carriages.
  Andueza, Francisco.
  Clarke, Ellen.
  Harding, Alexander.
  Harley, John.
  Munoz, Juan N.

BELIZE—Continued.

*Carriages—*Continued.
  O'Neal, James.
  Reyes, Marshal.

Chemists and druggists.
  Gray & Co., Thomas.
  Hunter, Alexander.

Exporters.
  Aikman, W. G. (India rubber, hides tortoise shell, and logwood).
  Beattie & Co. (mahogany and logwood).
  Belize Estate and Produce Company (mahogany, logwood, cocoanuts, tortoise shell, fustic, ziricote, and rubber).
  Binney & Co., William (logwood, tortoise shell, rubber, and sugar).
  Cramer & Co. (mahogany, logwood, hides, skins, India rubber, rosewood, and fustic).
  Harley, John (India rubber, fruit, and cocoanut).
  Heusner, Jacob (hides).
  Lind & Co. (hides, skins, sarsaparilla, and sponges.)
  Mutrie, Arthur and Currie (mahogany, logwood, sugar, India rubber, sarsaparilla, and skins).
  Steven Bros. & Co. (logwood, fustic, ziricote, mahogany, rum, and sugar.)

Grocers.
  Bernstein, Henry.
  Davidson, Henry.
  Harley, John.
  Ho Pun.
  Leon, Peter.
  Lopez, I. N.
  Muñoz, Juan.

BELIZE—Continued.

*Grocers—*Continued.
O'Neal, James.
Perez, Agustin.

Importers.
Aikman, W. G. (merchandise of all kinds).
Beattie & Co. (merchandise of all kinds).
Beatty, Alex. (provisions, etc.).
Beeks, Alfred (provisions, etc.).
Belize Estate and Produce Company (merchandise of all kinds).
Bernstein, H. (provisions, etc.).
Binney, Niven & Co. (merchandise of all kinds).
Brinton, A. H. (merchandise of all kinds).
Brodie & Co. (merchandise of all kinds).
Cramer & Co. (merchandise of all kinds).
Cuevas & Co. (drugs and oilmen's stores).
Cuthbert Bros. (merchandise of all kinds).
Gansz, Henry (merchandise of all kinds).
Gentle & Co., John (merchandise of all kinds).
Gray & Co. (drugs and oilmen's stores).
Harley, John (lumber, oilmen's stores, and provisions).
Heitler, Sigismund (provisions,etc.).
Heusner, Jacob (boots and shoes).
Ho Pun & Son (provisions, etc.).
Krug & Oswald (general merchandise).
Lind & Co., Henry (boots, shoes, and leather goods).
Moir & Jenkyns (drugs and oilmen's stores).
Morlan, A. E. (watches, clocks, jewelry,sewing machines,and notions).
Muñoz, Juan N. (provisions, etc.).
Mutrie, Arthur and Currie (general merchandise).

BELIZE—Continued.

*Importers—*Continued.
O'Neal, Jas. (provisions, etc.).
Pahmeyer & Co., C. (general merchandise).
Peters, Charles (provisions, etc.).
Stephen, Matthew (provisions, etc.).
Steven Bros. & Co. (general merchandise and lumber).
Trumbach, H. F. (provisions, etc.).
Vernon, C. M. (provisions, etc.).
Wolffsohn, Sally (provisions, etc.).

Jewelers.
Connair, John H.
Morlan, A. E.
Vega, M. F.

Printing offices.
"Angelus" Press.
Banham & Goodrich.
"Belize Independent."
Caines, R.
"Colonial Guardian" printing office.

Saddler.
MacLachlan, James.

Soda-water manufacturers.
Ganz, Henry.
Peters, Charles.
Vernon, Charles M

Undertakers.
Andueza, Francisco.
Fairweather, Benjamin.

Upholsterers.
Dennis, George.
Raboteau, George.

Watchmaker.
Mortan, A. E.

PUNTA GORDA.

Merchants.
Pearce, Levi (exporter of sugar).
Wells, D. S. (exporter of rosewood and ivory nuts, importer of general merchandise.)

STANN CREEK.

Importers of general merchandise.
Genico & Kuylen.

Dominica.

Exporters, general.
Bellot, G. L.
Bellot, John.
Garraway & Co., James.
Giraud & Co., L. A.
Hamilton, Henry.
Macintyre, Wm.
Riviere & Co., A. D.
Stedman & Co., Wm.
Tavernier, J. G.

Importers.
André, Wm. A.
Bellot, G. L.
Bellot, John.
Celestin, Augustin.
Dawbiney & Co., E. S.
Dupigny, W. J. A.
Duverney, Augustus.
Duverney, Eugene.
Emanuel, Augustus.

Importers—Continued.
Eriché, Wm. L.
Garraway & Co., Jas.
Giraud, Chas.
Giraud & Co., L. A.
Gordon, R. H.
Hamilton, Henry.
Joseph, Lucien.
Joseph, Benoît F.
Lionne, C.
Lockhart, A. R.
Macintyre, Wm.
Newman & Co., E.
O'Brien, Stephen.
Potter, F.
Riveiro & Co., D. O.
Riviere & Co., A. D.
Stedman & Co., Wm.
Tavernier, J. G.
Tavernier, J. F.

Falkland Islands.

STANLEY.

Importers.

The Falkland Islands Co. | Williams, Charles.

Grenada.

Banks.
Colonial Bank.
Grenada Savings Bank.

Exporters of cocoa.
Hubbard & Co., A.
Martin, Dean & Co.
Steele & Co., W.

Importers.
Beckwith, H. B. (dry goods, wines, etc.).
Franks, Antonio.
Franks, Samuel.
Hubbard & Co., A. (foodstuffs, lumber, etc.).

Importers—Continued.
Jardine, George.
La Mothe & Cassar. .
Marrast & Co., F. (dry goods, wines, etc.).
Martin, Dean & Co. (foodstuffs, lumber, etc.).
Murray, Wm.
McNielly & Co., John.
Simmons & Co., Wm.
Steele & Co., W. (foodstuffs, lumber, etc.).
Webster & Co., D. (dry goods, wines, etc.).

Jamaica.

ANNATTO BAY.

Bank.
 Colonial Bank (branch).

Merchants.
 Dias, I. C. (groceries and provisions).
 Henriques, F. C. (drugs).
 Henriques, Nathaniel (boots and shoes).

BLACK RIVER.

Exporters.
 Daly, R. B.
 Hendricks & Co.
 Isaacs, C. E. (general produce).
 Leyden Bros.

Importers.
 Clark, I. (millinery and drapery).
 Daly, R. B. (provisions).
 Hendricks & Co. (commission and general merchants).
 Isaacs, C. F.
 Leyden Bros.

Merchants.
 Hendricks & Co. (groceries and provisions).
 Leyden & Farquharson (boots and shoes, drugs, sewing machines).

BROWN'S TOWN.

Merchants.
 Delgado, C. P. (groceries and provisions).
 Levy, I. H. (general merchant and importer).

DRY HARBOR.

Merchants.
 Beverland, Robt. (drugs).
 Nash & Co. (drugs).

FALMOUTH.

Bank.
 Colonial Bank (branch).

Exporters.
 Kerr & Co., J. E.
 Kerr, Wm.
 Nunes & Co., R. B.
 Sloan, Mungo (island produce).

Importers.
 Delgado Bros. (foodstuffs and dry goods merchants).
 Kerr & Co., J. E.
 Lindo & Co., S. D.
 Nunes & Co., R. B.

Merchants.
 Delgado Bros. (drugs).
 Nunes, Robert (drugs, groceries, &c.).

KINGSTON.

Banks.
 Colonial Bank.
 Government Savings Bank.
 Penny Savings Bank.
 People's Discount and Deposit Company (limited).

Booksellers and stationers.
 Aarons, Alfred T.
 De Cordova & Co.

KINGSTON—Continued.

Booksellers and stationers—Continued.
De Souza, Mortimer C.
Gardner & Co., Aston W.
Hylton, Arthur.
Kerr & Co., J. W.
McCarthy, Justin.
McCartney & Co.
Rouse & Co.
Wesleyan Book Store.

Boots and shoes.
Alexander, M. M.
Bewley, Joseph.
Brandon, Joseph.
Burke, J. Milo.
Burrow, Joseph.
Cassis, John.
Dazevedo, Elias C.
Dick & Abbott.
Ellis & Co.
Hepburn, McCarthy & Co.
Joseph, S. Louis.
Largood, Thomas.
L'Azevedo, Elias C.
Lindo, Henry.
Malabre & Co., Arnold L.
Millingen, Charles.
Morales, A. H.
Motta, Daniel I.
Nathan & Co.
Parks & Burrows.
Pawsey & Co., Alfred.
Pinnock, Bailey & Co.
Recurero & Co., R.
Sargood, Thomas.
Silburn, J. C.
Sutherland, A. N.

Builder.
Roussfau, Paul L.

Carriage and wagon manufacturers and dealers.
Aguilar, Thos. N.
Brent, Alfred.
De Cordova & Son, G. J.
De Lonza, Reginald.
Goring, G.

KINGSTON—Continued.

Carriage and wagon manufacturers and dealers—Continued.
Hunt, A.
Martin & Spicer.
Turnbull, Mudon & Co.
Wales Bros.
Cattle food.
Myers, Fred L.
Cigars and tobacco.
Chacon & Co., L.
Duran & Co., S. V.
Mercado & Co., Lascelles de.
Coal.
McDowell, James H.
Soutar & Co.
Commission merchants.
Ahwe, Albert.
Alexander, M. M.
Boettcher & Co., G.
Bolton & Son, B.
Braham & Son, R. B.
Burke & Bro., G. Eustace.
Campbell, Geo. A.
Cody, H. W.
Colthirst & Co., Davidson.
De Cordova & Son, G. J.
Delgado, Son & Co.
Facey, Geo. S.
Fegan & Co., John C.
Finke & Co.
Fugner & Co., W. M. G.
George & Branday.
Iles, Henry A.
Jesurum, James A.
Levy & Co., Chas.
Lewis, G. C. H.
Lyons & Son, Emanuel.
McDowell, Jas. H.
Mercado & Co., Lascelles de.
Morais, Gerald A.
Schiller & Co.
Simon & Co.
Soutar & Co.
Stern, H.
Stevenson & Co., D.
Stines, B.
Wray & Nephew, J.

328 BRITISH COLONIES.

KINGSTON—Continued.

Drugs.

Anveay, P. E.
Bolton & Son.
Crossman, John M.
Crosswell, J. M.
Curphey & Co., Thos. J.
Evans, F. R.
Kinkead, Ed. D.
McCarthy, Justin.
McPherson & Co., W. R.
Mercado & Co., Lascelles de.
Pawsey & Co., Alfred.
Recuero, M. E.
Sautter, W. N.

Dry goods.

Aarons, Judith.
Alexander & Co., Frederick.
Anderson & Jacobsen.
Barrow, Chas. S.
Benjamin, P. A.
Bewley, Joseph.
Brandon, Jacob.
Burke, J. Milo.
Burrow, Joseph.
Cohen, Hyman.
Cox, Isaiah.
Da Costa, M. P.
Da Costa & Co., S. M.
Dazevedo, Elias C.
Dewdney & Co.
Dick & Abbott.
Ellis & Co.
Finke & Co.
Hepburn, McCarthy & Co.
Ledward, E. A.
Lindo, Henry.
Maduro, Brandon & Co.
Malabre & Co., Arnold L.
McCarthy, Justin.
McPherson & Co., W. R.
Millingen, Charles.
Morales, A. H.
Motta, Daniel I.
Nathan & Co.
Parks & Burrows.
Pawsey & Co., Alfred.
Pinnock, Bailey & Co.

KINGSTON—Continued.

Dry goods—Continued.

Sargood, Thomas.
Schiller & Co.
Sutherland, A. N.
Turnbul & Co.
Young & Co., W. G.

Furniture.

Aguilar, Thos. N.
Berry & Son, Alex.
Facey, Geo. L.
Fegan & Co., John C.
Hendricks, Mark C.
Turnbul, Mudon & Co.

General merchandise.

Aguilar, Thos. N.
Akin, Alexander.
Alexander, M. M.
Alexander, Thadeus J.
Ashenheim & Co., Solomon.
Colthirst & Co., Davidson.
Commercial Exchange.
Corcoso & Co., E.
De Cordova & Co.
Facey, Geo. S.
Fegan & Co.
Hendricks, Mark C.
Iles, Henry A.
Lordly & Son, A. J.
Malabre & Co., Arnold L.
McCarthy, Justin.
Mercado & Co., Lascelles de.
Mordecai & Co., A.
Munro, Archibald.
Stern, H.

Groceries and provisions.

Abrahams, Horatio.
Anvray, P. E.
Bevike & Bros., G. Eustace.
Boettcher & Co., G.
Cody, H. W.
Corcoso & Co., E.
Crosswell, John M.
Curphey & Co., Thos. J.
Delapenha, Uriah.
Delgado, Son & Co.
Delisser, Andrew.
Grant, Charles.

KINGSTON—Continued.

Groceries and provisions—Continued.
Hart, A. B.
Hart, John J.
Henriques, David P. C.
Kinkead, Ed. D.
Levy, Mose.
Levy & Co., Chas.
Lewis, G. C. H.
Lewis, J. J. G.
McMillan, A. C.
McPherson, W. G.
Mercado & Co., Lascelles de.
Millengen, Joseph.
Morrice, Alfred.
Myers, Fred. L.
Nunes, Theo.
Pinnock, Bailey & Co.
Recuero, M. E.
Saulter, W. N.
Scott, J. Watson.
Sehloss & Co., S. L.
Stevenson & Co., D.
White, Richard.

Haberdashers.
Lopez, jr., C. A.
Scott, Andrew M.

Hardware and agricultural implements.
Henderson & Co., David.
Hendriks, Mark C.
Lazarus & Co., Charles P.
Lyons & Son, Emanuel.
Malabre & Co., Arnold L.
Martin & Spicer.
Middleton & Co., J. W.

Hats.
Chipps, Scott & Co.

Importers.
Alexander, M. M.
Alexander, Thadeus J.
Ashenheim & Co., Solomon.
Colthirst & Co., Davidson.
Correosso & Co., F.
De Cordova & Co.
Fegan & Co., John C.
Gomes, Casseres & Co.
Iles, Henry A.

KINGSTON—Continued.

Importers—Continued.
Joseph, S. Louis.
Mercado & Co., Lascelles de.
Mordecai & Co., A.
Munro, Archibald.
Stern, H.
Sutherland, A. N.

Iron and brass founders.
Lazarus & Co., Charles P.

Ironmongers.
Dicks Bros.
Henderson & Co., David.
Lyons & Son, Emanuel.
Malabre & Co., Arnold.
Martin & Spicer.
Middleton & Co., J. W.

Jewelry and watches.
Alexander & Co., Frederick.
Burton, Charles.
Hylton, Arthur.
Martin & Spicer.
Mercado & Co., Lascelles de.
Milke & Bros., J. H.
Milke & Co., J. O.
Millholland, John.
Whitbourne, J. W.

Liquor dealers.
Crosswell, John M.
Desnoes & Son, Peter.
Finzi & Co., Daniel.
Haffdleen, Chas. T.
Henriques, David P. C.,
Leon & Co., Emil X.
McMillan, A. C.
Mercado & Co., Lascelles de.
Recuero, M. E.
Schloss & Co., S. L.
Simon & Co.
Sutherland, A. N.
Turnbul & Co.
West India Brewing Co.
Wray & Nephew, J.

Lumber.
Feurtado, Alex.
Lyons & Son, Emanuel.
Malabre & Co., Arnold L.

KINGSTON—Continued.

Mineral waters.
Da Costa & Co., S. M.
Fegan & Co., John C.
Martin & Spicer.

Musical instruments.
Berry & Son, Alexander.
Fegan & Co., John C.
Martin & Spicer.
Winkler & Co., Louis.

Photographers.
Bavastro, O.
Cleary, I. W.
Macpherson, R. J.
Marby, I. N.
Valdes & Co., I. B.

Produce dealers.
Jamaica Coöperation Fruit and Trading Company.
Jamaica Fruit and Vegetable Association.

Saddlery and harness.
Agton, T.
Da Costa, M. P.
McDonald, John.
Sinclair, Henry.

Sewing machines.
Da Costa, M. P.
Gomes, Casseres & Co.
Maduro, Brandon & Co.
Nathan & Co.
Recuero & Co., R.

Spectacles. •
Milke & Co., J. O.

- *Sugar.*
Correoso & Co., E.
Mercado & Co., Lascelles de.
Schloss & Co., S. L.

Tailors.
Arnaboldi, Chas. A.
Brock & Co., C. S.
Burke, J. Milo.
Lay & Couch.
Pawsey & Co., Alfred.

Unclassified.
Burley, J.

KINGSTON—Continued.

Unclassified—Continued.
Forwood, W. P.
Harrison, Thomas.
Jackson, Robert.
Levien & Sherlock.
Levy, George.
Verley & Co., Robinson.
Wood, Charles J.

Undertakers.
Aguilar, Thos. N.
Berry & Son, Alex.
Hendriks, Mark C.
Turnbull, Mudon & Co.

Wall paper.
Burke, John Milo.
McPherson & Co., W. R.
Nathan & Co.

LUCCA.

Merchants.
Browne & Co. (groceries and provisions).
Santfleben & Sons (drugs).

MANDEVILLE.

Merchants.
Braham, R. B.
Casseres, N. Gomez.
Casseres, B. D. J.
Isaacs, Lionel (drugs).
Sturridge & Co., Geo.

MONTEGO BAY.

Bank.
Colonial Bank.

Merchants.
Corrinaldi, G. L. P. (general merchant and importer).
Kerr & Co., J. E. (drugs, ale and beer, groceries and provisions).
Parkin, J. W.

MORANT BAY.

Merchants.
Cresser & Co. (drugs).
Marchalleck & Co., D. (groceries and provisions).
Mordecai & Co., I. J. (boots, shoes, drugs).

OLD HARBOR.

Merchants.

Delgado & Co. (groceries and provisions).

Melhado Bros. & Co. (groceries and provisions).

PORT ANTONIO.

Merchants.

Boston Fruit Co.

Cunningham, I. J. (groceries and provisions).

Gideon, David S. (drugs, boots and shoes).

Jamaica Fruit and Trading Co.

Mordecai, Lionel M. (drugs, boots and shoes, sewing machines).

PORT MARÍA.

Merchants.

Da Costa, A. L. (ale and beer, boots and shoes, drugs, groceries and provisions, sewing machines).

Goff & Co. (drugs, groceries and provisions).

Kerr & Co., J. E. (groceries, provisions and liquors).

Sweetland, A. L. (drugs).

PORT MORANT.

Merchants.

Carter & Co.

Crawford, R. W. (drugs).

ST. ANNS BAY.

Merchants.

Bravo Bros. & Co. (drugs).

Cotter, Silvester (drugs).

Fraser, L. L. (groceries and provisions).

Isaacs, Solomon.

Solomon & Co., M. (general merchandise).

SAV-LA-MAR.

Bank.

Colonial Bank.

Merchants.

Jones & Co., Herbert (drugs, groceries and provisions).

Leyden & Co. (drugs).

Neilson & Co. (general).

Segree, I. S. (drugs).

SPANISH TOWN.

Merchants.

Boettcher & Co., G.

Rees, G. H.

Montserrat.

Importers.
Burke, H.
Burke, P.
Collins, J. C.
Dyett, H.
Goodall, Jas. S.
Johnson, Mrs. E.
Irish, Geo. H.

Importers—Continued.
Hannan, R.
Lynch & Co.
Lynch, Jos. H.
Loving, J. M.
Walton, Wm.
Wilkin, Wm. H.
Wilkin, York.

Nevis.

Importers.
Bell, J. D.
Briggs, Joseph.
Burke, Wm. H.
Esdaile, C. P.
Damell, Wm. S.
Greaves, C. C.
Green, Wm. H.

Importers—Continued.
Gumbo, W.
James & Co., A.
Kirkwood & Co., R. R.
Maynard, Edward.
Pemberton, Wm.
Simmonds, Chas. H.
Van Romondt & Co., A.

St. Christopher or St. Kitts.

Importers and exporters.
Andrew, J. (dry goods).
Archer & Co., L. H. (general commission).
Berridge, T. P.
Branch, John.
Berkeley, J. H. H.
Ellis, E. J.
Delisle, E. S.
Farara, I. (lumber).
Fraites, A. (breadstuffs and provisions).
Fereira, Joaquin.
Gould, I. R. (breadstuffs and provisions).
Horne, George (dry goods).
Horsford & Co., S. L. (plantation supplies).
Kirkwood & Co., R. R. (dry goods and groceries).

Importers and exporters—Continued.
McKay, N.
McNish, T.
Meggs, M. (dry goods).
Napier, W. E. S.
Payson, Edward.
Pistana, E. (breadstuffs and provisions).
Procope, F. (breadstuffs and provisions).
Rodrigues, E. T. (breadstuffs and provisions).
Ryan, H. M.
Shelford, S.
Todd, E. G.
Wade & Abbott (breadstuffs, cooperage and lumber).
Wattley & Co. (general commission).
Williams, W. (dry goods).

Stª Lucia.

CASTRIES.

Bank.
Colonial Bank.
Merchants, general.
Augier & Plummer (dry goods).
Barnard & Co., Peter (general provisions and coal).
Belmar & Sons (dry goods).
Crawford & Monplasir (dry goods).
Du Boulay & Co. (dry goods).

CASTRIES—Continued.

Merchants, general—Continued.
Langellier & Co., Roger(dry goods, wines, etc.).
Macfarlane, jr., & Co. (provisions and general merchandise).
Macfarlane, Moffat & Co. (dry goods, wines, etc.).
Minvielle & Chastanet (coal, dry goods, provisions, etc.).

St. Vincent.

Importers.
Porter & Co., D. K.
Simmons & Co., C. J
Smith, Alexander.

Importers—Continued.
Smith, George.
Smith, William.
Wyllie, David.

Tobago.

SCARBOROUGH.

Importers of general merchandise.
Agard & Co., Geo.
Blakeley, jr., Thomas.
Carew & Hope.
Date, William.
Briggs, Augustus.
Hamilton, James.
Haynes, Hendy & Co.

SCARBOROUGH—Continued.

Importers of general merchandise—Cont'd.
Henderson & Co.
Heens & Co., Edward.
Isaacs & Co., S. B.
Lees, Benj.
McCall & Co., John.
Murdock, Richard.
Pautin, Henry.

Trinidad.

PORT OF SPAIN.

Ales, beer and porter.
Campbell, Hannay, Campbell & Co.
Clairmonte & Co.
Gordon, Grant & Co.
Schorner & Co.
Turnbull, Stewart & Co.

Breadstuffs and provisions.
Agostini & Co., Leon.
Ambard, L. F.
Archer & Co., Julian H.
Attale, Jules E.
Atwell, James.
Boissiere, Eugene.
Campbell, Hannay, Campbell & Co.
Cipriani, Jules.
Clairmonte & Co.
Cumming & Co., A.
Drennan & Co., J.
Futriner & Ramsay.
Gordon, Grant & Co.
Grell, Ellis.
Hayley & Co., C. L.
Lee Lum & Co.
Llanos & Co.
Michinaux, L. L.
New York and Bermudez Co.
Norman, W.
Ortiz, J. M.
Robertson, W. S.
Rodriguez, Sons & Co.
Schjolseth & Hollex.
Schock & Co., C.

PORT OF SPAIN—Continued.

Breadstuffs and provisions—Continued.
Schoener & Co.
Singuineau & Co.
Smith, M. H.
Tripp & Co., Edgar.
Turnbull, Stewart & Co.

Bookbinders.
Luce, E.
Spooner, Harry.

Boots and shoes.
Galt & Co.
Goodwille, G.
Herbert, M. H.
Miller, Bros.
Monceaux, H.
Wilson & Co.
Wilson, Son & Co.

Chinese and Japanese goods.
Lee Lum & Co.
Quong Lee & Co.

Cocoa merchants.
Anduzi & Co.
Borde Bros.
Carry, Leonard.
Centano, Leon.
Drago & Co., José.
Fabian & Son, Charles.
Ganteaume, Tinoco & Co.
Houghton & Co.
Kernahan, W.
Leotaud, C.
Llanos & Co.

PORT OF SPAIN—Continued.

Cocoa merchants—Continued.
Louis & Co.
Ponjados, Cipriano.
. Prada & Co., C.

Commission merchants.
Alston & Co.. George R.
Ambard, L. F.
Anduze & Co., J.
Bosch & Co.
Colonial Co. (Limited).
Finlayson & Co., T. A.
Grell, Ellis.
Harriman & Co., I. N.
Lambie, G.
Leotaud, C.
Lyon, I. C.
Michinaux, L. L.
New York & Bermudez Co.
Ross, W. S.
Rust, Randolph.
Schock & Co., C.
Spiers, George.
Stiven, Robert.
Toppin & Co., J. S.
Tripp & Co., Edgar.
Turnbull, Stewart & Co.
Wainwright, E. J.

Contractors and builders.
Graham, N. F.
Johnston, J. J.
Saurmann, Carl.
Turnbull, Stewart & Co.
Worrell, J.

Drugs, chemicals, confectionery, perfumes etc.
Alcazar, L. I.
Bock, C. O.
Boland, A. E.
Innis & Son, A. L.
Mills, W. H.
Ramsay, P. A.
Reis, J. F.
Richards & Co., Alfred.
Ross, W. C.
Silva & Co., J. D. de.
Taitt & Son.

PORT OF SPAIN—Continued.

Dry goods and general merchandise.
Alcazar, J.
Blanc & Co., J. M.
Boissiere & Park.
Bodu & Co., L.
D'Ade & Co.. J. G.
Delorme & Co.
Galt & Co.
Geoffroy, J.
Geoffroy, L.
Goodwille, Geo.
Herbert, M. H.
Hoadley, John.
Innis, Paul.
Johnston & Co., J. F.
Lafargue Bros.
Lamy, Arnold.
Lamy, Jules.
Metivier, J. R.
Miller Bros.
Miller, James.
Perreira & Co., S.
Skeoch, James.
Smith Bros. & Co.
Watronville, E.
Wilson & Co.
Wilson, Son & Co.

Founders.
Este, Patrick.
Malcomie, C.
Read, I.
Wishart, James.

Furniture.
Borberg, E.
D'Ade & Co., J. G.
Haley & Co., C. L.
Miller Bros.
Monceaux, H.
Todd & Sons, James.

Glassware, crockery and lamps.
Borberg, E.
Bourbon, H.
Deiroses, J. E.
Doyon, L.
Haley & Co., C. L.
Knox, Arnold.

PORT OF SPAIN—Continued.

Glassware, crockery, etc.—Continued.
Leon, Mathieu & Co.
Todd & Sons, James.
Traverno & Perez.

Groceries, canned goods, etc.
Baptista, Querino.
Brown, Frank.
Crouey & Co.
Haley & Co., C. L.
Haynes, Charles.
Knox, Arnold.
McGruer & Yuille.
Muir, Marshall & Co.
Rapsey, J. A.
Yuille, Andrew.

Hardware, saddlery, etc.
André, P. B.
Arnott, Lambie & Co.
Gerold & Sherer.
Hunter & Co.
Fitzwilliam & Co., George.
Léon, Mathieu & Co.
Nestor, A.
Turnbull, Stewart & Co.
Urich & Son, F.
Zurcher & Co., F.

Hides and horns.
Urich & Son, F.
Zurcher & Co., F.

Housefurnishing goods.
Borberg, E.
D'Ade & Co., J. G.
Haley & Co., C. L.
Knox, Arnold.
Miller Bros.
Miller, James.
Mouceaux, D.
Todd & Sons, James.

Importers and exporters.
Alcazar, John (dry goods).
Barcant & Co. (jewelry).
Bolland, Ant. E. (drugs).
Borberg, E. (glass and china ware).
Cabral Luiz, A. M. (provisions).
Clairmonte & Co.

S. Ex. 8, pt. 11——22

PORT OF SPAIN—Continued.

Importers and exporters—Continued.
Colonial Co. (Limited).
Crawford, F. E. (ironwork, brass castings, etc.).
Dalgleisch & Co. (dry goods).
Dècle, Alexander (clocks and watches).
Des Roses, Ernest (hardware).
Donnatien, John A. (jewelry).
Fabian & Son, Charles.
Fitzwilliam & Co., George (hardware).
Ford & Hutchinson (books, etc.).
Galt & Co. (boots, shoes, and dry goods).
Geoffroy & Co., J. (dry goods and ironmongery).
Gerold & Scherer (hardware).
Gibbs, Geo. B.
Gomez, J. M.
Goodwille, George (draper and outfitter).
Haley & Co., C. L. (ice, provisions, wines and spirits).
Harriman & Co., J. N.
Herbert, M. H. (dry goods, outfitter and tailor).
Hive, Adolphe (jewelry).
Hoadley, John (tailor and outfitter).
Hunter & Co. (hardware).
Miller Bros.
Miller, James (general stores).
Monceaux, H. (boots and shoes, hats, furniture, and pianos).
Muir, Marshall & Co. (stationery, etc.).
New York and Bermudas Co.
Ramsay, P. A. (drugs).
Ribeiro, Joaquim (provisions).
Ribeiro, Joseph J. (spirits).
Richards & Co., Alfred (drugs).
Ross, W. C. (drugs).
Schoener & Co. (general merchandise.)
Siegert & Sons., J. G. B.
Skeoch, James (dry goods).

PORT OF SPAIN—Continued.

Importers and exporters—Continued.

Smith Bros. & Co. (dry goods).
Strong, H. (pianos and music).
Taitt & Sons (drugs).
Todd & Sons, James (hardware, earthenware, and chinaware).
Toppin & Co., I. S. (provisions).
Traverso & Perez (watches and jewelry).
Tripp & Co., Edgar (general merchandise).
Urich & Son, F. (hardware).
Williamson, W. K. (photographic apparatus).
Wilson, Son & Co.

Jewelry, etc.

Barcant, C.
Beaupatre, M. Aumatre.
David, Leonidas.
Decle, sr., Alexander.
Decle, jr., Alexander.
Donnetieu, Alexander.
Georges, Paul.
Hire, Adolphe.
Marcano, J. B.
Renaud, Charles.
Todd & Sons, James.
Traverso & Perez.

Lumber.

Cumming & Co., A.
Gordon, Grant & Co.
Government Mills.
Graham, N. F.
Newbold, R. S.
Turnbull, Stewart & Co.

Merchant tailors.

Gonzales, Philip.
Goodwille, George.
Herbert, M. H.
Miller, James.

Musical instruments.

D'Ade & Co., J. G.
Monceaux, H.
Perreira & Co., S.
Strong, H.
Todd & Sons, James.

PORT OF SPAIN—Continued.

Photographers.

Cazabon, C.
Micheaux, L.
Morin, J.

Printers.

Lewis, Joseph.
Naughlin, T. R. N.
Rostant, Philip.

Shipbuilders.

Armstrong, H. W.
Charbonnier, J.
Harvey, James.
Thwaites, William.
Tronchin, J.

Trunks, etc

Guy, Edward.
Louisy, I.

SAN FERNANDO.

Commission merchants.

Allman, W. B.
Alston & Co., I. C. (dry goods, glassware, etc.).
Brown, Chas. (provisions).
Burt, A. (general merchandise).
Clerk, W. S. (draperies).
Cunningham, Thompson & Co. (general merchandise).
Dalgleish & Co., I. (dry goods).
Donawa, Grecian & Co., (dry goods).
Drennan & Co.
Edward, Philip (draperies).
Leoland & Knox.
Plowden, I. A. (general outfitter).
Robertson, W. S.
Tennants Agency.

Importers and exporters, general merchandise.

Bonyun, L. W.
Bourjonis, F.
Burt, A. H.
Cunningham, Thompson & Co.
Donawa, Grecian & Co.
Drennan & Co., J.
Dalgleish & Co., J.

SAN FERNANDO—Continued.

Importers and exporters, etc.—Continued.
Edward, Phillip.
Leoland & Knox.
Lewis, J. C.

SAN FERNANDO—Continued.

Importers and exporters, etc.—Continued.
Robertson, W. S.
Tennants Agency.
Turnbull, Ross & Co.

Turks Island.

COCKBURN HARBOR.

Importer of liquors.
Godet, Lewis J.

Manufacturers and exporters of salt.
Arthur, Walter G.
Godet, Lewis J.
Tatem, John W.

GRAND TURK.

Commission merchant.
Astwood, E. J. D.
Murphy, Jeremiah D.

Importers of drugs and chemicals.
Hutchings, J. Frank.
Hutchings, Hugh H.

Importers of dry goods.
Atwood, M. E.
Bascome, J. C.
Darrell, John W.
Frith, Joseph S.
Gardiner, Simeon A.
Glass, James M.
Lowe, Richard T.
Murphy, E. E.
Whitney, Albert E. A.
Whitney, D. St. Geo.

Importers of general merchandise.
Astwood, E. J. D.
Murphy, Jeremiah D.

Importers of groceries.
Astwood, M. E.
Darrell, John W.
Frith, Joseph S.
Gardiner, Simeon A.

GRAND TURK—Continued.

Importers of groceries—Continued.
Glass, James M.
Hinson, Cornelius R.
Lowe, Richard F.
Smith, F. Lindsay.
Whitney, Albert E. A.
Whitney, D. St. Geo.

Importers of liquors.
Astwood, William B.
Gardiner, William M.
Gardiner, Simeon A.

Importers of tools and machinery.
Astwood, E. J. D.
Murphy, Jeremiah D.

Manufacturers and exporters of fiber for cordage.
Astwood, E. J. D.

Manufacturers and exporters of salt.
Darrell, John W.
Durham, Joseph H.
Hinson, Cornelius R.
Murphy, Jeremiah D.
Smith, F. Lindsay.

SALT CAY.

Importers.
Harriott, Daniel F. (general merchandise).
Tatem, Anthony (dry goods, groceries and liquors).

Manufacturers and exporters of salt.
Harriott, Daniel F.
Tatem, Anthony.

DANISH WEST INDIES.

St. Croix or Santa Cruz.

CHRISTIANSTAD.

Bank.
Bank of St. Thomas.

Coal-importers.
Bartram Bros.

Dry and fancy goods.
De Chabert, H.
Frorup, N. E.
Gautier & Co.

General commission merchants.
Bartram Bros.
Heyliger, W. H.
McDougal & Co.

Provisions, wines, etc.
Armstrong & Co.
Creagh, A. G.
De Chabert, H.
Gautier & Co.
McEvoy, W.
Pentheny, W. L.
Roche, James W.
Taylor, James L.

FREDERICKSTAD.

Bank.
Colonial Bank.

FREDERICKSTAD—Continued.

Coal-importers.
Bartram Bros.

Dry and fancy goods.
Benjamin, E. L.
Ferris, R.
Henderson, A. E.
Iwerson, H. J.
Nielsen, R.
Russell Bros.
Smith, E.
Woods, W. B.

General commission merchants.
Armstrong & Co.
Bartram Bros.

Hardware.
Moore, T. M.

Provisions, wines, etc.
Fleming, W. H.
Golden, L. M.
Iwerson, H. J.
Nielsen, R.
Russell Bros.
Woods, W. B.

341

St. Thomas.

Banks.
Bank of St. Thomas.
Colonial Bank.
St. Thomas Savings Bank.

Booksellers and stationers.
Taylor, Charles E.
Wallöe, August.

Boots and shoes.
Gomez & Co., L.
Senior, R. D.

Cigars and tobacco.
Drejer & Co , F.

Commission merchants.
Abbott & Co., Jas. T.
Bach & Co.
Cameron & Co.
Jurgens & Co., J. F. D.
Lamb & Co.
Levi & Sons, Joseph.
McDougal & Co.
Sala & Co., J.
Smith & Co., G. W.

Distiller of bay oil.
Hassell, R. M.

Dry goods.
Beretta, G.
Bronsted & Co.
Carty & Co.
Castello & Co., W. B.
Daniel & Co.. C.
Delvalle & Co.
Fratelli, Copello & Co.
Levein, J.
Müller & Co., J.

Dry goods—Continued.
Pearson & Co., Charles.
Senior & Co., R.
Souffront, J. H.
Van Eps & Co., M.
White, Wm.

General provisions.
Fechtenburg & Co., J. H.
Fonseca, D. G.
Klingberg, Krebs & Co.

Hardware.
Cameron & Co.
Levi & Sons, Joseph.
McDougal & Co.

Importers and exporters.
Bornn, B.
Bronsted & Co.
Fechtenberg & Co., J. H.
Michelsen, H.
Philips & Co.
Pretto, D.
Raven & Co.
Riise, A. H.
Smith & Co., G. W.

Jewelers.
Bornn, B.
Corneiro, F. M.
Lagarde, A. de.

Photographers.
Fraas.
Giglioli, A.

Provisions, wines, etc.
Berg & Co., Louis.
Blasini, A. J.

ST. THOMAS—Continued.

Provisions, wines, etc.—Continued.
Burnot, Aug.
Delenois, Louis.
Estornel, Theodore.
Fechtenburg & Co., J. H.
Fidanque & Co., J.
Fonseca, D. G.
French & Co., O.
Jürgenson, D. H.
Klingberg, Krebs & Co.

ST. THOMAS—Continued.

Provisions, wines, etc.—Continued.
Lugo & Co., A.
Michelsen, H.
Pretto & Co., David.
Russell Bros.
Schroeder, E.
Toledano, S. H.
Toussaint, J. H., Suc.
Vauce & Co., A.

DUTCH COLONIES.

Curaçao.

CURAÇAO.

Banks.
> Banco de Hipotecas.
> Banco del Gobierno.

Chemists and druggists.
> Evertsz & Co., Hendrik.
> Jesurun, Frederico.
> Jones & Borchert.
> Meyer & Araujo.

Commission merchants.
> Boorn, Chris.
> Evertsz, C. & H.
> Fensohn & Co., Rivas.
> Hellmund & Co.
> Henriquez & Co., Edwards.
> Henriquez & Co., Penha.
> Jones, J. & H.
> Lima, H. A. de.
> Maduro, jr., & Co.
> Maduro & Sons, S. E. L.
> Oduber ó Hijos, Franco.
> Pietersz, J. J.
> Senior ó Hijo, Jeudah.
> Sola, M. de.
> Weeber, J.

Dry goods.
> Araujo, Elias.
> Baiz, David.
> Baiz, Prospero.
> Brandão & Marchena.
> Capriles & Co., A. D.
> Capriles, Elias.
> Capriles, Mord.

Dry goods—Continued.
> Capriles, Moses.
> Casseres jr., B. de.
> Castro, M. de.
> Correa Hermanos & Co.
> Correa, A. A.
> Correa, M. A.
> Curiel, Morris E.
> Curiel, Moses.
> Daal, H. M.
> Daal, M.
> Dania, R. N.
> Dys, J. E. van der.
> Evertsz, David.
> Evertsz, E. & J. M.
> Gorsira, J. P. E.
> Gorsira & Co., M. B.
> Gorsira, P. E.
> Haseth, C. Z. de.
> Henriquez, jr., D. D.
> Henriquez, jr., D. L.
> Henriquez & Co., Herman C.
> Henriquez, J. B.
> Henriquez, Mord C.
> Jesurun Bros.
> Jesurun, Benj.
> Jesurun, J. & D.
> Jutting ó Hijo, Chas.
> Leon & Ecker.
> Lima, jr., D. A. de.
> Lima, H. A. de.
> Maduro Bros.

CURAÇAO—Continued.

Dry goods—Continued.
 Maduro, M. S. L.
 Marchena & Co.
 Neuman, F. W.
 Obediento & Maal.
 Pardo, Jos. D.
 Penso, E. M.
 Penso, M. H.
 Pietersz & Co.
 Pinedo, Alvarez.
 Salas, Gabriel.
 Sideregts & Co.
 Valencia, D.
 Wederfoort, L.

Hardware.
 Ellis & Dania.
 Gorsira, C.
 Jones, James and Henry.
 Leyba & Co., Leon V.
 Salredo & Co., L.

Jeweler.
 Castro & Co., J. de.

Printers and publishers.
 Bethencourt é Hijos, A.
 Capriles, Aron.
 Neuman, C. J. and A. W.

Provisions.
 Baiz é Hijos, Isaac.
 Cordoze, M. and J.
 Correa, B. M. A.
 Curiel, M. F.

CURAÇAO—Continued.

Provisions—Continued.
 Curiel, M. P.
 De Sola, Jacob.
 De Veez, Henry.
 Evertsz, W. C.
 Gorsira & Maal.
 Hellmund, René.
 Henriquez, D. D.
 Henriquez, R. C.
 Jones, J. and H.
 Leyba & Co., Leon V.
 Mendez, A. M.
 Menleu, J. W. van der.
 Morisanto, Juan.
 Pietersz, H. W.
 Smith, L. B. (ice, lumber and salt).
 Sprock & Co.
 Valdeblanquez, M. C.
 Valencia, D.
 Welhous, J.
 Winkel, Christian.

Shipbuilders.
 Handel Maatschappy "Curaçao."
 Menleu, J. E. van der.

Stationers and booksellers.
 Bethencourt é Hijos, A
 Capriles, Aron.
 Neuman, C. J. and A. W.

Tailoring establishment.
 Ringeling, J. C.

St. Martin.

General merchants and importers.
Nisbet, H. O. (provisions).
Percival, H.
Richardson.
Rijnenberg.

General merchants and importers—Cont'd.
Romondt, C. M. van.
Romondt, Joseph van.
Romondt & Co., A. A. van.
Romondt & Co., D. C. van.

Dutch Guiana.

PARAMARIBO.

Bank.

Surinaamsche Bank (W. van Esveld, director).

Chemists and druggists.

Amson, L. C. van.
Amson, A. L. van.
Cabenda, W.
Coronel, M.
Gans, Mej. H. A.
Gilhuijs, H.
Hering, W. B.
Jesurun, A. M.
Klaverweide, J. J. O. S.
Leno, W. F. van der.
Meerten, J. E. van.
Seiler, G. B. J. K.
Stempel, C. van der.
Wesenhagen, A. L.

General merchants.

Alberga, S.
Amson, G. S. van.
Benjamins & Co., W.
Benjamins Gebrs.
Bixley, A. N.
Bloemendaal, I. J.
Bodeutsch, J. L.
Boer, D. de.
Bosmans, J. A.
Bromet & Co.
Bruggeman, P. A.
Brnijning, A.
Bueno, A. A.

PARAMARIBO—Continued.

General merchants—Continued.

Castilho, A. del.
Cohen & Drielsma.
Dranger, F. C. Curiel.
Emanuels, E. E.
Exel, G. B. van.
Ezechiels, J.
Fernandes, J.
Flu, P. C.
Fo-lin-Sin.
Fontaine, O.
Fuente, H. de la.
Goveia, M. J. de.
Haas, J.
Heilbron, G. P.
Heilbron, S. A.
Hoeffelman, J. P. A.
Horst, J. D.
Jong, Ma. A.
Leckie. M. J.
Leefmans, L. C.
Leijsner, R. H.
Levi, M.
Levi & Co., M. S.
Levie, S. J.
Lo Kioeng Schioe.
Loe Sack Sioe.
Lou, Aman.
Lou, Atsoen.
Louzada & Co., S.
Marcns, Erve J. L.
Mesquita, D. Bo. de.
Mesquita, W. Bo. de.

PARAMARIBO—Continued.

General merchants—Continued.

Muller-Pels, Wed. Henri.
Nahar, J. H.
Nassy, J. B. L.
Newsun, W. T.
Ong a Suie.
Parra, J. de la.
Pinto, E.
Pinto, J.
Pinto, W.
Polak, M. S.
Polak, S. M.
Poll, J. M.
Pos, J. H.
Pos, S. H.
Praag, Gebrs. van.
Praag, J. van.
Praag & Co., M. S. van.
Reelfs Gebrs.
Reminos, I. J.
Robles, J.
Robles, S. J.
Rodriguez & Co., José.
Salomons, Herman.
Salomons & Co., M. N. A.

PARAMARIBO—Continued.

General merchants—Continued.

Salomons & Co., J.
Salomons & Co., M. O.
Samson, B. M.
Samson, G. H.
Samson Gebrs.
Samuels, A.
Samuels, Jb.
Silva, Gebrs. da.
Strätei Esser & Co.
Stumpf, A. J. L.
Swift, S. M.
Taijtelbaum.
Tjon, Asam.
Vries, J. M. de.
Vries, Jacques de.
Wessels, J. J. P.
Wijngaarde, J. H.
Wong Gebrs.

Printers and publishers.

Erve, J. Morpurgo.
Heyde, B.
Labad & Zoon.
Pinto, A. J.

FRENCH COLONIES.

Guadeloupe.

BAHIE MAHAULT.

Sugar manufacturer.
Gerard frères.

BASSE TERRE.

Bank.
Banque de la Guadéloupe.
Banker.
Lacour, Arthur.
Druggists.
Beleurgey.
Maret-Mercier.
Maurice.
Souque.
Drg goods.
Daucourt, Alcide.
Duc, Frédéric.
Dufau, Léo.
Gratenel, A.
Jarrin frères.
Réaux frères.
Schmitt et Cognet.
Scauterey, G.
Hardware.
Colardeau.
Sauterey.
Importers.
Bailey & Lesaint.
Beoche, E.
Bonnet, R.
Bourjac, Alphonse.
Buffreuil & Macory.
Farreau, A.
Fleurot & Co., J.
Labordière, H.
Raimund, Am.
Tournier, L.

BASSE TERRE—Continued.

Lumber dealers.
Beoche et Cie.
Cabre et neveu.
Favreau, A.
Laurent & Co., Eugène.
Michaux, A.
Monchy, L. de.
Morau, Paul.

CAPESTERRE, GUADELOUPE.

Sugar manufacturer.
Hayot et Cie.

GRAND-BOURG, MARIE-GALANTE.

Dry goods.
Veuve Bonnet.
Sugar manufacturer.
Retz, Hippolyte de.

LE MOULE.

Bank.
Banque de la Guadéloupe.
Drugs.
Pic.
Rougé.
Dry goods.
Aimée, Ferdinand.
Dufau, Léo.
Isaac, Félicien.
Mabire et Cie., E.
Moringlane, A.
Réaux frères.
Tessonneau, J. B.
General merchants.
Duchassaing, de Fontbressin & Co.
Dufau, Léo.
Mabille, A.

349

LE MOULE—Continued.

*General merchants—*Continued.
Duchassaing de Fontbressin.
Stanley, Auguste.
Michaux, Alexandre.
Ricou, C.
Ricou, J.
Sergent, Alléaume & Co.
St. Alary, Evremont.
Vaugout, Benjamin.

MORNE À L'EAU.

Sugar manufacturer.
Compagnie Marseillaise.

PETIT-BOURG.

Sugar manufacturer.
Crédit Foncier Colonial.

PETIT-CANAL.

Sugar manufacturers.
Brumant, Beauperthuy et Cie.
Robin, Charles Magne.

POINTE-À-PITRE.

Banks.
Banque de la Guadéloupe.
Banque Transatlantique.

Druggists.
Capitaine.
Chambertrand.
Desgranges.
Duportail père et fils.
Duportail & Co., A.
Frossard.
Gédon, Emile.
Houillier.
Raymond.
Rommieu.
Sauvaire.

General commission merchants.
Boniface & Binet, Guérin.
Brumant, Beauperthuy & Co.
Carbonnel & Cie.
Collin de la Roncière, Numa.
Fleurot & Cie., Jules.
Hlie, E.
Japp, James.
La Barbe & Co., A.

POINTE-À-PITRE—Continued.

*General commission merchants—*Continued.
Lacroix et fils aîné, Amédée.
La Roncière, N. de.
Lévi, Théodore.
Monnerot et Cie., L.
Picard, A.
Romney & Seignoret.

Hardware.
Cabre et Cie., Adrian.
Dugard-Ducharmoy.
Gérard frères.
Honoré, Octave.
Lansac, H.
Melon & Co., A.

Ice companies.
American Ice Company.
R. Deumié Ice Factory.

Importers.
Advenant.
Aristo, Léodgard (boots and shoes, dry goods, confections, etc.).
Arsonneau, Nestor (dry goods, etc.).
Bailly et Cie.(provisions,wines, etc.).
Bertaud, Auguste (provisions).
Bourjac, Alphonse.
Bourjac, P. Ernest (dry goods).
Brumant, Beauperthuy & Co. (general merchandise).
Ducorp & Co., C.
Dufau et Cie., Léo (dry goods, etc.).
Fleurot & Co., J. (general merchandise).
Fleurot & Co.,E.(lumber merchants).
François-Julien, Saint-Eloi (dry goods).
Garlet, Emmanuel (dry goods).
Gobin, Emile (dry goods, etc.).
Honoré et Cie., François (dry goods, etc.).
Huet et Advenant (dry goods).
Mabire et Cie., Ernest (general merchandise).
Martialis.
Melse et Saint-Ange (dry goods, etc.).
Montcarel.

POINTE-À-PITRE—Continued.

Importers—Continued.

Moringlane, A.
Notly, Schmitt & Co.
Réaux frères.
Reynoird frères (dry goods).
Rodrigues, Honoré (dry goods, etc.).
Sarlat, Emanuel (dry goods).
Sauvaire et Cie. (lumber merchants).
Schmitt et Cognet (dry goods).
Tournier, L. (provisions).
Wolff (boots and shoes, etc.).

Jewelry.

Grellier, R.
Iphigénie, Denis.
Maugin & Co.

Liquors.

Bailly & Lesaint.
Beau, G.
Cardonnier, J.
Giraud, Léon.
Raimund, Amédée.

Ship chandler.

Wachter, A.

Sugar factories.

Alary, E. de St.
Brumant & Beauperthuy.
Cail & Co.
Chazelles, A. de.
Compagnie Sucrière Marseillaise.
Crédit Foncier.
Dubos frères.
Duchassaing, A.
Gérard frères.
Hayot & Co., Charles.
Pauvert et Cie., A.
Retz, H. de.
Sainte Anne.
Souques et Cie., E.

Timber merchants.

Champy, A.
Duchassaing, Joseph.
Fleurot & Co., E.
Laurent & Co., Eugène.
Léonard, Joseph.
Lévi, Théodore.
Pécholier.

POINTE-À-PITRE—Continued.

Wholesale provisions.

Bailly & Lesaint.
Bertaud, Auguste.
Bonnet, L.
Bourjac, Alphonse.
Brumant & Co., Emilien.
Buffrenil & Macary.
Dain, A. & G.
Dupuy, F.
Fertray.
Laborderie.
Lacroix, Edouard.
Lafages & Co., E. W.
Labongrais & Co., Leon de.
Lauriat.
Maston, Jean Baptiste.
Morizot et Cie.
Notly & Schmitt.
Poullin, Odillon.
Questel & Co., H.
Roger, G.
Sydambarom, Adolphe.
Tournier & Co., Léon.
Tuder, H.
Vergé, Merval.
Wachter, Albert.

PORT LOUIE.

Sugar manufacturers.

Société Sucrière Beauport.
Souques, Ernest.

SAINTE ANNE.

Sugar manufacturers.

Cail et Cie.
De Chazelles.
Dubos frères.

SAINTE FRANÇOISE.

Sugar manufacturer.

Héritiers Pauvert.

SAINTE ROSE.

Sugar manufacturer.

Crédit Foncier Colonial.

Martinique.

Banks.
Banque de la Martinique.

Commission merchants.
Aries et Cie., C.
Borde et fils.
Hurard, M.
Knight et fils aîné, L. T.
Lassière frères.
Marius, Coipel.
Plissoneaux et Cie.
Romondt, C. van.

Dry-goods merchants.
Coppier, J.
Grandmaison, H.
Lapignonne, R. et E.
Laurent et Cie., H.
Masson, F.
Reynoir frères.
St. Ange, E.

Fancy goods.
Collot, E.
Delsue, Madame.
Glondut, Madame des.
Grottes, Madame des.

Hardware.
Comairas et Cie.
Gérard frères.

Hatters.
Boissière, V.
Delsue, O.

Importers, general.
Bareme, A.
Caminade fi's, G.

Importers, general—Continued.
Coipel & Lawyer.
Cottrell, Joseph.
Decomio, L.
Dela, R.
De Lathifordière, P. M.
Delsue, O.
Lassère, An.
Massias de Boune, G.
Nassignac & Co., Paul.
Ninet, A. F.
Reacae, S. C.
Remy, J.
Reynaud, L.

Importers of—
Coal.
Borde et fils (coal and fertilizers).
Comairas & Co.
Knight et fils aîné, L. T.
Marius, Coipel.

Drugs, perfumery, etc.
Devin, Ad.
Lafosse, A.
St. Ange, Berte.

Dry goods, chinaware, notions, etc.
Barbe, G.
Coppier, J.
Declemy, J.
D'Olivet & Co.
Grandmaison, H.
Masson, F.
Reynoir frères.
St. Ange, E.

ST. PIERRE—Continued.

Hardware, metal goods, cordage, etc.
Beaufond & Co., L.
Comairas & Co.
Gérard frères.
Luny, C.
Palmer, M.

Jewelry, etc.
Croquet, P.
Du Lettasse, Godet.

Lumber, etc.
Berte, G. (staves).
Blaisemont, T. (lumber, etc.).
De Garrori & Avon (staves).
De Gentile & Co. (staves).
De Massias frères (lumber and building materials).
Hamlin & Son, I. H. (lumber, etc.).
Knight et fils ainé, L. T. (lumber, etc.).
Marius, Coipel (lumber, etc.).
Plissoneaux et Cie (lumber, etc.).
Raibaud et Cie., E. (staves).

Provisions, etc.
Alesandra, Joseph (American provisions, wheat, etc.).
Aries & Co., C. (American food products).
Bebet, Delmont.
Berte, G. (molasses).

S. Ex. 8, pt. 11——23

ST. PIERRE—Continued.

Provisions, etc.—Continued.
Blaisemont, T. (American food products).
Boudon, Th. (American provisions, wheat, etc.).
Caminade fils, G. (American provisions, wheat, etc.).
De Gentile & Co., H. A. (American food products).
Dela, R. (American provisions, wheat, etc.).
Depas de Gage & Co. (American food products).
Fouché, Virgil (wines, preserves, canned goods, etc.).
Grut, L. (American provisions, wheat, etc.).
Knight et fils ainé, L. T. (American flour).
Lassére, An. (general provisions).
Marius, Coipel (butter and fish).
Massignac, V. (American flour).
Minet, A. F. (American provisions, wheat, etc.).
Plissoneaux et Cie (butter and fish).
Van Romandt, Charles (American food products).

Sewing machines, oil stoves, and lamps.
Croquet, Armand.

St. Martin.

MARIGOT.

Merchants.
Becker & Morales.
Moreilhon, A.

MARIGOT—Continued.

Merchants—Continued.
Romondt, L. A. van.
Wager, Rey.

SPANISH COLONIES.

Cuba.

AGUACATE.

Boots and shoes.
Alvarez, José.
Calderón, Ramón.

Drugs.
Alvarez, Agapito.
Marin, Domingo.
Quian, José Carlos.

Saddlery and harness.
Alvarez, José.
Montero, Secundino.

Silk goods.
Gonzalez, Domingo.

Tobacco.
Alonso, Emiliano.
Jorba, José.
Serdeña, José.

ALQUIZAR.

Boots and shoes.
Lopez, Vicente.
Llorens, Miguel.
Rodriguez, Clemente.
Sanchez, José.

Drugs.
Martinez, Moné.

Groceries and provisions.
Alonso, Venancio.

BARACOA.

Bookseller.
Fernandez, José.

BARACOA—Continued.

Commission merchants.
Bonell & Ruiz.
Crespo, José A.
Cuervo, Arango.
Dumois & Co., H.
Gomez & Co., Francisco.
Soto, José María.
Tur, José.
Vidaillet, José.

Hardware.
José Pastor, Gonzalez.

Importers.
Cuervo & Co., Manuel (general merchandise).
Dumois & Co., H. (fruits).
Gomez & Co., Francisco N. (fruits).
Monés & Co. (fruits).
Tur, José (fruits).
Vidaillet, José (fruit).
Vidaillet & Monroig.

Jeweler.
Castro, Pedro Fornel.

Manufacturer of cocoanut oil, chocolate, etc.
Vidaillet, José.

Petroleum-refiners.
Vidaillet & Monroig.

Printing offices.
Castañón, César P.
Cuevas & Pera.
Timoned, José.

BARACOA—Continued.

Saddlery.
Soler, Enrique.
Tamayo, Patrocinio.

Silk goods.
Beruff, Angel.
Casanova Ruiz & Co.

Tobacco.
Albert, Carmelo.
Arrue, Miguel.
Berthlemy, Lizardo.
Cordero, Primitivo.
Fernando, Lino.
Osorio, Julio.
Rodriguez, Gabriel.

Undertakers.
Dominguez, Vicente.
Rodriguez, Francisco.

BATABANÓ AND HARBOR.

Boots and shoes.
Azarloza, Rufino, B.
Barceló, Juan.
Garnilla, Gregorio, B.
Pradera, Nicolás, H.
Ramirez, Francisco, B.
Rivero, Pedro, B.

Drugs.
Cortada, Benito, B.
Perez, Arístides, B.

Hardware.
Caballero & Co., H.
García, Cipriano, B.
Jaime, Francisco, H.
Martinez, Bernardo, B.

Notions.
Cereijo, Esperanza, H.

Saddlery.
Leon, Cristobal de, B.

Tailoring establishments.
Caridad, Pablo, H.
Lois, Felipe, H.

Tobacco.
Colmenares, José F., H.
Gomez, Francisco, B.

BATABANÓ AND HARBOR—Continued.

Tobacco—Continued.
Herrera, Francisco, B.
Monaga, Vidal, H.
Reynals, Ignacio, B.
Rodriguez, José R., B.
Roselló, Lorenzo, B.
Vazquez, Rosario, B.

Undertaker.
Rodriguez, Salvador.
B signifies Batabanó. H signifies harbor.

BEJUCAL.

Boots and shoes.
Alvarez, José.
Niebla, Manuel.
Pando, José María.
Simonte, Arturo.

Drugs.
Campos, Francisco.
Espinosa, José María.

Hardware.
Méndez, Felix.

Printing house.
Nicolás, Abad H.

Saddlery and harness.
Sierra, Faustino.

Tailoring establishment.
Mendivil, José.

Tobacco.
Alvarez, Francisco.
Fondevilla, Martinez.
Govantes, Francisco.
Perez, José.
Velasco, Antonio.

BOLONDRÓN.

Boots and shoes.
Campos, Alejandro.
Rodriguez, Felipa.
Romero, Luis.
Sanchez, Arturo.
Sang, Leon.

BOLONDRÓN—Continued.

Drugs.
Fernandez, Arturo.
Sanchez, M.
Telot, Julio.

Hardware.
Urrechaga, Rodrigo.

Saddlery.
Campos, Alejandro.
Gonzalez & Co.
Lezcano, Rafael.
Sanchez, Antonio.

Silversmiths.
Castellanos, Manuela.
Gras, Manuel.

Tobacco.
Ansman, Pedro.
Duarte, Juan.
Fernandez, Ramón.
García, Javier.
Ginés, Gregorio.
Valle, Zacarias.

CAIBARIÉN.

Boots and shoes.
Achón, Enrique.
Alegre & Bergues.
Cabo, Manuel.
Casasús, José.

Commission merchants.
Ariosa, Viuda de.
Garvalena & Co.
Zoraya & Co.

Drugs.
Bofill, Joaquin.

Furniture.
Cigoña, J. F.

General merchandise.
Barquinero, E.

Groceries and provisions.
Birba, Pedro.
Carabia & Co., G.
García, Domingo.
Lanza & Co.
Romañada & Hno., Antonio.

CAIBARIÉN—Continued.

Hardware.
Meade, Guarch & Co.

Hatter.
Alverdí, F.

Importers.
Alvarez & Co.
Meave Ymas & Co.
Zozarya & Co.

Printing house.
Sobrado & Jorge.

Silk goods.
Barrenas, C.

Silk goods and small hardware.
Alegre & Bergues.

Tailoring establishments.
Cao & San Pedro.
Cruz, R. de la.

Woven goods, cloths, etc.
Alvarez & Co.
Menendez, Soriano & Co.

CÁRDENAS.

Banks and bankers.
Balsells, J. & J.
Banco Español, Succursal.
Rabel & Co.
Rojas & Bacot.
Tellado, Mayol & Co.

Boots and shoes.
Diaz, Manuel.
Diaz Prieto, Manuel.
Faumith, Claudio.
Febles, Plácido.
Gilienan, Antonio.
Hoza, José de la.
Izquierdo, Dolores.
Lastra, Brea & Co.
Milian, María.
Sobrevié, Felipe.
Socias, Arnaldo.
Valero, Sobrevié.

CÁRDENAS—Continued.

Chinese goods.
Aship, Juan.
Loy Lay.
Young Leuy.

Coal.
Vieta, Ramón.

Commission merchants.
Balsells, J. & J.
Bringas, Pedro.
Hamel, J. B.
Muñiz & Garcia.
Pedemonte & Co.
Rabel & Co.
Rojas & Bacot.
Tellado, Mayol & Co.

Crockery and chinaware.
Alvarez & Co.
Gonzalez & Mori.

Drugs.
Barrinat Smith, Francisco.
Figueroa, Juan Fermin.
Herrero & Garcia, Emilio.
Planas Rodriguez, Manuel.
Saez, José María.

Foundry.
Labourdelle & Echegoyen.

Furniture.
Artigas & Co., José.
Madruga, Juan.
Martinez, Celedonio.
Mederos, Quintin.
Meras & Co.
Gonzalez, Morejon.

Groceries and provisions.
Alvarez & Cuervo.
Arango & Co.
Bermudez & Menendez.
Bermudez, Vega & Co.
Carol & Co.
Coto, Hermano & Co.
Gutierrez, Francisco.
Martinez, Manuel.
Pedemonte & Co.
Piñero, Juan.
Suarez, Villazon & Co.
Urbistondo & Co.

CÁRDENAS—Continued.

Hardware.
Alvarez & Co.
Arechaederra & Zabaleta.
Buñuell & Ruiz.
Larraurri & Co.
Linares & Pasch.
Maribona, Perez & Co.
Otero & Co.
Ruiz Austin, Leandro.
Torre & Framil.

Hatters.
Alcantara & hijos.
Castro Huergo, Pedro.
Fernández & Co., Francisco.
Ferrera & Co.
Mariño & Co.
Prieto, Carlos.
Rubira & Alvarez.
Soto Hevia, Pedro.

Hides and skins.
Crespo & Alvarez.
Diaz & Co.
Fernandez & Co.
Gutierrez, José.
Lastre, Brea & Co.
Nadal, Bartolomé.
Palacio, Pedro.
Pascual & Garcia.
Perez, José.
Signo & Lorenzo.
Villanueva, Ramón.

Importers.
Balsells, J. & J.
Barrinat, Roberto.
Cueto & Co.
Larraurri & Co.
Maribona, Perez & Co.
Suzerac & Sanvalle.
Tellado, Mayol & Co.

Jewelry.
Riestra, Vicente.
Sala, Esteban.

Manufacturers.
Arechavala, José (spirits).
Diaz, Echavarria & Co. (spirits).

CÁRDENÁS—Continued.

Manufacturers—Continued.
Domenech, Salvador (liqueurs).
Elizondo, Ometay & Co. (beer).
Lezcano & Co. (barrels).
Mesa, Juan (liqueurs).
Rosell, Viuda de (hogsheads).
Ruiz, Hilario (trunks).
Photographer.
Busto, Juan G.
Printing offices.
Martinez & Co., F.
Nuñez & Pagés.
Pestana, J.
Puig, Segundo.
Sancho, Juan M.
Trujillo, Enrique.
Saddlery.
Delgado & Perez, Tomas.
Gonzalez Santana, Vicente.
Hernandez, José.
Hernandez, Manuel Mederos.
Jiminez, Miguel.
Medero, Manuel.
Prieto Sanchez, Angel.
Roger, Ramón.
Viera Romero, Francisco.
Villanueva, Ramón.
Sewing machines.
Fernandez & Co., Guillermo.
Gutierrez Fernandez, José.
Lastra, Brea & Co.
Nadal Togores, Bartolomé.
Siguo & Lorenzo, José.
Villanueva & Ortiz, Ramón.
Silk goods and notions.
Bujan & Granda.
Campa & Co.
Garcia, Prudencio.
Lanza, Amalia.
Márquez, Juan.
Vales & Co., C.
Tobacco and cigars.
Bujan & Granda.
Fernandez, José.
Firigola, Pablo.

CÁRDENAS—Continued.

Tobacco and cigars—Continued.
Prado & Moya, José E.
Rotger, Guillermo.
Vales & Co.
Undertaker.
Cabezola, Hipólito.
Wood and clay.
Tolón & Co., S. T.
Vilá & Hnos.

CIENFUEGOS.

Boots and shoes.
Bálmaseda, Donato.
Bonza & Co., Cárlos.
Crespo, Antonio.
Fernandez, Andrés.
Fontela, Carlos.
García, José.
Hernandez, Antonio.
Irrebarregaray, Miguel.
Jiminez, Gabriel.
Martinez, Aniceto.
Muñoz, Andrés.
Ros Ferrer, Jaime.
Rosello, Gabriel.
Vilches, Antonio.
Vilches, Baldomero.
Chinese goods.
Alonso, Ignacio.
Cano, José.
Cervantes, Benito.
Lung & Co.
Coal merchants.
Ross & Co.
Crockery.
Gutierrez, Felipe.
Perez & Hno.
Drugs.
Figueroa, Dolores.
Figueroa, Leopoldo.
Figueroa, Rafael.
Gonzales, Francisco.
Novoa, Ramón.
Pedraja, Antonio.
Planas, Pedro.
Terry, José.

CIENFUEGOS—Continued.

Dry goods.
Cases & Co.
Castillo, Gregorio.
Garrido, Vicente.

Foundries.
Castello, Carlos.
Clarck, Diego.

Furniture.
Alvarez, Manuel.
Gomez & Co.
Gomez, Feliciano.
Gonzalo, Benito.
Ovies, Suarez & Co.
Villapol, José.

Groceries and provisions, wholesale.
Alvarez, Catcaño.
Alvarez, Llanos & Co.
Avello & Hno.
Cardona, Hartasánchez & Co.
Castaño & Intriago.
Francesch, Pons & Co.
Gándara & Hno.
García & Co.
Menéndez & Monte.
Planas Gil & Co.
Planas & Sanchez.
Pons & Co.

Hardware.
Arana, Perez & Co.
Cabruja & Robert.
Coperi, Antonio.
Llovio, José.
Palau, José.
Perez, Lorenzo.
Perez, Oluscoaga & Co.
Perez & Hermano.
Trujillo, Cárlos J.

Hatters.
Alvarez, Luis.
Barquin & Co.
Castrillón, Manuel.
Dorrego & Hermano.
Gonzalez Posada, Antonio.
Menendez, José.
Rodriguez, Francisco.
Sanjuan, Benito.

CIENFUEGOS—Continued.

Importers of—
Crockery, china, and glass ware.
Gutierrez, Felipe.

Dry goods.
Castillo, Gregorio.
Cazés & Co., Celestin.

Fancy ware, perfumery, basket ware, etc.
Torres & Co., J.
Villar & Co.

Hardware, cutlery, agricultural implements, etc.
Coppire, Antonio.
Llovio, José.
Perez, Olazcoaga & Co.
Trujillo, Carlos.

Provisions.
Cardona, Hartasánchez & Co.
Castaño, Nicolás, importer and exporter.
Francesch, Pons & Co.
Gándara & Hermano.
García & Co., importer and exporter.
Llano & Co., F.
Menendez & Mont.
Planas & Co., J.

Importers, general.
Cabrera & Acosta.
Cardona, Hartasánchez & Co.
Castaño & Intriago.
Castaño, Nicolas.
Castillo, G.
Cazes & Co., C.
Copperi, Antonio.
Francesch, Pons & Co.
Garcia & Co.
Gelhay Hermanos.
Murray, J. T.
Stillman, O. B.
Suarez & Co., Ovies.
Torres & Co., J.
Velasco & Ruiloba.
Yriondo Hermanos & Co.

Jewelers.
Bauriedel & Co.
D'Acosta, Antonio.
Villar & Co.

CIENFUEGOS—Continued.

Lumber and clay.
Castañer & Co.
Castaño & Co.
Garriga, Hno & Co.
Gomez & Co.

Manufacturers of cigars.
Alfonso & Co.
Avello, Sabino.
Borges, Ventura.
Cabrera, Joaquin.
Cabrera & Acosta.
Couto & Benito.
Fernandez, Serafin.
Fernandez & Co.
Gutierrez, Francisco.
Lorente, Gabriel.
Palacios & Co.
Rodriguez, Diego.
Sanchez, Manuel.
San Pedro & Co.
Suarez, Francisco.

Manufacturers, general.
Balta, José (soap).
Castillo, Cárlos (ice).
Castillo, Ramón (soda waters).
Estevez, Vicente (trunks).
Garcia, Francisco (chocolate).
Gomez, Manuel (liqueurs).
Guerra & Hermano (liqueurs).
Lavin & Co. (liqueurs).
Lopez, Manuel (liqueurs).
Osta Narciso (liqueurs).
Pagés, Pedro (ardent spirits).
Perez, Amaro (brooms).
Planos, Gil & Co. (chocolate).
Revuelta, Gavina (corn-meal).
Romagosa & Aulco (soda).
Salcines, Victor (brooms).
Santin, José (liqueurs).
Serpa, Ramón (trunks).
Suarez Alvarez, Ramón (liqueurs).
Suarez, Antonio R. (trunks).
Utset, Francisco (chocolate).

Merchants and bankers.
Avilés, J. & A.
Cardona, Hartasánchez & Co.

CIENFUEGOS—Continued.

Merchants and bankers—Continued.
Castaño & Intriago.
Dorticos, Teresa, Viuda de Terry.
Fowler & Co.
García & Co.
Hunicke, Federico.
Jova, José R.
Menendez & Co.
Peña & Co.
Robés, Faustino G.
Terry, Francisco & Emilio.
Torriente & Hnos.

Photographers.
Carbonell, José.
Cotera, Efasio.
Wigand, C.

Printing offices.
Amat, Federico.
Andrew, José Y.
Bayas, Fírmin.
Gamboa, Nicolás.
García, Ricardo.
Medin, Francisco.
Monteagudo, María.
Muñiz, Manuel.
Seguret, Federico.
Valero, Belisario.
Vila, Víctor.

Saddlery.
Echarte & Iribarregaray.
Loza, Adolfo.
Loza, Pastor.
Roselló, C.
Rupalé, Hipólito.

Small hardware and silk goods.
Alonso, José.
Anglada, Salvador.
Castillo, Gregorio.
Coca, Juan.
Gil, E.
Gonzalez & Gándara.
Llaguno & Sierra.
Rivas, Joaquin.
Torres & Co.
Villar & Co.

CIENFUEGOS—Continued.

Stationery.
Rodriguez, Benito.
Torres & Co., J.
Villar & Co.

Tobacco, leaf.
Avello, Sabino.
Cardona, Hartasánchez & Co.
Iglesias, Francisco.
Sanchez, Eloy.

Undertakers.
Alvarez & Goiri.
Alvarez & José.
Pujol, Juan.

COLÓN.

Boots and shoes.
Buena, Francisco.
Curbelo, Pedro.
Mendez, José.
Montoro & Hermano.
Rodriguez, José.
Vega & Hermano.
Velasquí, Juan.

Drugs.
Conde, F.
Gómez, Juan.
Valdés, Eduardo.
Xenes, Pablo.

Foundry.
Atkingson, Tío & Co.

Furniture.
Molinos, Pablo.

Groceries and provisions.
Lastra & Co.
Oroza, Bereijo, & Co.

Hardware.
García & Co.

Hatters.
Casoun, Segundo.
Fernandez & Co.
Rodriguez, Alvaro.

Manufacturers of cigars.
Las Horas, Angel.
Ramírez, José.

COLÓN—Continued.

Printing offices.
Loreto, Francisco.
Peña, Joaquin de la.

Sewing machines.
Molinos, Pablo.

Small hardware.
García, Prudencio.

Tinware.
García, Adolfo.
Inchaustiz, Juana.

Undertakers.
Corbella, José.
Rimbau, Pablo.
Santavalla, José.

GIBARA.

Bankers and merchants.
Beola & Co.
Longoria & Co.
Silva, Manuel.

Bookseller and stationer.
Bim, Martin.

Boots and shoes.
Gonzalez, Antonio.
Jimenez, Estéban.
Santiesteban, José A.
Torres, Viuda de.

Commission merchants.
Anguera, Federico.
Garrido & Co.
Torre & Co.

Drugs.
Munilla, Fermin.
Pardiñas, Francisco.

Dry goods.
Bolivar & Co.
Fernandez & Co., Sartorio.
Langoria, Benito.
Langoria, Demetrio.

Groceries and provisions.
Cabrera, Manuel.
García, Francisco.
Garrido & Co.
Martinez, Aja Manuel.
Muñiz, García & Co.

GIBARA—Continued.

ceries and provisions—Continued.
Peña & Co.
Roca, Martinez & Co.
Rosal & Sanchez.
Vecino, Juan.
orters.
Silva & Rodriguez.
nufacturers.
Gandara & Co. (liqueurs).
Guillaume, Pedro (liqueurs).
Riera & Co. (tobacco).
iting office.
Cuestra, Rafael.
llery.
Castillo, José.
goods.
Guarch & Co.
ersmiths and watchmakers.
Caramés, Manuel F.
Márquez, Abelardo.
ll hardware.
Magariño, Tomás.
ertaker.
Rodriguez, Francisco.

GUANABACOA.

and beer dealers.
Anedo, Rafael.
Ayats & Romaguera.
ts and shoes.
Bulfill, Tomás.
Fernández, Cárlos.
Longué, Sebastian.
Palacios, Francisco.
Perez, Dionisio.
Quintana, Juan.
gs.
Gonzalez, Antonio.
Herederos de Espinosa.
Montané, Domingo.
Suarez, Juan.
Tosar, Federico.
Valdés, Valenzuela.

GUANABACOA—Continued.

Furniture.
Guanche, Francisco.
Groceries and provisions.
Angel Castro.
Hardware, tools, etc.
Alió, Serafin.
Arronte, Baltasar.
Arronte, Diego.
Logoría, Agustin.
Mayol, Jaime (small hardware).
Piedra, Francisco.
Vicente, Crego (small hardware).
Hatters.
Agüero, Eugenio.
Fernandez, Carlos.
Mogro, Agustin.
Manufacturers of tobacco.
Alvarez, Genaro.
Arenal, Lucio.
Cazañas, Cesáreo.
Diaz, Ernesto.
Diaz, Francisco.
Grado, Emilio.
Granich, Juan.
Linares, Benjamin.
Miraben, José.
Muñiz, Antonio.
Muñiz, Manuel.
Murias, Pedro.
Printing establishments.
Huguet & Belarza, José.
Mauro Suárez, Juan.
Saddlery.
Fernandez, Nicolás.
Longue, Sebastian.
Palacio & Co.
Silk goods.
Hervas, Francisco.
Undertakers.
Chassagne, Cirilo.
Parejo, Benigno.
Ruiz & Ramos.

GUANAJAY.

Boots and shoes.
Gandía, Pánfilo.
García & Hermano.
Hernandez, Luciano.
López, Ramón.
Navarro, Juan.
Pedroso, Jorge.

Drugs.
Alvarez, Miguel.
Rojas, Enrique.
Zamora, Narciso.

Foundry.
Sanchez, Patricio.

Groceries and provisions.
García Barbón, Francisco.

Hardware.
Granda, Bernardo.
Lopez, Ambrosio.
Menendez, Santos.
Monet, Pedro Andres.
Sigarreta, Paulino.

Hatters.
Cairo, José.
García Blanco, Ramón.
García & Hno.
Fernandez, Antonio.
Fernandez, Barbón.

Jewelers.
Nuñez & Hno.

Manufacturers of tobacco.
Rodriguez, Manuel.

Printing office.
Rodriguez, Manuel.

Saddlery.
Alvarez, Manuel.

Sewing machines.
Fernández & Hermanos.

Small hardware.
Fábregas, Emilio.
Saavedra, Jacobo.

GUANE.

Boots and shoes.
Lopez, Fernando.
Lozano, Domingo.
Martinez, Bonifacio.
Muriedas, Justo.
Otega, Juan.
Santollo, Luis.

Drugs.
Fernandez, Miguel.
Rubio, Alejandro.

Hardware.
Bejarano, J. de la C.
Vico, José María.

GUANTÁNAMO.

Arms and ammunition.
Aguilar, Silvestre.
Cabal, Alfredo.
Juanneau, Constantino.

Bankers and merchants.
Baro & Hno.
Brauet & Co., C.
Brooks & Co.
Bueno & Co., J.

Boots and shoes.
Armesto & Vicens.
Carrey, Juan B.
Marqués, Francisco.
Martí, Viuda de.
Massó & Co.
Vicens & Co., Ramón.

China, glass ware, etc.
Adero & Co.
Callico & Co.
García, Juan.

Drugs.
Carcasés, Porfirio.
Guerra, Pedro.
Lacavalerie & Co., José.
Sierra, Estevan A.
Planas & Tur, Manuel.

Hardware.
Brauet & Co., C.
Escobar, Bernardo.

GUANTÂNAMO—Continued.

Hardware—Continued.
Esteban, José.
Juglada & Co., Arturo.
Larot, Julio.

Hats.
Pageó, Ramón.

Importers.
Soler & Co., P.

Manufacturers.
Beltrán, Salvador (bricks and tiles).
Cano, Francisco (bricks and tiles).
Duboc, Pedro (bricks and tiles).
García, Juan (hats).
Gaulhiac, Ernesto (lime).
Gaulhiac & Co., I. (ice).
Jacas & Co. (liqueurs).
López, Pedro (lime).
Mestre, Antonio (liqueurs).
Moné, Llorsas & Co. (liqueurs).
Planes, Sucesión S. (bricks and tiles).
Sánchez & Co. (bricks and tiles).
Soler, Esteban (lime).
Soler & Co., P. (liqueurs).

Provisions.
Callico, Gerónimo.
Gonzalez, Ramón.
Jacas & Co.
Mestre, Antonio.
Mola, Evaristo.
Moné, Pedro.
Moné, Llossas & Co.
Pi, Juan.
Rifa Hno & Co.
Rosés Hermanos & Co.
Soler & Co., Pablo.

Saddlery and harness.
Jalowasky, Eduardo.
Lobaina, María.
Prince, Juan.
Velez, Cárlos.

Small hardware and notions.
Aders & Co.
Garcia, Juan.

Sugars.
Bareó, J.

GUANTÁNAMO—Continued.

Sugars—Continued.
Brault & Co., C.
Brooks & Co.
Bueno & Co.

HAVANA.

Agricultural implements—importers.
Alvarez & Co., Benito.
Amat & Co.
Arambalza & Hno.
Ferran, Jorge.
Isasi & Co.
Uresandi, Alvarez & Co.

Arms and ammunition.
Fisher, Enrique.
Iriarte, José María.
Mayor & Arzola.
Romero, Antonio.
Romero, Faustino.
Uresandi, Alvarez & Co.

Banks and bankers.
Balcells & Co., J.
Bances, J. A.
Banco del Comercio.
Banco Español de la Isla de Cuba.
Borges & Co., J. M.
Bridat, Mont'ros & Co.
Codes, Loychate & Co.
Crédito Territorial Hipotecaria.
Gelats & Co., N.
Hidalgo & Co.
Lawton Brothers.
Piñón & Co., B.
Rafecas & Co., J.
Romero & Co., R.
Ruiz & Co., L.
Upmann & Co., H.
Wickes & Co., C. L.

Bookbinders.
Cortinas, José.
Fernandez & Co., P.
Howson Hnos.
Merelo, Cipriano.
Perez Villamil, Ramóna.
Ruiz & Hno.

HAVANA—Continued.

Bookbinders—Continued.
  Solana, B.
  Torroella & Lopez.

Booksellers.
  Alarcia & Co.
  Alorda, Viuda de.
  Chao, Alejandro.
  Fernandez Casona, Elias.
  Garcia Vazquez, Francisco.
  Gorzalez, Juan.
  Gutierrez, Julian.
  Gutierrez & Cueto.
  Lopez, Santiago.
  Martinez, Julian.
  Merino, José.
  Pozo ó Hijo, E.
  Pozo ó Hijo, Viuda de.
  Ricoy, Manuel.
  Riesch, Cárlos.
  Rodriguez, Ramos M.
  Sala, Clemente.
  Turbiano, José D.
  Turbiano, Rafael.
  Valdepares, José.
  Valle & Arribas, P. del.
  Villa, Viuda de Miguel.
  Wilson, Edwin W.

Boots and shoes.
  Albeae, Enriqueta.
  Arias, Bernardo.
  Assen, Pedro J.
  Basanta, Manuel.
  Boadella, Enrique.
  Cajeti, Antonio.
  Carbajal, Tiburcio.
  Carreras, Sebastian.
  Crucet, Juan.
  Cuesta, Angel.
  Diaz, Zoilo.
  Fusté, Juan.
  García, Andrés.
  García, Benito.
  García, Francisco.
  Garroti, Vicente.
  Gaspar, Francisco.
  Groset, Sebastian.

HAVANA—Continued.

Boots and shoes—Continued.
  Laiseca, Bernabé.
  Martin & Co.
  Mogica, José.
  Montané, Próspero.
  Naranjo & Vazquez.
  Noguera & Rosés.
  Pardiñas, Narciso.
  Paz, Ramón.
  Peñez, Ramón.
  Perez, Aniceto.
  Perez, José.
  Pla, Juan.
  Pol, Juan.
  Puig, Manuel.
  Riesgo, Isidro.
  Robles, Manuel.
  Rodriguez, Manuel.
  Rojas, Ignacio.
  Rubira, José.
  San-Pons, Joaquin.
  Torrado, Ramón F.
  Urzia, Mercedes.
  Vazquez, Francisco.

Chemicals.
  Anelle, J. T.
  Astudillo, Francisco.
  Caro, Antonio.
  Engel, Luis.
  Garrido, Ignacio.
  Herrera & Orúe.
  Quovedo, Benito.
  Sandoval, Aurelio.
  Vila & Vendrell.
  Zardoya, Maximino.

China and glass ware.
  Abascal, Valeriano.
  Alonso & Co.
  Argudin & Diaz.
  Callantes & Hnos.
  Cañizo, José S.
  Conejo, Angel.
  Diaz, Manuel.
  Fernandez & Co., Tomás.
  Gomez & Co.
  Humara & Co.

HAVANA—Continued.

China and glass ware—Continued.
Lavielle & Co., J.
Lopez, Hilario.
Martinez, Cárlos.
Ortiz, Pedro.
Ortiz, Rosendo.
Perez & Co.
Yarto & García.
Zapata, Vidaurrazaga & Larrate.

Chinese goods.
Alam & Asan.
Cham Dió.
Cong To Wo.
Lo Wing.
Luong Sang.
Weng, On & Co.
Wing, Tung.

Cigar and tobacco manufacturers.
Alvarez, Casimero.
Alvarez, Genaro.
Alvarez, Inocencio.
Alvarez & Alvarez.
Alvarez, Victor.
Alvarez & Co.
Alvarez & Co., Justo.
Alvarez & Co., Segundo.
Allones, Antonio.
Arce & Garcia.
Arenal, Lucio.
Arguelles & Co., R.
Arias, Pedro.
Arizaga, Vicente.
Azcano, Sebastian.
Bances & Lopez.
Barquinero, Adela.
Barranco & Co.
Barreto, Manuel.
Beci & Hno., M. de.
Bejar, Manuel.
Boher & Hno.
Bustamante, Manuel.
Bustillo & Hno.
Cabal, Francisco.
Calvo & Co.
Camacho, Manuel.
Cambas & Hno.

HAVANA—Continued.

Cigar and tobacco manufacturers—Cont'd.
Carreras, Cláudio.
Carvajal, Leopoldo.
Carvajal & Co.
Castillo, Gabino.
Celorio & Co., B.
Celorio & Mora.
Cocina, José.
Coll & Co., P.
Cortina & Gomez.
Cueto & Co., Juan.
Chao, Juan.
Diaz, Cristóbal.
Diaz & Alvarez.
Diaz, Tomás.
Diaz & Hno.
Diaz, Zóilo.
Dubróca, Ardadio.
Estanillo, Junco & Corujó.
Estanillo, P. Antonio.
Faedo & Co.
Faya, Faustino.
Fernandez, Corral & Co.
Fernandez, García Antonio.
Fernandez, José.
Fernandez & Fernandez.
Fernandez & García.
Fernandez & Palaez.
García, Candido.
García & Co., Ramón.
García, Gumersindo.
García, Manuel.
García & Co., Domingo.
García & Co., Marcelino.
Gener, José.
Godinez, Francisco.
Gonzalez, Gabriel.
Gonzalez, Ignacio & Onofre.
Gonzalez, José.
Gutierrez & Co.
Henry Clay & Bock & Co.
Herera, Dorotea.
Ilbaceta, José.
Inclan, Diaz & Co.
Larrea & Hno.
Looft & Co., Wm.
López, Antonio.

HAVANA—Continued.

Cigar and tobacco manufacturers—Cont'd.
Lopez, Bencomo M.
Lopez, Juan.
Lopez & Co.
Lopez & Co., Calixto.
Lopez & Co., Manuel.
Luque, Cristóbal F.
Maceda, José.
Marinas, Manuel.
Marinas & Posada.
Mendez, Francisco.
Mendia, Domingo.
Menendez, Francisco.
Menendez, José.
Mora & Co.
Morales & Co., José.
Moreda, Pedro.
Murias, Pedro.
Murias & Co., Felix.
Nogueira, Alfredo.
Olmo, Ignacio.
Ortiz & Hno.
Parrondo, Evaristo.
Partagás & Co., limited.
Peñeñori, Alvarez & Co.
Pereira, Manuel.
Pereda & Co., Luis.
Perez del Rio, Francisco.
Perez, Juan.
Perez, Sabino.
Pijuan, Viuda de.
Piñera & Hno., Rosendo.
Pino & Villamil.
Posada, José Antonio.
Rabell, Prudencio.
Ramirez, Angel.
Real, Tomás del.
Rencurrell, José M.
Rendueles, Rosendo.
Rivero, Manuel.
Rivero, Martinez & Co.
Rodriguez, Andrés.
Rodriguez, José.
Rodriguez, Melchor.
Rodriguez, Manuel F.
Rodriguez, Emilio.

HAVANA—Continued.

Cigar and tobacco manufacturers—Cont'd.
Rodriguez, Rosendo.
Roger, Viuda de Pedro.
Saavedra & Co., José.
Sanchez, Gabriel.
Sanchez & Co.
Selgas & Garcia.
Sosa, Manuel.
Suarez, Benito.
Suarez, Cayetano.
Suarez & Armas.
Tirado, Faustino.
Trotcha, Miguel.
Upmann & Co., H.
Valerio & Co., J.
Vales & Co., J.
Valle, Alejandro.
Valle & Co., M.
Ventura, Juan.
Yurre, Ignacio de.
Coal-dealers.
Artau, Gaspar.
Barrio & Coello.
Barceló & Cova.
Cao, José.
Capellá, Nonell & Sagaz.
Fernandez & Castrillón.
Gamiz, Pablo.
Lage, José.
Lopez, Pedro Paz.
Lopez, Ramón.
Llano & Hermano.
Piñero, Manuel.
Planiol, Fernandez & Co.
Commercial agents.
Artiaga, Luis (publications).
Betancourt, Frank A. (typewriters).
Corominas, Adolfo.
Extremera, José (Spanish newspapers).
Garrido, Francisco.
Hernandez, Domingo (machinery).
Marin, Ricardo (undertakers' supplies).
Molina & Alvarez, Nicolás (undertakers' supplies).

SPANISH COLONIES. 369

HAVANA—Continued.

Commercial agents—Continued.
Molinas & July (publications).
Pozo & Hijos, Viuda de (newspapers).
Reyling & Co. (railroad and building supplies).
Sala, Clemente (newspapers).
Tomati, Ambrosio (machinery).
Wilson, Ed. (foreign newspapers).

Commission merchants.

Alegret, José.
Alfonso, Pastor.
Almeida, N.
Alvarez, Juan.
Armand & Co., E.
Arrojo, Serafin.
Balcells & Co., J.
Bauces, J. A.
Barrios & Co.
Batista, Fernando.
Beck, C. E.
Berndes & Co., J. F.
Betancourt, Lucio.
Blanch & Co., C.
Brú, Alberto.
Bosselmann & Schroder.
Bridat, Mont'ros & Co.
Broderman, F. H.
Calvo & Co., M.
Camara, José J.
Carbó & Co.
Codés, Loxchato & Co.
Conill & Archbold.
Deulofeu, Hijo & Co.
Diez, Francisco,
Dominguez, Luis.
Droop, Otto D.
Dussag & Co.
Fabra & Co.
Falk, Rohlsen & Co
Fariñas & Hijos.
Fariñas, Pedro.
Fernandez, Carrillo & Co.
Francke, Hijos & Co.
Fuentes, Nicasio.
García, Serra & Co.
Gelats & Co., N.

S. Ex. 8, pt. 11——24

HAVANA—Continued.

Commission merchants—Continued.
Gomez, Joaquin.
Gonzalez, Palbo.
Giberga & Co., Samuel.
Gomez & Co., Manuel.
Gondie & Co., J.
Hamel & Co., Henry B.
Hayley & Co.
Hernandez, Pablo.
Hernandez, Ruperto.
Heydrich, Emilio.
Hidalgo & Co.
Higgins & Co.
Illas, Juan.
Jané & Co.
Jané & Co., Pascual.
Lange & Lemhardt.
Lawton Brothers.
Lay, Jorge.
Looft & Co., William.
Lopez, Guillermo.
Lopez & Co., Calixto.
Lozada, Andrés.
Marquette, jr., J. R.
Martinez & Co.
Martinez, Pinillos & Co.
Martinez, Tomás.
Matas, Juan Lino.
Mayos, Miguel.
Mena, Manuel.
Millington.
Moenck, D. H.
Moyarrieta, L.
Muller & Co.
Neo Pensado, Juan.
Neuhaus, Neumann & Co.
Noriega, Prudencio.
Ohmstedt, Enrique.
Ordetx, Julio.
Ordoñez Hnos.
Otamendi, Hermano & Co.
Pages, Pedro.
Pardiñas, Francisco.
Pastell, Miguel.
Perkins, Ricardo.
Perjol & Mayola.
Pinon & Co.

HAVANA—Continued.

Commission merchants—Continued.

Poblet & Casanueva.
Puig, Baldomero.
Rafecas & Co.
Rodriguez, Francisco Alvarez.
Rexach, Ulpiano.
Romero & Co., R.
Rovirosa, Francisco A.
Ruiz & Co., L.
San Juan, Francisco.
San Roman & Pita.
San Miguel, Manuel.
Santamaria, Rafael Perez.
Sobrinos de Herrera.
Sanchez, Antonio J.
Schmidt & Co.
Schwab & Tillmann.
Seidel, J. S.
Serpa, Antonio.
Serrapiñana, Enrique.
Serrapiñana and Heuser.
Someillan & Hijo.
Smith, Enriqué H.
Stevenson & Diaz.
Sturz & Co., B.
Suarez, Jacinto.
Truffin & Co.
Ubago & Hijo, Angel.
Upmann & Co., H.
Van Assche, Stroybant & Co.
Veiga, Solá & Co.
Varona, Enrique.
Veiga, Santiago.
Verdini, Francisco.
Villalonga, Narciso.
Vionnet & Co.
Wickes & Co., C. R.
Will Hermanos.
Zabala, J. D.
Zabarte, Candido.
Zendegui & Co.

Dealers in wood and clay.

Balbi, Domingo.
Carreras & Giol.
Diaz & Alvarez.
Diaz & Hno, Ladislao.

HAVANA—Continued.

Dealers in wood and clay—Continued.

Lens, Dosal & Co.
Ortoll, Bartolomé.
Planiol, Fernandez & Co.
Pons Hnos.
Rio & Co., J.
Rio & Perez, Andrés del.
Sureda & Roselló, Juan.
Tallería, Antonio C.
Vila, Antonio.

Distillers.

Alemany, Florencio.
Alvarez & Echeguren.
Ayarza, Gabriel.
Casanova, Pablo.
Castals & Garay.
Gil, Francisco.
González, Julian.
Menéndez & Domenech.
Miguel & Co., F.
Miró, F.
Otermin & Otamendi.
Oyarzabal & Co.
Peralta & Co., Camilo.
Quiroga & Co., E.
Rada, José Maria.
Romañá & Co.
Trespalacios, Aniceto.
Trueba & Hnos.
Vivanco, Braulio.

Drugs.

Alacan, Valentin.
Alvarez, Augusto.
Alvarez, Francisco.
Aragon, Ernesto.
Arnautó, Martin.
Bagner, José.
Barata, Miguel.
Barbero, Francisco.
Barrinat, Arturo.
Betancourt, Mauricio.
Bosque, Alfredo.
Bosque, Arturo C.
Botet, Ramón.
Brito, Benjamin L.
Bueno, J. A. Vedado.

HAVANA—Continued.

Drugs—Continued.

Cabrera, Felipe.
Cajigas, Juan.
Castellanos, Pedro.
Castells & Co.
Castro, Emilio de.
Castro, Pedro N. de.
Catalá, Viuda de.
Consuegra, Adolfo.
Consuegra, Ricardo.
Delgado, Manuel E. .
Diaz, Gabriel.
Diaz, José Guillermo.
Diaz, Joaquin.
Ecay, Manuel de J.
Estevez, José C.
Fernandez de Cordova, E. A.
Ferrer, J.
Fina, Ricardo.
Fontanills, Luis Felipe.
Formel, Julio Z.
Frias, Julio.
Gardáno, José.
Gomez de la Maza, José.
Gonzalez Curquejo, Antonio.
Guilhamelou, Cárlos.
Hernandez, Felix.
Hernandez, Ladislao.
Hernandez, Domingo.
Hierro, C. F.
Johnson, Manuel.
Larrazábal, Raimundo.
León, Viuda de Tomás.
Lopez, Clemente.
Lopez, Leopoldo.
Marquez, Luis J.
Martinez, Justo L.
Martinez, Tomás.
Maza, Ildefonso de la.
Maza, Miguel de la.
Militar.
O'Farrill, Gabriel.
Orts & Linares, Tomás.
Palú, Eduardo.
Pardiñas, Emilio.
Perez Carrillo, Alfredo.

HAVANA—Continued.

Drugs—Continued. ·

Perez, Mamerto.
Poey, Rodolfo.
Portocarrero, Manuel R.
Regueyra, Santiago.
Reyes, José.
Rodriguez Ecay, Gaspar.
Rodriguez, Manuel.
Rovira, José de J.
Ruiz, Viuda de.
Sanchez, Arturo.
Sarrá, José.
Sell & Guzmán, Manuel.
Silva, Francisco.
Solano & Molina, Manuel.
Torralbas, Antonio.
Tremoleda, Agustin.
Ulrici, Cárlos.
Valdes, José Belen.
Valdes, J. Tirso.
Villavicencio, Elígio N.
Villiers, Manuel.
Villiers & Suarez.
Xenes, Francisco.
Zardoya, Miximino.

Dry goods.

Alonso, Modesto.
Alvarez, Puente & Co.
Alvarez, Valdes & Co.
Arcos & Co., Angel A.
Arenas & Co., Juan F.
Arriaza & Selma.
Bandujo, Ramón.
Barbón, Hno. & Co.
Casuso & Dirube.
Cobo Hnos. & Co.
Diaz, Benito.
Doyle, Perez & Co.
Escandón, M.
Falk, Rohlsen & Co.
Fargas Hno. & Co.
Fernandez Hno. & Co.
Fernandez, Junquera & Co.
Galan & Co., José María.
Galindez, M. C.
Gamba & Co., F.

HAVANA—Continued.

Dry goods—Continued.

García Alvarez, José.
García Tuñón, Segundo.
Garrido, Calvo & Co.
Gomez & Sobrinos.
Goyenechea & Villanueva.
Grau, Lastra & Co.
Guezala, Cárlos.
Herrera, Manuel.
Herrero, Demetrio.
Ibañez & Co., L.
Inclan & Co.
Lenzano, Adolfo.
Lopez, San Pelayo & Co.
Maribona, García & Co.
Martinez, Rodriguez, Valdés & Co.
Maturana & Co., R.
Miquelarena, J. A.
Morante, Alfredo.
Nazabal, Ulacia & Co.
Pella, Martin F.
Prendes & Co.
Quirós, Loriente & Co.
Revuelta & Co.
Rodriguez, Gonzalez & Co.
Rodriguez, Martinez & Co.
Ruiz & Co.
Solís & Co., Francisco.
Somonte & Pola.
Suarez & García.
Sueyras, Pedro.
Taladrid & Hno.
Teran, Arénal & Co.
Valle & Co., G. del.
Villasuso, Muela & Co.
Zamanillo, Ricardo.

Electrical apparatus.

Morena, Manuel.
Morgue, Fernando.
Riquero, Francisco.

Engravers.

Arvier, Hipólito.
Bertolay, David.
Coopat, Eduardo (of jewelry).
Miarteni, Páblo (of precious stones).
Palmas, M. R. (of metals).

HAVANA—Continued.

Engravers—Continued.

Ruiz & Co., M.
Santa Coloma, J.
Sureda, Juan (of glass).
Taveira, Alfredo.
Torre, Nicasio de la.

Exporters of cigars and tobacco.

Bances, J. A.
Beck, C. E.
Bosselman & Schroder.
Broderman, F. H.
Carvajal & Co., L. H.
Clay, Bock & Co.
Gener, José.
Looft & Co., William.
Mayoz, Miguel.
Neuhaus, Neumann & Co.
Ordetx, Julio.
Upmann & Co., H.

Exporters of fruit.

Barrios & Co.
Betancourt, Ignacio.
Calafat, Antonio.
Gonzalez Lopez, Diego.
Leon, Bernardo.
Oliva, Julian R.

Exporters of old metals, rags, etc.

Hamel & Co., H. B.

Fans and umbrellas.

Amando, Andrés.
Carranza, Manuel (manufacturer).
Charavay & Lacoste (manufacturers).
Rivera, Antonio (manufacturer).
Rodriguez, José.
Tamarit, Antonio (manufacturer).

Foundries.

Baloyra, Manuel.
Estapó & Puig, Enrique.
Lambden, Amelia.
Madurell, José.
Velo, Angel.

Furniture.

Albo, Manuel.
Alonso, Antonio.

HAVANA—Continued.

Furniture—Continued.
Alvarez, Eduardo.
Baquiola, Juan B.
Betancourt, Cárlos.
Bombalier, J. J.
Borbollavy & Co., J.
Canelly & Hermano.
Carral & Fernandez.
Castillo, Florentino.
Cayón, Ramón.
Comas, José.
Fernandez, Antonio.
Fernandez, Franciscó.
Gándara & Co.
Hierro, Eladio.
Hourcade & Co.
Laburu, Antonio.
Martinez, Ricardo.
Maxenchs, José.
Pardo, Vicente.
Ponte, Manuel.
Quintana, Francisco.
Raventós, Mocesto.
Riera, Jaíme.
Rigol, Juan.
Rivera, Antonio.
Rodriguez, Manuel.
Rodriguez, Nicolás.
Rodriguez & Co.
Rodriguez & Reymunde.
Ros & Novoa.
Salgado, Mercédes.
Sanchez, Inocencio.
Suarez, Manuel.
Suarez & Co., Aurelio.
Suarez & Suarez, Manuel.
Tuero, Francisco.
Tuero & Tuero.
Vazquez & Hermano.
Villarnovo, Pedro.
*General commission merchants, importers
and exporters.*
Abascal, Valeriano.
Ablanedo, Polidoro.
Aguilera & Co.
Albertí & Dowling.
Albuerne, A. M.

HAVANA—Continued.

*General commission merchants, importers
and exporters*—Continued.
Amat & Co.
Amiel & Co.
Armand & Co., E.
Badia & Co.
Baguer & Co.
Balcells & Co., J.
Bances, J. A.
Barkhausen & Remmer.
Barrios & Co.
Basterrechea, José.
Bauriedel & Co., Federico.
Beck, C. E.
Berndes & Co., J. F.
Betancourt, Ernesto A.
Blanch & Co., C.
Bordenave & Co.
Bosselmann & Schroder.
Bridat, Mont'ros & Co.
Broderman, F. H.
Bulnes & Millás.
Calvo & Co., M.
Cámara, José I.
Carbó & Co.
Conill & Archbold.
Conill & Co.
Cordés, Loychate & Co.
Cuadra, Francisco.
Desvernine & Co.
Deulofeu, Hijo & Co.
Diago, Federico G.
Droop, Otto D.
Durán & Co.
Dussaq & Co.
Fabra & Co.
Falk, Rohlsen & Co.
Fernandez, Carrillo & Co.
Francke, Hijos & Co.
García, Eustoquio.
García, Serra & Co.
García & Trascastro.
Gelats & Co., N.
Geyer, Ricardo.
Giberga & Co., Samuel.
Gomez & Co., Manuel.
Gonzales Lopez, Diego.

HAVANA—Continued.

General commission merchants, importers and exporters—Continued.

Goudié & Co., J.
Grosch, H. V.
Hall, D. B.
Hamel & Co., Henri B.
Hayley & Co.
Heesch, Enrique.
Hernandez & Acosta.
Herrera, Sobrinos de.
Heydrich, Emilio.
Hidalgo & Co.
Higgins & Co.
Ibern & Hno., A.
Jané, Pascual & Co.
Jané & Co.
Jimenis, Alberto.
Jover, Francisco.
Lange & Leonhardt.
Larrabide & Fernandez.
Lawton Hnos.
Looft & Co., William.
Lopez & Co., Calixto.
Llata, Aurelio.
Marquette hijo, J. R.
Martinez Pinillos & Co., J. M. de.
Martinez & Co.
Mayoz, Miguel.
Medero, J.
Millington, J. F.
Moenck, D. H.
Mojarrieta, L.
Muller & Co.
Neuhaus, Neumann & Co.
Noriega, Prudencio.
Nuñez & Herrera.
Ohmstedt, Enrique.
Ordetx, Julio.
Ordoñez Hnos.
Otamendi, Hno. & Co.
Pagés, Pedro.
Perez Santamaría, Rafael.
Perkins, Ricardo.
Piñan & Ezquerro.
Piñon & Co., B.
Pigné, Agustin.
Pulido, José F.

HAVANA—Continued.

General commission merchants, importers and exporters—Continued.

Pujol & Mayola, José.
Rafecas & Co., J.
Rodriguez Alvarez, Francisco.
Romero & Co., R.
Rovirosa, Francisco A.
Ruiz & Co., L.
San Juan, Francisco.
San Roman & Pita.
Sanchez, Antonio J.
Schmidt & Co., F. C.
Schwab & Tillman.
Seidel, J. S.
Serpa, Antonio.
Serrapiñana, Enrique.
Serrapiñana & Henser.
Someillan & Hijo.
Smith, Enrique H.
Stevenson & Diaz.
Sturz & Co., B.
Suarez, Jacinto.
Truffin & Co., R.
Ubago & Hijo, Angel.
Upmann & Co., H.
Van Assche, Straybant & Co.
Veiga, Solá & Co.
Vionnet & Co.
Wickes & Co., C. R.
Will Hnos.
Zabala, J. D.
Zabarte, Cándido.
Zéndegui & Co.

Glass.

Baez & Hermano, Carlos.
Fernandez, Genaro.
Fernandez, Inocencio.
Lopez & Co., F.

Groceries and provisions.

Abascal & Co., F.
Abellano & Fuente.
Aguiar, Salvador.
Aguirre, Juan.
Alonso, Garin & Co.
Alonso, Jauma & Co.
Alonso Lavin, Francisco.
Alvarez & Co., Aurelio.

HAVANA—Continued.

Groceries and provisions—Continued.

Amiel & Co., Ignacio.
Arechaga, Ricardo.
Arxer, Benito.
Astorqui, Juan.
Avendaño, Paulino.
Baguer Hno. & Co.
Balaguer, José.
Barraqué & Co.
Beci & Hno.
Bedia & Co.
Berenguer & Negra.
Berriz, José M.
Bilbao & Co.
Blanch & Co., C.
Blanco, José.
Brocchi, Juan.
Bulnes & Millás.
Caño & Co.
Carbonell, Rosell & Co.
Cobo, Agustin.
Coca & Armengol.
Codina & Hno.
Coll, José.
Colom & Co.
Coro & Quesada.
Costa, Vives & Co.
De Beche, H.
Diaz, Manuel.
Echezarretta & Co., D.
Fabra & Co.
Fernandez, Canto & Co.
Fernandez, Garcia & Co.
Fernandez & Co., Eusebio.
Fernandez & Co., M.
Fors & Co.
Galban, Rio & Co.
Galbe & Hijo.
García, Castro & Co.
García, Cué & Co.
García, Landeras & Co.
García, Serra & Co.
Garri & Co., C.
Garviso, Hereds de J.
Gili, Quadreny & Co.
Gonzalez & Carreño.
Gonzalez & Co., J.

HAVANA—Continued.

Groceries and provisions—Continued.

Gutierrez, Arrese & Co.
Gutierrez & Co.
Herrera & Co., A.
Jané, Pascual & Co.
Larrea, Eguillor & Co.
Lezama & Larrea, J.
Loredo & Co., J.
Lloveras, Baldomero.
Martinez, Mendez & Co.
Menendez, Carratalá & Co.
Miró & Otero.
Muñiz & Co.
Nazabal & Co.
Otamendi Hno & Co.
Pastorino & Schultz.
Perez, Muniategui & Co.
Perez, Ortiz & Co.
Perez & Co., Ceferino.
Piñan & Ezquerro.
Pino, Juan L.
Pujol & Mayola, José.
Romagosa & Montejo.
Romaña, Juan.
Rossi, Romualdo.
Ruiz, S. G.
Ruiz & Co.
Salceda, Roda & Co.
San Roman & Pitá.
Santa Marina, J.
Sociedad Socorros Mútuos, Ejército y Armada.
Soler, Francisco.
Suero, Andés & Co.
Tabernilla & Sobrino.
Vega, Gregorio de la.
Veiret, Lorenzo & Co.
Villaverde & Co.
Yarto, Nemesio.

Groceries and provisions (finer class).

Alvarez & Coll.
Arechaga, Ricardo.
Berenguer & Negra.
Berriz, J. María.
Borrás & Llambés.
Canales, Fraga & Co.

376 SPANISH COLONIES.

HAVANA—Continued.

Groceries and provisions (finer class)—Con.
Carrera, Ricardo.
De Beche, H.
Fernandez, Cauto & Co.
Fuentes, Saturnino.
Gonzalez & Hno.
Gonzalo, Toribio de.
Masagné & Caviedes.
Mendy, Recalt & Co.
Miró, Isidro.
Miró, Juan.
Noguer, Juan.
Nolla, Miguel.
Remus & Baguer.
Salvat & Bustillo.
Seva, José R.
Zayas & Hno.

Hardware.
Aguilera & Garcia.
Aldecoa, Serrano & Co.
Alvarez & Co., B.
Alvarez & Co., Bernado.
Amat & Co.
Araluce, Martinez & Co.
Arambalza & Hno.
Builla & Co.
Cajigal & Co.
Ferran, Jorge.
Gutierrez, Alonso & Co.
Isasi & Co.
Larrazabal & Astuy.
Lastra & Co.
Martinez, Seña & Co.
Maza, Francisco de la.
Pardo, Ramón.
Perez, Ricardo.
Presa & Torres.
Prieto & Co.
Quintana, J.
Ramos & Castillo.
Soto & Co., A.
Tijero & Co.
Torre & Co., C.
Uresandi, Alvarez & Co.
Urquiola, Diaz & Co.
Vila & Coto.

HAVANA—Continued.

Hardware, agricultural.
Achagavia, Santiago
Armas, Eliseo.
Echavarría, Inés.
Fernandez, Francisco.
Ferreior, Manuel.
Ferreiro & Co.
García, Cándido.
García, Manuel.
García & García.
Iguzquiza, Angel.
León, Justo.
Lopez Seña, Juan.
Mendez, José.
Solá, Elvira.
Suarez, Francisco.
Villar, Antonio.

Importers of—
Chinese goods.
Alamy Asan.
Cham Dió.
Cong To Wo.
Lo Wing.
Wing Tung.
Coal.
Barrios & Co.
Calvo & Co., M.
Gomez, Pablo.
Drugs.
Gonsalves, Antonio.
Lobé & Torralba.
Sarrá, José.
Fancy goods.
Alvarez & Hermano.
Castro, Fernandez & Co.
Coll, Miguel.
Garcia & Hermano.
Gandasegui & Vega.
Sanchez & Hermano, F.
Taladrid & Hermano.
Furniture.
Gandara & Co.
Rigol, Juan.
Hardware.
Aguilera & García.
Amat & Co.
Arambalza & Co.

HAVANA—Continued.

Importers of—
. Hardware—Continued.
Diaz & Co., Urquiola.
Ferran, Jorge.
Gutierrez, Alouzo & Co.
Isasi & Co.
Lastra & Co.
Presa & Torres.
Tijero & Co.
Torre & Co., C.
Hats, and materials for manufacturing same.
Fernandez & Co., G.
Lopez, Ramón.
Menendez & Hno.
Ortiz & Avendaño.
Perajon, Hno. & Co.
Rubiera & Muñiz.
Trápaga & Puente.
Viadero & Co.
Horses.
Redding, W. H.
Lumber.
Duran & Co.
Jimenis, Alberto.
Mojarrieta, L.
Santamaria, Rafael Perez.
Sastre, Gabriel.
Machinery.
Alexander, H.
Amat & Co.
Cail & Co.
Cotiart, J. B.
Droop, Otto T.
Hyatt, George W.
Krajewski & Pesant.
Lawson Brothers.
Moenck, D. H.
Schawb & Tillmann.
Schmidt & Co., F. C.
Smith, James.
. Verastegui, Alberto.
Vionnet & Co.
Provisions, flour, etc.
Abascal & Co., F.
Baguer Hermano & Co.
Balaguer, José.

HAVANA—Continued.

Importers of—
Provisions, flour, etc.—Continued.
Barrios & Co.
Berenguer & Negra.
Blauch & Co., C.
Codina & Hermano.
Colom & Co.
Galvan, Rio & Co.
Goudie & Co., J.
Kicherer, J. E.
Lawton Brothers.
Mojarrieta, L.
Ruiz, S. G.
Truffin & Co., R.
Wick & Co., R.
Sewing machines.
Alvarez & Hinse.
Gonzalez & Co.
Sopeña & Co., José.
Xiquez, Felipe E.
Shoes and leather.
Aedo & Co., Viuda de.
Blanco, Tomás.
Diaz & Co., Mariano.
Estramy & Co., Dalman.
Garan, Mateó.
Martinez, Ramón.
Menendez, Rafael.
Torres & Co., J.
Veiga Solá & Co.
Vidal Hermanos.
Stationery.
Ruiz & Co., M.
Wilson, Edwin.
Watches and jewelry.
Bernard, A. B.
Cuervo, R. Fernandez.
Fischer, Enrique.
Hedman, Juan.
Hierro & Co.
Kramer & Co.
Masson, Emilio.
Odoñez Hermanos.
Oltmans, Guillermo.
Jewelers.
Alvarez, Francisco.
Bauriedel & Co., F.

HAVANA—Continued.

Jewelers—Continued.
Bernard, A. B.
Borbolla, J.
Carmona, Matías.
Cores & Hno.
Dufau, Esteban.
Fernandez Cuervo, Ramón.
Fernandez, Evelio.
García Corujedo Hnos.
Hierro & Co.
Ibern, Juan.
Jimenez, J.
Kramer & Co.
Laucha, Tomás.
Lopez, Santos.
Martinez, Gutierrez & Co.
Masson, Emilio.
Menendez, Francisco.
Ordoñez Hnos.
Palacio, Taracena & Co.
Sanchez & Hno.
Santa María, Bermudez & Co.
Sauter & Co., T. ·

Lamps, etc.
Alvarez, Saturnino.
Candales, Alonso & Co.
Loredo, Federico.
Masino, Enrique M.
Papiol, José.
Perez & Mendez.
Ramirez, A. P.
Rodriquez & Leiro.
Villadoniga, José.
Villaverde, Pedro.

Lithographers.
Abadens, Viuda de.
Caballero & Hijos, R.
Cuesta, Tiburcio V.
Fernandez, Rosendo.
García & Co., Manuel.
Guerra & Rius.
Lamy, E.
Lastra, Benito C.
Moré, Alvaro.
Navas, Francisco.
Palmas, M. R.
Sopeña, Silvino.

HAVANA—Continued.

Machinery.
Alexander, H. (importer).
Amat & Co. (importers).
Anderson, Juan R. (agent).
Cotiart, J. P. (importer).
Diaz Silveira, Tomás (commission).
Droop, Otto D. (commission).
Estany & Borrell (agents).
Heesch, Enrique (agent).
Heydrich, Emilio (agent).
Hyatt, G. W. (importer).
Krajewski & Pesant (engineers).
   Leblanc, Alfredo (importer).
Moenck, D. H. (agent).
Piqué, Agustin (agent).
Schmidt & Co., F. C. (importers).
Schwab & Tillmann (agents).
Supervielle, Juan B. (engineer).
Tatger, Juan (engineer).
Verastegui, Alberto (agent).
Vionnet & Co. (importers).

Manufacturers.
Alvarez & Gomez (coffins).
Ardavin, Joaquin (medals).
Arnavat, Luis (medals).
Baez & Hnos (screens and lamp shades).
Baudin, Francisco (trunks).
Barba, Manuel (brooms).
Benitez, Sobrino & Co. (vermicelli).
Bofill & Co. (crackers).
Brito & Llenrra (coffins).
Buch, Francisco (medals).
Cabal & Granda (loaf sugar and sirups).
Carballás, Dionisio (steelyards).
Carranza, Manuel (gloves).
Castro, Fernandez & Co. (envelopes and paper cartridges).
Crusellas, Carbonne & Co. (beer).
Crusellas, Hno & Co. (soap, candles, and perfumes).
Cuadrado, José (brooms).
Cuervo & Co. (mineral waters).
Cuesta, Manuel (canes).
Del Monte, Viuda de G. (trunks and valises).

HAVANA—Continued.

Manufacturers—Continued.

Diaz, Fernando (jackets).
Ezcofet, José (trunks and valises).
Fernandez, Francisco (small boats).
Fernandez, Generoso (mirrors and screens).
Fornells, Antonio (hat blocks).
Fornet, José (paper boxes).
Forteza, J. (billiard tables).
Galloso, José (trunks).
Gomez & Co., J. (crackers).
Gonzalez, José (loaf sugar).
Grovas, Alfredo (trunks).
Guddeman, M. F. (mineral water).
Heydrich & Co., A. (cordage).
Iglesias, Ramón (artificial coal).
Illa, Manuel (collars and cuffs).
Laplume & Diaz (champagne bis_cuits).
Lopez, A. (paper boxes).
Lopez, Aurelio (coffins).
Lopez, José C. (canes).
Llanos, José M. (hat linings).
Llinas, Antonio (window curtains).
Martinez, Antonio (hats).
Nadal, Narciso (billiard tables).
Perez, Francisco (trunks and valises).
Pomares, Pedro (hats).
Rabassa & Co. (brooms).
Rigol, Juan (furniture).
Roca, Emilio (trusses).
Roca & Varela (brooms).
Rodriguez Fernandez, José (boxes for guava preserves).
Roqué, Pablo (macaroni).
Rousset & Co., Ricardo (paper boxes).
Ruiz & Co., M. (rubber stamps).
Sabatés, Hno & Co. (soap, candles, and perfumes).
Sampayo, Martin (coffins).
Sariol, José (trunks and valises).
Urtiaga, Sabino (loaf sugar).
Valverde, Soriano & Co. (wax candles).
Varela & Rodriguez (mineral waters).
Vila, Lorenzo (gas fixtures).
Vilaró, José (soap and candles).

HAVANA—Continued.

Manufacturers—Continued.

Viloplana, Guerrero & Co. (English biscuit).
Zaldo, Carvajal & Co. (ice).
Zardon & Vallina (candles).

Manufacturers and dealers in matches.

Artiz, Zabaleta & Co. (manufacturers).
Coll & Co., P. (manufacturers and dealers).
Costa, Vives & Co.
Gispert, Antonio (manufacturer).
Hernandez, Urtiaga & Co.
Muguerza & Co. (manufacturers and dealers).
Perez Barañano, Diego.
Portas & de Pau (manufacturers and dealers).
Puig, Pedro.

Manufacturers of chocolate.

Baguer, José.
Iriarté, José María.
Martinez & Co.
Menendez, Villar & Co.
Perez, R.
Romero, Faustino.
Vilaplana, Guerrero & Co.

Manufacturers of preserves.

Estapé, José.
Gomez & Co., J.
Puig, J.
Rabentós, Francisco.
Viadero, Antonio.

Military goods.

Acea, Andrés.
Gutierrez, Bonifacio.
Pereda, José.
Sañudo Revuelta & Co.

Nautical, chemical, and scientific instruments.

Zarrabeitia & Azurmendi.

Optical instruments and supplies.

Alarcia, Manuel.
Alvarez & Hno.
Cuerov, Ramón F.

HAVANA—Continued.

Optical instruments and supplies—Cont'd.
Fischer, Enrique.
Gonzalez, A.
·Gonzalez, Rafael.
Kramer & Co.
Riquero, Francisco.
Sanchez & Hno., F.
Zarrabeitia & Azurmendi.

Orthopedical instruments.
Dominguez, Antonio.
Galvez Guillem Felipe.
Gallegos, Antonio.
Giralt, A.
Gros, José.
Martinez, Antonio.
Vega, Higinio A.

Paper-manufacturers.
Castro, Fernandez & Co.

Peltry, importers.
Aedo & Co., Viuda de.
Blanco, Tomás.
Dalmau Estrany & Co.
Diaz & Co., Mariano.
Fernandez & Narvaez.
Garau, Mateo.
Lliteras & Co.
Martinez, Juan.
Martinez, Ramón.
Martinez, Suarez.
Menendez, Rafael.
Ortiz & Hno.
Parets, Antelo & Co.
Pons & Co.
Torres & Co., J.
Veiga, Solá & Co.
Vidal Hnos.

Petroleum-refiner.
Agencias de las refinerías.

Photographers.
Castellote, Félix.
Cohner, S. A.
Maceo, N. E.
Mestre, Narciso.
Misa, Ignacio.
Rodriguez, José.
Suarez & Co., Viuda de.
Stenger, Francisco.

HAVANA—Continued.

Photographers' supplies.
Lopez & Co., J. S.

Pianos and musical instruments.
Curtis, T. J.
Esperez, Nicolás.
Lopez, Anselmo.
Marin Varona, A.
Pomares & Rivas.
Xiqués, Felipe E.

Pictures, mirrors, and paintings.
Balsa & Gottardi.
Fernández, Genaro.
Fernández Cibrian, Manuel.
Lecanda, Bernardo.
Pola & Co.
Valdés Castillo, Quintin.

Printing offices.
Abadens, Viuda de.
Alonso de Rivero, Herminia.
Alvarez & Co., A.
Arazoza, Francisco P.
Chao, Alejandro.
Farres, Juan.
Fernandez Casona, E.
Martinez, Saturnino.
Perez, Cayetano.
Puliado & Diaz.
Romero Rubio, M.
Ruiz & Hno.
Spencer Heredero de S. S.
Valdés, Teresa.

Saddlery, importers.
Arce, Vellon & Co.
Castillon, Briol & Soler.
García & Co.
Martinez, Juan.
Sala, José.
Vallés & Co., M. G.
Veiga, Solá & Co.

Sewing machines.
Alvarez & Hinse.
Fernandez, Constantino.
Gonzalez & Co.
Raño & Sobrino.
Solares, Luciano.

HAVANA—Continued.

Sewing machines—Continued.
Sopeña & Co.
Xiqués, Felipe E.

Silk goods, notions, and perfumery importers.
Ablanedo, Fernandez & Co.
Alvaréz & Perez.
Bidegajn, Prudencio.
Bulnes, Manuel F.
Castro, Fernandez & Co.
Coll, Miguel.
Del Monte, Viuda de G.
Fernandez Gomez, Angel.
Gandasegni & Vega.
García Corujédo Hno.
García & Hno.
Giral, Zorrilla.
Martin, José A.
Martinez & Co., R.
Medero, J.
Menendez, Villar & Co.
Perez del Molino, Luis.
Perez, Manuel P.
Pernas, Hno & Co.
Piélago & Co.
Pis & Co., C.
Rodriguez, Gonzalez & Co.
Saiz, Ovies & Co.
Sanchez & Hno, F.
Taladrid & Hno.
Tenreiro & Roldan.
Toca & Gomez.
Torresagasti.
Uriarte & San Martin.

Small hardware, notions, and perfumery.
Alvarez & Hno.
Blanco, Nicolás.
Castro & Co.
Doria & Milhau.
Dufau, E.
Fernandez, Evelio.
García Corujedo Hnos.
Hierro & Co.
Lambrini & Co.
Llanio & Muniz.
Palacio, Taracena & Co.

HAVANA—Continued.

Small hardware, notions, and perfumery—
Continued.
Reboredo & Co., J.
Sanchez, Manuel.
Sanchez, Roman.
Sanchez & Hno., F.
Valle & Co.
Wilson, Edwin W.

Stationery.
Barandiarán Hnos.
Bárcena & Co.
Canalejo & Xiqués.
Castro, Fernandez & Co.
Castro & Gutierrez.
Costa, Pablo M.
Chao, Alejandro.
Fernandez & Co., P.
Gomez, Ramón.
Gonzalez, Juan.
Gutierrez, Julian.
Gutierrez & Cueto.
Palmas, M. R.
Ruiz & Co.
Ruiz & Co., M.
Ruiz & Hno.
Solana & Co., B.
Torres & Co., J.
Uriarte & San Martin.
Valdepares, José.
Wilson, Edwin.

Sugar mills.
Bernavon, Vicente.
Nadal & Bernitez, Miguel.
Ugarte, José.
Villalba, Enriquez & Co.

Sugar-refiners.
Ordoñez Hnos.

Tinware.
Abad, María.
Abad, Tomás.
Alvarez, David.
Alvarez & Co.
Arcas, Andrés.
Armenteros, Socorro.
Baloyra, Manel.

HAVANA—Continued.

Tinware—Continued.
  Caballero, María.
  Duran, Eusebio.
  Fernandez, Joaquin.
  Fernandez, Narciso.
  Garcia, Antonio.
  Gilí, Antonio.
  Gonzalez, Cárlos.
  Gonzalez, José.
  Gual, Francisco.
  Gutierrez, Eustaqui.
  Hierro, Ceferino.
  Maruri, Federico.
  Menocal, Cárlos.
  Navarrete, Diego.
  Navarrete, Polonia.
  Paniagua, Juan.
  Perez & Mendez.
  Piñera, Cárlos.
  Piñera, Telesforo.
  Puenté, Joaquin.
  Rigual, José.
  Rocatagliata, Enrique.
  Rodriguez, Jaime.
  Rodriguez, Josefa.
  Rodriguez, Juan M.
  Triana, Francisco.

Tobacco, leaf.
  Acosta, Manuel.
  Aguiar, Rosendo.
  Alvarez, José.
  Allesta, Lorenzo.
  Arango, Ramón.
  Argudin, Manuel.
  Argüelles, Donato.
  Argüelles & Co., R.
  Bacallao, Antonio.
  Bernal, Juan.
  Bernheim & Son.
  Blanco, Ceballos & Co.
  Cadenaba, Gabriel.
  Cano & Hno.
  Carvajal, Leopoldo.
  Cepa, José.
  Cernuda, Joaquin.
  Cifuentes, Ramón.
  Codina, Jaime.

HAVANA—Continued.

Tobacco, leaf—Continued.
  Cueto, Manuel.
  Diaz Hnos.
  Echevesta, Joaquin.
  Fernandez & Hijo, Eugenio.
  Fernandez, Fernando.
  Fernandez Pulido, José.
  Fernandez, Ramón.
  Fernandez & Co., Joaquin.
  Fernandez & Ruiz.
  Font & Hijo.
  Garcia, Francisco.
  Garcia Hnos & Co.
  Garcia & Suarez.
  Garcia & Co., M.
  Gonzalez & Co., A.
  Gutierrez, Ramón.
  Hernandez, José.
  Iglesias, Manuel.
  Leon, Manuel.
  Lezama, José.
  Lopez & Co., Calixto.
  Lozano, Pendas & Co.
  Llerandi, José.
  Mantecon, Manuel.
  Marti & Co., J.
  Martinez, José.
  Marx Blun & Co.
  Menendez & Gonzalez.
  Muñiz & Hno.
  Navas, Lorenzo.
  Palacio, Gregorio.
  Paula, Luis & Co.
  Perez, Blanco & Co.
  Perez, Ehmer & Co.
  Prendez, Manuel.
  Puente & Co., J.
  Rabelo, Miguel.
  Rodriguez & Santalla.
  Salomon & Hno., G.
  Sanchez, Bartolomé.
  Santalla, Echevaria & Co.
  Santana, Nicolás.
  Suarez Cuétra, Manuel.
  Suarez, José Antonio.
  Torres, Pablo.
  Valdés, Manuel.

HAVANA—Continued.

Tobacco, leaf—Continued.
Valle, Pascual del.
Vega, Francisco.
Vega, José.
Vidal, Pio.
Viña, José de la.
Wagenfuehr, Eduardo A.
Undertakers.
Alvarez, R.
Caballero, Francisco.
Campos, Manuel.
Diaz, Felipe.
García, Ramón.
Gomez, Francisco.
Gomez, Juan A.
Guillot, Ricardo.
Gutierrez, Alejandro.
Infanzón, Matías.
Lopez, Serapio.
Lozano, Leandro.
Medina, Andrés.
Ramos, Adolfo.
Surís, Francisco.
Urrutia & Co.
Watches, importers.
Bernard, A. B.
Fernandez Cuervo, R.
Ordoñez Hnos.
Zarrabeitia & Azurmendi.
Wines and liquors.
Brocchi, Juan.
García & Trascastro.
Gil, Francisco.
Gonzalez, Santiago.
Muñoz, Manuel.
Noriega, Prudencio.
Parejo, J. M.
Rodriguez, Domingo.
Seijo & Hno.
Vega, Diego.
Vidal, Francisco.

HOLGUÍN.

Boots and shoes.
Alvarez, Juan R.
Cornet, Eleuterio.
Viña, Manuel.

HOLGUÍN—Continued.

Chinaware, books, etc.
Luque, Heliodoro.
Drugs.
Goya, Francisco.
Tamayo, Viuda de.
Groceries and provisions.
Camafreita, Vicente.
García, José A.
García, Juan.
Nates, Bolívar Manuel.
Perez, Alvarez & Co.
Importer.
Picaso, D. José.

ISABELA DE SAGUA.

Exporter of hides, bones, and woods.
Belt, Benjamin.
Importers of coal and cooperage.
García, Torres & Co.

JARUCO.

Boots and shoes.
Borjes, Agustin.
Drugs.
González, Rufino.
Páez, Julio María.
Rodriguez, Carlos.
Furniture.
Aguirre, Julian.
Hardware.
Castillo, Aquilino.
Jewelry and watches.
Delgado, José.

JOVELLANOS.

Boots and shoes.
Achin Apó, José.
Beltran, Agustin.
Echaide, Francisco.
Estevez, José.
Fernandez, Manuel.
Luna, Dolores.
Ruiloba, Ricardo.
Sobrenca, Valera.
Drugs.
Cadenas, Isidro.
Figueroa, Fermin.

JOVELLANOS—Continued.

Foundries.
Paniagua, Ricalt.
Ressler & Co.

Furniture.
Alboniga, Juan.

Hardware.
Murillo, Remigio.

Printing office.
Gonzalez, Cármen.

Tobacco leaf.
Santillano, Higinio.

Undertakers.
Rodriguez, Rafael.
Soto, José María.

LAS VUELTAS.

Boots and shoes.
Ferrer, Juan.
Rodriguez, Simón.
Visiedo, Miguel.

Drugs.
Hernandez, Enrique.
Hernandez, Manuel.
Nuche, Genaro.
Puget, José.

Sewing machines.
Lopez & Cortiñas.

MADRUGA.

Boots and shoes.
Almio, Gervasio.
Coll, Rafael.
García, José.
Pino, Anselmo.

Drugs.
Reyes, Manuel.

MANAGUA.

Boots and shoes.
Alvarez, Celestino.
Suarez, Manuel.

Drugs.
García, Emilia.

MARIANAO.

Drugs.
Cuesta, Severiano.
Iglesias, Abrahán.
Nuñez, Jorge.

MANZANILLO.

Boots and shoes.
Castropeña, Venacio.
Estrada, Roque.
Martinez, Paulino.
Mata, Laureano.
Mejia, Pedro.
Quesada, Clotilde.
Romeu, Juan.
Tamayo, Antonio.

Drugs.
Céspedes, P.
Mojarrieta, Miguel A.
Sanchez Sanz, Ramón.

Dry goods.
Almirall & Llopiz.
Vazquez & Co.

Foundries.
Fandiño, Juan.
Perez & Ibarra.

Groceries and provisions.
Aguirre, Emilio.
Coyani & Bruschini.
Menendez, Saturnino.
Planas & Hnos.
Sanchez, José.
Sisa, Feliciano.
Solis & Co.

Groceries and provisions, dry goods, crockery, etc.
Bonet, Asnaldo.
Granda Hno., Baltasar.
Guerrero & Co., Inocencio.
Martinez, Ramón García.
Merladet & Manday.
Planas, Miguel.
Plascoaga & Co., Perez.
Ramirez & Co.
Sandser, José Suarez.
Torres, Rafael.
Venecia, José.

MANZANILLO—Continued.

Hardware.
Brunell & Blanco, José.
Treserra & Guitart, Angel.
Urquijo & Carbajosa.

Hatter.
Vazquez, Marcelinó.

Importers.
Aces, Boeras & Co.
Beattie & Co.
Muñoz & Co., J.
Ramirez & Oro.
Rigney & Co., J.
Venecia, José M.

Merchants and bankers.
Boeras & Co.
Ferrer & Co.
Ferrer, Mori & Co.
Muñiz & Co., J.
Ramirez & Oro.
Roca Vivas Hnos.
Roca & Co.
Rouvira, Celestino.
Sanchez, José.
Segura, Guillermo.
Soler, Pedro.
Tornés, Rafael.
Venecia, José M.

Photographer.
Ochoa, Oscar.

Printers.
Fernández de Córdova, Fernando.
Fernández, Esteban.

Saddlery and shoes.
Celcis, Bonifacio.
Ginestá, Emilio Urgas.
Gonzalez, Salustiano.
Lagrista, Vicente Comas.
Tano, José Miranda.

Tobacco-manufacturers.
Gordillo, Emilio.
Merladet, Eusebio.
Planas & Gordillo.
Porro & Nuñez.

S. Ex. 8, pt. 11——·25

MATANZAS.

Arms and ammunition.
Mons, José María.
Rodriguez & Huo., Antonio.

Bankers and commission merchants.
Bea, Bellido & Co.
Brinkerhoff & Co.
Collado, Rufino.
Deetjen, C. L.
Galindez, Aldama & Co.
Heidegger & Co.
Juris & Garriga.
Lacerat, Pablo.
Molins, Emilio.
Zanetti, Dubois & Co.

Booksellers and stationers.
Albuerne, Manuel.
Carreño & Sobrino.
Rodriguez & Co.

Boots and shoes.
Betancourt, Ambrosio.
Calderin, Francisco.
Escolano, Francisco T.
Gayart, Francisco.
Hernandez, José.
Hernandez, Juan.
Herrero Monje, Domingo.
Lopez, Juan.
Ramón, Carolina.
Rodriguez & Rodriguez, Francisco.
Sanchez Hernandez, Pedro.
Sanchez, Pedro.
Sántana, Juan.
Silva, Domingo.

Crockery, etc.
Ampudia & Fuentes.
Ampudia & Mardonell.
Menéndez & Co.
Querol, Prudencio.
Rivas, Joaquin.
Rodriguez, Julio.
Sanchez & Quirós.
Schweyer, Alberto.
Tapia, Luis E.
Tomás, Vicente A.
Trelles, Jorge.

MATANZAS—Continued.

Crockery, etc.—Continued.
Ulmo, Andrés.
Valdés Anciano, José A.
Vera, Felix.
Zambrana, Manuel.

Coal.
Bea, Bellido & Co.
Galindez & Aldama.
Zambea, Juan.

Drugs.
Artiz & Zanetti.
Betancourt, Antonio.
Calle, Pedro de la.
Colfil Feliú, Joaquin.
Ginoulhiac, Eugenio.
Lecuona Madan, Domingo.
Lluria & Co.
Rusignol Miralles, Bernardo.
Sol, Digna América del.
Triolet, Ernesto.

Electric light company.
Hoffmann, Jorge, superintendent.

Furniture.
Angulo & Gil, Andrés.
Cabarrocas & Co.
Fernández, Josefa.
Fernández Lario, José.
García, Gregorio.
Gonzalez & Co., Manuel.
Romero & Villa.
Urcola, Sebastian.
Venero, Casimiro.

Groceries and provisions.
Abav & Hno.
Alvarez & Co.
Bariñó, Pons & Hijo.
Bernales, José.
Boada & Sobrino.
Cancela, Lino.
Cariezo & Co.
Grau & Co.
Martínez & Burset.
Ortiz & García, Angel.

Hardware.
Alegría & Hno.
Alvarez & Hipólito.

MATANZAS—Continued.

Hardware—Continued.
Amízaga & Co.
Bea, Bellido & Co.
Fernández Zorilla, Francisco.
Iturralde, Eugenio.
Ortiz & Gutierrez, Juan Francisco.
Rechaga, Pablo.
Rodríguez, N. Rechaga.

Importers.
Amezaga & Co.
Dubois, Zanetti & Co.
Gous, Pedro & Co.
Heidegger & Co.
Hoffmann & Co.
Laso, Gabriel.
Lluna, Francisco de.
Marzol, Adolfo.
Zanetti & Co.

Lumber and clay.
Amézaga, García & Co.
Galindez & Aldama, Antonio.
Zabala & Bea, José.

Manufacturers.
Arencibia, Manuel (flour).
Bellido, Heydrich & Co. (ice).
Benitez, Isabel (flour).
Cano, Gabriel (scales).
Dallí, Tomás (flour).
Durbase, Miguel (soap).
Galtraiht de Pérez, Elisa (brooms).
Hernaudez, Albnerue (liquors).
Inchaurtueta, José María (liquors and vinegar).
Josa & Co. (soap).
Luera, Antonio (soda water).
Maceda Sánchez, José (matches).
Marzol, Adolfo (liquors).
Méndez, Enriqno de (soda water).
Mons, José María (trusses).
Montero, Ramón (trunks).
Pérez, Josefa (liquors).
Pons & Co. (liquors).
Purcalla, Pablo (charcoal).
Rodríguez & Hno, Antonio.
Serna & Calero (candles).
Tejeiro, Balbino (trunks).

MATANZAS—Continued.

Manufacturers—Continued.
Valdés, Herederos de Adelaida (brooms).
Zardoya & Co., M. (liquors).

Photographers.
Hernandez, Junco & Co.
Otero, A.
Ruiz de Castro.

Sewing machines.
Collado, Benito.
Gutierrez & Co., Gerardo.
Salgueiro, Manuel.
Venero, Julian.

Small hardware.
Galvez & Rusignol.
Ruiz Diaz, Pedro.
Ruiz·Rodriguez & Co.
Soriano & Celeuja.
Sotelo, Estanislao.
Vila & Co., A.

Sugar and molasses.
Almirall, Peralta.
Amezaga, García & Co.
Bea, Bellido & Co.
Brinkerhoff & Co.
Capó, Simon.
Castañer, Joaquin.
Galindez & Aldama, Antonio.
Lersia, Manuel.
Sainz & Co., José.

Tobacco, leaf.
Aguirre, Hermano & Co.
Fuentes, Lorenzo.
García, José.
García, José de la Rosa.
Lombano, Cayetano.
Lombano & Hermano.
Martínez, Manuel de la Rosa.
Pérez Menéndez, Celestino.

MINAS.

Boots and shoes.
Lopez, Angel.
Miranda, Ramón.

Drugs.
Ferreras, Mariano.

MORÓN.

Drugs.
Arnaiz Fernandez, Segundo.

Printing office.
Cueto & Martinez, Antonio.

NUEVITAS.

Bookseller.
Calaforra, Primo.

Boots and shoes.
Quesada, Gil.

Crockery.
Calaforra, Primo.

Drugs.
Fornos Perez, J.
Moya, Antonio.

Groceries and provisions.
Rodriguez Alonso, J.
Rodriguez, José.
Tomeu, Janer & Co.

Hardware.
Rodriguez, José.

Importers.
Gibbs, Ricardo.
Rodriguez, Vicente & Co.
Tomeu & Co., F.
Yriarte Hno & Co.

Merchants and bankers.
Rodriguez, Vicente & Co.
Sanchez Adan, Bernabé.
Tomeu, Janer & Co.

Printing office.
Arrebola, Vicente.

Undertakers.
Ferrer, Bartolomé.
Varona, Gregorio.

PINAR DEL RIO.

Bankers.
Suárez, Girbal & Co.

Booksellers and stationers.
Fernandez, Agapito.
Fernandez, Guerra & Hno.
Gil, José María.
Gonzalez & Hno.
Mijores, Marcos.

PINAR DEL RIO—Continued.

Boots and shoes.
  Castro, Domingo.
  Morales, Jacinto.
  Paban, José.
  Puig, Domingo.
  Santamaría, Luis.

Cigar-manufacturer.
  Mijares, Julian.

Crockery.
  Fernández, Paulino.
  Rodriguez, Eleuterio.
  Rodriguez, F. Ricardo.
  Sanchez & Barrero.

Drugs.
  Dominguez & Legorburu, Dolores.
  García Suárez, José.
  Porta, Alfredo.
  Rodriguez, Jacinto.
  Rodriguez Sanpedro, Manual.
  Vila, Tito.

Groceries and provisions.
  Diaz Lopez, Francisco.
  Gonzalez & Hno.
  Lopez & Co., G.
  Sordo & Co., A.
  Suárez, Girbal & Co.
  Viñas, Prieto & Co.

Hardware.
  Diaz & Lopez, Francisco.
  Fernandez, Paulino.
  Rodriguez, Eleuterio.
  Rodriguez, F. Ricardo.
  Solarez, Luis.
  Sordo & Co., A.

Hatters.
  Alonso & Co., Manuel.
  Carriles & Co., Lucio.
  Cobian & Alea.
  Gonzalez & Hno.
  Guerra & Hno.
  Navarro & Vigueira.

Photographer.
  Antonio Pi.

Printing offices.
  Fernández & Vives.
  Ruiz, Angel.

PINAR DEL RIO—Continued.

Sewing machines.
  Alonso & Co., Manuel.
  Carriles & Co., Lucio.
  Gonzalez & Hnos., J.
  Lopez & Co., Saturnino.
  Menendez & Co., Constantino.
  Navarro & Vigueira.
  Suarez, Girbal & Co.

Silk goods.
  Alonso & Co., Manuel.
  Carriles & Co., Lucio.
  Gonzalez & Hnos., J.
  Rodriguez, Anastasio.

Small hardware and notions.
  Fernandez, Agapito.
  Fernandez, Paulino.
  Gonzalez & Hno.
  Guerra & Hno., F.
  Mijares, Marcos.
  Rodriguez, Atanasio.

Tailoring houses.
  Alonso & Co., Manuel.
  Carriles & Co., Lucio.
  Lopez & Co.
  Navarro & Vigueira.

Undertaker.
  Bertran, José.

PLACETAS.

Boots and shoes.
  Rodriguez, Rafael.

Drugs.
  Fumero, Nicolás.
  Pérez, Lorenzo G.
  Tejeda, Diego.

Importers.
  Castañon, Leandro.
  Fortun, José M.

Printing offices.
  Castañon, L.
  Lagomasino, L.

Small hardware and notions.
  Moa, Ramón.

PUERTO DEL PADRE.

Boots and shoes.
Gonzalez, Catalino.
Lopez, F.
Negrete, José.
Risco, Carlos.

Groceries and provisions.
Martinez & Querol.
Rodriguez & Pereda.

Timber.
Miguel Tomás & Co.
Zenon, Torrens & Co.

PUERTO PRÍNCIPE.

Arms and ammunition.
Gonzalez, Luciano.
Lavadens, Juan.
Zayas, Adriano.

Banks.
Banco Agrícola.
Banco Español de la Isla de Cuba.

Books.
Ginferre, Isidro.
García, José Serapio.

Drugs.
Betancourt, Fernando.
Blanco, Alberto W.
Casas, Alfredo.
Herrera, Enrique.
Mendez, Salustiano.
Ramirez, Francisco.
Socarrás, Aurelio.

Electric-light company.
Ruiz Toledo Muñoz, Ramón, superintendent.

Furniture.
Torres Alvarez, José.

Groceries and provisions.
Cásares, Blas.
Gonzalez Celis, Juan.
Margenats & Burzoza.
Rodriguez & Co., Isaac.

Importer.
Roura, Ramón.

PUERTO PRÍNCIPE—Continued.

Manufacturers.
Fernandez, Santos (tobacco).
Forcadas, Salvador (bricks).
Lopez, Segundo (liquors).
Mas & Margenats (chocolate).
Mestre & Pijuan (liquors).
Rodriguez & Co., A. (tobacco).

Photographer.
Delmonte, Rafael.
Fernández & Naranjo.

Sewing machines.
Cabada & Co.
Gonzalez Solares, Rudesindo.
Maribona & Hno.
Pagés, Benito.

Silk goods.
Rodriguez & Hno.

Tobacco, leaf.
Oyer & Robert, José.
Vidal & Robert, José.

RANCHO VELOZ.

Boots and shoes.
Azcarrate, Cecilio.
Martinez & Co., Manuel.

Drugs.
Figueroa Martí, Enrique.

REGLA.

Coal.
Barrios & Coello.
Mendez, Benito.

Drugs.
Avila, José G.
Denias, Bernardíno.
Echavarría, Antonio.
Gonzalez, Polonia.

Foundry.
Bartalot, Tomás.

Hardware.
Cajigas & Co.

Lumber.
Mocunill, Batet & Co.

REGLA—Continued.

Manufacturers.
Amesnea & García (soap).
Diaz, Antonio (rope).
Ferrol & Co. (soap).
Giralt, José (rope).
Lopez, Fernando (chocolate).

Refiners of petroleum.
Herederos de Moré & Co.

Undertakers.
Bonet, Francisco.
Chassague, Cirilo.

SAGUA LA GRANDE.

Bank.
Banco Español, Sucursal.

Bankers and commission merchants (importers and exporters).
Amézega & Co.
Arronte, Manuel.
Arronte & Co.
Corrales Hnos.
La Condesa, Viuda de Casa-Moré.
Larrondo & Co.
Millares, Radelat & Co.
Mora, Oña & Co.
Prieto & Co.
Puente, Arenas & Co.

Books and stationery.
Ramos, Miguel.

Drugs.
Figueroa, Alfredo.
López, Luis.
Oña, Eugenio.
Prieto, Alberto.
Roa, Camilo.

Foundry.
Bustillo, Antonio.

Furniture.
Blanco & Rivas.
Gispert, Martin.
Pita, Juan.

Groceries and provisions.
Aróstegui & Alzúa.
Ciriz, Fernandez & Co. (importers).
Corrales & Hno.

SAGUA LA GRANDE—Continued.

Groceries and provisions—Continued.
De Leon, King & Co. (importers).
Gallegos, Lucio & Co.
Gonzalez & Hno.
Menendez & Concha (importers).
Noriega & Co.
Perez & Co., Manuel.
Puente, Arenas & Co. (importers).
Radelat & Arenas (importers).

Hardware.
Carbonell & Hijos.
Joirin & Nadal.
Lorenzo & Co., J.
Maribona, Laya & Co. (importers).
Ramirez, Inés.

Hatters.
García & Fernández.
Lapuente, Domingo.

Importer of hides, honey, bones, and woods.
Pelletier, Antonio.

Lumber.
Escandon & Co.
Llacuno, Diego.

Photographer.
Alvarez, Eduardo.

Silk goods and notions.
Andreu, Victor.
Cabeza & Primo.
Gutierrez, Felipe.

Undertakers.
Chavez & Parajuelos.
Ponce de Leon, Luis.

SAN ANTONIO.

Drugs.
Esparolini, Blas.
Fernández Cadena, F.
Luna, Genaro.

Furniture.
Gómez, Eliseo.

Groceries and provisions.
Perez Capote, José María.

Hardware.
Gómez, Eliseo.
Tejedor & Alonso.

SPANISH COLONIES. **391**

SAN ANTONIO—Continued.

Hatter.
Rodriguez, Bernardo.

Silk goods and notions.
Argüelles, Agustin.
Carranza, Rudesindo.
Gómez, Eliseo.
Guiterrez, C. Manuel.

Undertaker.
Ebra, Rafael.

SAN JOSÉ DE LAS LAJAS.

Drugs.
Fernandez, Tomás.
Hernandez, Celestino.

SAN JUAN DE LOS REMEDIOS.

Crockery, etc.
Pascua, Rodriguez & Co.

Drugs.
Escobar, Luis A.
Gonzalez, Joaquin.
Pujet, Esteban.
Rio, Joaquin del.

Hides and skins.
Bidegaray & Co.

Small hardware.
Fuentes Pando, Manuel.
García, Manuel R.
Valdés, Juan Bautista.

Undertaker.
Testar, Alejandro.

SANCTI SPIRITUS.

Drugs.
Barceló, Viuda de Francisco.
Galí Diaz, Ferreol.
García Cañizares, José.
Rabell Marin, Francisco J.
Trelles Figueroa, Landelino.

Furniture.
Nawmann Schröeder, Federico.

Merchant and banker.
Gruppe, Agusto.

SANCTI SPIRITUS—Continued.

Photographer.
Trelles Figueroa, José.

Printing offices.
Canto Cueto, Cárlos.
Toboada & Hno.

Small hardware.
Alvarez Miranda, Eduardo.
Blasón Correa, Luis.

Undertakers.
Torres & Co., Salustiano.

SANTA CLARA.

Bankers.
García & Co., C. A.

Boots and shoes.
Calzadilla, Marcelino.
Leon, Rufino de.
Meulener, Fernando.
Perez, Federico.
Ulacia & Hijos, D.

Cigars and tobacco.
Fernández Vega, S.
Ramos, Eduardo.
Vizcaino, Miguel.

Drugs.
Acosta, José F.
Cristo, Juan N.
Onis, J.
Silva, Rafael J.
Torrens, Miguel A.

Hardware and crockery.
Bengochea, Manuel.
Calvo, Domingo.
García & Co., C. A.
Gonzalez del Valle, José.

Hatters.
Blanco, Francisco.
Calvo, Juan C.
Fernández, Rafael.
Fernández, V.
Martinez & Cruz.

Jewelers and watchmakers.
Benitez, José.
Meulener, Agustin.
Tobió, José María.
Valdés, Antonio.

SANTA CLARA—Continued.

Lumber.
García & Co., C. A.

Photographer.
Valdés León, Antonio.

Printing offices.
Alemán, José B.
Bengochea, Manuel M.
Casañas & Fernández.
Muñiz, M.

Small hardware.
Anido, Antonio.
Olavarrieta, Serafín.
Ruiz, Aurelio.

Tobacco, leaf.
González Coya, Sabino.

Undertakers.
Dupuy, Beltrán.
Pérez, Manuel.

SANTA CRUZ.

Importers and exporters.
Voigt & Hencke.

SANTIAGO DE CUBA.

Booksellers.
Aders & Co.
Lopez & Co.
Perez Dubrull, Enrique.

Boots and shoes.
Arias & Co.
Campo & Co.
Coll & Hermano (importers).
Comas, Juan (importer).
Flaguer & Co. (importers.)

Crockery and glassware.
Idel, Castillo & Co.
Valiente, Ricardo.

Drugs.
Bottino, Luis Carlos.
Causse, Emiliano.
Guerrero, Antonio M.
Martinez, Alfredo.
Millan, Miguel.
Padró Greñán, Tomás.

SANTIAGO DE CUBA—Continued.

Drugs—Continued.
Padró, Jaíme.
Padró, Tomás.
Planas & Co., Manuel.
Quintana, Ambrosio.
Ramirez Ortiz, Juan.
Trenard, Teobaldo.

Dry goods.
Herrera, Martinez & Co.
Hill & Casas.
Sánchez & Hno.
Serradell & Co.

Exporters and commission merchants.
Brooks & Co. (sugar).
Bueno & Co., J. (sugar, mahogany,
and cedar).
Castillo & Co., J. del (woods).
Cuevas, J. (general merchandise).
Ferrer, J. F. (general products and
manganese ore).
Hill & Casas (tobacco on commis-
sion).
Inglada, Arturo (tobacco on commis-
sion.)
Marques Hnos. & Co. (woods, as
agents).
Mas & Co. (tobacco on commission
and manganese ore).
Masfarrol, Manuel (cocoanuts).
Schumann & Co. (woods).

Flour.
Cuevas, J.
Ferrer, J. F.
Ros & Co., E.
Schumann & Co.

Foundries.
Arragon, A.
Empresa del Ferrocarril.

Furniture.
Casals, Enrique.

Groceries and provisions.
Abascal & Co.
Berenguer, José.
Bruna, Antonio.
Castillo & Co., J. del.

SANTIAGO DE CUBA—Continued.

Groceries and provisions—Continued.
Eguilior, José María.
Ferrer, J. F.
Font, Pedro.
Jaíme & Lluhiz.
Llopiz, Enrique.
Lluhi & Co.
Mas & Co.
Miret Crespo & Co.
Ros & Co., Eligio.
. Salas & Fornello.
Trillas & Co.

Haberdashers.
Carreño & Sirgo.
Castillo & Suarez.

Hardware.
Brauet & Co.
Camp & Badillo.
Font & Falp.
Inglada & Co., Arturo.
Juglada, A.
Llovet & Boix.
Llovet & Co., J.
Márquez Hno. & Co.
Mustelier, Asunción.
Soler & Francoli.

Hats.
Arias, Manuel.
Balart, Domingo.
Catalá & Costa.

Importers.
Bueno & Co., J.
Brooks & Co.
Hill & Casas.
Inglada & Co., Arturo.
Marquez Hnos. & Co.
Martinez, Herrera & Co.
Mitchel, José.
Trillas & Co.
Valiente, Ricardo.

Lumber.
Cardonne, Pablo.
Hereaux, Oscar & Emilio.

Manufacturers.
Bacardi & Co. (liquors).
Bermúdez Hermida (candles).

SANTIAGO DE CUBA—Continued.

Manufacturers—Continued.
Camps & Co., C. (liquors).
Crossi, Mestre & Co. (liquors).
Hernandez, Reguera (conserves).
Misser, José (candles and conserves).
Reaud, Alfredo (ice).
Rifá Huos. (macaroni).
Rovira & Guillaume (liquors).
Sarabia & Hno. (conserves).
Torres, José (cigars).
Trenard & Muiry (tiles).
Vidal, V. (soap).

Merchants and bankers.
Bosch & Co.
Brauet & Co.
Brooks & Co.
Bueno & Co.
Inglada & Co.
Mas & Co.
Ros & Co.
Saenz & Co.
Shumann & Co.

Photographers.
Babastro, R.
Baxarias, Manuel.
Desquiron, Antonio.
Ortiz, Pedro.

Printing offices.
Massana & Co.
Morales, Manuel.

Saddlery, importers.
Coll & Hermanos.
Comas, Juan.
Flaguer & Co.
Rio & Hermanos.

Sewing machines and lamps.
Flaguer & Co.
Rio Hermanos.
Valiente, Ricardo.

Silk goods.
Aders & Co.
D'John, David S.
Felise & Roget.
Fuertes & Co.
Gené, M.
Martí, Diaz & Co.

394 SPANISH COLONIES.

SANTIAGO DE CUBA—Continued.

Tailoring houses.
Castillo & Suarez.
Castillo, Manuel.
Corredor & Hnos.
Magrans & Co.
Marino, El.
Palomo & Rubio.
Planas & Co.

Tobacco-manufacturers.
Fabré, Bartolomé.
Massana & Co.
Mestre & Mestre, Ramón.
Polanco, Camps & Co.
Rovira & Guillaume.
Yofré Hnos.

Undertakers.
Bravo Carreoso, Elígio.
Casamor, Justo.
Corona, Benigno.
Ruis, Luis Felipe.

TRINIDAD.

Drugs.
Baslida, Julio.
Cailá, J.
Mascorto, Narciso.

Furniture.
Torres, Domingo.

Groceries and provisions.
Fuente, Martinez & Co.
Garmendía, Victoriano.
Perez & Co., Gabriel.
Rubiés, Jaime.
Vila & Portilla.

Merchants and bankers.
Meyer, Thode & Co.
Schmidt & Co., Guillermo.
Vila & Portilla.

TRINIDAD—Continued.

Printing offices.
Diario, El.
Iznaga, Mariano.
Sociedad Anónima.

TRUJILLO.

Importers.
Castillo, Prospero.
Julia, José.

UNIÓN DE REYES.

Drugs.
Lastres, Nestor.
Telot, Jorge.

Foundry.
Marcelin & Co.

VICTORIA DE LAS TUNAS.

Groceries and provisions.
Fajardo & Cardona.
Fernández, Emilio.

VILLA DE GÜINES.

Drugs.
Espinosa, Joaquin.
Fernández Guerrero, Tomás.
Moreno, Eduardo.

Hardware.
Aldecoa, Juan Antonio.
Garzon, Esteban.

Photographer.
Flores, Emilio.

Printing office.
Cuesta & Renduoles, Valentin.

Puerto Rico.

AGUADILLA.

Coffee merchants and exporters.
Arana, Antonio C.
Arana, Felipe.
Colon, Sebastian.
Delgado, Antonio.
Feo, Serapio.
Frontera, Guillermo.
Luigi, Pablo.
Marqué, Miguel.
Oliver & Delgado.
Paoli, Domingo.
Torres, Santiago.
Viella Hnos.

Commission merchants.
Buttmann & Co.
Esteves, J. F.
Martinez, J. R. M.
Schnabel & Co.
Silva & Co.
Valle Koppische & Co.

Druggists and chemists.
Iturrino Hnos.
Navas, Jorge M.
Picornell, Salvador.

Furniture.
Belfors, Juan.
Call, José B.
Morales, Antonio.

General merchandise, wholesale.
Acevedo & Co., V.
Arbona, Juan.
Canals, Coll & Co.
Carbonell, Agustin.

AGUADILLA—Continued.

General merchandise, wholesale—Cont'd.
Castañer, Juan.
García, Garbino.
Gonzalez, Felipe.
Gonzalez, Tomás.
Lacaroz, Nicolás.
Marquez & Co.
Marquez, Miguel.
Martinez, Braulio.
Mayol & Suan.
Mendez, Aurelio.
Mendez, Justo.
Novoa, Ramón.
Rios, Pedro.
Suan & Co.
Torres, Juan.
Vidal, Pablo.
Vilella Hnos.

Importers and retail merchants.
Boscio & Co.
Deliz & Co., J. M.
Deliz & Toro.
Diaz, Toró.
Llumet Hermanos.
Martinez, J. R. M.
Mitjans Hermanos.
Peña & Rodriguez.
Rofols, J. L.
Rubio, Ernesto.
Santiesleban & Chavarri, P.

Jewelers.
Aramburo, Pedro.
Gonzaga, Luis.

ARECIBO.

Drugs.
Hijalmarson, Cárlos.
Perez, Manuel.
Rivera, José Ramón.
Silva, Rafael Gabino.

General importers.
Ahumada & Co.
Bahr & Co.
Balseyro & Co., Benigno.
Ledesma & Co., G.
Muro, Ruperto.
Nones & Co.
Roses & Co.
Rupert & Co., M.

Groceries and provisions, wholesale.
Galanes & García.
Ledesma, Francisco.
Morales, José.
Pericas & Co.
Rupert & Co., M.
Vilamil, Ramón.

Ship chandlery and naval stores.
Ahumada & Co.
Balseyro & Co., B.
Muro, Ruperto.
Nones & Co.

Undertakers.
Lopez, José.
Pereira, Juan.

FAJARDO.

Bird & Co., J.
Cintrón, L. M.
Véve, Vinde de.

GUAYAMA.

Bankers.
Amoros Hermanos.
Cano & Co.

Bookbinders.
Castillo & Luzunares.

Booksellers and stationers.
Capo, José.
Castillo & Luzunares.

GUAYAMA—Continued.

Drugs.
Bruno, Cárlos.
Bruno, Julio S.
Bruno, Nicolas.
Dominguez, C.
Dominguez, Tomás.
Massanet, Juan B.

Dry goods, etc.
Balbas, Tomás.
Capo, Juan Ignacio.
Cevedanes, Manuel.
Escñat, José.
Fuster, Rafael.

General importers.
Cano & Co., Tomás.
Cantiño, Jenaro.
Fernández, Vicente.
Grau, Antonio.
Lopez, Manuel.
Morazani Hermanos.
Sanguinety, José.

Hardware.
Caussade, Juan.
Girod & Co.
Rovira, Francisco.

Printing office.
Castillo & Luzunares.

Sugar merchants and shippers.
Cabassa, Luis P.
Capo, Juan Ignacio.
Gual Hermanos.
Lopez, Francisco.
Lopez, Julian.
Massó, Felix.
Moret, Clemente.
Texidor, J. M.
Vazquez, Rafael.
Villodas, Joaquin.
Virilla, Pedro.
Vives, Juan.

ISABELA.

Goigel é hijos.
Rafols, J. L.

LARIS.

General merchants.

Canals Coll & Co.
Juan, Pedro.
Lecaroz &.Co
Marquez & Co.
Mayol & Juan.
Vidal, Pablo.
Vilella Hermanos.

MAYAGUEZ.

Bankers.

Badrena & Co., M.
Bages & Co., F.
Barahona, Blaines & Co.
Boothby & Co.
Cartagena, José.
Cuyar, Pratts & Co.
Palmer, Santiago R.

Booksellers and stationers.

Enrique, Dick.
Mantilla & Co.

Commission merchants.

Badrena & Co., M. (provisions).
Bages & Co., F. (dry goods).
Blanes, Francisco (dry goods).
Cuyar & Pratts (dry goods).
Kraemer & Co. (general merchandise).
Moral, Gonzalez & Co. (general merchandise).
Nieva & Co., P. (iron and steel ware).
Plaja & Bravo (general merchandise).
Schulze & Co. (general merchandise).
Suan & Co., S. (iron and steel ware).
Victori & Co. (provisions).

Drugs.

Gatell & Co.
Manzano, Manuel.
Monagas, Carlos.
Mulet, Guillermo.
Saliva Hnos.

MAYAGUEZ—Continued.

Dry goods, etc.

Ahedo & Peña, Miguel.
Bages & Co., F.
Barbona, Jaime.
Caco, Jacinto.
Cancio & Lopez.
Casteñer, Sebastian.
Gonze, Pablo.
Martinez, Ramón.
Pietri, Pablo.
Ramirez, Pedro.
Revera & Rodriguez.
Sancho, Sard & Co.
Sitjes & Co., J.

Furniture.

Berga, Pablo.
Castro, José.

General merchants, importing and exporting.

Aduana, J.
Badrena & Co., M.
Bages & Co.
Barahona, C.
Blanes & Co.
Blanes, Francisco.
Boothby & Co.
Cuyar, Pratts & Co.
Esmoris Hermanos.
Fernandez & Co.
Gomila, Antonio.
Guio, Francisco Molina.
Haws & Co.
Infanson, Felix.
Kraemer & Co.
Lopez, Gonzalez & Co.
Moral, Gonzalez & Co.
Mulet, Guillermo.
Nieva & Co., P.
Pluja & Bravo.
Roberts, Adolfo.
Sancho, Sard & Co.
Schultz & Co.
Torrabello & Co., J.
Victori, Polegri & Co.

MAYAGUEZ—Continued.

Groceries and provisions, wholesale.
Bengoa & Co., M.
Homar, Guillermo.
Martinez Hnos.
Quiñones, Miguel.
Rodriguez, José García.

Hardware.
Blanes & Co.
Nieva & Co., P.
Vigo, Mendes.

Ice-manufacturers.
Lopez, Besosa & Co.

Importers.
Badrena & Co., M.
Fernandez & Co.
Kraemer & Co.
Sard, Antonio.

Jewelers.
Grau, Tomás.
Rivera, Antonio.

Lithographer,
Rodek, H.

Lumber.
Fornabels & Co., P.
Vidal, Isidro.

Photographers.
Alonso, Rudolfo.
Lyon, Eduardo.

Undertakers.
Berga & Co., Andres.
Gutierrez & Co., José.
Marcias & Co., José.

MOCA.

General merchants.
Miranda, Juan.
Pagan, Viuda de.

PEPINO.

General merchants.
Arocana, Pedro.
Cabrero, J. M. & S.
Lauruaga & Co.
Ortila, Lorenzo.

PONCE.

Banks and bankers.
Armstrong & Co.
Caja de Ahorros.
Gandaria, Brigaro & Co.

Bookbinders.
Campius, A.
Revera, Luis.

Booksellers and stationers.
Lopez, Manuel.
Melendez, José.
Otero, Olimpio.

Brickmakers and dealers in building material.
Arabia, Narciso.
Bigay, Salvador.
Gonzalez, U.
Pigeu, Salvador.

Coffee-shippers.
Gandaria, Bregaro & Co.
Salazar & Co., E. P.
Sauri, Subira & Co.

Commission merchants.
Armstrong, Carlos.
Blasini Hermanos.
Bregaro & Co.
Cortada, Ramon.
Kraemer & Co.
Mayol Hermanos & Co.
Miller, T. B.
Morales & Co.

Druggists.
Arrillaga, Juan Bautista.
Ferrer, José.
Fiol, Francisco.
Subirá, Manuel.
Valle & Cancio.

Electrical apparatus.
Vidaurre & Co., J.

Foundries.
Graham & Co.
Querejeta Hnos.

General merchants, wholesale.
Armstrong & Co.
Gandaria, Brigaro & Co.
Mayorel & Co.

PONCE—Continued.

General merchants, wholesale—Continued.
Mirandes Hnos.
Molinas & Co., A. E.
Pellegrini Hnos.
Salazar & Co.
Sauri, Subira & Co.
Schuck & Co.
Torres & Hijo.
Valdecilla & Co.
Vidal & Co.

Groceries and provisions, wholesale.
Angulo, Fernando.
Canto, José.
Codo & Co.
Leon & García.
Mayal Hnos.
Morales, M.

Ice-manufacturer.
Hoffmann, Otto.

Importers and retailers of provisions.
Cot & Co., P.
Fernandez & Co., F.
Gilet, Juan.
Mayoral, Antonio.
Olivio & Co.
Pons & Co., J.
Puente, Luzaro.
Snau & Co.

Importers of dry goods and hardware.
Calone & Co., Mercado.
Cortada, Manuel.
Emanuelli & Co.
Forest Hermanos.
Lucchetti & Co., A.
Milau & Co.
Mirandez, Luiz.
Molina, Antonio.
Pellegrini Hermanos.
Rivas, Gumersindo.
Subiña & Co., Trujillo.
Tarrats, Reverter & Co.
Toro & Co., R.
Vidal & Co.

Lumber merchants.
Hedella & Co.

PONCE—Continued.

Lumber merchants—Continued.
Perez Guerra & Co.
Porrata, Doria & Co.

Photographer.
Molina, M.

Pianos and musical instruments.
Aspiroz, M.
Carreras, P. G.
Castiner, Pedro.
Forns, José.
Otero, O.

Printers and publishers.
El Comercio.
El Vapor.
Lopez, Manuel.
Velazquez, L. R.

Ship chandlery, etc.
Gandaria, Brogaro & Co.
Salazar & Co.

Undertakers.
Carreras, Pedro G.
Santamaría, Antonio.
Toro, Antonio.

SAN JUAN.

Banks and bankers.
Banco Crédito Mercantil.
Cabrera Hnos.
Chavarri & Co.
Ezquiaga Sobrinos.
Fedderson & Co.
Izquierdo & Co., J. M.
Ludwig, Duplace.
Mullenhorf & Korber.
Sala & Co., Suce. de J.
Silva, José T.
Vijande & Co.

Bookbinders.
Anfosso & Co., J.
Gonzalez & Co.

Booksellers and stationers.
Acosta, José J., successor.
Font, José Gonzalez.
Gonzalez & Co.

SAN JUAN—Continued.

Booksellers and stationers—Continued.
  Lynn, A., sucr. de Moris.
  Sanjurjo Vidal, B. F.

Boots, shoes, etc.
  Bordoy, sucr. de.
  Pieras, Marcos.
  Piza Hermanos.
  Rubert Hermanos.

Chocolate manufacturers.
  Carbonell, Covas & Co.
  Dorado & Co.
  Olivas & Co. •

Cigar-manufacturers.
  Martinez, Emetrio.
  Portela & Lomba.
  Somahano, Paulino.

Commission merchants.
  Baró & Co.
  Crosas, Andres.
  Duplace, Ludwig.
  Ezquiaga, Sobrinos de.
  Finlay Brothers.
  Izquierdo &Co., J. M.
  Latimer & Fernandez.
  Lopez, Villamil & Co.
  Müllenhoff & Körber.
  Ochoa & Hermano, J.
  Palacios & Co.
  Quevedo & Hess, sucr.
  Rauschenplat, A.
  Rubert Hermanos.
  Silva, José T.
  Torner Hermanos.
  Trigo, Ctvidanes & Co.
  Vicente & Co.
  Vijande & Co.

Distilleries.
  Duplace, Ludwig.
  Guiardo, J. Vidal.
  Quevedo & Hess, sucrs. de.

Drugs.
  Blanco, José M.
  Danbon, Juan.
  Gallardo & Co.
  Guillermetz, Fidel.

SAN JUAN—Continued.

Dry goods.
  Ahumada & Co.
  Arana, Trueba & Co.
  Chavarri & Co.
  Duplace, Ludwig.
  Font, Vidal & Co.
  Hernaiz & Co.
  Hernaiz & Co., J., sucr.
  Mendizábal & Co.
  Miralles, Pablo.
  Orcasitas & Co., sucr.
  Peña & Co., J.
  Villar, Fabian & Co.
  Zalduondo & Valle.

Fancy goods, toys, etc.
  "Ambos Mundos."
  Gardon, Ramon.
  Jaúregui, Antonino.
  Lentini & Co.
  Marceau, Celina.
  Vicente, Manuel.

Foundries.
  Portilla, Sobrinos de.
  San Felix, Apolinaria.

Furniture.
  Margarida & Co.
  Masjuan & Co.
  Monclova & Co., A.
  Noa & Valle.

Groceries and provisions.
  Alonso, S.
  Barcelo & Pernjo.
  Bolivar & Co., G.
  Bozzo & Hijos, L.
  Caldas & Co.
  Cerecedo Hermanos & Co.
  Duplace, Ludwig.
  Egozcue & Clos.
  Gaviño, Vicente & Co.
  Gonzalez & Alonso.
  Gonzalez & Perez.
  Lopez, Villamil & Co.
  Luiña, & Co., Sobrinos de.
  Ochoa & Hermanos, J.
  Palacios & Co.
  Serra & Co.

Groceries and provisions—Continued.
Torner Hermanos.
Trigo, Cividanes & Co.
Vicente & Co.

Hardware, crockery, etc.
Armas & Jiménez.
Baró & Co.
Matienzo, J.
Mayol & Co., A.
Noell & Co., P.
Quijano, J. Gonzalez.
Rodriguez, Cleavert & Co.
Simonet, B.
Vergara, Antonio.

Hatters.
Gonzalez, Augustin.
Quiñones, José F.
Suarez, Angel.

Ice-manufacturer.
Besosa & Co.
Goyco & Co.

Importers and exporters.
Ahumada & Co.
Alberti, Nicolas.
"Ambos Mundos."
Arana, Trueba & Co.
Armas & Jiménez.
Barceló & Perujo.
Baró & Co.
Blanco, José Maria.
Bolivar & Co., G.
Bordoy, sucr. de.
Boschetti, Clemente.
Bozzo & Hijos, L.
Caldas & Co.
Cerecedo Hnos.
Chavarri & Co.
Crosas, Andres.
Danbon, Juan.
Duplace, Ludwig.
Egozcue & Clos.
Ezquiaga, Sobrinos de.
Font, Vidal & Co.
Fuentes, José R.
Gallardo & Co.
Gardon, Ramon.

S. Ex. 8, pt. 11——26

Importers and exporters—Continued.
Gaviño, Vicente & Co.
Gonzalez & Alonso.
Guillermetz, Fidel.
Hernaiz & Co., J., sucr.
Izquierdo & Co., J. M.
Jauregui, Antonino.
Latimer & Fernández.
Lentini & Co.
Lopez, Villamil & Co.
Luina & Co., Sobrinos de.
Lynn, A., sucr. de Moris.
Marcean, Celina.
Martienzo, Julian.
Mayol & Co., A.
Mendizábal & Co.
Miralles, Pablo.
Müllenoff & Körber.
Musa, A.
Noell & Co., P.
Ochoa & Hno., J.
Orcasitas & Co., sucr.
Palacios & Co.
Peña & Co.
Pieras, Marcos.
Piza Hermanos.
Quevedo & Hess, sucr.
Quijano, J. Gonzales.
Rauschenplat, A.
Rodriguez, Cleavert & Co.
Rubert Hnos.
Serra & Co.
Silva, José T.
Simonet, B.
Torner Hnos.
Trigo, Cividanes & Co.
Vergara, Antonio.
Vicente, Manuel.
Vicente & Co.
Vijande & Co.
Villar, Fabian & Co.
Zalduondo & Valle.

Jewelers.
Alberti, Nicolas.
Boschetti, Clemente.
Lentini & Co.

SAN JUAN—Continued.

Jewelers—Continued.
Musa, A.
Tinaud, Grato.

Lumber.
Crosas, Andres.
Daubon & Co.
Latimer & Fernandez.
Margary & Co., R.

Match manufactory.
Bolivar & Co., G.

Military equipments.
Claudio, José.
Matens, Juan.

Paper and stationery, wholesale.
Acosta, José J.
Anfosso & Co., F.
Gonzalez & Co.
Gonzalez, José Font.
Lynn, A., sucr. de Moris.

Photographers.
Alonzo, Feliciano.
Alonzo, José J.
Cepero, Eduardo L.

Pianos, etc.
Agullo, José.
Delgado, Pedro.

Printing offices.
Anfosso & Co., J.

SAN JUAN—Continued.

Printing offices—Continued.
Gonzalez & Co.
Lynn, A., sucr. do Moris.

Sewing machines.
Melon & Co., S.

Ship chandlers.
Crosas, Andres.
Latimer & Fernandez.

Tailors.
Lopez, Julio.
Montes, Rosendo.
Rodriguez, José.
Roig, Rafael.

Tobacconists.
Apellániz, Juan.
Apellániz Hijos Sánchez.
Fuentes, José R.
Gandier, José A.
Lomba, Luciano.
Lopex, Pablo I.
Martinez, Hemeterio.
Merino & Co., Manuel.
Pardo, Felix
Portela & Co.

Undertakers.
Aquino, Tomás.
Llanger, Carambot L.
Mesa, Moreno & Co.

NEWSPAPER DIRECTORY.

Mexico.

AGUASCALIENTES, AGUASCALIENTES.

Weeklies.
El Republicano.
Soldado de la Fé.

Semi-monthly.
La Gaceta Pública.

Monthly.
El Instructor.

Not specified.
El Porvenir.

ALAMOS, SONORA.

Semi-monthly.
El Artesano.

ALJOJUCA, PUEBLA.

Semi-monthly.
El Ensayo.

ALVARADO, VERACRUZ.

Weekly.
El Defensor del Pueblo.

APAN, HIDALGO.

Weekly.
El Gallito.

ATOYAC, HIDALGO.

Weekly.
El Regenerador.

CAMPECHE, CAMPECHE.

Weekly.
Reproductor Campechino.

Semi-monthly.
Diario Oficial.

Not specified.
La Esperanza.

CELAYA, GUANAJUATO.

Monthly.
La Unión.

Not specified.
La Voz de Celaya.

CHALCO, MEXICO.

Not specified.
La Aurora Política.

CHIHUAHUA, CHIHUAHUA.

Daily.
El Chihuahuense.

Weeklies.
El Estado de Chihuahua.
La Avispa.
Libertad Católica.
Revista de Chihuahua.

Semi-monthly.
El Boletin Municipal.

Not specified.
El Constitucional.
El Paso del Norte.
El Progresista.

CHILCHIHUITES, ZACATECAS.

Weekly.
El Mosquito.

CHILPANCINGO, GUERRERO.

Weekly.
La Voz del Sur.
Semi-monthly.
Periódico Oficial.
Not specified.
El Porvenir del Sur.

CIUDAD GUERRERO, TAMAULIPAS.

Weekly.
El Correo del Bravo.

CIUDAD GUZMAN, JALISCO.

Not specified.
El Pensamiento.

CIUDAD MIER, TAMAULIPAS.

Weekly.
El Obrero.

CIUDAD VICTORIA, TAMAULIPAS.

Weekly.
El Eco del Centro.
Semi-monthly.
Periódico Oficial.

COATEPEC, VERACRUZ.

Weekly.
El Faro.
Monthly.
La Biblioteca Escolar.

COCULA, GUERRERO.

Weekly.
El Buscapiés.

COLIMA, COLIMA.

Weeklies.
El Estado de Colima.
La Revista Judicial.

COLIMA, COLIMA—Continued.

Semi-monthlies.
El Renacimiento.
La Lira de Occidente.
La Voz del Progreso.
Not specified.
El Costeno.
La Voz del Pacífico.

CORDOBA, VERACRUZ.

Weekly.
Boletin Cantonal.
Monthly.
Revista de la Sociedad José M. Mena.
Not specified.
Obrero Cordobes.

CUERNAVACA, MORELOS.

Weekly.
El Orden.

CULIACÁN, SINALOA.

Weeklies.
El Estado de Sinaloa.
El Occidental.
La Razón.
Not specified.
El Continental.
La Gaceta Sinaloense.

CUNDUACÁN, TABASCO.

Semi-monthly.
El Eco del Pueblo.

DOLORES HIDALGO, GUANAJUATO

Weekly.
El Anunciador Comercial.

DURANGO, DURANGO.

Weeklies.
Boletin Municipal.
El Domingo.
El Eco de Durango.
Semi-monthlies.
Hojas Sueltas.
Periódicos Oficiales.

ENCARNACIÓN DE DIAZ, JALISCO.

Weekly.
El Pigmeo.

GUADALAJARA, JALISCO.

Daily.
Diario de Jalisco.
Weeklies.
El Litigante.
El Mercurio Occidental.
El Tapatío.
Jalisco Ilustrado.
La Gaceta Mercantil.
La Justicia Tapatía.
La Sombra de Cuauhtemoc.
Semi-monthlies.
Colección de Documentos Ecclesiásti-
cos.
El Cantonal.
El Testigo.
Investigador Médico
Juan Panadero.
La Linterna de Diógenes.
La Palmera del Valle.
La Religión y la Sociedad.
La República Literaria.
Provincia de Jalisco.
Monthlies.
El Expositor Bíblico.
El Mentor de los Niños.
La Espada de Dámocles.
La Niñez.
La Revista Mercantil.
Not specified.
Bandera de Jalisco.
El Cascabel.
Las Clases Productoras.

GUANAJUATO, GUANAJUATO.

Weeklies.
Don Gregorito.
La Voz de Guanajuato.
Semi-monthlies.
El Foro Guanajuatense.
Periódico Oficial.

GUANAJUATO, GUANAJUATO—Continued.

Not specified.
El Artesano.
El Jurado.
La Bandera Blanca.

GUAYMAS, SONORA.

Weekly.
El Tráfico.
Semi-monthly.
Colegio, El Progreso.
Monthlies.
Boletin Municipal.
El Obrero.
El Regenerador.
La Instrucción Pública.
Not specified.
El Correo del Pacífico.
El Monitor del Comercio.

GUERRERO, TAMAULIPAS.

Not specified.
El Correo del Bravo.
El Obrero.

HERMOSILLO, SONORA.

Weeklies.
El Sábado.
La Constitución.
Not specified.
Correo del Comercio.

HIDALGO DEL PARRAL, CHIHUAHUA.

Weekly.
El Parral.

HUAMANTLA, TLAXCALA.

Monthly.
La Filípica.

HUATUSCO, VERACRUZ.

Weekly.
La Voz de Huatusco.
Semi-monthly.
El Progresista.

IGUALA, GUERRERO.

Weekly.
La Alianza de Acatempan.

IRAPUATO, GUANAJUATO.

Weekly.
El Avisador.

Semi-monthly.
El Comercio del Bajio.

ISLA DEL CÁRMEN, CAMPECHE.

Weekly.
Periódico Oficial.

IXTAPAN DEL ORO, MEXICO.

Not specified.
El Heraldo.

IZAMÁL, YUCATAN.

Weekly.
El Centro.

Semi-monthly.
La Voluntad Popular.

JALAPA, VERACRUZ.

Weekly.
El Estudio.

Semi-monthlies.
Bandera Veracruzana.
Colección de Lecciones Clínicas.
México Intelectual.

Tri-weekly.
Periódico Oficial.

Monthlies.
El Sol.
Revista de Ciencias Médicas.

Not specified.
Defensor del Pueblo.

LAGOS, JALISCO.

Weekly.
El Defensor del Pueblo.

LAMPAZOS DE NARANJO, NUEVO LEÓN.

Semi-monthly.
El Dia.

LA PAZ, TERRITORY OF LOWER CALIFORNIA.

Weekly.
Boletin Oficial.

Not specified.
El Criterio Público.
La Baja California.

LA PIEDAD, MICHOACAN.

Monthly.
El Destello.

LA UNIÓN, JALISCO.

Weekly.
El Campesino.

LEON, GUANAJUATO.

Weekly.
El Pueblo Católico.

Not specified.
El Sol de Mayo.
La Era Nueva.

LOS ALAMOS, SONORA.

Not specified.
Voz de Alamos.

MAGDALENA, SONORA.

Weekly.
La Voz del Estado.

Semi-monthly.
El Chicote.

MATAMOROS, TAMAULIPAS.

Weekly.
La Unión Obrera.

Semi-monthlies.
El Amigo del Pueblo.
El Cronista.

Tri-weeklies.
El Sol de Mayo.
La Revista del Norte.

Monthly.
El Ramo de Olivo.

Not specified.
El Progreso.

MAZATLAN, SINALOA.

Daily.
El Correo de la Tarde.
Weeklies.
El Colegio Independencia.
El Láico.
El Pacífico.
La Píldora.
Semi-monthly.
El Bisemanal.
Monthly.
El Precursor.
Not specified.
El Continental.
El Monitor del Pacífico.
El Obrero del Occidente.

MERIDA, YUCATAN.

Dailies.
El Alva.
El Telégrama.
Weeklies.
El Municipio.
La Razón Social.
La Sombra de Zepeda.
Semi-monthlies.
El Eco del Comercio.
J. Jacinto Cuevas.
La Escuela Primaria.
Tri-weeklies.
La Razón del Pueblo.
La Revista de Mérida.
Not specified.
El Honor Nacional.
El Pueblo Yucateo.
La Revista de Mérida.
Los Derechos del Pueblo.

MEXICO, FEDERAL DISTRICT.

Dailies.
Diario Oficial.
El Anunciador Mexicano.
El Diario del Hogar.
- El Liberal Español.
El Monitor Republicano.

MEXICO, FEDERAL DISTRICT—Continued.

Dailie —Continued.
El Mundo.
El Municipio Libre.
El Nacional.
El Partido Liberal.
El Tiempo.
El Universal.
La Bolsa Mercantil.
La Caridad.
La Patria.
La Política.
La Voz de España.
La Voz de México.
Siglo XIX.
The Two Republics.
Trait d'Union.
Weeklies.
Boletin Ecclesiástico.
Boletin Taurino.
Convención Radical Obrera.
Courrier de Mexique.
El Abogado Christiano Ilustrado.
El Agente Minero Mexicano.
El Album de la Patria.
El Anglo-Americano.
El Arte de la Lidia.
El Avisador Comercial.
El Combate.
El Correo Español.
El Correo de las Señoras.
El Economista Mexicano.
El Escolar Mexicano.
El Estudio.
El Financiero Mexicano.
El Hijo del Ahuizote.
El Porvenir de México.
El Progreso.
El Resúmen.
El Telón.
Guia Práctica de Derecho.
La Escuela de Jurisprudencia.
La Familia.
La Federación.
La Germania.
La Revista Financiera Mexicana.
La Semana Mercantil.

MEXICO, FEDERAL DISTRICT—Continued.

Weeklies—Continued.
La Voz de Hipócrates.
La Voz de La Nación.
Los Estados.
Revista de México.

Semi-monthlies.
El Bien Social.
El Día.
El Faro.
Gaceta Médica de México.
Revista de Legislación y Jurisprudencia.
Revista Jurídica del Estado de México.
Revista Militar Mexicana.
Revista Telegráfica Mexicana.

Monthlies.
Boletin de la Santa Familia.
El Boletin Masónico.
El Evangelista Mexicano.
El Micrófono.
La Luz.
Revista Latino-Americana.

Not specified.
Centinela Española.
El Comercio del Golfo.
El Correo del Lunes.
El Correo Universal.
El Cronista de Méjico.
El Eco del Pueblo.
El Expreso Mercantil.
El Foro.
El Nacional.
El Noticioso.
El Porvenir Nacional.
El Republicano.
El Siglo Diez y Nuevo.
El Vigilante.
Industria Alemana.
Instrucción.
La Constitución.
La Cooperación.
La Evolución.
La Libertad.
La Opinión Nacional.

MEXICO, FEDERAL DISTRICT—Continued.

Not specified—Continued.
La Paz.
La Paz Pública.
La Prensa.
La República.
La Revista Agrícola.
La Voz de Anahuac.
La Vanguardia.
La Ilustración Espírita.

MIER, TAMAULIPAS.

Not specified.
El Unionista.
La Brisa.

MONTEMORELOS, NUEVO LEON.

Semi-monthly.
La Vanguardia Fronteriza.

MONTEREY, NUEVO LEON.

Daily.
La Defensa del Pueblo.

Weekly.
La Voz de Nuevo León.

Semi-monthly.
Periódico Oficial.

Monthly.
El Obrero.

Not specified.
El Renacimiento.

MORELIA, MICHOACAN.

Weeklies.
La Familia Católica.
La Revista Católica.
Luz de Verdades Católicas.
Pierrot.

Semi-monthly.
Gaceta Oficial.

Not specified.
El Municipal.
La Unión.

NUEVO LAREDO, TAMAULIPAS.

Weeklics.
El Domingo.
El Duende.
El Orden.
Not specified.
La Redención.

OAXACA, OAXACA.

Weekly.
El Estudio.
Not specified.
Periódico Oficial.

ORIZABA, VERACRUZ

Weeklies.
El Siglo que Acaba.
La Primavera.
Semi-monthlies.
Boletin Municipal.
El Eco de la Juventud.
El Reproductor.
Monthlies.
Boletin de la Sociedad Sánchez y Oropeza.
Boletin del Círculo Espiritista Paz y Progreso.
Not specified.
El Conciliador.
El Gladiator.
La Justicia.

PACHUCA, HIDALGO.

Weeklies.
El Explorador.
El Hidalguense.
El Instituto.
El Obrero.
La Tribuna.
Periódico Oficial.
Not specified.
Eco de Hidalgo.
El Bucaro.

PARRAL, CHIHUAHUA.

Not specified.
El Orden.

PASO DEL NORTE, CHIHUAHUA.

Weeklies.
El Eco.
La Revista Internacional.

PATZCUARO, MICHOACAN.

Semi-monthly.
La Municipalidad.

PENJAMO, GUANAJUATO.

Semi-monthly.
La Patria de Hidalgo.

POCHUTLA, OAXACA.

Semi-monthly.
El Avisador de Puerto Angel.

PUEBLA, PUEBLA.

Weeklies.
Boletin Municipal.
El Amigo de la Verdad.
El Monitor do Puebla.
La Justicia.
Semi-monthlies.
El Comercio de Puebla.
El Cruzado.
Tri-weekly.
Periódico Oficial.
Monthly.
Observaciones Meteorólogicas.
Not specified.
El Hijo del Obrero.
El Verbo.
La Bandera Blanca.
La Emulacion.
La Luz.
La Palabra Libre.
Página Teatral.

PUEBLO VIEJO, VERACRUZ.

Weekly.
Defensor del Pueblo.

PURUÁNDIRO, MICHOACAN.

Semi-monthly.
Angel del Hogar.

QUERETARO, QUERETARO.

Weekly.
La Sombra de Arteaga.

ROSARIO, SINALOA.

Weekly.
El Sur de Sinaloa.
Not specified.
El Látigo.

SALAMANCA, GUANAJUATO.

Not specified.
La Simiente del Bien.

SALTILLO, COAHUILA.

Weekly.
El Libre Exámen.
La Instrucción.
Semi-monthly.
El Coahuilense.
Monthly.
El Alivio del Mundo.
Not specified.
El Periódico Oficial.
La Sombra del Fuente.

SAN CRISTOBAL, CHIAPAS.

Not specified.
El Demócrata.
Periódico Oficial del Estado de Chiapas.

SAN JUAN BAUTISTA, TABASCO.

Weeklies.
El Independiente.
La Opinión Pública.
Semi-monthlies.
El Comercio.
El Mensajero.
La Central.
La Escuela Católica.
La Siesta del Obrero.
Periódico Oficial.
Monthly.
La Bandera Roja.

SAN JUAN BAUTISTA, TABASCO—Continued

Not specified.
La Unión Democrática.
La Unión Liberal.

SAN LUIS POTOSI, SAN LUIS POTOSI.

Daily.
El Estandarte.
Weekly.
El Correo de San Luis.
Semi-monthlies.
El Anunciador Comercial.
La Esperanza.
Not specified.
El Minero Potosino.
El Obrero Potosino.
El Republicano.
El Telégrama.
Instrucción Primaria.
La Industria.
La Unión Democrática.

SAN MARTIN TEXMELUCAN, PUEBLA.

Weekly.
El Periquito.

SAN MIGUEL DE ALLENDE, GUANAJUATO.

Not specified.
El Fenix.

SANTA ROSALIA, CHIHUAHUA.

Semi-monthly.
La Gaceta Municipal.

TACUBAYA, FEDERAL DISTRICT.

Semi-monthly.
Boletin Bibliográfico y Escolar.

TAMPICO, TAMAULIPAS.

Weekly.
El Porvenir.
Not specified.
El Semanario.

TEHUACAN, PUEBLA.

Weekly.
El Dia.
Not specified.
El Verbo.

TEKAX, YUCATAN.

Not specified.
El Fronterizo.

TELOLOAPAN, VERACRUZ.

Not specified.
El Eco de Aldama.

TENANCINGO, MEXICO.

Semi-monthly.
La Enseñanza Católica.

TENANGO DEL VALLE, MEXICO.

Semi-monthly.
La Liga Escolar.

TEPIC, JALISCO.

Not specified.
Aurora del Trabajo.

TEPIC, TERRITORY OF TEPIC.

Weeklies.
Lucifer.
Periódico Oficial.
Revista Comercial de Tepic.
Semi-monthly.
La Juventud.

TEQUILA, JALISCO.

Semi-monthly.
El Imparcial.

TLACOTALPAM, VERACRUZ.

Weekly.
El Correo de Sotavento.
Monthly.
La Luz.
Not specified.
La Razón.

TLALUEPANTA, MEXICO.

Not specified.
Sombra de Mirafuentes.

TLAXCALA, TLAXCALA.

Weekly.
El Estado de Tlaxcala.
Not specified.
Derechos del Pueblo.

TOLUCA, MEXICO.

Weeklies.
Boletin de la Lonja Agrícola Mercantil.
El Pueblo.
El Regenerador.
La Juventud Liberal.
Semi-monthly.
Gaceta Oficial.
Monthly.
La Antigua Fé.
Not specified.
La Democracia.
Sombra de Riva Palacio.

TULA, TAMAULIPAS.

Weekly.
El Tultico.

TULANCINGO, HIDALGO.

Weekly.
El Ideal.

URES, SONORA.

Semi-monthly.
El Eco del Valle.

URIQUE, CHIHUAHUA.

Not specified.
El Artesano.

VERACRUZ, VERACRUZ.

Dailies.
El Diario Comercial.
El Ferro-Carril.

VERACRUZ, VERACRUZ—Continued.

Weeklies.
El Moscardón.
El Mosquito.

Semi-monthly.
El Centinela del Golfo.
El Zenzontle de Zempoala.

Monthly.
La Verdad.

VILLA LERDO, DURANGO.

Weekly.
La Luciérnaga.

YZAMAL, YUCATAN.

Not specified.
El Microscopio.

ZACATECAS, ZACATECAS.

Weeklies.
El Imparcial.
El Meteoro.
La Rosa del Tepeyac.

Semi-monthlies.
Crónica Municipal.
Defensor de la Constitución.

Not specified.
Bien Social.
Crónica Zacatecana.
El Barretero.

ZAMORA, MICHOACAN.

Weekly.
Don Barbarito.

ZONGOLICA, VERACRUZ.

Semi-monthly.
El Eco de la Montaña.

Costa Rica.

CARTAGO.

El Cometa.

SAN JOSÉ.

Central American Reporter.
El Costa Ricense.

SAN JOSÉ—Continued.

El Ferro-Carril.
El Imparcial.
El Partido Constitucional.
La Gaceta Diario Oficial.
La Prensa Libre.

Guatemala.

CHIQUIMULA.

El Oriental.
La Lira Americana.

COBAN.

El Quezal.

GUATEMALA.

Boletin de la Exposición.
Diario de Centro América.
El Amigo del Pueblo.
El Censor.
El Correo de la Tarde.
El Guatemalteco.
El Imparcial.

GUATEMALA—Continued.

El Oriente.
El Porvenir.
Gaceta de Guatemala.
La Opinión Nacional.
La Semana.

QUEZALTENANGC.

El Bien Público.

SACATEPEQUEZ.

El Adelante.
El Alacran.
La Zumba.

413

Honduras.

CHOLUTECA.

La Verdad.

COMAYAGUA.

El Diario.
El Orden.

JUTACALPA, OLANCHO.

El Eco.

SANTA BARBARA.

El Progreso.

SANTA ROSA, COPAN.

El Copaneco.

TEGUCIGALPA.

El Monitor.
El Orden.
Gaceta Oficial.
Honduras Mining Journal.
La Nación.
La Paz.
La República.

TRUJILLO.

La Voz de Trujillo.

YORO.

La Nueva Era.

Nicaragua.

CHINANDEGA.

El Amigo del Pueblo.

GRANADA.

El Centro Americano.

LEON.

El Ateneo.
El Crepúsculo.
El Municipio.
El Principio.
La Avispa.
La Verdad.

MANAGUA.

Diario de la Capital.
El Diario Nicaragüense.
El Porvenir.
Gaceta Oficial.
La Patria.
La Reconciliación.

RIVAS.

El Album.
El Termómetro.

Salvador.

CHALATENANGO.

El Fígaro.

CHALCHUAPA.

El Patriota.

SAN MIGUEL.

La Aspiración.
La Revista Universitaria.

SAN SALVADOR.

Diario Oficial.
El Boletin Oficial.
El Correo Militar.
El Correo Nacional.
El Gymnasio.
El Heraldo.
El Municipio Salvadoreño.

SAN SALVADOR—Continued.

El Pueblo.
La Discusión.
La Federación.
La Juventud.
La Linterna.

SANTA NA.A

El Boletin Municipal.
La Idea.
La Palanca.

TUCUAPA.

El Agricultor.

USULUTAN.

El Triunfo.

Argentine Republic.

Anales de la Sociedad Rural Argentina.
Anales del Círculo Médico Argentino.
Argentinisches Tageblatt.
Argentinisches Wochenblatt.
Boletin de la Unión Industrial.
Boletin del Departamento Nacional de Agricultura.
Boletin del Instituto Geográfico Argentino.
Boletin Industrial.
Boletin Judicial.
Boletin Mensual de Estadística Política de la Capital.
Boletin Mensual de la Cámara Italiana de Comercio y Artes.
Boletin Oficial Masónico.
Buenos Aires Handels-Zeitung.
Constancia.
Correo de las Niñas.
Deutsche La Plata Zeitung.
Diario de Buenos Aires.
Don Quijote.
El Argentino.
El Asegurador Argentino.
El Boletin.
El Censor.
El Comercio de la Plata.
El Comercio Universal Unido.
El Correo Español.
El Diario.
El Escolar Argentino.
El Extrangero.

El Foro Argentino.
El Mosquito.
El Nacional.
El Obrero.
El Porvenir.
El Sastre.
El Sud-Americano.
Gazeta Portugueza.
Guia Comercial de la Capital.
Guia Kraft.
Guia Mensual de Kidd.
Guia Mensual do Mackern.
Guia Penser del Viajero.
L'Amico del Popolo.
La Educación.
La Elegancia Porteña.
La Libertad.
La Nación.
La Nazione Italiana.
La Pampa.
La Patria.
La Patria Ilustrada.
La Patria Italiana.
La Perla de la Plata.
La Plata Post.
La Prensa.
La República.
La Tribuna.
Laurak-Bat.
La Viti-Vinícola, Revista Mensual.
La Voz de la Iglesia.
Le Courrier de la Plata.
Lecturas Católicas.

416

ARGENTINE REPUBLIC—Continued.

BUENOS AIRES—Continued.

Le Petit Journal.
L'Eco delle Società Italiane.
L'Italo Argentino.
L'Operario Italiano.
Revista del Centro Científico Litera-
rio.
Revista del Paraguay.
Revista Farmacéutica.
Revista Ilustrada del Rio de la Plata.
Revista Jurídica.
Revista Mercantil.
Revista Patriótica del Pasado Argen-
tino.
Sud América.
The Buenos Aires Herald.
The Standard.
The Southern Cross.
Vorwärts.

CATAMARCA.
La Unión.

CORDOBA.
El Agricultor Industrial.
El Eco de Córdoba.
El Interior.

S. Ex. 8, pt. 11——27

ARGENTINE REPUBLIC—Continued.

CORDOBA—Continued.

El Progreso.
El Pueblo.

JUJUY.
La Democracia.

MENDOZA.
El Constitucional.

ROSARIO, SANTA FE.
El Independiente.

SALTA.
La Situación.

SAN JUAN.
La Unión.

SAN LUIZ.
El Boletin Oficial.

TUCUMAN.
El Argentino.
Los Debates.

Bolivia.

Brazil.

ALEGRETE, RIO GRANDE DO SUL.

Gazeta de Alegrete.

ALEMQUER, ESTADO DO PARÁ.

Gazeta de Alemquer.

ANGRA DOS REIS, ESTADO DO RIO DE JANEIRO.

A Gazeta de Angra.
O Angrense.

ARACAJU, SERGIPE.

A Ordem.
Diario de Sergipe.
Diario Popular.
Gazeta de Aracajú.
Jornal de Sergipe.
O Americano.
O Conservador.
O Democrata.
O Facho.
O Guarany.
O Libertador.
O Sergipe.

ARAGUAYA, GOYAZ.

Bocayuva.
Diario Official.
Estado de Goyaz.
O Commercio.
O Tribuno.
Tribuno Livre.

ASSU, RIO GRANDE DO NORTE.

O Conservador.

ATTERADO, MINAS GERAES.

Aurora Atteradense.

BAEPENDY, MINAS GERAES.

A Estrella.
O Baependyeno.

BAGÉ, RIO GRANDE DO SUL.

Cruzeiro do Sul.

BARBACENA, MINAS GERAES.

Gazeta de Barbacena.

BARRA MANSA, ESTADO DO RIO DE JANEIRO

A Gazeta de Barra Mansa.
Aurora Barramansense.
Gazeta Barramansense.

BATURITÉ, ESTADO DO CEARÁ.

A Gazeta de Baturité.
O Baturitense.
O Combate.

BLUMENAU, SANTA CATHARINA.

Blumenauer Zeitung.

BOCAINA, SÃO PAULO.

Echo Municipal.
Gazeta da Bocaina.

BRAGANÇA, SÃO PAULO.

Bragancense.
Correio Bragantino.

BRAZIL—Continued.

CACHOEIRA, BAHIA.

A Gazeta do Bocaina.
A Ordem.
O Americano.
O Cachoeirano.
O Guarany.

CALDAS, MINAS GERAES.

Gazeta de Caldas.
O Caldense.

CAMPANHA, MINAS GERAES.

O Colombo.

CAMPANHA DA PRINCEZA, MINAS GERAES.

Monitor Sul Mineiro.

CAMPINAS, SÃO PAULO.

Correio de Campinas.
Diario de Campinas.
Livro Azul.

CAMPOS, ESTADO DO RIO DE JANEIRO.

Diario de Campos.
Gazeta de Campos.
Monitor Campista.

CANAVIEIRAS, PARANA.

O Municipio.

CANTAGALLO, ESTADO DO RIO DE JANEIRO.

Correio de Cantagallo.
O Voto Livre.

CARANGOLA, ESTADO DO RIO DE JANEIRO.

O Carangolense.

CASA BRANCA, PARANA.

Oeste de São Paulo.

CONSERVATORIA, ESTADO DO RIO DE JANEIRO.

O Conservatoriense.

BRAZIL—Continued.

CORUMBA, MATTO GROSSO.

O Corumbaense.
O Iniciador.

CURITIBA, PARANA.

A Republica.
A Provincia do Paraná.
Commercio do Paraná.
Gazeta Paranaense.
Jornal do Commercio.
O Discipulo.
O Livre Paraná.
O Patriota.
O Realismo.

CUYABA, MATTO GROSSO.

A Brisa.
A Situação.
O Estado de Matto Grosso.
O Expectador.

DESTERRO, SANTA CATHARINA.

A Matraca.
A Regeneração.
A Republica.
Jornal do Commercio.
O Conservador.
O Despertador.

DIAMANTINA, MINAS GERAES.

A Voz do Provo.

ESTANCIA, SERGIPE.

A Gazetinha.
O Commercial.

FEIRA DE SANTANNA, BAHIA.

O Commercial.
O Conservador.
O Vigilante.

FORTALEZA, ESTADO DO CEARA.

A Constituição.
A Ordem.
Diario da Tarde.
Gazeta do Norte.
O Cearense.
O Libertador.

BRAZIL—Continued,

GUARATINGUETA, SÃO PAULO.

Estrella do Norte.
Gazeta do Norte.
Gazetinha.
Parahyba.

ITAJUBA, MINAS GERAES.

Gazeta Commercial.
O Itajubá.
Rio Branco.

ITAPEMIRIM, ESPIRITO SANTO.

A Gazeta do Itapemirim.

JAGUARÃO, RIO GRANDE DO SUL.

A Ordem.
A Tribuna.
O Tempo.

JOINVILLE, SANTA CATHARINA.

Gazeta de Joinville.
O Globo.

JUIZ DE FORA, MINAS GERAES.

O Pharol.

LAGUNA, SANTA CATHARINA.

A Verdade.
O Municipio.
O Trabalho.

LIVRAMENTO, RIO GRANDE DO SUL.

Correio do Sul, Mercantil.
Echo da Fronteira.

MACAHE, ESTADO DO RIO DE JANEIRO.

Gazeta Popular.
O Conservador.
O Constitucional.
O Diario Popular.
Tribuna do Povo.

MACEIO, ALAGOAS.

A Barboleta.
Camaragibe.
Diario das Alagoas.
Diario de Manhã.
Gazeta de Noticias.
Jornal das Alagoas.
O Liberal.
O Orbe.

BRAZIL—Continued.

MANAOS, ESTADO DO AMAZONAS.

Baixo Amazonas.
O Amazonas.
O Commercio do Amazonas.

MARAGOGIPE, BAHIA.

O Democrata.
O Labaro.

MOCOCA, SÃO PAULO.

Monitor Paulista.

MOGY-MIRIM, SÃO PAULO.

Gazeta de Mogy-Mirim.
O Independente.

NATAL, RIO GRANDE DO NORTE.

Correio de Natal.
Correio Official.
O Liberal.

NAZARETH, BAHIA.

Opinão Liberal.
O Regenerador.

NICTHEROY, ESTADO DO RIO DE JANEIRO.

Fluminense.

OURO PRETO, MINAS GERAES.

A Epoca.
O Estado de Minas.
O Trabalho.

PÃO DE ASSUCAR, ALAGOAS.

O Trabalho.

PARA, ESTADO DO PARA.

Democracia.
Diario do Gram-Pará.
O Liberal.
Provincia do Pará.

PARAHYBA, PARAHYBA.

Correio Official.
Jornal da Parahyba.
O Conservador.
O Liberal Parahybano.
O Mercantil.
O Parahyba.

BRAZIL—Continued.

PARAIZO, MINAS GERAES.

O Oriente.

PARANAGUA, PARANA.

Itibere.
Violeta.

PASSOS, MINAS GERAES.

Gazeta de Passos.

PELOTAS, RIO GRANDE DO SUL.

A Discussão.
Correio Mercantil.
Diario de Pelotas.
O Commercio.

PENEDO, ALAGOAS.

Jornal do Penedo.
O Conservador Penedense.
Ó Progresso.

PERNAMBUCO, PERNAMBUCO.

Diario de Pernambuco.
Jornal de Recife.

PETROPOLIS, ESTADO DO RIO DE JANEIRO.

Arauto.
O Mercantil.

PILAR, ALAGOAS.

Jornal do Pilar.

PINAR DO RIO DE PEIXE, MINAS GERAES.

A Luz.

PONSO-ALEGRE, MINAS GERAES.

Livro do Povo.

PORTO ALEGRE, RIO GRANDE DO SUL.

A' Federação.
A Reforma.
Deutsche Zeitung.
Diario de Porto Alegre.
Jornal do Commercio.
Koseritz Deutsche Zeitung.

BRAZIL.—Continued.

PORTO ALEGRE, RIO GRANDE DO SUL—Cont'd.

L' Italiano.
O Mercantil.
O Rio Grande.

RIO DE JANEIRO.

Cidade do Rio.
Diario de Noticias.
Diario Official.
Gazeta da Tarde.
Gazeta de Noticias.
Jornal do Brazil.
Jornal do Commercio.
Novidades.
O Brazil.
O Paiz.
O Tempo.
The Rio News.

RIO GRANDE, RIO GRANDE DO SUL.

Diario do Rio Grande.
Echo do Sul.
Gazeta Mercantil.
O Artista.
O Commercial

RIO NOVO, MINAS GERAES.

A Gazeta do Rio Novo.
Diario do Rio Novo.
Rio Novense.

SANT' AMARO.

Echo Sant' Amarense.

SANT' ANNA, ESTADO DO CEARA.

Municipio de Sant' Anna.

S. M. MAGDALENA, ESTADO DO RIO DE JANEIRO.

Echo de Magdalena.

SANTOS, SÃO PAULO.

Correio de Santos.
Diario de Santos.

BRAZIL—Continued.

SÃO CARLOS DO PINHAL, SÃO PAULO.

Diario de São Carlos.
São Carlense.

SÃO FIDELIO, ESTADO DO RIO DE JANEIRO.

O Monitor Fidelense.

SÃO GABRIEL, RIO GRANDE DO SUL.

Revista Gabrielense.

SÃO JOSE DOS CAMPOS, SÃO PAULO.

A Vida.

SÃO JOÃO DA BARRA, ESTADO DO RIO DE JANEIRO.

O São João da Barra.
Progresista.

SAO JOÃO DEL REI, MINAS GERAES.

O Arauto de Minas.

SÃO JOSE D'ALEN PARAHYBA, MINAS GERAES.

Correio de São José.

SÃO LEOPOLDO, RIO GRANDE DO SUL.

Deutsches Volksblatt.

SÃO LUIZ, ALAGOAS.

O Municipio.

SÃO MIGUEL DE CAMPOS, ALAGOAS.

A Palavra de Deus.

SÃO PAULO, SÃO PAULO.

Correio Paulistano.
Diario de Noticias.
Diario Popular.
Estado de S. Paulo.
Gazeta do Povo.
O Mercantil.

SÃO SALVADOR, BAHIA.

Diario de Noticias.
Gazeta da Bahia.

BRAZIL—Continued.

SÃO SALVADOR, BAHIA—Continued.

O Pensamento.
O Preceptor.

SAPUCAIA, ESTADO DO RIO DE JANEIRO.

O Sapucaiense.

SOBRAL, ESTADO DO CEARÁ.

Gazeta de Sobral.
O Sobralense.

THEREZINA, PIAUHY.

A Epoca.
A Floresta.
O Crepusculo.
O Cri-Cri.

UBERABA, MINAS GERAES.

A Gazeta de Uberaba.
Monitor Uberabense.

URUGUAYANA, RIO GRANDE DO SUL.

O Commercial.
O Commercio.
O Guarany.

VALENÇA, ESTADO DO RIO DE JANEIRO.

Gazeta de Valença.
O Tempo.
Tribuna de Valença.

VASSOURAS, ESTADO DO RIO DE JANEIRO.

Gazeta de Vassouras.
O Municipio.
O Vassourense.

VICTORIA, ESPIRITO SANTO.

O Espirito Santense.
O Estado de Espirito Santo.
O Horizonte.
Vasco Coitinho.

VIGIA, ESTADO DO PARÁ.

Baixo Amazonas.
Liberal de Vigia.
O Despertador.

Chile.

El Chilote.

ANGELES.

El Laja.

ANTOFAGASTA.

El Eco del Desierto.
El Pueblo Chileno.

ARANCO.

La Frontera.

CANQUENES.

El Maule.

CARACOLES.

La Patria.

CARRIZAL.

El Eco de Carrizal.

CHAÑARAL.

El Pueblo.

CHILLAN.

El Telégrafo.
La Discusión.

CONCEPCIÓN.

El Autonomista.
La Libertad Católica.
Revista del Sur.

COPIAPÓ.

El Amigo del País.
El Atacama.
El Constituyente.
El Copiapino.

COQUIMBO.

Comercio de la Serena.
El Comercio.
El Coquimbo.
El Progreso.
La Reforma.

CURICO.

El Curicano.
El Sufragio.

ELQUL

La Voz.

ILLAPEL.

La Ley.

IQUIQUE.

El Nacional.
El Veintenno de Mayo.
La Patria.
La Voz Chilena.

LINARES.

El Progreso.
Los Principios.

LOTA.

El Lota.
La Esmeralda.

MELIPILLA.

El Melipilla.

OVALLE.

El Tamaya.
La Libertad.

PARRAL.

La Decentralisación.

CHILE—Continued.

PETORCA.

El Comercio.

QUILLOTA.

El Correo.

RANCAGUA.

El Fenix.
El Lantaro.
El Rancagua.

RENGO.

El Canpolican.

SAN BERNARDO.

El Cachopoal.
El Maipío.

SAN CARLOS.

El Nuble.
La Epoca.

SAN FELIPE.

El Censor.
El Comercio.

SAN FERNANDO.

El Pueblo.
La Juventud.

SANTA ROZA.

El Andinó.

SANTIAGO.

Diario de Avisos.
El Ferro-Carril.
El Heraldo.
El Independiente.
El Porvenir.
Estrella de Chile.
La Nación.
La Republica.
Las Novedades.
Libertad Electoral.
Los Tiempos.

CHILE—Continued.

SANTIAGO—Continued.

Nuevo Ferro-Carril.
Revista Literaria.

SERENA.

El Coquimbo.
El Progreso.
La Reforma.

TALCA.

La Libertad.
La Opinión.
El Progreso.

TALTAL.

El Salitrero.

TOCOPILLA.

El Loa.

TOLTEN.

El Biobio.

TOMÉ.

El Faro.

VALDIVIA.

La Libertad.
La Verdad.

VALLENAR.

La Acción.

VALPARAISO.

El Comercio.
El Heraldo.
El Mercurio.
El Trabajo.
La Patria.
La Unión.
Mercurio del Vapor.
The Chilian Times.

YUMBAL.

El Yumbal.

Colombia.

El Anunciador.
El Promotor.
La Hoja Noticiosa.
La Opinión.
La Revista Mercantil.
La Tribuna.
La Verdad.
La Voz.
La Voz del Artesano.
The Shipping List.

BOGOTÁ.

Diario de Cundinarca.
El Correo de Coloba.
El Correo Nacional.
El Heraldo.
El Liberal.
El Tradicionista.
La Nación.
La Velada.

CARTAGENA.

El Agrícola.
El Diario Bolivar.
El Fonagrafo.
El Mercurio.
426

CARTAGENA—Continued.

El Noticioso.
Los Estados Unidos.

CUCUTA.

El Eco.
El Negocio.

MEDELLIN.

El Estado.
La Golondrina.
Registro Oficial.

PANAMÁ.

El Canal.
El Cronista.
El Hispano-Americano.
El Mercurio.
El Observador.
El Percursor.
La Estrella de Panamá.
Star and Herald

SAN JOSÉ DE CÍRCUTA.

El Mortero.

SANTA MARTA.

El Magdalena.

Ecuador.

Comercial.
Diario de Avisos.
El Comercio.
El Eco Industrial.
El Globo.
El Porvenir Nacional.
El Tiempo.
El Trabajador.

GUAYAQUIL—Continued.

La Nación.
Liberal.
Los Andes.

QUITO.

El Fenix.
El Municipio.
El Nacional.
El Telégrama.

Paraguay.

ASUNCIÓN.

Diario Oficial.
El Republicano.
La Libertad.

Peru.

AREQUIPA.
El Eco del Misti.
La Bolsa.

CALLAO.
El Callao.
El Mercurio.
El Porvenir.

CUZCO.

El Heraldo.

HUAREZ.
La Autonomia de Aucacho.

Uruguay.

URUGUAY—Continued.

MONTEVIDEO—Continued.

Revista de Ciencias.
Revista de la Academia.
Revista de la Sociedad Liga Profesional.
Revista del Uruguay.
The Montevideo Times.

PAYSANDÚ.

El Paysandú.
El Pueblo.

RIVERA.

El Partido Colorado.

ROCHA.

La Ley.

URUGUAY—Continued.

SALTO.

El Porvenir.
El Progreso.

SAN EUGENIO,

La Justicia.

SAN JOSÉ.

El Constitucional.
La Libertad.
La Trinidad.

TACUAREMBO.

El Pueblo.

Venezuela.

ARAGUA.

El Seminario.

ASUNCIÓN.

El Esfuerzo.
La Epoca.

BARCELONA.

El Cometa.
El Iris.

BARINAS.

El Zamorano.

BARQUISIMETO.

El Ateneo.

BOCANÓ.

El Progresista.

CALABOZO.

La Situación.

CARÁCAS.

El Angel Guardian.
El Apóstol Liberal.
El Boletin de la Agencia Pumar.
El Boletin del Ministerio de Obras Públicas.
El Boletin Militar.
El Carácter.
El Cojo.
El Correo de Carácas.
El Cronista.
El Diablo.
El Diario de Avisos.
El Deber Profesional.

CARÁCAS—Continued.

El Eco Industrial.
El Granuja.
El Hogar Doméstico.
El Intransigente.
El Iris de la Fé.
El Luchador.
El Mensajero del Corazón de Jesús.
El Monitor.
El Noticiero.
El Padre Cobos.
El Partido Democrático.
El Pueblo.
El Radical.
El Siglo.
El Sol de América.
El Testigo.
El Tribuno.
La Campaña.
La Clínica de los Niños Pobres.
La Gaceta de los Hospitales.
La Gaceta Municipal.
La Gaceta Oficial.
La Guillotina.
La Ilustración.
La Linterna.
La Opinión Nacional.
La Rehabilitación.
La Religión.
La República.
La Revista Mercantil.
La Revista Universal Ilustrada.
La Unión Médica.

CARUPONA.

El Bien Público.

VENEZUELA—Continued.

CIUDAD BOLIVAR.

El Bolivarense.
El Patriota.
El Revindicador.
El Siglo.
La Opinión de Guayana.
La Siempreviva.

CORO.

La Industria.

CUMANÁ.

La Gaceta Oficial.

GUAYANA.

La Opinión Nacional.

LA GUAYRA.

El Diario de La Guayra.

LA VICTORIA.

La Voz de Aragua.

MARACAIBO.

Boletin Comercial.
Ecos de Zulia.
El Posto del Comercio.

MATURIN.

La Voz de Maturin.

MERIDA.

La Semana.

NUEVA BARCELONA.

El Cometa.

PETARE.

El Avila.

ES PÍRITU DE BARCELONA.

El Iris.

VENEZUELA—Continued.

PUERTO CABELLO.

El Correo Porteño.
El Diario Comercial.
El Diario Mercantil.
El Fuerte.
La Voz Pública.

QUIBOR.

El Eco.

SAN CARLOS.

Gaceta de Tachira.

SAN CRISTOBAL.

El Porvenir.
La Posta Mercantil.

SAN FELIPE.

El Porvenir.

SAN FERNANDO.

El Criterio.
El Eco de Apure.

TARIBA.

El Gabinete.
La Unión Liberal.

TOCUYO.

Año Nuevo.
El Tiempo.

TRUJILLO.

El Trujillano.

VALENCIA.

Avisador Comercial.
El Civismo.
La Voz Pública.

VICTORIA.

El Escolar.

British Guiana.

GEORGETOWN.

A União Portugueza.
The Argosy.
The Berbice Gazette.
The Colonist.
The Daily Chronicle.
The Echo.
The Gold Mining Gazette.
The Mercantile Intelligencer.
The Monthly Greeting.

GEORGETOWN—Continued.

The Official Gazette.
The Reflector.
The St. Andrew's Magazine.
The Villager.

NEW AMSTERDAM.

Berbice Gazette.
Penny Weekly.

British Honduras.

BELIZE.

El Sol.
The Angelus.
The Belize Diocesan and Parish Ga-
zette.

BELIZE—Continued.

The Belize Independent.
The Colonial Guardian.
The Government Gazette.

432

Cuba.

S. Ex. 8, pt. 11——28

433

CUBA—Continued.

Boletin Oficial de la Provincia.
Boletin Oficial de Voluntarios.
Crónica Médico-Quirúrgica.
Diario de la Marina.
Diario del Ejército.
Eco de Cuba.
Eco de Galicia.
Eco Montañés.
El Centinela.
El Comercio.
El Economista Antillano.
El Español.
El Estudio.
El Fígaro.
El Gil Blás.
El Heraldo de Asturias.
El Hogar.
El León Español.
El Liberal.
El Observador.
El País.
El Pitcher.
El Progreso Militar.
El Score.
El Tabaco.
El Triunfo.
Gaceta de la Habana.
Havana Price Current (English).
Havana Weekly Report (English).
La Caricatura.
La Casualidad.
La Confianza.
La Discusión.
La Evolución.
La Fraternidad.
La Habana Elegante.
La Humanitaria.
La Iberia.
La Libertad.
La Lucha.
La Política.
La Tarde.
La Tribuna.
La Unión Constitucional.

CUBA—Continued.

Laurac Bat.
La Voz de Cuba.
Reportorio Médico-Farmacéutico.
Revista Cubana.
Revista de Agricultura.
Revista de Ciencias Médicas.
Revista de Estudiantes.
Revista Economica.
Revista del Foro.
Revista Mercantil.

HOLGUIN.

Cuba Española.
La Doctrina.

JARUCO.

El Jaruqueño.

MANZANILLO.

El Canto.
El Liberal. -
La Unión.

MATANZAS.

Aurora del Yumurí.
Boletin Oficial.
El Constitucional.
El Diario.
La Juventud Liberal.
El Ramillette.

NUEVITAS.

El Rivereño.

PINAR DEL RIO.

Boletin Oficial.
El Alerta.
El Boletin.
El Constitucional.
La Alborada.
La Fraternidad.
La Idea.
Paz y Concordia.

CUBA—Continued.

PLACETAS.

La Industria.

PUERTO PRÍNCIPE.

Boletin Oficial.
Eco del Porvenir.
El Fanal.
El Pueblo.
El Progreso.

REMEDIOS.

El León Español.

SAGUA.

El Comercio.
El Productor.
La Alborada.
La Luz.

SAN ANTONIO.

La Situación.

SANCTI SPIRITUS.

El Aprendiz.
El Espirituano.
El Fenix.
El País.
Guzman de Alfereche.
La Buena Nueva.
La Fraternidad.

SAN JOSÉ DE LAS LAJAS.

La Justicia.

CUBA—Continued.

SAN JUAN DE LOS REMEDIOS.

El Centro de Recreo.
El Popular.
La Idea.

SANTA CLARA.

El Boletin Oficial.
El Combate.
El Eco de las Villas.
El Pabellón Español.
El Trabajo.
La Bella Unión.

SANTIAGO DE CUBA.

Avisador Comercial.
Bandera Española.
Bien Público.
Boletin Comercial.
Boletin Oficial de la Provincia.
Boletin Oficial Eclesiástico.
Espíritu del Siglo XIX.
Machete.
Patria.
Revista Jurídico Notarial.
Triunfo.

TRINIDAD.

El Diario.
El Imparcial.
El Telégrafo.

UNIÓN DE REYES.

La Voz del Pueblo.

Curaçao.

WILLEMSTAD.

El Imparcial.

Guadeloupe.

BASSE-TERRE.

Journal Officiel.

POINTE-À-PITRE.

Le Courrier de la Guadeloupe.
Le Progrès.
La Vérité.

Jamaica.

FALMOUTH.

The Falmouth Gazette.

KINGSTON.

Gall's News Letter.
Jamaica Christian Chronicle.
The Baptist Reporter.
The Budget.
The Colonial Standard.
The Evening Express.
The Gleaner.
The Gospeler.
The Jamaica Churchman.
The Jamaica Congregational Magazine.

436

KINGSTON—Continued.

The Jamaica Gazette
The Jamaica Post.
The Jamaica Prices Current.
The Journal of Commerce.
The Methodist Messenger.
The Moravian.
The Police Gazette.
The St. Michael's Magazine.
The Victoria Quarterly.
Tri-Weekly Gleaner.

MONTEGO BAY.

The Nineteenth Century.

Martinique.

Le Moniteur de la Martinique.
La Petite France.

La Défense Coloniale.
Le Propagateur.
Les Antilles.
Les Colonies.

Puerto Rico.

HUMACAO.

El Peregrino.

MAYAGUEZ.

Diario de Avisos.
La Razón.

PONCE.

La Avispa.
Revista Mercantil.

SAN JUAN.

Boletin Mercantil.
El Buscapié.
Gaceta de Puerto Rico.

YAUCO.

El Movimiento.

ST. THOMAS.

Tidende.

447

Santo Domingo.

PUERTO PLATA.

El Porvenir.
El Propagador.

SAMANA.

El Eco de Samana.

448

SAN DOMINGO.

Auras del Ozama.
Eco de la Opinión.
El Boletin del Comercio.
Gaceta Oficial.

SANTIAGO.

La Voz de Santiago.

www.ingramcontent.com/pod-product-compliance
Lightning Source LLC
Chambersburg PA
CBHW031828270326
41932CB00008B/587